PLATINUM EDITION

1

Series Director: Diane Larsen-Freeman

GRAMMAR DIMENSIONS

TEACHER'S EDITION

Victoria Badalamenti
University of California
Santa Barbara

Carolyn Henner Stanchina
California State University
Fullerton

HH Heinle & Heinle
Thomson Learning™

Australia • Canada • Denmark • Japan • Mexico • New Zealand
Philippines • Puerto Rico • Singapore • Spain • United Kingdom • United States

Acquisitions Editor: Eric Bredenberg
Senior Developmental Editor: Amy Lawler
Production Editor: Michael Burggren
Senior Marketing Manager: Charlotte Sturdy
Manufacturing Coordinator: Mary Beth Hennebury
Composition/Project Management: The PRD Group, Inc.
Text Design: Sue Gerould, Perspectives
Cover Design: Hannus Design Associates
Printer: Phoenix Color

Heinle & Heinle Publishers
20 Park Plaza
Boston, MA 02116

AUSTRALIA/NEW ZEALAND:
Nelson/Thomson Learning
102 Dodds Street
South Melbourne
Victoria 3205 Australia

CANADA:
Nelson/Thomson Learning
1120 Birchmount Road
Scarborough, Ontario
Canada M1K 5G4

UK/EUROPE/MIDDLE EAST:
Thomson Learning
Berkshire House
168-173 High Holborn
London, WC1V 7AA, United Kingdom

LATIN AMERICA:
Thomson Learning
Seneca, 53
Colonia Polanco
11560 México D.F. México

SPAIN:
Thomson Learning
Calle Magallanes, 25
28015-Madrid
Espana

ASIA (excluding Japan):
Thomson Learning
60 Albert Street #15-01
Albert Complex
Singapore 189969

JAPAN:
Thomson Learning
Palaceside Building, 5F
1-1-1 Hitotsubashi, Chiyoda-ku
Tokyo 100 0003, Japan

ISBN: 0-8384-0267-4

This book is printed on acid-free recycled paper.

Printed in the United States of America
1 2 3 4 5 6 7 8 9 04 03 02 01 00

Teacher's Edition Contents

Contents

iv

Introduction

A Word from Diane Larsen-Freeman, Series Director

Before ***Grammar Dimensions*** was published, teachers would always ask me, "What is the role of grammar in a communicative approach?" These teachers recognized the importance of teaching grammar, but they associated grammar with form and communication with meaning, and thus could not see how the two easily fit together. ***Grammar Dimensions*** was created to help teachers and students appreciate the fact that grammar is not just about form. While grammar does indeed involve form, in order to communicate, language users also need to know the meaning of the forms and when to use them appropriately. In fact, it is sometimes not the form, but the *meaning* or *appropriate use* of a grammatical structure that represents the greatest long-term learning challenge for students. For instance, learning when it is appropriate to use the present perfect tense instead of the past tense, or being able to use two-word or phrasal verbs meaningfully, represent formidable challenges for ESL students.

The three dimensions of form, meaning, and use can be depicted in a pie chart with their interrelationship illustrated by the three arrows:

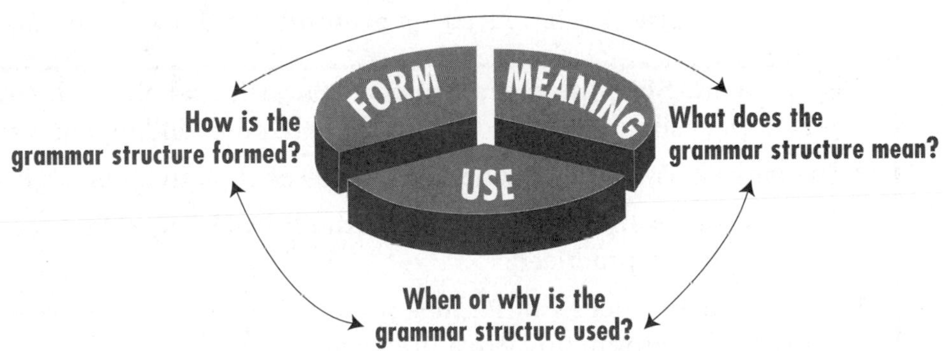
FORM
MEANING
USE
How is the grammar structure formed?
What does the grammar structure mean?
When or why is the grammar structure used?

Helping students learn to use grammatical structures accurately, meaningfully, and appropriately is the fundamental goal of ***Grammar Dimensions.*** It is consistent with the goal of helping students to communicate meaningfully in English, and one that recognizes the undeniable interdependence of grammar and communication.

Enjoy the Platinum Edition!

To learn more about form, meaning, and use, read ***The Grammar Book: An ESL/EFL Teacher's Course,*** Second Edition, by Marianne Celce-Murcia and Diane Larsen-Freeman, also from Heinle & Heinle. It helps both prospective and practicing teachers of ESL/EFL enhance their understanding of English grammar, expand their skills in linguistic analysis, and develop a pedagogical approach to teaching English grammar that builds on the three dimensions. ISBN: 0-8384-4725-2.

Welcome to Grammar Dimensions, Platinum Edition!

The most comprehensive communicative grammar series available.

Updated and revised, ***Grammar Dimensions, Platinum Edition,*** makes teaching grammar easy and more effective than ever. Clear grammar explanations, a wealth of exercises, lively communicative activities, technology resources, and fully annotated Teacher's Editions help both beginning and experienced teachers give their students the practice and skills they need to communicate accurately, meaningfully, and appropriately.

Grammar Dimensions, Platinum Edition is:

Communicative	• Students practice the **form, meaning,** and **use** of each grammar structure. • **Improved! A variety of communicative activities** helps students practice grammar and communication in tandem, eliciting self-expression and personalized practice. • Students learn to communicate accurately, meaningfully, and appropriately.
Comprehensive	• **Improved!** Grammar is presented in **clear charts.** • **A wealth of exercises** helps students practice and master their new language. • **The Workbook** provides extra practice and helps students prepare for the TOEFL® Test. • **Engaging listening activities** on audiocassette further reinforce the target structure. • **New! Enclosed CD-ROM** includes over 500 activities and gives students even more practice in mastering grammar and its use in language. **FREE!**
Clear	• **Improved! Simplified grammar explanations** help both students and teachers easily understand and comprehend each language structure. • **Improved! A fresh new design** makes each activity engaging. • **New! Communicative activities** ("the Purple Pages") are now labeled with the skill being practiced. • **New!** The Teacher's Edition has **page references** for the Student Book and Workbook, minimizing extra preparation time.

User Friendly for Students	• **Contextualized grammar explanations and examples** help students understand the target language. • **New! Goals** at the beginning of each unit focus students' attention on the learning they will do. • **Sample phrases and sentences** model the appropriate use of the structure.
User Friendly for Teachers	• **New!** Teacher's Edition now contains answers, tests, tape scripts, and complete, **step-by-step teaching suggestions** for every activity. • **New!** "Purple Page" activities are now labeled with the skill. • **Improved! A tight integration** among the Student Book, the Workbook, and the Teacher's Edition make extension activities easy to do.
Flexible	• Instructors can use the units in order or as set by their curriculum. • Exercises can be used in order or as needed by the students. • "Purple Page" activities can be used at the end of the unit or interspersed throughout the unit.
Effective	Students who learn the form, meaning, and use of each grammar structure will be able to communicate more accurately, meaningfully, and appropriately.

Grammar Dimensions, Platinum Edition

In ***Grammar Dimensions, Platinum Edition,*** students progress from the sentence level to the discourse level, and learn to communicate appropriately at all levels.

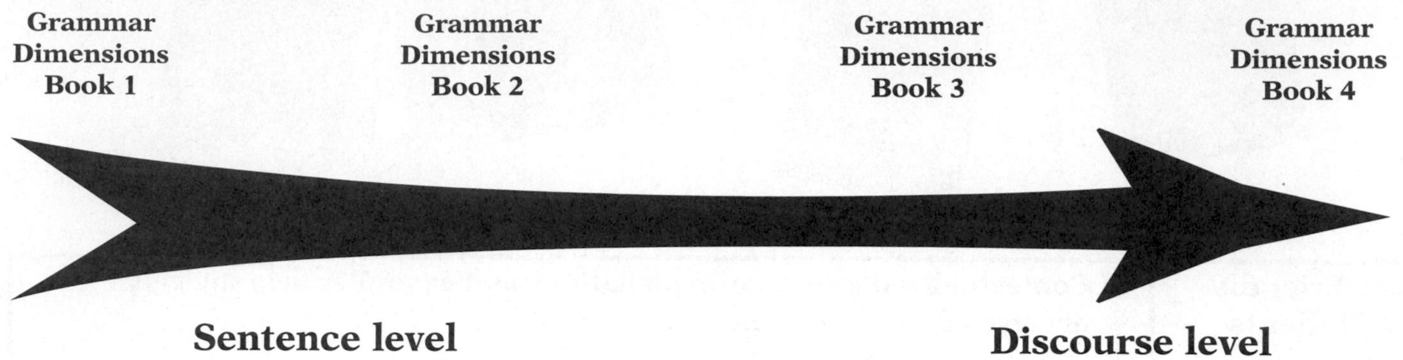

	Grammar Dimensions, Book 1	Grammar Dimensions, Book 2	Grammar Dimensions, Book 3	Grammar Dimensions, Book 4
Level	High beginning	Intermediate	High intermediate	Advanced
Grammar level	Sentence and subsentence level	Sentence and subsentence level	Discourse level	Discourse level
Primary language and communication focus	Semantic notions such as *time* and *place*	Social functions, such as *making requests* and *seeking permission*	Cohesion and coherence at the discourse level	Academic and technical discourse
Major skill focus	Listening and speaking	Listening and speaking	Reading and writing	Reading and writing
Outcome	Students form accurate, meaningful, and appropriate structures at the sentence level.	Students form accurate, meaningful, and appropriate structures at the sentence level.	Students learn how accurate, meaningful, and appropriate grammatical structures contribute to the organization of language above the simple sentence.	Students learn how accurate, meaningful, and appropriate grammatical structures contribute to the organization of language above the simple sentence.

Unit Organization

Used with or without the Workbook and the *Grammar 3D* CD-ROM, ***Grammar Dimensions*** Student Book units are designed to be clear, comprehensive, flexible, and communicative.

Goals	• **Focus students' attention** on the learning they will do in each chapter.
Opening Task	• **Contextualizes** the target grammatical structure. • **Enables teachers to diagnose** their students' performance and identify the aspect of the structure with which their students have the most difficulty. • **Provides a roadmap** for the grammar points students need to work on in that unit.
Focus Boxes	• **Present the form, meaning,** or **use** of a particular grammatical structure. • **Focus students' attention** to a particular feature of the target structure. Each rule or explanation is preceded by examples, so teachers can have students work inductively to try to discover the rule on their own.
Exercises	• Provide a wealth of opportunity to **practice** the form and meaning of the grammar structures. • Help students develop the skill of **"grammaring"**—the ability to use structures accurately, meaningfully, and appropriately. • Are varied, thematically coherent, but purposeful. • Give students many opportunities to personalize and own the language.
Communicative Activities ("The Purple Pages")	• Help students practice **grammar and communication in tandem.** • **Are engaging!** • Encourage students to **use their new language** both inside and outside the classroom. • Provide an opportunity to **practice reading, writing, listening, and speaking skills,** helping students realize the communicative value of the grammar they are learning.

Student Book Supplements

Audiocassettes	• **Provide listening activities for** each unit so students can practice listening to **grammar structures in context.**
Workbooks	• **Provide additional exercises** for each grammar point presented in the student text. • Offer question types found on the **TOEFL**® Test.
CD-ROM	• *Grammar 3D* **provides additional practice** for 34 of the key grammar structures found in the text series. • Offers over **500 activities** for beginning to advanced students. • **Provides an instructional "help page"** that allows students to access grammar explanations at any point. • **Provides feedback** that helps students understand their errors and guides them toward correct answers. • **Free** with each Student Book!
Teacher's Editions	• **Facilitate teaching** by providing in one place notes and examples, answer keys to the Student Book and Workbook, page references to all of the components, the tapescript for the audiocassette activities, and tests with answer keys for each unit. • **Minimize teacher preparation time** by providing step-by-step teaching suggestions for every focus box and activity in the Student Book.

The ***Grammar Dimensions, Platinum Edition*** Student Books and the additional components help teachers teach and students learn to use English grammar structures in communication accurately, meaningfully, and appropriately.

Introduction

A Word from Diane Larsen-Freeman, Series Director

Before ***Grammar Dimensions*** was published, teachers would always ask me, "What is the role of grammar in a communicative approach?" These teachers recognized the importance of teaching grammar, but they associated grammar with form and communication with meaning, and thus could not see how the two easily fit together. ***Grammar Dimensions*** was created to help teachers and students appreciate the fact that grammar is not just about form. While grammar does indeed involve form, in order to communicate, language users also need to know the meaning of the forms and when to use them appropriately. In fact, it is sometimes not the form, but the *meaning* or *appropriate use* of a grammatical structure that represents the greatest long-term learning challenge for students. For instance, learning when it is appropriate to use the present perfect tense instead of the past tense, or being able to use two-word or phrasal verbs meaningfully, represent formidable challenges for ESL students.

The three dimensions of form, meaning, and use can be depicted in a pie chart with their interrelationship illustrated by the three arrows:

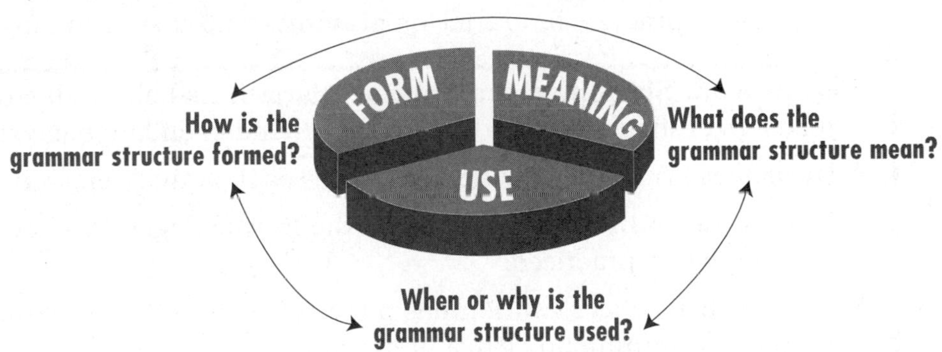
FORM
MEANING
USE
How is the grammar structure formed?
What does the grammar structure mean?
When or why is the grammar structure used?

Helping students learn to use grammatical structures accurately, meaningfully, and appropriately is the fundamental goal of ***Grammar Dimensions.*** It is consistent with the goal of helping students to communicate meaningfully in English, and one that recognizes the undeniable interdependence of grammar and communication.

Enjoy the Platinum Edition!

To learn more about form, meaning, and use, read ***The Grammar Book: An ESL/EFL Teacher's Course,*** Second Edition, by Marianne Celce-Murcia and Diane Larsen-Freeman, also from Heinle & Heinle. It helps both prospective and practicing teachers of ESL/EFL enhance their understanding of English grammar, expand their skills in linguistic analysis, and develop a pedagogical approach to teaching English grammar that builds on the three dimensions. ISBN: 0-8384-4725-2.

Welcome to Grammar Dimensions, Platinum Edition!

The most comprehensive communicative grammar series available.

Updated and revised, ***Grammar Dimensions, Platinum Edition,*** makes teaching grammar easy and more effective than ever. Clear grammar explanations, a wealth of exercises, lively communicative activities, technology resources, and fully annotated Teacher's Editions help both beginning and experienced teachers give their students the practice and skills they need to communicate accurately, meaningfully, and appropriately.

Grammar Dimensions, Platinum Edition is:

Communicative	• Students practice the **form, meaning,** and **use** of each grammar structure. • **Improved! A variety of communicative activities** helps students practice grammar and communication in tandem, eliciting self-expression and personalized practice. • Students learn to communicate accurately, meaningfully, and appropriately.
Comprehensive	• **Improved!** Grammar is presented in **clear charts.** • **A wealth of exercises** helps students practice and master their new language. • **The Workbook** provides extra practice and helps students prepare for the TOEFL® Test. • **Engaging listening activities** on audiocassette further reinforce the target structure. • **New! Enclosed CD-ROM** includes over 500 activities and gives students even more practice in mastering grammar and its use in language. **FREE!**
Clear	• **Improved! Simplified grammar explanations** help both students and teachers easily understand and comprehend each language structure. • **Improved! A fresh new design** makes each activity engaging. • **New! Communicative activities** ("the Purple Pages") are now labeled with the skill being practiced. • **New!** The Teacher's Edition has **page references** for the Student Book and Workbook, minimizing extra preparation time.

General Teaching Suggestions

OPENING TASK

Our time with our students is very precious. We must seek ways to put it to their best advantage. In order to do this, you need to learn what your students know and don't know how to do. This will allow you to target what you teach to what your students don't know, and therefore, need to learn. This is the major purpose of the opening task. You should be able to obtain invaluable information about your students' learning needs from "reading" (closely observing) your students as they go about doing the task. Each task has been constructed so that students will need to use the target structures in order to complete it.

As the students are focused on completing the task, you are freed to learn as much as you can about your students' learning needs. It will probably be best if after you have introduced the task (making sure students know what they are being asked to do), you have the students carry out as much of the task as they can by themselves. This will allow you to more closely observe your students' performance.

One way of doing this is to circulate in the classroom and "eavesdrop" on small group discussions. Take mental or written notes on your observations. Pay particular attention to how accurate, meaningful, and appropriate your students' use of the target structures is. Hold up the form, meaning, and use pie chart in your mind and see if you can determine where they have been successful, and where they need help. At this point, it is probably better if you refrain from any error correction. The tasks are supposed to encourage students to work meaningfully without concern that they will be interrupted, evaluated, or corrected. The only exception might be the need to remind students to work in English if they are using another language.

Sometimes the tasks involve individual written performances. When this is the case, study carefully what your students write. It, too, can provide valuable clues about what they can and cannot do. In many cases, students will want to hear each other's solutions to the questions or problems posed in the task. This provides yet another excellent opportunity for you to listen to your students and learn what has been easy for them and what has been difficult.

Of course, as with anything, different difficulties are likely to arise for different students. To cope with differing learning needs, you may consider grouping students with similar problems in class and giving each group different exercises to work through and/or different homework assignments. Another possibility is to group students in such a way that students who already know certain aspects of the target structure are grouped with other students who don't. In this way, students can learn from one another as they work through the focus boxes and exercises. If you do group students in this manner, however, it is important that each student be given a role in the group, so that students who are struggling with the content can still be contributing members of the group. For example, give these students the assignment of recording the group's answers, or reporting them to another group or to the whole class.

Obviously, if students demonstrate no ability to use the target structures required in completing the task, you will need to work systematically through the unit. It may be the case, though, that you will discover that students do not need to attend to all the focus boxes or do all the exercises; this makes your teaching more efficient.

Don't hesitate to alter tasks to fit your timetable. For example, have your students do only part of the task, or have them do one of the communicative activities at the end of the unit, if you feel that the opening task would not work as well. Other teachers have found it helpful to have students do the task twice—first for diagnostic purposes and second after students have worked through a unit in order to determine how much they have progressed.

All in all, what we are trying to achieve is an optimal use of the time we have available by identifying teachable moments when the students need to and are ready to learn.

FOCUS BOXES

The focus boxes feature the form, meaning, and use facts concerning the target structure that are appropriate for students at a given level of instruction. By treating one aspect of the structure at a time, followed by exercises providing practice, the focus boxes allow students to develop step-by-step a better understanding of, and an ability to use, the structure accurately, meaningfully, and appropriately.

Use student performance on the opening task as a bridge to the focus boxes. One way to do this is to write students' responses to the task on the blackboard, eliciting or supplying the target structures as they are needed. By going back and pointing out the target structures and asking questions about their form, meaning, or use, you may be able to induce the rules in the focus boxes (not all at once, of course). At this point, you may want students to consult the relevant focus box in order to confirm the generalizations they have just made. On the other hand, if the students have arrived at the generalizations you feel they need to know, you may simply want to call their attention to the appropriate focus boxes for them to refer to for homework or when needed.

If you prefer a more deductive approach, you could go right to the first or appropriate focus box after the students have completed the task. You could present it orally to students or read it while they listen or read along silently with you. Alternatively, you could have the students read the focus boxes for homework or silently in class. You could help them when they do not understand something. You could check their understanding by asking students to come up with additional examples to supplement the ones in the focus box or asking them to compare how the material in this focus box differs from one earlier in the unit or from those in a related unit that they have completed.

A variation on this is to ask students individually or in pairs to present the information in a focus box to another pair of students, or even to the whole class, adding a few new examples of their own. Teaching something to others is a great way to learn!

Another possible way of teaching the focus boxes is not to present them at all, but rather to assign students the exercises that go along with them. The focus boxes can be used for reference purposes as the students work their way through the exercises. In this way, the material becomes more meaningful to students because they will need to access and understand it in order to do something with it.

EXERCISES

At least one exercise follows each focus box. There is a wide variety of exercises in *Grammar Dimensions*. There are both comprehension and production exercises. Comprehension exercises work on students' awareness and understanding. Production exercises develop students' skill in using the structures.

There are exercises that are consistent with the theme of the task and ones that introduce students to new themes and vocabulary in order to provide variety and to foster students' ability to transfer their learning to new contexts. There are personalized exercises, in which students use their own background knowledge or opinions to answer questions, and ones where students use the information that is supplied in order to complete the exercise.

Then, too, although general directions are provided for each exercise, there is a great deal of flexibility in how the exercises can be handled. Some exercises, such as information gaps, call for pairwork. Others are amenable to many different student configurations: individual, pair, small group, whole class; so you will need to decide what works best for a particular exercise and particular group of students. For instance, some students prefer to work individually at first and then get together with others to go over their answers. The variety of possible student configurations that the exercises permit allows students' differing learning styles to be catered to.

Sometimes you can choose freely whether to have students do an exercise orally or in writing. At other times, an exercise will work better in one modality than another because of the modality in which the structure normally occurs. Some exercises may be done in class, others for homework, and still others skipped all together. Don't forget to consult the Workbook for additional exercises.

There are also many options for how exercise answers can be checked. For example:

1. You can circulate while students are doing an exercise in class and spot-check.
2. You can go over the exercise afterwards as a whole class with each student being called on to supply an answer.
3. Exercises can be done individually and then pairs of students can get together to check their answers with each other. Where a difference of opinion occurs, you (or another pair of students) can act as a referee.
4. Different students, pairs, or groups of students can be assigned different parts of an exercise. For example, the first group does #'s 1–5, the second group does #6–10, etc. The groups post their answers on newsprint or butcher block paper and everyone circulates at the end noting the answers and asking questions.
5. A variation of #4 is to have one student from each group get together and present to the other students the exercise answers that his or her group came up with.
6. You can prepare a handout with the answers, and each student corrects his or her answers individually.
7. You can collect the written work, and make a list of common errors. You can put the errors on an overhead transparency and show it to the students during the next class and have them correct the errors together.

There are both closed and open-ended answers to questions. With closed questions, there is a single right answer. This is the most common type of question in Books 1 and 2. In Books 3 and 4, while closed questions still prevail, sometimes open-ended questions, for which there are no definitive answers, are used. Nuances of the language and contextual differences are such that it is sometimes difficult to say definitively what the single best answer is. The point is that students should understand that they have choices, but they also need to understand the consequences of their choices, i.e., they should be able to explain why they have chosen a particular answer. In many of these cases a "most likely" interpretation (based on English native speaker responses) has been indicated in the answer key, but no feasible opinion offered by your students should be discounted. Giving students an opportunity to defend their answers encourages students to form their own hypotheses about the appropriate use of certain grammar structures and to test these hypotheses through continued observation and analysis.

"USE YOUR ENGLISH" ACTIVITIES

In the "Use Your English" activities section of each unit (the purple pages), students can apply the language discussed in the unit to wider contexts and integrate it with the language they already know. Many activities give students more control over what they want to say or write than the exercises, and offer them more opportunities to express their own points of view across a range of topics. Most of the activities are quite open-ended in that they lend themselves to being done with structures covered in the unit, but they do not absolutely require their use.

The activities section is also designed to give instructors a variety of options. Since time is limited, you probably will not be able to have students do all the activities. You might choose two to do or ask your students to choose ones that they would prefer. Perhaps different groups of students could do different activities and then report on their experience to the whole class. Like the exercises, the activities can be adapted for use with different group configurations and different modalities.

If you are teaching in a program that is skill-based, you might want to collaborate with your colleagues and distribute the activities among yourselves. For example, the writing teacher could assign the activities that involve a written report, the teacher of listening could work on the listening activities during his or her class periods, or the teacher of speaking could work with students on activities where students are supposed to make an oral presentation.

Although the activities are meant to be culminating, it is also possible to intersperse them among the exercises. Sometimes an activity provides a particularly useful follow-up to an exercise. And we have already mentioned that certain activities might work well in place of the recommended opening task. Also, it may be useful to go back to a previous unit and do an activity for review purposes. This is especially useful at the beginning of a new, but related, unit.

The activities are an integral part of each unit because they not only provide students with opportunities to stretch their language use, but as with the opening task, they also provide you with the opportunity to observe your students' language use in action. In this way, activities can be informal holistic assessment measures encouraging students to show you how well they can use the target structures communicatively. Any persistent problems that still exist at this point can be noted for follow-up at a later time when students are more ready to deal with them.

As you can see, *Grammar Dimensions* is meant to provide you with a great deal of flexibility so that you can provide quality instruction appropriate for your class. We encourage you to experiment with different aspects of the material in order to best meet the needs of your unique group of students.

Unit 1

UNIT OVERVIEW

Unit 1, Unit 2, and Unit 3 are devoted to the verb *be.* Unit 1 focuses on affirmative statements and subject pronouns within the context of nationalities, countries, and ethnicity. The world map on page 3 is an essential resource for this unit, and can also be used elsewhere.

UNIT GOALS

Each Opening Task is designed to be used inductively, and to show you whether students (Ss) can understand and/or use the target structure accurately and appropriately. To maximize this diagnostic potential of the Opening Task, do not review the Unit Goals with Ss until after they have completed and reviewed the task. Reviewing the Unit Goals in a deductive fashion first will give the target structure away, thereby undermining the diagnostic function of the task.

OPENING TASK

The **Opening Task** contextualizes the target structure and has Ss use the structure in some meaningful way, allowing the teacher to diagnose Ss' level of mastery of the target structure. For a more complete discussion of the Opening Task, see page xxiii of this Teacher's Edition.

The purpose of this particular task is to create an authentic communicative context (nationalities and places of origin) in which Ss can use the verb *be.* The Ss' attention should be focused on *meaning* at this point.

SETTING UP THE TASK

These photos are contextualized so that Ss can match them to the appropriate introductions even if they know very little language.

SUGGESTIONS

1. Put a large world map on the board.
2. If you have done an introductory activity prior to doing this unit, ask Ss to locate their home countries on the map as a warm-up. Make two columns on the board: Countries Nationalities. Write information about your Ss.

UNIT 1

THE VERB *BE*

Affirmative Statements, Subject Pronouns

UNIT GOALS:

- To use correct forms of the verb *be* in affirmative statements
- To use subject pronouns
- To use correct forms of contractions with subjects and the verb *be*
- To introduce and greet people formally and informally in English

OPENING TASK
Introductions

STEP 1 Match the introductions to the pictures.

A.

B.

C.

D.

E.

F.

1. "Hello. My name is Monique. I'm French. I'm from Paris."
2. "I'm Chen. I'm Chinese. I'm from Beijing."
3. "We're the Mendoza family. This is my wife Maria. I'm Carlos. Our daughters' names are Rosita and Raquel."
4. "Hi. I'm Genya. I'm Russian. I'm from Moscow."
5. "I'm Fernando and this is Isabel. We are married. We are Colombian. We're from Bogota."
6. "Hi. My name is Oumar and this is my brother Alioune. We're from Senegal. Senegal is in West Africa."

STEP 2 Look at Monique's information card. Then complete the information card about yourself. Introduce yourself to the class.

Information Card

Name: Monique Delande
Country: France
Nationality: French
Age: 28 years old
Married/Divorced/Single: Single

Information Card

Name: ________
Country: ________
Nationality: ________
Age: ________
Married/Divorced/Single: ________

My name is ________ .
I am from ________ .
I'm ________ .
I'm ________ years old.
I'm ________ .

ANSWER KEY

Opening Task

Step 1

1. d 2. c 3. f 4. a 5. b 6. e

CONDUCTING THE TASK

Step 1 

If you use this unit as your first lesson to get Ss to introduce themselves to each other, encourage pairs to do the matching first, by guessing if necessary. Do not call attention to the verb *be* at this point. Check answers with the whole class. Have Ss explain their choices.

Step 2 

1. Familiarize Ss with the information card. Ask questions like: *What's the person's name? What's her first name? Her last name? What country is she from?, Is she married? Single? Divorced?* etc. You will need to explain first and last name, and to define single, married, divorced. Remember that most Ss use last name, first name when introducing themselves.
2. If you feel your Ss are capable, skip the third box and have them introduce themselves using the second box.
3. Listen to the language Ss produce in Step 2 and take notes on errors. Though the verb *be* is provided in box three, Ss may still make errors as they are focusing on meaningful communication and not on correct form.

REVIEWING THE TASK

Use your notes on sentences Ss produced to present the form of *be* using the focus boxes that follow. Ss' errors will allow you to begin to assess what they know and what they need to work on.

FOCUS 1

SUGGESTIONS 

1. This is a seemingly simple focus box. However, it provides a very important introduction to S-V fulfillment (i.e., every verb must have a subject, unless it's an imperative form), S-V word order, and S-V agreement. Write the focus box on he board or present it on an overhead projector.
2. Have Ss read the sentences aloud.
3. To proceed inductively, have Ss observe the sentence patterns, give you the S-V rules, and tell you why the verb *be* changes.
4. To work more deductively, point out the S-V word order and the singular-plural changes.
5. If Ss notice the contraction "*I'm*" in the task, explain this and have them look at "*We're*" in the task as well. Tell them that Focus 3 deals with these contractions.

Exercise 1

Exercises following each focus provide meaningful practice with the grammar item presented in that particular box. For a more complete discussion of how to use the exercises, see page xxv of this Teacher's Edition.

This particular exercise can be done individually or as pairwork. It has Ss identify the target structure without asking them to produce it yet.

Workbook Exs. 1, p. 1
Answers: TE p. 526

FOCUS **1** FORM

▶ *Be*: Affirmative Statements

SUBJECT	VERB *Be*		
Monique She Paris The city of Paris	is	single. from Paris. in France. beautiful.	singular (one)
Fernando and Isabel They The people in Colombia	are	Colombian. married. friendly.	plural (more than one)

EXERCISE 1

Fill in the blanks with the verb *be* or a name.

1. Genya ____is____ from Russia.
2. Fernando and Isabel ______________ married.
3. ______________ is from the People's Republic of China.
4. Monique ______________ twenty-eight years old.
5. Rosita and Raquel ______________ sisters.
6. ______________ are from Senegal.
7. Genya ______________ divorced.
8. The Mendozas ______________ Mexican.
9. ______________ is from France.
10. Moscow ______________ in Russia.

2 UNIT 1

ANSWER KEY

Exercise 1

Singular forms are underlined; plural forms are italicized.

1. My name is Monique. I'm French. I'm from Paris.
2. I'm Chen. I'm Chinese. I'm from Beijing.
3. *We're* the Mendoza family. This is my wife Maria. I'm Carlos. *Our daughters' names are* Rosita and Raquel.
4. I'm Genya. I'm Russian. I'm from Moscow.
5. I'm Fernando and this is Isabel. *We are* married. *We are* Colombian. *We're* from Bogotá.
6. My name is Oumar and this is my brother Alioune. *We're* from Senegal. Senegal is in West Africa.

EXERCISE 2

Use the world map to complete each sentence. The first one has been done for you.

Continents/Regions

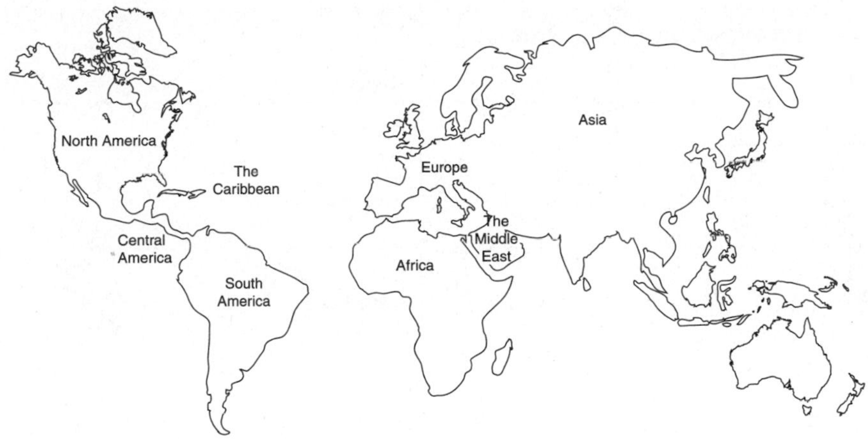

1. Japan is in Asia.
2. The Dominican Republic ________________.
3. Senegal and Nigeria ________________.
4. Honduras and El Salvador ________________.
5. Peru and Ecuador ________________.
6. Bangladesh ________________.
7. Israel ________________.
8. Canada ________________.
9. Italy and Greece ________________.

Now write two sentences of your own.

10. ________________________________
11. ________________________________

Exercise 2

SUGGESTIONS

1. Have Ss identify the continents and geographic regions on the world map on page 3 before doing this exercise.
2. If you have a more detailed world map that you can put on the board, ask Ss to come to the board to locate the places in this exercise and their home countries.
3. Have Ss write their own sentences on large pieces of paper or on the blackboard so that you can check them. Or have them work in pairs and dictate their sentences to each other.

EXPANSION

Depending on the home countries of your Ss or their interests, supply a list of countries and have Ss work in groups to determine in which part of the world these countries are found. This might elicit discussion and debate—in particular: Egypt (Middle East or Africa?), Turkey (Europe or Asia?).

Workbook Exs. 2, p. 2
Answers: TE p. 526

ANSWER KEY

Exercise 2

2. The Dominican Republic is in the Caribbean. **3.** Senegal and Nigeria are in Africa. **4.** Honduras and El Salvador are in Central America. **5.** Peru and Ecuador are in South America. **6.** Bangladesh is in Asia. **7.** Israel is in the Middle East. **8.** Canada is in North America. **9.** Italy and Greece are in Europe.

FOCUS 2

1. Have Ss study the chart individually for a few minutes. Be prepared to clarify the meaning of the pronouns: *We* (the speaker is included in the group), *You* (for speaking directly to a group), *They* (for speaking about a group). You can demonstrate this visually by using groups of students in the room. Students will practice this in Exercise 4.
2. Make sure Ss understand *anaphoric reference,* that is, how a subject pronoun is used to refer to a noun or noun phrase in a previous sentence (*Chen is Chinese. He is from Beijing. Carlos and Maria are Mexican. They're* married.). This will prepare them for other instances of anaphoric reference; see, for example, Unit 6, Focus 2 regarding the use of object pronouns as a cohesive device. Make statements about Ss in the class and ask them what the subject pronoun is referring to. For example, *Jose and Maria are South American. They are from Ecuador.* Draw an arrow from "they" to "Jose and Maria."

Exercise 3

This exercise focuses Ss' attention on the meaning of the subject pronouns. The pictures should allow Ss to distinguish between *we, you, they, he, she,* and *you* (singular and plural).

FOCUS 2

Subject Pronouns with *Be*

SUBJECT PRONOUN	VERB *Be*	
I	am	single.
You	are	married.
He She It	is	Brazilian.
We You They	are	from Korea.

Note: Use subject pronouns only after you know the subject.
Chen is Chinese. He is from Beijing.

EXERCISE 3

Read the dialogues. Fill in the blanks with a subject pronoun. The first one has been done for you.

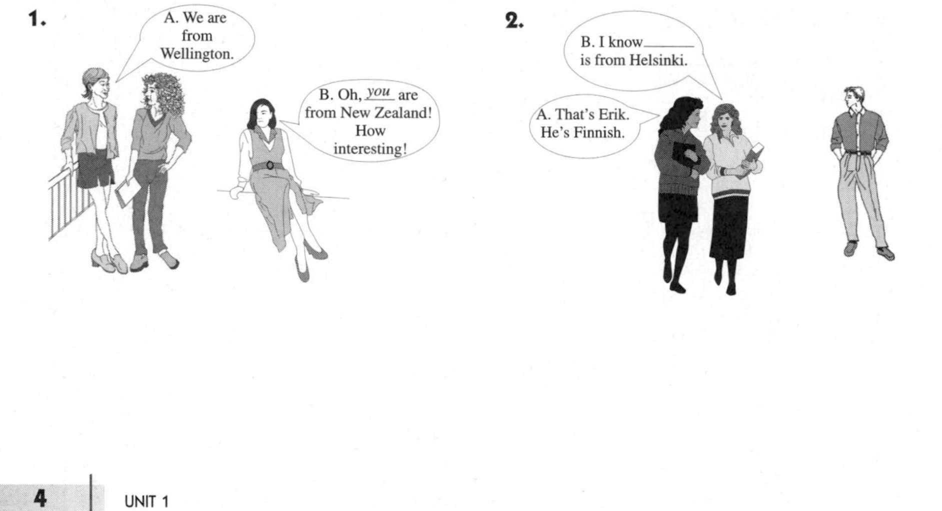

1.
A. We are from Wellington.
B. Oh, *you* are from New Zealand! How interesting!
2.
B. I know_____ is from Helsinki.
A. That's Erik. He's Finnish.

ANSWER KEY

Exercise 3

1. you **2.** He **3.** They **4.** You **5.** She **6.** I

EXERCISE 4

The subject pronouns in the sentences below are not correct. Circle the incorrect pronouns and write the correct sentences in the blanks.

1.	Miyuki and Seung are from Asia.	(You) are Asian.	They are Asian.
2.	John is thirty years old.	She is from Cyprus.	___
3.	You and Hamid are Algerian.	They are from Algiers.	___
4.	Port-au-Prince is in Haiti.	She is the capital city.	___
5.	Clemente and I are from Rome.	They are Italian.	___
6.	Pedro and Miguel are from Puebla.	You are Mexican.	___
7.	Ayelet and Amir are from Tel Aviv.	We are Israeli.	___

EXERCISE 5

Information Gap. Here is a list of students in an English-as-a-Second-Language (ESL) class. Work with a partner. You look at List A on the next page and make a statement about student number 1 on your list. Your partner looks at List B on page A-14 and makes a second statement with a subject pronoun about student number 1.

EXAMPLE: **You say:** Mario is from Peru.
Your partner says: He is Peruvian.

Exercise 4

This exercise addresses problems with anaphoric reference: the subject pronouns do not match the nouns they refer to. Encourage Ss to find the noun phrase in each of the first sentences. Have them correct the subject pronouns. Make sure they understand #3 *You and Hamid = you* (speaker excluded), #5 *Clemente and I = We* (speaker included).

Exercise 5 

This is an Information Gap exercise. Student A has one set of information and Student B has another set of information on page A-14 of the book. Each student has to transmit the information to his/her partner so they can complete the chart. The names are divided into male and female so that Ss know whether to use *he or she.*

1. Demonstrate by having two Ss do the first two items aloud.
2. Go around the room and help Ss if necessary.

ANSWER KEY

Exercise 4

2. He **3.** You **4.** It **5.** We **6.** They **7.** They

Exercise 5

1. Mario is from Peru. He is Peruvian. **2.** Mohammed is Moroccan. He is from Morocco. **3.** Hideki and Yoshi are from Japan. They are Japanese. **4.** Leonardo is Dominican. He is from the Dominican Republic. **5.** Oumar is from Senegal. He is Senegalese. **6.** Lilik is Indonesian. She is from Indonesia. **7.** Krystyna is from Poland. She is Polish. **8.** Liisa and Katja are Finnish. They are from Finland. **9.** Belén is from Spain. She is Spanish. **10.** Margarita and Dalia are Brazilian. They are from Brazil.

List A

Men	Country	Nationality
1. Mario	Peru	
2. Mohammed		Moroccan
3. Hideki and Yoshi	Japan	
4. Leonardo		Dominican
5. Oumar	Senegal	
Women		
6. Lilik		Indonesian
7. Krystyna	Poland	
8. Liisa and Katja		Finnish
9. Belen	Spain	
10. Margarita and Dalia		Brazilian

EXERCISE 6

Make summary statements about the students in the ESL class in Exercise 5. Use the continents/regions and countries below.

▶ **EXAMPLE:** Africa

Two students are from Africa. One is from Morocco and one is from Senegal.

1. Africa

____

2. Asia

____

3. Europe

____

4. South America

____

5. Dominican Republic

____

6. Finland

____

Exercise 6

1. Have Ss write their statements. Encourage group members to correct each other.
2. While the groups complete this exercise, have a pair of Ss put the summary statements on the blackboard. This allows you to work on corrections and have Ss check answers.

Workbook Exs. 3 and 4, pgs. 2-3. Answers: TE p. 526.

ANSWER KEY

Exercise 6

2. Three students are from Asia. Two are from Japan and one is from Indonesia. **3.** Four students are from Europe. One is from Poland and one is from Spain. Two are from Finland. (Note: Poland is actually considered to be part of Central Europe now.). **4.** Three students are from South America. Two are from Brazil and one is from Ecuador. **5.** One student is from the Dominican Republic. **6.** Two students are from Finland.

FOCUS **3**

Contraction with *Be*

SUBJECT PRONOUN + *Be*		*Be* CONTRACTIONS	
I am You are He is She is It is We are You are They are	American.	I'm You're He's She's It's We're You're They're	from the United States.

EXERCISE 7

Think about the people and places in this unit. Match the people and places on the left with the information on the right. Make two statements aloud. Use the name in the first statement and the subject pronoun and *Be* contraction in the second statement.

▶ **EXAMPLE:** **1.** Genya is Russian. 2. She's divorced.

1. Genya	a. Colombia/the capital
2. Japan	b. sisters/Mexican
3. Chen	c. Russian/divorced
4. Fernando and Isabel	d. an island/in the Caribbean
5. Monique	e. Chinese/twenty-five years old
6. Moscow	f. brothers/from Senegal
7. Bogotá	g. Russia/the capital
8. Rosita and Raquel	h. French/from Paris
9. Haiti	i. Colombian/married
10. Oumar and Alioune	j. an island/in the Pacific Ocean

FOCUS 3

Point out the proper position of the apostrophe, as Ss tend to write this as a comma.

SUGGESTION

1. After Ss have studied the chart, ask them to close their books.

2. Write the eight subject pronouns on the board under one column and the forms of the verb *be* (*am, are,* and *is*) under another column in random order. Ask different Ss match the subject pronouns with the correct form of the verb and make sentences.

Exercise 7

1. Have Ss match people and places individually first.

2. Pair Ss up and have them take turns making the first statement using the name, and the second statement using the subject pronoun and *be* contraction.

ANSWER KEY

Exercise 7

2. (j) Japan is an island. It's in the Pacific Ocean. **3.** (e) Chen is Chinese. He's 25 years old. **4.** (i) Fernando and Isabel are Colombian. They're married. **5.** (h) Monique is French. She's from Paris. **6.** (g) Moscow is in Russia. It's the capital. **7.** (a) Bogota is in Colombia. It's the capital. **8.** (b) Rosita and Raquel are sisters. They're Mexican. **9.** (d) Haiti is an island. It's in the Caribbean. **10.** (f) Oumar and Alioune are brothers. They're from Senegal.

Exercise 8

This exercise can be done individually or as pairwork. It has Ss identify the target structure. Point out that the subject can be a person, a place, or an inanimate object.

Exercise 9

1. Ask Ss which famous people they know and what they are famous for. Write useful vocabulary on the board to enable Ss to do the exercise: *a rock/pop star; a political leader; a singer; opera singers; baseball player.*
2. Do this exercise as a whole class so that Ss can share their background knowledge and agree or disagree with the facts.

EXPANSION

You could elicit negative statements (e.g., *Gabriel Garcia Marquez isn't an actor. He's a writer.*), depending on how much your class already knows and how much you feel you can introduce at this point.

Workbook Ex. 5, p. 3.
Answers: TE p. 526

EXERCISE 8

Go back to the Opening Task on page 1. Underline all the singular subjects and the verb *be*. Circle all the plural subjects and the verb *be*.

▶ **EXAMPLE:** My name is Monique.
We're the Mendoza family.

EXERCISE 9

Choose information from Columns A and B that matches each famous person or group of people. Then make two statements.

▶ **EXAMPLE:** Madonna is American. She's a pop singer.

	A	B
Famous People	**Nationality**	**Occupation**
1. Madonna	Tibetan	Opera singers
2. Arnold Schwarzenegger	South African	An actress
3. The Rolling Stones	Canadian	A baseball player
4. Nelson Mandela	Dominican	An actor
5. Dalai Lama	French	A writer
6. Luciano Pavarotti & Cecilia Bartoli	Italian	A country music singer
7. Gabriel Garcia Marquez	British	A pop singer
8. Catherine Deneuve	Colombian	A political leader
9. Sammy Sosa	American	A religious leader
10. Shania Twain	Austrian	Rock singers

ANSWER KEY

Exercise 8

1. My name is Monique. I'm French. I'm from Paris.
2. I'm Chen. I'm Chinese. I'm from Beijing.
3. We're the Mendoza family. This is my wife Maria. I'm Carlos and these are our children Rosita and Raquel. They're twins.
4. I'm Genya. I'm Russian. I'm from Moscow.
5. I'm Fernando and this is Isabel. We are married. We are Colombian. We're from Bogotá.
6. My name is Oumar and this is my brother Alioune. We're from Senegal. Senegal is in West Africa.

Exercise 9

2. Arnold Schwarzenegger is Austrian. He's an actor. **3.** The Rolling Stones are British. They're rock singers. **4.** Mandela is South African. He's a political leader. **5.** The Dali Lama is Tibetan. He's a religious leader. **6.** Pavarotti and Bartoli are Italian. They're opera singers. **7.** Marquez is Colombian. He's a writer. **8.** Deneuve is French. She's an actress. **9.** Sosa is Dominican. He's a baseball player. **10.** Twain is Canadian. She's a country music singer.

FOCUS **4**

Introductions and Greetings

Introductions

EXAMPLES	EXPLANATIONS
(a) Hello. My name's Gustavo. I'm from the Philippines.  (b) Hi! I'm Jennifer Brown. I'm from Florida. Please call me Jenny. 	Introducing yourself
(c) Susan: Hello, John. This is Mario Ortiz. He's from the Philippines. John: Hi, Mario. Nice to meet you. Mario: Nice to meet you too, John. 	Introducing another person
(d) Jeff: Hi, my name is Jeff Jones. I'm from California. What is your name? Alicia: Alicia Torres. Jeff: Where are you from, Alicia? Alicia: I'm from Chile. Jeff: Oh, really? Nice to meet you. 	Meeting someone for the first time

FOCUS 4

SUGGESTIONS

1. To introduce this focus, go around the classroom and introduce yourself to a couple of Ss. Ask Ss what you are doing.
2. Ask Ss to read (a) and (b).
3. Ask Ss to introduce themselves to the person next to them.
4. Follow the same procedure with (c) and (d).
5. Get Ss to role-play introducing themselves and each other.
6. To practice greetings, have Ss cover the right-hand side of the box and read (e), (f), and (g). Elicit the differences in register. Discuss formal and informal greetings. For example, if Ss went for job interviews and used informal language, this would be inappropriate.
7. Point out the use of titles in greetings. Assign Ss roles and have them role-play the greetings. Discuss their performance in terms of correctness and appropriateness.

Greetings

EXAMPLES	EXPLANATIONS
(e) Ms. Chen: Good morning, Mr. Brown. Mr. Brown: Good morning, Ms. Chen. How are you today? Ms. Chen: I'm fine, thank you. How are you? **(f)** Bill: Hello, Lautaro. How's everything? Lautaro: Fine thanks, Bill. And how are you? **(g)** Jake: Hi, Yoshi. How are you doing? Yoshi: O.K., Jake. How about you? Jake: Not bad.	Greetings can be formal or informal (very friendly). Formal ↕ Informal
(h) Hello, Ms. Smith. **(i)** NOT: Hello, Ms. Susan Smith. Hello, Ms. Susan.	Use a title *(Mr., Mrs., Ms., Dr., Professor)* with a family name (last name), not with the full name, not with the first name.

Exercise 10
Encourage Ss to use other vocabulary as well if they can. *This is Yoshi. He's from Japan. He's Japanese. He's from Osaka.* Make sure Ss are audible and comprehensible.

Exercise 11
Have students work individually or in pairs to reconstruct these short interactions. Ask for volunteers to role-play each example in front of the class.

Workbook Exs. 6 & 7, p. 4.
Answers: TE p. 526

EXERCISE 10
Introduce the person next to you to the class.

▶ **EXAMPLE:** This is Yoshi. He's from Japan.

EXERCISE 11
Fill in the blanks in the conversation.

▶ **EXAMPLE:** Susan: I'm Susan Wilson from New York.

Jim: Nice to meet you Susan. My name is Jim. I'm from California.

1. **Fred:** Hello. I'm Fred.

   Phillippe: ______________, Fred. ______________ Phillippe.

2. **Lilik:** Hi! I'm Lilik. ______________ ?
Demos: My name's Demos.
Lilik: ______________ ?
Demos: Greece. ______________ ?
Lilik: I'm from Indonesia.

3. **Michael:** Hi, Gregg. ______________ Jane.
Gregg: Hello, Jane. ______________ ?
Jane: Fine, thanks. ______________ ?
Gregg: Great!

UNIT GOAL REVIEW

Now ask Ss to look at the goals on the opening page of the unit. Help them understand how much they have accomplished in each area. Ask them if they have any questions about what they have learned so far.

ANSWER KEY

Exercise 11

1. Hello/Hi
   I'm/My name is.
2. What's your name?
   Where are you from?
   And you/Where are you from?
3. This is Jane.
   How are you?
   And you/How are you?

USE YOUR ENGLISH

Note: These "purple" pages at the end of each unit contain more open-ended communicative activities designed to get Ss to apply what they have learned in less structured contexts. They can be used at any time during the unit, interspersed with the exercises for variety. For a more complete discussion of how to implement the *Use Your English* activities, see page xxvi of this Teacher's Edition.

Activity 1

Step 1

Put the list of your Ss on the board to help Ss write their summary statements.

Step 2

1. Ss can work individually or in pairs.
2. While Ss are working, have individual Ss write their summary statements on the board or butcher block paper.
3. Ask Ss to help you identify and correct any errors.

VARIATION

Have Ss make pie charts or do percentages to show the make-up of the class. *45% of the students are Asian.*

Activity 2

While Ss are writing, go around and check their work. Or assign this activity as homework.

VARIATION

To get Ss out of their seats, collect all the papers and put them up around the room. Ss then walk around and write the name of the student they think wrote the sentences.

Use Your English

ACTIVITY 1: WRITING

STEP 1 Make a list of all the students in your class. Make a list of the countries they come from and their nationalities.

Names	Countries	Nationalities

STEP 2 Write summary statements about the students in your class with the information from Step 1.

▶ **EXAMPLES:** Two students are Colombian.
Six students are from Asia.

ACTIVITY 2: WRITING/LISTENING

On a piece of paper write three sentences about yourself. Do not write your name on the paper. Give the paper to your teacher. Your teacher reads each paper and the class guesses who the person is.

▶ **EXAMPLE:** I am twenty-two years old. I'm from North Africa. I'm Algerian.

ACTIVITY 3: WRITING/SPEAKING

Work with a partner. Go back to your information card in the Opening Task on page 1. Exchange your information card with your partner. Introduce your partner to the class.

▶ **EXAMPLE:** This is Maria Gomez. She is from Mexico City. She is twenty-five years old. She is married.

ACTIVITY 4: SPEAKING

Role-play with a partner.

1. You are a student. Greet your professor in school.
2. Greet your classmate.
3. Greet your boss at work.
4. Introduce your partner to another student.

ACTIVITY 5: LISTENING

Listen and decide. Three different people greet Mr. Maxwell Forbes, a bank manager, at a job interview. In two of the conversations, the greetings are wrong. Who gets the job? Circle the person who gets the job.

1. Mr. Blake 2. Ms. Robbins 3. Kevin Dobbs

ANSWER KEY

Activity 5
Ms. Robbins gets the job. Mr. Blake is inappropriate because he calls the bank manager by his first name. Kevin Dobbs makes a mistake by saying "Mr." without the last name.

Activity 3
While Ss are introducing their partners, ask the class to take notes on any mistakes they hear. Write the incorrect sentences on the board and have the class correct them.

Activity 4
1. Give Ss time to prepare and correct their introductions before they present them to the class.
2. Ask the class for feedback on the grammatical accuracy as well as on the appropriateness of register (formal/informal). You could include other criteria in this feedback, such as comprehensibility and audibility.

EXPANSION
Create an assessment grid on the board. Elicit from them or give them the criteria above. Then have them assess each other, or assess themselves.

VARIATION
Tape record Ss' role-plays. Note the error types on an assessment sheet and work on correcting them in class or for homework.

Activity 5 
Play textbook audio. The tapescript for this listening appears on p. 544 of this book. Play the tape more than once if necessary.

The test for this unit can be found on pp. 448–449 of this book. The answers can be found on p. 450.

Unit 2

UNIT OVERVIEW

Unit 2 introduces yes/no questions with the verb *be*, negative statements and *be* + adjective.

UNIT GOALS

Each Opening Task is designed to be used inductively and to show you whether students (Ss) can understand and/or use the target structure accurately and appropriately. To maximize this diagnostic potential, do not review the Unit Goals with Ss until after they have completed and reviewed the task. Reviewing the Unit Goals in a deductive fashion first will give the target structure away, thereby undermining the diagnostic function of the task.

OPENING TASK

This **Opening Task** exposes Ss to the target structure without asking them to produce it. Even if they don't understand the yes/no questions at this point, they can still do the matching by using a lexical strategy (focusing on the vocabulary items they recognize) and deriving meaning from the pictures. How Ss do this task will tell you how much they already know.

SETTING UP THE TASK

1. Bring in the classified section of a newspaper to familiarize Ss with these kinds of ads and their various purposes.
2. Teach key vocabulary items such as *dating, employment agency, kitchen, dr. = doctor, body/health* before Ss begin the task. Encourage Ss to guess the meanings of new words in context rather than use their dictionaries.

UNIT 2

THE VERB *BE*

Yes/No Questions, *Be* + Adjective, Negative Statements

UNIT GOALS:

- To ask *yes/no* questions with the verb *be* and give short answers
- To use the verb *be* with adjectives
- To make negative statements and contractions with *be*

OPENING TASK

Asking Personal Questions

STEP 1 Here are some advertisements from the newspaper. Match each advertisement to the correct advertisers on the next page.

Are you single? Are you lonely? Are you ready to meet someone?
Call1-800-555-LOVE

A.

Is English hard for you? It isn't at our school. It's easy and fun!
Enroll now! Call ENG-LISH

B.

Are you sad? Are you nervous? Are you worried? You are not alone. I can help. Call 554-HELP

C.

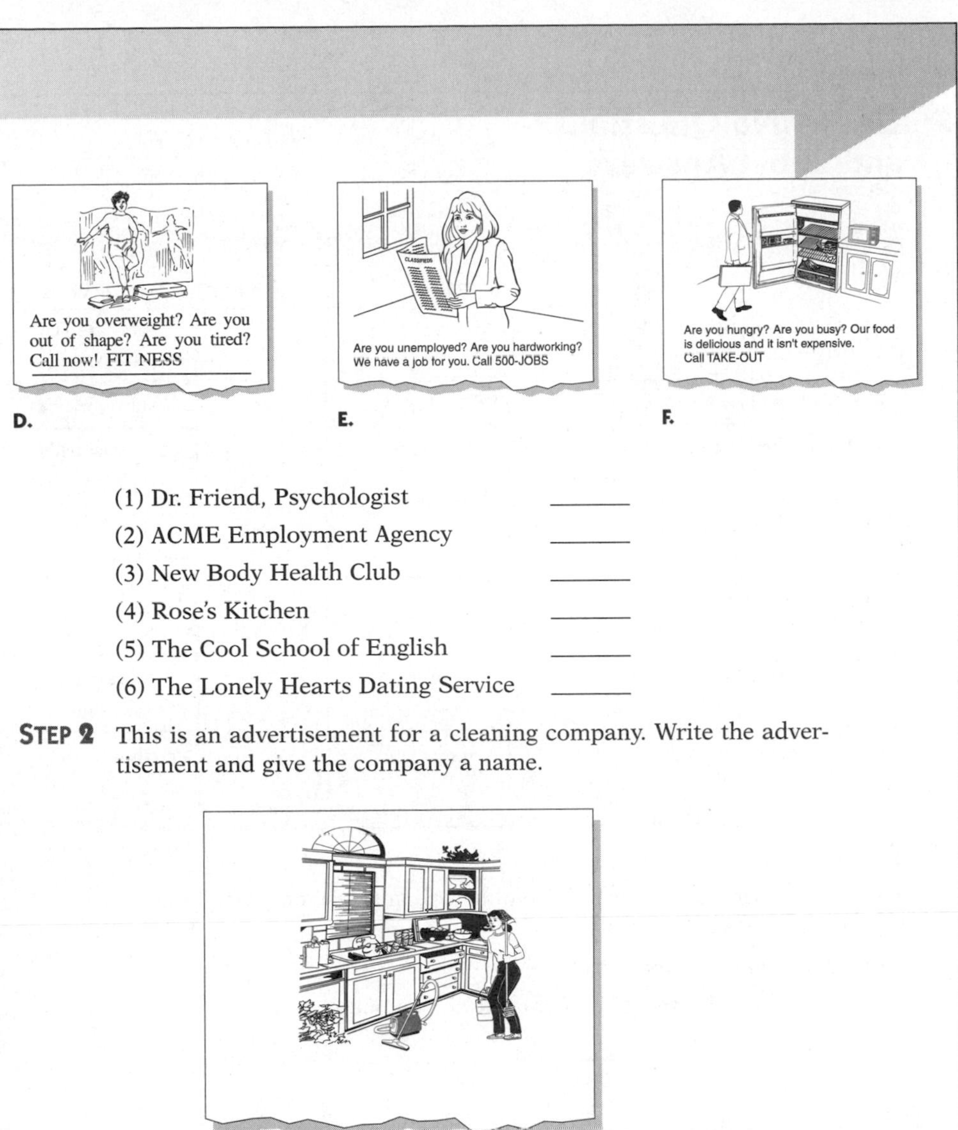

Are you overweight? Are you out of shape? Are you tired? Call now! FIT NESS
Are you unemployed? Are you hardworking? We have a job for you. Call 500-JOBS
Are you hungry? Are you busy? Our food is delicious and it isn't expensive. Call TAKE-OUT
D.
E.
F.
(1) Dr. Friend, Psychologist ______
(2) ACME Employment Agency ______
(3) New Body Health Club ______
(4) Rose's Kitchen ______
(5) The Cool School of English ______
(6) The Lonely Hearts Dating Service ______
STEP 2 This is an advertisement for a cleaning company. Write the advertisement and give the company a name.

CONDUCTING THE TASK

Step 1 

Focus on ad A first with the whole class. Ask Ss to describe the people. *Are they sad? Are they happy? Are they in love?* Have Ss match picture A to the correct advertiser. Then have them complete the task in pairs.

Step 2

Have each pair write an ad for the advertiser represented by this picture.

REVIEWING THE TASK

1. Ask pairs to read the ads aloud and tell which advertiser the ad refers to.

2. Have pairs write their ads on the board. Have the class choose the best advertisement and tell why it's the best. Use the questions in the ads in Step 1 and 2 to introduce the form of yes/no questions when you do Focus 1.

ANSWER KEY

Opening Task

Step 1

1. C **2.** E **3.** D **4.** F **5.** B **6.** A

Step 2

Possible answers:
Is your house messy?
Is your house dirty?
Are you busy and tired?
Call us! The Dustbusters!
We Clean.

FOCUS 1

Both types of negative contractions are presented here so that Ss can practice the form. In Focus 3, the difference in use will be introduced. Point out that there is no negative contraction of *NOT* in *I am not* (b).

SUGGESTIONS:

1. Have Ss read the chart silently. Then ask Ss other questions to see if they can answer correctly: *Are you hungry? Is Maria from Guatemala? Is English easy? Are you and your partner single? Are English grammar rules difficult?*

Exercise 1

As a follow-up, ask Ss questions about their partners—*"Is your partner unhappy about his/her pronunciation?" "Is English hard for your partner?"*

FOCUS **1**

Be: *Yes/No* Questions and Short Answers

YES/NO QUESTIONS	SHORT ANSWERS			
	Affirmative		Negative Contractions	
(a) Am I hardworking?	Yes,	you are.	No,	you aren't. you're not.
(b) Are you nervous?		I am.		I'm not.
(c) Is he/she lonely?		he/she is.		he/she isn't. he's/she's not.
(d) Is English difficult?		it is.		it isn't. it's not.
(e) Are we out of shape?		you are.		you aren't. you're not.
(f) Are you single?		we are.		we aren't. we're not.
(g) Are verbs difficult?		they are.		they aren't. they're not.

EXERCISE 1

Ask your partner *yes/no* questions from the Opening Task on pages 14 and 15. Use short answers and contractions.

EXAMPLE: **You:** Are you single?

Your Partner: Yes, I am. **OR** No, I'm not.

EXERCISE 2
Read the conversations. Fill in the blanks with *yes/no* questions or short answers.

1. **A:** Hello, this is the New Body Health Club.
   B: Hello, ________________ you open on Sundays?
   A: Yes, ________________ ________________. We're open from seven in the morning until ten at night.
2. **Mitch:** Hello, my name is Mitch Brown. ________________ you Karen Jones?
   Karen: Yes, ________________ ________________.
   Mitch: I got your telephone number from the Lonely Hearts Dating Service. How are you, Karen?
   Karen: Fine, thanks. And you?
   Mitch: Not bad, thanks. ________________ ________________ free tonight?
   Karen: No, I'm sorry, ________________ ________________. How about tomorrow?
   Mitch: Great!
3. **A:** Hello, is this Dr. Friend's office?
   B: Yes, ________________ ________________.
   A: ________________ Dr. Friend busy? I need to speak to him.
   B: Just a minute, please.
4. **Secretary:** Cool School of English. May I help you?
   Hui Chen: Yes, I'd like some information about your classes, please.
   Secretary: What would you like to know?
   Hui Chen: ________________ the classes big?
   Secretary: No, ________________ ________________. We have only ten students in a class.
   Hui Chen: ________________ the teachers good?
   Secretary: Yes, ________________ ________________. All the teachers are excellent.
   Hui Chen: ________________ the tuition expensive?
   Secretary: No, ________________ ________________. It's only $800 for ten weeks.
   Hui Chen: O.K. Thank you very much.
   Secretary: You're welcome. Goodbye.

Exercise 2 
Pairs who finish early can put the correct answers on the board.

EXPANSION
Have Ss role-play these dialogues. Work on grammar and pronunciation (including stress and intonation).

Workbook Exs. 1 & 2, p. 5.
Answers: TE p. 526.

ANSWER KEY

Exercise 2
1. B: are A: we are **2.** Are; I am; are you; I'm not **3.** It is; Is **4.** Are; they aren't, Are, they are; Is; it isn't/it's not

FOCUS 2

1. Ask Ss to read the examples silently.

2. Elicit or provide more examples of *be* + adjective and write them on the board. For example: *The students are intelligent. The book is interesting.*
3. Point out that adjectives do not take "s" in the plural.

Exercise 3

Have Ss call out the adjectives they circled. Write them on butcher block paper or on the board so you can keep a list of adjectives as they come up.

SUGGESTION

Encourage Ss to keep an adjective list in their notebooks. Help them organize this list in a way that will facilitate memorization and recall: adjectives about people, pairs of opposite adjectives, etc.

Exercise 4 

This is an information gap exercise. Demonstrate the example provided with a student. Make sure Ss don't look at each other's set of pictures. Check answers with the whole class.

SUGGESTION

Start an index card file by writing an adjective on one side of the card and its opposite on the other side. Use these cards as quick warm-ups at the beginning of class.

Workbook Exs. 3 & 4, pp. 6-8.
Answers: TE p. 526.

FOCUS 2

Be + Adjective

EXAMPLES	EXPLANATIONS
(a) Dr. Friend is **busy**. (b) The health club is **open**. (c) Verbs are **difficult**.	An adjective describes a person, place, or thing. Adjectives can come after the verb *be*.
(d) They are **excellent**. (e) NOT: They are excellents.	Do not put "s" on the adjective when the subject is plural (more than one).
(f) The classes are **very good**.	*Very* makes the adjective stronger. *Very* can come before most adjectives.

EXERCISE 3

Go back to the Opening Task on pages 14 and 15 and circle all the adjectives.

▶ **EXAMPLE:** Are you (single)? Are you (lonely)?

EXERCISE 4

Information Gap. Work with a partner. You have two pictures: A and B. Your partner has one picture on page A-15. Ask your partner a question about his/her picture using the adjective in parentheses. Which picture does your partner have: A or B? You circle the correct picture.

▶ **EXAMPLE:** You look at pictures A and B. You look at the adjective.

Picture A **Picture B** **(young)**

You say: Is he young?
Your partner says: No, he isn't. He's old.
You circle picture A.

ANSWER KEY

Exercise 3
A. single; lonely; ready **B.** hard; easy; fun **C.** sad; nervous; worried; alone **D.** overweight; out of shape; tired **E.** unemployed; hardworking **F.** busy; hungry; delicious; expensive.

	Picture A	Picture B	Adjective
2.			(thin)
3.			(weak)
4.			(neat)
5.			(nervous)
6.			(healthy)
7.			(poor)
8.			(serious)
9.			(lazy)
10.			(sad)

Opposites

funny	sick	hardworking	happy	rich	calm
old ✓	strong	overweight	tall	messy	

The Verb *Be*: *Yes/No* Questions, *Be* + Adjective, Negative Statement 19

ANSWER KEY

Exercise 4

2. Is he thin? No, he isn't. He's overweight.
3. Is she weak? No, she isn't. She's strong.
4. Is she neat? No, she isn't. She's messy.
5. Is he nervous? Yes, he is. **6.** Is she healthy? No, she isn't. She's sick. **7.** Is he poor? Yes, he is. **8.** Is he serious? No, he isn't. He's funny. **9.** Is she lazy? No, she isn't. She's hardworking. **10.** Is he sad? No, he isn't. He's happy.

Exercise 5

Have Ss do this exercise individually and then check answers with a partner.

Exercise 6 

This is an information gap exercise in which Ss must exchange information in order to complete their charts. Exercise 6 will prepare Ss for Activity 4.

SUGGESTIONS

1. Have Ss check their answers by looking at their partners' charts.
2. With the whole class, summarize by asking Ss to describe Cindy and Gloria.

EXERCISE 5

Mark Heller is single and lonely. He wants a girlfriend. He puts this advertisement in the newspaper. Fill in the blanks with *am* or *are*. Use contractions where possible.

1) I'm/I am 28 years old. (2) ________ 6′2″ tall. (3) ________ single. (4) ________ handsome and athletic. (5) ________ romantic. (6) ________ (negative) shy. (7) ________ you under 30? (8) ________ you tall? (9) ________ you outgoing? (10) ________ ready for a serious relationship? Then call me: (718) 555-7954.

EXERCISE 6

Information Gap. Two women answer Mark's advertisement. Work with a partner. You have information about Cindy in Chart A and your partner has information about Shelly in Chart B on page A-16. Ask each other *yes/no* questions to find the information that you do not have in your chart. Then put a check in the correct place.

EXAMPLE: **You:** Is Shelly tall?
Your Partner: Yes, she is.
Your Partner: Is Cindy tall?
You: No, she isn't.

Chart A

	CINDY 24 years old	**SHELLY** 30 years old
1. Height		
tall		
average height		
short	✓	
2. Weight		
thin	✓	
average weight		
heavy		

ANSWER KEY

Exercise 5
2. I am/I'm **3.** I am/I'm **4.** I am/I'm
5. I am/I'm **6.** I am not/I'm not **7.** Are
8. Are **9.** Are **10.** Are

3. Personality		
shy		
friendly	✓	
quiet		
talkative	✓	
neat		
messy	✓	
funny	✓	
serious		
nervous	✓	
calm		

EXERCISE 7

Ask a partner questions with the adjectives below.

talkative	funny	neat	lazy	messy
energetic	calm	strong	serious	shy

▶ **EXAMPLE:** **You:** Are you talkative?

Your Partner: Yes, I am. **OR** No, I'm not.

EXERCISE 8

What do you **like** about your partner? Write five statements.

▶ **EXAMPLE:** My partner is funny. He's energetic.

____

____

____

____

____

Exercise 7

Answers will vary.

SUGGESTIONS

1. Encourage Ss to ask questions of their own with other adjectives from this unit.
2. Have Ss share what they learned about their partner with the class.

Exercise 8

Exercises like this are essential for creating a cohesive group and a positive working atmosphere.
Answers will vary.

SUGGESTION

1. Have Ss write individually.
2. Pick 3 Ss to write their statements on the board. Encourage the class to check for errors.

FOCUS 3

Both the contraction of the subject and *be* and the contraction of *be* + *not* are presented here again. There is slight difference in use between the two: when the verb *be* is contracted and followed by *not* as a full word, it makes a stronger negative that is used to contradict or correct someone. It is important even for lower level Ss to become aware of use differences.

1. Have Ss read the chart silently.
2. Make sure Ss understand the point about using the full form *"not"* to correct or contradict. Give examples using yourself or your Ss. Say about yourself: *I am very old/short.* Ss say: *No, you're not. You're very young/tall.* Say about Ss: *He's from Ecuador.* Ss say: *No, he's not. He's from Chile.*

Exercise 9 

This exercise clearly illustrates the emphatic negative with *not.* Make sure Ss use emphatic intonation when correcting their partners. *His last name's NOT Yu-ho. It's Oh.*

SUGGESTION

Rewrite these cards in careless handwriting so that the information is not so clear. For example, on card #1, write 23 so that it could be read as 25, and so on.

FOCUS **3**

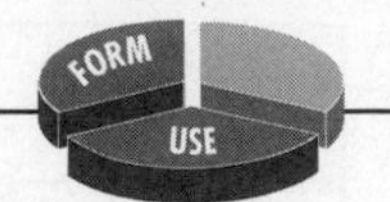

▶ *Be*: Negative Statements and Contractions

NEGATIVE STATEMENT	CONTRACTION OF [SUBJECT + *BE*] + NOT	CONTRACTION OF [*BE* + *NOT*]
I am not shy.	I'm not shy.	*
You are not old.	You're not old.	You aren't old.
He / She / It } is not ready.	He's / She's / It's } not ready.	He / She / It } isn't ready.
We / You / They } are not nervous.	We're / You're / They're } not nervous.	We / You / They } aren't nervous.

Note: The contraction of [subject + *be*] followed by *not* (*he's not*) makes a negative statement stronger than a negative contraction of [*be* + not] (*he isn't*).

EXERCISE 9

Read the statements below each ID (identification) card. If the information is correct, say "That's right." If the information is not correct, make a negative statement with the *be* contraction + *not* and a correct affirmative statement.

▶ **EXAMPLE:** 1. His last name is Yu-ho.
His last name's not Yu-ho.
It's Oh.

Last Name:	Oh
First Name:	Yu-ho
Country:	Taiwan
Nationality:	Taiwanese
Age:	23
Marital Status:	single

1. His last name is Yu-ho.
2. He is Korean.
3. He's twenty-five.
4. He's single.

Last Name:	Ryperman
First Name:	Aline
Country:	Holland
Nationality:	Dutch
Age:	32
Marital Status:	married

5. Her first name is Alice.
6. She's from Germany.
7. She is Dutch.
8. She's fifty-two.

ANSWER KEY

Exercise 9
2. He's not Korean. He's Taiwanese. **3.** He's not 25. He's 23. **4.** That's right **5.** Her first name's not Alice. It's Aline. **6.** She's not from Germany. She's from Holland. **7.** That's right. **8.** She's not 52. She's 32. **9.** His first name's not Mafegna. It's Abiy. His last name is Mafegna. **10.** He's not Indian. He's Ethiopian. **11.** That's right. **12.** He's not married. He's single. **13.** Jehad's not Jordanian. He's Lebanese. **14.** He's not 29. He's 27. **15.** That's right.

Last Name:	Mafegna
First Name:	Abiy
Country:	Ethiopia
Nationality:	Ethiopian
Age:	30
Marital Status:	single

Last Name:	Shram
First Name:	Jehad
Country:	Lebanon
Nationality:	Lebanese
Age:	27
Marital Status:	single

9. His first name is Mafegna.
10. He's Indian.
11. He's thirty.
12. He's married.
13. Jehad is Jordanian.
14. He is twenty-nine.
15. He's single.

EXERCISE 10

Complete each dialogue with an affirmative or a negative statement and an adjective from the list below.

Adjectives:					
delicious	smart	ugly	beautiful	selfish	boring

1. **Ann:** I'm short. I (a) ________________ fat.
I (b) ________________ ugly.
Marilyn: No, you (c) ________________.
You (d) ________________, Ann!

2. **Woman:** This dinner is terrible! I'm sorry.
Guest: No, it (a) ________________.
It's (b) ________________!

3. **Mike:** Sam, I (a) ________________ nervous about this test. I (b) ________________ stupid, Sam!
Sam: No, you (c) ________________, Mike. You (d) ________________! Your average is 98!

Exercise 10

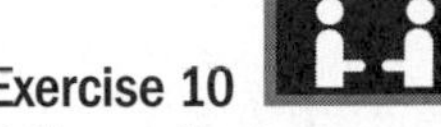

Both negative forms can be used here, though *"not"* is preferable.

1. Do the first one with the class to make sure they know how to work.
2. Have them perform the dialogues in front of the class with a partner.
3. Discuss grammar and pronunciation, stress/intonation, comprehensibility, and audibility.

Workbook Exs. 5 & 6, p. 8.
Answers: TE p. 526.

4. 

Sally: You know Jill, I'm in love with Jack. He (a) ________________ exciting and generous.

Jill: Exciting and generous??? No, he (b) ________________. He (c) ________________ and (d) ________________.

5. **Salesperson:** That dress is perfect on you.

Customer: Perfect? Oh no, it (a) ________________. It (b) ________________.

UNIT GOAL REVIEW

Now ask Ss to look at the goals on the opening page of the unit. Help them understand how much they have accomplished in each area. Ask them if they have any questions about what they have learned so far.

ANSWER KEY

Exercise 10

1. a. I'm/I am
   b. I'm/I am
   c. You're not/You aren't
   d. You're beautiful/You are beautiful.
2. a. it's not/it isn't
   b. It's delicious!
3. a. I am/I'm
   b. I am/I'm
   c. you're not/you aren't
   d. You're smart!/You are smart!
4. a. He is/He's
   b. he's not/he isn't.
   c. he's boring
   d. and (he's) selfish
5. a. it is not/it's not/it isn't
   b. It's ugly.

Use Your English

ACTIVITY 1: SPEAKING/WRITING

Work with a partner. Make true statements with the subjects and adjectives below. Use the affirmative or negative form of the verb *be*. The pair with the most correct sentences wins.

▶ **EXAMPLE:** The United States is big.

SUBJECT	BE	ADJECTIVE	
My country		happy	difficult
I		single	rich
My classmates		tall	poor
The President		young	lonely
The United States		old	strong
My friends		beautiful	small
My father		smart	easy
English		big	powerful
My sister/brother		important	intelligent
		healthy	friendly

USE YOUR ENGLISH

Note: These "purple" pages at the end of each unit contain more open-ended communicative activities designed to get Ss to apply what they have learned in less-structured contexts. They can be used at any time during the unit, interspersed with the exercises for variety. For a more complete discussion of how to implement the *Use Your English* activities, see page xxvi of this Teacher's Edition.

Activity 1

SUGGESTIONS

1. Set a time limit here (20 minutes).
2. Have pairs write sentences on butcher block paper so you can see how many sentences each pair wrote. Determine the winners. Point out that the subject "the United States" is singular and requires the singular form of the verb *be.*
3. Encourage Ss to use other adjectives if they can.

Activity 2

1. Have Ss check column A individually.

2. As Ss ask each other questions, offer help as needed.
3. If you feel Ss are ready, you can introduce *and* and *but* and perhaps *both* so Ss can say, *We are both shy. My partner is funny, but I'm serious.*
4. Have pairs present their similarities and differences to the class.

ACTIVITY 2: SPEAKING/WRITING

STEP 1 Check all the adjectives that describe you.

Adjective	Column A: You	Column B: Your Partner
shy		
quiet		
talkative		
romantic		
practical		
athletic		
lazy		
healthy		
funny		
friendly		
serious		
messy		
neat		

STEP 2 Ask your partner *yes/no* questions with the adjectives in the box. Check the adjectives in Column B.

▶ **EXAMPLE:** **You ask:** Are you shy?
Your partner answers: Yes, I am. **OR** No, I'm not.

STEP 3 Write three ways you and your partner are similar and three ways you are different.

▶ **EXAMPLE:**

Similar	Different
1. We are both athletic.	1. My partner is romantic. I'm practical.
2. We are both healthy.	2. He's serious. I'm funny.
________	________
________	________
________	________

ACTIVITY 3: WRITING

Write your own personal advertisement for the newspaper or write one for a friend who is single.

▶ **EXAMPLE:** My name is ____________________

I'm ____________________ (nationality).

I'm ____________________ years old.

I'm ____________________ (adjective).

I'm ____________________ (adjective).

And I'm ____________________ (adjective).

Are you ____________________ (adjective)?

Are you ____________________ (adjective)?

PLEASE CALL ME!

ACTIVITY 4: SPEAKING

Look at your answers to Exercise 6. Who is the best woman for Mark? Discuss your reasons.

ACTIVITY 5: LISTENING/ SPEAKING

STEP 1 Consuela is at the Cool School of English to register for classes. Listen to the conversation and look at the questions below. Check Yes or No.

	Yes	No
1. Is Consuela a new student?		
2. Is Consuela an intermediate-level student?		
3. Is Consuela interested in morning classes?		

STEP 2 With a partner, ask and answer the questions. If the answer is no, make a true statement.

STEP 3 Role-play the conversation.

Activity 3

Ss can refer to Exercise 5 if they need help.

SUGGESTION

Collect all the personal ads and create a classified ad column, but leave the name of the student blank. Bring the ad column back to class. Have Ss read the ads and fill in the missing names, or choose the person they would like to date (or become friends with/get to know)!

VARIATION

Give your class's ads to another class and have the other Ss respond in writing. Or, arrange to have the two classes meet and pair up the Ss who were interested in each other. Let them role-play telephone calls to each other. Decide on criteria for evaluating those conversations.

Activity 4

Have Ss work in groups of 3 or 4 to find the best woman for Mark. Have a spokesperson from each group explain the group's decision to the class. If other groups disagree, have them express their opinions using negative contractions.

Activity 5

Play textbook audio. The tapescript for this listening appears on p. 544 of this book.

SUGGESTION

Before Step 3, play the tape several more times and have Ss concentrate on pronunciation and intonation.

The test for this unit can be found on pp. 451–452 of this book. The answers can be found on p. 453.

ANSWER KEY

Activity 5

Step 1: **1.** Yes **2.** No **3.** Yes

Unit 3

UNIT OVERVIEW

Students (Ss) are introduced to *Wh*- question words and prepositions of location in Unit 3. In addition, Ss learn how to talk about the weather and the time.

UNIT GOALS

Each Opening Task is designed to be used inductively and to show you whether Ss can understand and/or use the target structure accurately and appropriately. To maximize this diagnostic potential of the Opening Task, do not review the Unit Goals with Ss until after they have completed and reviewed the task. Reviewing the Unit Goals in a deductive fashion first will give the target structure away, thereby undermining the diagnostic function of the task.

OPENING TASK

The **Opening Task** challenges Ss to understand the target structures.

For this particular task, as in Units 1 and 2, Ss can use lexical clues and the four photos to do the matching and guess the meanings of the *wh*-words. By observing how Ss perform the task, you will see if they have prior knowledge of the target structures.

SETTING UP THE TASK

1. Elicit Ss' background knowledge by using the world map on page 3 or a large map placed in the front of the room. Have Ss in groups identify the photographs and the countries they represent.

UNIT 3

THE VERB *BE*

Wh-Question Words, *It* with Time and Weather, and Prepositions of Location

UNIT GOALS:

- To ask *Wh*-questions with the verb *be*
- To use *it* to talk about the weather and the time
- To use prepositions of location

OPENING TASK

Test Your World Knowledge

The Pyramids of Egypt

The Himalayas

The Kremlin

Pope John Paul II

STEP 1 Match the questions with the answers.

Questions	Answers
1. Who is the head of the Catholic Church? →	**a.** It's a river.
2. Where is the Kremlin?	**b.** the Pope
3. What's the Amazon?	**c.** It's 12:00 noon.
4. How is the weather in Argentina in June?	**d.** about 4,700 years old
5. Where are the Himalayas?	**e.** It's between Mexico and South America.
6. When is Thanksgiving in the United States?	**f.** It's cold.
7. It's 9 A.M.* in California. What time is it in Boston?	**g.** North America, South America, Africa, Asia, Australia, Europe, and Antarctica
8. How old are the Pyramids in Egypt?	**h.** because it is Independence Day
9. Where is Central America?	**i.** the last Thursday in November
10. Why is July 4th special in the United States?	**j.** It's in the Czech Republic, on the Vultava River.
11. What are the names of the seven continents?	**k.** in Moscow
12. Where is Prague?	**l.** in India, Nepal, and Tibet

*A.M.: in the morning

STEP 2 Make up two questions of your own. Ask your classmates the questions.

ANSWER KEY

Opening Task
2. k 3. a 4. f 5. l 6. i 7. c
8. d 9. e 10. h 11. g 12. j

CONDUCTING THE TASK

Step 1  

Allow Ss to pool their background knowledge for this task, working in pairs or groups of three.

VARIATION

To get Ss out of their seats, put all questions and answers on index cards. Give one card to each student. Have each student find his/her match. By asking the *wh*-questions. This could also be done in two teams.

Step 2

This step allows Ss to show off a bit of their own knowledge, and allows you to see whether they know how to make *wh*-questions. Have Ss work individually or in pairs and write additional questions. Walk around the room monitoring.

REVIEWING THE TASK

1. Have pairs call out their answers. Ask Ss to locate the places on the world map.
2. Have pairs put their questions on the board. Make this into a game with Ss answering the questions. Use their questions later when you introduce the form of *wh*-questions.

FOCUS 1

1. Have Ss study the chart.
2. Provide other examples of *wh* questions: *What is Peru? (a country); Where is California? (in the U.S.); How is the weather in your country at this time of year?; When is Independence Day in your country?; What time is it now?; Why are you here?*

FOCUS **1**

Wh-Question Words with Be

Some *wh*-question words are: *what, where, who, when, how, what time, how old,* and *why.* Use *Wh*-question words to ask for specific information.

QUESTION WORD	*BE*	SUBJECT	ANSWER	MEANING
What	is 's	the Amazon?	a river	THING
Where	are	the Himalayas?	in India, Nepal, and Tibet	PLACE
Who	is 's	the head of the Catholic Church?	the Pope	PEOPLE
How	is 's	the weather in Argentina in June?	It's cold.	CONDITIONS
When	is 's	Thanksgiving in the United States?	the last Thursday in November	TIME
What time	is	it in New York?	It's 12:00.	TIME ON A CLOCK
How old	are	the Pyramids in Egypt?	about 4,700 years old	AGE
Why	is 's	July 4th special in the United States?	because it is Independence Day	REASON

Exercise 1

Have Ss do this individually. They can check their answers with a partner, or with the class.

EXERCISE 1

Fill in the blanks with one of these *wh*-question words: *what, where, how, who, when, how old, what time,* and *why.*

Questions	**Answers**
1. How old is the Great Wall of China?	about 2,200 years old

2. _______________ are the authors of *Grammar Dimensions, Book I*? — Victoria Badalamenti and Carolyn Henner Stanchina
3. _______________ is Morocco? — in Africa
4. _______________ is the weather in the summer in Washington, D.C.? — It's hot.
5. _______________ is the capital of Belgium? — Brussels
6. _______________ is the first day of summer? — June 21st
7. It's 10 A.M.* in Boston. _______________ is it in Barcelona? — It's 4:00 P.M.*
8. _______________ is Independence Day in France? — July 14th
9. _______________ are you in this class? — to learn English
10. _______________ are the Nile and the Mississippi? — rivers

*A.M. = morning *P.M. = afternoon, evening, night

EXERCISE 2

Match the question in Column A to the answer in Column B. Write the letter in the blank on the left.

	Column A	Column B
d	1. What's your name?	a. October 17th.
______	2. Where are you from?	b. I'm Turkish.
______	3. What is the capital of your country?	c. To study English.
______	4. What's your nationality?	d. Mehmet.
______	5. How old are you?	e. It's Ankara.
______	6. When's your birthday?	f. I'm twenty-five.
______	7. Why are you here?	g. Fine, thanks.
______	8. How are you today?	h. Istanbul.

Exercise 2

VARIATION

Ss can do this exercise in two teams. Divide the class in half—one team asks the question; the other answers. Point out that in some cultures certain questions are not considered polite (for example, #5) and that Ss must be careful whom they ask this question to.

ANSWER KEY

Exercise 1

2. Who 3. Where 4. How
5. What 6. When/What 7. What time
8. When 9. Why 10. What

Exercise 2

2. h 3. e
4. b 5. f
6. a 7. c 8. g

Exercise 3 

SUGGESTION

Have 2 or 3 pairs role-play this conversation for the class.

EXPANSION

1. Have Ss re-create situations where they would want to start conversations (for example: on an airplane, at a party). Give them time to write new conversations. Go around the room to assist them.
2. Let them perform these new conversations for the class. Evaluate performances in terms of correctness and appropriateness.

Exercise 4

Answers will vary. Ss can work individually or in pairs. Walk around and help when necessary.

VARIATION

Make this exercise into a class activity by having Ss work in teams. One team asks the other team a *who* question. If the group answers correctly, they get five points. The object is for the teams to ask difficult questions that the others can't answer easily.

Workbook Ex. 1, p. 10.
Answers: TE p. 527.

Now choose two of these questions. Memorize them. Go around the room and ask five other people your questions. They ask you their questions.

EXERCISE 3

Starting a Conversation at a Bus Stop: Write *wh*-questions in the blanks.

Carlos: Excuse me, (1) ______________ please?
Maria: It's 10:15.
Carlos: Thank you. (2)______________?
Maria: Maria (3) ______________?
Carlos: My name is Carlos.
Maria: (4) ______________?
Carlos: I'm from Mexico.
Maria: (5) ______________ your hometown?
Carlos: Mexico City.
Maria: (6) ______________ in Mexico at this time of year?
Carlos: It's warm and sunny in Mexico now.
Maria: (7) ______________?
Carlos: I'm here to study English. (8) ______________ my English?
Maria: Your English is not bad.
Carlos: Thank you.
Maria: Here's the bus.
Carlos: O.K. Bye!
Maria: Bye! Good Luck!

EXERCISE 4

Write five questions about students in the class with the question word *who*. Then ask your partner the questions.

▶ **EXAMPLES:** *Who's from Asia?*
Who is twenty-five years old?
Who's tall?

ANSWER KEY

Exercise 3

1. What time is it?
2. What's your name?
3. What's your name?
4. Where are you from?
5. What's your home town?
6. How's the weather?
7. Why are you here?
8. How's my English?

FOCUS **2**

How to Ask Questions about English

When you need to ask about a word in English, you say:

(a) **What** is the meaning of *crowded?*

(b) **What** is the spelling of *crowded?*

(c) **What** is the pronunciation of *c-r-o-w-d-e-d?*

EXERCISE 5

Read the paragraph below about Vancouver. Underline the words you don't know or can't pronounce. Ask your teacher or classmates questions.

▶ **EXAMPLE:** What is the meaning of crowded?

Vancouver is a city in Canada. It's on the Pacific coast. The city is magnificent. It is clean and open. It isn't crowded. Almost three-quarters of the population are of British ancestry. Other ethnic groups are the Chinese, French, Japanese, and East Indians. As a result, the food in Vancouver is varied and delicious. It is a wonderful place for a vacation.

FOCUS **3**

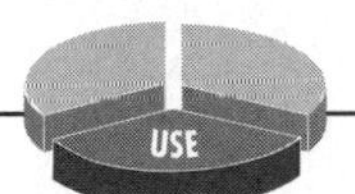

Using *It* to Talk about the Weather

QUESTIONS	ANSWERS		
How's the weather in Montreal?	**It's** sunny **It's** hot	in the	summer.
	It's cold **It's** snowy		winter.
	It's cloudy **It's** rainy		spring.
	It's windy **It's** cool		fall.
What's the temperature today?	**It's** 77 degrees Fahrenheit/25 degrees Celsius.		

FOCUS 2

This is the first use box on communication strategies in the book. Its purpose is to teach Ss how to appeal to other speakers in order to get information about English. Although these may not be the most idiomatic expressions for asking about English (see unit 9 on simple present questions), it is important that Ss begin to learn strategies as early as possible. Encourage Ss to use these strategies in other activities as well. Put these questions up at the front of the room so you can point to them when Ss need to use them.

Exercise 5

Answers may vary. Start Ss off by looking at the first two sentences in the paragraph. Encourage them to ask questions. Then have Ss work in pairs. Check as a whole class.

Workbook Ex. 2, pp. 11–13.
Answers: TE p. 527.

FOCUS 3

1. Ask Ss about the weather in the place where they are presently living.

2. Whatever expressions Ss call out should be written on the board.
3. Have Ss read the chart.
4. Ask additional questions about the weather in Ss' home countries during different seasons.
5. Have Ss ask each other questions about weather.

SUGGESTION

To convert Celsius to Fahrenheit, use the formula: $9/5 \times$ Celsius $+ 32$. Familiarize Ss with the American system of measurement. This is a good opportunity to tell Ss that normal body temperature is approximately 98.6 degrees Fahrenheit, and not 37 degrees! This could be comforting if they had to take their temperature!

Exercise 6 

This is an information gap exercise. Have Ss do this sitting back to back, with each student looking at either Map A or Map B. Make sure Ss take turns. Afterwards, ask Ss to look at their partner's map to check the information they wrote down.

EXPANSION

1. Give Ss a map of the U.S. and have them create their own weather map so they can get further practice using these questions.
2. Bring in taped weather reports and have Ss listen selectively to see if they can recognize any of the weather terminology. (Videotapes are always easier for Ss to understand because of the visual support. To focus purely on auditory comprehension, have Ss listen with their eyes closed or their backs to the screen, and show the video later.)

Workbook Exs. 3 & 4, p. 13–14.
Answers: TE p. 527.

EXERCISE 6

Information Gap. Work with a partner. You look at Map A and your partner looks at Map B (on page A-17). You have some information about the weather in the different cities on Map A. Your partner has different information on Map B. Ask each other questions to find out the missing information. Take turns asking questions.

MAP A

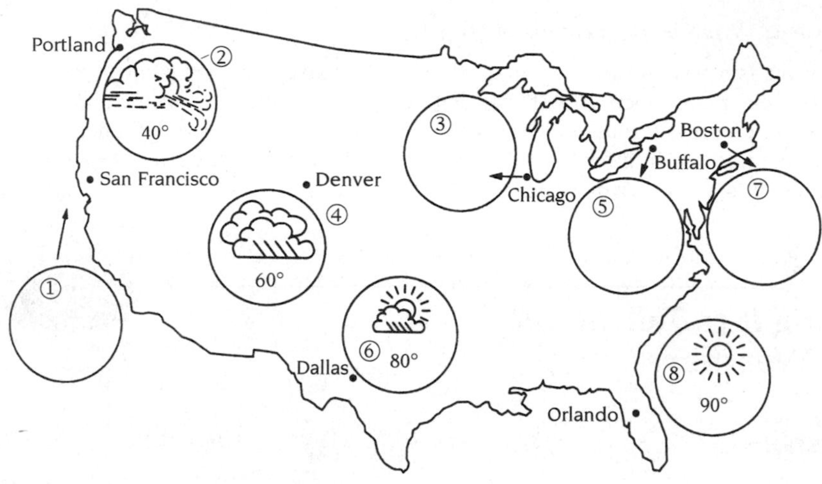

▶ **EXAMPLE:** **You:** ① How's the weather in San Francisco today?
Your Partner: It's sunny.
You: What's the temperature?
Your Partner: It's 65 degrees.

FOCUS **4**

Using *It* to Talk about Time

WHAT TIME IS IT?

3:00	**It's** three o'clock. **It's** three.	
3:05	**It's** five after three.	
3:15	**It's** three-fifteen. **It's** a quarter past three. **It's** a quarter after three.	
3:30	**It's** three-thirty. **It's** half past three.	
3:45	**It's** three forty-five. **It's** a quarter to four.	

FOCUS 4

1. Ask Ss to cover the text in the focus box and see if they can tell the time by looking at the clocks.
2. Have them uncover the text. Go through the various ways to state the time.
3. Have Ss practice telling the time with their partners. You can provide additional clock faces or draw them on the board.

WHAT TIME IS IT?

3:50	**It's** three-fifty. **It's** ten to four.	
12:00	**It's** twelve o'clock. **It's** noon. **It's** midnight.	

Exercise 7 

Have a pair of Ss do this exercise at the blackboard. The rest of the class can use their clocks to check their answers.

EXERCISE 7

Information Gap. Work with a partner. You look at the times on Chart B on page A-17. Say the time in different ways. Your partner draws the time on the clocks below.

▶ **EXAMPLE:** **You:** 1. (6:30) It's six thirty. It's half past six.

Your partner: 

Chart A

1. 
2. 
3. 
4. 
5. 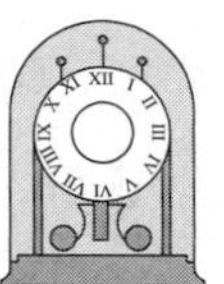
6. 
7. 
8. 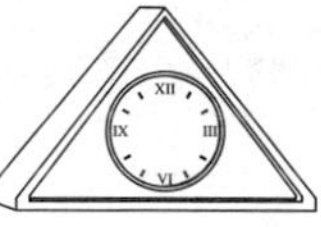

ANSWER KEY

Exercise 7

1. It's eleven thirty. It's half past eleven. **2.** It's eight fifteen. It's a quarter after/past eight. **3.** It's seven thirty-five. It's twenty-five to eight. **4.** It's nine forty-five. It's a quarter to ten. **5.** It's one fifty-five. It's five to 2. **6.** It's three-ten. It's ten after/past three. **7.** It's two-forty. It's twenty to three. **8.** It's five-twenty. It's twenty past/after five.

EXERCISE 8

Look at the map of the time zones in the United States. Ask and answer the questions.

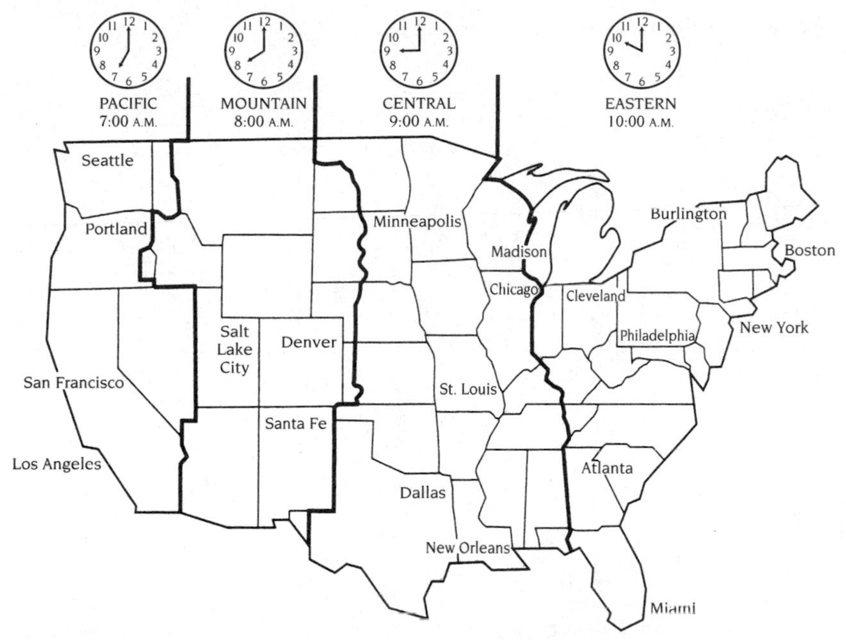

1. It's 7:00 A.M. in San Francisco. What time is it in Philadelphia? ______.
2. It's 10:45 P.M. in Miami. What time is it in Salt Lake City? ______.
3. It's 6:50 P.M. in Minneapolis. What time is it in New Orleans? ______.
4. It's 10:30 P.M. in Santa Fe. What time is it in Chicago? ______.
5. It's 2:15 A.M. in Los Angeles. What time is it in Boston? ______.
6. It's 9:10 A.M. in Dallas. What time is it in Portland? ______.
7. It's 10:20 A.M. in Atlanta. What time is it in Denver? ______.
8. It's 10:05 A.M. in Seattle. What time is it in Cleveland? ______.

Now make five questions of your own for your partner to answer.

Exercise 8

Familiarize Ss with the concept of time zones in the U.S. They may have heard of these zones on television. Ask *What time zone is Boston in? Denver?*

Workbook Ex. 5, pp. 14–15.
Answers: TE p. 527.

ANSWER KEY

Exercise 8

1. It's 10:00 A.M. **2.** It's 8:45 P.M. **3.** It's 6:50 P.M. **4.** It's 11:30 P.M. **5.** It's 5:15 A.M. **6.** It's 7:10 A.M. **7.** It's 8:20 A.M. **8.** It's 1:05 P.M.

FOCUS 5

Prepositions of location are introduced in this unit because they are used when answering questions with *where*.

1. Have Ss read the chart silently.
2. Then use objects or people in the classroom to demonstrate the meaning of the prepositions. Point out the difference between *near, next to,* and *opposite.*

FOCUS **5**

Prepositions of Location

Prepositions of location tell where something is.

COMMON PREPOSITIONS OF LOCATION		
The ball is **in** the box.	The ball is **on** the box.	The ball is **above** the box.
The ball is **next to** the box.	The ball is **in back of** the box.	The ball is **under** the box.
The ball is **near** the box. It isn't next to the box.	The ball is **behind** the box.	The ball is **opposite** the box.
The ball is **between** the two boxes.	The ball is **in front of** the box.	

SUBJECT +	*Be* +	PREPOSITIONAL PHRASE (PREPOSITION + NOUN)
Prague	is	**in** the Czech Republic.
It	's	**on** the Vultava River.
The hotel	is	**near** the Vultava River.

EXERCISE 9

Sally and her family are in Prague, in the Czech Republic. Read the postcard and circle the prepositions of location. Who wrote this postcard?

Hi everybody. Here we are in Prague, the capital city of the Czech Republic. It is a beautiful city in Central Europe. I am between Ken and Jirka, our Czech friend. In this photo, we are at a cafe next to the Charles Bridge. Michele is trying to hide; she's camera shy! And right across from the cafe is a souvenir shop. Prague is very popular during the summer. Many tourists come here to visit. The couple next to us is from Italy. They love Prague too!

Exercise 9

SUGGESTIONS

1. Have Ss look at the postcard and read silently, circling the prepositions of location.
2. They should understand that Sally wrote this postcard.

ANSWER KEY

Exercise 9

in Prague; *in* Central Europe; *between* Ken and Jirka; *In* this; *at* a café; *next to* the; *across* from the café; *next to* us;

Exercise 10 

SUGGESTIONS

1. Have Ss identify and label the objects and furniture in the room before they ask the questions.
2. Have Ss sit back to back while doing the exercise.
3. Have Ss draw the objects or write the name of each object in its place in the illustration, and then check their drawings.

Workbook Exs. 6, 7, & 8, pp. 16–19.
Answers: TE p. 527.

EXERCISE 10

Information Gap. You cannot find items 1–6 in Picture A. Your partner cannot find items 7–12 in Picture B on page A-18. Ask each other questions with *where*.

▶ **EXAMPLE:** **Student A asks**: 1. Where are my slippers?
Student B says: They're under the sofa.

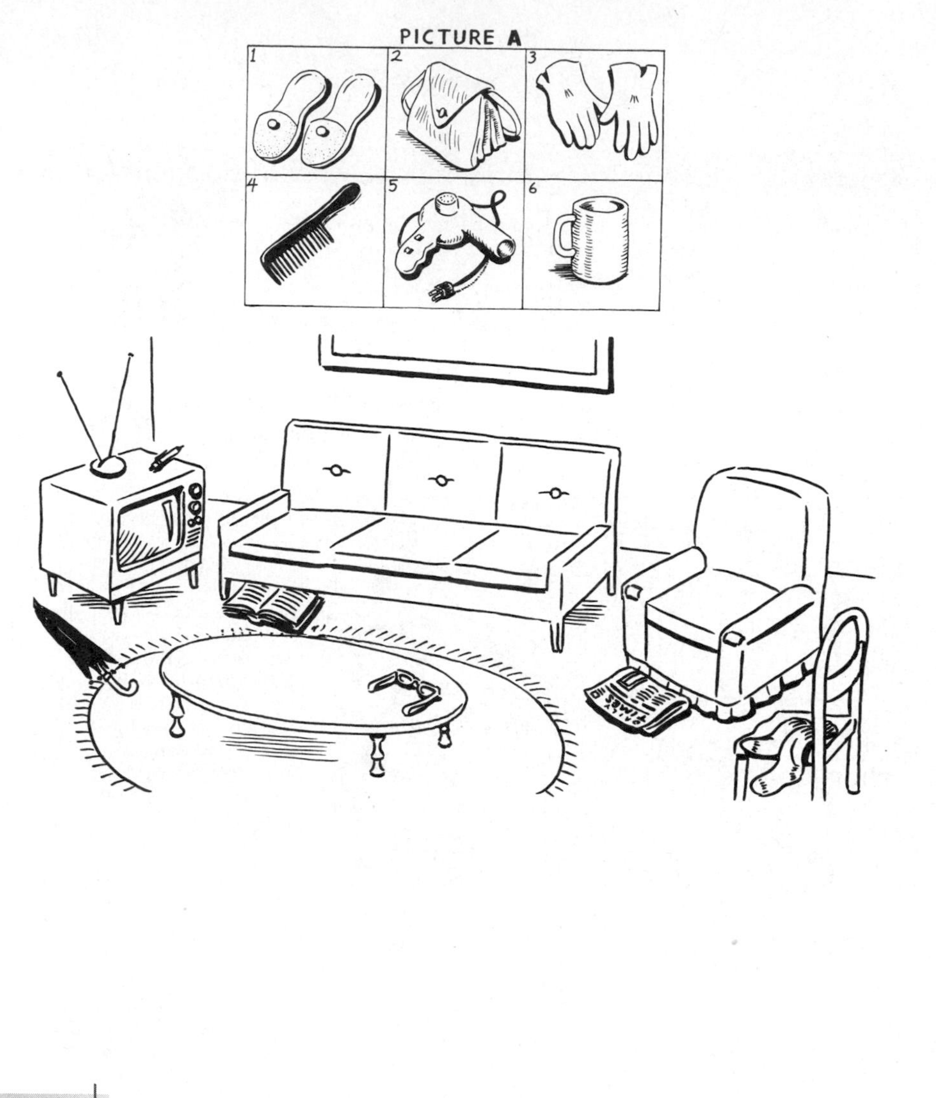

ANSWER KEY

Exercise 10

Answers may vary. Possible answers:
1. The slippers are under the sofa. **2.** The bag is behind/in back of the chair. **3.** The gloves are on the armchair. **4.** The comb is on the rug/next to the table. **5.** The hair dryer is under the armchair. **6.** The cup is on the television. **7.** The book is under the sofa. **8.** The newspaper is next to/in front of the armchair. **9.** The umbrella is next to/near the television. **10.** The glasses are on the table. **11.** The pen is on the television. **12.** The socks are on the chair.

EXERCISE 11

This is a map of your neighborhood. The names of the places are missing. Read the sentences and fill in the names of the places on the map. The first one has been done for you.

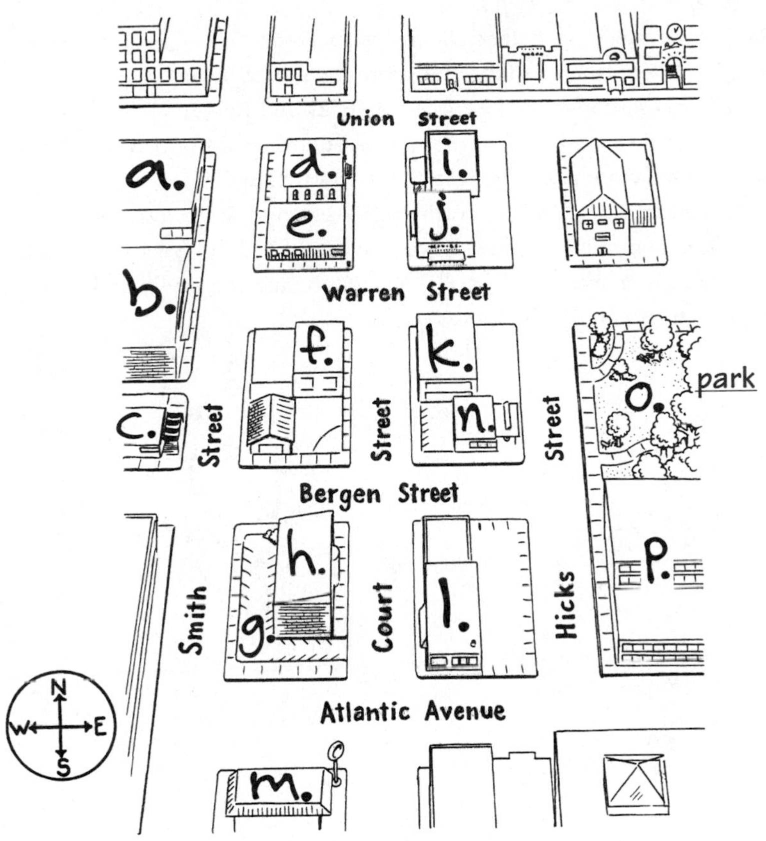

1. The park is on the corner of Hicks and Warren Street.
2. The hospital is next to the park.
3. The bank is on the southwest corner of Court Street and Union.

Exercise 11

Familiarize Ss with the streets on the map and with expressions such as *on the corner of. . . , on the west side of. . . , on the southwest corner of. . . .* Do the first couple of examples to demonstrate.

ANSWER KEY

Exercise 11

2. P **3.** D **4.** E **5.** J **6.** i **7.** h
8. g **9.** l **10.** N **11.** K **12.** F **13.** C
14. A **15.** b **16.** M

4. The drugstore is next to the bank.
5. The candy store is across the street from the drugstore on Court Street.
6. The video store is near the candy store.
7. The movie theater is on the west side of Court Street between Bergen and Atlantic.
8. The parking lot is behind the movie theater.
9. The bakery is across the street from the movie theater.
10. The gas station is on the corner of Hicks and Bergen.
11. The hardware store is on the southeast corner of Court Street and Warren.
12. The bookstore is across from the hardware store.
13. The newsstand is on the corner of Bergen and Smith Streets.
14. The pet store is on the southwest corner of Union Street and Smith Street.
15. The supermarket is between the pet store and the newsstand on Smith Street.
16. The diner is on Atlantic Avenue.

UNIT GOAL REVIEW

Now, ask Ss to look at the goals on the opening page of the unit. Help them understand how much they have accomplished in each area. Ask them if they have any questions about what they have learned so far.

Use Your English

ACTIVITY 1: SPEAKING

TEST YOUR KNOWLEDGE GAME

Get into two teams.

STEP 1 Team 1 chooses a category and an amount of money. Team 2 asks a question with *what* or *where*. If Team 1 answers correctly, they get the money.

STEP 2 Team 2 chooses a category and an amount of money. Team 1 asks a question with *what* or *where*. If Team 2 answers correctly, they get the money. The team with the most money at the end wins.

▶ **EXAMPLES:** **Step 1.**
Team 1: Monuments for $30.
Team 2: Where is the Colosseum?
Team 1: It's in Rome, Italy.

	Categories				
Amount $$$	**Monuments**	**Capitals**	**Countries**	**Continents**	**Rivers, Mts, Deserts**
Question	**Where is/are**	**What's the capital of**	**Where's**	**Where's**	**Where is/are**
$10	The Eiffel Tower	Afghanistan	Managua	Canada	The Sahara Desert
$20	The Great Wall	Greece	Nagasaki	Chile	The Rocky Mts.
$30	The Colosseum	Israel	Budapest	India	The Amazon River
$40	The Pyramids	Peru	Capetown	Egypt	Mount Everest
$50	The Taj Mahal	Turkey	Zurich	Portugal	The Nile River

ANSWER KEY

Paris, France	Kabul	Nicaragua	North America	Africa
The People's Republic of China	Athens	Japan	South America	The U.S. and Canada
Rome, Italy	Jerusalem	Hungary	Asia	South America
Egypt	Lima	South Africa	Africa	Nepal
India	Ankara	Switzerland	Western Europe	Africa

USE YOUR ENGLISH

Note: These "purple" pages at the end of each unit contain more open-ended communicative activities designed to get Ss to apply what they have learned in less-structured contexts. They can be used at any time during the unit, interspersed with the exercises for variety. For a more complete discussion of how to implement the *Use Your English* activities, see page xxvi of this Teacher's Edition.

Activity 1 

1. This is a variation of the game "Jeopardy." Ss work in two large groups. If your class is very large, form smaller groups of 4, so they can pool their ideas and answer the questions.
2. The answers for the last column (Rivers, Mountains, and Deserts) may vary since some of these places might not be in one particular country (the Rocky Mountains are in the U.S. and in Canada).
3. Provide a map so Ss can check their answers.
4. Yes/no questions with *be* can be recycled here (*Is the Nile River in Egypt?*).

Activity 2 

Step 1

Have Ss choose partners. However, let them work individually first to write their questions. Walk around to assist. Then pair Ss up to ask their questions. Ss must communicate this information to each other in order to be prepared for Step 2.

Step 2

Ss use the information they gathered in Step 1 for this writing assignment.

VARIATION

Ss could put together a small class newspaper about their hometowns. They could also create posters, adding photos or other realia to go along with the text. Put the posters around the room and have an "international day" event.

ACTIVITY 2: SPEAKING/WRITING

STEP 1 Ask a classmate about his or her hometown. Ask questions with *is/are* . . . or *wh*-question words.

▶ **EXAMPLE:** **You:** Where are you from? **Your Partner:** Acapulco.
Where's Acapulco? It's in Mexico.
How is the weather? It's hot in the summer and mild in the winter.
Are the people friendly? Yes, they are.

The words in the box will help you:

Weather	People	Other
hot warm mild cold sunny dry humid rainy cloudy	happy friendly hard-working cold religious outgoing quiet rich poor	expensive cheap small big crowded delicious safe dangerous clean

STEP 2 Write about your partner's hometown.

▶ **EXAMPLE:** My classmate is from Mexico City. Mexico City is the capital of Mexico. Mexico City is big. It is crowded. It is hot in the summer. People are friendly. The food is delicious.

Activity 3

Play textbook audio. The tapescript for this listening appears on p. 544 of this book.

Play the tape more than once.

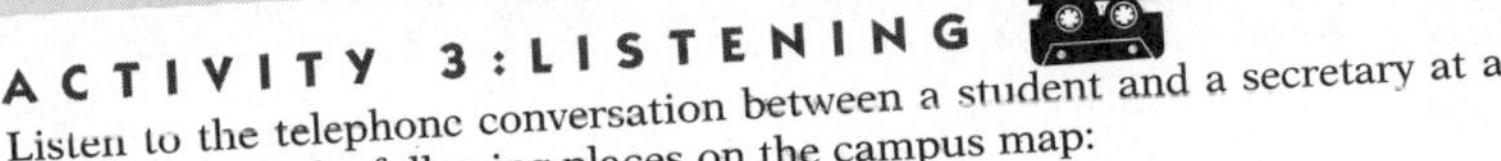

Listen to the telephone conversation between a student and a secretary at a college. Fill in the following places on the campus map:

- Parking Lot B
- Administration Building
- library
- bookstore
- English as a Second Language Department
- auditorium
- cafeteria

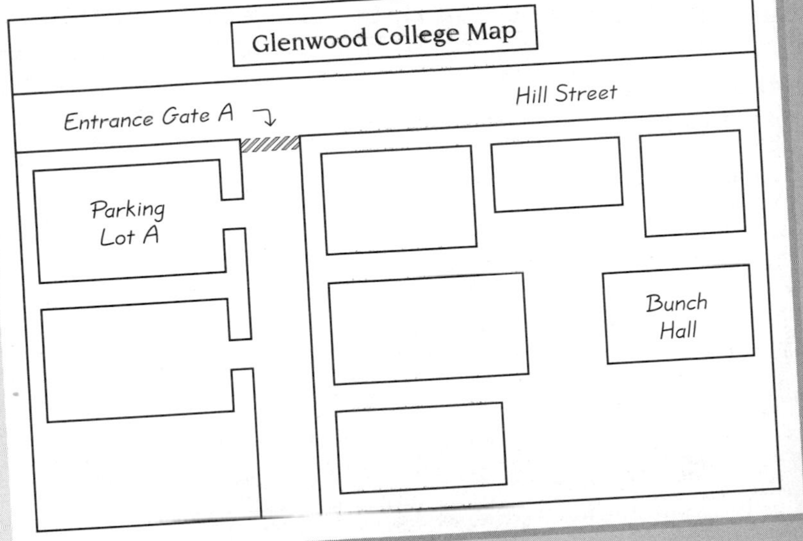

ACTIVITY 4: SPEAKING/WRITING

Draw a map of your hometown or the place where you live now. Describe your map to your partner. Then write down the description, using prepositions.

▶ **EXAMPLES:** This is my house. It's on Main Street. The drugstore is on the corner of Main and 1st Avenue. The supermarket is opposite the drugstore.

Activity 4

Ss can draw a map or bring in detailed photographs if they have any. Collect their descriptions and analyze their errors.

The test for this unit can be found on p. 454–455 of this book. The answers can be found on p. 456.

TOEFL Test Preparation Exercises for Units 1–3 can be found on pp. 20–22. The answers are on p. 527 of this book.

ANSWER KEY

Activity 3

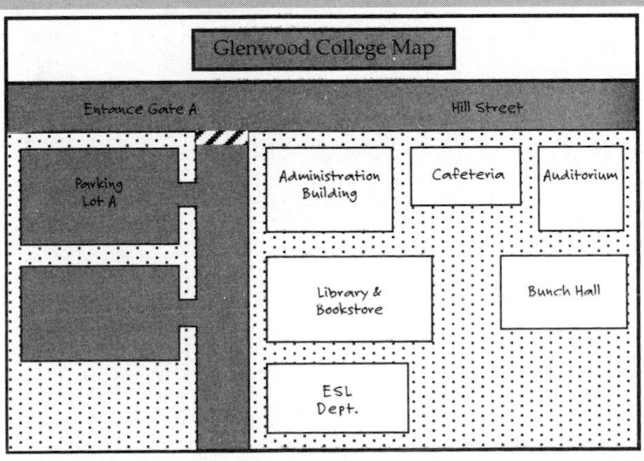

Unit 4

UNIT OVERVIEW

Unit 4 presents count and noncount nouns. *Be* + adjective is expanded here to include *be* + adjective + noun.

UNIT GOALS

To maximize the diagnostic potential of the Opening Task, do not review the Unit Goals with students (Ss) until after they have completed and reviewed the task.

OPENING TASK

SETTING UP THE TASK

Elicit vocabulary using the photograph. Write vocabulary on the board. You can refer to it later to discuss count and noncount nouns.

UNIT 4

NOUNS

Count and Noncount Nouns, *Be* + Adjective + Noun

UNIT GOALS:

- To understand the difference between count and noncount nouns
- To use *a/an* with singular count nouns
- To know how to spell and pronounce regular plural nouns
- To know how to form the irregular plurals of nouns
- To ask questions with *how much* . . .
- To make statements with *be* + *adjective* + *noun*

OPENING TASK

Categories

STEP 1 Write each word in the box in one of the three circles below.

milk	dresses	cash
dollars	bread	a shoe
a shirt	cents	an egg

Category

1. Food

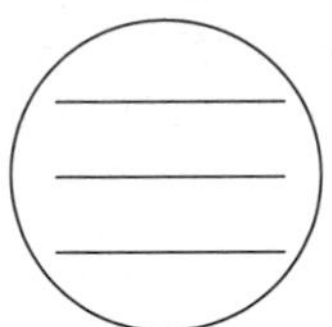

3. Money

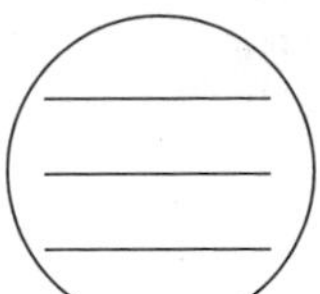

2. Clothing

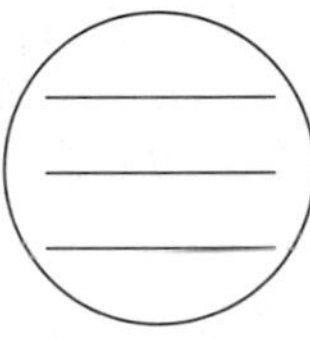

STEP 2 Now the same words from above are in different categories. Write a name for each category. Note: The new categories are types of nouns.

1. ______
   - a shirt
   - a shoe
   - an egg

3. ______
   - milk
   - bread
   - cash

2. ______
   - dollars
   - cents
   - dresses

ANSWER KEY

Step 1

1. Food: milk, bread, an egg
2. Clothing: a shirt, dresses, a shoe
3. Money: dollars, cents, cash

Step 2

1. Singular Count Nouns
2. Plural Count Nouns
3. Noncount Nouns

CONDUCTING THE TASK

Step 1

Students are asked to group the nouns in semantic categories. This is a focus on Meaning. Ss can do this step individually or in pairs.

Step 2

Ss are given a new grouping—this time in grammatical categories—count nouns (singular, plural) and noncount nouns. Step 2 will tell you which Ss already know something about count and noncount nouns and which Ss don't. If none of your Ss know the categories, ask them to observe carefully. How are the words in these three circles different? Give them some hints. *These words (dollars, cents, dresses) have "s" at the end. How are they different from "a shirt, a shoe, an egg"? How is "milk, bread and cash" different from these other two groups?* Try to get Ss to derive a rule first.

REVIEWING THE TASK

count nouns → singular nouns / plural nouns

Put the categories of count and noncount nouns, with examples of each, on the board to use when you introduce the first focus box.

FOCUS 1

Presentations of count/noncount nouns tend to be confusing when they imply that nouns are inherently count or noncount. In fact, while some nouns are always noncount (information, advice), in most cases it is how we view the object that determines how we choose the noun. This explains why some nouns can be both count and noncount. For example, *fruit* viewed as a mass—as one entity, is usually noncount. *The fruit in the bowl is delicious.* However, if viewed as individual or separate entities, we can use it as a count noun. *I eat two fruits a day.* Further discussion of this can be found in Unit 11 on quantifiers. For the sake of simplicity and clarity at this level, the count/noncount distinction is drawn less subtly for the students.

SUGGESTIONS

1. Explain the focus box introduction: the difference between seeing something as one entity and seeing something as separate individual parts. Money is a good example because even though we all know we can count money, when we think of money, we think of a lump sum, not of the components of that sum.
2. Have students read the examples and explanations. Provide other examples of count nouns *(chairs, desks, pens, students)* and noncount nouns *(furniture, information, coffee, fruit).*

Exercise 1

Have Ss do this exercise individually. Check answers as a class.

SUGGESTION

Go back to the list of words you elicited using the photograph in the Opening Task. Ask Ss to indicate if the words are count or noncount.

Workbook Ex. 1, p. 23.
Answers: TE p. 527.

FOCUS **1**

Count Nouns and Noncount Nouns

Money

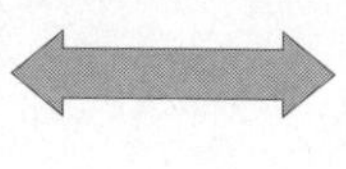

Coins

We can see things as whole or as separate things we can count. We use noncount nouns like *money* when we see a thing as whole. We use count nouns like *coins* when we refer to things we can count.

EXAMPLES		EXPLANATIONS
Count Nouns SINGULAR an egg a dress	 PLURAL eggs dresses	**Things we can count** Count nouns take *a/an* in the singular. They take *-s* or *-es* in the plural.
Noncount Nouns money cash clothing		**Things we don't count** Noncount nouns have one form. They are not singular, not plural.

EXERCISE 1

Look at the list of words from the Opening Task. Check count or noncount.

	COUNT NOUN	NONCOUNT NOUN
food		
milk		
egg		
bread		
clothing		
dresses		
shirt		

ANSWER KEY

Exercise 1

Count Nouns: (an) egg, dresses, (a) shirt, (a) shoe, dollars, cents; Noncount: food, milk, bread, clothing, money, cash

	COUNT NOUN	NONCOUNT NOUN
shoe		
money		
dollars		
cents		
cash		

FOCUS **2**

A/An with Singular Count Nouns

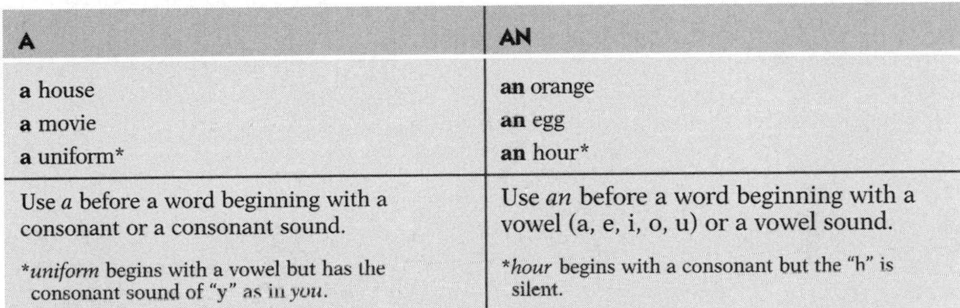

A	AN
a house **a** movie **a** uniform*	**an** orange **an** egg **an** hour*
Use *a* before a word beginning with a consonant or a consonant sound. **uniform* begins with a vowel but has the consonant sound of "y" as in *you*.	Use *an* before a word beginning with a vowel (a, e, i, o, u) or a vowel sound. **hour* begins with a consonant but the "h" is silent.

EXERCISE 2

List the words below under the correct categories. Then, read your lists to your partner with *a* or *an*.

earring	bed	watch	necklace
dormitory	table	apple	house
orange ✓	apartment	ring	desk
armchair	banana	pear	hotel

Fruit	Furniture	Jewelry	Housing
an orange	______	______	______
______	______	______	______
______	______	______	______
______	______	______	______

FOCUS 2

Get Ss to figure out the rule.

1. Have them close their books.
2. Put the words in the box on the board.
3. Ask Ss to read them aloud and find the difference between *a* and *an*
4. Have them read the explanation in the book. Provide additional examples if need be: *a hospital, an herb.*

Exercise 2 

EXPANSIONS

1. This exercise lends itself to pronunciation practice. Have Ss read these words aloud and assess their own and their classmates' pronunciation. Expect different language groups to have different problems. Tape record the students.
2. Have Ss add two new items to each category and also include *a/an.*

ANSWER KEY

Exercise 2

Fruit: an orange, a banana, an apple, a pear; Furniture: an armchair, a bed, a table, a desk; Jewelry: an earring, a watch, a ring, a necklace; Housing: a dormitory, an apartment, a house, a hotel

Exercise 3

SUGGESTION

Have Ss take turns reading these sentences out of order. The rest of the class must show they understand which picture number each student is talking about. This will motivate Ss to listen to each other and will encourage them to aim for comprehensibility.

EXPANSION

Have Ss make sentences about the occupations of people in their families. Provide examples: *My mother is a professor.*

EXERCISE 3

For each picture write a sentence to show the person's occupation. Use *a/an.*

▶ **EXAMPLES:**

He's a waiter.

She's an athlete.

1. actor

2. secretary

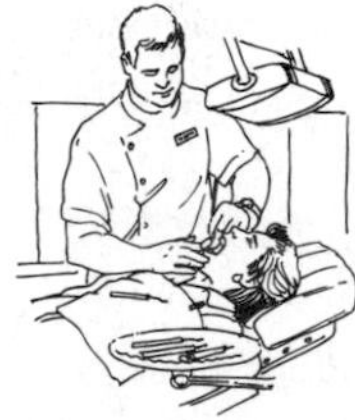

3. dentist

4. cashier

5. engineer

6. doctor

ANSWER KEY

Exercise 3

1. He's an actor. **2.** She's a secretary. **3.** He's a dentist. **4.** She's a cashier. **5.** She's an engineer. **6.** He's a doctor. **7.** He's a nurse. **8.** He's a hairdresser. **9.** He's a flight attendant. **10.** She's an accountant.

7. nurse

8. hairdresser

9. flight attendant

10. accountant

EXERCISE 4

Test your knowledge. Work with a partner. You read the question on the left. Your partner finds the answer on the right and reads it using *a/an*.

▶ **EXAMPLE:** **You:** What's Poland?

Your Partner: (m) It's a country.

1.	What's Poland?	**a.**	It's _____ continent.
2.	What is Thanksgiving?	**b.**	It's _____ car.
3.	What is the Atlantic?	**c.**	It's _____ hour.
4.	What is Puerto Rico?	**d.**	It's _____ clock.
5.	What's the Sahara?	**e.**	It's _____ river.
6.	What is Africa?	**f.**	It's _____ island.
7.	What's New York?	**g.**	It's _____ holiday in the United States and Canada.
8.	What's the Concorde?	**h.**	It's _____ museum.
9.	What's Big Ben?	**i.**	It's _____ university.
10.	What is the Louvre?	**j.**	It's _____ ocean.
11.	What is Harvard?	**k.**	It's _____ city.
12.	What's sixty minutes?	**l.**	It's _____ airplane.
13.	What's a Mercedes?	**m.**	It's _____ country.
14.	What's the Amazon?	**n.**	It's _____ desert.

Exercise 4 

Working in pairs or small groups, Ss benefit from each other's background knowledge.

SUGGESTION

After completeing the exercises, have Ss re-read the answers aloud to reinforce pronunciation.

Workbook Ex. 2, p. 24.
Answers: TE p. 527.

ANSWER KEY

Exercise 4

2. a holiday (g); **3.** an ocean (j) **4.** an island (f) **5.** a desert (n) **6.** a continent (a) **7.** a city (k) **8.** an airplane (l) **9.** a clock (d) **10.** a museum (h) **11.** a university (i) **12.** an hour (c) **13.** a car (b) **14.** a river (e)

FOCUS 3

Advise Ss to re-read and memorize the rules at home. In the meantime, allow them to keep the chart handy as they do Exercises 5 and 6.

SUGGESTION

Combine Focus Boxes 3 and 4, working on spelling and pronunciation simultaneously to incorporate pronunciation practice, beginning with Exercise 5.

FOCUS **3**

Spelling of Regular Plural Count Nouns

SINGULAR	PLURAL	EXPLANATIONS
(a) a car a book	two cars three books	To make the plural form of most count nouns, add *-s*.
(b) a boy a radio	four boys two radios	Nouns that end in: vowel + *y* vowel + *o* Plural form: add *-s*.
(c) a class a sandwich a dish a box	two classes two sandwiches two dishes three boxes	Nouns that end in: *ss* *ch* *sh* *x* Plural form: add *-es*.
(d) a potato a tomato	six potatoes four tomatoes	Nouns that end in: consonant + *o* Plural form: add *-es*.
(e) a baby a city	babies cities	Nouns that end in: consonant + *y* Plural form: change *y* to *i*, add *-es*.
(f) a thief a life	two thieves three lives	Nouns that end in: *f* or *fe* Plural form: change *f* to *v*, add *-es*. Exceptions: *chief—chiefs* *chef—chefs*

EXERCISE 5

Write the plural form of the words below.

1. party	parties		**7.** wife	________
2. shoe	________		**8.** watch	________
3. fox	________		**9.** leaf	________
4. dictionary	________		**10.** lady	________
5. week	________		**11.** month	________
6. glass	________		**12.** key	________

EXERCISE 6

Complete the sentences with the plural of one of the nouns in the box.

desert	city	story	holiday ✓	university	state
river	mountain	country	continent	company	ocean

1. Thanksgiving and Christmas are holidays.
2. The Atlantic and the Pacific are ________.
3. Africa and Asia are ________.
4. Princeton and Yale are ________.
5. IBM and Sony are ________.
6. "Cinderella" and "Beauty and the Beast" are ________.
7. The Alps are ________.
8. Colombia and Venezuela are ________ in South America.
9. Colorado and Vermont are ________ in the United States.
10. Vienna and Oslo are two ________ in Europe.
11. The Sahara and the Gobi are ________.
12. The Amazon and the Nile are ________.

Exercise 5

As Ss work, walk around and check. If you have introduced pronunciation rules, call on Ss to say the plural forms of these words.

Exercise 6

Allow Ss to share background knowledge. Have them write their answers on the board. Check spelling as a class.

Workbook Exs. 3, p. 24–25.
Answers: TE p. 527.

ANSWER KEY

Exercise 5

2. shoes 3. foxes 4. dictionaries 5. weeks 6. glasses 7. wives 8. watches 9. leaves 10. ladies 11. months 12. keys

Exercise 6

2. oceans 3. continents 4. universities 5. companies 6. stories 7. mountains 8. countries 9. states 10. cities 11. deserts 12. rivers

FOCUS 4

1. Tell Ss to put their hands on their throats and say the word "lips." They will not feel a vibration: the sound is voiceless.
2. Do the same and say the word "legs." They will feel a vibration: the sound is voiced.
3. Have Ss practice the plurals aloud with each other. Point out that the words in "c" have an extra syllable.

SUGGESTION

If some Ss have difficulty feeling a vibration in the throat, have them cover their ears as they make these sounds. Voiced sounds will produce a buzzing sensation.

Exercise 7

Have Ss say the plurals aloud and write the words in the correct columns. Allow them to refer to Focus 4 if necessary. To reinforce pronunciation, write the exercise on the board and do as a class.

FOCUS 4

Regular Plural Nouns: Pronunciation of Final *-s*, and *-es*

EXAMPLES	EXPLANATIONS
(a) books, students, groups months, desks, cats	/S/ Final *-s* is pronounced /s/ after voiceless sounds.*
(b) beds, rooms, lives years, days, dogs	/Z/ Final *-s* is pronounced /z/ after voiced sounds.**
(c) classes, faces exercises, sizes dishes, wishes sandwiches, watches colleges, pages class-es	/IZ/ Final *-es* is pronounced /iz/ after "s" sounds "z" sounds "sh" sounds "ch" sounds "ge/dge" sounds This adds an extra syllable to the noun.
	*Voiceless sounds: /p/t/k/f/th. **Voiced sounds: /b/d/g/v/m/n/l/r/ and vowels.

EXERCISE 7

Make the words below plural. Then, write each word in the correct pronunciation group on the next page. Read each group aloud.

✔ book	radio	dress	house	ticket	rule
thing	horse	head	list	bus	cup
car	train	boat	church	peach	hat

ANSWER KEY

Exercise 7

/s/: books, boats, lists, tickets, cups, hats
/z/: things, cars, trains, heads, rules, radios
/IZ/: horses, dresses, churches, houses, peaches, buses

/S/	/Z/	/IZ/
books		

EXERCISE 8

Look at the list of common measurements. Make the measurement on the right plural. Then, read the statements aloud using the verb *equals*.

▶ **EXAMPLE:** 98.6 degrees Fahrenheit = 37 degree_s___ Celsius.

98.6 degrees Fahrenheit equals 37 degrees Celsius.

1. one foot = 12 inch____
2. one pound = 16 ounce____
3. one minute = 60 second____
4. one hour = 60 minute____
5. one day = 24 hour____
6. one year = 365 day____
7. one quart = 2 pint____
8. one gallon = 4 quart____
9. one inch = 2½ centimeter____
10. one kilo = 2.2 pound____

EXERCISE 9

Rhymes. Make the nouns in italics plural. Then, read the rhymes aloud.

1. **On Education**

   Word____, sentence____, exercise____, rule____,
   Dictionary____, textbook____, page____, school____,
   Classroom____, teacher____, student____, —all *jewel____*
   Of education, these are the *tool____*.

2. **On Age**

   Day____, week____, month____, year____.
   Getting old? Please, no *tear____*!!!

3. **On Imports**

   The *shoe____* are Brazilian,
   The *glove____* are Italian,
   The *chef____* are from France;
   from South America—the salsa dance.
   The *toy____* are Chinese,
   The *camera____* are Japanese:
   Tell me, what's American, please?

Exercise 8

This exercise helps Ss convert to a new system of measurement (the nonmetric system) while practicing pronunciation. Use realia such as rulers, one-lb. cans of coffee, quart containers, clocks, etc., to facilitate this transition.

1. Have Ss figure out their height, weight, arm length, waist size, etc.
2. Have pairs check with the whole group.
3. As Ss call out the answers, list the words under the /s/, /z/ and /IZ/ columns on the board.

Exercise 9

Have pairs monitor each other's pronunciation. Walk around and listen to plurals, as well as to stress and intonation. ("*Getting old?* = rising intonation.) Practice with the whole class.

SUGGESTION

Have Ss tape record themselves so they can listen back and evaluate their pronunciation.

Workbook Exs. 4 & 5, p. 25.
Answers: TE p. 528.

ANSWER KEY

Exercise 8

1. inches 2. ounces 3. seconds 4. minutes 5. hours 6. days 7. pints 8. quarts 9. centimeters 10. pounds

Exercise 9

1. Words, sentences, exercises, rules; Dictionaries, textbooks, pages, schools; Classrooms, teachers, students, all jewels; Of education, these are the tools. 2. Days, weeks, months, years; Please, no tears! 3. The shoes; The gloves; The chefs; The toys; The cameras.

FOCUS 5

Before Ss look at this box, give them the singular nouns, and ask if they know the plural forms. Then refer them to the chart in Focus 5.

FOCUS **5**

Irregular Plural Nouns

EXAMPLES			EXPLANATIONS
(a)	child man woman foot tooth mouse person	children men women feet teeth mice people	Some nouns change spelling in the plural.
(b)	a deer a sheep a fish	two deer three sheep four fish	Some nouns do not change in the plural.
(c)	scissors pajamas eyeglasses shorts clothes pants		Some nouns are always plural. They have no singular form.

EXERCISE 10

STEP 1 Work in pairs. Match each noun to the correct part of the picture by asking questions. Use *a/an* when necessary.

STEP 2 Then label the picture.

▶ **EXAMPLES:** What's number 1? An eyebrow.
What's number 2? Toes.

eyebrow	sunglasses	teeth	lips	nose	ear
hand	fingers	arm	tee shirt	shorts	feet
toes	sandal	freckles	baseball cap	eye	hair

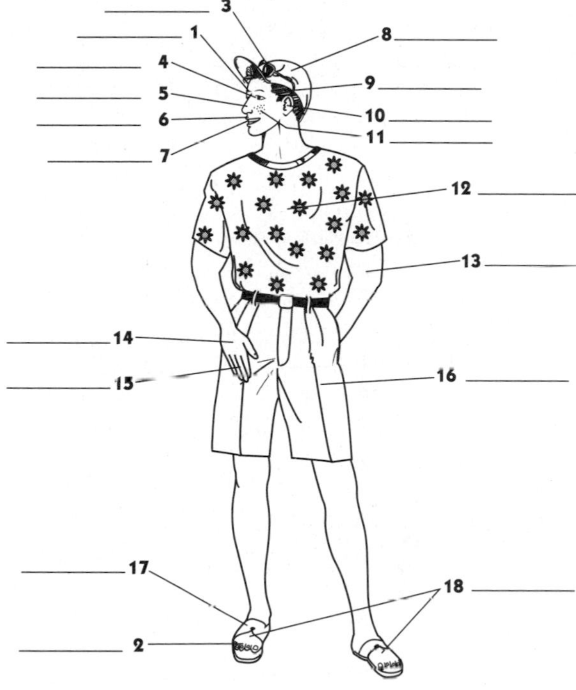

Exercise 10 

Familiarize Ss with the drawing. Walk around listening for correct pronunciation of plurals.

Workbook Ex. 6, p.26.
Answers: TE p. 528.

ANSWER KEY

Exercise 10

3. sunglasses
4. an eye
5. a nose
6. lips
7. teeth
8. a baseball cap
9. hair
10. an ear
11. freckles
12. a tee shirt
13. an arm
14. a hand
15. fingers
16. shorts
17. a sandal
18. feet

FOCUS 6

Have Ss read the examples and say whether the nouns are count or noncount. Point out the differences between the two. You may also do this inductively by putting the sentences in two columns on the board and asking what the differences between count and noncount are.

EXPANSION

Have Ss choose 3 of the common noncount nouns in the box and write sentences. Provide sample sentences yourself: *Traffic in this city is terrible. Pollution is also a problem.*

FOCUS 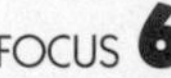

Count and Noncount Nouns

COUNT NOUNS	NONCOUNT NOUNS
Can take *a/an* or *one* in the singular. **(a)** It's a job. **(b)** I'm on vacation for one week.	Cannot take *a/an* or *one* in the singular. **(c)** It's work.
Can take *-s* or *-es* in the plural. **(d)** They are earrings. **(e)** They're watches.	Cannot take *-s* or *-es.* **(f)** It's jewelry.
Can take a singular or plural verb. **(g)** It is a table. **(h)** They are chairs.	Always take a singular verb. **(i)** Furniture is expensive.
To ask about prices with count nouns, use: **(j)** How much is a television set in Taiwan? (singular) **(k)** How much are newspapers in Russia? (plural)	To ask about prices with noncount nouns, use: **(l)** How much is gas in Italy?

Some Common Noncount Nouns

advice	electricity	help	mail	salt
bacon	fish	homework	milk	sugar
bread	food	information	money	tea
cheese	fruit	jewelry	music	traffic
clothing	furniture	love	news	transportation
coffee	garbage	luck	pollution	water
crime	hair	luggage	rice	work

EXERCISE 11

Donald is an international student arriving in Wisconsin with his wife. Read his conversations. Check count or noncount for each underlined noun.

		COUNT	NONCOUNT
1. Donald is at the airport with his wife.			
Donald: It's cold here in Wisconsin.			
a. I need warm clothing.	**a.**	______	______
b. Where's my coat?	**b.**	______	______
Wife: c. It's in the black suitcase.	**c.**	______	______
Donald: d. Where is the luggage?	**d.**	______	______
Wife: It's still on the plane!			
2. Donald is at the University of Wisconsin.			
Secretary: a. Donald, here are three letters for you.	**a.**	______	______
Donald: b. Thank you. Mail from home is very important to me.	**b.**	______	______
3. Donald is with an American student.			
Donald: a. How's the food in the cafeteria?	**a.**	______	______
Student: b. The vegetables are good.	**b.**	______	______
c. The fruit is fresh.	**c.**	______	______
d. The meat is terrible.	**d.**	______	______

EXERCISE 12

Work with a partner. Use the words below to ask questions about the country your partner comes from.

▶ **EXAMPLE:** hamburgers/popular/in . . .?
Are hamburgers popular in Russia?
Yes, they are.
OR No, they aren't.

1. pizza/popular/in . . .?
2. fruit/cheap/in . . .?
3. cars/big/in . . .?
4. electricity/cheap/in . . .?
5. American music/popular/in . . .?
6. rent/expensive/in . . .?
7. families/big/in . . .?
8. taxes/high/in . . .?
9. public transportation/good/in . . .?
10. American movies/popular/in . . .?

Now ask five questions about the price of the following items in your partner's country using: *How much is/are?*

hamburgers	public transportation	rent
gas	movies	a local telephone call
fruit	a daily newspaper	a CD (compact disc)

Exercise 11 

Ss should recognize some of these nouns from Focus Boxes 1 and 6. They can also use the verb *be* (singular/plural) as clues in determining whether a noun is count or noncount. Have Ss perform these dialogues.

Exercise 12  

This exercise should provoke a lot of discussion.

1. Have Ss share their answers; make a chart on the board so that the information from various countries can be easily compared. *Gas is cheap in the U.S. It's very expensive in Europe.* Correct any errors.
2. Have students write the questions they make with *"How much is/are"* on the board. Have the class make comparative statements.

VARIATION

Do this exercise as a class survey. Give each student one question to ask. Each student walks around the room and asks his/her question to each of the other students. Each student then provides a summary of the information he/she gathered to share with the class.

Workbook Exs. 7, 8, & 9, pp. 26–28.
Answers: TE p. 528.

ANSWER KEY

Exercise 11
1. a. noncount, b. count, c. count, d. noncount **2.** a. count, b. noncount **3.** a. noncount, b. count, c. noncount, d. noncount

Exercise 12
1. Is pizza **2.** Is fruit **3.** Are cars **4.** Is electricity **5.** Is American music **6.** Is rent **7.** Are families **8.** Are taxes **9.** Is public transportation **10.** Are American movies

FOCUS 7

SUGGESTIONS

1. Use sentence (a) and put each word on an index card.
2. Scramble the cards and have a student put them in the correct order on the board.
3. Ask questions like, *"Why did you put 'private' before 'university'?"*
4. Do the same with the other examples.

Elicit or provide a rule governing be + adjective + noun.

FOCUS **7**

Be + Adjective + Noun

EXAMPLES	EXPLANATIONS
(a) Princeton and Yale are **private** universities.	An adjective can come before the noun.
(b) They are **excellent** colleges.	Do not put *-s* on the adjective when the noun is plural.
(c) It's **a** large university. (d) English is **a** universal language.	Use *a* before an adjective with a consonant or a consonant sound.
(e) He's **an** "A" student. (f) She's **an** honor student.	Use *an* before an adjective with a vowel sound.
(g) Psychology is a **very** interesting subject.	Put *very* before most adjectives to make the adjectives stronger.

Exercise 13

Answers may vary. Encourage Ss to use other adjectives if they wish.

SUGGESTION

Bring in photos of each of these places or a large map of the U.S. to motivate Ss and give them a sense of the diversity of tourist spots in the U.S. Encourage them to make statements about other places they know.

Workbook Ex. 10, p. 29.
Answers: TE p. 528.

UNIT GOAL REVIEW

Now, ask Ss to look at the goals on the opening page of the unit. Help them understand how much they have accomplished in each area. Ask them if they have any questions about what they have learned so far.

EXERCISE 13

Tour the United States. Choose an adjective from the box. Make sentences using *be + adjective + noun*. You can also use *very*. Remember: you can use an adjective more than once.

beautiful	exciting	spectacular	famous
small	crowded	expensive	tall
huge	popular	long	important

EXAMPLE: Disneyworld <u>is a very popular</u> place in Florida.

1. The Twin Towers ________________ buildings in New York City.
2. The Golden Gate ________________ bridge in San Francisco.
3. The Keys ________________ islands off the coast of Florida.
4. The Mississippi ________________ river flowing from Minnesota to the Gulf of Mexico.
5. Bryce and Zion ________________ national parks in Utah.
6. Niagara Falls ________________ waterfall between the U.S. and Canada.
7. The Lincoln Memorial ________________ monument in Washington.
8. Alaska and Hawaii ________________ vacation spots in the U.S.

ANSWER KEY

Exercise 13
1. are very tall **2.** is a very long **3.** are beautiful/small/popular **4.** is a very long **5.** are very beautiful/popular/spectacular **6.** is a very famous/spectacular/beautiful **7.** is a very huge/popular/famous **8.** are very beautiful/exciting/crowded/popular/spectacular

Use Your English

ACTIVITY 1: WRITING/SPEAKING

CATEGORIZING GAME.

STEP 1 Get into two teams. Write the words in the box in the correct categories below.

STEP 2 Then, next to each word, write C for count nouns and NC for noncount nouns.

STEP 3 Each correct answer is one point. The team with the most points wins. Find the winning team.

shirts	ears	coffee	shoes	feet	tea
toothpaste	underwear	lemonade	soap	coat	rice
cheese	shampoo	bread	jacket	eyes	head
hair	toothbrush	juice	beans	milk	pizza
soda	hairbrush	hamburger	socks	towels	arm

Things to Wear

shirts C

Things to Eat

Things to Drink

Things in the Bathroom

Parts of the Body

USE YOUR ENGLISH

For a complete discussion of how to implement the *Use Your English* activities, see page xxvi of this Teacher's Edition.

Activity 1

Step 1

Make sure Ss understand the categories on the cards before doing the activity. Set a time limit of 10 minutes. There should be 6 words under each category.

Step 2

Also set a time limit for this step—approximately 10 minutes. Help Ss as needed.

Step 3 

Write the categories on the board and have five Ss write up the answers. Have each team correct their list and count their points.

SUGGESTION

Ask Ss to think of another 2 words they could add to each category.

VARIATION

Create additional categories that are more specific to your Ss. Examples: *Things You Find in School* (students, chalk, blackboard, books) , *Things in a Handbag* (keys, money, wallet, make-up, tissue), *Things at a Party* (cake, games, soda, food, people) , *Things in a House* (bedroom, closet, dust, kitchen, electricity).

Activity 2

1. Have Ss work in groups, writing their lists on butcher block paper.
2. Put the paper up in the front of the room and compare lists.
3. Have Ss identify the count and noncount nouns.
4. Have Ss judge whose party seems the most exciting, and/or who seems the most prepared for their party.

Activity 3

1. Have Ss first complete the chart individually.
2. Have them share their answers in groups. Go around the room listening for problems with count/noncount nouns.
3. Write any errors you hear on the board and ask Ss to correct these when they have completed the activity.

Activity 4

Play textbook audio. The tapescript for this listening appears on p. 545 of this book.

Step 1

You might have to play the tape a couple of times, but each time you play it elicit what Ss heard and write answers on the board. Each successive playing should add more information and facilitate their understanding.

Step 2

Walk around and listen for correct pronunciation and whether Ss are using count or noncount nouns. Keep a list of mistakes for Ss on an error correction sheet.

Step 3

Tape record Ss' role-plays and have them listen and comment on corrections.

ACTIVITY 2: SPEAKING

Plan a party for the class. Get into groups. Each group plans what they are going to bring to the party under the following categories.

Food **Drinks** **Entertainment**

Compare your plans with the other groups'. Which group has the best plan?

ACTIVITY 3: SPEAKING

Tell your classmates what you have for:

Breakfast	Lunch	Dinners	Snack
coffee			
cereal			
orange juice			

ACTIVITY 4: LISTENING/SPEAKING

STEP 1 Listen to what kind of pizza the woman orders.

STEP 2 Check (✔) what the woman wants on the pizza. Then mark C for count nouns and NC for noncount nouns.

❑ cheese ______ ❑ pepperoni ______
❑ tomatoes ______ ❑ mushrooms ______
❑ olives ______ ❑ anchovies ______
❑ peppers ______ ❑ onions ______

STEP 3 Ask a classmate about his or her favorite pizza.

STEP 4 Role play. Telephone the pizza store with your order.

62 | UNIT 4

ACTIVITY 5: SPEAKING

Work in groups. Bring in a picture of friends or family. Talk about your friends or family members to your group.

▶ **EXAMPLE:** I have two brothers. Juan is an engineer. Carlos is a student.

ACTIVITY 6: SPEAKING

Work with a partner. Bring in a clothing catalogue. You have $200 and you need to buy some clothes for a party. Here are some things you might look for:

Checklist:

Shoes ______	socks/stockings ______
Pants ______	jacket ______
Shirt ______	belt ______
Blouse $27	dress ______
Skirt ______	hat ______
Tie ______	vest ______

▶ **EXAMPLE:** You (looking in the catalogue): "I want to buy the blouse on page 52."

Your Partner: "How much is it?"

You: "It's $27.00."

Your Partner: (Write down $27 next to the blouse on the checklist. Make sure your total isn't over $200.)

Activity 5 

Encourage Ss to bring in photographs of their family and friends. Demonstrate by talking about your own photograph.

EXPANSION

1. Have individual Ss write a description for the photograph they brought. Collect these descriptions and use for correction.
2. Post photos and written descriptions in different places around the room, like an art gallery. Ss walk around and match descriptions to photos.

Activity 6

Ss may have difficulty finding clothing catalogues on their own. Bring some into class yourself.

The test for this unit can be found on p. 457–458 of this book. The answers can be found on p. 459.

Unit 5

UNIT OVERVIEW

Unit 5 is an introduction to the more typical verb pattern: verbs that use the auxiliary *do/does* to form negatives and questions. The focus on the verb *have* is, therefore, a very important preparation for students (Ss). It comes in contrast to the first three units on the verb *be*. It also recycles the knowledge of count/noncount nouns Ss gained in Unit 4. *Some/any* are presented in a straightforward, simplified way(See notes on Focus 4). Ss will also practice two speech acts in this unit: making polite requests and describing people.

The theme of this unit is modern vs. traditional lifestyles. The intention here is not for Ss to judge each culture; rather, for them to reflect on modern culture and its influence on their own cultures, (good or bad) while learning the verb *have*.

UNIT GOALS

To maximize the diagnostic potential of the Opening Task, do not review the Unit Goals with Ss until after they have completed and reviewed the task.

OPENING TASK SETTING UP THE TASK

1. Introduce the concept of modern and traditional cultures. You can do this most effectively by showing National Geographic photographs of traditional peoples around the world. Ask Ss for the names of traditional cultures from their home countries or other traditional groups they may know of.

UNIT 5

THE VERB *HAVE*

Affirmative and Negative Statements, Questions and Short Answers, *Some/Any*

UNIT GOALS:

- To make affirmative statements with the verb *have*
- To make negative statements with *do*
- To ask *yes/no* questions with *do* and give short answers
- To use *some/any*
- To ask for something politely
- To use the verb *have* to describe people

OPENING TASK

Modern and Traditional Lifestyles

Look at the photographs of two Inuit women in North Canada, and at the chart on the next page. Check (✔) and say the things you think Mary has. Check and say the things you think Nilaulaq and her husband have.

Mary

Nilaulaq

	Mary	Nilaulaq (Nila) and her husband, Napachee
1. a house		
2. an Inuit name		
3. Inuit clothing		
4. dogs		
5. furniture		
6. electricity		
7. fresh fish		
8. a bed		
9. a tent		
10. canned food		

In the photographs, who has a traditional lifestyle? Who has a modern lifestyle? Say why.

1. ________________________ a traditional lifestyle.
2. ________________________ a modern lifestyle.

2. Introduce the Inuit from Northern Canada. Use the world map.
3. Pre-teach some of the vocabulary in the chart before asking Ss to do the task. The photographs will help you.

The names are authentic Inuit names. Use Nila for Nilaulaq.

CONDUCTING THE TASK

Walk around while Ss are working to see if they are using the verb *have* in questions or in statements. Take notes.

REVIEWING THE TASK

Check as a class, and answer the two questions: *Who has a traditional/modern lifestyle?* Elicit as much language from your Ss as you can. Listen to see if any Ss are already able to make negative statements or questions using *do/does*. Determining how much they already know will dictate how much of this unit you will need to work on with them.

ANSWER KEY

Opening Task

Mary: a house, furniture, electricity, a bed, canned food; Nila & her husband: an Inuit name, Inuit clothing, dogs, fresh fish, a tent

1. Nila and her husband have a traditional lifestyle.
2. Mary has a modern lifestyle.

FOCUS 1

Focus 1 shows subject-verb word order and the singular-plural distinction. You may already have derived this structure from the Ss during the task. If so, just review the box quickly. If not, have Ss read the statements in the box, silently or aloud. To be more explicit, tell Ss that the singular *"has"* is used for the third person singular subjects (*he, she it*).

Exercise 1

In A and B, Ss make statements about what they know. In C, they make logical conclusions using what they know. You may need to help Ss with vocabulary. Ss can do this exercise individually or in pairs.

Workbook Ex. 1, p. 30–32.
Answers: TE p. 528.

FOCUS **1**

FORM MEANING

▶ *Have* and *Has:* Affirmative Statements

The verb *to have* means to own or possess.

SUBJECT	VERB	
I You	have	a telephone.
He She It Mary	has	
We You They (Nila & Napachee)	have	children.

EXERCISE 1

Fill in the blanks about Nilaulaq and Mary with *have* or *has*. Read the sentences aloud.

A. Nilaulaq ___has___ an Inuit name. She _______________ a husband. He _______________ an Inuit name too. They _______________ two children. They _______________ two dogs. Nilaulaq is proud. She says, "I _______________ a beautiful family."

B. Mary _______________ wallpaper in her house. Mary _______________ a clock. She _______________ photographs and a map. She _______________ furniture. She _______________ canned food on the shelf.

C. Modern Inuit people live in towns. The towns _______________ stores. Modern Inuit people _______________ money. They _______________ jobs.

ANSWER KEY

Exercise 1

A. has, has, has, have, have, have
B. has, has, has, has, has
C. have, have, have

FOCUS **2**

Have: Negative Statements and Contractions

EXAMPLES	DO/DOES	BASE FROM OF VERB	
I You We They Nilaulaq and her husband	do not (don't)	have	a telephone.
He She It Nilaulaq	does not (doesn't)		

EXERCISE 2

What are some differences between traditional and modern families? Make the words below into sentences with *has/have* or *doesn't have/don't have.*

Traditional families are big.

1. They/many children.
2. They also/grandmothers and grandfathers living with them.
3. In a traditional family, only the father/a job.
4. The mother/a job.
5. The children/a babysitter.

Modern families are different.

6. Sometimes they/only two people.
7. Sometimes the parents/one or two children.
8. Sometimes, they/children.

Now make four sentences of your own about modern families.

9. ______________________________
10. ______________________________
11. ______________________________
12. ______________________________

FOCUS 2

1. Emphasize the difference between *be* and *have* in the negative: *have* requires the help of *do* to form the negative, but *be* does not. Remember that *do/does* is very challenging for Ss at this level.
2. Remind Ss that negative contractions are the commonly used form. Full-word negatives are used for emphasis—to contradict or correct.

Exercise 2

Ss often come from very traditional families. This exercise gives them an awareness of different family structures as well as some tools to talk about family.

Workbook Ex. 2, p. 32–33.
Answers: TE p. 528.

ANSWER KEY

Exercise 2

1. They have many children. **2.** They also have grandmothers and grandfathers living with them. **3.** . . . , only the father has a job. **4.** The mother doesn't have a job. **5.** The children don't have a babysitter. **6.** Sometimes they have only two people. **7.** Sometimes the parents have one or two children. **8.** Sometimes they don't have children.

FOCUS 3

SUGGESTIONS

1. Review the word order for questions with the verb *be;* contrast this with the insertion of *do/does* for the verb *have.* Examples: *Are you married? Do you have any children?* Tell Ss that most English verbs work like the verb *have.*
2. Point out that the question: *Have you a telephone?* is common in British English, but uncommon in American English.
3. Emphasize the fact that *does* is for third person singular subjects and that the verb *have* remains in the base form in a question, no matter what the subject.
4. Have Ss read the questions aloud. Discuss the intonation of yes/no questions.
5. Go over the short answers. Tell Ss that these are the most common responses to yes/no questions.

Exercise 3

Ss must stand up and walk around the room actively seeking information from one another. They must keep asking these questions until they find at least one classmate who says "yes" for each item. This provides practice with questions, short answers and with count/noncount nouns. They may also ask you the questions.

SUGGESTIONS

1. Make sure Ss understand all vocabulary items before you begin.
2. You may want to add other items of particular relevance to your Ss (an English-English dictionary, a student (F-1) visa).
3. Go around the room; monitor & correct Ss if necessary.

FOCUS 3

Have: Yes/No questions and Short Answers

DO/DOES	SUBJECT	HAVE	
Do	I you we they Nilaulaq and Napachee	have	children?
Does	he she it Mary		

AFFIRMATIVE SHORT ANSWERS		
Yes,	I you we they	**do.**
	he she it	**does.**

NEGATIVE SHORT ANSWERS		
No,	I you we they	**do not. (don't)**
	he she it	**does not. (doesn't)**

EXERCISE 3

Find Someone Who

Ask your classmates if they have the things on the left. Write the names of the students who say "yes."

▶ **EXAMPLE:** Do you have a cordless telephone?
Yes, I do. **OR** No, I don't.

Things	**Students' Names**
1. a cordless telephone	______________
2. pets	______________
3. a car	______________
4. children	______________

ANSWER KEY

Exercise 3

Answers will vary. All start with "Do you have . . . ?

5. relatives in this country ______________________
6. a job ______________________
7. English-speaking friends ______________________
8. a bicycle ______________________
9. a driver's license ______________________
10. a video cassette recorder (VCR) ______________________

EXERCISE 4

Work with a partner. Take turns asking and answering questions. Make questions about the Inuit people in the Opening Task. Use short answers.

▶ **EXAMPLE:** **You:** Does Mary have a house?
Your Partner: Yes, she does.

1. Nila/children
2. Mary/bed
3. Napachee/boat.
4. Nila/wallpaper in her house
5. Nila/furniture
6. Mary/an Inuit name
7. Nila/a television set
8. Mary/canned food

EXERCISE 5

Work with a partner. Write questions using the words on the next page. Try to answer the questions by looking at the pictures below. Then, read the text and check your answers to the questions.

Horse and carriage in Lancaster, Pennsylvania

Daniel

An Amish family

John Lapp

ANSWER KEY

Exercise 4

1. Does Nila have children? Yes, she does.
2. Does Mary have a bed? Yes, she does.
3. Does Napachee have a boat? Yes, he does.
4. Does Nila have wallpaper in her house? No, she doesn't. 5. Does Nila have furniture? No, she doesn't. 6. Does Mary have an Inuit name? No, she doesn't. 7. Does Nila have a television set? No, she doesn't. 8. Does Mary have canned food? Yes, she does.

Exercise 4  

VARIATION

1. Divide the class into two teams.
2. Have each team ask the other a question.
3. Alternate teams. Let Ss refer back to the photos in the Opening Task if necessary. Encourage Ss to correct each other.

Exercise 5

Exercise 5 presents a new context within the theme of traditional lifestyles. This exercise is designed to reflect the reading process. Ss begin by building background knowledge as a pre-reading phase for this short reading passage.

1. Briefly introduce the traditional culture of the Amish. (Most likely, these people are mennonites, since the Amish do not allow themselves to be photographed.) Using the photos, elicit vocabulary
2. Have Ss first look at the cues and write questions.
3. Check the questions as a class.
4. Have them look at the photographs and generate hypotheses about the Amish in order to answer the questions.
5. Then have them read the passage in order to confirm or disconfirm their expectations.
6. Go over the answers as a class. Tell your Ss that reading this way can help them improve their comprehension.

VARIATION

Have Ss look at the pictures and read the text first. Then have them write and answer the questions. This is a more traditional model of reading; one which tests rather than teaches.

Workbook Exs. 3 & 4, p. 33–34.
Answers: TE p. 528.

Questions

▶ **EXAMPLE:** An Amish man/car?

You: Does an Amish man have a car?

Your Partner: No, he doesn't.

1. Amish people/a simple life? ______________________? ______________________.
2. Amish women/jewelry? ______________________? ______________________.
3. An Amish home/electricity? ______________________? ______________________.
4. An Amish farmer/horses? ______________________? ______________________.
5. An Amish home/telephone? ______________________? ______________________.
6. Amish people/their own language? ______________________? ______________________.
7. An Amish child/computer? ______________________? ______________________.
8. Amish people/colorful clothing? ______________________? ______________________.
9. An Amish home/television? ______________________? ______________________.
10. Amish children/special teachers? ______________________? ______________________.
11. Amish children/school after eighth grade? ______________________? ______________________.
12. Amish people/a modern lifestyle? ______________________? ______________________.

The Amish are a special group of Americans. There are about 85,000 Amish people in the United States. They have their own language. They also have a simple way of life.

The Amish are farmers, but they don't have machines on their farms. They have horses. They do not have electricity or telephones in their homes.

The Amish are called "the plain people." They wear dark clothing. The men all have beards and wear hats. The women wear long dresses and hats.

Amish children have one-room schoolhouses. They have Amish teachers. They have no school after the eighth grade. The Amish have a very traditional lifestyle.

ANSWER KEY

Exercise 5

1. Do Amish people have a simple life? Yes, they do.
2. Do Amish women have jewelry? No, they don't.
3. Does an Amish home have electricity? No, it doesn't.
4. Does an Amish farmer have horses? Yes, he does.
5. Does an Amish home have a telephone? No, it doesn't.
6. Do Amish people have their own language? Yes, they do.
7. Does an Amish child have a computer? No, he/she doesn't.
8. Do Amish people have colorful clothing? No, they don't.
9. Does an Amish home have a television? No, it doesn't.
10. Do Amish children have special teachers? Yes, they do.
11. Do Amish children go to shcool after eighth grade? No, they don't.
12. Do Amish people have a modern lifestyle? No, they don't.

FOCUS 4

Some/Any

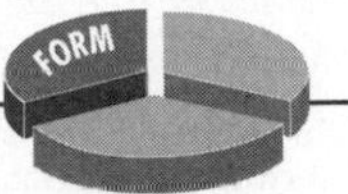

EXAMPLES			EXPLANATIONS
STATEMENT	(a)	The children have **some** books.	Use *some* in statements (with plural count nouns and noncount nouns).
	(b)	They have **some** money.	
NEGATIVE	(c)	They don't have **any** books.	Use *any* in negative statements (with plural count nouns and noncount nouns).
	(d)	She doesn't have **any** money.	
QUESTION	(e)	Do they have **any** books?	Use *any* in questions (with plural count nouns and noncount nouns.)
	(f)	Does she have **any** money?	

EXERCISE 6

Complete the rhyme with *some* or *any.*

I don't have (1) ____________ time today.
I have (2) ____________ problems to solve.
I have (3) ____________ bills to pay.
Do you have (4) ____________ time to play?
I have (5) ____________ places to go.
I have (6) ____________ people to see.
Do you have (7) ____________ advice for me?
Yes, I do: "Slow down!"

FOCUS 4

1. Focus 4 deals only with the form of *some/any.* If you choose to explain the meaning explicitly, remember that *some* refers to an indefinite quantity—it means more than nothing, but implies not a lot, or not all. (We also use *some* in questions when we expect the answer to that question to be "yes." *Do you have some sugar? Sure.*)
2. Be sure that Ss see that *some* and *any* are used only with plural count or noncount nouns.

VARIATION

One way to present this focus box is to have Ss guess the contents of the teacher's bag; or the teacher can talk about the contents using *some/any* and write examples on the board from that context. Realia may help, especially with plural count and noncount nouns.

Exercise 6

Have Ss do this exercise individually.

VARIATION

Use this exercise as a jazz chant. Work on question intonation and rhythm. Have Ss recite the rhyme in small groups. Start slowly and gradually increase speed. Clap to set the rhythm and keep everyone together at first.

ANSWER KEY

Exercise 6

1. any **2.** some **3.** some **4.** any
5. some **6.** some **7.** any

Exercise 7

This exercise gives Ss practice using *some* in affirmative statements and *any* in negative statements, within the context of the Amish. Have Ss do this all together as a class or in small groups. Each student reads a statement, says "True" or "False" and corrects the statement. Encourage Ss to correct each other.

Workbook Ex. 5, p. 35.
Answers: TE p. 528

EXERCISE 7

Read the sentence. Say if it is true or not true. If it's not true, change it to make a true sentence.

▶ **EXAMPLES:** John Lapp has some electrical machines on his farm.
False. He doesn't have any electrical machines on his farm.
The Amish people have a close community.
True.

1. Daniel has some colorful T-shirts.
2. John Lapp's wife has some expensive jewelry.
3. The Amish people have different ideas about education.
4. The Amish have very big telephone bills.
5. Amish schools have some non-Amish teachers.
6. Amish people have strong religious beliefs.
7. The Amish people have some very different habits.
8. The Amish people have some problems with modern lifestyles.
9. The Amish people have some beautiful farmland in the state of Pennsylvania.
10. Amish children have some experience in the outside world.

72 UNIT 5

ANSWER KEY

Exercise 7

1. False. Daniel doesn't have any colorful T-shirts. **2.** False. John Lapp's wife doesn't have any expensive jewelry. **3.** True. **4.** False. The Amish don't have any big telephone bills. (They don't have any telephones!) **5.** False. Amish schools don't have any non-Amish teachers. **6.** True **7.** True **8.** True **9.** True **10.** False. Amish children don't have any experience in the outside world.

FOCUS **5**

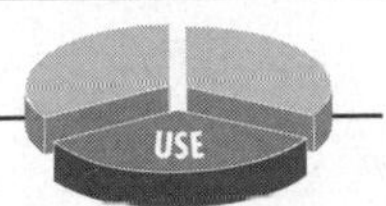

Asking for Something Politely

Use *Do you have . . .* ? to ask for something politely.

EXAMPLES	EXPLANATIONS
Use: **(a)** Do you have an eraser? **Answer** **(b)** Yes, I do. **OR** Sure.	• to ask for something politely.
Use: **(c)** Excuse me, do you have the time? **Answer** **(d)** No, I don't. **OR** Sorry, I don't.	• to stop a person and ask for something.

EXERCISE 8

Work in pairs. You need to borrow five items from your partner. Keep asking questions until you get the five items. The words in the box may help you.

▶ **EXAMPLE:** Do you have an eraser? Yes, I do. **OR** Do you have any gum? Sorry, no I don't.

Eraser	Gum	Notebook
Pen	Whiteout	Piece of paper
Pencil	Stapler	English-English dictionary
Calculator	Ruler	Electronic dictionary
Stamp	Quarter (25 cents)	Change
Tissue	Pencil sharpener	Aspirin

FOCUS 5

This Use box has Ss practice count/noncount nouns and teaches them to make and respond to polite requests. Go over vocabulary first.

SUGGESTIONS

There are two ways to proceed:

1. For an inductive approach, have Ss do Exercise 8 before reading the focus box. Listen to the language they produce. Discuss errors with the class. Then refer them if necessary to Focus Box 5.
2. For a deductive approach, have Ss read the Focus Box first. Then do Exercise 8.

Exercise 8 

Have Ss practice making the questions. Be sure they use the correct article *a/an.*

VARIATION

Make this exercise into a contest: the student who gets all five items first wins.

Workbook Exs. 6 & 7, p. 35–36.
Answers: TE p. 529.

ANSWER KEY

Exercise 8

Do you have: a pen, a pencil, a calculator, a stamp, a tissue, any gum, any whiteout, a stapler, a ruler, a quarter (25 cents), a pencil sharpener, a notebook, a piece of paper, an English-English dictionary, an electronic dictionary, any change, an/any aspirin.

FOCUS 6

This use box teaches Ss how to describe people (while incorporating count/noncount nouns.) Use your Ss or photographs to illustrate descriptive language. Add any relevant features not included here.

FOCUS 6

USE

▶ Using *Have* to Describe People

He **has** short hair.
He **has** a mustache.

HAIR COLOR	HAIR LENGTH	HAIR TYPE	OTHER	EYE COLOR
dark light black brown red blond gray white	long short medium-length	straight wavy curly	a mustache a beard bangs freckles	black brown blue green gray hazel

Exercise 9

Have Ss do this exercise individually.

EXERCISE 9

You need to seat these guests at the dinner table below. Match each description to the correct photograph. Write the number of the photograph on the correct name card at the table.

Photographs:

1.

2.

3.

4.

5.

6.

Descriptions:

a. Rodrigo has a mustache and short, dark, curly hair. He wears glasses. He has an oval face and bushy eyebrows. He's at the head of the table on the left side.

b. Opposite Rodrigo is Chita. Chita is exotic. She has big, round, happy eyes. She has a diamond in her nose. Her hair is dark and she has two shoulder-length braids.

c. Theresa is to the left of Rodrigo. She has short, dark hair and bangs. She has dark round eyes.

d. Next to Theresa is Gonzalo. Gonzalo has a kind face. He has a beard and mustache. His hair and beard are dark, but a little grey. He has bright, round eyes.

e. Across from Theresa is Karl. Karl is almost bald. He has a white mustache and beard. He has wrinkles in his forehead. He has a long, narrow face.

f. Across from Gonzalo and next to Karl is Dominique. Dominique is a very cute woman. She has short hair. It's light brown. She has thin eyebrows and high cheek bones. She has a nice smile.

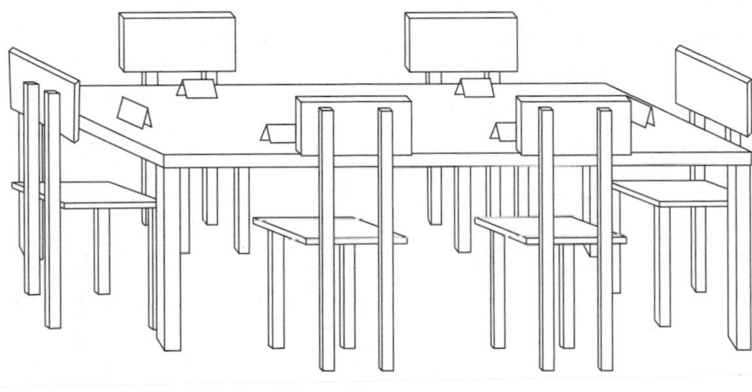

ANSWER KEY

Exercise 9

1. b **2.** f **3.** d **4.** e **5.** a **6.** c

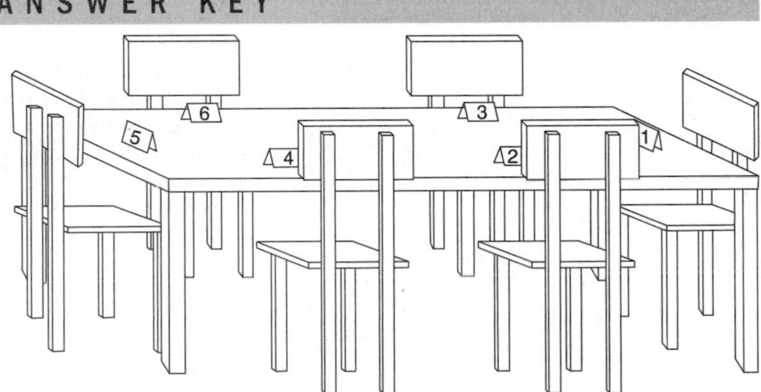

Exercise 10

This exercise opposes the verbs *be* and *have* as a review. Ss will have to recognize *be* + adjective, *be* + adjective + noun, and descriptions with *have*. Expect some confusion between *be* and *have* at this point. Check answers as a class and restate rules if necessary.

Workbook Ex. 8, p. 37–38.
Answers: TE p. 529

Exercise 11

This is the first exercise where Ss are asked to identify and correct errors. These are errors commonly made by beginning level ESL Ss. It is a good idea to get Ss in the habit of evaluating their language and correcting errors.

UNIT GOAL REVIEW

Now ask Ss to look at the goals on the opening page of the unit. Help them understand how much they have accomplished in each area. Ask them if they have any questions about what they have learned so far.

EXERCISE 10

Look at the photographs of Mary and Nilaulaq and of the Amish on pages 64, 65, and 69. Fill in the blanks with *be* or *have* and the correct nouns.

1. John Lapp is Amish.
   a. He ___is___ married.
   b. He __________ long __________.
   c. He __________ a long __________.

2. a. Nilaulaq __________ an Inuit name.
   b. She __________ long black __________.
   c. She __________ a nice smile.

3. a. Daniel __________ a young Amish boy.
   b. He __________ long blond hair.
   c. He __________ bangs.

4. a. Mary __________ a modern Inuit woman.
   b. Mary __________ a round face.
   c. She __________ dark hair.

EXERCISE 11

Correct the mistakes in the sentences.

1. He ~~have~~ has a car.
2. She have not a house.
3. He no have a TV set.
4. He doesn't is rich.
5. She doesn't has children.
6. Does he has a sister?
7. Does she is an Inuit?
8. Excuse me, have you change?

76 | UNIT 5

ANSWER KEY

Exercise 10

1. He has long hair. He has a long beard. 2. Nilaulaq has an Inuit name. She has long black hair. She has a nice smile. 3. Daniel is a young Amish boy. He has long blond hair. He has bangs. 4. Mary is a modern Inuit woman. Mary has a round face. She has dark hair.

Exercise 11

2. She doesn't have a house. 3. He doesn't have a TV set. 4. He isn't rich. 5. She doesn't have any children. 6. Does he have a sister? 7. Is she an Inuit? 8. Excuse me, do you have any change?

Use Your English

ACTIVITY 1: WRITING/SPEAKING

WHO IS HE OR SHE?

Write a description of one of your classmates. Do not write the person's name. Read your description to the class. Your classmates guess who it is.

▶ **EXAMPLE:** This student is tall. He has short black hair. He has brown eyes. He has a mustache. Who is he?

ACTIVITY 2: WRITING/SPEAKING

Think of a person or people you know with traditional lifestyles. Write about these people. Write about what they look like. Tell how their lives are different. Tell what they have and what they don't have. Then make an oral presentation to the class.

ACTIVITY 3: RESEARCH

Go to the library and take out a book about the Inuit, the Amish, or another culture you want to learn about. Write down five new things you have learned about what they have and don't have. Report to the class.

USE YOUR ENGLISH

For a more complete discussion of how to implement the *Use Your English* activities, see page xxvi of this Teacher's Edition.

Activity 1

SUGGESTION

If your Ss are predominantly from the same ethnic group, try to add other features to these descriptions; for example, face shape, or even nonphysical features such as earrings (*he has an earring in his left ear*), or clothing (*he has a red shirt on. . .*).

Activity 2

Allow Ss from the same home country to work together. Encourage them to talk about groups with traditional lifestyles in their home countries today: possibly ethnic minority groups, women, religious groups, etc. Then have each group make a presentation to the class.

Activity 3

SUGGESTIONS

1. Advise Ss to check the children's or young adult section of the library to do this research. They may also use the Internet.
2. Try to have them define which group they want to research and formulate some questions they want answered. With specific information to look for, Ss can scan through library books for key words and concepts before attempting to read for detail. This strategy will facilitate the reading task
3. Ss should choose to work on this individually or in small groups.
   Allow them some time to rehearse before reporting their findings to the class.

Activity 4

This activity gives Ss an opportunity to make cultural comparisons and evaluate certain cultural institutions.

SUGGESTIONS

1. Be sure that Ss understand all the terms on the list before you begin.
2. Add other terms that are relevant to your population—health clubs, psychotherapists, etc.
3. Encourage Ss to express their opinions and check to see that they all understand each other.

Activity 5 

Play textbook audio. The tapescript for this listening appears on p. 545 of this book. Play the tape more than once. You can also use the tape to focus on pronunciation/intonation.

ACTIVITY 4: SPEAKING

Work in groups. These are aspects of United States culture. Do you have them in your country today? What is your opinion of these things? Discuss this with your group.

▶ **EXAMPLE:** In my country today, we have fast-food restaurants. I like them because the food is good and not expensive.

or

I don't like them because the food is not good and we have no time to talk.

- fast-food restaurants
- take-out restaurants
- 24-hour supermarkets
- cell phones
- social security
- daycare centers
- nursing homes
- health insurance

ACTIVITY 5: LISTENING/SPEAKING

STEP 1 Listen to this news report. Then fill in the blanks with information from the news report.

In Zorlik—*Not Any*	**On the American airplanes—*Some***
______________	______________
______________	______________
______________	______________

STEP 2 With a partner, ask and answer questions about the information above. Use *some* and *any*.

ANSWER KEY

Activity 5

See Tapescript for answers.

ACTIVITY 6: SPEAKING

STEP 1 **The Dream List** Look at the Dream List and choose five items you want in your life, or think of some others. Write the items in the chart.

A beautiful house	A car	A computer
15 minutes of fame	Some freedom	An interesting job
Some help in English	A spouse	Some money
Some good friends	A good education	Some free time
Some excitement in my life	Some good luck	Some advice for a problem

My Dream List	Classmate #1	Classmate #2	Classmate #3
1.			
2.			
3.			
4.			
5.			

STEP 2 Find three other students who want the same items.

▶ **EXAMPLE:** You: What do you want?

Classmate #1: I want some free time. I also want some good friends.

Activity 6

EXPANSION

To maximize this activity, encourage Ss to go beyond Step 2, to find out why they want these things in life. Have them ask each other questions that lead them to elaborate on their responses.

The test for this unit can be found on p. 460–461 of this book. The answers can be found on p. 462.

Unit 6

UNIT OVERVIEW

Unit 6 combines a focus on demonstratives and possessives. Many new count/noncount nouns are introduced in everyday contexts such as food, clothing, hobbies, and family relationships. Students (Ss) are taught how to increase their vocabulary by using demonstratives to ask what things are.

UNIT GOALS

To maximize the diagnostic potential of the task, do not review the Unit Goals with Ss until after they have completed and reviewed the task.

OPENING TASK

SETTING UP THE TASK

This task incorporates two different target structures in a problem-solving situation.

1. Since the purpose of Step 1 is to elicit demonstratives and observe whether and how well Ss can use them, do not pre-teach the food items on the tray. You may want to give Ss an overview of the task right from the start. If so, point out that the problem to solve is in Step 3: *Where are the vegetarians?* Ask if anyone knows the definition of "vegetarian" and can give examples of foods vegetarians eat. Or, you may choose to wait and explain this right before Ss begin working on Step 3.
2. Make sure Ss see the numbers on the tables.

CONDUCTING THE TASK

Step 1 

1. While Ss ask each other questions, go around the room to see if any Ss are using demonstratives and if they know the vocabulary.
2. Write their questions and answers on the board as they work. If you hear them using both demonstrative pronouns (Example: *What's <u>this</u>?*) and determiners (*What's <u>that</u> thing?*), list these separately. You can come back to these and correct them later.
3. Review the names of all the foods before going on to Step 2.

UNIT 6

THIS/THAT/THESE/THOSE AND POSSESSIVES

UNIT GOALS:

- To use *this, that, these, those* correctly
- To ask what things are
- To use possessive nouns, adjectives, and pronouns
- To ask questions with *whose*

OPENING TASK

Wally the Waiter

Wally the waiter is new at his job.

STEP 1 Ask your partner questions to name all the foods on Wally's tray.

STEP 2 Read the conversation.

Wally: Uh, excuse me, whose steak is this?

Charles: It's not ours. Maybe it's theirs at the next table.

Wally: Oh, I'm sorry. Is this your soup?

Charles: Yes, it is.

Wally: Then this bread is yours too . . . and what about these french fries?

Jim: No, they aren't ours. The french fries are theirs, too.

Wally: This salad?

Jim: Yes, that's mine.

Wally: And the pizza?

Charles: That's his pizza.

Wally: Is the hamburger for this table?

Charles: No, it isn't. But those strawberries are.

Wally: I'm very sorry. Today is my first day on this job. I'm a little confused.

Jim: No problem. But those are our sodas too, please.

Wally: Sure, thanks again for your patience!

STEP 3 Try to help Wally remember whose foods these are. Where are the vegetarians—Table 1 or Table 2?

Foods	Charles	Jim	Table 2
a. sodas	❑	❑	❑
b. hamburger	❑	❑	❑
c. french fries	❑	❑	❑
d. strawberries	❑	❑	❑
e. salad	❑	❑	❑
f. steak	❑	❑	❑
g. soup	❑	❑	❑
h. pizza	❑	❑	❑
i. bread	❑	❑	❑

Step 2

1. Advise Ss to read the whole conversation once; then read it a second time and check the correct boxes in Step 3.
2. Show Ss how to use context clues (*yes,no, not*) to compensate for any possessives they may not know. Example: in the following interaction, *Whose steak is this? It's not ours. Oh, I'm sorry.* . . Ss can use the clues: *not* and *I'm sorry* to infer meaning, even if they do not understand *ours*.

COMPLETING THE TASK

1. Ask Ss to make statements aloud telling which food is for whom. Example: *The hamburger is Table 2's*. Write their correct and incorrect statements on separate boards.
2. Have them solve the problem: Where are the vegetarians?

REVIEWING THE TASK

Return to what you wrote on the board. Have Ss observe the language they produced and try to see patterns. Allow them to discuss their hypotheses. Review count/noncount nouns. Then go over the Unit Goals.

ANSWER KEY

Opening Task

Step 3

Answers may vary.

a. They're Jim and Charles' sodas./They're Charles and Jim's sodas.
The sodas are Jim and Charles.' The sodas are Charles and Jim's.

b. It's table 2's hamburger./ The hamburger is table 2's . . .

c. They're table 2's french fries./The french fries are table 2's

d. They're Jim and Charles'; They're Charles and Jim's strawberries./The strawberries are Charles and Jim's./The strawberries are Jim and Charles'.

e. It's Jim's salad./The salad is Jim's.

f. It's table 2's steak./The steak is table 2's.

g. It's Charles' soup./The soup is Charles.'

h. It's Jim's pizza./ The pizza is Jim's.

i. It's Charles' bread./The bread is Charles.'

The vegetarians are at Table 1.

FOCUS 1

Both demonstrative pronouns (*This is a hamburger*) and demonstrative determiners (*This Italian bread is cheap*) are included in this focus box.

1. Show proximity and distance visually by placing objects around the room close to and far from the Ss.
2. Point out that demonstratives agree in number with the noun phrases they refer to or precede. In this way, they are unlike adjectives, which do not agree in number with the noun phrases they precede. Examples: *This desk is near me. That desk is far from me. These papers are near me. Those papers are far from me.*

Exercise 1 

While Ss are identifying the target structure in context, see if they can tell the difference between the pronouns and the determiners. Make two separate lists on the board.

Exercise 2

This exercise can be done independently. Ss will have to pay attention to the near/far and the count/noncount distinction.
Encourage them to correct each other.

FOCUS **1**

This, These, That, Those

NEAR SPEAKER	FAR FROM SPEAKER
Singular	
(a) **This** is a hamburger. (b) **This** hamburger is good.	(c) **That** is a steak. (d) **That** steak is delicious.
Plural	
(e) **These** are baked potatoes. (f) **These** baked potatoes are hot.	(g) **Those** are french fries. (h) **Those** french fries are salty.
Noncount	
(i) **This** is Italian bread. (j) **This** Italian bread is cheap.	(k) **That** is French bread. (l) **That** French bread is expensive.

EXERCISE 1

Go back to the Opening Task on page 81. Find at least five sentences with *this, these, that,* and *those*. Write them below.

1. ______________________
2. ______________________
3. ______________________
4. ______________________
5. ______________________

EXERCISE 2

Are the things in the pictures on the next page singular, plural, or noncount? Are the things near or far from the speaker? Fill in the blanks with *this/that/these/those* and the correct form of the verb *be*.

ANSWER KEY

Exercise 1

1. Uh, excuse me, whose steak is this?
2. Is this your soup?
3. Then this bread is yours too. . . and what about these French fries?
4. This salad?
5. Yes, that's mine.
6. That's his pizza.
7. Is the hamburger for this table?
8. But those strawberries are.
9. Today is my first day on this job.
10. But those are our sodas too.

Pronouns	Determiners
Whose steak is this? Is this your soup? That's mine. That's his pizza. Those are our sodas too.	This bread is yours too. . . and what about these french fries? This salad Is the hamburger for this table? those strawberries are . . . Today is my first day on this job.

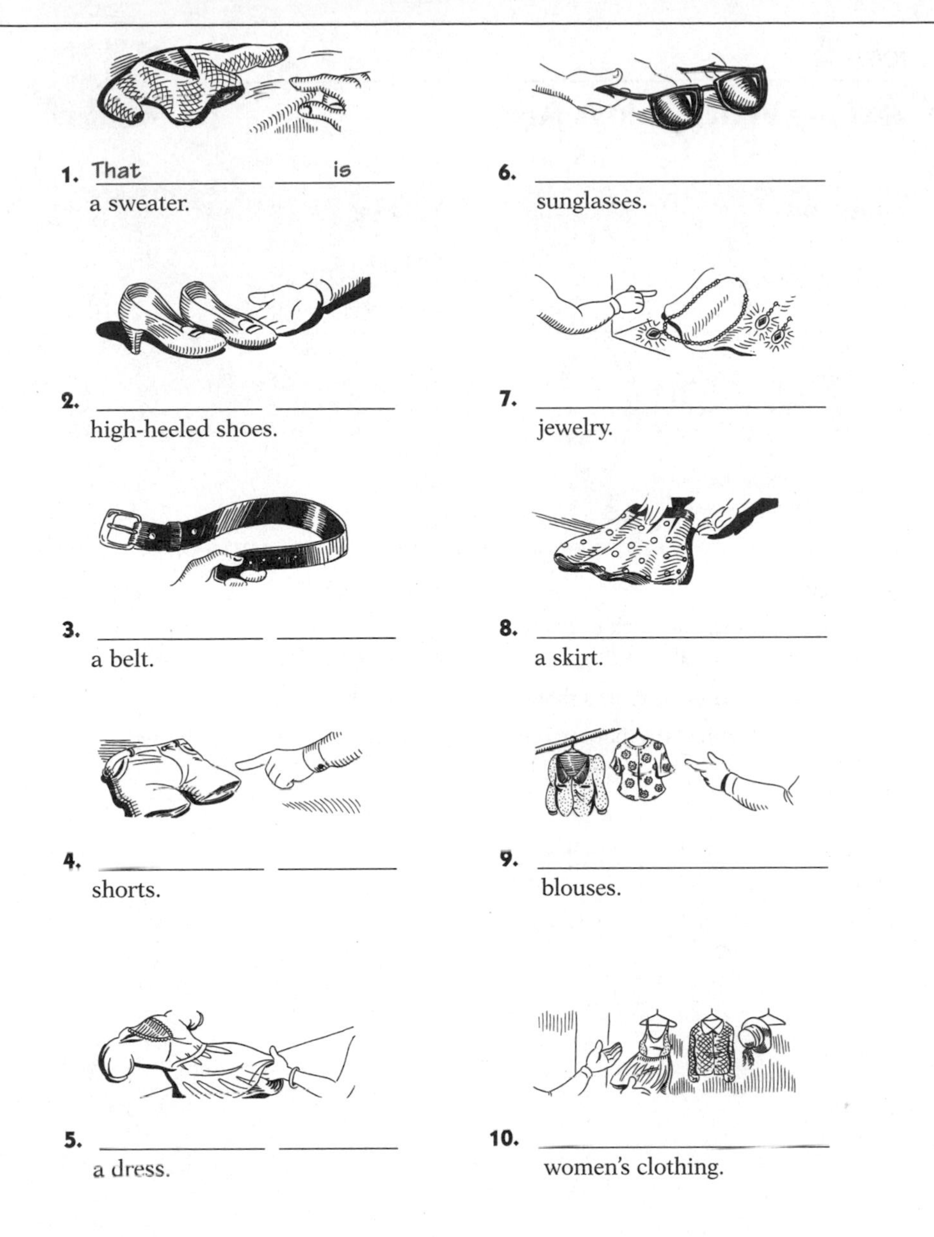

ANSWER KEY

Exercise 2

2. These are **3.** This is **4.** Those are
5. This is **6.** These are **7.** That is
8. This is **9.** Those are **10.** That is

FOCUS 2

Ss need this simple strategy to learn the words for the things they see around them.

SUGGESTIONS

1. Use visuals placed around the room to support the examples.
2. Have Ss read the examples aloud.
3. Point out that in the answers, we often use subject pronouns (*It, They*) instead of demonstratives.

Exercise 3 

1. As a vocabulary review, recycle the pictures in Exercise 2 . Or bring in other items of clothing, or pictures of items of clothing.
2. Place them around the room and have Ss ask each other what each item is. Work on pronunciation.

FOCUS **2**

Asking What Things Are

QUESTIONS	ANSWERS
(a) What's **this**? / **that**	**Singular** **It's a** sandwich. **It's an** egg.
(b) What are **these**? / **those**	**Plural** **They are** french fries. **They're** cookies.
(c) What's **this** dish? / **that** dish?	**Noncount** **It's** soup.

EXERCISE 3

Work with a partner. Go back to Exercise 2. Partner A asks questions about the items of clothing. Use *What's this/that? What are these/those*? Partner B responds.

EXAMPLES: **Partner A:** What's that? **Partner B:** It's a sweater.
Partner A: What are these? **Partner B:** They're high-heeled shoes.

ANSWER KEY

Exercise 3

3. What's this? It's a belt. **4.** What are those? They're shorts. **5.** What's this? It's a dress. **6.** What are these? They're sunglasses. **7.** What's that? It's jewelry. **8.** What's this? It's a skirt. **9.** What are those? They're blouses. **10.** What's that? It's women's clothing.

EXERCISE 4

This is Maria's first American party. She doesn't know about American food. She asks her American friend, Chris, about the food on the table.

Ask questions with *what*. Then fill in the subject, verb, and *a/an* where necessary. Then match each sentence to the picture.

			Letter in the Picture
1.	What's this? It's a	hamburger.	d
2.		hot dog.	
3.		french fries	
4.		ketchup.	
5.		pizza.	
6.		sandwich.	
7.		doughnuts.	
8.		cookies.	
9.		muffin.	
10.		ice cream cone.	

Exercise 4 

First decide which objects are near/far from Maria and Chris. Then have Ss do the exercise.

Workbook Ex. 2, p. 40.
Answers; TE p. 529.

ANSWER KEY

Exercise 4

2. What's that? Its a hot dog. . . i
3. What are those? They're. . . j
4. What's this? It's (a) . . . c
5. What's that? Its (a) . . . f
6. What's this? It's a . . . e
7. What are these? They're . . . a
8. What are those? They're . . . g
9. What's this? It's a . . .b
10. What's that? It's a . . . h

FOCUS 3

SUGGESTIONS

1. Emphasize the position of the apostrophe:
   -The aspotrophe indicates singular/ plural:
   The boy's dog vs. The boys' dog.
   -The aspotrophe is not a comma
2. Emphasize the order of the nouns. Some Ss will make the wrong noun possessive: *The dog's boy* instead of *The boy's dog.*
3. Have Ss read examples aloud. Work on the pronunciation of possessive nouns.

Exercise 5 

Ss should make two statements: one using proper nouns and one using common nouns. For clarification:
Common nouns may vary: #1: The couple's hobby. . . ,
The man and woman's hobby. . . ,
The girl and boy's hobby. . . ,

FOCUS **3**

Possessive Nouns

EXAMPLES	EXPLANATIONS
(a) The boy has a dog. The **boy's dog** is small. (b) Carol has a magazine. **Carol's magazine** is on the table.	Add an apostrophe (**'**) and **-s** to a singular noun.
(c) The boss has an office. The **boss's office** is big. The **boss' office** is neat. (d) Charles has a sister. **Charles's** sister is twenty-six. **Charles'** sister is successful.	Add an apostrophe (**'**) and **-s** or just an apostrophe (**'**) to singular nouns and names that end in **-s.**
(e) The waiters have trays. The **waiters' trays** are heavy.	Add only an apostrophe (**'**) at the end of a plural noun.
(f) The **children's school** is near here. (g) **Women's clothing** is cheap here.	Add apostrophe (**'**) **-s** to irregular plural nouns.
(h) Paul and **Mary's dog** is friendly. (i) My mother-in-**law's cookies** are delicious.	For two or more subjects or a subject with hyphens **(-)**, add **'-s** at the end of last noun.

EXERCISE 5

A *hobby* is an activity we do in our free time. Look at the pictures. Match each person to a hobby. Complete the statement using possessive nouns.

▶ **EXAMPLE:**

BERNIE

a. Bernie's hobby is photography.
b. The man's hobby is photography.

HOBBIES			
photography	playing the piano	hiking	reading
gardening	dancing	astronomy	collecting stamps
traveling	surfing the Internet		

1. JULIO & KARLA

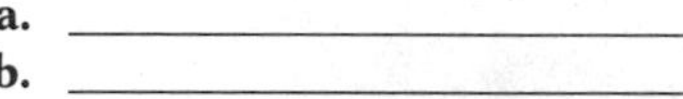

a. ______________________
b. ______________________

2. CHRIS

a. ______________________
b. ______________________

3. CAROL

a. ______________________
b. ______________________

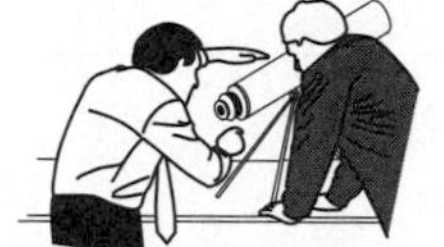

4. JOEL & EUGENE

a. ______________________
b. ______________________

5. ALEXIS

a. ______________________
b. ______________________

EXPANSION

Have Ss write their names and their own hobbies on index cards. Collect and redistribute them. Have them make statements about each other's hobbies.

Workbook Ex. 3, p. 41–42.
Answers: TE p. 529.

6. DONALD

a. ______________________
b. ______________________

7. JUDY, ELLEN & GINA

a. ______________________
b. ______________________

8. ALICE

a. ______________________
b. ______________________

9. SONIA & TOMMY

a. ______________________
b. ______________________

ANSWER KEY

Exercise 5

1. a. Julio and Karla's hobby is dancing.
   b. The couple's hobby is dancing./The man and woman's hobby is dancing.
2. a. Chris' hobby is reading.
   b. The young boy's hobby is reading.
3. a. Carol's hobby is gardening.
   b. The woman's hobby is gardening.
4. a. Joel and Eugene's hobby is astronomy.
   b. The men's hobby is astronomy.
5. a. Alexis' hobby is surfing the Internet.
   b. The girl's hobby is surfing the Internet.
6. a. Donald's hobby is playing the piano.
   b. The teenage boy's hobby is playing the piano.
7. a. Judy, Ellen, and Gina's hobby is hiking.
   b. The girls' hobby is hiking.
8. a. Alice's hobby is traveling.
   b. The young woman's hobby is traveling.
9. a. Sonia and Tommy's hobby is collecting stamps.
   b. The children's hobby is collecting stamps.

EXERCISE 6

This is Charles' family tree. Read the sentences. Write each person's relationship to Charles under the name in the box.

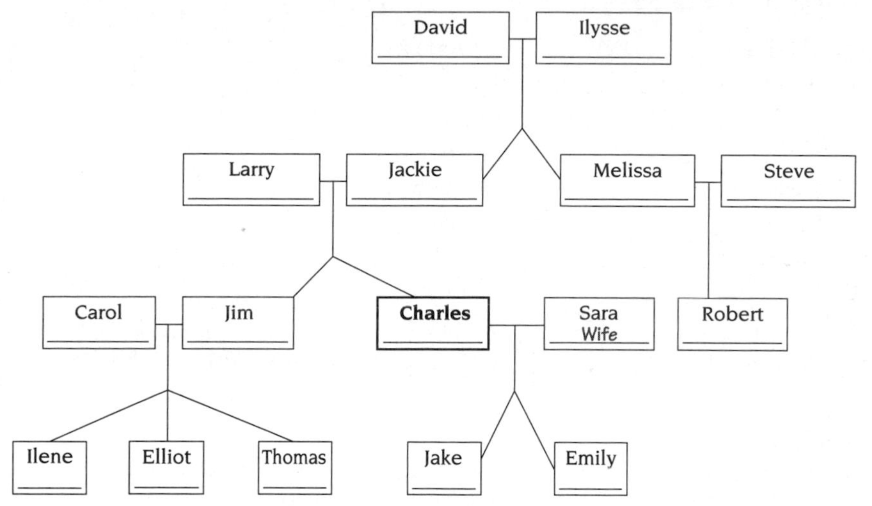

1. Sara is Charles' wife.
2. Emily is Sara and Charles' daughter.
3. Jake is Sara and Charles' son.
4. Jim is Charles' brother.
5. Carol is Charles' sister-in-law.
6. Elliot and Thomas are Charles' nephews.
7. Ilene is Charles' niece.
8. Melissa is Charles' aunt.
9. Steve is Charles' uncle.
10. Robert is Charles' cousin.
11. Jackie is Charles' mother.
12. Larry is Charles' father.
13. David is Charles' grandfather.
14. Ilysse is Charles' grandmother.

Exercise 6

This exercise teaches Ss the vocabulary of family relationships and prepares them for Exercise 7. Put the family tree on the board or on an OHP, to provide a visual representation of these relationships.

ANSWER KEY

Exercise 6

David	- grandfather
Ilysse	- grandmother
Larry	- father
Jackie	- mother
Melissa	- aunt
Steve	- uncle
Carol	- sister-in-law
Jim	- brother
Sara	- wife
Robert	- cousin
Ilene	- niece
Elliot	- nephew
Thomas	- nephew
Jake	- son
Emily	- daughter

Exercise 7 

Refer Ss to the family tree in Exercise 6. Correct answers as a class.

Workbook Exs. 4 & 5, pp. 43–44.
Answers: TE p. 529.

Exercise 8

The position of the apostrophe is very confusing to Ss. Remind them that the position of the apostrophe indicates singular/plural, showing how many people (one person or more than one person) have something. Do this exercise as a class and encourage Ss to correct each other.

EXERCISE 7

Write the correct possessive nouns in the blanks. Say each sentence aloud.

▶ **EXAMPLE:** Sara is Charles' wife.

1. Charles is __________ brother.
2. David is __________ father.
3. Emily is __________ sister.
4. Jim is __________ husband.
5. Melissa is __________ daughter.
6. Elliot is __________ cousin.
7. Charles is __________ uncle.
8. Jake is __________ nephew.
9. Carol is __________ sister-in-law.
10. Ilysse is __________ mother-in-law.

EXERCISE 8

Look carefully at the apostrophes in the sentences below. How many people are there in each sentence? How many dogs? Check *one* or *more than one* for each sentence.

	How many people?		How many dogs?	
	One	**More than one**	**One**	**More than one**
1. My daughter's dog is big.	✔	____	✔	____
2. My daughters' dogs big.	____	____	____	____
3. My son's dog is big.	____	____	____	____
4. My sons' dogs are big.	____	____	____	____
5. My sons' dog is big.	____	____	____	____
6. My son's dogs are big.	____	____	____	____
7. My children's dog is big.	____	____	____	____
8. My children's dogs are big.	____	____	____	____

ANSWER KEY

Exercise 7
1. Jim's
2. Jackie and Melissa's
3. Jake's
4. Carol's
5. David and Ilysse's
6. Jake and Emily's
7. Ilene, Elliot and Thomas'
8. Carol and Jim's
9. Sara and Charles'
10. Steve and Larry's

Exercise 8
2. More than one; More than one 3. One; One 4. More than one; More than one 5. More than one; One 6. One; More than one 7. More than one; One 8. More than one; More than one

FOCUS **4**

Possessive Adjectives, Pronouns

POSSESSIVE ADJECTIVES		POSSESSIVE PRONOUNS	
My	car is new.	The car is	**mine**.
Your	house is beautiful.	The house is	**yours**.
His	dog is old.	The dog is	**his**.
Its	fur is white.	(**Its** cannot be a possessive pronoun.)	
Her	jewelry is expensive.	The jewelry is	**hers**.
Our	children are cute.	The children are	**ours**.
Their	television is big.	The television is	**theirs**.

NOTES: Do not confuse a possessive adjective (*its*) with the contraction of *it* + *is* (*it's*). **Example:** I have a Siamese cat. **Its** a pure breed. It's eyes are deep blue.

Use possessive adjectives with parts of the body.

My hair is black. **Your** eyes are blue.

EXERCISE 9

Fill in each blank with a possessive adjective or possessive pronoun.

1.

Man: Excuse me, miss. Is this _______________ scarf?

Woman: No, it's not _______________. I have _______________ scarf, thanks.

Man: Oh, I'm sorry. By the way, what's _______________ name?

Woman: Anna. What's _______________?

FOCUS 4

1. Ss often make mistakes such as: *My sister and his husband. . ."* because they assume that the possessive adjective agrees with the noun phrase that follows (*husband* is a masculine word in some languages). Emphasize that the possessive word depends on the person who has the thing or the relationship (*My sister has a husband. Her husband is 40 years old.*).
2. Point out that a possessive adjective (determiner) is not like other adjectives in that it cannot be preceded by an article (*My dog is cute.* NOT: *The my dog is cute.*).
3. Make sure Ss know the difference between *its* (possessive) and *it's* (S-V, contraction of *it is*).

GRAMMAR NOTE

1. *His* is the same whether it is a possessive adjective or a possessive pronoun: *His dog is old./The dog is his.*
2. All possessive pronouns end in *s*, except *mine.*
3. *Its* doesn't occur as a possessive pronoun.

EXPANSION

1. Refer to your Ss to show the use of possessives with body parts: *Your eyes are blue. Mine are brown.*
2. As an entire class activity, Ss write their names on slips of paper, which are placed in a hat, box, or the like. Each student takes a paper, writes a description of that person and reads it to the class.
3. The class guesses which student that person is.

Workbook Ex. 7, p. 45–46.
Answers: TE p. 529.

Exercise 9

Discuss the pictures first to be sure that Ss understand the situations and vocabulary (for example, in #5: SS must understand *genes*). Have Ss role-play the mini-dialogues.

EXPANSION

Ask Ss to continue these dialogues and perform them in class, and compare their outcomes with those of the other groups.

2.

Couple 1: Pardon me, but these are ________________ seats.

Couple 2: I don't think so. These are ________________ seats. Here are ________________ tickets.

Couple 1: We're very sorry. It's ________________ mistake.

3.

Girl 1: Are these ________________ glasses?

Girl 2: No, they're ________________. She really needs ________________ glasses to read the board.

4.

Police Officer: Is this ________________ car, young man?

Young Man: Yes, it is, sir.

Police Officer: Where is ________________ registration?

Young Man: It's right here in ______________ wallet, with ____________ license.

ANSWER KEY

Exercise 9

1. Is this your scarf? No, it's not mine. I have my scarf. . . .what's your name? What's yours? **2.** these are our seats. These are our seats. Here are our tickets. It's our mistake. **3.** Are these your glasses? No, they're hers. She really needs her glasses to read the board. **4.** Is this your car, young man? Where is your registration? It's right here in my wallet with my license. **5.** Who's your new friend? He has his own website. Zack's parents have their own computer company. Maybe computers are in his/their genes!

5.

Boy #1: Who's ______________ new friend?

Boy #2: That's Zack. He's a real computer wiz. He has ______________ own website. Zack's parents have ______________ own computer company. Maybe computers are in ______________ genes!

EXERCISE 10

Fill in each blank with a possessive word (a possessive adjective or a possessive pronoun). Then look at the two dogs. Whose dog is A? Whose dog is B?

Many people have pets. (1) ___Their___ pets are very important to them. Charles' family loves pets. (2) ______________ children have a dog. Emily says the dog is (3) ______________ ; Jake says the dog is (4) ______________ . (5) ______________ dog is small. (6) ______________ legs are short, (7) ______________ ears are long. It's very cute.

Charles' parents have a dog too. They introduce their dog: "This is (8) ______________ dog. (9) ______________ name is Buck. He's strong. (10) ______________ nose is flat. (11) ______________ fur is short. We love Buck. He's part of (12) ______________ family."

A. This is ______________ dog. **B.** This is ______________ dog.

Exercise 10

You might point out to Ss that we use *it* to talk about animals when we do not know if they are male or female. Once we know the sex, we can use *his* or *her.*

EXPANSION

Have Ss bring in pictures of their own pets and talk about them.

Workbook Exs. 6 & 8, pp. 44–47.
Answers: TE p. 529.

ANSWER KEY

Exercise 10

2. His **3.** hers **4.** his **5.** Their **6.** His/Its **7.** His/Its **8.** our **9.** His/Its **10.** His/Its **11.** His/Its **12.** our

A. This is Emily and Jake's dog./This is Charles' dog. This is Charles' family's dog.
B. This is Charles' parents' dog.

FOCUS 5

Have Ss read the examples aloud and notice the range of responses. Stress the distinction between *Whose* (possessive) and *Who's* (S-V). Examples: *Who's from Africa in our class?*
Who's married?
Whose umbrella is on the floor?
Whose books are these?

Exercise 11 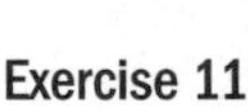 

Ss can also do this exercise in pairs. Go around the room listening and correcting Ss as they work.

Workbook Ex. 9, p. 47–48.
Answers; TE p. 529.

FOCUS **5**

Questions with *Whose*

Use *whose* to ask who owns or possesses something.

WHOSE	NOUN	VERB		ANSWERS
Whose	dog	is	this?	It's Carol's dog. It's her dog. It's hers. Carol's.
Whose	glasses	are	these?	They're Jim's glasses. They're his glasses. They're his. Jim's.

EXAMPLES	EXPLANATIONS
(a) **Who's** she? My sister. (b) **Whose** car is that? Mine.	Do not confuse *who's* and *whose*. *Who's* and *whose* have the same pronunciation. *Who's* = *who is*. *Whose* asks about who owns something.

EXERCISE 11

Ask questions with *whose* to find out who owns each object. Answer in two ways as in the example.

▶ **EXAMPLE:** Whose hammer is this?
It's Jackie's hammer. It's hers.

A. John is a hairdresser.

B. Jackie is a carpenter

C. Jim is a secretary

D. Pierre and Daniel are cooks

1. spoon

2. pencil sharpener

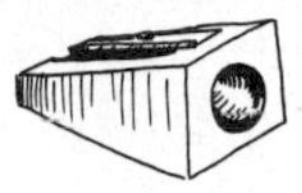

3. shampoo

4. screwdriver

5. computer

6. comb

7. hammer

8. hairbrush

9. sauce pan

10. scissors

11. envelope

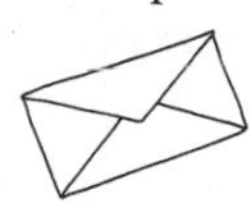

12. can opener

13. ladder

14. nails

15. frying pan

16. paperclip

ANSWER KEY

Exercise 11

1. 1. It's Pierre and Daniel's . . . It's theirs **2.** It's Jim's . . . It's his **3.** It's John's . . . It's his **4.** It's Jackie's . . . It's hers **5.** It's Jim's . . . It's his **6.** It's John's . . . It's his **7.** It's Jackie's . . . It's hers **8.** It's John's . . . It's his **9.** It's Pierre and Daniels' . . . It's theirs **10.** They're John's . . . They're his **11.** It's Jim's . . . It's his **12.** It's Pierre and Daniels's/It's theirs **13.** It's Jackie's . . . It's hers **14.** They're Jackie's . . . They're hers **15.** It's Pierre and Daniel's . . . It's theirs **16.** It's Jim's . . . It's his

Exercise 12

Have Ss do this exercise individually and then check as a class.

UNIT GOALS REVIEW

Discuss with Ss the Unit Goals on page 80. Which goals have they achieved? Which goals are they still working on?

USE YOUR ENGLISH

For a more complete discussion of how to implement the *Use Your English* activities, see page xxvi of this Teacher's Edition.

Activity 1

EXPANSION

1. Challenge Ss to make other types of statements using possessives in Step 2: *My partner's aunt is in the U.S. His aunt's family has a dog. . . ,* etc.
2. Have a poster session in class where some Ss post their family trees and others circulate, learning about their classmates' families.

Activity 2

EXPANSION:

Ask Ss to bring in culture-specific or unfamiliar items so that they can ask :*Whose is this? /Whose are these?* and then *What is it?/What are they?* (For example: silver bracelets for India, chopsticks for Japan, China, Korea.)

EXERCISE 12

Correct the mistakes in the following sentences.

1. This is Jim magazine.
2. Charles is married. Sara is her wife.
3. That computer is her's.
4. Is Jim the brother of Charles?
5. Who's son-in-law is Charles?
6. Charles and Sara have two children. Jake and Emily are theirs children.
7. What's that name's man?
8. The Larry's dog is small.
9. Whose hungry?
10. This dogs are cute.
11. A: Is this the dog's food?
    B: Yes, that's its.
12. The teacher has chalk on the face.

Use Your English

ACTIVITY 1: WRITING

STEP 1 Draw your family tree.

STEP 2 Ask a classmate about his or her family tree. Draw your classmate's family tree. Then write five sentences about your classmate's family.

ACTIVITY 2: SPEAKING

The teacher asks each student to put a personal object into a bag. One student picks an object and asks, "Whose is this?" The class guesses who the owner is. If the class is not correct, the owner says, "It's mine."

96 UNIT 6

ANSWER KEY

Exercise 12

1. This is Jim's magazine. **2.** Sara is his wife. **3.** That computer is hers. **4.** Is Jim Charles' brother? **5.** Whose son-in-law is Charles? **6.** Jake and Emily are their children. **7.** What's that man's name? **8.** Larry's dog is small. **9.** Who's hungry? **10.** These dogs are cute. **11.** Yes, it is./ Yes, that's his/hers. **12.** The teacher has chalk on his/her face.

ACTIVITY 3: SPEAKING/WRITING

STEP 1 Bring something to class from your country or another country you know that is special (something you eat, something you wear, something people use, etc.). Tell the class about the special thing. Tell why it is special.

▶ **EXAMPLES:** This is a special dress. It's for a wedding.
These are ankle bracelets from India.
They're made of silver.

STEP 2 Choose one of the objects from the class presentations. Write about it.

ACTIVITY 4: SPEAKING

Bring in a menu from an American restaurant. Ask questions about the foods on the menu. Role-play a dialogue between a confused waiter (like Wally) and two customers in a restaurant.

ACTIVITY 5: LISTENING

STEP 1 Listen to the conversation. What are the people talking about?

STEP 2 Listen again. In the chart, write *this/that/these* or *those* next to each thing. Then check (✔) if each thing is *near* or *far from* the speaker.

This/that/these/those?		*Near*	*Far from*
1. these	chairs	✔	
2.	table		
3.	lamp		
4.	pictures		
5.	statue		
6.	sofa		

ANSWER KEY

Activity 5
See tapescript for answers.

Activity 3

These items could also be ordinary things: a ring, a photograph, a key, but with some special significance to the speaker.

Activity 4

SUGGESTIONS

1. Asking and answering questions about food provides practice describing. See how well Ss do this. You may need to correct some imaginative descriptions!
2. Set your classroom up as a restaurant. Refer Ss back to the dialogue in the Opening Task. If possible, explain to Ss that the waiter is going to take orders and then make mistakes when serving the food, as in the dialogue. Ss will have to correct the waiter. If this is too challenging for Ss, have them simply role-play the restaurant scene. Record the role-plays and play back the tape for evaluation and correction.

Activity 5

Play textbook audio. The tapescript for this listening appears on p. 545 of this book.

The test for this unit can be found on p. 463–464 of this book. The answers are on p.465.

TOEFL Test Preparation Exercises for Units 4–6 can be found on p. 49–51.

The answers are on p. 530 of this book.

Unit 7

UNIT OVERVIEW

This unit illustrates the "given-new" discourse rule in English; that is, the ordering of information in a sentence so that the new information is postponed. Unit 7 also deals with the article system: the use of the indefinite article to introduce new information with the structure *there* + *be*, as well as other uses.

UNIT GOALS

To maximize the diagnostic potential of the task, do not review the Unit Goals with students (Ss) until after they have completed and reviewed the task.

OPENING TASK
SETTING UP THE TASK

Look at the picture and the statements. Have Ss identify the items in the room: desk, bookshelves, etc.

CONDUCTING THE TASK

1. Put Ss in pairs or groups of 3 to decide what kind of person lives in this apartment.

UNIT 7

THERE IS/THERE ARE, A/AN VERSUS THE

UNIT GOALS:

- To understand the meaning of *there* + *be*
- To know when to use *there* + *be* to focus on new information
- To make affirmative and negative statements, and *yes/no* questions with *there* + *be*
- To choose between *a/an* and *the*

OPENING TASK

Whose Apartment is This?

Read the statements on the next page. Then circle the type of person you think lives in this apartment. Give reasons for your choices.

1. The person | is a man. | is a woman.
2. The person | has a baby. | doesn't have a baby.
3. The person | has a pet. | doesn't have a pet.
4. The person | is athletic. | is not athletic.
5. The person | drinks coffee. | doesn't drink coffee.
6. The person | is well-educated. | is not well-educated.
7. The person | likes music. | doesn't like music.
8. The person | is on a diet. | is not on a diet.

I think this person is a man/woman because ... List your reasons.

2. Have Ss write their reasons for their choices. This is how you will see if and to what extent they know how to use *there* + *be*. Expect them to write sentences such as:
   - *have a cat under the bed*
   - *there no have baby toys*
   - *there's the coffee pot on the stove*
   - *is a cat under the bed*
   - *a cat is under the bed*

Write Ss' statements on the board, both the correct and the incorrect ones. Organize the board so that all correct statements are listed together and incorrect statements are grouped by error type. For example, group all statements without subjects, such as: *is a cat under the bed* together. Or group all statements using definite articles, such as: *there's the coffee pot on the stove.* You will use these later as a bridge to the target structure.

COMPLETING THE TASK

Go over the answers and decide who lives there.

REVIEWING THE TASK

Let Ss evaluate the sentences on the board. They will be discussing form/meaning and use at this point. Some Ss may have learned this and will give you enough to begin formulating rules or patterns, and correcting these hypotheses. If you cannot elicit enough from them, move on to Focuses 1 and 2 and then come back to correct their hypotheses.

ANSWER KEY

Opening Task

Answers may vary here.

1. is a woman. (There's women's clothing in the closet.)
2. doesn't have a baby. (There's no crib/There are no baby toys.)
3. has a pet. (There's a cat under the bed.)
4. is athletic. (There's an exercise bicycle in the room.)
5. drinks coffee. (There's a coffee pot on the stove.)
6. is well-educated. (There are many books on the shelves.)
7. likes music. (There are many CDs on the shelves.)
8. is not on a diet. (There's a cake on the counter.)

FOCUS 1

Explain to Ss that we place new information at the end of the sentence when:

a. talking about existence or location
b. describing something
c. talking about something for the first time

This discourse rule explains why a native speaker would spontaneously say, *"There's a cat under the bed,"* and NOT *"A cat is under the bed."*

Exercise 1

Ss have to make a discourse choice here. Both statements are grammatically correct, but only one is appropriate in this context.

Workbook Ex. 1, p. 52.
Answers: TE, p. 530

FOCUS **1**

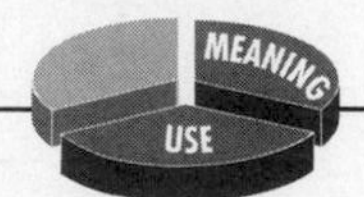

There + Be

EXAMPLES	EXPLANATIONS
(a) **There are** a lot of things in the apartment.	Use *there + be:* • to show something or somebody exists.
(b) **There is** a cat under the bed.	• to show something or somebody's location.
(c) **There is** a mouse in the house. There's a mouse in the house. NOT: A mouse is in the house.	• when you talk about something or somebody for the first time.
(d) **There are** two men in the picture below. **They are** not happy.	Do not confuse *there are* and *they are.*

EXERCISE 1

Circle (a) or (b) for the correct sentence.

EXAMPLE: (a) Two men are in this picture.
(b) There are two men in this picture. [circled]

1. An angry restaurant customer says,
   (a) "Waiter, a fly is in my soup."
   (b) "Waiter, there's a fly in my soup."
2. The waiter answers,
   (a) "Sorry, sir. There's more soup in the kitchen."
   (b) "Sorry, sir. More soup is in the kitchen."
3. The customer gets the bill. He says,
   (a) "Waiter, a mistake is on the bill."
   (b) "Waiter, there's a mistake on the bill."

ANSWER KEY

Exercise 1
1. b **2.** a **3.** b

FOCUS **2**

There Is/There Are

FORM

The form of the *be* verb depends on the noun phrase that follows it.

THERE + *BE*	NOUN PHRASE		EXPLANATIONS
(a) **There is**	an angry man	at the table.	singular count noun
(b) **There are**	two people	in the restaurant.	plural count noun
(c) **There is**	soup	in his dish.	noncount noun
(d) **There is**	a dining room, kitchen, and restroom	in this restaurant.	When there is more than one noun, *be* agrees with the first noun.

Contraction: *There is* = *There's.*

EXERCISE 2

Go back to the Opening Task on page 98. Write sentences about the picture with *there is/are* and the words below.

EXAMPLE: one bed in the apartment
There's one bed in the apartment.

1. a tennis racquet in the closet
2. high-heeled shoes in the closet
3. women's clothing in the closet
4. sneakers in the closet
5. a coat in the closet
6. CDs on the shelf
7. a CD player on the shelf
8. books on the shelf
9. women's jewelry in the box on the table
10. coffee in the coffee pot
11. a big cake on the counter
12. an exercise bicycle in the apartment
13. an expensive rug on the floor
14. two pillows on the bed

FOCUS 2

This focus box shows how to postpone new information using *there* as a dummy subject. *There* is in the subject position in front of the verb *be*, followed by a noun phrase headed by an indefinite article. The verb *be* agrees with the noun phrase that follows it. Teaching the structure this way reinforces English S-V word order, and makes it easier for Ss to understand question formation: *Is there a cat under the bed?* (Otherwise we'd have to say that the noun phrase is really the subject, even though it comes after the verb in these statements!)

SUGGESTIONS

1. If you were able to elicit most of these rules from Ss during the task, skip them or review them quickly and move on to the exercises.
2. If you prefer a deductive approach, go over the examples and explanations with the Ss and then have them do the exercises.

Exercise 2

Ss can do this orally or in writing. Put their sentences on the board to correct for
- omission of *there*
- use of *have* instead of *be*
- noun errors
- article errors, etc.

ANSWER KEY

Exercise 2
1. There's 2. There are 3. There's 4. There are 5. There's 6. There are 7. There's 8. There are 9. There's 10. There's 11. There's 12. There's 13. There's 14. There are

Exercise 3 

This exercise gives Ss a chance to use the structure for a real purpose—to describe a scene that others must draw. Put their drawings up around the room to see if they're accurate, funny, artistic, etc.

Workbook Ex. 2, p. 53.
Answers: TE, p. 530

EXERCISE 3

STEP 1 Get into groups. Choose one student to read the following sentences. Listen to the description and draw the picture.

1. There's a table in the center of the room.
2. There are two chairs at the table—one at each end.
3. There's a tablecloth on the table.
4. There's a plate on each end of the table. On one plate, there's a steak and potatoes.
5. The other plate is empty. There's only a napkin.
6. Next to the empty plate, there's an empty glass.
7. Next to the plate with food, there's a half-full glass.
8. There's a bottle of water on the right side of the table. The bottle is half full.
9. There is a vase in the center of the table.
10. There are eight flowers on the floor next to the table.

STEP 2 Compare your drawings. Whose is correct? Who is a good artist?

STEP 3 Choose the best title for your picture.

A. A Wonderful Dinner
B. Disappointed Again!
C. Always Eat Your Vegetables

ANSWER KEY

Exercise 3
Step 3
The best title is "B."

FOCUS **3**

There Isn't/There Aren't/ There's No/There Are No

THERE	BE + NOT		TYPE OF NOUN
There	isn't	a vase on the table.	singular count noun
There	aren't	any children in this restaurant.	plural count noun
There	isn't	any water on the table.	noncount noun

THERE	BE	NO	
There	is	no	vase on the table.
There	are	no	children in the restaurant.
There	's	no	water on the table.

EXERCISE 4

Go back to the Opening Task on page 98. Make sentences with *there is/are, there isn't/there aren't,* or *there's no/there are no* with the words below.

▶ **EXAMPLE:** There isn't an armchair in the apartment.
OR There's no armchair in the apartment.

1. television set
2. rug
3. men's clothing
4. computer
5. window
6. desk
7. books
8. toys
9. exercise bicycle
10. plants
11. coffee pot
12. ties

FOCUS 3

Ss will tend to say *There no are children* instead of *There are no children.* Emphasize that NO always comes after the verb *be, before the noun phrase.*

Exercise 4

This exercise can be done orally or in writing.

ANSWER KEY

Exercise 4

1. There isn't a ... /There's no ... **2.** There's a ... **3.** There isn't any ... /There's no ... **4.** There's a ... **5.** There isn't a ... / There's no ... **6.** There's a ... **7.** There are ... **8.** There aren't any ... There are no ... **9.** There's an ... **10.** There aren't any ... / There are no ... **11.** There's a ... **12.** There aren't any .../ There are no

Exercise 5

Elicit or provide a definition of *Utopia* (*A perfect place*).

VARIATION

1. To make this exercise more challenging, eliminate the checks in the yes/no columns and let Ss judge what *Utopia* has and doesn't have.
2. Write each item (parks, crime, etc.) on an index card.
3. Have Ss choose a card and make an appropriate statement.
4. Add items to this list.

Examples: police officers, amusement parks, pollution, restaurants, laws, beggars, etc.

Exercise 6

1. Elicit or provide a definition of *politician* and discuss the context of a campaign speech.
2. Have Ss read the text quickly first, to familiarize themselves with the content and enhance their predictive ability.

EXPANSION

Have Ss role-play this as an interview between a journalist and the Mayor.

Workbook Ex. 3, p. 54.
Answers: TE, p. 530

EXERCISE 5

Use the information in the chart below about the city Utopia. Write sentences with *there is/are, there isn't/there aren't,* or *there's no/there are no.*

EXAMPLE: In Utopia, there aren't any guns.
In Utopia, there are no guns.

THE CITY OF UTOPIA

	Yes	No		Yes	No
1. guns		✔	6. universities	✔	
2. public transportation	✔		7. noise		✔
3. crime		✔	8. jobs	✔	
4. museums	✔		9. parks	✔	
5. traffic problems		✔	10. poor people		✔

EXERCISE 6

Read the politician's speech about the city of Utopia. Fill in the blanks with *there is/are, there isn't/there aren't,* or *there's no/there are no.*

Good evening, Ladies and Gentlemen. I am the Mayor of Utopia. I am here tonight to talk about our wonderful city.

Today, (1) ___there are___ 50,000 people in our city. We are all happy. (2) ________ problems in our city.

(3) ________ jobs for all our people. (4) ________ good schools for the children. (5) ________ nice houses for all our families. The houses are comfortable. They aren't expensive.

(6) ________ homeless people on our streets. Our streets are safe. (7) ________ crime here. (8) ________ drugs. Our streets are clean. (9) ________ garbage on the streets. (10) ________ pollution.

(11) ________ many museums, theaters, and parks in our city. (12) ________ entertainment for everyone. (13) ________ good and cheap public transportation for everyone.

(14) ________ many reasons why Utopia is a great city! (15) ________ a good quality of life here in Utopia. And don't forget: (16) ________ an election this year. I want to be your Mayor for four more years. Are you happy in Utopia? Then (17) ________ only one thing to do: VOTE FOR ME, your Mayor Lucas Lime, on November sixth!

ANSWER KEY

Exercise 5

1. There are no guns./ There aren't any guns. **2.** There's public transportation. **3.** There's no crime./ There isn't any crime. **4.** There are museums. **5.** There are no traffic problems./ There aren't any traffic problems. **6.** There are universities. **7.** There's no noise./ There isn't any noise. **8.** There are jobs. **9.** There are parks. **10.** There are no poor people./ There aren't any poor people.

Exercise 6

2. There aren't any/There are no **3.** There are **4.** There are **5.** There are **6.** There are no/There aren't any **7.** There is no/There isn't any **8.** There are no/There aren't any **9.** There is no/There isn't any **10.** There is no/There isn't any **11.** There are **12.** There is/There's **13.** There is/ There's **14.** There are **15.** There is/There's **16.** There is/There's **17.** There is/There's

FOCUS **4**

Yes/No Questions with *There Is/There Are*

YES/NO QUESTIONS	SHORT ANSWERS	TYPE OF NOUN
(a) **Is there** a computer in the room?	Yes, there is. No, there isn't.	singular count noun
(b) **Are there** any books on the shelves?	Yes, there are. No, there aren't.	plural count noun
(c) **Is there** any jewelry in the box?	Yes, there is. No there isn't.	noncount noun

EXERCISE 7

Complete the questions for each picture.

1. Are there ________ any messages for me?

3. ________ any food in here, Mom?

2. ________ a doctor in the house?

4. Excuse me, ________ a post office near here?

FOCUS 4

SUGGESTIONS

If you have presented *there* as holding the subject position (as described in Focus 2), this structure should be easier for Ss. If not, focus on word order by giving many examples of questions with *there* + *be.* Examples: *Are there any Middle Eastern students in our class? / Is there a language laboratory in this building?,* etc.

2. Be sure Ss do not omit *there* in the questions. Example: *Is a computer in the room?*
3. Have them read the examples aloud.
4. Review count/noncount nouns.

Exercise 7

EXPANSION

Have Ss role-play these situations in pairs, embellishing the dialogues.

5. ________________ any tickets available for the 10:00 show?

6. ________________ any room for me?

7. ________________ any more instructions in the box?

8. ________________ any mail for me?

9. ________________ any small sizes?

10. ________________ a seat for me?

ANSWER KEY

Exercise 7

2. Is there **3.** Is there **4.** Is there **5.** Are there **6.** Is there **7.** Are there **8.** Is there **9.** Are there **10.** Is there

EXERCISE 8

Test your knowledge. Ask your partner *yes/no* questions with *Is there/Are there* and the words below.

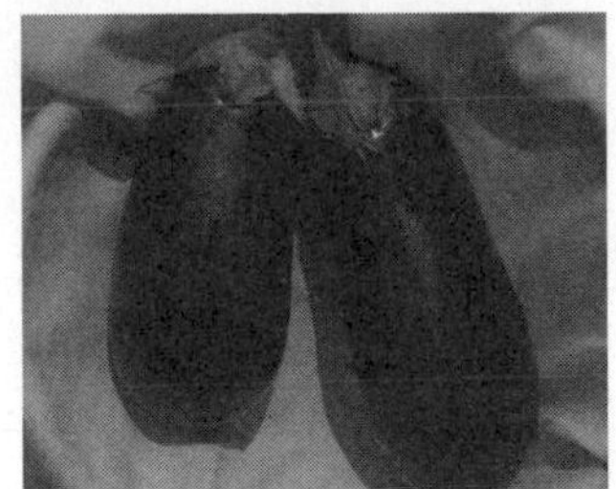

▶ **EXAMPLE:** eggs in an eggplant?
Are there any eggs in an eggplant?
No, there aren't.

1. rain in a desert
2. two billion people in China
3. fifty-two states in the United States
4. earthquakes in Japan
5. billions of stars in the sky
6. life on the moon
7. trees at the North Pole
8. cure for the common cold

FOCUS **5**

USE

Choosing *A/An* or *The*

A/An and *the* are articles. *A/An* are indefinite articles (see Unit 4). *The* is the definite article.

A/AN	*THE*
Use only with singular count nouns. **(a)** Susan has **a** bicycle.	Use with all nouns. **(b)** **The** bicycle is new. *(singular)* **(c)** **The** books are on the shelf. *(plural)* **(d)** **The** jewelry is in the box. *(noncount)*
Use to talk about a person or thing for the first time. **(e)** Susan has **a** necklace.	Use the second time you talk about a person or thing. **(f)** Susan has a necklace. **The** necklace is beautiful.
Use to classify people, animals, and things. **(g)** She is **an** investment banker.	Use when both speakers know which noun they are talking about. **(h)** When's **the** party? It's at 8:00.
	Use when the noun is the only one. **(i)** **The** sun is hot.

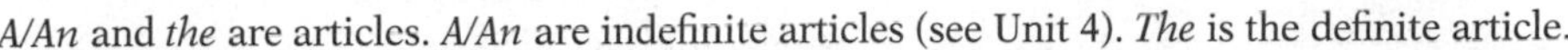

Exercise 8

SUGGESTIONS

1. Have Ss work in pairs or as a class. Ss will need to use their own background knowledge to answer these questions.
2. Encourage Ss to add questions.
3. Review *any.*

Workbook Ex. 4, p. 55.
Answers: TE, p. 530

FOCUS 5

SUGGESTIONS

1. If you prefer to work inductively, have Ss first do Exercises 9 and 10, which illustrate the different uses of *a/the.* Correct the exercises and have the Ss derive the rules: *a* for classification and first mention; *the* for second mention, for knowledge shared by the speakers, and for nouns that are unique.
2. To work deductively, go through the rules in the focus box and then move on to the exercises.

ANSWER KEY

Exercise 8
1. Is there any... ? No, there isn't. **2.** Are there... ? No, there aren't. There are one billion... **3.** Are there... ? No, there aren't. There are 50... **4.** Are there any... ? Yes, there are... **5.** Are there... ? Yes, there are... **6.** Is there any... ? Maybe, I don't know... **7.** Are there any... ? No, there aren't... **8.** Is there a... ? No, there isn't.

Exercise 9 

EXPANSION

Have Ss role-play these dialogues.

EXERCISE 9

Look at the pictures. Fill in the blanks with *a/an* or *the*.

1. **Nurse:** It's _______________ girl!
   Congratulations, Mr. Spade.

2. **Passenger:** Boy, it's hot. Do you have ___________ air conditioner in this car?
   Driver: Yes, but _______________ air conditioner doesn't work. Sorry about that!

3. **Husband:** What's in _______________ box?
   Wife: I have _______________ surprise for you.
   Husband: What's _______________ surprise?
   Wife: Open it!

4. **Man:** Do you have _______________ room for tonight?
   Clerk: Sorry, sir. _______________ motel is full tonight.

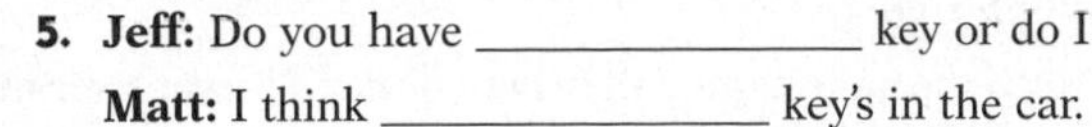

5. **Jeff:** Do you have ________________ key or do I?

   Matt: I think ________________ key's in the car.

6. **Receptionist:** Take your feet off ________________ table, please young man!

7. **Woman:** Who is it?

   Mailman: It's ________________ mailman, Mrs. Wallace. Here's your mail.

   Woman: Thanks, Mr. Brown. Have a good day!

ANSWER KEY

Exercise 9

1. a **2.** an; the **3.** the; a; the **4.** a; the
5. the; the **6.** the **7.** the

Exercise 10

Have Ss check their answers with a partner.

Workbook Ex. 5, p. 56.
Answers: TE, p. 530

EXERCISE 10

Read the paragraph. Fill in *a/an* or *the.* Then answer the question: *Who is Susan's brother-in-law?* (Refer to Unit 6.)

Susan owns (1) ________________ neighborhood restaurant. (2) ________________ restaurant is very small. It has (3) ________________ cook, (4) ________________ cashier, and (5) ________________ waiter. Susan is (6) ________________ boss. Susan has (7) ________________ excellent cook in (8) ________________ kitchen: her mother! Susan has (9) ________________ sister. Her sister is (10) ________________ cashier in (11) ________________ restaurant. Her sister's husband is (12) ________________ waiter. Susan's sister is (13) ________________ good cashier, but her brother-in-law is not (14) ________________ very good waiter. He doesn't have (15) ________________ good memory and is always confused. This is (16) ________________ big problem for Susan.

ANSWER KEY

Exercise 10

1. a 2. the 3. a 4. a 5. a 6. the 7. an 8. the 9. a 10. the 11. the 12. the 13. a 14. a 15. a 16. a

EXERCISE 11

Correct the mistakes in the following sentences.

1. It's a picture on a wall.
2. There are a bathroom, a kitchen, and a living room in my house.
3. There have three bedrooms and two bathrooms in the apartment.
4. Is a good restaurant in my neighborhood.
5. There aren't milk in the refrigerator.
6. In my picture, have one woman and two men.
7. Are homeless people in your city?
8. Is there a jewelry in Susan's apartment?
9. Susan owns a restaurant.
   Really? Where is a restaurant?
10. Are there any museums in your town?
    Yes, they are.
11. Excuse me, is there the men's room in this restaurant?
12. Do you have any children?
    Yes, I have the daughter.
13. Are there pollution in your city?
14. There no are women in the restaurant.
15. There are no any poor people in Utopia.

Exercise 11

Error correction exercises are designed to raise Ss' awareness of their errors and help them monitor themselves. Refer Ss to the appropriate focus boxes if necessary. Ss can work individually and then correct these as a class.

UNIT GOALS REVIEW

Discuss with Ss the Unit Goals on page 98. Which goals have they achieved? Which ones are they still working on?

ANSWER KEY

Exercise 11

1. There's a picture on the wall. **2.** There's a bathroom, a kitchen, and a living room in my house. **3.** There are three bedrooms and two bathrooms ... **4.** There's a good restaurant ... **5.** There isn't any milk in... /There's no milk in... **6.** In my picture, there is one woman and two men. **7.** Are there (any) homeless people in your city? **8.** Is there any jewelry... ? /**9.** Where is the restaurant? **10.** Are there any museums in your town? Yes, there are. **11.** ... is there a men's room in this restaurant? **12.** Do you have any children? Yes, I have a daughter. **13.** Is there any pollution...? **14.** There are no women in ... /There aren't any women **15.** There are no poor people... /There aren't any poor people...

USE YOUR ENGLISH

For a more complete discussion of how to implement the *Use Your English* activities, see page xxvi of this Teacher's Edition.

Activity 1

A simple way to do this activity is to have both Ss look at both pictures. Focusing on picture B, they tell how it is different from picture A, and write sentences together. Go around to check their sentences. Correct sentences as a class.

VARIATION

To make this activity more challenging, have each student look at only one picture and describe it to a partner. Ss have to find the differences by working them out orally. You can still have them write their sentences, and correct them as a class.

Use Your English

ACTIVITY 1: WRITING/SPEAKING

Work with a partner. Look at the two pictures. Find eight differences and write sentences with *there is/isn't* or *there are/aren't*. Compare your sentences with those of another pair of students.

▶ **EXAMPLE:** In picture A, there is a dog. In picture B, there's a cat.

Picture A

Picture B

ANSWER KEY

Activity 1:
Possible answers:

1. There are two thieves in Pix. A. There's only one thief in B.
2. There are pictures on the wall in A. There are no pictures in B.
3. In Pix. A there's a door on the left. In Pix. B there's a door on the right.
4. There are two young children in Pix. A. There are two teenagers in Pix. B.
5. There's a foot stool in Pix. A. There's no foot stool in Pix. B.
6. There are two women in Pix. A .There are two men in Pix. B.
7. There's a large hutch/chest in Pix. A./There's no hutch/chest in pix.B
8. There's a chess board in Pix. B/There's no chess board in Pix. A.
9. There's a grandmother in Pix. A. There's a grandfather in Pix. B.
10. There's a dog in Pix. A. There's a cat in Pix. B.

ACTIVITY 2: SPEAKING

Find out about your partner's neighborhood.

STEP 1 Ask questions with *Is there . . .? Are there . . .?* Check **Yes** or **No** in the chart.

▶ **EXAMPLE:** A: Is there a hospital in your neighborhood?
B: Yes, there is. **OR** No, there isn't.

	Yes	No
supermarkets		
movie theaters		
bookstore		
hospital		
bank		
fast-food restaurants		
gas station		
post office		
public library		
schools		
crime		
coffee shop		
trees		
public transportation		

STEP 2 Tell the class or group about your classmate's neighborhood.

Activity 2

EXPANSIONS

1. Extend this list with items relevant to your Ss and location.
2. In Step 2, Ss can decide whose neighborhood is the most pleasant, or try to persuade someone to move to their neighborhood.

Activity 3 

Encourage Ss to add other categories to the survey: major/profession, religion, life goals, etc. Ss can work in pairs or small groups and then pool their information. Put a large grid on the board so that Ss can write sentences for Step 2.

ACTIVITY 3: SPEAKING/WRITING

STEP 1 Use the categories below to find out about your classmates. Fill in the blanks with numbers of students.

Total number of classmates ________

Sex: Male ________ Female ________

Physical Characteristics: Dark eyes ________ Blue/Green eyes ____

Women with short hair ________ Women with long hair ________

Nationalities: ________

Personalities: Shy ________ Outgoing ________

Marital Status: Married ________ Single ________

Add your own categories.

STEP 2 Write sentences about your classmates.

▶ **EXAMPLE:** There are ten Mexicans, two Chinese, three Koreans, one Vietnamese, and one Brazilian in my class.

Activity 4

Let Ss try a pre-writing phase: generate vocabulary, images of their special places (maybe using photographs), feelings they have there. Help them write a coherent paragraph.

ACTIVITY 4: WRITING

Think of a place that's important to you. Write a short description of this place.

▶ **EXAMPLE:** There's an island off the coast of Sicily called Filicudi. There aren't many houses on the island.

Activity 5

This gives Ss a chance to write for a real purpose. Teach them the format of a letter, either before or after they write.

SUGGESTIONS

1. As in Activity 4, allow them a pre-writing phase.
2. Collect their letters and create an error correction sheet.
3. Share the best, the most interesting, or the most problematic letters with the whole class. Send these letters to the appropriate parties, if possible.

ACTIVITY 5: WRITING

Write a letter to the mayor of your city. Write about the problems in your city or neighborhood.

▶ **EXAMPLE:** Dear Mr. Mayor,
I live in ________. There are many problems in my neighborhood.

ACTIVITY 6: LISTENING

STEP 1 Listen to Tom's description of his neighborhood and write in the places on the map.

Tom's apartment

STEP 2 Work with a partner. Ask about these places in Tom's neighborhood:

1. police station
2. supermarket
3. banks
4. gas station
5. laundromat
6. mini-market
7. library
8. schools

▶ **EXAMPLE:** Is there a police station?
No, there isn't.

There Is/There Are, A/An versus *The* **115**

Activity 6 

Play textbook audio. The tapescript for this listening appears on p. 545 of this book.

The test for this unit can be found on p. 466–467 of this book. The answers are on p. 468.

Unit 8

UNIT OVERVIEW

The simple present is introduced before the present progressive so that Students (Ss) will not overgeneralize the progressive aspect and fail to understand the form and use of the simple present. Ss have already learned the verb *have*, which should help them with the forms in this unit.

UNIT GOALS

To maximize the diagnostic potential of the Opening Task, do not review the Unit Goals with Ss until after they have completed and reviewed the task.

OPENING TASK
SETTING UP THE TASK

Pre-teach any vocabulary you think Ss will not know. Possible unfamiliar words may include: *skip*, *rush*, *nap*, *take-out restaurant*.

UNIT 8

SIMPLE PRESENT TENSE

Affirmative and Negative Statements, Time Expressions:
In/On/At, Like/Need/Want

UNIT GOALS:

- To make affirmative and negative statements using the simple present tense
- To know how to spell and pronounce the third person singular form of verbs in the simple present tense
- To use frequency and time expressions
- To use the simple present tense to:
  -talk about habits and routines
  -talk about things that are always true
  -talk about what you like, want, or need

OPENING TASK
Looking at Healthy and Unhealthy Habits

Fran Tic and Rhee Lakst are university students. Fran attends a large university in California and Rhee goes to a small New England school in Massachusetts.

STEP 1 Look at a typical day in their lives. Whose life is healthier? Whose lifestyle is more stressful? Why? Discuss this with a partner.

A Typical Day in the Life of:		
	Fran Tic	**Rhee Lakst**
6:30 A.M.	Wake up and skip breakfast	
7:30 A.M.	Rush to subway station	Wake up and eat breakfast
8:30 A.M.	Go to class	
9:30 A.M.		Walk to school
10:30 A.M.		Go to class
12:30 P.M.	Eat a fast lunch, study in the library	Eat lunch with friends in the cafeteria
1:30 P.M.		Go to work
2:30 P.M.	Rush to work	
4:30 P.M.	Work out in the gym	Go home and take a nap
5:30 P.M.	Meet with her study group	
6:30 P.M.		Buy dinner at a take-out restaurant
7:30 P.M.	Go grocery shopping	Study
8:30 P.M.	Cook dinner at home	Watch TV
10:30 P.M.	Go out with friends	Have milk and cookies and go to bed
12:30 A.M.	Go to bed	

STEP 2 Write statements to complete the chart about the healthy and unhealthy/stressful things Fran and Rhee do.

	Healthy Things They Do	**Unhealthy/Stressful Things They Do**
Fran	*Fran goes to the gym.*	*Fran skips breakfast.*
Rhee		
Fran and Rhee		

ANSWER KEY

Step 2

Healthy Things They Do:
Fran cooks dinner./Fran goes out with friends.
Rhee eats breakfast./Rhee eats 3 meals a day.
Rhee walks to school./Rhee takes naps.
Fran and Rhee (both) exercise.
Fran and Rhee (both) spend time with friends.

Unhealthy Things/Stressful Things They Do:
Fran rushes to work.
Fran goes to bed late and wakes up early. Fran skips breakfast.
Rhee has milk and cookies before bed.
Fran and Rhee (both) worry about school.

CONDUCTING THE TASK

Step 1 

Have Ss work in pairs or small groups to answer the questions: *Whose life is healthier? Whose life is more stressful?* Go around the room listening. This is the beginning of your diagnostic phase.

Step 2 

Check Ss' work as they write; have them put both correct and incorrect sentences on the board.

VARIATION

To make this Opening Task more challenging, reproduce the chart in Step 1, but do not give Ss the chart in Step 2. Having no model to follow, Ss will generate whatever language they know. This will allow you to do a true diagnosis.

REVIEWING THE TASK

Use Ss' sentences to begin your focus on form. If you chose not to give Ss the chart in Step 2 of the task, you may get a broader array of error types. These could include errors in form: *She is go to school;* and in use: *She is going to school*. You will need to analyze these errors and present the rules as feedback on what the Ss have produced.
NOTE: Fran Tic = Frantic ; RheeLakst = Relaxed

FOCUS 1

If Ss were able to derive the form from Step 2 of the task, go over this quickly.

Exercise 1

Ss can do this exercise individually.

VARIATION

To make it more challenging, hide the names and have Ss fill in the name(s) and verbs as a whole class.

FOCUS **1**

Simple Present Tense: Affirmative Statements

SUBJECT	VERB
I You* We They	work.
He She It	work**s**.

*Both singular and plural.

EXERCISE 1

Compare Fran and Rhee's lifestyles. Circle the correct form of the verb in each statement.

1. Fran (lead/leads) a busy life in a big city.
2. Rhee (live/lives) a quiet life in a small city.
3. Fran and Rhee both (like/likes) their colleges.
4. Fran (fill/fills) her schedule with many activities.
5. Rhee (need/needs) time to rest during the day.
6. Fran and Rhee (worry/worries) about their grades.
7. They both (work/works) part-time.
8. Fran (sleep/sleeps) about 6 hours a night.
9. Fran (drink/drinks) coffee every night to stay awake.
10. Fran (skip/skips) meals.
11. Rhee (get/gets) a good night's sleep.
12. Rhee (eat/eats) regular meals.
13. Fran and Rhee (study/studies) hard.
14. Fran (exercise/exercises) every day.
15. Rhee (walk/walks) to school.
16. Fran (make/makes) time for her friends.
17. Rhee (spend/spends) a lot of time alone.
18. Fran and Rhee (enjoy/enjoys) their independence.

ANSWER KEY

Exercise 1

1. Fran leads 2. Rhee lives 3. Fran and Rhee both like 4. Fran fills 5. Rhee needs 6. Fran and Rhee worry 7. They both work 8. Fran sleeps 9. Fran drinks coffee 10. Fran skips 11. Rhee gets 12. Rhee eats 13. Fran and Rhee study 14. Fran exercises 15. Rhee walks 16. Fran makes 17. Rhee spends 18. Fran and Rhee enjoy

EXERCISE 2

Go back to the chart in Step 2 of the Opening Task. Correct the statements you wrote.

FOCUS **2**

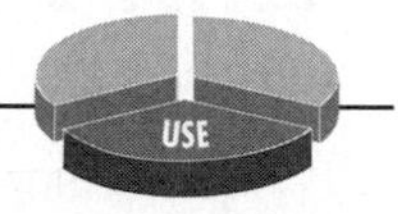

Talking about Habits and Routines

EXAMPLES	EXPLANATION
(a) Fran and Rhee **listen** to music together. (b) Fran **goes** to the gym every afternoon.	Use the simple present tense to talk about habits or things that happen again and again.

EXERCISE 3

Match the occupations with what the people do. Use the correct verb forms and make statements aloud.

EXAMPLE: A doctor takes care of sick people.

1.	A doctor	**a.**	repair cars
2.	Construction workers	**b.**	protect people
3.	A mechanic	**c.**	answer the telephone
4.	Air traffic controllers	**d.**	take care of sick people
5.	A receptionist	**e.**	build houses
6.	Taxi drivers	**f.**	direct airplanes
7.	Police officers	**g.**	work in emergencies
8.	A fire fighter	**h.**	take passengers to different places

Which of these jobs are the most stressful? Explain why.

Exercise 2

You may already have done this after the task. If so, move on to Focus 2.

Workbook Ex. 1, p. 57.
Answers: TE, p. 530

FOCUS 2

Although the affirmative form is very simple, the use of the simple present is difficult. Ask Ss to talk about their own habits and routines when doing this. Write their sentences on the board and check the use. (For example, Ss might say, "*I get married,*" indicating that they do not understand the use of the simple present tense.)

Exercise 3

SUGGESTIONS

1. Bring in photos to show each of the occupations. Allow Ss to work in small groups.
2. Have them write sentences to justify their views on the most stressful jobs. Write them on the board and correct.

EXPANSION

Add other occupations to the list: mother, teacher, etc . . .

Workbook Exs. 2 & 3, p. 58–59.
Answers: TE, p. 530

ANSWER KEY

Exercise 3

2. e . . . build houses **3.** a . . . repairs cars **4.** f . . . direct airplanes **5.** c . . . answers the telephone **6.** h . . . take passengers **7.** b . . . protect **8.** g . . . works

FOCUS 3

Pronunciation is a challenging aspect of this tense. Remind Ss that the third person singular form of verbs ending in *sh, ch, x, z,* or ss has an extra syllable. Review the voiced/voiceless distinction presented in Unit 4.

FOCUS **3**

Third Person Singular: Spelling and Pronunciation

BASE FORM OF VERB	SPELLING	PRONUNCIATION
1. The final sound of the verb is "voiceless" (for example: p/t/k/f/s/th): **sleep**	Add *-s.* He **sleeps** eight hours every night.	/s/
2. The final sound of the verb is "voiced" (for example: b/d/g/v/m/n/l/r or a vowel): **prepare**	Add *-s.* He **prepares** dinner.	/z/
3. The verb ends in **sh, ch, x, z,** or **ss**: **watch**	Add *-es.* He **watches** TV.	This adds another syllable to the verb. /IZ/
4. The verb ends in a consonant +**y**: **hurry**	Change *y* to *i* and add *-es.* She **hurries** home.	/z/
5. The verb ends in a vowel +**y**: **play**	Add *-s.* He **plays** tennis on Saturday.	/z/
6. Irregular Forms: **have** **go** **do**	Rhee **has** a job. She **goes** to work every day. Fran **does** the dishes.	/z/

EXERCISE 4

The pictures of Lazy Louie and his wife Hannah are not in the correct order. Number the pictures in the correct order. Then write the number of the picture next to the sentences below.

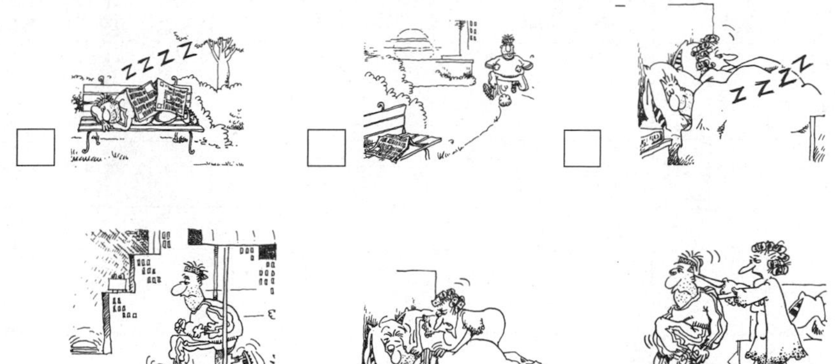

______ **A.** Poor lazy Louie leaves the house and goes jogging.

______ **B.** He lies down on the bench and says, "Finally, I am free!" Then he goes to sleep.

______ **C.** Lazy Louie hates exercise. He wants to sleep, but he gets up. He puts on his clothes and sneakers with his eyes closed. Hannah pushes him out of the house.

______ **D.** Lazy Louie loves to sleep. He dreams about sleeping! But he snores all the time and his wife gets no sleep. Hannah is tired and needs to do something.

______ **E.** He runs to the park and finds his favorite bench.

______ **F.** Hannah finds a way to get Louie out of bed. She wakes him at 6:45 every morning. He continues to sleep. She shakes him. She shouts in his ear, "Time to get up! You need your exercise, dear!"

Exercise 4

1. Have Ss work in groups to figure out what's happening and to put these pictures in order.
2. Elicit or pre-teach any problematic vocabulary.
3. Have them match each picture to a sentence.

VARIATIONS

1. Enlarge the pictures and put each on a card. Put Ss in groups of six. Each student takes only one card and describes that card to the group. After hearing all the descriptions, the group puts the pictures into the correct sequence.
2. For a more inductive approach, have Ss put the pictures into the correct sequence and write their own stories before looking at the text. Put their stories up around the room and correct them. Then have them compare their stories to the one given here. Add any new verbs to the list in Exercise 5.

ANSWER KEY

Exercise 4

The pictures are set up as follows:

6 5 1
4 2 3

The correct sequence of the story is:
D,F,C,A,E,B

Exercise 5

Ss can read these verbs aloud, or they can listen to you read them and check their answers.

EXERCISE 5

Here is a list of third-person singular verbs from the story about Lazy Louie. Check (✔) the sound you hear at the end of the verb. Then read the verbs aloud.

Verb	/s/	/z/	/iz/
1. loves		✔	
2. dreams			
3. snores			
4. gets			
5. needs			
6. finds			
7. wakes			
8. continues			
9. shakes			
10. shouts			
11. hates			
12. wants			
13. puts			
14. pushes			
15. leaves			
16. goes			
17. runs			
18. lies			
19. says			

ANSWER KEY

Exercise 5

2. dreams /z/ **3.** snores /z/ **4.** gets /s/ **5.** needs /z/ **6.** finds /z/ **7.** wakes /s/ **8.** continues /z/ **9.** shakes /s/ **10.** shouts /s/ **11.** hates /s/ **12.** wants /s/ **13.** puts /s/ **14.** pushes /IZ/ **15.** leaves /z/ **16.** goes /z/ **17.** runs /z/ **18.** lies /z/ **19.** says /z/

EXERCISE 6

Sit in a circle. The first person in the circle starts to tell the story of Louie and Hannah and the next continues, and so on all around the circle. The pictures in Exercise 4 and the verb list in Exercise 5 will help you.

FOCUS **4**

Frequency and Time Expressions

EXAMPLES				EXPLANATIONS
every morning/afternoon/evening/night every day/week/year every summer/winter/spring/fall all the time once a week twice a month three times a year				*Frequency expressions* tell how often we do something.
in	+	the morning the afternoon the evening	more general ↑	*Time expressions* tell when we do something.
in	+	June 1969 the summer		
on	+	Wednesday(s) March 17 the weekend		
at	+	7:30 night noon	↓ more specific	

Exercise 6

Answers will vary. Encourage Ss to go beyond the given text in the retelling.

EXPANSION

Record them and play back the tape to evaluate and correct pronunciation.

Workbook Exs. 4 & 5, pp. 59–60
Answers: TE, p. 530

FOCUS 4

This focus covers the meaning of frequency and time expressions. Ask Ss to make statements about themselves to see if they understand the meanings. Give examples about yourself: *I take a vacation three times a year.*

Exercise 7

Elicit or provide a definition of *urban*. Ss can work individually.

Workbook Ex. 6, p. 61.
Answers: TE, p. 531

EXERCISE 7

Lifestyles of Urban Kids. Fill in the blanks with a frequency or time expression.

Michele and Nadia live in a big city. They get up (1) ______________ 6:00 (2) ______________ day of the week, but not (3) ______________ weekends. (4) ______________ Saturdays, they get up (5) ______________ 8:00. They go to dancing school (6) ______________ Saturday morning for 3 hours. (7) ______________ the afternoon, they go to swimming lessons. (8) ______________ 5:30, they take art lessons at the local college. (9) ______________ Saturday nights, they go out with friends. (10) ______________ , on Sunday morning, they sleep late. They have breakfast (11) ______________ 12:00 noon! They do homework (12) ______________ the afternoon. They talk on the phone and read their e-mails (13) ______________ the evening. These big city kids are busy (14) ______________ .

ANSWER KEY

Exercise 7

1. at **2.** every **3.** on **4.** On **5.** at **6.** every / on **7.** In **8.** At **9.** On **10.** Once a week, / Every week, **11.** at **12.** in **13.** in **14.** all the time

FOCUS **5**

Frequency and Time Expressions

EXAMPLES	EXPLANATIONS
(a) They cook dinner **every night.** (b) She gets up at 7:00 **every morning.**	Frequency and time expressions usually come at the end of a sentence.
(c) They cook dinner **every night at 7:00.** (d) They cook dinner **at seven every night.**	When there is both a frequency and a time expression in one sentence, the frequency expression can come before or after the time expression.
(e) **Once a week,** they go out to eat. (f) **On weekends,** they stay in.	Frequency and time expressions can sometimes come at the beginning of a sentence. Use a comma (,) after the expressions at the beginning of a sentence.
(g) I work **on Saturdays.** (h) I work **Saturdays.** (i) I work **on July 4th.** (j) I work **July 4th.**	With days and dates, *on* is not necessary.

EXERCISE 8

Make true statements about yourself using the time and frequency expressions below and the simple present tense.

EXAMPLE: once a week

You say: I go to the library once a week.

1. once a week
2. every weekend
3. twice a week
4. on my birthday
5. once a year
6. at 7:30 in the morning
7. on Friday nights
8. in September
9. in the summer
10. all the time
11. on December 31
12. at 6:00

FOCUS 5

This form focus covers the position of frequency and time expressions. Cover up the "Explanations" column and see if Ss can derive the rules by reading the examples.

Exercise 8

Answers will vary. Check that Ss do not say, for example, *I once a year go on vacation.* Have Ss write their sentences on the board and check them.

Exercise 9

This exercise is a good opportunity to go over expressions that take *make* or *do: do the laundry, do the dishes, vs. make the bed, make dinner,* etc. as well as expressions with go: go jogging, go out for breakfast, go to bed, go to the movies, etc.

Workbook Exs. 7 & 8, pp. 62–63.
Answers: TE, p. 531

EXERCISE 9

Look at Wendy's weekly schedule. Then fill in the blanks in the exercise with the simple present tense or a frequency or time expression.

	Monday	Tuesday	Wednesday	Thursday	Friday
7:00	wake up				
7:30	eat breakfast at home				go out for breakfast
9:30	teach French	go jogging	teach French	do aerobics	teach French
12:00	eat lunch at school	eat lunch at home	eat lunch at school	eat lunch at home	attend meetings
3:00	play tennis	prepare lessons	play tennis	go food shopping	clean apartment
6:00	meet a friend for dinner	go to cooking class	go to the movies	take dancing lessons	go out with friends
8:00	do the laundry	use the Internet	read the newspaper	prepare lessons	
10:30	go to bed early				
12:00					go to bed

1. Wendy <u>goes food shopping</u> on Thursday afternoon.
2. Wendy cleans her apartment <u>on Friday afternoon</u>.
3. Wendy ________________ every day at 7:00.
4. She eats breakfast at home ________________ .
5. Once a week, on Friday mornings, she ________________ .
6. She ________________ three times a week.
7. She does aerobics ________________ .
8. She eats lunch at school ________________ .
9. She attends meetings ________________ .
10. She eats lunch at home ________________ .
11. She goes to cooking class ________________ .

ANSWER KEY

Exercise 9
3. wakes up **4.** four days a week/four times a week; on Monday(s), Tuesday(s), Wednesday(s), Thursday(s) **5.** goes out for breakfast **6.** teaches French **7.** once a week; on Thursday(s) **8.** two days a week/twice a week; on Monday(s) and Wednesday(s) **9.** on Friday(s) **10.** On Tuesday(s) and Thursday(s); twice a week; two times/days a week **11.** on Tuesday(s); once a week **12.** on Wednesday(s); on Wednesday night; once a week **13.** goes out with friends **14.** four days/times a week; on Monday(s), Tuesday(s), Wednesday(s), and Thursday(s) **15.** goes to bed **16.** on Monday(s); once a week **17.** prepares lessons

12. She reads ________________ .
13. On Friday evening, she ________________ .
14. She goes to bed early ________________ .
15. She ________________ at midnight on Friday.
16. She does the laundry ________________ .
17. She ________________ at 8:00 on Thursday night.

Now make three more statements about Wendy's schedule.

18. ____ .
19. ____ .
20. ____ .

FOCUS 6

Simple Present: Negative Statements

SUBJECT	DO/DOES NOT	BASE FORM OF VERB
I You* We They Jim and Peter	do not don't	work.
He She It Mary	does not doesn't	

*Both singular and plural

FOCUS 6

Ss have already had the negative form (in Unit 4.) This should be a review.

Exercise 10
Answers will vary.

EXPANSION
Have Ss add other health factors to this list.

EXERCISE 10

Do you have a healthy life? Check (✔) Yes or No.

	Yes	No
1. I smoke.	_____	_____
2. I exercise every day.	_____	_____
3. I drink three or more cans of soda every day.	_____	_____
4. I eat fruit and vegetables.	_____	_____
5. I eat fast food every day.	_____	_____
6. I live a quiet life.	_____	_____
7. I go to bed late.	_____	_____
8. I skip meals.	_____	_____
9. I feel tired every day.	_____	_____
10. I eat red meat every day.	_____	_____
11. I cook fresh food at home.	_____	_____
12. I find time to relax.	_____	_____
13. I overeat.	_____	_____
14. I worry all the time.	_____	_____

Now look at your partner's **Yes** and **No** checks. Tell the class why your partner has a healthy or unhealthy life.

▶ **EXAMPLE:** My partner has a very healthy life. He doesn't smoke. He exercises every day.

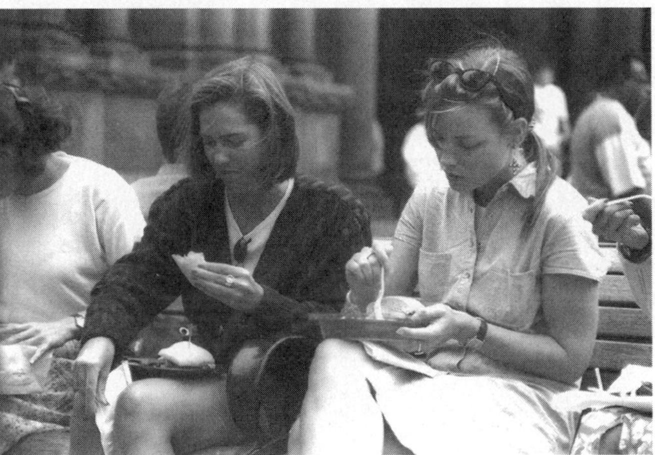

EXERCISE 11

For each verb below, make a negative statement about Fran or Rhee.

▶ **EXAMPLE:** skip meals

Rhee doesn't skip meals.

1. go to bed late
2. get a good night's sleep
3. have a healthy diet
4. take naps
5. have milk and cookies every night
6. take time to relax
7. cook
8. skip breakfast
9. eat breakfast
10. go to the gym

Exercise 11

Ss must refer to the two women in the task to do this. All statements are negative, but Ss must make each statement true by supplying the correct name.

Workbook Ex. 9, p. 63–64.
Answers: TE, p. 531

ANSWER KEY

Exercise 11

1. Rhee doesn't go to bed late **2.** Fran doesn't get a good night's sleep **3.** Rhee doesn't have a healthy diet **4.** Fran doesn't take naps **5.** Fran doesn't have milk and cookies every night **6.** Fran doesn't take time to relax **7.** Rhee doesn't cook **8.** Rhee doesn't skip breakfast **9.** Fran doesn't eat breakfast **10.** Rhee doesn't go to the gym.

FOCUS 7

This focus is about making generalizations. Have Ss brainstorm other examples, such as: *Water freezes at 32°F.*

FOCUS **7**

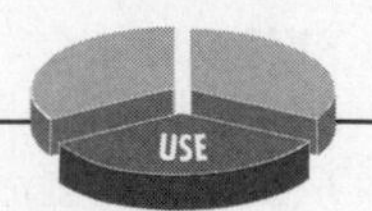

▶ Talking about Things that Are Always True

EXAMPLES	EXPLANATION
(a) The sun **rises** in the East. (b) A healthy person **enjoys** life. (c) A healthy person **doesn't use** drugs.	Use the simple present to make statements about things that always happen or things that are always true.

Exercise 12 

Allow Ss to pool their knowledge in pairs or groups to figure out these definitions.

EXERCISE 12

Use the simple present affirmative or negative to complete the definitions of the new words below.

1. Workaholics (love) ____love____ to work all the time.
2. Vegetarians (eat) ____________ meat.
3. Couch potatoes (sit) ____________ in front of the TV all the time.
4. An alcoholic (drink) ____________ a lot of wine, beer, or liquor every day.
5. A pacifist (like) ____________ war.
6. An insomniac (sleep) ____________ at night.
7. A stressed person (worry) ____________ a lot.
8. A health-conscious person (care) ____________ about his or her health.
9. Environmentalists (like) ____________ pollution.

Exercise 13

SUGGESTION

Have Ss discuss the photograph and identify all the technological gadgets. Then have Ss read through the whole text once before they begin to fill in the blanks. This will give them the general context and allow them to make the inferences they need to choose affirmative or negative forms. Have them work individually; check with the whole class.

EXPANSION

Have them discuss the stress factors in their own lives.

Workbook Ex. 10, p. 65.
Answers: TE, p. 531

EXERCISE 13

Fill in the blanks. Use the simple present affirmative or negative of the verbs in parentheses.

ANSWER KEY

Exercise 12
2. don't eat 3. sit 4. drinks 5. doesn't like 6. doesn't sleep 7. worries 8. cares 9. don't like

Today, many Americans are under stress. They (move) (1) ___move___ at a fast pace. They (work) (2) ________ all the time. They often (work) (3) ________ overtime. People (have) (4) ________ time for themselves or their families. An average worker (have) (5) ________ too much work and (have) (6) ________ enough time to finish it. As a result, many Americans (take) (7) ________ vacations.

Why are Americans so busy all the time? One reason is modern technology. Modern technology (keep) (8) ________ us busy and (give) (9) ________ us stress. Technology (let) (10) ________ us relax. We (wear) (11) ________ beepers. We (use) (12) ________ fax machines to send messages fast. We (take) (13) ________ time to rest. Even on Sundays, many stores (stay) (14) ________ open and people (go shopping) (15) ________ . Today, stress is one of the top reasons why Americans (get) (16) ________ sick.

ANSWER KEY

Exercise 13
2) work **3)** work **4)** don't have **5)** has **6)** doesn't have **7)** don't take **8)** keeps **9)** gives **10)** doesn't let **11)** wear **12)** use **13)** don't take **14)** stay **15)** go shopping **16)** get

FOCUS 8

The challenge here is the form:

	want	
I	*like*	*to go.*
	need	

Many Ss will translate this as: *I want go/I want that you go*, so they need a lot of practice with this.

Exercise 14 

Encourage Ss to make other statements about these pictures.

Workbook Ex. 11, p. 66
Answers: TE, p. 531

FOCUS **8**

Like, Want, Need

EXAMPLES	EXPLANATIONS
I { **like** / **want** / **need** } coffee.	Subject + Verb + Noun
I { **like** / **want** / **need** } to drink coffee.	Subject + Verb + Infinitive
(a) I love animals. I **want** a cat. **(b)** I love Joel. I **want** to marry him.	*Want* expresses desire.
(c) I have a headache. I **need** some medicine. **(d)** You don't look well. You **need** to see a doctor.	*Need* expresses something that is necessary.

EXERCISE 14

What do these people need? Write one sentence with *need* + noun and another sentence with want + infinitive. Use the nouns and verbs in the box.

EXAMPLE:

He needs some flour.
He wants to bake some cookies.

Nouns	Verbs
cup of coffee	write down a message
hammer	hang a picture
a quarter	fix a broken cup
peace and quiet	paint a room
pen	wake up
glue	get some sleep
a can of paint	make a telephone call

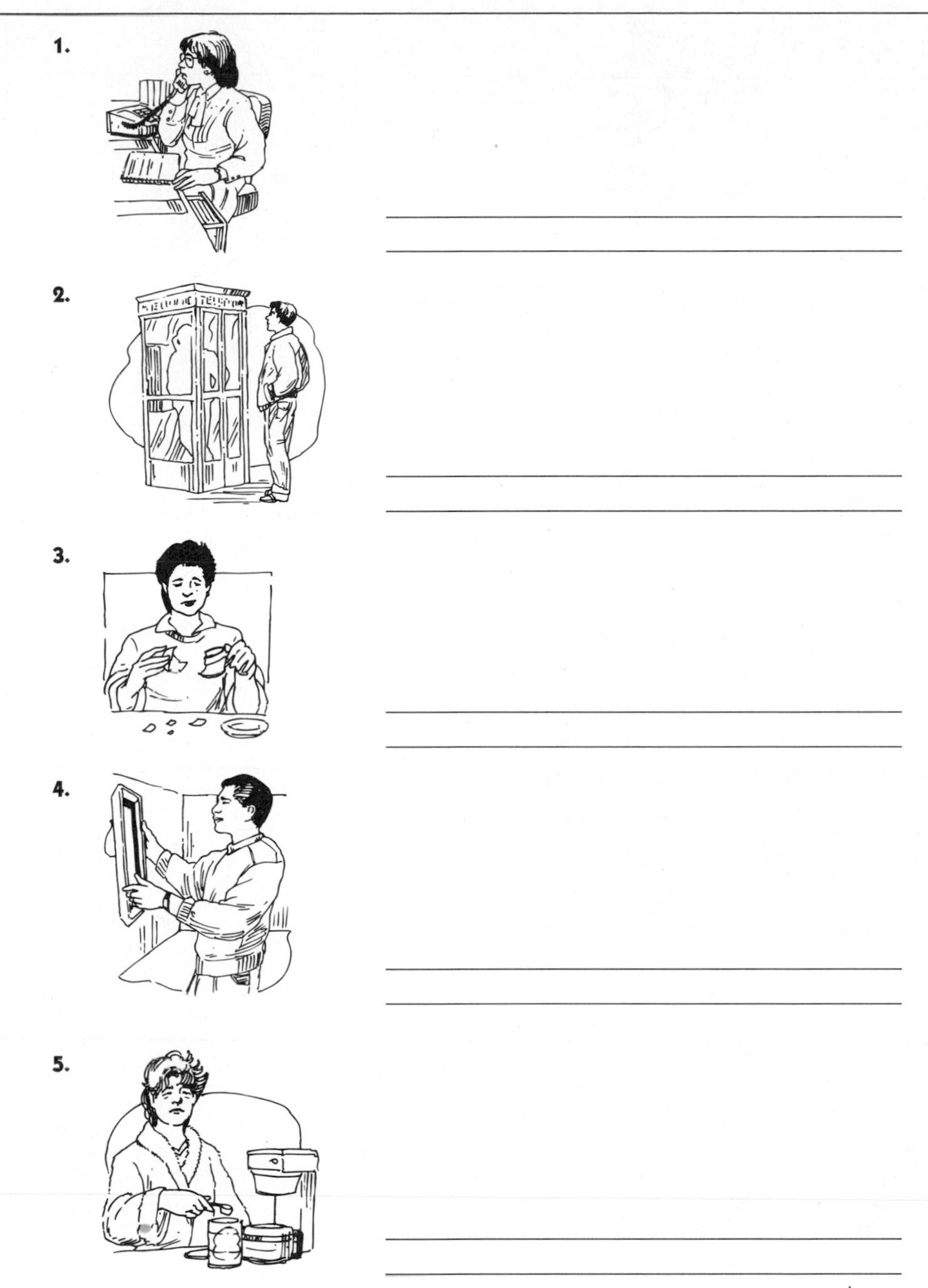

ANSWER KEY

Exercise 14

1. She needs a pen. She wants to write down a message **2.** He needs a quarter. He wants to make a telephone call **3.** She needs some glue. She wants to fix a broken cup **4.** He needs a hammer. He wants to hang a picture **5.** She needs a cup of coffee. She wants to wake up **6.** He needs some peace and quiet. He wants to get some sleep **7.** She needs a can of paint. She wants to paint the room.

6.

7.

Exercise 15

Have Ss work individually. This exercise could be done for homework.

EXERCISE 15

Correct the mistakes in the following sentences.

1. She is smile every day.
2. He every day takes a walk.
3. He finish his dinner every night.
4. He don't cook dinner on Sundays.
5. We are study in the library on Saturdays.
6. She don't work on Tuesdays.
5. English classes begin at September.
8. She need a pen to write.
9. He want to make a sandwich.
10. Wendy plays tennis on 3:00.

UNIT GOALS REVIEW

Ask Ss to look at the goals on the opening page of the unit. Help them understand how much they have accomplished in each area. Ask them if they still have any questions about what they have learned so far.

ANSWER KEY

Exercise 15

1. She smiles every day. **2.** He takes a walk every day./Every day, he takes a walk. **3.** He finishes his dinner every night. **4.** He doesn't cook dinner on Sundays. **5.** We study in the library on Saturdays. **6.** She doesn't work on Tuesdays. **7.** English classes begin in September. **8.** She needs a pen to write. **9.** He wants to make a sandwich. **10.** Wendy plays tennis at 3:00.

Use Your English

ACTIVITY 1: SPEAKING

Who is a person you admire? Tell your partner about this person. Then answer questions your partner may have.

▶ **EXAMPLE:** I admire my mother. She loves our family. She enjoys her work. She cooks great food. She doesn't get angry.

Tell your partner about a person you are worried about. Then answer the questions your partner may have.

▶ **EXAMPLE:** I am worried about my friend. He doesn't eat healthy food. He doesn't exercise. He doesn't sleep. He sits in front of the TV all the time.

ACTIVITY 2: WRITING/SPEAKING

What do you and your partner have in common? Write two affirmative statements and two negative statements with *like* for each of the categories below. Share your sentences with your partner and find out what you both have in common. Report your results to the class.

Music	Books	Food
I like to listen to classical music. I also like rock. I don't like rap. I don't like to listen to opera.		
Movies	**Sports**	**Cars**

USE YOUR ENGLISH

Activity 1

Give Ss time to think about what they want to say; perhaps by making a list or brainstorming.

VARIATION

This can also be done as a writing activity. Then have Ss respond to each other's writing.

Activity 2

VARIATION

Change or add to these categories to make them more relevant for your Ss.

Activity 3

To maximize class time, ask Ss to do Step 1 for homework. Step 2 is more interactive. Have Ss focus on unusual or surprising things their partners do, and report these to the class.

Activity 4

1. Group Ss from the same home country together to brainstorm. Go around checking their statements.
2. Put the interesting ones on the board, separating the correct from the incorrect.
3. After correcting the errors, discuss the habits of people in different countries.
4. Encourage Ss to ask each other questions. This will produce fascinating exchanges and lead you into Unit 9 on question formation.

ACTIVITY 3: WRITING/SPEAKING

STEP 1 Fill out your own daily schedule using only the base form of the verb.

My schedule:

	Mon.	Tues.	Wed.	Thurs.	Fri.	Sat.	Sun.
Morning		6:00 go jogging					
Afternoon				3:00 go to the library			
Evening					8:00 go bowling		

STEP 2 Exchange your schedule with a partner. Write several sentences about your partner's habits and routines. Report to the class.

▶ **EXAMPLE:** My partner wakes up at 10:00 on Sundays.

My schedule:

	Mon.	Tues.	Wed.	Thurs.	Fri.	Sat.	Sun.
Morning							10:00 wake up
Afternoon							
Evening							

ACTIVITY 4: WRITING/SPEAKING

Write ten statements about the habits of people in the country you come from. Share your information with your classmates. Compare the habits of people in different countries.

▶ **EXAMPLES:**
1. In Korea, women don't change their names when they get married.
   people eat rice every day.
   men go into the army.
2. In China, people like to exercise in the morning.
   people go to work by bicycle.
3. In Italy, people eat pasta.

ACTIVITY 5: SPEAKING

What is a typical day for you?
Look at the activities below and say how much time you spend on each activity.

sleep ___	eat ___	work ___
study in school ___	exercise ___	clean my room ___
watch TV ___	do homework ___	talk on the phone ___
commute ___	cook ___	get dressed ___
other ___		

Get into a group and talk about each activity. What is the average time the group spends on each activity? Each group should report to the class.

▶ **EXAMPLE:** In our group, everyone sleeps eight hours a night.

ACTIVITY 6: LISTENING 

Listen to the two people talk about their jobs. Complete the chart.

S = Sunday
M = Monday
T = Tuesday
W = Wednesday
T = Thursday
F = Friday
S = Saturday

Job	Start	Circle workdays	Work on Sundays?
1.		S M T W T F S	
2.		S M T W T F S	

Which job do you like? 1 or 2? Why?

Activity 5

SUGGESTION

Add other categories. Have Ss work individually and then share their answers with their group. The group decides who has a healthy/stressed out lifestyle. Make a chart on the board showing how most people spend their time. Come back to the question in the task and discuss lifestyles.

Activity 6 

Play textbook audio. The tapescript for this listening appears on p. 545 of this book. Play the tape more than once, if necessary.

The test for this unit can be found on p. 469–470 of this book. The answers are on p. 471.

ANSWER KEY

Activity 6

1. farmer, 5:00, SMTWTFS, yes
2. computer programmer, _, MTWTF, No

Unit 9

UNIT OVERVIEW

In contextualizing the simple present tense, questions, and adverbs of frequency, much of this unit deals with language learning habits and strategies, problems adjusting to a new language, and so on. The goal is to raise students' (Ss') awareness, both of themselves as learners, and of language learning styles and strategies. This is a good time to have Ss begin a language learning journal in which they reflect on their own learning process and difficulties.

UNIT GOALS

To maximize the diagnostic potential of the Opening Task, do not review the Unit Goals with Ss until after they have completed and reviewed the task.

OPENING TASK

SETTING UP THE TASK

Instead of reading the text first, as a pre-reading activity, have Ss work in pairs or groups to define the good language learner. Discuss their ideas and elaborate vocabulary. See if they can formulate questions at this point. Remember that they had an introduction to questions in Unit 5. Put their questions on the board.

UNIT 9

SIMPLE PRESENT TENSE

Yes/No Questions, Adverbs of Frequency, *Wh*-Questions

UNIT GOALS:

- To ask *yes/no* and *Wh*-questions in the simple present tense
- To understand the meaning and correct position of adverbs of frequency
- To ask questions with *who* and *whom*
- To ask for information about English

OPENING TASK

What Do Good Language Learners Do?

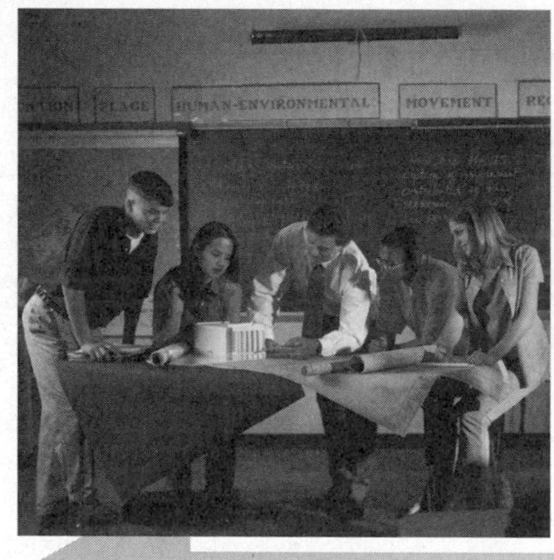

You are all "language learners" in this class. But are you **good** language learners? What is a good language learner? What does a good language learner do?

STEP 1 Read the text below. Do you think you are a good language learner?

Good language learners think about how to learn. They try to use the new language every day. They read, write, and listen to the new language. They find people to speak to. When they don't understand, they don't get nervous. They try to guess the meanings of new words and expressions. They always ask questions about the language. They find ways to remember new words. They try to use new words and expressions in sentences. They listen to correct pronunciation. They repeat words out loud. They sometimes talk to themselves in the new language. They also think about grammar. They try to understand how the new language works.

Good language learners know that learning a new language is not easy. They don't feel bad when they make mistakes. They try to understand their problems in the new language. They review every day.

STEP 2 With a partner, make up five comprehension questions about this text. For example: Do good language learners think about how to learn? Does a good language learner practice the new language? Then ask another pair of students the questions.

CONDUCTING THE TASK

Step 1

Have Ss read the text.

Step 2

If they have already formulated some questions, just add the new ones to those already on the board.

COMPLETING THE TASK

Have each pair ask another pair the questions. If there are discrepancies in the answers, go back to the text to re-read and clarify.

REVIEWING THE TASK

Look at their questions on the board. Remind them that they had a focus on questions in Unit 5. Correct their errors and move on to Focus 1.

FOCUS 1

Review question formation and short answers with reference to Unit 5: *Have.*

Exercise 1

This exercise lists some behaviors that can make Ss more successful and autonomous as learners. Discuss the strategies of good language learners. Have Ss begin to use these strategies (i.e., organizing lists of new words, keeping a journal, etc.)

VARIATION

This exercise can be done as a Find Someone Who ... activity

FOCUS **1**

Simple Present: *Yes/No* Questions

DO/DOES	SUBJECT	BASE FORM OF VERB	SHORT ANSWERS	
			Affirmative	**Negative**
Do	I you we they	work?	Yes, you / I / we / they do.	No, you / I / we / they do not. / don't.
Does	he she it		Yes, he / she / it does.	No, he / she / it does not. / doesn't.

EXERCISE 1

Are your classmates good language learners?

Ask one classmate *yes/no* questions with the words below. Then ask another classmate the questions.

EXAMPLE: **You:** Do you speak English outside of class?
Classmate: Yes, I do./No, I don't.

	Classmate 1 Yes	Classmate 1 No	Classmate 2 Yes	Classmate 2 No
1. speak English outside of class				
2. practice pronunciation				
3. ask people to correct your English				
4. ask people questions about English				
5. watch TV in English				
6. guess the meaning of new words				
7. make lists of new words				
8. read something in English every day				
9. write something in English every day				
10. think about grammar				

Discuss your answers with the class. Decide who is a good language learner.

ANSWER KEY

Exercise 1

1. Do you speak English outside of class? **2.** Do you practice pronunciation? **3.** Do you ask people to correct your English? **4.** Do you ask people questions about English? **5.** Do you watch TV in English? **6.** Do you guess the meaning of new words? **7.** Do you make lists of new words? **8.** Do you read something in English every day? **9.** Do you write something in English every day? **10.** Do you think about grammar?

EXERCISE 2

Information Gap

Nahal and Sang-Woo are two different types of language learners. Work with a partner to find out how they are different. Student A looks at the chart below. Student B looks at the chart on page A-19. Ask and answer questions to complete your chart.

▶ **EXAMPLE:** **Student A:** Does Nahal want to meet English-speaking people?
Student B: Yes, she does.
Student B: Does Sang-Woo want to meet English-speaking people?
Student A: No, he doesn't.

Student A:

	Nahal		**Sang-Woo**	
	Yes	**No**	**Yes**	**No**
1. like to learn English	✔			
2. want to meet English-speaking people				✔
3. feel nervous when speaking English		✔		
4. like to work in groups			✔	
5. need grammar rules to learn English	✔			
6. learn by speaking and listening to English				✔
7. learn by reading and writing English		✔		
8. learn slowly, step by step			✔	
9. try new ways of learning	✔			

EXERCISE 3

What kind of language learner are you?
Look at Exercise 2 and write statements about yourself.

▶ **EXAMPLE:** I like to learn English. I want to meet English-speaking people. I don't feel nervous when speaking English.

Exercise 2 

This exercise focuses on the *affective* dimension of learning: attitudes, the role of anxiety, motivation, and cooperation. It introduces learning styles: whether a learner is detail-oriented or holistic; dependent on a step-by-step presentation or able to figure out how language works while using it. It also addresses sensory preferences: auditory or visual. Exercise 2 can be done in pairs, or as two teams.

Exercise 3

The purpose of this follow-up to Exercise 2 is to allow Ss to see themselves as learners. Ss can write their answers and discuss them in groups or as a class. If you prefer to continue practicing question formation, pair Ss up and have them ask each other these questions. Encourages Ss to add their own statements or questions.

ANSWER KEY

Exercise 2

1. Does Nahal like . . . Yes, she does. Does SangWoo? Yes, he does **2.** Does Nahal want . . . Yes, she does. Does SangWoo . . . No, he doesn't **3.** Does Nahal feel . . . No, she doesn't. Does SangWoo . . . Yes, he does **4.** Does Nahal like . . . Yes, she does. Does SangWoo . . . Yes, he does **5.** Does Nahal need . . . Yes, she does. Does SangWoo . . . Yes, he does **6.** Does Nahal learn . . . Yes, she does. Does SangWoo . . . No, he doesn't **7.** Does Nahal learn . . . No, she doesn't. Does SangWoo . . . Yes, he does **8.** Does Nahal learn . . . No, she doesn't. Does SangWoo . . . Yes, he does **9.** Does Nahal try . . . Yes, she does. Does SangWoo . . . No, he doesn't.

Exercise 3

Answers will vary.

Exercise 4 

These questions about personal habits will prepare Ss for Activity 2, in which they will try to find a compatible roommate in the class. Encourage Ss to ask additional questions that would be interesting and relevant. Example: *Do you smoke?*

EXERCISE 4

What are some of your personal habits? Ask a partner *yes/no* questions with the words below. Check *yes* or *no*. Then your partner asks you.

▶ **EXAMPLE:** **You:** Do you wake up early?
Your Partner: Yes, I do./No, I don't.

	Your Partner's Answers Yes	No
1. wake up early	______	______
2. watch TV a lot	______	______
3. listen to loud music	______	______
4. cook	______	______
5. have parties on weekends	______	______
6. make friends easily	______	______
7. go to bed late	______	______
8. talk on the telephone a lot	______	______
9. study hard	______	______
10. clean your apartment every week	______	______

Exercise 5

EXPANSION

Turn this into a class discussion about issues such as the cost of education, the teaching of religion in public schools, the teaching of moral values, the separation of boys and girls in school, the wearing of uniforms, etc.

EXERCISE 5

Read about students in the United States.

(1) In the United States, a child usually starts kindergarten at age five. (2) In public schools, boys and girls study together. (3) Children go to school five days a week. (4) They don't go to school on Saturdays. (5) They go to school from 8:30 a.m. to 3:00 p.m. (6) They don't wear uniforms. (7) In public schools, children do not study religion.

(8) In high school, some students take difficult exams to enter college. (9) A private college costs a lot of money. (10) The government doesn't pay for private colleges. (11) Many parents pay for their children's education. (12) Many students work after school to help pay for college.

ANSWER KEY

Exercise 4

1. Do you wake up early? **2.** Do you watch TV a lot? **3.** Do you listen to loud music? **4.** Do you cook? **5.** Do you have parties on weekends? **6.** Do you make friends easily? **7.** Do you go to bed late? **8.** Do you talk on the telephone a lot? **9.** Do you study hard? **10.** Do you clean your apartment every week?

Write twelve *yes/no* questions from the sentences marked 1–12 in the reading. Interview a classmate about his or her country with the questions you wrote. Compare students in the United States to students in your home countries.

QUESTIONS

1. Does a child usually start kindergarten at age five in your country ?
2. Do boys and girls usually study together ?
3. ______ ?
4. ______ ?
5. ______ ?
6. ______ ?
7. ______ ?
8. ______ ?
9. ______ ?
10. ______ ?
11. ______ ?
11. ______ ?
12. ______ ?

Now write five sentences about school in your partner's home country.

1. In Korea, a child usually starts kindergarten at age four or five.
2. ______
3. ______
4. ______
5. ______

ANSWER KEY

Exercise 5

3. Do children go to school five days a week? **4.** Do children go to school on Saturdays? **5.** Do they go to school from 8:30 to 3:00? **6.** Do they wear uniforms in school? **7.** Do children study religion in public schools? **8.** In high school, does a student take difficult exams to enter college? **9.** Does a private school/college cost a lot of money? **10.** Does the government pay for private colleges? **11.** Do parents pay for their children's education? **12.** Do students work after school to help pay for college? Statements 1–5 will vary.

FOCUS 2

Since the meanings of adverbs of frequency are very relative, it is difficult to assign exact percentages to all of them. Focus 2 presents them in order of decreasing frequency.

Workbook Exs. 1 & 2, pp. 67–69.
Answers: TE, p. 531.

Exercise 6

This is not a rote exercise; Ss must read the whole context in order to know which adverb of frequency to choose.

FOCUS **2**

Adverbs of Frequency

Adverbs of frequency tell how often something happens.

QUESTION: HOW OFTEN DOES NAHAL WATCH TELEVISION?			
	always		100%
	almost always		↑
	usually		
Nahal	**often/frequently**	watches television.	
	sometimes		
	seldom/rarely		↓
	never		0%

EXERCISE 6

Read the questions and answers. Circle the correct adverbs of frequency.

▶ **EXAMPLE:** **Q:** Does Belinda read English/American newspapers?
A: She (often/seldom) reads an English or American newspaper. She buys one every morning.

1. **Q:** Does Hamid ever use his hands when he speaks English?
   A: He (never/always) uses his hands. His hands help him explain things.
2. **Q:** Does Belinda ever guess the meanings of words?
   A: She (never/always) guesses the meanings of new words. She uses her dictionary all the time.
3. **Q:** Does Hamid ever think in English?
   A: He (never/usually) thinks in his own language first. Then he translates his words into English.
4. **Q:** Does Belinda ever sing in English?
   A: She (often/seldom) sings in English. She doesn't like to sing.
5. **Q:** Does Hamid ever write letters in English?
   A: He has an American friend in Boston. He misses him. He (rarely/sometimes) writes letters to him in English.
6. **Q:** Does Belinda ever make telephone calls in English?
   A: She lives with her aunt. Her aunt speaks English. Her aunt makes the phone calls. Belinda (never/always) makes phone calls in English.

ANSWER KEY

Exercise 6

1. always **2.** never **3.** usually
4. seldom **5.** sometimes **6.** never
7. usually **8.** always

7. Q: Does Belinda ever talk to herself in English?
A: She likes English. She (usually/rarely) talks to herself in English.

8. Q: Does Hamid ever think about how English works?
A: He thinks grammar is very interesting. He (never/always) tries to understand how English works.

EXERCISE 7

The chart below shows learning habits and adverbs of frequency. Check the box that is true for you.

Learning Habits	Adverbs of Frequency						
	Always	**Almost always**	**Usually**	**Often/ Frequently**	**Sometimes**	**Seldom/ Rarely**	**Never**
1. use a dictionary							
2. make telephone calls in English							
3. speak to native speakers							
4. discuss learning problems with classmates							
5. practice English pronunciation							
6. record my voice on tape							
7. read books or newspapers in English							
8. ask questions about English							
9. think in English							
10. dream in English							

Exercise 7

This context gets Ss to reflect on their own learning habits. Answers are personal and will vary. The focus here is only on meaning. After Focus 3, Ss will come back to this exercise and write the statements that describe their own learning habits

FOCUS 3

Have Ss read the examples aloud. Point out the difference between the verb *be* and other verbs, with regard to the position of adverbs of frequency.

Exercise 8

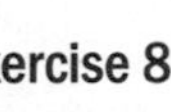

Check the position of the adverbs of frequency in Ss' statements.

Exercise 9

Ss can do this orally or in writing. Use this exercise as a springboard for discussion of educational practices in different cultures. Such a discussion could help Ss understand and adjust to their new classroom situation. Answers will vary.

Workbook Exs. 3 & 4, p. 69–70.
Answers: TE, p. 531

FOCUS **3**

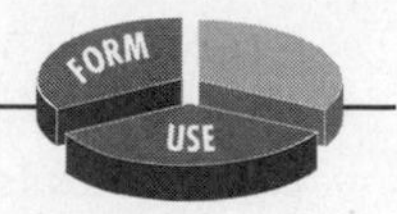

Position of Adverbs of Frequency

EXAMPLES	EXPLANATIONS
(a) They **always** come to class. (b) He **sometimes** asks questions in class. (c) He **never** asks questions.	Adverbs of frequency usually come between the subject and the verb.
(d) **Sometimes** I ask questions in class. (e) That's not true. He asks questions **often.**	Some adverbs of frequency can come at the beginning or at the end of a sentence for emphasis.
(f) They **are always** in class. (g) **I am never** late to class.	Adverbs of frequency come after the verb *be*.

EXERCISE 8

Go back to the chart in Exercise 7. Exchange books with a partner. Write statements about your partner's learning habits using adverbs of frequency.

▶ **EXAMPLES:** He always uses a dictionary.
She rarely speaks to native speakers.

EXERCISE 9

Make true statements about your home country by adding an adverb of frequency.

Name of country: ______________________________

In schools in my home country:

1. The students are of the same nationality.
   The students are usually of the same nationality.
2. The teachers are women.
   ____
3. Teachers hit students.
   ____

4. Teachers are young.

____

5. Teachers give homework.

____

6. Teachers are relaxed and friendly.

____

7. Students work together to learn.

____

8. The classrooms are noisy.

____

9. Students take tests.

____

10. Students cheat on tests.

____

Now discuss what you think is true for the United States.

FOCUS 4

With the exception of *how often* and *whom*, all of these *wh*-question words were presented in Unit 3. *Who/whom* is presented separately in Focus 5. Have Ss read the questions aloud. Elicit answers to each question to review meanings and illustrate possible answers such as:

a) You teach the class
b) I review new vocabulary in the evening
c) We begin class at 9:00
d) They study in an intensive English program
e) He needs English because he wants to go to an American university
f) She gets to school by bus
g) She talks to native speakers every day
h) He meets his friends.

NOTE: For the sake of simplification, we have not included *wh*-questions with post-posed prepositions: *for whom; to whom did you write that letter?* You might, however, decide to do this if you feel the class is ready.

Exercise 10

Ss can do this matching exercise individually, or work with a partner to ask and answer the questions.

FOCUS **4**

Simple Present: *Wh*-Questions

Wh-QUESTION WORD	DO/DOES	SUBJECT	BASE FORM OF VERB	
(a) **What**	**do**	I	**do**	in class?
(b) **When**	**do**	you	**review**	new vocabulary?
(c) **What time**	**do**	we	**begin**	class?
(d) **Where**	**do**	they	**study**	English?
(e) **Why**	**does**	he	**need**	English?
(f) **How**	**does**	she	**get**	to school?
(g) **How often**	**does**	Maria	**talk to**	native speakers of English?
(h) **Who(m)**	**does**	George	**meet**	after school?

EXERCISE 10

Match each question to its answer. Write the letter on the line.

_f_ 1. Why does he need English?	a. on weekends
___ 2. When does the semester begin?	b. by car
___ 3. What do they do in class?	c. at the City University of New York
___ 4. What time does your class start?	d. They speak, read, write, and listen to English.
___ 5. Where does he study English?	e. at 8:30
___ 6. How often does he speak English?	f. because he wants to go to college in the United States
___ 7. When does she go out with her American friends?	g. on September 10th
___ 8. How does he go home?	h. every day

ANSWER KEY

Exercise 10

2. g **3.** d **4.** e **5.** c **6.** h
7. a **8.** b

EXERCISE 11

Read the story of a student named Denise. Write *Wh*-questions with the words in parentheses. Then read the story again and take turns asking a partner the questions and answering them aloud.

Denise is a Haitian student in Washington, D.C. She speaks three languages—Creole, French, and English. She wants to be a bilingual teacher. Her English is very good, but she speaks with an accent. Sometimes people don't understand her when she speaks. She often meets her Haitian friends to talk about her problem. Denise feels embarrassed and seldom speaks English. She feels angry at Americans. She says Americans only speak English. They don't understand the problems people have when they learn a new language.

▶ **EXAMPLE:** (Denise/live) Where does Denise live ______?

1. (Denise/come from) ______?
2. (Denise/want to be) ______?
3. (Denise/speak English) ______?
4. (Denise/feel when she speaks English) ______?
5. (Denise/feel this way) ______?
6. (Denise/feel angry) ______?

Now ask two questions of your own about the story.

7. ______?
8. ______?

Exercise 11

This exercise deals with the frustrations of using a new language.

EXPANSION

Have your Ss write a questionnaire on this topic. Give them the opportunity to go around to other ESL classrooms and survey the Ss there. Have them gather statistics on Ss' experiences and feelings about English, and report their findings to the class. This could lead to the school publication of a written report as well.

Workbook Exs. 5 & 6, pp. 70–72.
Answers: TE, p. 531.

ANSWER KEY

Exercise 11

1. Where does Denise come from? **2.** What does Denise want to be? **3.** Does Denise speak English?/ Does Denise speak English well?/How well does Denise speak English? **4.** How does Denise feel when. . . **5.** Why does Denise feel. . . **6.** Why does Denise feel. . .

FOCUS 5

1. Present these questions on the board with other examples showing *who/what* without *do/does*, as the subject of a question:
   -*Who knows the answer?*
   -*What helps you learn?*
   or other examples relevant to your own Ss:
   Who speaks every day?
   Who works after class?
   What comes after V in the English alphabet?
   Help Ss differentiate *who/whom* when the question is clearly about the object, but the speaker has to choose between being formal or informal.

Examples

Whom do you look like?
Who do you look like? Your mother or your father?

Exercise 12

Ss need to distinguish between WHO (subject) and WHOM (object). They can do this exercise individually.
After Ss have done this exercise, have them focus on #4,5,8. Point out the use of the auxiliary *do* after *whom.*

FOCUS **5**

Wh-Questions with *Who/Whom*

EXAMPLES	EXPLANATIONS
(a) Q: **Who** usually meets her friends? A: Denise. (b) Q: **Who** speaks Creole? A: Denise and her Haitian friends.	*Who* asks a question about the **subject** (Denise) of the sentence. Do not use *do/does.*
(c) Q: **Who(m)** does Denise meet? A: Denise meets her friends.	*Who(m)* asks a question about the **object** (her friends) of the sentence.
(d) **Whom** does Denise call on Sundays? (e) **Who** does Denise call on Sundays?	Formal written English Informal or spoken English
(f) Q: **What** goes up but never comes down? A: Your age!	*What* can also be the subject of a question. Do not use *do/does* in this case.

EXERCISE 12

Fill in the blanks with *who* or *whom.*

EXAMPLE: ___Who___ speaks English?
___Who(m)___ do you call every week?

1. ____________ likes English?
2. ____________ avoids English?
3. ____________ bites his or her nails before a test?
4. ____________ do you meet after class?
5. ____________ do you usually visit on weekends?
6. ____________ makes mistakes in English?
7. ____________ do you call at night?
8. ____________ understands the difference between *who* and *whom*?
9. ____________ helps you with English?

ANSWER KEY

Exercise 12

1. Who 2. Who 3. Who 4. Whom
5. Whom 6. Who 7. Whom 8. Who
9. Who

EXERCISE 13

Read about immigrant families in the United States.

Many families immigrate to the United States. At the beginning, the parents often have problems. They don't speak English. They don't learn English fast. The children usually learn English before the parents, so they translate for their parents. The children always help their parents. Sometimes, the children pay the rent to the landlords. They often talk with doctors about their parents' health. The children take their parents to job interviews. They solve the family's problems. This is a big responsibility for the children, and they feel important. But their parents sometimes feel sad and helpless. Life is often difficult for new immigrant families.

Fill in the blanks with *who* (subject) or *whom* (object). Then answer the questions.

▶ **EXAMPLES:** Q: ___Who___ learns English before the parents?

A: The children (learn English before the parents.)

Q: ___Whom___ do the children help?

A: (The children help) their parents.

1. ______________ translates for the parents?
2. ______________ helps the parents?
3. ______________ do the children pay the rent to?
4. ______________ do the children often talk to about their parents' health?
5. ______________ do the children take to job interviews?
6. ______________ solves the family's problems?
7. ______________ feels important?
8. ______________ feels sad and helpless?

Exercise 13

VARIATION

Instead of having Ss read and answer the questions in this sequence, have Ss fill in *who/whom* in the questions first. Then teach them to **scan** the text for the answers to these questions.

EXPANSION

Some of your Ss may have been, or may still be, in similar situations. Discuss this as a class.

Workbook Exs. 7 & 8, pp. 72–73.
Answers: TE, p. 531

ANSWER KEY

Exercise 13

1. Who 2. Who 3. Whom 4. Whom
5. Whom 6. Who 7. Who 8. Who

FOCUS 6

The purpose of this focus box is to enhance Ss' ability to use communication strategies (introduced in Unit 3, Focus 2). They need to compensate for their lack of linguistic knowledge, either by asking questions about English (a-b-c-d), or by using a circumlocution strategy (e-f). These strategies should be given names and reinforced in class whenever possible.

Exercise 14

Do this exercise as a class.

EXPANSION

Write new words on index cards. Ss choose cards and have to ask: *What does it mean? How do you spell it? How do you pronounce it? How do you say the opposite of . . . ?* Elicit or provide answers. Ss will continue to practice this strategy in Unit 14, Focus 3.

Workbook Exs. 9 & 10, pp. 74–75.
Answers: TE, pp. 531–532.

FOCUS **6**

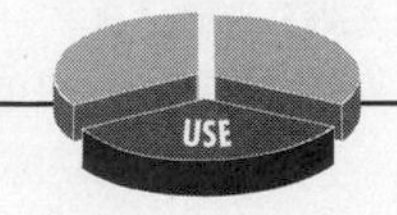

Getting Information about English

In a new language, you do not always know the words to say what you want. When you have a problem, ask for help.

EXAMPLES	EXPLANATIONS
You say: **(a)** What does the word *decision* mean? **(b)** What does *strategy* mean?	**When you:** • want to know the **meaning** of a word.
(c) How do you spell *remember?*	• want to know the **spelling** of a word.
(d) How do you pronounce *communicate?*	• want to know the **pronunciation** of a word.
(e) How do you say *a machine to clean floors?* **(f)** How do you say *the opposite of happy?*	• don't know the word for something, and you want to communicate your meaning and learn new words.

EXERCISE 14

Ask *Wh*-questions for the answers below.

EXAMPLE: **Q:** How do you say *special shoes you wear in the house*?
A: You say *slippers.*

1. **Q:** ______________________________?
   A: You pronounce it lǽŋ-gwIdz.
2. **Q:** ______________________________?
   A: The word *guess* means you don't know the answer, but you try to find the answer in your head.
3. **Q:** ______________________________?
   A: You say *thin.*
4. **Q:** ______________________________?
   A: You spell it: *c-o-m-m-u-n-i-c-a-t-e.*

ANSWER KEY

Exercise 14
1. How do you pronounce "language"?
2. What does the word "guess" mean?
3. How do you say the opposite of "fat"?/ "heavy"? **4.** How do you spell "communicate"? **5.** What does the word "strategy" mean?

5. **Q:** ____?

A: *Strategy* means an action or actions you take to achieve a goal; for example. to learn English.

EXERCISE 15

Correct the mistakes in the following sentences.

1. Is he read books?
2. Do they good students?
3. What means *routines?*
4. I watch sometimes TV.
5. How often you listen to nativc speakers of English?
6. Does he studies in the library?
7. What does the class on Mondays?
8. How you say *not correct?*
9. I am never make mistakes.
10. Why you feel embarrassed to speak English?

Exercise 15

Have Ss work on this exercise individually, then compare answers with a partner or correct as a class.

UNIT GOALS REVIEW

Ask Ss to look at the goals on the opening page of the unit. Help them understand how much they have accomplished in each area. Ask them if they still have any questions about what they have learned so far.

ANSWER KEY

Exercise 15

1. Does he read books? **2.** Are they good students? **3.** What does "routines" mean? **4.** I sometimes watch TV **5.** How often do you listen **6.** Does he study **7.** What does the class do on Mondays? **8.** How do you say **9.** I never make mistakes **10.** Why do you feel embarrassed

USE YOUR ENGLISH

For a more complete discussion of how to implement the Use Your English Activities, see page xxiv of this Teacher's Edition.

Activity 1

Pair Ss from different home countries, if possible.

1. Go around while Ss are working. Check their questions. Put unclear or incorrect questions on the board. Go over these before they go on to the next step.
2. As Ss report their findings, organize this information in a semantic map on the board: *Roles-Habits-Routines.* Add other categories if necessary. Discuss the results.

Activity 2

Ss can refer back to Exercise 4 or make up new questions of their own. This can be done in pairs, or as a Find Someone Who activity.

VARIATION

Have each student choose another whom they think would be a compatible roommate. They ask each other their questions to confirm their compatibility. If they turn out to be incompatible, they must choose another classmate and try the questions again. They get two chances to find a roommate. The most compatible pair (with the most questions answered favorably) wins a prize.

Activity 3

Help Ss define categories. Use those mentioned in this unit or new ones—government, family structure, roles of men and women, dating habits, eating habits, etc.

VARIATION

Ss can write this report in short paragraphs instead of presenting the information orally.

Use Your English

ACTIVITY 1: WRITING/SPEAKING

Work with a partner.

STEP 1 Write at least ten questions you have about family life in your partner's country. Include people's roles, habits, and routines.

STEP 2 Ask each other questions about family life in your countries. Find five similarities and five differences in family life. Report to the class.

▶ **EXAMPLES:**

	Same	Different
Do women make important family decisions?	______	______
What decisions do women make?	______	______
Do men cook at home?	______	______
Who cooks?	______	______

ACTIVITY 2: WRITING/SPEAKING

Find the perfect roommate. You want to share an apartment with another student. Write ten questions to ask your classmates. Find a good "roommate" in your class.

▶ **EXAMPLES:**
- *Do you smoke?*
- *What time do you get up?*

ACTIVITY 3: WRITING/SPEAKING

What do you know about the countries your classmates come from? Write ten questions about customs, habits, etc. Find a classmate who comes from a different country and ask the questions. Then report to the class.

▶ **EXAMPLES:** *What do people usually do on weekends?*
How often do people go to the movies?
How do people usually celebrate their birthdays?

ACTIVITY 4: WRITING/SPEAKING

United States Knowledge Quiz

STEP 1 Get into two teams. Write ten *Wh*-questions in the simple present that test knowledge about the United States.

STEP 2 Team A asks Team B the first question. Team B can discuss the question before they answer. Then Team B asks Team A the second question and so on.

Score: Score 1 point for each grammatically correct question. Score 1 point for each correct answer. The team with the most points is the winner.

▶ **EXAMPLES:** Where does the President of the United States live?
When do Americans vote?

ACTIVITY 5: WRITING

Write about the educational system in your native country. Answer these questions:

- What do students usually do?
- What do teachers usually do?
- What are the differences between the school system in your country and in the United States?

ACTIVITY 6: LISTENING/SPEAKING 

STEP 1 Listen to the conversation between Pedro and Yuko. Who is the hard-working student?

STEP 2 Listen again. Make a list of the things Pedro and Yuko do on Sundays.

Pedro	Yuko
________	________
________	________
________	________
________	________

STEP 3 Role-play the conversation with a partner.

Activity 4

Assist Ss in formulating questions. Questions can be about things they know or about things they would like to know about the U.S. even if they don't know the answers yet. You may have to supply the answers. During Step 1, check to see that Ss' questions are clear and correct. For Step 2, assign a score keeper.

Activity 5

Try to have Ss organize a coherent paragraph with topic and support. For example: *The school systems in my home country and the U.S. are similar in two ways—the roles of teachers and the roles of students . . . etc.*

Activity 6 

Play textbook audio. The tapescript for this unit can be found on p. 545 of this book.

The test for this unit can be found on p. 472–473 of this book.
The answers are on p. 474.

TOEFL Test Preparation Exercises for Units 7–9 can be found on pp. 76–78 of the workbook.
The answers can be found on TE p. 532.

ANSWER KEY

Activity 6

Step 1: Yuko is the hard-working student.
Step 2: Pedro plays tennis, meets friends, goes out for a meal, and does homework. Yuko stays home, watches TV, and does homework.

Unit 10

UNIT OVERVIEW

Although students (Ss) may learn to form imperatives easily, they will often use them inappropriately, and this can cause misunderstanding. Since the challenge in imperatives lies in how they are used, the Opening Task evokes functions of the imperatives in various social situations.

UNIT GOALS

Do not give the target structure away before Ss have done the task. Introduce the goals listed on this page after they have completed the task.

OPENING TASK
SETTING UP THE TASK

Have Ss discuss in pairs or groups what is happening in each picture.

UNIT 10

IMPERATIVES AND PREPOSITIONS OF DIRECTION

UNIT GOALS:

- To make affirmative and negative imperatives
- To understand the many functions of imperatives
- To use prepositions of direction
- To give directions

OPENING TASK

Who Says What?

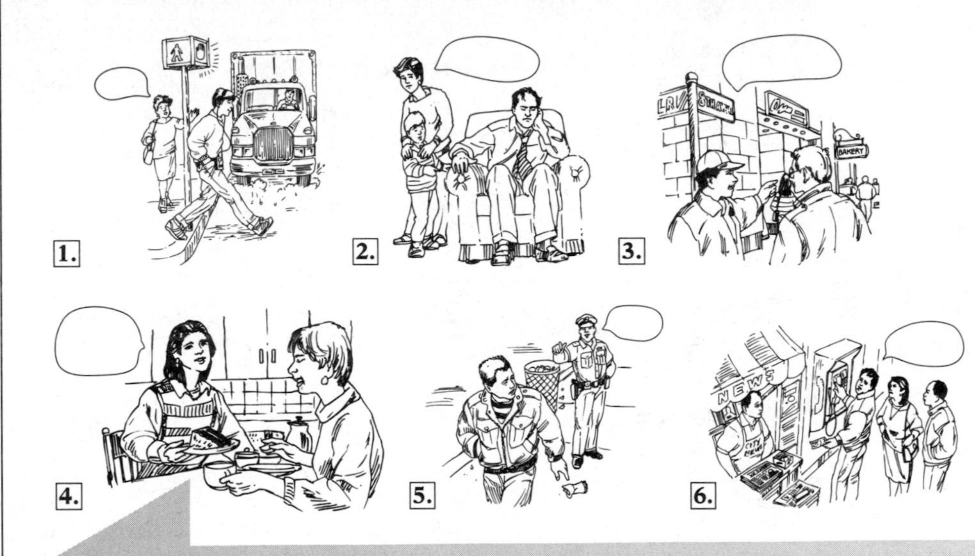

STEP 1 Match each statement to a picture.

		Picture Number
(a)	"Please give me change for a dollar, Sir."	_____
(b)	"Have a piece of cake with your coffee, Mary."	_____
(c)	"Don't ask your father now. He's very angry."	_____
(d)	"Don't throw your litter on the street. Pick it up!"	_____
(e)	"Go straight down Eighth Avenue and turn left at the bakery."	_____
(f)	"Watch out!"	_____

STEP 2 What is the mother saying? Write her words.

CONDUCTING THE TASK

Step 1

Ask Ss to write their own captions in each bubble. This will show you if they know the form/use of imperatives. According to what Ss produce, you can (a) ask them to match each statement to a picture, or (b) have them compare their statements to those in Step 1.

Step 2  

Write each pair's imperative statement on the board. Write the correct statements on one side and the incorrect statements on the other. Use these sentences to introduce the form of the imperative.

ANSWER KEY

Opening Task

a. 6 b. *4* c. *2* d. *5* e. *3* f. *1*

Step 2

Don't touch that pot on the stove! Be careful—that's hot! Watch out. That's hot!

FOCUS 1

1. Write the affirmative and negative imperatives on the board.
2. Point out that there is no subject in imperatives. We only use "You" when we want to make the imperative more emphatic.
3. Point out that we use "Do not ..." as opposed to the contraction "Don't" to make an imperative statement more emphatic.
4. Explain that it is important to say "Please" with imperatives, especially when the speaker is not in a position of authority.

Exercise 1

Review answers with the whole class.

Workbook Ex. 1, p. 79–80.
Answer: TE, p. 532

FOCUS **1** FORM

Imperatives: Affirmative and Negative

Affirmative

BASE FORM OF VERB	
(a) **Have**	a piece of cake
(b) **Give**	me change for a dollar.

Negative

DO NOT/DON'T + BASE FORM OF VERB	
(c) **Do not throw**	your litter on the street.
(d) **Don't ask**	your father now.

Polite imperatives

(e) **Please give** me change for a dollar.
(f) **Please don't do** that again.
(g) **Don't do** that again, **please.**

NOTE: Don't use a subject with imperatives:
Have a piece of cake. **NOT:** ~~*You*~~ *have a piece of cake.*

EXERCISE 1

Go back to the Opening Task on pages 156–157. Underline all the affirmative imperative verbs and circle all the negative imperative verbs.

▶ **EXAMPLE:** "Please give me change for a dollar, Sir."

ANSWER KEY

Exercise 1

Answers that should be underlined (affirmative imperatives) are underlined; those that should be circled (negative imperatives) are italicized.

a. Please give me change for a dollar.
b. Have a piece of cake with your coffee.
c. *Don't ask* your father now.
d. *Don't throw* your litter. Pick it up!
e. Go straight down ... and turn left.
f. Watch out!

FOCUS 2

Uses of Imperatives

Imperatives have different uses or functions. Look at the pictures and notice what the imperative does in each situation.

a.

d.

b.

e.

c.

f.

FOCUS 2

The challenge of imperatives is knowing how to use them appropriately. Exercises 2, 3, and 4 present different functions or "speech acts" realized with imperatives.

SUGGESTIONS

1. Write the uses in Focus 2 on the board in random order (*give an order, give directions,* etc.).
2. Have a student read the first bubble (*"Don't worry. Relax."*) and match it to the use.

IMPERATIVE	USE
(a) "Don't worry. Relax."	Give advice or make a suggestion.
(b) "Be careful!"	Give a warning when there is danger.
(c) "Make a right at the corner."	Give directions or instructions.
(d) "Please give me some aspirin, Mom."	Make a polite request.
(e) "Have some coffee, dear."	Offer something politely.
(f) "Don't come home late again!"	Give an order.

Exercise 2

Have Ss do this exercise individually and check as a class.

EXPANSION

Give additional examples for Ss to match with a Use. (Imperative: *Go home and take a nap!* Purpose: Advice. Please *lend me a pen.* Purpose: Polite request.)

Workbook Ex. 2, p. 81.
Answers: TE, p. 532

EXERCISE 2

Look back at the Opening Task on pages 156–157. Write the number of the picture that matches each use.

Use	Picture Number
A. Give advice	2
B. Give an order	
C. Give a warning when there is danger	
D. Make a polite request	
E. Offer something politely	
F. Give directions	

Exercise 3

The function of the imperative in this exercise is giving instructions. After Ss have done the exercise, ask them to identify the use, to reinforce the notion that imperatives have different functions.

EXERCISE 3

Fill in each blank with an affirmative or negative imperative.

use	keep	drink	be	drive
wear	obey	leave	look	use

ANSWER KEY

Exercise 2
A. 2 B. 5 C. 1 D. 6 E. 4 F. 3

Exercise 3
1. Be 2. Look 3. Use 4. Obey 5. Leave 6. Wear/Use 7. Don't drive 8. Don't drink 9. Use 10. Keep

To be a good driver, remember these rules:

1. ________________ prepared to stop.

2. ________________ at the road ahead.

3. ________________ your rearview mirrors.

4. ________________ the speed limit.

5. ________________ space between your car and the car in front of you.

6. ________________ your seat belt.

7. ________________ if you are very tired or are on medication.

8. ________________ and drive.

9. ________________ your horn to warn others of danger.

10. ________________ your car in good condition.

Exercise 4

VARIATION

1. Put each sentence on the left and each response on the right on separate pieces of paper.
2. Divide the class in half.
3. Give one half of the Ss the sentences on the left and the other half the responses on the right.
4. Have Ss walk around saying their statements and trying to find the appropriate response.
5. Have pairs stay together and repeat their sentences and responses out loud so all Ss can check.

FOCUS 3

1. To sensitize Ss to the inappropriate use of imperatives, pretend you are a student and start giving orders to other Ss such as *"Give me your book." "Open the window." "Don't sit in the back of the room—move to the front."*
2. Ask Ss how they felt when you spoke to them that way.

3. Write the orders on the board and point out that though the sentences are grammatically correct, something was wrong in how they were used.
4. Elicit the fact that if used inappropriately, imperatives are considered rude.
5. Looking at the examples in the box, discuss the relationships between the speakers and the situation.

EXERCISE 4

Work with a partner. You read each sentence on the left. Your partner gives an appropriate response from the right.

1. I don't like my landlord.	**a.** Go on a diet.
2. I have a headache.	**b.** Go to the dentist.
3. I am overweight.	**c.** Make friends with your classmates.
4. I have the hiccups.	**d.** Move to a different apartment.
5. I have a toothache.	**e.** Call home.
6. I don't have any friends here.	**f.** Go to bed early.
7. I feel tired every morning.	**g.** Practice speaking to native speakers.
8. I miss my family.	**h.** Hold your breath for two minutes.
9. I worry too much.	**i.** Take it easy.
10. I can't speak English very well.	**j.** Take some aspirin.

FOCUS **3**

Using Imperatives Appropriately

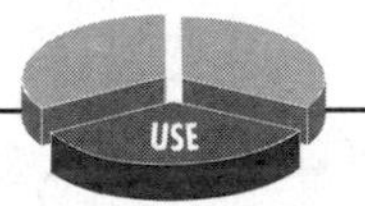

EXAMPLES	EXPLANATIONS
(a) Police Officer to driver: "Show me your license."	Use an imperative when: • the speaker has the right or authority to tell the listener to do something.
(b) A teacher to a teacher: "Pass me that book, please."	• the speaker and the listener are equals; for example, they work together.

ANSWER KEY

Exercise 4

1. d **2.** j **3.** a **4.** h **5.** b **6.** c
7. f **8.** e **9.** i **10.** g

EXERCISE 5

Check (✔) Yes if the imperative is appropriate in each situation. Check (✔) No if the imperative is not appropriate.

Situation	Imperative	Yes	No
1. A student says to a teacher:	"Give me my paper."		
2. A student says to a classmate:	"Wait for me after class."		
3. A man stops you on the street. He says:	"Hey, mister. Tell me the time."		
4. A worker says to his boss:	"Don't bother me now. I'm busy."		
5. You get into a taxi and say:	"Take me to the airport, and please hurry!"		
6. A father says to his teenage son:	"Turn down that music! I can't take it anymore!"		

FOCUS **4**

MEANING

Prepositions of Direction: *To, Away From, On (to), Off (of), In (to), Out of*

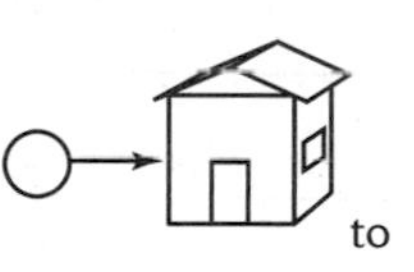

to

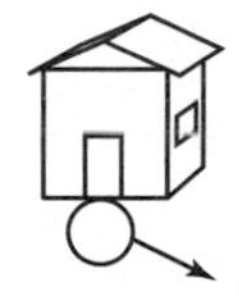

away from

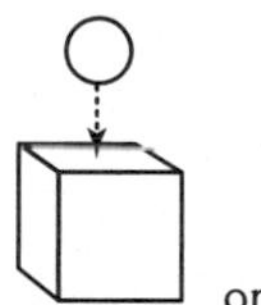

on(to)

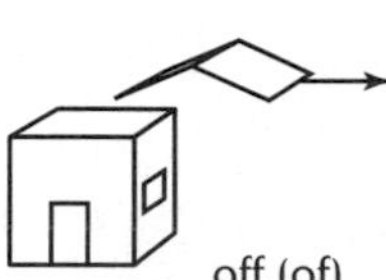

off (of)

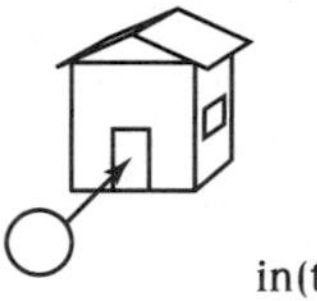

in(to)

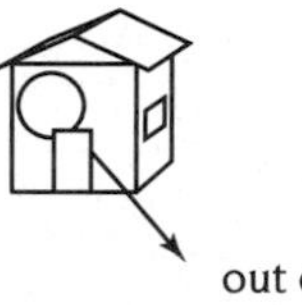

out of

EXAMPLES	EXPLANATIONS
(a) He gets **in (to)** the car. (b) He gets **on** the bus. (c) He gets **out of** the taxi. (d) He gets **off of** the train.	Prepositions of direction show movement. For cars, taxis, and vans, use *in (to)* and *out of*. For buses, trains, and planes, use *on (to)* and *off (of)*.

Exercise 5

These situations could generate a great deal of discussion, especially of cultural differences. Encourage Ss to explain their answers.

Workbook Exs. 3 & 4, p. 82.
Answers: TE, p. 532.

FOCUS 4

1. Refresh Ss' memory of prepositions of location (Unit 3)
2. Explain that prepositions of location talk about position or place and are used with position verbs (*be, live*).
3. Have Ss look at Focus 4. Go over the meanings of the prepositions of direction. Give examples in class if necessary, Simon-says style: *Walk out of the room. Move away from the window.* Explain how prepositions of direction are used with verbs of motion (*walk, run, jump, go*).

VARIATIONS

1. Bring in some photographs or pictures illustrating movement.
2. If possible, use video to illustrate these prepositions of direction.
3. Go directly to Exercise 6 to show how prepositions of direction are used with verbs of motion. Elicit prepositions of direction.

ANSWER KEY

Exercise 5

1. No (Speaker and listener are not equals) **2.** Yes (Two Ss are equals.) **3.** No (The address "Hey, mister" is impolite; raw imperative is rude.) **4.** No (Worker and boss are not equals.) **5.** Yes (In this situation, it is understood that it is an emergency and the driver probably wouldn't be offended. Also, "please" is used.) **6.** Yes (A father has the authority to tell his son to do something.)

Exercise 6

Have Ss do this exercise individually.

EXPANSION

Have Ss cover the text and explain the sequence of pictures from memory. Encourage Ss to supply the prepositions quickly and naturally.

EXERCISE 6

Here is a story about the hard life of a mouse. Fill in the blanks with a preposition of direction from Focus 4.

1. The mouse comes _______________ his hole.

2. The cat jumps _______________ the table.

3. The mouse runs _______________ the cheese.

4. The cat jumps _______________ the table and runs after the mouse.

5. The mouse runs _______________ the cat.

6. The mouse runs _______________ his hole.

ANSWER KEY

Exercise 6

1. out of **2.** on (to) **3.** to **4.** off (of)
5. away from **6.** into

Prepositions of Direction: *Up, Down, Across, Along, Around, Over, Through, Past*

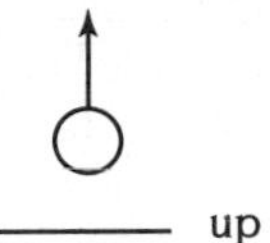

up

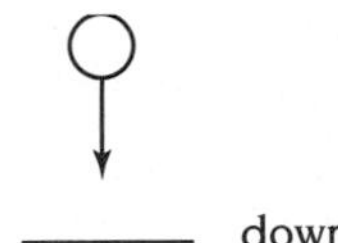

down

across

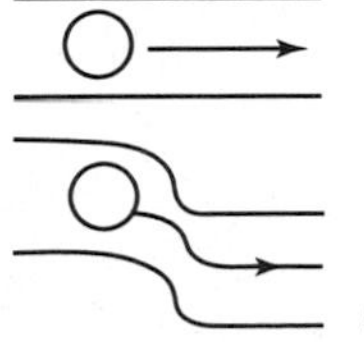

along

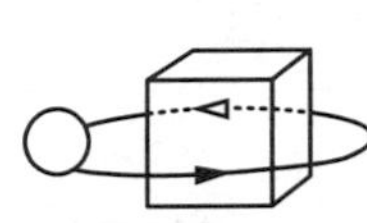

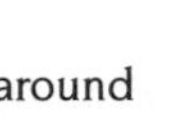

around

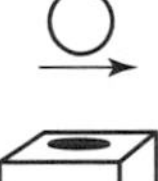

over

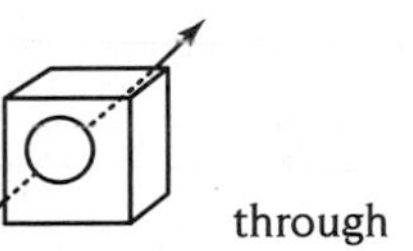

through

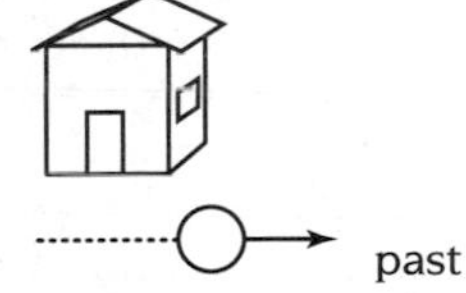

past

FOCUS 5

SUGGESTION

Try miming these prepositions of direction or asking Ss to do so. Have the class verbalize what each mime means (walk "up the stairs" "down the stairs" "across the room" "around a student").

VARIATION

Use pictures or videos to present the meanings of prepositions of direction, or discuss them.

Workbook Exs. 5 & 6, pp.83–84.
Answers: TE, p. 532

Exercise 7

Have Ss do this exercise individually.

EXPANSION

Have Ss cover the text and explain the sequence of pictures from memory.

Workbook Ex. 7, p. 85.
Answers: TE, p. 532

EXERCISE 7

Here is a story about the hard life of a cat. Fill in the blanks with a preposition of direction from Focus 5.

1. The cat sees the dog. He runs ________________ the field.

2. He runs ________________ the grass.

3. He runs ________________ the bridge.

4. He climbs ________________ the tree.

5. The dog barks and runs ________________ the tree.

6. The dog's owner arrives and puts a leash on the dog. The cat climbs ________________ the tree.

7. The cat walks ________________ the dog.

8. He walks ________________ the road with a smile on his face.

ANSWER KEY

Exercise 7

Some answers may vary. **1.** across **2.** through **3.** over/across **4.** up **5.** around **6.** down **7.** past **8.** along/down/up

FOCUS **6**

USE

Giving Directions

Look at the map and read the conversation below.

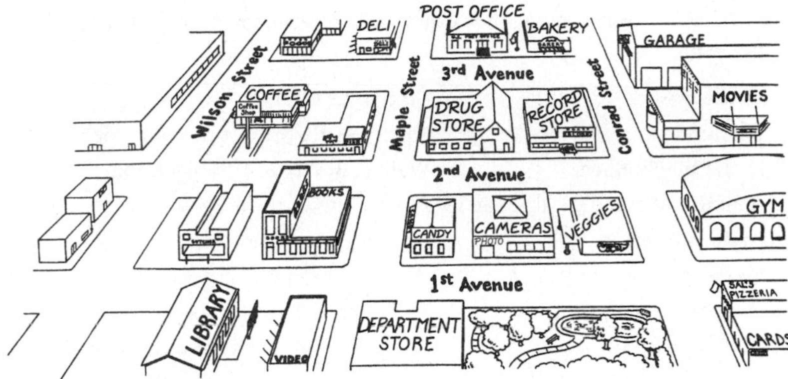

(Person A is at the bakery.)

A: Excuse me, how do I get to the department store?

B: Walk **down** Conrad Street until you get to First Avenue. Then turn **right** at the corner. Go **straight**. Walk one block. The department store is on the corner on the left.

EXERCISE 8

Look at the map in Focus 6. Follow the directions. Then answer the questions.

EXAMPLE: You are at the record store on the corner of Second Avenue and Conrad Street. Walk down Conrad Street until you get to Third Avenue. Turn left at the corner. Walk one block. Cross Third Avenue. This place is on the right. Where are you? Answer: *At the Post Office*.

1. You are at the bakery. Walk down Conrad Street and make a right on Second Avenue. Go straight and make a left on Maple Street. Walk across the street. Where are you? ______________
2. You come out of the coffee shop on Second Avenue. Walk down Second Avenue and go two blocks. Turn right on Conrad Street. Go straight until you get to First Avenue. Make a left. Walk into the building on your right. Where are you? ______________

FOCUS 6

Giving directions is an authentic way for Ss to practice prepositions of direction.

1. Familiarize Ss with the streets and places on the map.
2. Elicit prepositions of location by asking where each place is (e.g., *The bakery is on the corner of Conrad Street and Third Avenue. It's next to ...*)
3. Have two Ss read the dialogue aloud.

ANSWER KEY

Exercise 8

1. at the bookstore 2. At Sal's Pizzeria
3. At the garage

Exercise 9

This exercise offers an alternative, interactive way of checking if Ss really understand prepositions of direction.

VARIATION

Have a student mime one of the two commands in front of the class. The class then says which imperative it is.

EXPANSION

Have Ss write additional commands using prepositions of direction. They can add these to the list in the book or tell their classmates to act them out.

UNIT GOAL REVIEW

Ask Ss to look at the goals on the opening page of the unit again. Help them understand how much they have accomplished in each area. Ask them if there are any questions they still have about what they have learned so far.

3. You are at the library on First Avenue. Walk up Wilson Street. Make a right on Third Avenue. Go straight for two blocks. Then make a left on Conrad Street. Go across the street from the bakery. Where are you? ________________

Now write two sets of directions and questions of your own.

EXERCISE 9

Work with a partner. Take turns giving the commands. Your partner acts out the commands you give.

1. Step off the bus.	Step onto the bus.
2. Put your hand into your pocket.	Take your hand out of your pocket.
3. Walk to the blackboard.	Walk away from the blackboard.
4. Put a pencil into the desk drawer.	Put a pencil on the desk.
5. Climb up a mountain.	Climb down a mountain.
6. Walk on the grass.	Walk through tall grass.
7. Walk away from your classmate.	Walk around your classmate.
8. Walk past a group of people.	Walk through a group of people.
9. Walk across the room.	Step over a book on the floor.

Use Your English

ACTIVITY 1: WRITING/SPEAKING

DO'S AND DON'TS

STEP 1 Make a list of *do's* and *don'ts* for someone who plans to travel to your country or the United States.

▶ **EXAMPLE:** Korea

	DO'S	DON'TS
Hand and body movements	Bow to say goodbye.	Don't touch or pat a man on the back—only if you are very good friends.
Eating		
Manners for a guest at a person's house		
Other		

STEP 2 Make an oral presentation of the *do's* and *don'ts* to your class.

USE YOUR ENGLISH

For a more complete discussion of how to use the activities, see p. xxvi of this Teachers' Edition.

Activity 1 

This activity should provoke a lot of discussion about cross-cultural values and customs. Use this time to inform Ss about American customs (e.g., *Shake hands when you greet someone; Leave a 15% tip in restaurants.*)

SUGGESTIONS

1. Have Ss sit in culturally homogeneous groups so they can generate imperatives about their particular cultures and then present them to the class.
2. Or, have Ss work in multicultural groups so they can exchange information with each other.
3. Put up butcher block paper with the general categories (hand and body movements, eating, etc.) so Ss can walk around the room and write up their imperatives. This also gives you a chance to work on correction.

VARIATION

Step 2

Have Ss write a *do's and dont's* book about the cultures they represent.

Activity 2

Read Ss the problem in the example, or give another one. Example: *I am nervous about speaking English.* Have them generate advice.

Compare the kinds of advice each of the pairs came up with. This can lead to an interesting cross-cultural discussion. If Ss do this activity in writing, collect the papers to check how well Ss have understood. Put the errors on an error correction sheet to use in the next class.

Activity 3

SUGGESTIONS

1. Bring in magazines so Ss can cut out pictures to create their booklets. Display the booklets when Ss have finished.
2. Have Ss identify the imperatives in the booklets.

VARIATION

To make this into an amusing activity, use titles such as "How Not to Learn English," "How Not to Meet People," "How to Annoy People in Movie Theaters."

Activity 4

SUGGESTIONS

1. Have certain destinations in mind. Give each group the same destination so Ss can compare the directions they write.
2. Make this into a competition so that the first group that gets to the destination wins.

ACTIVITY 2: WRITING/SPEAKING

PROBLEMS AND ADVICE

STEP 1 Write down three problems you have.

STEP 2 Work with a partner. Tell your partner your problems.

STEP 3 Your partner gives you advice.

▶ **EXAMPLE:** **You:** I can't sleep at night.
Your Partner: Drink a cup of hot milk.

Problems	Advice
1.	
2.	
3.	

ACTIVITY 3: WRITING

Work in a group. Create an information booklet to give advice to new students in the United States. Choose from the ideas below.

- How to Learn English
- How to Find a Job
- How to Do Well in School
- How to Find an Apartment
- How to Meet People

ACTIVITY 4: WRITING/SPEAKING

DIRECTIONS GAME

STEP 1 Work in groups of two or three. Write directions for someone to go to different parts of the building you are in (restrooms, snack bar, etc.).

▶ **EXAMPLE:** *Go out of the room. Turn left and go to the end of the corridor. Turn right. It's on the right.*

STEP 2 Ask the rest of the class to find out where your directions lead.

ACTIVITY 5: RESEARCH

Look around your neighborhood or your home. Find imperatives in public notices and signs. Discuss the meaning of the notices.

SAVE ENERGY!
RECYCLE OLD NEWSPAPERS.

Learn English the Easy Way
Register now.

DO NOT WALK ON THE GRASS

NO PARKING

ACTIVITY 6: LISTENING/SPEAKING

REMEDIES

STEP 1 Listen to the three different remedies. Match the remedy to one of the titles below.

Remedies

(a) ______ How to cure a headache

(b) ______ How to cure a cold

(c) ______ How to treat a burn

STEP 2 Describe a remedy you know.

Activity 5

SUGGESTIONS

1. Ask Ss to bring in their own notices or to copy notices they might find on trains or buses or in public places. They could also bring in instructions to electronic devices or appliances they have at home.
2. Have Ss post their findings around the room and ask them to identify the imperatives.

Activity 6

Play textbook audio. The transcript for this listening appears on p. 546 of this book. Play the tape more than once, if necessary. You can also, after completing the activity, use the tape to focus on pronunciation and intonation.

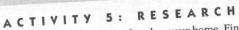

The test for this unit can be found on pp.475–476 of this book.
The answers can be found on p. 477.

ANSWER KEY

Activity 6
Step 1: **(a)** 3 **(b)** 1 **(c)** 2

Unit 11

UNIT OVERVIEW

In working on quantifiers, students (Ss) will review count/noncount nouns (Unit 4). They will also learn a great deal of new vocabulary related to a healthy diet and environment.

UNIT GOALS

To maximize the diagnostic potential of the Opening Tasks, do not review the Unit Goals with Ss until after they have completed and reviewed the task.

OPENING TASK
SETTING UP THE TASK

Explain *calories, fat,* and *cholesterol* in foods. Have Ss read the explanations. Bring in actual products or containers (yogurt, cereal, snack foods, soft drinks, etc.).

UNIT 11

QUANTIFIERS

UNIT GOALS:

- To understand the meaning of quantifiers
- To choose between *a few* and *few, a little* and *little*
- To use the correct form of quantifiers with count/noncount nouns
- To ask questions with *How many . . . , How much . . .*
- To understand the meaning of measure words

OPENING TASK
Who Eats a Healthy Breakfast?

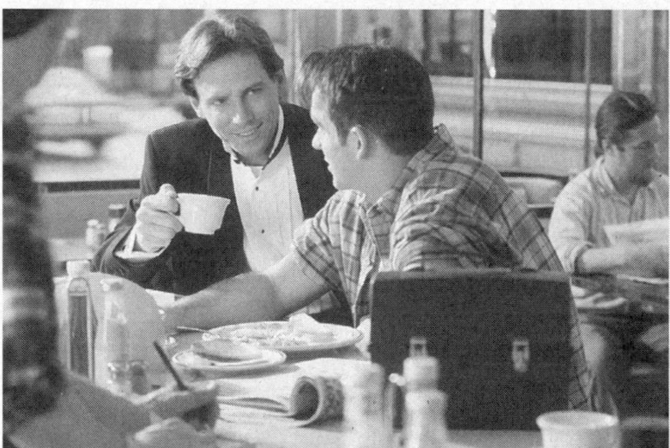

The chart on page 173 shows the number of **calories** and the amount of **fat** and **cholesterol** in the foods Billy, Juanita, and Brad eat for breakfast every day.

Calories are the amount of energy a food produces in the body. To lose weight, we need to reduce our calories.

There is **fat** in foods like butter, cheese, and meat. Too much fat is bad for your health.

There is **cholesterol** in foods like eggs, butter, and cheese. Too much cholesterol can give you heart disease.

STEP 1 Look at the chart and answer the questions.

	Calories	Fat (grams)	Cholesterol (milligrams)
Billy			
eggs (3)	140	9.8	399
sausages (2)	180	16.3	48
muffin	170	4.6	9
whole milk	165	8	30
Brad			
cereal	80	1.1	0
orange juice	80	0	0
nonfat milk	85	0	0
banana (1)	130	less than 1	0
Juanita			
pancakes (3)	410	9.2	21
vanilla milkshake	290	13	10
doughnuts (2)	240	20	18

1. Is there a lot of fat in Juanita's breakfast?
2. Who eats a breakfast with only a little fat?
3. Whose breakfast has a lot of calories?
4. Are there any calories in Brad's breakfast?
5. How much cholesterol is there in each breakfast?
6. Which foods don't have any cholesterol?
7. Which foods have little fat?
8. Which food has a lot of cholesterol?

STEP 2 Whose breakfast is healthy? Write three sentences to explain why.

________________________ has a healthy breakfast.

1. ________________________ calories.
2. ________________________ fat.
3. ________________________ cholesterol.

ANSWER KEY

Opening Task
1. Yes **2.** Brad **3.** Billy's and Juanita's **4.** Yes (cereal = 80, orange juice = 80, nonfat milk = 85, banana = 130 **5.** Billy = 486, Brad = 0, Juanita = 49 **6.** cereal, orange juice, nonfat milk, bananas **7.** cereal, orange juice, nonfat milk, bananas **8.** eggs, sausages, whole milk, pancakes, doughnuts.

Step 2:
Brad has a healthy breakfast.
1. His breakfast doesn't have many calories/ has only a few calories./There aren't many calories in his breakfast. **2.** He eats very little fat for breakfast. **3.** There's no cholesterol in his breakfast. He has no cholesterol.

CONDUCTING THE TASK

Step 1

familiarize Ss with the chart by asking such questions as *How many calories do eggs have?* Have Ss work in pairs to answer the questions. Walk around to see whether Ss are generating answers with quantifiers.

Step 2

The sentences Ss write will show you how well they know the target structure.

COMPLETING THE TASK

Write Ss' sentences on the board. Answer the question in Step 2. *Whose breakfast is healthy?*

REVIEWING THE TASK

You can either: (a) Go on to Focus 1 for a review of count/noncount nouns, and do Focus 2 before reviewing the task; or (b) Go directly to Focus 2 and review count/noncount nouns at the same time as you present the quantifiers. Correct Ss' sentences from Step 2 after Focus 2.

FOCUS 1

If you need to review count and noncount nouns from Unit 4, have Ss look at the examples in the chart and explain the differences. Elicit their hypotheses by asking questions such as *What articles are used with count and noncount nouns? What form of the verb is used with count and noncount nouns?*

Exercise 1

Have Ss do this exercise individually and then check with a partner.

Workbook Ex. 1, p. 86.
Answers: TE, p. 533.

FOCUS **1**

Review of Count and Noncount Nouns

EXAMPLES	EXPLANATIONS
(a) Billy eats a **muffin** and an **egg**. (b) Brad likes **pancakes.** (c) Billy eats three **eggs.** (d) There is a **fast-food restaurant** near here. (e) There are a lot of **calories** in a **milkshake.** (f) How many **eggs** does Billy eat?	**Count nouns:** • can have *a/an* in front of them. • can have plural forms. • can have a number in front of them. • can take singular or plural verbs. • can be in questions with *how many.*
(g) **Cereal** is healthy. (h) He eats **bread** and **butter.** (i) It has a little **cholesterol.** (j) Nonfat **milk** is good for you. (k) How much **cholesterol** does an egg have?	**Noncount nouns:** • can't have *a/an* in front of them. • can't have plural forms. • can't have a number in front of them. • can't take plural verbs. • can be in questions with *how much.*

EXERCISE 1

Go back to the Opening Task on page 173. Make a list of the count and noncount nouns.

Count Nouns	Noncount Nouns
eggs	milk

ANSWER KEY

Exercise 1

Count Nouns: eggs, sausages, muffin, banana, pancakes, milkshake, doughnut.
Noncount Nouns: whole milk, cereal, orange juice, nonfat milk.

FOCUS **2**

Quantifiers

Quantifiers are words or phrases that show how many things or how much of something we have.

Positive Meaning

COUNT NOUNS				
		Quantifiers		
(a)	There are	**many**	eggs	in the refrigerator.
(b)	There are	**a lot of**	apples	
(c)	There are	**some**	carrots	
(d)	There are	**a few**	oranges	
NONCOUNT NOUNS				
		Quantifiers		
(e)	There is	**a lot of**	milk*	in the refrigerator.
(f)	There is	**some**	juice	
(g)	There is	**a little**	cake	

NOT: There is much milk in the refrigerator. Do not use *much* in affirmative statements.

Negative Meaning

COUNT NOUNS				
		Quantifiers		
(h)	There aren't	**many**	oranges	in the refrigerator.
(i)	There aren't	**a lot of**	oranges	
(j)	There are	**few**	tomatoes	
(k)	There aren't	**any**	onions	
(l)	There are	**no**	onions	
NONCOUNT NOUNS				
		Quantifiers		
(m)	There isn't	**much**	cake*	in the refrigerator.
(n)	There isn't	**a lot of**	cake	
(o)	There is	**little**	coffee	
(p)	There isn't	**any**	jam	
(q)	There is	**no**	jam	

*Use *much* in negative statements.

FOCUS 2

1. Ask Ss to count the number of eggs in the refrigerator. Then have them read sentence (a).
2. Continue having them judge how much of each food there is and read the corresponding sentences aloud.
3. Point out that *much* is not used in affirmative sentences.
4. Correct Ss' sentences from Step 2 of the Opening Task, if you have not done so.

Exercise 2

This exercise demonstrates the relative nature of quantifiers where meaning depends on the speaker and on the context. For example, in #1, we give "d," *Carlos has a lot of money in the bank* as the answer. For some Ss, "c" might also be possible if they think that $500 is a lot of money.

EXERCISE 2

Match the picture to the statement. Write the letter next to each statement.

A.

Community Bank January 31
Account #536
Debits: $325.00
Credits: $325.00
Balance: $ ____.00

B.

Community Bank January 31
Account #741
Debits: $458.31
Credits: $958.31
Balance: $ 500.00

C.

Community Bank January 31
Account #289
Debits: $312.80
Credits: $412.80
Balance: $100.00

D.

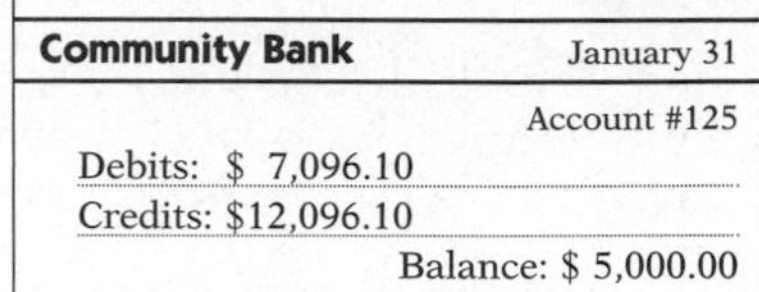
Community Bank January 31
Account #125
Debits: $ 7,096.10
Credits: $12,096.10
Balance: $ 5,000.00

__d__ **1.** Carlos has a lot of money in the bank.
_______ **2.** François has a little money in the bank.
_______ **3.** Kim has no money in the bank.
_______ **4.** Lee has some money in the bank.

E. 

F. 

G. 

_______ **5.** The Greens have a lot of plants in their home.
_______ **6.** The Smiths don't have any plants.
_______ **7.** The Taylors have a few plants.

H. 

I. 

J. 

_______ **8.** Jody has no friends.
_______ **9.** Irene has a few friends.
_______ **10.** Helene has many friends.

ANSWER KEY

Exercise 2

1. d **2.** c **3.** a **4.** b **5.** g **6.** e.
7. f **8.** j **9.** i **10.** h **11.** l **12.** m
13. k

K.

L.

M.

________ **11.** Bill has a lot of hair.
________ **12.** Jim doesn't have any hair.
________ **13.** Albert has a little hair.

EXERCISE 3

Cross out the incorrect quantifier in each sentence.

▶ **EXAMPLE:** My new apartment has ~~many~~ / some / a lot of furniture.

1. Middletown has a lot of / a little / a few pollution.
2. The teacher gives us some / many / a little homework.
3. Billy has a little / a few / many girlfriends.
4. Mario speaks much / three / a few languages.
5. Majid has a lot of / a little / many money.

Exercise 3

When going over the answers, ask Ss to explain why the incorrect quantifier is wrong. (Example: #1—*Pollution* is noncount).

ANSWER KEY

Exercise 3
1. a few **2.** many **3.** a little **4.** much
5. many

Exercise 4 

Have each group present their answers. This will lead into interesting discussions.

EXPANSION

Have Ss make a true statement for the "False" answers. (e.g., #3—*There are no calories in diet soda. There are many calories in soda.*)

Exercise 5

Remember that *much* is not used in affirmative sentences. (#3, #4, #7, #8)

Workbook Exs. 2 & 3, pp. 87–88.
Answers: TE, p. 533.

EXERCISE 4

Test your knowledge about food. Check *True* or *False*. Then compare your answers to your partner's answers.

	True	False
1. There are no calories in water.	✓	
2. There's a lot of salt in fast food.		
3. There are no calories in soda.		
4. There's a lot of fat in cheese.		
5. There are few calories in a small baked potato.		
6. There's little cholesterol in fish.		
7. There are few vitamins in orange juice.		
8. There's some fat in low-fat yogurt.		
9. There isn't any sugar in fruit.		
10. There's a little caffeine in herbal tea.		

EXERCISE 5

Use the chart in the Opening Task on page 173 to complete the statements by adding quantifiers.

1. Doughnuts have ___a lot of___ calories.
2. A banana doesn't have ____________ calories.
3. There is ____________ cholesterol in eggs.
4. There is ____________ cholesterol in a muffin.
5. There is ____________ fat in bananas.
6. Orange juice has ____________ calories.
7. Sausages have ____________ fat.
8. Eggs and pancakes have ____________ fat.
9. There are ____________ calories in cereal.
10. There is ____________ cholesterol in orange juice.
11. There is ____________ fat in cereal.
12. There is ____________ fat in whole milk.

ANSWER KEY

Exercise 4

2. True **3.** False **4.** True **5.** True **6.** True **7.** False **8.** True **9.** False **10.** False

Exercise 5

1. a lot of/many **2.** many **3.** a lot of **4.** a lot of/some **5.** very little, a little **6.** some **7.** a lot of **8.** a lot of **9.** some **10.** no **11.** very little/a little **12.** a lot of

FOCUS **3**

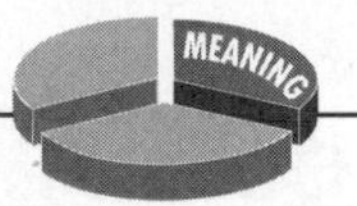

A Few/Few, A Little/Little

EXAMPLES	EXPLANATIONS
(a) She has **a few** books. = She has *some* books. **(b)** I have **a little** time. = I have *some* time.	*A few* and *a little* have a positive meaning for the speaker. The speaker means: *some,* or more than zero (a sufficient quantity).
(c) They have **few** books. = They don't have many books. **(d)** They have **little** time. = They don't have much time.	*Few* and *little* have a negative meaning for the speaker. The speaker means: *not much, not many,* almost zero (an insufficient quantity).

EXERCISE 6

Linda and Kathy are both Americans living in Europe for a year. Their experiences are very different. Fill in the blanks with *few/a few* or *little/a little.*

Linda is very lonely. She doesn't have a full-time job. She has (1) ___few___ friends and (2) ______________ money. She works part-time as a baby sitter. She doesn't like this kind of work. She has (3) ______________ patience for children. She speaks very (4) ______________ Spanish.

Kathy loves to live in different countries. She speaks (5) ______________ languages. She goes to a language school in Spain and she has (6) ______________ very close friends. Kathy learns (7) ______________ Spanish every day. She also works as a baby sitter and makes (8) ______________ extra money. Kathy works hard, but she always has (9) ______________ time to go out and have fun. She has (10) ______________ problems in Spain.

FOCUS 3

The meaning difference between *a few/few* and *a little/little* is difficult for Ss. Both *a few* and *a little* suggest that there is a sufficient quantity and connote a positive meaning. *Few* and *little* suggest that there is an insufficient quantity. To convey this distinction to Ss, give a couple of dollars to one student and only 25 cents to another. Ask them to go buy a cup of coffee. Elicit from the class: *Student 1 can buy a cup of coffee. He/She has a little money. Student 2 can't buy coffee because he/she has very little money.*

Exercise 6

Have Ss do this exercise individually and then check with a partner.

Workbook Ex. 4, p. 88.
Answers: TE, p. 533.

ANSWER KEY

Exercise 6

2. little **3.** little **4.** little **5.** a few **6.** a few **7.** a little **8.** a little **9.** a little **10.** few

FOCUS 4

1. To work inductively, give Ss a few minutes to ask their classmates questions about their family, school, work, or home. Use their questions to present Focus 4.
2. To work deductively, have Ss read the focus box and go on to Exercise 7.

FOCUS 4

Questions with *How Many* and *How Much*

QUESTION			ANSWER	EXPLANATIONS
How many	**Count Noun**			
(a) **How many**	universities	are there?	A lot.	Use *How many* with **count nouns.**
(b) **How many**	brothers	do you have?	Two.	
(c) **How many**	oranges	do you eat every week?	A few.	
How much	**Noncount Noun**			
(d) **How much**	money	do you have in your account?	$200	Use *How much* with **noncount nouns.**
(e) **How much**	time	do you have?	Not much.	
(f) **How much**	gas	do you need?	Five gallons.	

Exercise 7

VARIATION

Have Ss ask each other the questions. Ask the class if the questions and answers are correct.

EXERCISE 7

Go back to the Opening Task on page 173. Make questions with *how much* or *how many.* Then answer the questions.

1. ___How many___ pancakes does Juanita usually eat for breakfast?
2. ___How much___ juice does Brad drink?
3. ______________ eggs does Billy have?
4. ______________ cholesterol is there in three eggs?
5. ______________ calories are there in a vanilla milkshake?
6. ______________ cholesterol is there in a bowl of cereal?
7. ______________ fat is there in two doughnuts?
8. ______________ calories are there in three pancakes?
9. ______________ sausages does Billy eat?
10. ______________ money does Brad spend on breakfast?

Exercise 8 

Have Ss do this exercise individually, then read the dialogues aloud in pairs. Answers may vary.

EXERCISE 8

Fill in the blanks with *how much* or *how many* or a quantifier (*a lot, a little, some, any, much, many*). Then read the conversations aloud.

ANSWER KEY

Exercise 7
1. How many—3 **2.** How much—one glass **3.** How many—3 **4.** How much—399 mg. **5.** How many—290 **6.** How much—none **7.** How much—20 gms **8.** How many—410 **9.** How many—2 **10.** How much—I don't know

1. **Mom:** How was school today, dear?
   Child: O.K., Mom . . .
   Mom: (a) ______________ homework do you have tonight?
   Child: I have (b) ______________ homework—three compositions plus a spelling test tomorrow!
   Mom: Don't worry, I have (c) ______________ time to help you tonight.
2. **Doctor:** Please remember to take this medicine, Mr. Josephson.
   Patient: (a) ______________ medicine do I need to take every day?
   Doctor: These are pills. You need three red pills a day, one after every meal. And you need two blue pills a day, one in the morning and one before bed.
   Patient: Say that again, please . . . (b) ______________ red pills? (c) ______________ blue pills? And (d) ______________ pills do I need to take in all?
   Doctor: Three red pills and two blue pills. Five pills a day in all. Take these for a week. Then call me.
   Patient: O.K. Thanks, Doctor.

EXERCISE 9

Ask your partner questions about a city he or she knows. First ask a *yes/no* question. Then ask a question with *how many* or *how much.*

1. skyscrapers — Are there any skyscrapers in your city? How many skyscrapers are there?
2. crime — Is there any crime in your city? How much crime is there?
3. noise
4. universities
5. pollution
6. trash on the streets
7. parks
8. poor people
9. traffic
10. museums
11. beaches
12. American fast-food restaurants
13. public transportation
14. shopping malls
15. hospitals

Exercise 9

Choose a student in class to demonstrate how to do this exercise. Have Ss take notes on what their partners say. Then have each pair tell what they learned about their partner's city.

Workbook Ex. 5, p. 89.
Answers: TE, p. 533.

ANSWER KEY

Exercise 8

1. a. How much **b.** a lot of **c.** a. lot of/some/a little **2. a.** How much **b.** How many **c.** How many **d.** How many

Exercise 9

3. Is there any noise? How much noise...? **4.** Are there any universities? How many universities are there? **5.** Is there any? How much? **6.** Is there any? How much? **7.** Are there any? How many? **8.** Are there any? How many? **9.** Is there any? How much? **10.** Are there any? How many? **11.** Are there any? How many? **12.** Are there any? How many? **13.** Is there any? How much? **14.** Are there any? How many? **15.** Are there any? How many?

FOCUS 5

Bring in realia (empty containers, bottles etc.) or pictures from supermarket flyers to help explain these measure words.

VARIATIONS

1. Another way to present this is to have a list of measure words in one column on the board and a list of the items in random order on the right. Have Ss match the measure word with the item.
2. Put measure words on individual cards and write items on the board. Ask Ss to match the measure word with the item.

Exercise 10

If it is difficult to give specific measurements to some of the container sizes—a quart, half gallon, or gallon of oil—take all acceptable answers.

FOCUS **5**

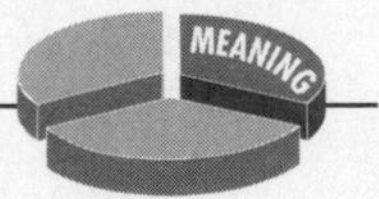

▶ Measure Words

Measure words change the way we see a thing. A measure word before a noncount noun tells us about the specific quantity.

▶ **EXAMPLES:** I have a lot of coffee. (coffee = noncount noun)
I have four cans of coffee. (specific quantity)

a **can** of tuna a **jar** of jam a **tube** of toothpaste	a **box** of cereal a **bottle** of beer a **bag** of sugar	Containers
a **slice** of pizza a **piece** of pie	a **glass** of milk a **cup** of coffee	Portions
a **cup** of flour a **pint** of ice cream a **teaspoon** of salt	a **quart** of milk a **pound** of sugar a **gallon** of water	Specific quantities
a **head** of lettuce a **sheet** of paper	a **loaf** of bread a **bar** of soap	Other
a **bag** of apples a **pound** of onions **BUT:** a **dozen** eggs **NOT:** a dozen of eggs	a **can** of beans a **box** of chocolates **five thousand** people **NOT:** five thousand of people	Measure words can also be used with count nouns.

EXERCISE 10

Here is Maggie at the checkout counter. Write down her shopping list on the next page. Use measure words in the list.

Shopping List

a pound of	coffee	____________	oil
____________	milk	____________	soda
____________	rice	____________	bread
____________	soup	____________	soap
____________	toothpaste	____________	lettuce
____________	candy	____________	toilet paper
____________	eggs	____________	beef
____________	butter	____________	peanut butter

EXERCISE 11

How much food do you have in your refrigerator? Use measure words to tell your classmates what you have.

▶ **EXAMPLE:** *I have a quart of milk.*

EXERCISE 12

Correct the mistakes in the following sentences.

1. **Jane:** Can I talk to you for a minute?
   Kevin: Sure, I have little time.
2. John has much friends.
3. How many money do you have?
4. My teacher gives us many homeworks.
5. Her hairs are black.
6. Elsie is in great shape. She runs few miles a day.
7. We don't sell no newspapers here.
8. There are much stores in this city.
9. I would like some informations please.
10. My best friend gives me many advices.
11. This school has little students.
12. We have few time to finish this book.

Exercise 11

Go around and check as Ss are doing this exercise individually. Then have them share their answers with a partner. See who in the class has the fullest refrigerator or the healthiest foods in the refrigerator!

Workbook Ex. 6, p. 90.
Answers: TE, p. 533.

Exercise 12

Ss can do this exercise individually or in pairs.

UNIT GOAL REVIEW

Ask Ss to look at the goals on the opening page of the unit again. Help them understand how much they have accomplished in each area. Ask them if there are any questions they still have about what they have learned so far.

ANSWER KEY

Exercise 10

A half gallon of milk, a 5-lb bag of rice, two cans of soup, a tube of toothpaste, a $\frac{1}{2}$ pound bag of candy, a dozen eggs, a half pound of butter, a quart/gallon of oil, a bottle of soda, a loaf of bread, a bar of soap, a head of lettuce, two rolls of toilet paper, a pound of beef, a jar of peanut butter.

Exercise 12

1. a little time **2.** many/a lot of friends **3.** How much money **4.** a lot of homework **5.** Her hair is black **6.** a few miles **7.** any newspapers **8.** many/a lot of **9.** some information **10.** some/a lot of advice **11.** few Ss **12.** little time

USE YOUR ENGLISH

For a more complete discussion of how to use the activities, see p. xxvi of this Teacher's Edition.

Activity 1 

Practice making each question first with the whole class. Then have Ss work in groups. Ss can decide who has the healthiest diet in the group, and present this person to the class, explaining why: *Joel has the healthiest diet. He doesn't use a lot of sugar. He eats a lot of fruit and* vegetables.

Use Your English

ACTIVITY 1: SPEAKING

FOOD HABIT SURVEY

Ask three students questions with *how much* and *how many* to complete the chart.

▶ **EXAMPLES:** How much coffee do you drink a day?
I drink three cups a day.
How much sugar do you put in your coffee?
Two teaspoons.

	Student 1	Student 2	Student 3
cups of coffee or tea/drink/a day			
teaspoons of sugar/put in coffee or tea			
meat/eat/a week			
fish/eat/a week			
soda/drink/a day			
money/spend on food/a week			
bread/eat/a day			
fruit/eat/a day			
salt/put on food			
glasses of water/drink/a day			
eggs/eat/a week			
meals/have/a day			
other			
other			

184 UNIT 11

ACTIVITY 2: SPEAKING

Play a circle game with all the students in the class. Make a statement starting with "I want to buy . . ." One student says an item that begins with the letter A and uses a measure word. The second student repeats the statement and adds a second item that starts with the letter B. The third student does the same and adds on an item with the letter C, and so on.

▶ **EXAMPLE:** **Student 1:** I want to buy a bag of apples.

Student 2: I want to buy a bag of apples and a loaf of bread.

Student 3: I want to buy a bag of apples, a loaf of bread, and a head of cabbage.

ACTIVITY 3: WRITING/SPEAKING

Choose a recipe you like and write the ingredients without writing the quantity. The other students ask you questions with *how much* and *how many* to fill in the exact quantity. Make a book of the class' favorite recipes.

▶ **EXAMPLE:** Recipe: *Italian Tomato Sauce*

Ingredients: tomatoes
onions
garlic
oil
salt and pepper

Questions: How many tomatoes do you use?
How many onions do you use?
How much garlic is there?
How much oil do you use?
How much salt do you add?

Activity 2

If you have a very large class, it might be too time-consuming to do this circle game. Divide the class into two or more groups and have circles going on simultaneously. This activity is a lot of fun and challenges Ss to remember all the information.

SUGGESTION

Keep track of mistakes by designating a note taker for each group to make sure items are correctly restated.

Activity 3 

Introduce this activity by writing the ingredients on the board and having Ss ask you questions with *how much* and *how many.*

SUGGESTIONS

1. Have Ss write the ingredients for their recipes on butcher block paper so they can put them up in front of the class.
2. Have Ss create their own international cookbook with their recipes.
3. Have an international day when Ss bring in their dishes and tell the class how they prepared them.

Activity 4

Ask Ss to bring in real food items or labels if they can. Have them write summary statements about the nutrition facts or ingredients and present what they learned to the class. Since manufacturers in other countries are not always required to divulge this information, Ss can learn a lot about what they eat by doing this activity.

SUGGESTION

Specify what type of food Ss should research—one group could do research on snack foods, another group on fast foods, another on ethnic dishes common to Ss in the class.

ACTIVITY 4: RESEARCH

Go to a supermarket. Look at three food labels. Write the nutrition facts on the chart below.

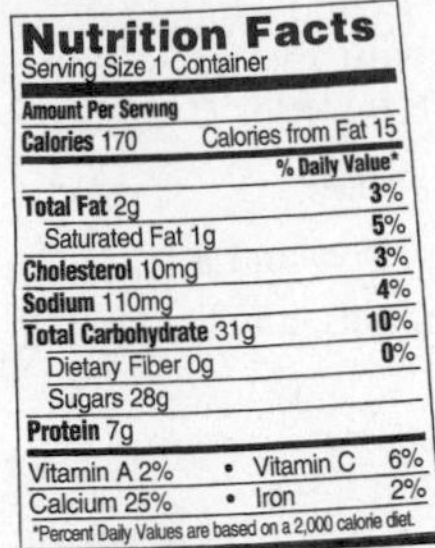

Nutrition Facts

Serving Size 1 Container

Amount Per Serving	
Calories 170	Calories from Fat 15
	% Daily Value*
Total Fat 2g	3%
Saturated Fat 1g	5%
Cholesterol 10mg	3%
Sodium 110mg	4%
Total Carbohydrate 31g	10%
Dietary Fiber 0g	0%
Sugars 28g	
Protein 7g	
Vitamin A 2% • Vitamin C	6%
Calcium 25% • Iron	2%

*Percent Daily Values are based on a 2,000 calorie diet.

	Example	Label 1	Label 2	Label 3
Food	yogurt			
Calories per serving	170			
Fat	2g			
Cholesterol	10 mg			
Sodium	110 mg			
Sugars	28g			
Protein	7g			

Tell the class about the foods. Are they healthy or not?

ACTIVITY 5: WRITING

Your friend wants to come and live where you are living now. Write a letter to your friend explaining why this is or is not a good idea. Use the vocabulary in the box to help you.

▶ **EXAMPLE:** I live in a really wonderful neighborhood. There isn't much crime. There are a lot of trees and parks. There are many good restaurants.

crime	parks	trees
traffic	hospitals	flowers
noise	houses	grass
spacious apartments	bookstores	drugstores
good restaurants	movie theaters	job
clean streets	ethnic markets	good schools
people from my country	friendly neighbors	open spaces

ACTIVITY 6: LISTENING 

Sara is calling a supermarket. She has a shopping order.

STEP 1 Listen to her order and check the things she wants.

STEP 2 Listen again. Write the amount she wants.

_______ onions	_______ potatoes	_______ carrots
_______ milk	_______ water	_______ yogurt
_______ lettuce	_______ cabbage	_______ tomatoes
_______ tuna	_______ eggs	_______ oil

Activity 5

SUGGESTIONS

1. The vocabulary provided here should not restrict Ss in their writing. They should express their own true feelings in this letter. Give them 15 minutes or so as a pre-writing period: Let them brainstorm, make lists, or freewrite to generate ideas.
2. Pair Ss to read each other's letters and offer feedback as to clarity, focus, and development. How helpful will this letter be to a friend? Have Ss revise their letters if you feel they could benefit from this.
3. Collect and evaluate Ss' letters to see if they still have problems with quantifiers. Create error correction sheets from these mistakes.

Activity 6 

Play textbook audio. The tapescript for this listening appears on p. 546 of this book. It may be helpful to play the tape more than once: the first time, Ss listen for the main idea; after that they listen for specific details.

The test for this unit can be found on pp. 478–479 of this book.
The answers can be found on p. 490.

ANSWER KEY

Activity 6

Steps 1 and 2: Five pounds of onions, five pounds of potatoes, a bunch of carrots, a half gallon of milk, a head of cabbage, two pints of yoghurt, two cans of tuna, a dozen eggs, a bottle of olive oil

Unit 12

UNIT OVERVIEW

This unit teaches students (Ss) to qualify people's habits and behaviors by using adverbs of manner. It shows them how to focus their comments either on the person or on the action.

UNIT GOALS

To maximize the diagnostic potential of the Opening Task, do not review the Unit Goals with Ss until after they have completed and reviewed the Opening Task.

OPENING TASK
SETTING UP THE TASK

1. Make sure Ss are familiar with the concept of life insurance. Discuss the fact that companies can refuse to insure people if they're high risks. Go over all challenging vocabulary.
2. Ask Ss questions about the information in the insurance record (*Is Bill Rogers single or married? How old is he? How tall is he? Is he in good health?*).

UNIT 12

ADVERBS OF MANNER

UNIT GOALS:

- To understand the meaning of adverbs of manner
- To know the position of adverbs of manner in a sentence
- To know how to spell adverbs of manner
- To focus on either an action or a person

OPENING TASK

Do You Want to Give Bill Rogers Life Insurance?

STEP 1 You work for a life insurance company. Look at Bill Rogers' record and read the sentences below. Check *True* or *False*.

Long Life Insurance Company
Health and Accident Record

Name:	Bill Rogers	Sex:	Male
Date of Birth:	9/20/48	Marital Status:	Single
Height:	5'7"	Weight:	225 pounds
Health Information:	Heart Problems Smokes 2 packs a day		

Previous Offenses: Speeding: 5/19/92, 8/15/96
Not stopping at a red light: 7/14/89, 9/21/93, 12/31/94, 7/4/95
Drunk driving: 12/31/95
Crashing into a wall: 3/17/96

	True	False
1. Bill is a careful driver.		
2. He drives slowly.		
3. He drives carelessly.		
4. He is a big eater.		
5. He drives fast.		
6. He drinks excessively.		
7. He eats moderately.		
8. He is a heavy smoker.		
9. He takes his health seriously.		
10. He lives dangerously.		

STEP 2 Work with a group. Are you going to give Bill Rogers life insurance? Explain why or why not.

CONDUCTING THE TASK

Have Ss work individually, checking *true* or *false*.

Step 2 

Have them work in groups to do Step 2. Though these adverbs are in the Opening Task, Ss will be focusing on meaning, not form, at this point. Ask the groups to write their reasons so you can assess their use of adverbs of manner.

COMPLETING THE TASK

Have all groups share their opinions of Bill Rogers, and explain why they will/won't give him life insurance. Listen to their language. Write interesting or problematic statements on the board.

REVIEWING THE TASK

Look at Focus 1 for the form and position of an adverb of manner (as compared to that of an adjective). Correct Ss' sentences on the board.

ANSWER KEY

Opening Task
1. False 2. False 3. True 4. True
5. True 6. True 7. False 8. True
9. False 10. True

FOCUS 1

Put sentences (a) and (b) on the board. Ask Ss what word "*careful*" describes and what word "*carefully*" describes.

SUGGESTION

Provide a few more examples that contrast adjectives and adverbs: loud/loudly, quiet/quietly, cheerful/cheerfully. Follow the structures of (a), (b), (c). Use Ss' names or real situations.

Exercise 1

Ss can do this exercise individually or in pairs.

Workbook Exs. 1 & 2, pp. 91–92.
Answers: TE, p. 533.

FOCUS 2

To present the spelling rules inductively, write the adjective and adverb forms on the board and have Ss generate the rules. Go over the exceptions. These are very confusing for Ss. Have Ss read the examples aloud.

FOCUS **1**

Adverbs of Manner

EXAMPLES	EXPLANATIONS
(a) He is a **careful** driver.	*Careful* is an adjective. It describes the noun *driver*. The adjective goes before the noun.
(b) He drives **carefully**.	*Carefully* is an adverb of manner. It describes the verb *drive*. The adverb answers the question "how?" The adverb goes after the verb.
(c) He drives his car **carefully**. NOT: He drives carefully his car.	When there is an object after the verb, the adverb goes after the object (*his car*).

EXERCISE 1

Go back to the Opening Task on page 189. Underline all the adjectives and circle all the adverbs of manner.

EXAMPLE: Bill is a careful driver.
He drives (slowly).

FOCUS **2**

FORM

Spelling of Adverbs of Manner

ADJECTIVE	ADVERB	RULE
slow beautiful	slowly beautifully	Add *-ly*.
heavy	heavily	Adjectives that end in *-y*: change *y* to *i* and add *-ly*.
fantastic	fantastically	Adjectives that end with *-ic*: add *-ally*.
terrible	terribly	Adjectives that end with *-le*: drop the *-e*, and add-*y*.

ANSWER KEY

Exercise 1
Adjectives are underlined and adverbs are italicized.

3. *carelessly* 4. big 5. *fast* 6. *excessively* 7. *Moderately* 8. heavy 9. *seriously* 10. *dangerously*

EXAMPLES		EXPLANATIONS
(a) She's a **fast** driver. (c) We have an **early** dinner. (e) We eat a **late** lunch. (g) We are **hard** workers.	(b) She drives **fast**. (d) We have dinner **early**. (f) We eat lunch **late**. (h) We work **hard**.	Some adverbs have the same form as adjectives.
(i) Joel's a **good** cook.	(j) He cooks **well**.	Some adverbs are irregular.
(k) He works **hard**. (l) He **hardly** works.		Do not confuse *hard* with *hardly*. In example (l), *hardly* is an adverb of frequency. It means "he doesn't work very much."
(m) She is lovely. (n) Marco is lonely. (o) That dress is ugly. (p) Maria is friendly. (q) The party is lively.		Some words that end in *-ly* are not adverbs. They are adjectives.

EXERCISE 2

Find three sentences that describe each occupation. Write the letters next to the occupation.

Occupations

1. I am a teacher. ___c___ ______ ______
2. I am a lawyer. ______ ______ ______
3. I am an artist. ______ ______ ______
4. I am the Secretary General of the United Nations. ______ ______ ______

a. I respond to medical emergencies very quickly.
b. I defend my clients successfully.
c. I prepare lessons carefully.
d. I draw beautifully.
e. I take care of international problems urgently.
f. I give medical treatment to people carefully.
g. I paint well.
h. I speak three languages fluently.
i. I stay at the office very late.
j. I drive very fast.

Exercise 2

In Exercises 2 and 3, Ss are not required to spell the adverbs of manner, only to understand their meaning. Call attention to their spelling as well.

ANSWER KEY

Exercise 2

1. c, k, n **2.** b, i, m **3.** d, g, l **4.** e, h, o
5. a, f, j.

5. I am an emergency medical technician in an ambulance. ______ ______ ______

k. I talk to my students politely
l. I use colors creatively.
m. I study the law constantly.
n. I write on the blackboard neatly.
o. I act diplomatically.

Exercise 3

Ss can work individually or in pairs.

SUGGESTION

This exercise also lends itself to dramatic reading aloud. Have Ss practice saying these sentences aloud in a manner that matches the adverb.

VARIATION

You can reverse these directions and have Ss say the sentences in different ways and have other Ss guess the adverb.

EXERCISE 3

How are the speakers saying the sentences below? Match each sentence with the best adverb. Write the adverb in the blank.

▶ **EXAMPLE:** "Shhh, don't say a word." she said quietly.

politely	sadly	nervously	quickly	shyly
incorrectly	impolitely	happily	angrily	kindly

1. "I just got engaged!" she said ________________.
2. "My dog just died," he said ________________.
3. "I'm in a hurry," she said ________________.
4. "I no make mistakes," he said ________________.
5. "May I make a telephone call?" she asked ________________.
6. "Bring me a menu, fast!" he said ________________.
7. "This is the last time I'm telling you! Clean up your room!" she said ________________.
8. "WWWWWWWWWWill yyyyou mmmmmmmmmarry mmmmmm-mmmmme?" he asked ________________.
9. "Please, don't ask me to speak in front of the class," she said ________________.
10. "Can I help you?" he asked ________________.

Exercise 4

Ss must spell the adverbs in Exercises 4 and 5. Have Ss write their answers on the board. Check spelling.

EXERCISE 4

Read each statement. Use the adjective in parentheses to make another statement with an adverb.

▶ **EXAMPLE:** My son is a safe driver. (careful)
My son drives carefully.

1. Baryshnikov is an excellent dancer. (graceful)

____

ANSWER KEY

Exercise 3

1. happily 2. sadly 3. quickly
4. incorrectly 5. politely 6. impolitely
7. angrily 8. nervously 9. shyly
10. kindly

Exercise 4

1. dances gracefully 2. runs fast
3. teaches us patiently 4. speaks effectively
5. sings beautifully 6. work diligently
7. behaves politely 8. learn quickly
9. paint sloppily 10. thinks quickly/clearly

2. Uta Pippig is a great runner. (fast)

3. My father is a good teacher. (patient)

4. The President is a good speaker. (effective)

5. Andrea Bocelli is a wonderful singer. (beautiful)

6. Teachers are hard workers. (diligent)

7. He is a well-behaved child. (polite)

8. Some students are fast learners. (quick)

9. These painters are messy workers. (sloppy)

10. She is a good thinker. (quick/clear)

EXERCISE 5

Work with a partner. Take turns asking and answering the questions below. The first one has been done for you.

1. Why is Carrie an excellent teacher?
   (a) speak/slow
   She speaks slowly.
   (b) pronounce words/clear
   (c) prepare/careful
2. Why is Mark a good secretary?
   (a) type/fast
   (b) answer the phone/ polite
   (c) take message/accurate
3. Why is Mike a good truck driver?
   (a) drive/slow
   (b) respond/quick
   (c) drive/defensive

Exercise 5 

EXPANSION

Have Ss ask their own questions about each other or people they know. They can use the same words as in the exercise or use others. Encourage them to think of their friends and family's occupations.

Workbook Ex. 3, p. 93.
Answers: TE, p. 533.

ANSWER KEY

Exercise 5
1. **b.** She pronounces words clearly. **c.** She prepares carefully. 2. **a.** He types fast. **b.** He answers the phone politely. **c.** He takes messages accurately. 3. **a.** He drives slowly. **b.** He responds quickly. **c.** He drives defensively. 4. **a.** She sings well. **b.** She dances energetically. **c.** She performs enthusiastically. 5. **a.** She studies hard. **b.** She guesses intelligently. **c.** She asks questions constantly.

4. Why is Gloria Estefan a popular performer?
   (a) sing/good
   (b) dance/energetic
   (c) perform (enthusiastic)
5. Why is Miyuki a good language learner?
   (a) study/hard
   (b) guess/intelligent
   (c) ask questions/constant

FOCUS 3

The main point of this use box is to show how to shift emphasis to either the performer or the activity by using an adjective or an adverb. Additional examples: *I am a good language learner. I speak several languages fluently.*

FOCUS **3**

Talking about a Person or an Action

EXAMPLES	EXPLANATIONS
(a) Isabelle Allende is a **good** writer.	When you want to say something about a person, place, or thing, use an adjective.
(b) Isabelle Allende **writes** well.	When you want to say something about a verb or action, use an adverb.
(c) She is a **very good** writer. (d) She writes **very well**.	You can use *very* in front of most adjectives or adverbs.

EXERCISE 6

Do these sentences focus on the person or the action? Check the correct column.

	Person	Action
1. Meryl Streep is a fantastic actress.		
2. My students learn easily.		
3. Steven reads slowly.		
4. Karl's a fast runner.		
5. My children are good cooks.		
6. Bill Rogers drives carelessly.		
7. My accountant is an honest person.		
8. Anh speaks to his parents impolitely.		
9. Linda dresses beautifully.		
10. Your friend is a generous person.		

EXERCISE 7

Read the statements below. Write one sentence that focuses on the person and another that focuses on the action.

▶ **EXAMPLE:** Can you believe it! Jeryl is the winner of the race! (runner)

She is a great runner. She runs very fast.

1. Just look at Joe! He finishes one cigarette and then lights up another. (smoker)
____
2. My mom cooks a great meal every night. She loves to make new dishes. (cook)
____
3. Gloria goes to work at 8:00 in the morning and leaves at 6:00 in the evening. She never takes a break. (worker)
____
4. Nancy manages a large ESL program. She has a staff of over 50 people. (manager)
____
5. Bob can sing, dance, and play the piano too. (performer)
____

Exercise 6

Ss can do this exercise individually.

Exercise 7

EXPANSION

Encourage Ss to write sentences like these about each other without using any names. Have the class guess whom they are referring to.

ANSWER KEY

Exercise 6

1. Person 2. Action 3. Action 4. Person 5. Person 6. Action 7. Person 8. Action 9. Action 10. Person

Exercise 7

1. He's a heavy smoker. He smokes heavily. 2. She's a great/fantastic/ creative cook. She cooks well. 3. She's a hard/diligent worker. She works hard/diligently. 4. She's a good/ an excellent manager. She manages people effectively. 5. He's a good/great/ wonderful performer. He performs well.

Exercise 8

If you have Ss write sentences, you can collect them to check their understanding of adjectives and adverbs.

Workbook Exs. 4, 5, & 6, pp. 94–96.
Answers: TE, pp. 533–534.

Exercise 9

Ss can do this exercise individually.

UNIT GOAL REVIEW

Ask Ss to look at the goals on the opening page of the unit again. Help them understand how much they have accomplished in each area. Ask them if there are any questions they still have about what they have learned so far.

EXERCISE 8

Read each sentence and give two or three reasons why the sentence is true. Use adverbs in your reasons.

▶ **EXAMPLE:** I don't want Henry to drive me downtown.

Reasons: He doesn't drive very carefully.
He drives very fast.
He's a careless driver.

1. I'm already late. I don't want Harold to drive me to school.
2. I can't understand Bruce when he speaks.
3. Patricia is now the chef at that expensive restaurant downtown.
4. Rose is a great friend.
5. Lucia is a good language learner.
6. Ms. Wu is a great boss.

EXERCISE 9

Correct the mistakes in the following sentences.

1. Sarah comes to work in a suit every day. She dresses elegant.
2. Melanie speaks fluently French.
3. Sam studies three hours every night. He studies hardly.
4. Dinner starts at 8:00. They always arrive at 9:30. They always come very lately.
5. Johan plays the piano very good.
6. She speaks slow.
7. She sings lovely.
8. The city traffic is heavily.

ANSWER KEY

Exercise 8

Answers may vary. **1.** Harold's a slow driver. He drives very slowly. He doesn't drive very fast. **2.** Bruce speaks very fast. He doesn't speak very clearly. He doesn't speak loudly. **3.** Patricia cooks very well. She presents food creatively. She combines ingredients perfectly. **4.** Rose treats her friends kindly. She behaves considerately. She listens attentively. **5.** Lucia studies hard. She guesses intelligently. She speaks fluently. **6.** Ms. Wu manages people fairly. She works hard.

Exercise 9

1. She dresses elegantly. **2.** Melanie speaks French fluently. **3.** He studies hard. **4.** They always come very late. **5.** Johan plays the piano very well. **6.** She speaks slowly. **7.** She sings sweetly/beautifully. She's a lovely singer. **8.** The city traffic is heavy.

Use Your English

ACTIVITY 1: SPEAKING

Work in a group. One person in the group chooses an adverb of manner, but does not tell the other students the adverb. The students in the group tell the person to do something "in that manner." The person mimes the action and the other students guess the adverb.

▶ **EXAMPLE:**
1. The first student chooses the adverb *slowly*.
2. Students in the group say: "Walk to the door in that manner."
3. The first student mimes.
4. Students in the group guess: *slowly*.

(Example adverbs: *slowly, fast, nervously, happily, angrily, loudly, sadly, romantically, passionately*.)

ACTIVITY 2: SPEAKING

Work in a group. Are you a good student? A good mother? A good friend? A good worker? Choose one and give your group five reasons to explain why or why not.

▶ **EXAMPLE:** I'm a very good student. I study hard. . .

ACTIVITY 3: SPEAKING

Think about the Opening Task on pages 188–189. Interview your partner. Role-play a conversation between an insurance agent and a person like Bill Rogers. The person tries to convince the agent to give him/her insurance. Then explain to the class why your partner can or cannot get insurance easily.

ACTIVITY 4: LISTENING/SPEAKING

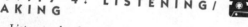

STEP 1 Listen to the three people. What are their occupations? Choose from the occupations below.

waiter   salesperson   flight attendant   doctor   receptionist

STEP 2 Describe an occupation to the class. The class guesses the occupation.

ANSWER KEY

Activity 4
Step 1: 1. salesperson 2. doctor 3. flight attendant

USE YOUR ENGLISH

For a more complete discussion of how to use the activities, see p. xxvi of this Teacher's Edition.

Activity 1

SUGGESTIONS

1. To play this game with the whole class, have about twenty adverbs written on index cards for Ss to choose from. Make sure the designated student understands the adverb.
2. Encourage the class to come up with interesting "orders" to give the student (*Sing a song in that manner. Brush your teeth. Shake hands,* etc.).
3. At the end of the game, have Ss review by saying what each student does (*Johan walks to the door slowly. Maria sings a song passionately*.)

Activity 2

EXPANSION

Have Ss write a paragraph about someone they know who is a good student, a good parent, a good friend, etc. They will need to explain why they value this person, using adjectives or adverbs of manner.

Activity 3

To help pairs with their interviews, first have the class brainstorm questions and write them on the board. *Do you smoke? How much do you smoke? How old are you? Do you have any medical problems?* At the end of the activity, tally how many Ss were able to get insurance.

Activity 4

Play textbook audio. The tapescript for this listening appears on p. 546 of this book.

The test for this unit can be found on pp. 481–482 of this book.
The answers can be found on p. 483.

TOEFL Test Preparation Exercises for Units 10–12 can be found on pp. 97–99 of the workbook.
The answers can be found on p. 534 of this book.

Unit 13

UNIT OVERVIEW

Much of this unit has a cultural context—it is about the customs associated with major life events or with simple everyday living. It will lend itself to a lot of cultural comparisons and discussion.

UNIT GOALS

To maximize this diagnostic potential of the Opening Tasks, do not review the Unit Goals with students (Ss) until after they have completed and reviewed the Opening Task.

OPENING TASK
SETTING UP THE TASK

Quickly go over the vocabulary on the next page. Discuss the types of gifts Ss give/receive and the occasions when gift-giving occurs.

UNIT 13

DIRECT AND INDIRECT OBJECTS, DIRECT AND INDIRECT OBJECT PRONOUNS

UNIT GOALS:

- To use direct objects and direct object pronouns correctly
- To use indirect objects correctly
- To form two sentence patterns with indirect objects
- To know where to place the indirect object in a sentence to focus on new information
- To know which verbs do not omit *to* with indirect objects

OPENING TASK

Giving Gifts

STEP 1 You need to give gifts to the people on your list below. Look at the gifts you have and decide which gift you want to give to each person.

Gifts

A. 
Camera

B. 
Flowers

C. 
Toaster

D. 
Doll

E. 
Earrings

F. 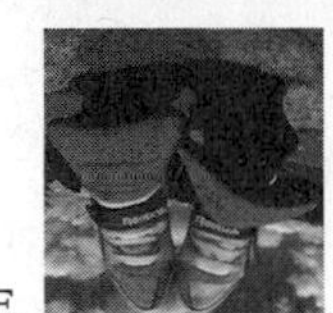
Running Shoes

G. 
Compact Disc Player

People

1. a single thirty-five-year-old athletic male friend
2. your sixty-three-year-old grandmother
3. your friend's four-year-old daughter
4. an artistic twenty-seven-year-old friend
5. your mother
6. your music-loving boyfriend/girlfriend
7. a newlywed couple

STEP 2 Tell a partner which gift you want to give each person and why.

▶ **EXAMPLE:** I want to give the earrings to my mother because she loves jewelry.

CONDUCTING THE TASK

Ss can do this task individually and then share their decisions with a partner, or they can work in groups where they have to come to a consensus. Go around listening to the language they use and take notes.

COMPLETING THE TASK

Discuss Ss' answers and their reasons.

REVIEWING THE TASK 

When you sum up the activity, write Ss' answers on the board and use this to present the form of direct and indirect objects.

FOCUS 1

Ask Ss questions about what kinds of things they love, such as music, food, movies, etc. Write their statements on the board. Then have Ss read the examples and explanations in the focus box.

Exercise 1

To assist Ss, ask them to identify the subject-verb in each sentence first.

Workbook Exs. 1 & 2, pp. 100–101.
Answers: TE, p. 534.

FOCUS **1**

▶ Direct Objects

EXAMPLES			EXPLANATIONS
Subject	Verb	Direct Object	
(a) My friend	sings.		Some sentences have only a subject and a verb.
(b) He	loves	music.	Some sentences have a subject, a verb, and an object.
(c) He	buys	compact discs.	A direct object answers the question "What?" *Compact discs* is the direct object.
(d) He	loves	the Beatles.	A direct object also answers the question "Who(m)?" *The Beatles* is the direct object.

EXERCISE 1

Underline the direct object in each sentence below.

▶ **EXAMPLE:** My friend loves sports.

1. My grandmother loves flowers. She always has fresh flowers on the dining room table.
2. Andrea and Bob have a new home.
3. My mother adores jewelry.
4. My friend's daughter has a doll collection. She owns ten different dolls.
5. Akiko takes beautiful pictures.
6. My friend enjoys classical music. She prefers Mozart.
7. In my family, we always celebrate our birthdays together.

ANSWER KEY

Exercise 1

1. flowers, fresh flowers **2.** a new home **3.** jewelry **4.** a doll collection, ten different dolls **5.** beautiful pictures **6.** classical music, Mozart **7.** our birthdays

FOCUS 2

Direct Object Pronouns

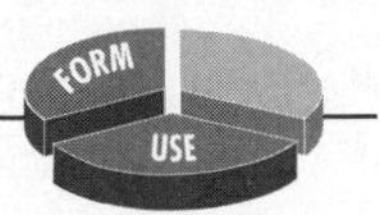

EXAMPLES	EXPLANATIONS
Subject **Verb** **Direct Object** **(a)** My mother loves my father. **(b)** My mother loves him.	The direct object can also be a pronoun.
(c) My mother loves **my father.** She thinks about **him** all the time. **(d)** My father loves **my mother**. He thinks about **her** all the time.	Object pronouns refer to a noun that comes before. In (c), *him* refers to "my father." In (d), *her* refers to "my mother."

SUBJECT	VERB	OBJECT	SUBJECT	VERB	OBJECT PRONOUN
I You	need	a friend.	She	likes	me. you.
He She It	needs				him. her. it.
We You They	need				us. you. them.

EXERCISE 2

Fill in the correct subject or object pronouns.

1. My grandmother is a very special person. (a) _______________ has a vegetable garden in her backyard. (b) _______________ plants tomatoes, cucumbers, eggplant, leeks, and carrots. She picks (c) _______________ fresh every day. We love her fresh vegetables. (d) _______________ taste delicious. We eat (e) _______________ in salads and soup. Her vegetable garden gives (f) _______________ great pleasure.
2. Mariela and Juan are newlyweds. (a) _______________ have a new

FOCUS 2

Go over subject and object pronouns. Explain or review anaphoric reference by showing how object pronouns refer to noun phrases in an earlier part of the text.

SUGGESTION

When doing reading or writing activities with Ss, ask them to point out object pronouns and tell what they refer to.

Exercise 2

In order to complete this exercise, Ss must understand how object pronouns are used for anaphoric reference, particularly 1 *c* and *e*, 2 *c*, *d*, *e*, *f*, and 3 *b* and *c*. Have them read each paragraph once before filling in the pronouns.

ANSWER KEY

Exercise 2

1. a. She **b.** She **c.** them **d.** They **e.** them **f.** us **2. a.** They **b.** they **c.** it **d.** them **e.** her **f.** him...
3. a. I **b.** it **c.** It **d.** me

home, and (b) _______________ really love (c) _______________.
Their appliances are on order, but they don't have (d) _______________
yet, so Mariela and Juan have a lot of work to do. He helps
(e) _______________ with the cooking. She helps
(f) _______________ with the laundry.

3. Sally: Billy, do you like heavy metal music?
Billy: (a) _______________ love (b) _______________!
Sally: Really? I hate heavy metal. (c) _______________ bothers
(d) _______________. I hate all that noise.

Exercise 3

This exercise contrasts subject and object pronouns. The story line continues through Exercise 4. Make sure Ss understand the love triangle.

EXERCISE 3

This is a story about three people in a love triangle. Maggie has a steady boyfriend, Ted. She also has a male friend, Jim. Read the text below. Cross out the incorrect pronouns and write the correct pronouns above them.

Maggie loves her boyfriend, Ted. She also likes Jim. (1) Jim works with ~~she~~ her. (2) She sees he every day. (3) She sometimes invites he to dinner. (4) She likes to talk with he. (5) Maggie doesn't love Jim, but Jim loves she. (6) Jim thinks about she all the time. Jim knows about Ted, but Ted doesn't know about Jim. Ted is very jealous. (7) So, Maggie can't tell he about Jim. (8) Maggie doesn't want to leave he. But she cares for both Ted and Jim. She doesn't know what to do. (9) She doesn't want to hurt they. She says to herself, "What's wrong with me? (10) Ted loves I and I love he. (11) Jim is my friend and I like to be with he. So what can I do?"

ANSWER KEY

Exercise 3

2. She sees <u>him</u>... 3. invites <u>him</u>... 4. with <u>him</u>... 5. loves <u>her</u>... 6. thinks about <u>her</u>... 7. tell <u>him</u>... 8. leave <u>him</u>... 9. hurt <u>them</u>... 10. loves <u>me</u> and I love <u>him</u> 11. like to be with <u>him</u>

EXERCISE 4

Ted finds out about Jim. He talks to Maggie on the phone late one night. Fill in the correct object pronouns.

1. **Ted:** Hello, Maggie. Do you remember (a) ___me___ ?
   Maggie: Of course, I remember (b) ________ , Ted. You're my boyfriend!
2. **Ted:** I know about Jim, Maggie.
   Maggie: What? You know about (a) ________ ?
3. **Ted:** That's right, Maggie. I know everything about (a) ________ .
   Maggie: How do you know?
   Ted: John—your secretary—told me. I meet (b) ________ for lunch sometimes. He knows about (c) ________ and Jim.
4. **Ted:** Jim can't come between (a) ________ , Maggie.
   Maggie: I know, Ted. Don't worry. I don't love (b) ________ . We're just friends.
   Ted: Do you love (c) ________ ?
   Maggie: Of course, I love (d) ________ , Ted. I want to marry (e) ________ .
5. **Ted:** Then you can't see (a) ________ so much, Maggie.
   Maggie: Ted, please trust (b) ________ .

EXERCISE 5

Ask your partner questions with *how often*. Your partner answers with object pronouns.

▶ **EXAMPLE:** **You:** How often do you call your parents?
Your Partner: I call them every week.

1. clean your room?
2. do your laundry?
3. see your dentist?
4. buy the newspaper?
5. cut your nails?
6. wash your hair?
7. visit your friends?
8. drink coffee?
9. do the grocery shopping?
10. watch the news?

Exercise 4 

Ask Ss to practice the dialogue aloud with a partner.

EXPANSION

Have Ss create endings to resolve the issue in this conversation and compare them.

Exercise 5 

Answers may vary. Each begins with "**How often ...** "

Workbook Ex. 3, p. 101.
Answers: TE, p. 534.

ANSWER KEY

Exercise 4

1. b. you 2. a. him 3. a. him b. him c. you 4. a. us b. him c. me d. you e. you 5. a. him b. me

FOCUS 3

1. Put the sentences on the board and ask Ss to identify the subject, verb, direct object.
2. Explain the function of the indirect object.
3. Provide other examples of verbs that can be used with "for" such as *do, make, repair*. Write *"I wrote a letter <u>to</u> my friend. I wrote a letter <u>for</u> my friend. She speaks to all of us. She speaks for all of us."* Ask Ss to explain the difference.

Exercise 6

Answers may vary. Have some Ss write their answers either on the board or on butcher block paper. Correct errors with the whole class.

Exercise 7

EXPANSION

Have Ss make their own New Year's resolutions orally or in writing and share them with the class.

FOCUS **3**

▶ Indirect Objects

EXAMPLES					EXPLANATION
	Subject	Verb	Direct Object	Indirect Object	
(a)	I	want to give	the toaster	to **the newlyweds.**	Some sentences have two objects: a direct object and an indirect object. *The toaster* is the direct object. It tells **what** I want to give. *The newlyweds* is the indirect object. It tells **to whom** I want to give the toaster.
(b)	I	buy	flowers	for **my grandmother.**	*My grandmother* is the indirect object. It tells **for whom** I buy flowers.
(c)	I	want to give	the toaster	to **the newlyweds.**	The indirect object can be a noun or a pronoun.
(d)	I	want to give	the toaster	to **them.**	
(e) I cook **for** my grandmother. **(f)** I want to give the earrings **to** my mother.					***For* and *To*** *For* tells us one person does the action to help or please another person. *To* tells us about the direction of the action: The earrings go from you to your mother.

EXERCISE 6

Write sentences telling what you want to give to each of the people in the Opening Task. Underline the direct object and circle the indirect object. Then tell why you want to give that item to that person.

▶ **EXAMPLE:** I want to give <u>the toaster</u> to the (newlyweds.) They have a new home and don't have any appliances.

EXERCISE 7

New Year's Resolutions. Every January 1st, North Americans decide to change their lives and do things differently. Read the following resolutions. Change each underlined noun to a pronoun. Then add the information in parentheses. Read the statements aloud.

▶ **EXAMPLE:** Every year, I give <u>my father</u> a tie. (golf clubs)
This year, I want to give him golf clubs.

1. Used car salesman:
I always sell my customers bad cars. (good cars)
This year, I want to . . .
2. Child away at college:
I always write to my parents once a month. (once a week)
This year, I want to . . .
3. People with money problems:
Every year, the bank sends my husband and me a big credit card bill. (a very small bill)
This year, I want the bank to . . .
4. Boyfriend:
I usually buy my girlfriend flowers for her birthday. (a diamond ring)
This year, I want to . . .
5. Teenager:
Sometimes I lie to my mother. (tell the truth)
This year, I want to . . .
6. Mother:
I never have time to read to my children at night. (every night)
This year, I want to . . .
7. Student:
I always give my homework to the teacher late. (on time)
This semester, I want to . . .
8. Friend:
Every year, I lend money to you and your brother. (lend money)
This year, I don't want to . . .

Now say three things you want to do differently this year.

ANSWER KEY

Exercise 7

1. sell them good cars **2.** write to them once a week **3.** send us a very small bill **4.** buy her a diamond ring **5.** tell her the truth **6.** read to them every night **7.** give my homework to him/her on time **8.** lend money to you

FOCUS 4

1. Have Ss close their books.
2. Write sentences (*a*) and (*d*) on the board.
3. Ask Ss to generate sentences substituting an indirect object pronoun for the indirect object.
4. Ask Ss to substitute a direct object pronoun for the direct object. Emphasize that the word order stays the same in all these sentences: S-V-D.O.-I.O.

EXPANSION

Encourage Ss to go beyond this exercise and discuss birthday customs in their home countries or families. You could actually do Activity 5 here.

FOCUS **4**

▶ Position of the Indirect Object

All verbs that take indirect objects can follow Pattern A.

Pattern A

SUBJECT	VERB	DIRECT OBJECT	INDIRECT OBJECT
(a) I	give	presents	to my mother on her birthday.
(b) I	give	presents	to her.
(c) I	give	them	to her.
(d) We	make	a party	for our twin daughters on their birthday.
(e) We	make	a party	for them.
(f) We	make	it	for them.

Some of these verbs also follow Pattern B. In Pattern B, put the indirect object before the direct object. Do not use *to* or *for*.

Pattern B

SUBJECT	VERB	DIRECT OBJECT	INDIRECT OBJECT
(g) People	send	their friends	birthday cards.
(h) People	send	them	birthday cards.
(i) I	make	my friends	birthday cakes.
(j) I	make	them	birthday cakes.

NOTE: Do not put an indirect object pronoun before a direct object pronoun.
I make my friend a cake.
I make her a cake.

NOT: I make her it.

Some verbs that follow both Pattern A and B

bake	do	hand	offer	sell	tell
bring	find	lend	pass	send	throw
buy	get	mail	pay	show	write
cook	give	make	read	teach	

EXERCISE 8

Work with a partner. Write sentences about North American customs with the words below.

BIRTH: When a baby is born:

1. mother / flowers / the / to / give / friends
   Friends give flowers to the mother.
2. cigars / gives / friends / father / his / the
3. send / and / parents / friends / family / to / birth / announcements / their / the
4. baby / family / friends / gifts / the / buy / and
5. knit / for / grandmothers / sweaters / new / the / baby
6. grandfathers / for / toys / make / baby / the
7. child / the / the / parents / everything / give

ENGAGEMENT/MARRIAGE: When a couple gets engaged or married:

8. diamond / man / a / woman / the / gives / ring / the / to / sometimes
9. friends / couple / an / party / the / for / have / engagement
10. gifts / woman / give / friends / at the party / the
11. at the wedding / to / couple / gifts / give / the guests / the

DEATH: When someone dies:

12. send / family / some / flowers / people / the
13. people / special cards / the / send / family / to
14. some / to / give / people / money / charities
15. some / food / for / family / bring / people / the

Exercise 8 

This exercise should generate some discussion about American customs compared to those in other countries.

VARIATION

1. Prepare this sentence scramble in advance by writing each word in the sentence on an index card.
2. Put each sentence in an envelope that indicates the number of the sentence.
3. Have Ss work in pairs, unscrambling the sentence and then writing the sentence on a piece of paper.
4. Give each pair a new envelope. Once Ss have unscrambled the sentences, ask them to restate the sentences using the alternate pattern.

Workbook Exs. 4 & 5, pp. 102–103. Answers: TE, p. 534.

ANSWER KEY

Exercise 8

2. The father gives his friends cigars. **3.** The parents send birth announcements to their friends and family. **4.** Friends and family buy the baby gifts. **5.** Grandmothers knit sweaters for the new baby. **6.** Grandfathers make toys for the baby. **7.** The parents give the child everything. **8.** The man sometimes gives a diamond ring to the woman. **9.** Friends have an engagement party for the couple. **10.** Friends give the woman gifts at the party. **11.** The guests give gifts to the couple at the wedding. **12.** Some people send the family flowers. **13.** People send special cards to the family. **14.** Some people give money to charities. **15.** Some people bring food for the family.

FOCUS 5

This use box focuses on the rule governing the position of given and new information. Although both sentences are grammatically correct, they are not interchangeable when used in context. The answer to the question "*Whom do you give earrings to?*" would most naturally be, "*I give them/the earrings/to my mother,*" because "my mother" is the new information. Likewise, the answer to question "B"—"*What do you usually give your mother?*" would be "*I usually give my mother earrings.*" Here "earrings" is the new information and would go at the end of the sentence. The two exercises that follow provide specific contexts in which learners need to make these discourse choices, shifting the focus of the sentence.

Exercise 9 

When checking answers, ask Ss to identify the new information, and use direct and indirect object pronouns.

FOCUS **5**

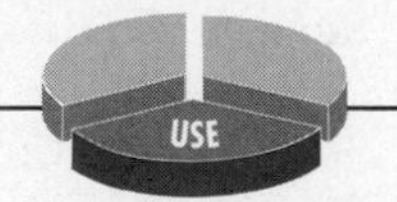

Position of New Information

New information comes at the end of a sentence. You can write these sentences in two different ways. Both are grammatically correct, but the emphasis is different.

EXAMPLES	EXPLANATIONS
(a) Whom do you give earrings to? I usually give earrings to **my mother.**	The emphasis is on **who(m)**. *My mother* is the new information.
(b) What do you usually give your mother? I usually give my mother **earrings**	The emphasis is on **what.** *Earrings* is the new information.

EXERCISE 9

Answer the following questions. The new information is in parentheses ( ).

EXAMPLES: Who(m) do you usually give presents to at Christmas? (my family)

I usually give presents to my family.

What do you usually give your father? (a good book)

I usually give him a good book.

1. Who(m) do you want to give presents to at work? (three of my co-workers)
2. What do you usually give your parents for their anniversary? (tickets to a play)
3. Who(m) do you tell jokes to? (my friend)
4. What do you send your sister every year? (some photographs)
5. Does she teach English to your brother or sister? (my brother)
6. Which story do you usually read to your little sister—"Cinderella" or "Snow White"? ("Cinderella")
7. Who(m) do you need to mail the application to? (the admissions office)
8. What do you usually buy for your son on his birthday? (compact discs)

ANSWER KEY

Exercise 9

1. I want to give presents to three of my co-workers. **2.** I usually give them tickets to a play. **3.** I tell jokes to my friend. **4.** I send her some photographs. **5.** She teaches English to my brother. **6.** I usually read her "Cinderella." **7.** I need to mail it/the application/to the admissions office. **8.** I usually buy him compact discs.

EXERCISE 10

Choose the best sentence.

▶ **EXAMPLE:** You are waiting for a friend in front of a restaurant.
You do not have your watch. You want to know the time.
You see someone coming. You ask him:
(a) Could you please tell me the time? (circled)
(b) Could you please tell the time to me?

1. You are alone at a restaurant. You finish your meal. You see the waiter. You ask him:
(a) Could you please give the check to me?
(b) Could you please give me the check?
2. You are celebrating someone's birthday with a group of friends. You finish your meal. You want to be sure you pay the check. You tell the waiter:
(a) Please give the check to me.
(b) Please give me the check.
3. What do your children usually do for you on Mother's Day?
(a) They usually serve breakfast in bed to me.
(b) They usually serve me breakfast in bed.
4. You are at a friend's house for dinner. The food needs salt. You say:
(a) Please pass me the salt.
(b) Please pass the salt to me.
5. You realize you don't have any money for the bus. You ask a friend:
(a) Could you lend a dollar to me?
(b) Could you lend me a dollar?
6. You are in class. It is very noisy. You say to a classmate:
(a) Do me a favor. Please close the door.
(b) Do a favor for me. Please close the door.
7. Why does your class look so sad on Mondays?
(a) because our teacher gives us a lot of homework on weekends.
(b) because our teacher gives a lot of homework to us on weekends.
8. You want to apply to the City University. You have the application form in your hand. The Director is helping you.
Director: (a) Please send the application form to the City University.
(b) Please send the City University the application form.

Exercise 10

EXPANSION

Ask each group to make up two or three situations and sentence pairs like these.

Workbook Exs. 6 & 7, pp. 104–105.
Answers: TE, p. 534

ANSWER KEY

Exercise 10

1. b **2.** a **3.** b **4.** a **5.** b **6.** a
7. a **8.** a **9.** b **10.** b

9. You come home from the supermarket. Your car is full of groceries. You need help. You say to your roommate:
   (a) Can you please give a hand to me?
   (b) Can you please give me a hand?
10. There are three children at a table. They are finishing a box of cookies. A fourth child sees them and runs toward them. The child says:
   (a) Wait! Save me one!
   (b) Wait! Save one for me!

FOCUS 6

Provide Ss with other sentences that follow Pattern A only *(Introduce your friend to me, please. You need to report your results to the class.)* Here Ss identify and label S, V, DO, and IO.

FOCUS **6**

Verbs that Do Not Omit *To* with Indirect Objects

EXAMPLES	EXPLANATION
S + V + D.O. + I.O. (a) My mother reads stories to us. S + V + I.O. + D.O. (b) My mother reads us stories.	Many verbs follow both Pattern A and B. (See Focus 4)
D.O. + I.O. (c) The teacher explains the grammar to us. (d) NOT: The teacher explains us the grammar.	Some verbs only follow Pattern A.
carry *clean* *describe* *do* *explain* *fix* *introduce* *open* *prepare* *repair* *repeat* *report* *shy* *solve* *spell*	Verbs that follow Pattern A ONLY. Do not omit *to/for.*

EXERCISE 11

Read the following sentence or question pairs aloud. Check any sentence that is not possible. In some pairs, both patterns are possible.

▶ **EXAMPLE 1:**
Pattern A: My husband sends flowers to me every Valentine's Day.
Pattern B: My husband sends me flowers every Valentine's Day.
(Both patterns are possible.)

▶ **EXAMPLE 2:**
Pattern A: The teacher always repeats the question to the class.
NOT: Pattern B: The teacher always repeats the class the question.

	Pattern A	Pattern B
1.	Tell the truth to me.	Tell me the truth.
2.	Please explain the problem to me.	Please explain me the problem.
3.	Spell that word for me, please.	Spell me that word, please.
4.	I need to report the accident to the insurance company.	I need to report the insurance company the accident.
5.	My father usually reads a story to my little brother every night.	My father usually reads my little brother a story every night.
6.	He always opens the door for me.	He always opens me the door.
7.	Let me introduce my friend to you.	Let me introduce you my friend.
8.	Cynthia gives her old clothes to a charity.	Cynthia gives a charity her old clothes.
9.	The students write letters to their parents every week.	The students write their parents letters every week.
10.	Please repeat the instructions to the class.	Please repeat the class the instructions.
11.	Can you describe your hometown to me?	Can you describe me your hometown?
12.	Can you carry that bag for me?	Can you carry me that bag?

Exercise 11 

This exercise can be done individually or in pairs. You might also encourage Ss to do these orally with their partners.

Workbook Ex. 8, pp. 105–106.
Answers: p. 534.

UNIT GOAL REVIEW

Ask Ss to look at the goals on the opening page of the unit again. Help them understand how much they have accomplished in each area. Ask them if there are any questions they still have about what they have learned so far.

ANSWER KEY

Exercise 11
1. Both are possible **2.** Only Pattern A **3.** Only Pattern A **4.** Only A **5.** Both are possible **6.** Only A **7.** Only A **8.** Both **9.** Both **10.** Only A **11.** Only A **12.** Only A

USE YOUR ENGLISH

For a more complete discussion of how to use the activities, see p. xxvi of this Teacher's Edition.

Activity 1 

Have Ss work in groups to write their clues. Play the game as a whole class by having one group give another group the clues.

Activity 2

Have Ss brainstorm as many occupations as they can in groups and write each one on a separate piece of paper. Collect the papers and have each student choose one or two.

VARIATION

This activity can be done with other themes such as food, hobbies, entertainment, etc.

Use Your English

ACTIVITY 1: SPEAKING

Think of the different things people have. Then give clues so that your classmates can guess the objects.

▶ **EXAMPLE:** **Clues:** The Japanese make a lot of them. We drive them. What are they?
Answer: Cars!

ACTIVITY 2: SPEAKING

STEP 1 Write down the names of ten occupations on ten pieces of paper.

STEP 2 Choose one piece of paper and make sentences for the class so they can guess what the occupation is. You get one point for each sentence you make.

STEP 3 When the class guesses the occupation, another student picks a piece of paper. The person with the most points at the end wins.

▶ **EXAMPLE:** (You choose "firefighter.")
You say: *This person wears a hat.*
He or she drives a big vehicle.
He or she saves people's lives.

ACTIVITY 3: WRITING/SPEAKING

STEP 1 Each person in the class writes down a personal habit—good or bad.

STEP 2 Each person reads his or her statement to the class.

STEP 3 The class asks questions to find out more information. (Possible habits: playing with your hair, tapping your feet.)

▶ **EXAMPLE:** **You:** *I bite my fingernails.*
Class: *Why do you bite them?*
You: *Because I'm nervous!*

ACTIVITY 4: SPEAKING

What customs do you have in your country for events such as birth, engagement, marriage, death? Tell the class what people do in your country.

▶ **EXAMPLE:** In Chile, when a baby is born . . .
when a couple gets married . . .
when someone dies . . .
when a person turns thirteen . . .
OTHER . . .

Activity 3

Have the class generate a list of personal habits first and write them on the board.

EXPANSION

This activity can be done using cultural customs—holidays, habits, etc.

Activity 4

EXPANSION

Turn this activity into an International Customs Day event with Ss creating posters for different occasions. Have Ss walk around the room learning about the different customs.

VARIATION

Have Ss create culture pamphlets with the information they've gathered.

Activity 5

After doing this activity, have Ss reiterate the commands. *Lend some money to Maria.*

ACTIVITY 5: SPEAKING

Work in a small group. On small slips of paper, write the numbers 1 to 16 and put them in an envelope. One person in the class is the "caller" and only he or she looks at the grid below. The first student picks a number from the envelope. The caller calls out the command in that square for the student to follow. Then a second student picks out a number and the caller calls out the command. Continue until all the commands are given.

▶ **EXAMPLE:** You pick the number 7.
Caller: Lend some money to Maria.

1. Whisper a secret to the person next to you.	2. Give a penny to the person on your left.	3. Write a funny message to someone in your group.	4. Hand your wallet to the person on your right.
5. Make a paper airplane for the person across from you.	6. Tell a funny joke to someone.	7. Lend some money to a person in your group.	8. Describe a friend to someone.
9. Explain indirect objects to a person near you.	10. Tell your age to the person on your right.	11. Introduce the person on your left to the person on your right.	12. Offer a piece of gum to someone.
13. Teach your classmates how to say "I love you" in your language.	14. Open the door for someone in the class.	15. Throw your pen to the person across from you.	16. Pass a secret message to one person in your group.

ACTIVITY 6: LISTENING/ SPEAKING

STEP 1 Listen to the conversation between Linda and Amy. Then read the statements below. Check True or False.

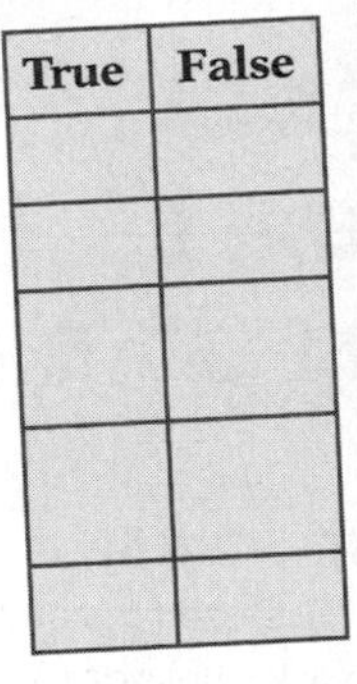

	True	False
1. Linda is giving her mother perfume on Mother's Day.		
2. Linda's mother tells her what gift she wants.		
3. Amy's mother always tells her daughter what gift she wants.		
4. Linda's father only takes Linda's mother to a restaurant on Mother's Day.		
5. Linda's father does not buy his wife a gift.		

STEP 2 Compare your answers with a partner's. If a statement is false, make a true statement.

STEP 3 Tell your classmates what you do and give to a person on a special day like Mother's Day or a birthday.

Activity 6 

Play textbook audio. The tapescript for this listening appears on p. 546 of this book.

EXPANSION

After completing the activity, you could use the tape to focus on pronunciation and intonation.

The test for this unit can be found on pp. 484–486 of this book.
The answers can be found on p. 487

ANSWER KEY

Activity 6

Step 1: 1. T 2. F 3. F 4. F 5. F

Unit 14

UNIT OVERVIEW

Can is the first modal verb to be presented in this book. Its use here is limited to talking about ability. *Can* and *be able to* are contrasted with *know how to* for expressing natural or learned ability. *Can* is introduced as a tool for getting information about English. The sentence connectors *and*, *but*, *so*, and *or* are also presented in this unit.

UNIT GOALS

To maximize the diagnostic potential of the Opening Task, do not review the Unit Goals with students (Ss) until after they have completed and reviewed the Opening Task.

OPENING TASK
SETTING UP THE TASK

This "Find Someone Who" task is designed to show you who can use *can* to make questions and statements. Familiarize Ss with the actions in each photograph.

CONDUCTING THE TASK
Step 1

Have Ss walk around the room asking questions to each other. If the person says "yes," they can write the name of the student under the picture. Be sure Ss understand that if they receive a "no" answer they cannot write a name under the picture. Encourage them to get as many different names as possible.

UNIT 14

CAN, KNOW HOW TO, BE ABLE TO, CONNECTORS: AND/BUT/SO/OR

UNIT GOALS:

- To use *can* to express ability
- To ask questions with *can*
- To ask for help with English using *can*
- To understand the difference between *can/know how to/be able to* for expressing learned or natural ability
- To use sentence connectors: *and, but, so,* and *or* correctly

OPENING TASK
Find Someone Who Can . . .

STEP 1 Find someone in your class who can do these things:

1. dance

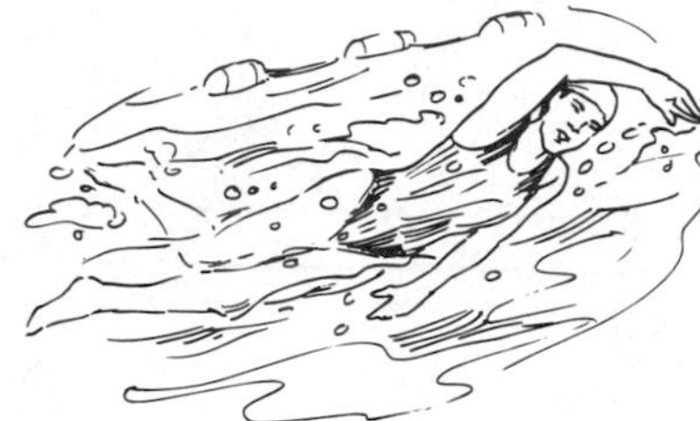
2. swim

3. draw

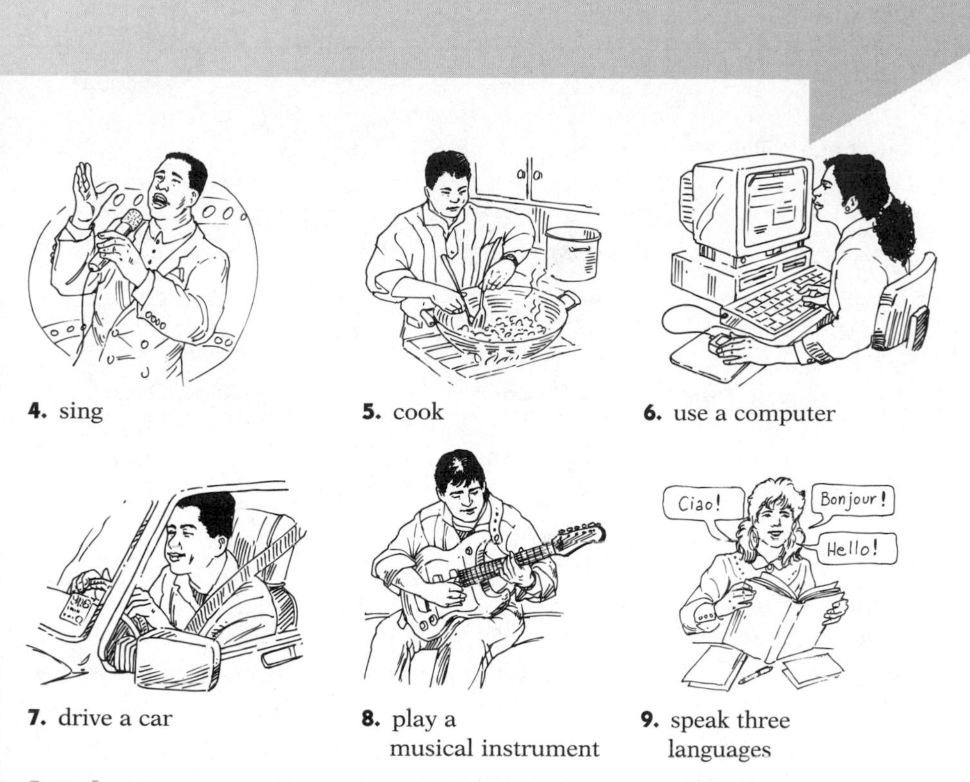

4. sing **5.** cook **6.** use a computer

7. drive a car **8.** play a musical instrument **9.** speak three languages

STEP 2 Report to the class what you know about your classmates. Who is the most versatile person in the class? Who can do the most?

Step 2

Ask Ss who the most versatile person in the class is. Ask that student to list all the things he/she can do.

REVIEWING THE TASK

Encourage the class to ask the student additional questions *(Can you sing well? What kind of songs can you sing? What kind of musical instrument can you play?)*. Use the information obtained to present the target structure at the end of the Opening Task.

FOCUS 1

1. Although this is not mentioned in the student text, you can explain that *can* is a special kind of verb called a modal verb. Point out that *can* does not change form with different subjects (i.e., we do not add "s" to the verb in the third person singular) and that we do not use "to" after *can*.
2. Practice the pronunciation of *can* and *can't*. Say a sentence aloud (*I can swim*). Have Ss raise one finger if they hear *can* (/kən/) and two fingers if they hear *can't* (/kænt/). Then have Ss practice sentence pairs like this with partners.

VARIATION

1. To work on contextualized sentence pairs, write out statements on index cards and give one card to each student.
2. Have one student make a statement and a second student respond to it accordingly. For example: Student 1: "*I can't meet you after class today*." Student 2: "*Why not?*"; Student 1: "*I can meet you after class today*." Student 2: "*Great! I'll be there at 3:30*."

Exercise 1

Have Ss share their answers with the class. Practice the same finger-raising technique described above for pronunciation.

FOCUS **1**

Can

Can expresses ability.

AFFIRMATIVE	NEGATIVE	NEGATIVE CONTRACTION
I You He She **can** speak English. We You They	I You He She **cannot** We speak Chinese. You They	I You He She **can't** speak French. We You They
(a) She can DANCE. **(b)** He can SING.	In the affirmative, we pronounce *can* as /kən/ and stress the base form of the verb.	
(c) He CAN'T DANCE. **(d)** She CAN'T SING.	In the negative, we stress both *can't* and the base form of the verb.	

EXERCISE 1

Go back to the Opening Task on pages 216-217. With a partner, take turns saying what you can or can't do.

▶ **EXAMPLES:** I can cook.
I can't play a musical instrument.

EXERCISE 2

Make affirmative or negative statements about the pictures. The first one has been done for you.

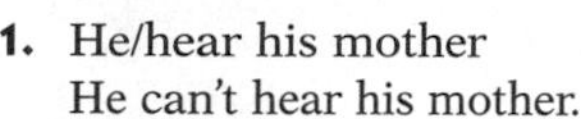

1. He/hear his mother
   He can't hear his mother.
2. She/swim
3. They/play basketball

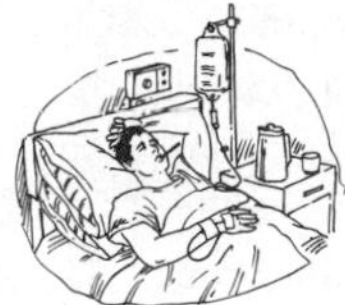

4. She/open the jar
5. He/walk
6. He/go to work

7. They/see the screen
8. They/speak Korean

EXERCISE 3

What can you do in English? Check *Yes* or *No*.

	Yes	No
1. I can introduce someone.		
2. I can ask about prices.		
3. I can describe people and places.		
4. I can make a polite request.		
5. I can give directions.		
6. I can give advice.		
7. I can ask for information about English.		

Now, exchange books with a partner. Tell what your partner can or can't do in English.

▶ **EXAMPLE:** My partner can introduce someone.

Exercise 2

After each statement ask "why" to enrich Ss' vocabulary and encourage them to produce more language.

Exercise 3

This self-assessment grid contains all the speech acts that have been presented in Use boxes up to this point.

EXPANSION

As a follow-up, ask Ss to role-play different situations to practice their interactive skills.

Workbook Ex. 1, pp. 107–109.
Answers: TE, p. 535

ANSWER KEY

Exercise 2

2. She can swim. **3.** They can play basketball. **4.** She can't open the jar. **5.** He can't walk. **6.** He can't go to work. **7.** They can't see the screen. **8.** They can speak Korean.

FOCUS 2

Point out that modals like *can* do not take the auxiliary *do*. Use the prompts in the Opening Task to ask Ss questions with *can*. *(Can you dance? Can you swim?)* Have Ss answer, *"Yes, I can" or "No, I can't."*

Exercise 4

This exercise will prompt lively discussion. When checking responses, have Ss elaborate on their answers.

VARIATION

Put a sign saying "Women" on one wall, another sign "Men" on another wall, and a third with "Both" on a third wall. Have one student ask question #1; the others walk to the sign representing their position, and discuss the issue in their group. Have a representative from this group report on what was said. In doing this, Ss will be making more statements with *can*.

FOCUS 2

Questions with *Can*

(a) **Can** you use a computer?
Yes, I can. No, I can't.
(b) **Can** he cook?
Yes, he can. No, he can't.

(c) What **can** he cook?
He can boil water!
(d) Who **can** cook in your family?
My mother can.
My father can't.

EXERCISE 4

STEP 1 Write *yes/no* questions with *can*. Then, under *Your Response,* check *Yes* or *No* to give your opinion about each question. Leave the columns under *Total* blank for now.

	Your Response		Total	
	Yes	No	Yes	No
1. a woman/work as a firefighter *Can a woman work as a firefighter?* ?				
2. women/fight bravely in wars ________________?				
3. a man/be a good nurse ________________?				
4. men/raise children ________________?				
5. women/be good police officers ________________?				

ANSWER KEY

Exercise 4
2. Can women fight bravely in wars? **3.** Can a man be a good nurse? **4.** Can men raise children? **5.** Can women be good police officers? **6.** Can a woman be a construction worker? **7.** Can a man keep house neatly? **8.** Can a woman be a good president of a country? **9.** Can men communicate successfully with women?

	Your Response		Total	
	Yes	No	Yes	No
6. a woman/be a construction worker ________________?				
7. a man/keep house neatly ________________?				
8. a woman/be a good president of a country ________________?				
9. men/communicate successfully with women ________________?				

STEP 2 Go back to Step 1. Read the questions aloud. Do a survey in your class. Count how many students say "yes" and how many say "no." Write the *total* number of Yes and No answers in the *Total* column. Do you agree or disagree with your classmates? Give reasons for your answers.

▶ **EXAMPLE:** Women can be good police officers.

They can help people in trouble. They can use guns when necessary.

EXERCISE 5

Work in a group of four to six people. Take turns asking the following questions.

▶ **EXAMPLES:** **a.** Who/type? — Who can type? **b.** How fast/type? — How fast can you type?

1. **a.** Who/cook? **b.** What/cook?
2. **a.** Who/speak three languages? **b.** What languages/speak?
3. **a.** Who/play a musical instrument? **b.** What/play?
4. **a.** Who/sew? **b.** What/sew?
5. **a.** Who/fix a car? **b.** What/fix?
6. **a.** Who/draw? **b.** What/draw?
7. **a.** Who/run a marathon? **b.** How fast/run a marathon?

SUGGESTION FOR STEP 2

On butcher block paper, write summary statements of the classes' responses – *The majority of the class thinks . . . The women in the class think . . . The men in the class . . .*

Exercise 5 

The questions being generated here move from the more general (*Who can type?*) to the more specific (*How fast can you type?*). The "**b**" questions are follow-up questions directed at an individual in the group and can include a variety of possibilities.

Workbook Exs. 2, 3, & 4, pp. 109–110. Answers: TE, p. 535.

ANSWER KEY

Exercise 5

1. a. Who can cook? **b.** What can you cook? **2. a.** Who can speak three languages? **b.** What languages can you speak? **3. a.** Who can play a musical instrument? **b.** What instrument can you play? **4. a.** Who can sew? **b.** What can you sew? **5. a.** Who can fix a car? **b.** What can you fix? **6. a.** Who can draw? **b.** How well/what can you draw? **7. a.** Who can run a marathon? **b.** How fast can you run?

FOCUS 3

These two communication strategies will allow Ss to take more risks and avoid dropping out of conversations when they have difficulty expressing themselves. The first is a means of checking the accuracy of one's own speech. The second is a means of compensating for what one doesn't know how to say in English. It teaches Ss how to use gestures and mime to get their meaning across and learn more language. Encourage Ss to use these strategies as much as possible.

EXPANSION

This is a good opportunity to teach circumlocution; that is, teach Ss to keep talking, explaining, defining, etc., until the listener grasps their meaning and offers help. This is how Ss learn to negotiate meaning.

FOCUS **3**

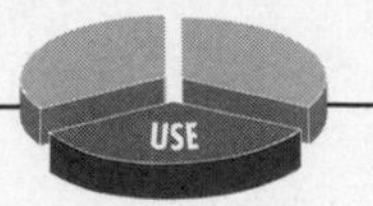

Asking for Help with English

EXAMPLES	EXPLANATIONS
(a) **Can I say,** "She can to swim" **in English?**	When you are not sure your English is correct, use the expression: *Can I say . . . in English?*
(b) **How can I say, ". . ." in English?**	When you don't know how to say something in English, ask the question: *How can I say, ". . ." in English?*
	And then explain your meaning: Use your hands to show "tremendous." Use your face to show "sour." Use your whole body to show actions like "sweeping."

EXERCISE 6

Look at the pictures. First mime each action and then ask your classmates questions to find out how to say each word.

▶ **EXAMPLE:** How can I say (*mime the action*) in English?

1. 
2. 
3.   
4. 
5. 
6. 

FOCUS **4**

Expressing Ability: *Can, Know How to,* and *Be Able to*

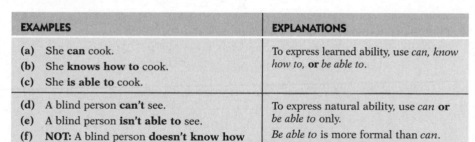

EXAMPLES	EXPLANATIONS
(a) She **can** cook. (b) She **knows how to** cook. (c) She **is able to** cook.	To express learned ability, use *can, know how to,* **or** *be able to*.
(d) A blind person **can't** see. (e) A blind person **isn't able to** see. (f) **NOT:** A blind person **doesn't know how to** see.	To express natural ability, use *can* **or** *be able to* only. *Be able to* is more formal than *can*. Use *be able to* in all tenses; not *can*.

Exercise 6

EXPANSIONS

1. Have Ss come up with a few mimes themselves.
2. Cut out pictures from magazines and give them to Ss so they can practice these strategies.

Workbook Ex. 5, p. 111.
Answers: TE, p. 535

FOCUS 4

This focus box distinguishes between learned ability and natural ability. As for form, it contrasts the negative – *I can't, I'm not able to* with *I don't know how to.*

1. Have Ss read the examples that express learned ability. Point out that we can use *be able to* in all tenses, but we can only use *can* in present (and *could* in past) tense to express ability.
2. Then read *d, e,* and *f* and give examples of other verbs that express natural ability (*hear, live, grow*) and explain that we cannot use *know how to* here.
3. Point out the use of *do/does* with *know how to* as opposed to *can*.

Exercise 7

Ss can do this exercise individually or in pairs.

Exercise 8 

Discuss the pictures and have Ss read the conversation once to get some contextual information. Go over important vocabulary such as *temporary, pay raise* ...

Ask pairs to perform the dialogue in front of the class.

EXERCISE 7

Make affirmative or negative statements with the words below. To express learned ability, make one statement with *can* and one statement with *know how to*. To express natural ability, make only one statement with can.

▶ **EXAMPLES:** **a.** fix/a flat tire

I can fix a flat tire.

I know how to fix a flat tire.

b. see/without glasses

I can see without glasses.

1. A blind person/see
2. A dog/live for twenty-five years
3. Infants/walk
4. A deaf person/hear
5. Fish/breathe on land
6. Mechanics/fix cars
7. Men/take care of babies
8. A man/have a baby
9. Doctors/cure some diseases
10. Roses/grow without water

EXERCISE 8

Fill in the blanks with the affirmative or negative forms of *can* or *be able to*.

Fran: Hello, Vanna. How are you today?

Vanna: I'm sorry to say I'm still not well, Fran. My back still hurts. I (1) can sit up now, but I (2) am not able to walk very well.

Fran: What? You mean you (3) ______ come in to work today? Vanna, I (4) ______ do my work without you. I (5) ______ use my computer. I (6) ______ find any of my papers. I (7) ______ remember any of my appointments. This office is a mess. I (8) ______ do all this work myself.

ANSWER KEY

Exercise 7

1. A blind person can't see. (Natural Ability) **2.** A dog can live ... (Natural Ability) **3.** Infants can't walk/don't know how to walk. (Learned Ability) **4.** A deaf person can't hear. (Natural Ability) **5.** Fish can't breathe on land. (Natural Ability) **6.** Mechanics can fix cars/know how to fix cars. (Learned Ability) **7.** Men can take care of babies/know how to take care of babies. (Learned Ability) **8.** A man can't have a baby. (Natural Ability) **9.** Doctors can cure some diseases/know how to cure some diseases. (Learned Ability) **10.** Roses can't grow without water. (Natural Ability)

Exercise 8

3. can't/are not able to **4.** can't/am not able to **5.** can't/am not able to **6.** can't/am not able to **7.** can't/am not able to **8.** can't/am not able to **9.** can **10.** can't/isn't able to **11.** can't **12.** can/are able to **13.** can't/am not able to **14.** can/am able to

Vanna: What about your temporary secretary? What (9) _______________ he do?

Fran: This temporary secretary is terrible. He (10) _______________ do anything. He (11) _______________ even make a good cup of coffee! I need you here, Vanna. Only you (12) _______________ do everything in this office.

Vanna: Well, Fran, do you remember our conversation about my pay raise?

Fran: O.K., O.K., Vanna. You can have your raise. But please come in today!

Vanna: O.K., calm down, Fran, and listen to me. I (13) _______________ come in to the office this morning, but I (14) _______________ come in this afternoon.

Vanna: Oh . . . thank you, Vanna . . . See you later.

EXERCISE 9

Test your knowledge. Make *Yes/No* questions and discuss your answers.

EXAMPLES: people/live without food for six months

Can people live without food for six months?

Yes, they can.

No, they can't.

Are people able to live without food for six months?

Yes, they are.

No, they aren't.

1. a computer/think
2. smoking/cause cancer
3. an airplane/fly from New York to Paris in four hours
4. a person/run twenty-five miles an hour
5. a river/flow uphill
6. we/communicate with people from other planets
7. a person/learn a language in one week
8. modern medicine/cure AIDS
9. a two-year old child/read
10. the United Nations/stop wars
11. you/think of any more questions

Exercise 9

SUGGESTIONS

This exercise can be done in pairs, teams, or as a whole class. To simplify this exercise, ask Ss to make questions only with *can* or only with *be able to*. These questions should provoke interesting discussions.

Workbook Exs. 6 & 7, p. 111.
Answers: TE, p. 535.

ANSWER KEY

Exercise 9

1. Can a computer think?/ Is a computer able to think? **2.** Can smoking cause cancer? **3.** Can an airplane fly...? **4.** Can a person run...?/...Is a person able to run...? **5.** Can a river flow...? **6.** Can we communicate...?/Are we able to communicate...? **7.** Can a person learn...? **8.** Can modern medicine cure ...?/ Is modern medicine able to cure...? **9.** Can a two-year-old child read?/ Is a two-year-old child able to read? **10.** Can the United Nations stop...? Is the United Nations able to stop...? **12.** Can you think...?/Are you able to think...?

FOCUS 5

1. To present this focus box inductively, write the two complete clauses in (a), (b), (c), and (d) on the board, leaving out the connectors.
2. Write the words *and, but, so,* and *or* in random order on the other side.
3. Ask Ss to define the relationship between the two clauses (*How can we put these two parts of the sentence together?*) and choose the connector that fits.
4. Review the focus box.

Exercise 10

Answers will vary. Have Ss write their sentences on the board. Check with the whole class.

FOCUS **5**

Sentence Connectors: *And/But/So/Or*

And, but, so, and **or** are sentence connectors. We use them to connect two complete sentences.

EXAMPLES	EXPLANATIONS
(a) I can rollerskate **and** I can ski.	**And** adds information.
(b) I can dance, **but** I can't sing. He can swim, **but** his brother can't.	**But** shows contrast.
(c) I can't cook, **so** I often go out to eat.	**So** gives a result.
(d) You can go **or** you can stay.	**Or** gives a choice.
(e) I can speak English, but I can't speak Spanish. (f) I can speak Spanish, and my sister can speak Japanese.	When you connect two complete sentences, use a comma (,) before the connector.
(g) I can say it in English, or I can say it in French. (h) I can say it in English or French.	When the subject is the same for the two verbs, it is not necessary to repeat the subject or *can*. Do not use a comma.

EXERCISE 10

What can you do? Write sentences about yourself with *can* or *know how to* with *and* or *but*.

▶ **EXAMPLE:** use a typewriter/use a computer

I can use a typewriter, but I can't use a computer.

I can use a typewriter and a computer.

1. rollerskate/rollerblade
2. ride a bicycle/drive a car
3. use a camera/use a video camera
4. use a telephone/use a fax machine
5. cook rice/cook Chinese food
6. sew a button/sew a dress
7. walk fast/run fast
8. swim/dive

Now make three statements of your own:

9. ____________________

10. ____________________

11. ____________________

EXERCISE 11

Look back at the pictures in Exercise 2. Fill in the blanks with *and, but,* or *so.*

1. (Look at Picture 7 in Exercise 2)

Bob and Andrea love the movies, (a) __but__ they are often too busy to go to the movies on Saturdays. They usually go to the first show on Sundays. On Sunday afternoon, the tickets are half-price, (b) __________ the theater is very crowded. There is one woman in the audience who is always a problem. Today, Bob and Andrea are behind her. The woman has very bushy hair, (c) __________ Bob and Andrea can't see the movie screen. She loves popcorn (d) __________ eats it non-stop during the movie. Popcorn is delicious, (e) __________ it is also very noisy, (f) __________ Bob and Andrea can't hear the movie. Sometimes they think it's better to stay home and rent a movie!

2. (Look at Picture 6 in Exercise 2)

Larry is in the hospital. He has a high fever, (a) __________ he is very sick. The doctor wants him to stay in the hospital, (b) __________ Larry wants to go home. The doctor says he needs to rest, (c) __________ Larry wants to go back to work. He is bored in the hospital, (d) __________ he misses his family. He is unhappy, (e) __________ he decides to leave.

3. (Look at Picture 1 in Exercise 2)

Tommy loves to listen to loud music, (a) __________ his mom hates his music. Tommy's mom has a headache, (b) __________ she asks Tommy to use his walkman. Tommy has a walkman, (c) __________ he can't use it. It's broken.

Exercise 11

Let Ss read through each text once so that they get some background knowledge. Have them determine the relationships between sentences before choosing the connecting words.

Workbook Ex. 8, p. 112.
Answers: TE, p. 535.

ANSWER KEY

Exercise 11

1. b. so, **c.** so, **d.** and **e.** but, **f.** so
2. a. and **b.** but, **c.** but, **d.** and
e. so **3. a.** but, **b.** so, **c.** but

Exercise 12 

Ss will practice using *or* to make a choice. Have pairs share their plans with the class.

EXERCISE 12

You want to spend a Saturday with a classmate. Choose a partner. Ask each other questions to decide what kind of day you want to have.

STEP 1 Ask each other the six questions given.

▶ **EXAMPLE:** **You:** Do you want to meet early for breakfast or wait until later to meet?

Your Partner: Let's meet early for breakfast.

1. meet early for breakfast/wait until later to meet
2. skip lunch/have a picnic lunch
3. go to a museum/spend some time outdoors (in a park or at the beach)
4. go on the Internet/play soccer
5. cook dinner together/eat out
6. rent a video/go to a movie

STEP 2 Now add three questions of your own.

UNIT GOAL REVIEW

Ask Ss to look at the goals on the opening page of the unit again. Help them understand how much they have accomplished in each area. Ask them if there are any questions they still have about what they have learned so far.

ANSWER KEY

Exercise 12

2. Do you want to skip lunch or have a picnic lunch? **3.** Do you want to go to a museum or spend some time outdoors? **4.** Do you want to go on the Internet or play soccer? **5.** Do you want to cook dinner together or eat out? **6.** Do you want to rent a video or go to a movie?

Use Your English

ACTIVITY 1: SPEAKING

Read the job advertisement in the newspaper for a baby sitter. Interview your partner for the job. Ask questions with *can, know how to,* and *be able to.*

▶ **EXAMPLES:** Do you know how to cook?
Can you work full-time?

142 Employment

WANTED: Baby sitter ★
Responsible person. Full-time work five days a week 8:00-5:00, some evenings and weekends. Must speak English and be able to drive. Laundry, light housekeeping, and cooking required. Experience with children necessary. References requested.

Chemist ★
Stable, fast-growing company seeks chemist for formulation of industrial

ACTIVITY 2: WRITING

What can you do that your parents or other people you know cannot do? Write six sentences.

▶ **EXAMPLES:** My mother can't ride a bicycle, but I can.
My sister knows how to sew, but I don't.

ACTIVITY 3: WRITING/SPEAKING

Do you think it's better to be a man or a woman? Write as many reasons as you can for your opinion and then discuss them.

▶ **EXAMPLE:** It's better to be a woman. A woman can have children.

USE YOUR ENGLISH

For a more complete discussion of how to use the activities, see p. xxvi of this Teacher's Edition.

Activity 1 

Bring in real job advertisements from the classifieds to familiarize Ss with ads.

EXPANSION

Try to find ads that would be suitable to your student population. Or have Ss cut out ads from the classifieds that appeal to them. Discuss abbreviations and new vocabulary. Have them write questions and role-play job interviews. They could also respond to the ads in writing, telling what they are able to do.

Activity 2

Collect Ss' papers so you can do error correction. Expect some cnofusion with the short forms: I *can/can't* and *I do/don't.*

Activity 3 

This activity will provoke a lot of discussion. Give Ss time to brainstorm ideas, either individually, or in groups, or both.

VARIATIONS

1. Tape record the group discussion and create an error correction sheet from the mistakes made.
2. Divide the class in half. Do this activity as a mini-debate.

Activity 4

Have Ss create a list of occupations to choose from and elaborate on the tasks and responsibilities of each one. Have each student choose one and state his/her abilities.

VARIATION

Have Ss simulate a heated discussion between two friends. One friend tries to persuade the other that (a) he/she is qualified for a certain job, (b) he/she is unable to do a certain job.

Activity 5

VARIATION

This activity could be done as a bingo game. Add a few more boxes to the grid to create 16 or 25 squares. Each student has a grid and walks around the room using the suggested procedure. The goal of the game is to get all "yes" answers from different Ss either vertically, horizontally, or diagonally. The first student to get all "yes" answers shouts out "Bingo!" and wins the game.

ACTIVITY 4: SPEAKING

Make a list of ten jobs.

Say what you can or are able to do. The class decides what job is good for you. Use *and* and *but*.

▶ **EXAMPLE:** **You say:** I can help sick people, and get along with them. I am able to follow directions.
Your group: Then you can be a nurse!

ACTIVITY 5: SPEAKING

STEP 1 Ask a classmate if he or she can do one of the activities in the box below.

▶ **EXAMPLE:** Can you touch your toes without bending your knees?

STEP 2 If the person says *yes*, write his/her name in the box. Then go to another student and ask another question.

If the person says *no*, ask the other questions until he or she says *yes*. Then write his or her name in the box.

STEP 3 Each student who answered *yes* must perform the action in the box!

touch your toes without bending your knees ______	dance ______	whistle ______
sing a song in English ______	say "Hello" in four languages ______	tell a joke in English ______
draw a horse ______	pronounce the word "Psychology" ______	juggle ______

230 UNIT 14

ACTIVITY 6: LISTENING/ SPEAKING 

STEP 1 Listen to Ken's interview for a job. Then answer the questions. Check *Yes* or *No*.

	Yes	No
1. Ken can speak French, Spanish, and German.		
2. Ken can stay in another country for a year.		
3. Ken can drive.		
4. Ken can use computers.		
5. Ken can sell computers.		
6. Ken can repair computers.		

STEP 2 Discuss with your classmates.

1. What kind of job is the interview for?
2. Can Ken get the job? Why or why not?

Activity 6 

Play textbook audio. The tapescript for this listening appears on p. 546 of this book.

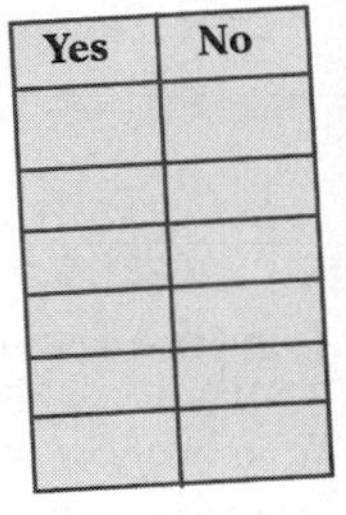

The test for this unit can be found on pp. 488–490 of this book.
The answers can be found on p. 491.

ANSWER KEY

Activity 6

1. Yes 2. No 3. Yes 4. Yes 5. Yes
6. No

Unit 15

UNIT OVERVIEW

The present progressive is often introduced before the simple present tense in many texts because it is relatively easy to form once the verb *be* has been acquired and because its meaning is tangible and easy to demonstrate. However, to avoid overgeneralization, the present progressive is introduced well after the simple present in this book. You may choose to introduce this structure at any given point in your semester. Thematically, this unit deals with the roles of men and women in modern American society.

UNIT GOALS

To maximize the diagnostic potential of the Opening Task, do not review the Unit Goals with students (Ss) until after they have completed and reviewed the Opening Task.

OPENING TASK
SETTING UP THE TASK

Work as a whole class first. Familiarize Ss with the vocabulary on the next page. Ask them to describe what's happening in the picture and why they think the scene looks this way. Try to elicit generalizations in the simple present as well as statements in the present progressive. Listen to the language Ss use. Take notes on correct and incorrect statements to put on the board later.

UNIT 15

PRESENT PROGRESSIVE TENSE

UNIT GOALS:

- To make affirmative and negative statements in the present progressive tense
- To know how to spell verbs ending in *-ing*
- To choose between the simple present and the present progressive
- To know which verbs are not usually used in the progressive
- To ask *yes/no* questions in the present progressive

OPENING TASK
A Bad Day at the Harrisons'

Robin's babysitter cannot come today, so her husband Regis is staying at home and taking care of the children and the house.

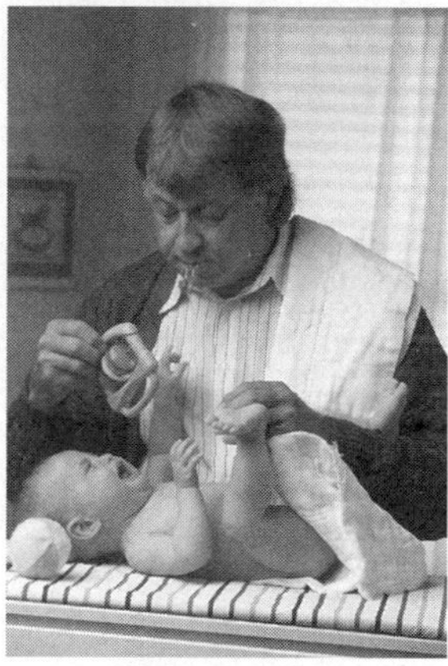

Why is Regis having a bad day today?

Talk about what is happening in the picture using the subjects on the left and the verbs in the box.

the food	bark
Suzy	play cowboy on his father's back
the telephone	burn on the stove
the baby and the dog	go crazy
the baby	watch TV
Jimmy	cry
the dog	ring
Regis	fight over a toy

CONDUCTING THE TASK

Have Ss work in groups to write what's happening in the picture, using the prompts as well as the sentences generated by the class. Ask Ss to write their hypotheses as to why poor Regis is having such a bad day today.

COMPLETING THE TASK

Go around the room and observe what they're writing. Write both correct and incorrect statements on the board. Distinguish between Form errors: *The food is burn on the stove. The food burning on the stove*, and Use errors: *The food burns on the stove*.

REVIEWING THE TASK

When all statements (including your notes) have been put up on the board, ask Ss to look at and evaluate them. Are they grammatically correct? Are they used correctly? This will allow you to bridge to form and use problems. Then you can come back to each focus as needed.

ANSWER KEY

Opening Task

The food is burning on the stove. Suzy is watching TV. The telephone is ringing. The baby and the dog are fighting over a toy. The baby is crying. Jimmy is playing cowboy on his father's back. The dog is barking. Regis is going crazy.

FOCUS 1

This focus box presents the form, meaning, and use of the present progressive.

1. Emphasize that the present progressive talks about actions in progress, actions that are happening right now, or actions that are not completed. Contrast this with the simple present tense used to talk about habits and routines. (This will be done again in Focus 4.) Provide other examples: *I wear glasses/I'm wearing my glasses now. I teach English/I'm teaching you a new lesson now. I speak 3 languages. I'm speaking English now.*
2. In presenting the form, have Ss generate all forms of the verb *be* and then introduce the progressive by showing the base form of the verb + *ing.*

FOCUS **1**

Present Progressive: Affirmative Statements

EXAMPLES	EXPLANATIONS
(a) The food **is burning.** **(b)** The baby **is crying.** **(c)** The dog and the baby **are fighting.**	Use the present progressive to talk about an action that is happening right now; an action in progress.
now *right now* *at the moment*	Use these time expressions with the present progressive.

SUBJECT	*BE*	BASE FORM OF THE VERB + *-ING*
I	am	
You	are	
He She It	is	working.
We You They	are	

Affirmative Contractions

SUBJECT + *BE* CONTRACTION	BASE FORM OF THE VERB + *-ING*
I'm	working.
You're	
He's She's It's	
We're You're They're	

EXERCISE 1

Underline all the present progressive verbs in the text.

▶ **EXAMPLE:** Regis isn't having a good day.

Today is not a normal day at the Harrisons'. Usually, Robin's babysitter comes at 3:00 when Robin leaves for work. But today, Robin is attending an all-day meeting at the college, and her babysitter can't come. So Regis is spending the day at home. He's taking care of the children and the house. He's trying very hard, but everything is going wrong. Regis isn't having a good day. Actually, poor Regis is going crazy. He's thinking about Robin. He's learning something today. It's not easy to stay home with the children. He's beginning to understand this.

Exercise 1

This exercise implicity opposes the simple and progressive Form and Use. Focus on both, especially statements like: Robin is attending an all-day meeting at the college...," which refer to actions that are not habitual, not generally true, not the norm. Students can do this exercise individually.

Workbook Exs. 1–3, pp. 113–115.
Answers: TE, pp. 535–536.

ANSWER KEY

Exercise 1
is attending . . ., is spending . . ., He's taking care of . . ., He's trying . . ., is going . . ., isn't having . . ., is going . . ., He's thinking . . ., He's learning . . ., He's beginning

FOCUS 2

SUGGESTIONS

1. To work deductively, present each rule separately and give Ss additional examples. (For rule #1-*bite, wake, take;* #2-*pay, mix, grow,* #3-*perMIT;* #4-*tie;* #5-*teach, meet, hold).*
2. To work inductively, present the various examples and have Ss come up with the rules.

FOCUS **2**

Spelling of Verbs Ending in *-ing*

VERB END	RULE	EXAMPLES	
1. consonant + *e*	Drop the *-e*, add *-ing*.	write	writing
2. consonant + vowel + consonant (one syllable verbs)	Double the consonant, add *-ing*.	sit	sitting
Exception: verbs that end in *-w*, *-x*, and *-y*.	Do not double *w*, *x*, and *y*.	show fix play	showing fixing playing
3. consonant + vowel + consonant. The verb has more than one syllable, and the stress is on the last syllable.	Double the consonant, add *-ing*.	beGIN forGET	beginning forgetting
If the stress is not on the last syllable	Do not double the consonant.	LISten HAPpen	listening happening
4. *-ie*	Change *-ie* to *y*, add *-ing*.	lie die	lying dying
5. All other verbs	Add *-ing* to the base form of verb.	talk study do agree	talking studying doing agreeing

Exercise 2

When Ss finish the exercise, have them refer to the rule in focus box 2 which governs each example.

EXERCISE 2

Fill in the blanks with the present progressive.

Today's a normal day at the Harrisons'. It is 4:00. Robin (1) ______________ (prepare) dinner in the kitchen. She (2) ______________ (slice) onions and (3) ______________ (wipe) the tears from her eyes. The house is quiet, so she (4) ______________ (listen) to some music. She (5) ______________ (think) about her class tonight. She (6) ______________ (wait) for her babysitter to arrive. The baby (7) ______________ (sleep). The dog (8) ______________ (lie) on the floor and (9) ______________

ANSWER KEY

Exercise 2

1. is preparing **2.** is slicing **3.** is wiping **4.** is listening **5.** is thinking **6.** is waiting **7.** is sleeping **8.** is lying **9.** is chewing **10.** is playing **11.** is cleaning **12.** is happening (chew) on a bone. Jimmy (10) _______________ (play) with his toys. Suzy (11) _______________ (clean) her room. Nothing unusual (12) ___________ (happen). Everything is under control.

EXERCISE 3

Who's talking? Fill in the blanks with the present progressive of the verb. Then match each statement to a picture.

▶ **EXAMPLE:** "You're ___driving___ (drive) me crazy. Turn off the TV!"

1. "That crazy dog _______________ (bite) me!"

a.

2. "I _______________ (walk) into a zoo!"

b.

3. "Quiet! You _______________ (make) a lot of noise. I can't hear the TV."

c.

4. "Stop that, Jimmy. You _______________ (hurt) me."

d.

Exercise 3

After Ss fill in the blanks, have them say which rule each statement exemplifies.

Workbook Ex. 4, pp. 115–116
Answers: TE, p. 536.

ANSWER KEY

Exercise 3

1. is biting (f) **2.** am walking (d) **3.** are making (e) **4.** are hurting (b) **5.** is burning (a) **6.** am dying, are killing (c)

5. "Oh no! The food _____________ (burn)!"

e.

6. "I _____________ (die) to take off my shoes.
My feet ___________ (kill) me."

f.

FOCUS 3

Refer Ss back to Unit 2, Focus 3 (p. 22): *Be:* Negative Statements and Contractions. They should already know how to contract the verb *be* and not and how to contract the subject pronoun with *be*. Point out that there is no negative contraction with *I am not*, only *be* contraction + *not (I'm not)*.

FOCUS 3

Present Progressive: Negative Statements

SUBJECT + *BE* + *NOT*			NEGATIVE CONTRACTION			BE CONTRACTION + *NOT*	
I	am	not working.	*		working.	I'm	not working.
You	are		You	aren't		You're	
He She It	is		He She It	isn't		He's She's It's	
We You They	are		We You They	aren't		We're You're They're	

*There is no standard English contraction with *I am not.*

EXERCISE 4

Make negative statements using contractions.

▶ **EXAMPLE:** Robin/take care of the children today
Robin isn't taking care of the children today.

1. Robin/wear comfortable shoes today
2. Robin's babysitter/come today
3. The baby and the dog/get along
4. Regis/relax
5. The children/listen to Regis
6. Suzy/do her homework
7. Suzy/help Regis
8. Regis/pay attention to the dinner on the stove
9. Regis/laugh
10. Regis/enjoy his children today

EXERCISE 5

Look at the picture. Make affirmative or negative statements.

▶ **EXAMPLES:** Mrs. Bainbridge ___is having___ (have) a party at her home this evening.
Mrs. Bainbridge ___isn't talking___ (talk) to her guests at the moment.

Mrs. Bainbridge is having a party at her home this evening. The guests (1) ______________ (talk) in the living room. But Mr. and Mrs. Parker (2)______________ (talk) to the other guests. They (3) ______________ (enjoy) the party. They (4) ______________ (feel) very bored right now. They (5) ______________ (think of) a way to escape. Mrs. Bainbridge (6) ______________ (stand) in the doorway. She (7) ______________ (turn) her back to the Parkers. The Parkers (8) ______________ (leave), but they (9) ______________ (leave) by the front door. Mr. and Mrs. Parker (10) ______________ (climb) out of the bedroom window. Mr. Parker (11) ______________ (hold) his hat between his teeth. He (12) ______________ (help) Mrs. Parker climb out. Mr. and Mrs. Parker (13) ______________ (say) good-bye to the other guests.

Exercise 4

Have Ss say these answers aloud. Check pronunciation. Again, be sure Ss understand that these statements express a departure from the norm in the Harrison family.

Exercise 5

SUGGESTIONS

1. Have Ss talk about what's happening in the picture first.
2. After Ss have done the exercise, have them retell the story to each other to practice pronunciation of contractions.

Workbook Exs. 5–7, pp. 117–119.
Answers: TE, p. 536.

ANSWER KEY

Exercise 4

1. isn't wearing, Robin's not wearing **2.** isn't coming, babysitter's not coming **3.** aren't getting along **4.** Regis isn't relaxing, is not relaxing **5.** aren't listening **6.** Suzy isn't doing, Suzy's not doing **7.** Suzy isn't helping. Suzy's not helping **8.** Regis isn't paying, Regis's not paying **9.** Regis isn't laughing. Regis's not laughing **10.** Regis isn't enjoying, Regis's not enjoying

Exercise 5

1. are talking **2.** aren't talking **3.** aren't enjoying **4.** are feeling/They're feeling
5. are thinking of/They're thinking of
6. is standing/Mrs. Bainbridge's standing
7. is turning/She's turning **8.** are leaving
9. aren't leaving/They're not leaving
10. are climbing **11.** is holding/Mr. Parker's holding **12.** is helping/He's helping
13. aren't saying

FOCUS 4

1. Have Ss read the different uses of the simple present and present progressive.
2. Point out the time expressions used with each.
3. Explain that the present progressive is used not only with (a) actions in progress at the moment, but also with (b) temporary actions that are not habitual or that go on for a specific period of time (*You are studying English this semester. This week we're learning the present progressive tense.*), and (c) for changing, evolving situations (*People are traveling a lot these days.*).

Exercise 6

Have Ss explain the uses they're choosing for each statement.

FOCUS **4**

USE

Choosing Simple Present or Present Progressive

The simple present and the present progressive have different uses.

USE THE SIMPLE PRESENT FOR:	USE THE PRESENT PROGRESSIVE FOR:
• **habits and repeated actions** **(a)** Suzy usually does her homework in the afternoon. • **things that are true in general** **(c)** Women usually take care of children.	• **actions in progress now** **(b)** Suzy's watching TV right now. • **actions that are temporary, not habitual** **(d)** Regis is taking care of the children to-day • **situations that are changing** **(e)** These days, men are spending more time with their children.
Time Expressions *always* — *rarely* *often* — *never* *usually* — *every day* *sometimes* — *once a week* *seldom* — *on the weekends*	**Time Expressions** *right now* — *now* *today* — *at the moment* *this week* — *this evening* *this year* — *this month* *these days* — *nowadays*

EXERCISE 6

Read each statement on the next page. If the statement is in the simple present, make a second statement in the present progressive. If the statement is in the present progressive, make a second statement in the simple present. Discuss the differences in meaning.

ANSWER KEY

Exercise 6
Answers may vary.
2. a. Robin usually cooks dinner.
3. b. Robin isn't taking care of the children today. Regis is taking care of the children today.
4. a. Regis usually goes to work/Regis usually works. Regis doesn't usually spend the day at home. Robin usually spends the day at home
5. b. The babysitter isn't taking care of the children today. Regis is taking care of the children today. **6. a.** The baby and the dog don't usually fight. **7. b.** Regis is going crazy right now.

Simple Present	Present Progressive
1a. Suzy usually does her homework in the evening.	1b. Tonight she isn't doing her homework. She's watching cartoons.
2a. ______________	2b. Tonight, Robin isn't cooking dinner.
3a. Robin usually takes care of the children.	3b. ______________
4a. ______________	4b. Today, Regis is spending the day at home.
5a. The babysitter usually takes care of the children when Robin goes to work.	5b. ______________
6a. ______________	6b. Right now, the baby and the dog are fighting.
7a. The babysitter usually doesn't go crazy.	7b. ______________

EXERCISE 7

Make sentences with *these days, nowadays,* or *today* to show changing situations in the United States.

▶ **EXAMPLE:** women/get more education

These days, women are getting more education.

1. Women/get good jobs
2. Fifty percent of American women/ work outside the home
3. Women/earn money
4. Women/become more independent
5. Men/share the work in the home
6. Husbands/help their wives
7. Fathers/spend more time with their children
8. The roles of men and women/ change

Add two sentences of your own.

9. ______________________________
10. ______________________________

Exercise 7 

EXPANSION

Ss can work in groups (culturally homogeneous, if possible) to make statements about the changing roles of men and women in their home countries. Have Ss write their own sentences on the board. Correct errors as a class.

Workbook Exs. 8–9, pp. 120–121. Answers: TE, p. 536.

ANSWER KEY

Exercise 7

Answers may vary. Possible answers:
1. These days, women are getting good jobs **2.** Today, fifty percent of American women are working outside the home **3.** These days, women are earning money **4.** These days, women are becoming more independent **5.** Nowadays, men are sharing the work in the home **6.** Today, husbands are helping their wives **7.** These days, fathers are spending time with their children **8.** Today the roles of men and women are changing.

FOCUS 5

Read the categories for stative verbs and the examples. Provide additional examples. *I know you. NOT: I am knowing you. This sandwich tastes delicious. NOT: This sandwich is tasting delicious. I understand English. NOT: I'm understanding English.* The stative verbs in the simple present in *h*, *j*, and *l* relate to the states in the chart above. When used in the progressive, these verbs describe actions in progress. This is difficult for beginning Ss, so provide enough examples to illustrate the difference. *A. Maria has a baby. vs. Maria is having a baby (is pregnant or giving birth right now). B. I see him. vs. I'm seeing him (dating).*

FOCUS **5**

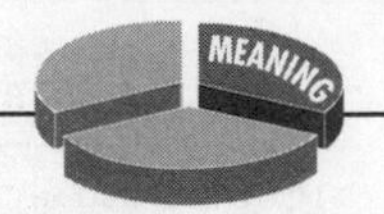

Verbs Not Usually Used in the Progressive

There are some verbs we usually do not use in the present progressive. These verbs are *not* action verbs. They are called nonprogressive (or stative) verbs.

EXAMPLES	NONPROGRESSIVE (STATIVE) VERBS
(a) Robin **loves** her job. (b) **NOT:** Robin is loving her job. (c) The children **need** help. (d) **NOT:** The children are needing help.	**FEELINGS AND EMOTIONS** *(like, love, hate, prefer, want, need)*
(e) Regis **understands** his wife.	**MENTAL STATES** *(think, believe, understand, seem, forget, remember, know, mean)*
(f) Regis **hears** the telephone ringing.	**SENSES** *(hear, see, smell, taste, feel, sound)*
(g) Robin and Regis **own** a house.	**POSSESSION** *(belong, own, have)*

There are some stative verbs you can use in the present progressive, but they have a different meaning.

SIMPLE PRESENT	PRESENT PROGRESSIVE
(h) I **think** you're a good student. (*Think* means "believe.")	(i) I **am thinking** about you now. (Here *thinking* shows a mental action.)
(j) I **have** two cars. (*Have* means "possess.")	(k) I'**m having** a good time. (*Have* describes the experience.)
(l) This soup **tastes** delicious. (*Taste* means "has a delicious flavor.")	(m) I'**m tasting** the soup. (*Taste* here means the action of putting soup in one's mouth.)

EXERCISE 8

Fill in the blanks with the present progressive or simple present form of the verb. Read the dialogues aloud. Use contractions.

▶ **EXAMPLE:** **Regis:** _I'm going_ (go) crazy in this house.
Robin: _I think_ (think) you need a vacation!

1. **Regis:** Suzy, I need your help here.
   Suzy: But, Dad, you (a) ______________ (need) my help every five minutes! I (b) ______________ (watch) TV right now!
2. It is 3:00. The telephone rings.
   Regis: Hello.
   Laura: Hello, Regis. What are you doing home in the middle of the afternoon?
   Regis: Oh, hi, Laura. I know I (a) ______________ (be) never home in the afternoon, but today I (b) ______________ (try) to be a househusband!
   Laura: Oh really? Where's Robin?
   Regis: Robin (c) ______________ (attend) a meeting at the college, so I (d) ______________ (take care of) the kids.
3. Jimmy interrupts Regis's telephone conversation:
   Regis: Hold on a minute, Laura . . . Jimmy (a) ______________ (pull) on my leg! Jimmy, I (b) ______________ (talk) to Mommy's friend Laura right now. You (c) ______________ (know) Laura. She (d) ______________ (come) to see Mommy every week. Now, just wait a minute, please . . .
   Laura: Is everything O.K., Regis?
   Regis: Oh, yes, Laura, don't worry. We (e) ______________ (do) just fine. Talk to you later; bye!
4. It is 5:30. The telephone rings.
   Regis: Hello.
   Robin: Hi, honey! The meeting (a) ______________ (be) over. I (b) ______________ (be) on my way home. What (c) ______________ (happen)? I hope the children (d) ______________ (behave).

Exercise 8

After Ss have filled in the blanks, ask them to explain why the present simple is used in 1.*a*, 3.*c* and *d*, 4.*f*, and *h*. Also ask why the progressive form is used with *have* in 4.*g*.

EXPANSION

Have the class role-play these situations.

ANSWER KEY

Exercise 8

1. **a.** need, **b.** I'm watching 2. **a.** am, **b.** am trying, **c.** is attending, **d.** am taking care of 3. **a.** is pulling, **b.** am talking, **c.** know, **d.** comes, **e.** are doing 4. **a.** is, **b.** am, **c.** is happening/'s happening? **d.** are behaving, **e.** are behaving, **f.** yell, **g.** am not having, **h.** sound

Exercise 9 

1. Ss will need help with vocabulary to describe what each person is doing (e.g., #8 *She's staring out the window.* #11 *He's sweating*). Walk around while pairs are working. Assist them with vocabulary. Or, elicit or provide infinitive forms before Ss begin this exercise.

2. Review the answers with the whole class and write new vocabulary on the board.

Workbook Ex. 10, pp. 121–122.
Answers: TE, p. 536.

Regis: They (e) ______________ (behave) like wild animals, Robin. I (f) ______________ (yell) at them all the time, but they don't listen to me. I (g) ______________ (not/have) a very good day today. Please come home soon!

Robin: You (h) ______________ (sound) terrible! Can I bring anything home, dear?

Regis: Yes, a bottle of aspirin!

EXERCISE 9

Work with a partner. Choose any picture (do not go in order). Describe the picture by making one statement with *seem, look,* or *feel* and an adjective from the box. Make another statement with the present progressive to say what the person is doing. Your partner must guess the number of the picture you are talking about. Take turns.

▶ **EXAMPLE:** **You say:** The woman looks nervous. She's smoking five cigarettes at one time.

Your partner says: Picture Number 5.

sad	sick	scared	tired
angry	happy	cold	hot
bored	surprised	nervous ✓	confused

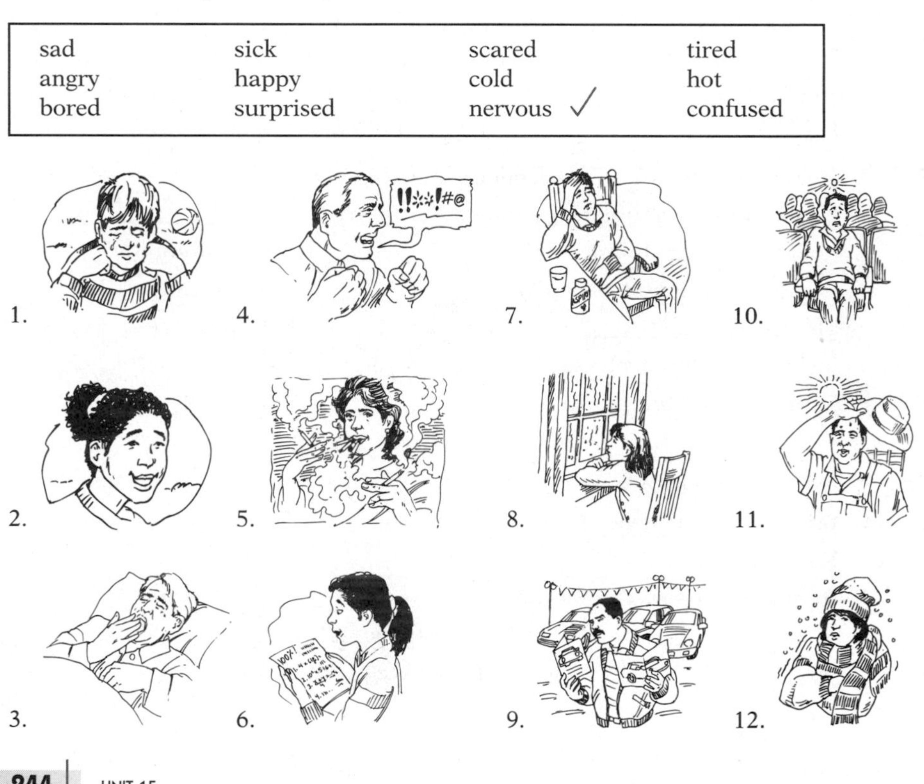

ANSWER KEY

Exercise 9

Answers may vary. Possible answers:
1. The boy looks/seems sad. He's crying. **2.** The woman looks/seems happy. She's smiling. **3.** The man looks/seems tired. He's yawning. **4.** The man looks/seems angry. He's clenching his fists and swearing. **5.** The woman looks/seems nervous. She's smoking frantically. **6.** The girl looks/seems surprised. She's looking at her test grade. She got 100% on her test. **7.** The boy looks/seems sick. He's holding his head and his stomach. He's taking medicine. **8.** The girl looks bored. She's staring out the window. **9.** The man looks/seems confused. He's reading about new cars. He's trying to decide on a new car. **10.** The man looks/seems scared. He's watching a horror movie./He's holding onto his chair. **11.** The man looks/seems hot. He's sweating. **12.** The boy looks/seems cold. He's shivering.

FOCUS 6

Present Progressive: *Yes/No* Questions and Short Answers

YES/NO QUESTIONS			SHORT ANSWERS					
Am	I		Yes,	you	are.	No,	you	aren't
Are	you		Yes,	I	am.	No,	I'm	not.
Is	he she it	working?	Yes,	he she it	is.	No,	he she it	isn't.
Are	you we they		Yes,	we you they	are.	No,	we you they	aren't.

EXERCISE 10

Refer to the picture in the Opening Task on page 233. With a partner, take turns asking and answering questions about the Harrisons. Give short answers. Use the verbs from the box below.

EXAMPLE: Suzy/ . . . /her father
You: Is Suzy helping her father?
Your Partner: No, she isn't.

watch	ring	play	bite	come
enjoy	burn	help	fight	smile

1. children / their father
2. the baby and the dog/ . . .
3. Suzy / TV
4. their dinner/ . . .
5. the phone/ . . .
6. Jimmy / cowboy
7. the dog / Regis
8. Robin / home
9. Robin
10. Regis/his children

FOCUS 6

Have Ss study the chart. Then ask them relevant yes/no questions (e.g., *Are you enjoying this class? Is Mario daydreaming? Are Susana and Ling paying attention?*)

Exercise 10

Have pairs alternate asking questions with every other number.

ANSWER KEY

Exercise 10

1. Are the children helping their father? No, they aren't./They're not. **2.** Are the baby and the dog fighting? Yes, they are. **3.** Is Suzy watching TV? Yes, she is. **4.** Is their dinner burning? Yes, it is. **5.** Is the phone ringing? Yes, it is. **6.** Is Jimmy playing cowboy? Yes, he is. **7.** Is the dog biting Regis? Yes, he is. **8.** Is Robin coming home? Yes, she is. **9.** Is Robin smiling? No, she isn't/She's not. **10.** Is Regis watching his children? Yes, he is.

Exercise 11 

VARIATION

This exercise can be done as a class survey. Give one question to each student. Have them walk around and ask everyone in the class their questions. Each student then makes summary statements about their question. (e.g., *Everyone is enjoying this English class. Seventy-five percent of the Ss think their English is improving.*)

Workbook Ex. 11, pp. 122–123.
Answers: TE, p. 536.

EXERCISE 11

Work with a partner. Ask each other *yes/no* questions about your lives these days. Check *Yes* or *No*.

▶ **EXAMPLES:** a. enjoy English class
Are you enjoying your English class?
b. your English/improve
Is your English improving?

	You		Your Partner	
	Yes	No	Yes	No
1. enjoy English class?				
2. your English/improve?				
3. take any other classes?				
4. learn a lot?				
5. get good grades?				
6. make progress?				
7. do a lot of homework?				
8. cook for yourself?				
9. go out with friends?				
10. meet lots of new people?				
11. eat well?				
12. sleep well?				
13. exercise?				
14. work after school?				

ANSWER KEY

Exercise 11

Answers may vary. **1.** Are you enjoying? **2.** Is your English improving? **3.** Are you taking any...? **4.** Are you learning a lot ...? **5.** Are you getting...? **6.** Are you making...? **7.** Are you doing...? **8.** Are you cooking...? **9.** Are you going out...? **10.** Are you meeting...? **11.** Are you eating...? **12.** Are you sleeping...? **13.** Are you getting...?/Are you exercising...? **14.** Are you working...?

FOCUS **7**

Present Progressive: *Wh*-Questions

WH-WORD	*BE*	SUBJECT	VERB + *-ING*	ANSWERS
What	am	I	doing?	(You're) getting ready for the beach.
When **Where** **Why** **How**	are	you	going?	(I'm going) at 2:00. (We're going) to Malibu Beach. (We're going) because we don't have school today. (We're going) by car.
Who(m)	is	she	meeting?	(She's meeting) her friends.
Who	is		going with us?	Clara (is going with us).

Who is asking about the subject.

EXERCISE 12

Write the question that asks for the underlined information.

1. Q: *Who is watching television?*
   A: Suzy is watching television.
2. Q: *Who(m) is Regis taking care of tonight?*
   A: Regis is taking care of the children.
3. Q: ______________________
   A: The baby and the dog are fighting because they both want the toy.
4. Q: ______________________
   A: Robin is meeting her colleagues at the college.
5. Q: ______________________
   A: Robin's thinking that she's lucky to be at work!
6. Q: ______________________
   A: They're eating peanut butter and jelly sandwiches for dinner because Regis' dinner is burnt.

FOCUS 7

These *wh*-questions should be a review (Unit 9, Focuses 4 and 5). Try doing Exercise 12 directly to see how much Ss remember. Come back to Focus 7 if necessary. Ask Ss relevant *wh*-questions (e.g., *Why are you studying English? What are you planning to do in life?*)

Exercise 12

Have Ss write the questions on the board. Check especially for problems with *who* questions. Ask Ss to identify the *who* questions that ask about the subject (#1, 7, and 12).

Workbook Ex. 12, pp. 123–124. Answers: TE, p. 536.

ANSWER KEY

Exercise 12

3. Why are the baby and the dog fighting? **4.** Who(m) is Robin meeting at the college? **5.** What is Robin thinking? **6.** Why are the children eating peanut butter and jelly sandwiches ? **7.** Who is watching the children? **8.** Why is Regis taking aspirin? **9.** Where is Robin's meeting taking place? **10.** When is Robin coming home? **11.** How is Regis feeling right now? **12.** Who is making a lot of noise?

7. Q: ______________________________

A: Regis is watching the children today.

8. Q: ______________________________

A: Regis is taking two aspirin because he has a terrible headache.

9. Q: ______________________________

A: Robin's meeting is taking place at the college.

10. Q: ______________________________

A: Robin is coming home right now.

11. Q: ______________________________

A: Regis is feeling very tired right now.

12. Q: ______________________________

A: The children are making a lot of noise.

Exercise 13

These are common errors with the present progressive tense. Ss can work individually or in pairs. You can also assign this for homework.

EXERCISE 13

Correct the mistakes in the following sentences.

▶ **EXAMPLE:** Is the pizza tasting good?
Does the pizza taste good?

1. The baby and the dog are fight.
2. He's having a new TV.
3. Why you are working today?
4. Are you needing my help?
5. What Robin is thinking?
6. Is she believing him?
7. Right now, he plays cowboy on his father's back.
8. The soup is smelling delicious.
9. Where you are going?
10. People no are saving money nowadays.
11. You working hard these days.
12. How you doing today?

UNIT GOAL REVIEW

Ask Ss to look at the goals on the opening page of the unit again. Help them understand how much they have accomplished in each area. Ask them if there are any questions they still have about what they have learned so far.

ANSWER KEY

Exercise 13

1. The baby and the dog are fighting **2.** He has a new TV **3.** Why are you working today? **4.** Do you need my help? **5.** What is Robin thinking? **6.** Does she believe him? **7.** Right now, he is playing cowboy on his father's back **8.** The soup smells delicious **9.** Where are you going? **10.** People are not saving money nowadays **11.** You are working hard these days **12.** How are you doing today?

Use Your English

ACTIVITY 1: SPEAKING/WRITING

Your teacher will divide the class into two groups.

STEP 1 Group A should look at the statements in Column A. One student at a time will mime an action. Students in Group B must guess the action. Group B students can ask questions of Group A. Then Group B mimes statements from Column B and Group A guesses the actions.

Column A

1. You are opening the lid of a jar. The lid is on very tight.
3. You are watching a very funny TV show.
5. You are trying to sleep and a mosquito is bothering you.
7. You are crossing a busy street. You are holding a young child by the hand and carrying a bag of groceries in the other hand.
9. You are trying to thread a needle, but you're having trouble finding the eye of the needle.

Column B

2. You are reading a very sad story.
4. You are watching your country's soccer team playing in the final game of the World Cup.
6. You are sitting at the bar in a noisy disco. At the other side of the bar, there is someone you like. You are trying to get that person's attention.
8. You are a dinner guest at a friend's house. Your friend is not a good cook. You don't like the food!
10. You are cutting up onions to cook dinner.

STEP 2 Make up three situations like those above. Write each situation on a separate piece of paper and put all the situations in a hat. Every student will then pick a situation and mime it for the others to guess.

USE YOUR ENGLISH

For a more complete discussion of how to use the activities, see p. xxvi of this Teacher's Edition.

Activity 1

Have Ss generate as many statements as possible until they get the right one.

SUGGESTION

As Ss are miming, have a student write what they are doing on the board, or have the class write, so you can check their statements.

VARIATION 

Ask Ss to work in pairs with each pair miming an action and the second pair trying to guess what it is.

Activity 2

Let Ss share their information in small groups or with the class. Comparing the roles of all these people in different cultures will constitute an interesting class discussion.

EXPANSION

Have Ss follow up this discussion by writing a paragraph with topic and support.

Activity 3

Play textbook audio. The tapescript for this listening appears on p. 547 of this book. Play the tape more than once if necessary.

ACTIVITY 2: WRITING

In this unit, we see that family life is changing in the United States. Is family life changing in your home country or in a country that you know? Write sentences expressing habits and things that are generally true or things that are changing. Discuss your statements in a group or with the whole class.

Mothers . . .	Grandparents . . .
Fathers . . .	Couples . . .
Children . . .	Men . . .
Teenagers . . .	Women . . .

ACTIVITY 3: LISTENING/SPEAKING

LISTEN AND DECIDE

STEP 1 Look at the three pictures. Listen to the conversation. Decide which picture fits the description. Check A, B, or C.

A.

B.

C.

The woman is describing Picture A _______ B _______ C _______

STEP 2 Describe the other two girls in the picture.

250 UNIT 15

ANSWER KEY

Activity 3

The woman is discussing picture C.

ACTIVITY 4: WRITING/SPEAKING

STEP 1 Look at the picture. Give this person a name, nationality, occupation, age, and so on. Write a story about this person. What is the woman doing? Where is she? How does she look? What is she thinking about? Why is she there?

STEP 2 Tell the class your story.

Activity 4

This is a creative activity where Ss have to use their imagination to tell a story.

SUGGESTION

Have Ss brainstorm in small groups as a pre-writing activity. They need to agree on the details and story line.

VARIATIONS

1. Have Ss write their stories as groups, and then share with the class.
2. Have Ss write their stories individually and then share with a group or the whole class. Ask the class to choose the "best" stories.
3. Select some of the stories and type them out. Use them to focus both on writing strengths and on weaknesses—focus, development, coherence, organization, and grammar.
4. Record Ss retelling their stories. Use the tape for correcting grammar and pronunciation.
5. This activity can be repeated with fascinating results by providing Ss with National Geographic-type photographs showing people in their own cultural contexts.

The test for this unit can be found on pp. 492–493 of this book. The answers can be found on p. 494.

TOEFL Test Preparation Exercises for Units 13–15 can be found on pp. 125–127 of the workbook. The answers are found on p. 537 of this book.

Unit 16

UNIT OVERVIEW

Adjective phrases are introduced here in order to prepare students (Ss) to understand and use adjective clauses later (see Book 2). While there is no unifying theme in this unit, in terms of language functions, Ss will be doing a lot of *describing* and *identifying* using adjective phrases, *another/the other, other(s)/the other(s)*, and intensifiers.

UNIT GOALS

To maximize the diagnostic potential of the Opening Task, do not review the Unit Goals with Ss until after they have completed and reviewed the Opening Task.

OPENING TASK
SETTING UP THE TASK

The point of this Task is to get Ss to generate sentences such as, *The man in the suit and tie is the school principal*. Elicit or provide vocabulary first: *ladle, microscope, thermometer, paintbrush, stopwatch.*

CONDUCTING THE TASK

1. Work either with the entire class to elicit statements about the people at P.S. 31, or have Ss work in groups to identify who's who.

2. Put Ss' statements 1–6 on the board. Organize the board so that any statements with correct adjective phrases are grouped together.
3. Check answers.
4. To make the Opening Task more challenging, do not show Ss the model in 1.

UNIT 16

ADJECTIVE PHRASES

Another, The Other, Other(s), The Other(s), and Intensifiers

UNIT GOALS:

- To understand and know how to use adjective phrases
- To ask questions with *which*
- To understand and use *another, the other, other(s),* and *the other(s)*
- To use intensifiers with adjectives

OPENING TASK
Meeting the Staff at P.S. 31

Identify the people below only by describing them. Do not point to the picture or say the letter. Say what each person does at P.S. 31.

1. The man in the suit and tie is the school principal.

2. ______________ teaches science.

3. ______________ is the school nurse.

4. ______________ is the girls' basketball coach.

5. ______________ works in the school cafeteria.

6. ______________ teaches art.

REVIEWING THE TASK

Focus on the form in Ss' statements, and analyze the problems in the incorrect statements. Do not discourage Ss from using adjective *clauses*; if they seem to know these, incorporate them into your presentation. Use your analysis of errors to move on to Focus 1.

ANSWER KEY

Opening Task (answers may vary)
2. The man with the microscope/with the books teaches science. **3.** The woman with the thermometer is the school nurse. **4.** The woman with the stop watch/on the bench is the girls' basketball coach. **5.** The man with the ladle works in the school cafeteria. **6.** The woman with the paintbrush teaches art.

FOCUS 1

Point out that adjective phrases follow the nouns they describe. An adjective phrase consists of a preposition and a noun phrase: *in the suit*. The verb in the sentence agrees with the subject, not with the noun in the adjective phrase.
Example: *The bag with the books is (NOT: are) mine*. Call Ss' attention to the article shift; this change from indefinite to definite article occurs because the adjective phrase is used to identify/specify the noun(s).

Exercise 1

The purpose of this exercise is simply to have Ss identify the target structure and Subject-Verb. Ss can do this individually.

FOCUS **1**

Adjective Phrases

EXAMPLES			EXPLANATIONS
Noun	Adjective Phrase	Verb	
(a) The man (b) The food	**in the suit** **on the table**	is the school principal. is delicious.	Adjective phrases are groups of words that describe nouns.
The woman is in a white coat. The woman is the school nurse. (c) The woman **in the white coat** is the school nurse.			Adjective phrases combine two sentences.
(d) The **man** with the books **is** the science teacher.			The verb agrees with the subject, not with the noun in the adjective phrase.

EXERCISE 1

Put parentheses around the adjective phrases. Underline the subject and the verb in each sentence.

▶ **EXAMPLE:** The man (in the suit) works in an office.

1. The man in the suit and tie is the school principal.
2. The man with the books and microscope is the science teacher.
3. The woman in the white coat is the school nurse.
4. The woman with the stopwatch is the girls' basketball coach.
5. The man with the white hat works in the school cafeteria.
6. The woman with the easel and paints is the art teacher.
7. The people on page 252 work at P.S. 31.

ANSWER KEY

Exercise 1

1. The man (in the suit and tie) is 2. The man (with the books and microscope) is ... 3. The woman (in the white coat) is ...
4. The woman (with the stopwatch) is ...
5. The man (with the white hat) works ...
6. The woman (with the easel and paints) is ...
7. The people (on page 252) work ...

EXERCISE 2
Ten of the people below sit in specific chairs on the next page. Match each person to a chair. Then write a sentence with an adjective phrase. The first one has been done for you.

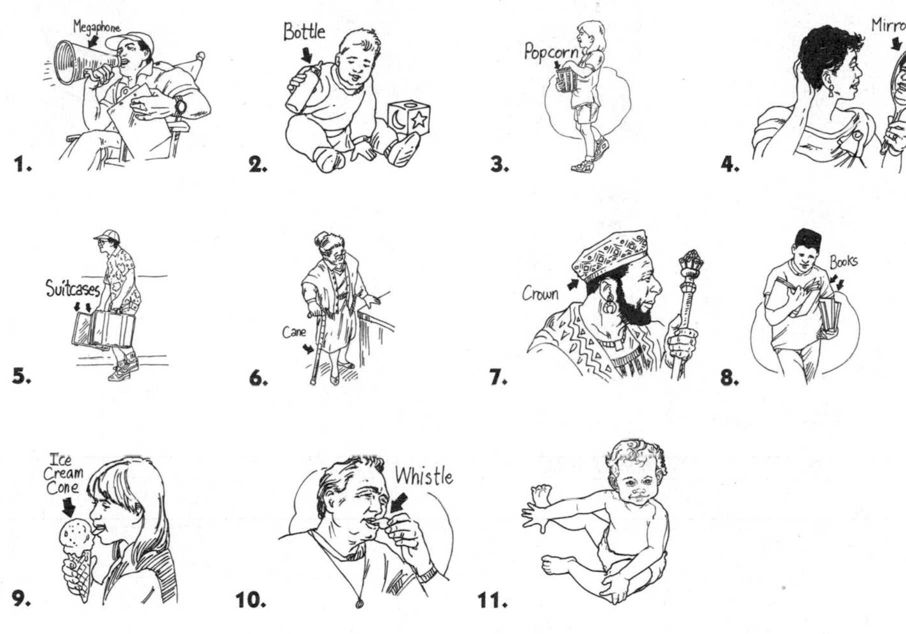

Exercise 2

All the necessary vocabulary is given here to facilitate the matching. Ss can do this individually and check their sentences as a class. (Note: there is no chair for the baby in # 11!)

VARIATION

Have Ss discuss this exercise in pairs to reinforce the structure orally.

ANSWER KEY

Exercise 2

2. The baby with the bottle sits in chair G.
3. The girl with the popcorn sits in chair C.
4. The woman with the mirror sits in chair D.
5. The man with the suitcases sits in chair H.
6. The woman with the cane sits in chair I.
7. The man with the crown sits in chair A.
8. The boy with the books sits in chair F.
9. The girl with the ice cream sits in chair J.
10. The man with the whistle sits in chair E.

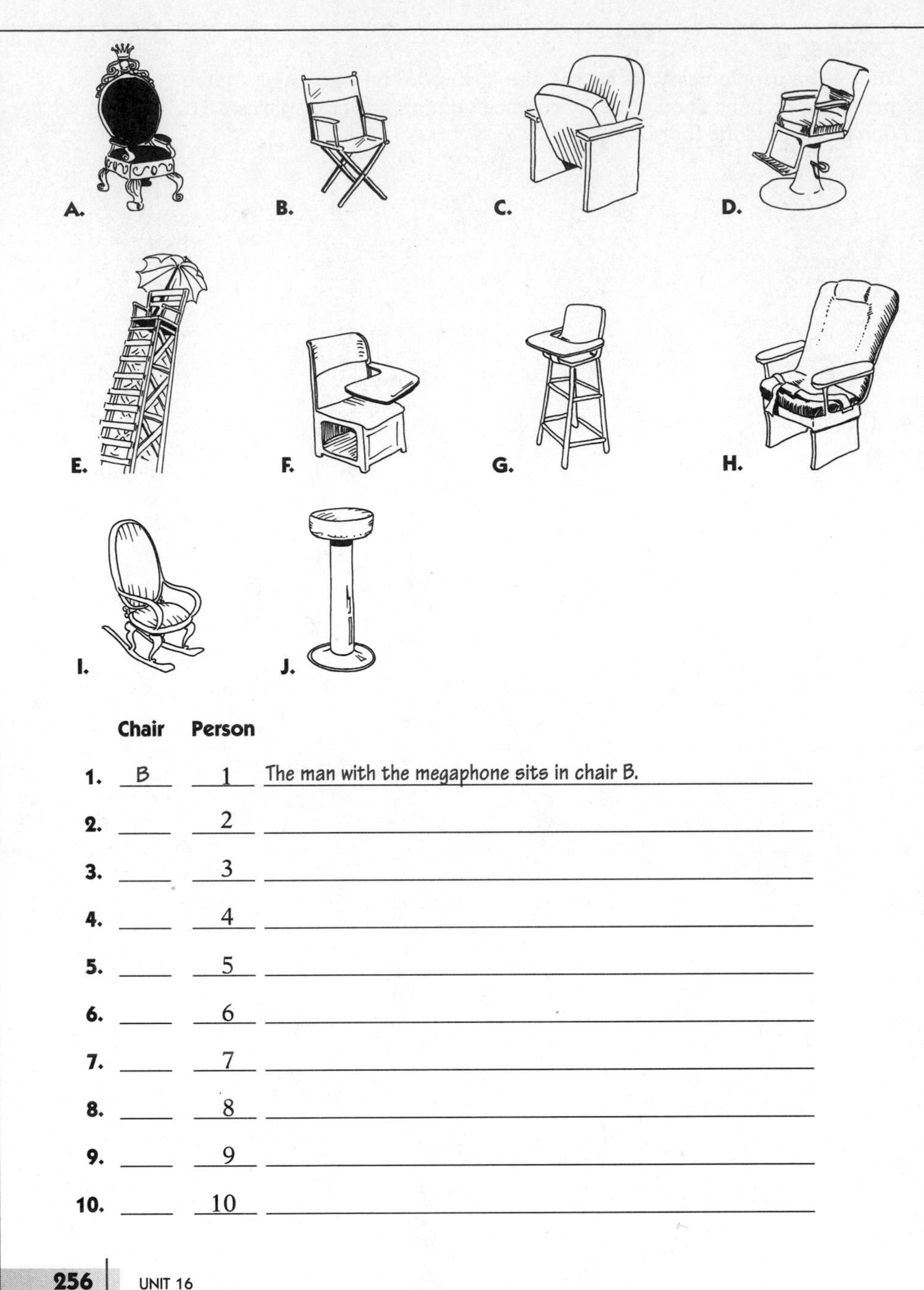

	Chair	Person	
1.	B	1	The man with the megaphone sits in chair B.
2.		2	
3.		3	
4.		4	
5.		5	
6.		6	
7.		7	
8.		8	
9.		9	
10.		10	

256 UNIT 16

EXERCISE 3

Combine each of the sentence pairs into one sentence using an adjective phrase. Then find the person in the picture and write the number of your sentence on the person.

Kindergarten Chaos

1. The girl has a bow in her hair. She is kicking her partner.
   The girl with the bow in her hair is kicking her partner.
2. The boy has a striped shirt and black pants. He is throwing a paper airplane across the room.
   ____
3. The girls are near the window. They are waving to their friends outside.
   ____
4. The boy is in a baseball uniform. He is standing on the teacher's desk.
   ____

Exercise 3

Ss can do this exercise individually and check their combined sentences, or do it in pairs.

Focus on the article shift from ***a*** to ***the*** when the sentences are combined. Example: *The boy is in **a** baseball uniform. He is standing on the teacher's desk = The boy in **the** baseball uniform is standing...* (There is only one boy in a baseball uniform... That boy is standing on the teacher's desk.)

EXPANSION

Tell Ss to imagine that the principal has called all the parents and asked them to come pick up their children. Since the principal does not know all the children's names, each parent must identify his/her child by describing that child. Have Ss role-play. Example: *My child is the boy in the baseball uniform...*

Workbook Exs. 1,2, & 3, pp. 128–130. Answers: TE, pp. 537.

ANSWER KEY

Exercise 3

2. The boy in the striped shirt and black pants is throwing a paper airplane across the room. **3.** The girls near the window are waving to their friends outside. **4.** The boy in the baseball uniform is standing on the teacher's desk. **5.** The boys in the back of the room are fighting. **6.** The boy in the corner is reading. **7.** The boy in the closet is crying. **8.** The girl with the walkman is singing. **9.** The man with the rope around him is the new teacher. **10.** The man in the suit and tie is the school principal.

5. The boys are in the back of the room. They are fighting.

____

6. The boy is in the corner. He is reading.

____

7. The boy is in the closet. He is crying.

____

8. The girl has a Walkman. She is singing.

____

9. The man has a rope around him. He is the new teacher.

____

10. The man is in a suit and tie. He is the school principal.

____

FOCUS **2**

Questions with *Which*

EXAMPLES	EXPLANATIONS
(a) **Which** woman is wearing a white coat? the school nurse (b) **Which** teachers are women? the coach and the art teacher	Use *which* when there is a choice between two or more people or things.
(c) **Which** coat do you like, Mom? I like the black **one**. (d) **Which** shoes do you like, Dad? the brown **ones**	Substitute the words *one* or *ones* for nouns so you do not repeat the noun.
(e) **Which** shoes do you want? the ones **in the window**	You can also use adjective phrases after *one* and *ones*.

FOCUS 2

Have Ss read the examples and explanations. To reinforce this structure, come back to either the Opening Task or Exercise 2. Have Ss ask each other questions with ***which*** and answer them using adjective phrases. Model an example or two with a student.

Example:

1. ***Q:*** *Which teacher is the coach?*

A: The woman with the stopwatch (is the coach).

2. ***Q:*** *Which man sits in the lifeguard's chair?*

A: The one with the whistle (sits in the lifeguard's chair).

Exercise 4

VARIATIONS

1. Have Ss write each *which* question and answer.
2. Have Ss role-play the entire telephone call. Record them and replay the tape to focus on the target structure, pronunciation, stress, and intonation.

EXERCISE 4

Julie's house was robbed. She is very upset, and is talking to her husband on the phone, describing the damage. Work with a partner. Find the differences between the pictures. You say Julie's statements. Your partner is the husband, and asks questions to get more specific information.

▶ **EXAMPLE:** **Julie:** The window is broken.

Husband: Which window?

Julie: The one over the kitchen sink.

BEFORE

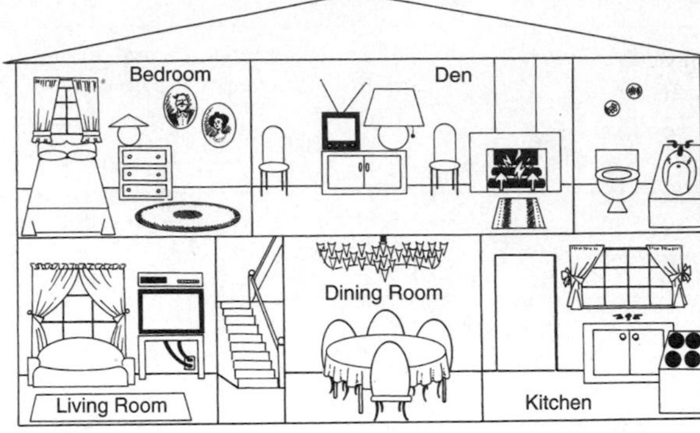

AFTER

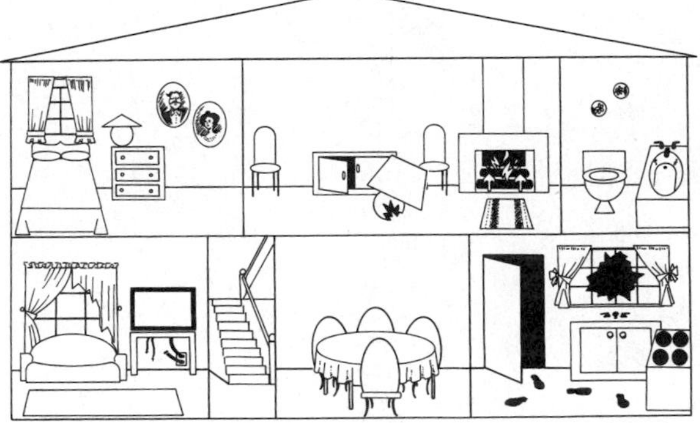

1. The floor is dirty.
2. The curtains are torn.
3. The TV is missing.
4. The door is open.
5. The lamp is broken.
6. The VCR is missing.
7. The cabinet is empty.
8. The rug is missing.
9. The chandelier is gone.

ANSWER KEY

Exercise 4

1. Which floor is dirty?/the one in the kitchen 2. Which curtains are torn?/the ones in the living room 3. Which TV is missing?/the one in the den 4. Which door is open?/the one in the kitchen 5. Which lamp is broken?/the one in the den 6. Which VCR is missing?/The one in the living room 7. Which cabinet is empty?/the one in the den 8. Which rug is missing?/the one in the bedroom 9. Which chandelier is gone?/the one in the dining room.

FOCUS **3**

Another, The Other, Other(s), The Other(s)

	ADJECTIVE	PRONOUN	MEANING
A: I'm hungry. B: Here. Have a cookie. A: I am still hungry. Can I have **another** cookie? (Can I have **another**?)	**another** cookie	**another**	one more cookie; one more from a group
B: There are no more cookies in the box. A: There are two **other boxes** in the closet. (There are two **others** in the closet.)	**other** boxes	**others**	more than one more
A: I found one box. Where is **the other box**? (Where is **the other**?) B: **The other box** is behind it.	**the other** box	**the other**	the one you spoke about; the last one in a group
A: How many more cookies can I have? B: You can have one more. **The other cookies** are for me! (**The others** are for me!)	**the other** cookies	**the others**	the ones you spoke about; the last ones in a group

FOCUS 3

1. Emphasize the two important distinctions in this focus box:
   A. Another is used with singular nouns. Other is used with plural nouns
   B. Another is nonspecific; it can refer to ***any*** other ...
   Example: *I want to learn another language.*
   The other is specific, unique; it is used when the noun is the ***only other*** one, or when speaker and listener both know what is being referred to.
   Example: *There are two languages I want to learn. One is Spanish; the other is Korean.*
2. Have Ss read the examples aloud.

Exercise 5

Ss can do Exercise 5 individually or in pairs.

SUGGESTIONS

1. Since Exercises 5, 6, and 8 deal with extraterrestrial life, preface Exercise 5 with a short discussion of life on other planets, how Ss imagine it, and what questions they would ask someone from another planet. This discussion will also prepare Ss for Exercise 9.
2. Have Ss role-play the dialogue.

EXPANSION

Check to see if Ss understand the humor in the pun "intelligent life on Earth," or in the gentle mocking of American culture in these exercises:

a. American consumerism: "Americans like to buy things."

b. America's love/hate relationship with its lawyers:
Thor: "We don't have any lawyers, I'm happy to say."
Soaprah: "That sounds great to me too!"

c. The TV talk show host's obligation to pause for commercials: "Let's stop for a station break." As a follow-up, bring in some simple lawyer jokes for Ss to tell each other, and videos of TV commercial breaks for Ss to use as listening comprehension practice.

EXERCISE 5

Thor is visiting Earth from another planet. Ed Toppil interviews Thor on television. Fill in the blanks with *another, the other, other(s),* or *the other(s).*

Ed: We on Earth are really excited to know there is (1) ______________ planet out there, Thor. Many of us know there are (2) ______________, but we are not able to find them. Do you know of any (3) ______________ planets?

Thor: Yes, we do. We know two (4) ______________: Limbix and Cardiax. I have photos of the people from both of (5) ______________ planets.

The Limbix are the ones on the left. The Cardiax are (6) ______________ ones. We also now know the planet Earth. We are sure there are (7) ______________ out there, but (8) ______________ are very far away.

Ed: I am surprised that you speak English so well, Thor. Do the Thoraxes have (9) ______________ language too?

Thor: Yes, of course. We speak Thoracic, but English is a universal language, you know, so we all learn it in school. People on (10) ______________ two planets speak English too!

Ed: So what brings you to Earth?

Thor: Well, Ed, we are looking for (11) ______________ intelligent beings in the universe.

Ed: On Earth?!! I don't know if you can find many intelligent beings on Earth, Thor! But we can discuss this at (12) ______________ time. Right now, let's stop for a station break.

ANSWER KEY

Exercise 5

1. another **2.** others **3.** other **4.** others **5.** the other **6.** the other **7.** others **8.** the others **9.** another **10.** the other **11.** other **12.** another

EXERCISE 6

Thor tours America. Fill in *another, other(s),* or the *other(s).*

1. **Ed:** You only have one tie, Thor. You need to buy (a) ______________ one.
   Thor: Why?
   Ed: Because Americans are consumers. They like to buy things.
   Thor: But I don't like any (b) ______________ ties here.
   Ed: O.K. Look at (c) ______________ over there. Maybe you can find (d) ______________ one.

2. Thor is in a candy store with a child:
   Thor: Which candy is good here?
   Child: This one is good, but first taste (a) ______________ one in the brown and green paper. It's out of this world!
   Thor: Hmmmm, excellent. Is it O.K. to take (b) ______________ one?

3. **Soaprah:** So, Thor, tell us about your family. Are you married?
   Thor: Yes. I am, and I have two children. One is a specialist in interplanetary communication and (a) ______________ owns a spaceship factory.
   Soaprah: And what does your wife do?
   Thor: My wife is a spaceship pilot.
   Soaprah: What about (b) ______________ people on Thorax? What do they do?
   Thor: (c) ______________ do different jobs. We have doctors, teachers, artists, and so on. We don't have any tax collectors.
   Soaprah: Are there any (d) ______________ professions you don't have?
   Thor: We don't have any lawyers, I'm happy to say.
   Soaprah: That sounds great to me too!
   Thor: Do you have any (e) ______________ questions?
   Soaprah: I have a million (f) ______________ questions! But our time is up. It was nice meeting you, Thor. Thanks so much for coming.

Exercise 6

Ss can do this exercise individually and then role-play the dialogues.

VARIATION

For these three mini-interviews, break Ss up so that at least two pairs are working on the same interview. Have Ss read their interviews aloud and check with each other.

EXPANSION

Encourage Ss to make up their own potential interviews with people from other planets. To do so, they need either to pinpoint an aspect of American culture or to choose an aspect of their own native culture that they want to poke fun at.

Workbook Ex. 6, p. 132.
Answers: TE, p. 537.

ANSWER KEY

Exercise 6

1. a. another b. other c. the others d. another 2. a. the other b. another 3. a. the other b. the other c. The others d. other e. other f. other

FOCUS 4

Point out:

1. the difference in formality between ***rather*** and ***pretty***
   Example: The teacher says: *This exam is rather difficult.*
   A student says: *That test is pretty hard!*
2. the possible use of ***very*** in negative contexts
   Example: *Studying English the night before a test isn't a very good idea.*
3. the position of ***quite***
   Example: *You are quite a good class. You learn fast.*
4. the difference between ***quite*** (intensifier) and ***quiet*** (adjective)
   Example: *He is quite a good writer, but he is very quiet in class.* Emphasize the difference in pronunciation as well: *quite* has one syllable, *quiet* has two.

FOCUS **4**

Intensifiers

Intensifiers are words that make adjectives more or less strong.

SUBJECT	*BE*	INTENSIFIER	ADJECTIVE
(a) Earth	is	very	beautiful.
(b) The people on Thorax	are	quite	similar.
(c) The people on Earth	are	rather/pretty* fairly	different.
(d) Thorax	isn't	very**	beautiful.

Pretty has the same meaning as rather, but is very informal.
**Very* is the only intensifier we use in negative sentences.

SUBJECT	*BE*	ARTICLE	INTENSIFIER	ADJECTIVE	NOUN
(e) Earth	is	a	very	special	place.
(f) Thorax	is	a	rather/pretty* fairly	small	planet.
(g) Thorax	isn't	a	very**	attractive	place.

SUBJECT	*BE*	INTENSIFIER	ARTICLE	ADJECTIVE	NOUN
(h) Thorax	is	quite	a	small	planet.

EXERCISE 7

Test Thor's knowledge. How many of the objects can Thor (and you) guess?

1. This is fairly long and thin.
   People eat it.
   It is very popular in Italy.
   What is it? ______________________

2. This is a liquid.
   People usually drink it hot.
   They like its rather strong, rich smell.
   It's brown.
   What is it? ______________________

3. This is an electrical appliance.
   It is quite common in people's homes.
   Sometimes it is very hot.
   You put bread into it.
   What is it? ______________________

4. This is very cold.
   It's also pretty hard.
   People put it in drinks on hot days.
   It's quite slippery.
   What is it? ______________________

5. This is quite a big metal box.
   It's electrical and pretty practical.
   It's very useful in tall buildings.
   People go inside the box.
   The box goes up and down.
   What is it? ______________________

6. This is a very popular piece of plastic.
   It isn't very big.
   With it, we can buy rather expensive things without cash.
   What is it? ______________________

Exercise 7

Ss can do this exercise individually or in pairs. If they work in pairs, have one student read and the other guess the object. Have them alternate, reading and guessing four descriptions each.

EXPANSION

Have each pair write their own descriptions for the class to guess. (Activity 6, which is similar to this exercise, can be done now as a follow-up, or later, if you prefer to go in order).

ANSWER KEY

Exercise 7

1. spaghetti 2. coffee 3. a toaster
4. ice 5. an elevator 6. a credit card
7. chocolate 8. a rainbow

7. There are different kinds of candy.
All of them are good.
But this one is very special.
It comes in brown or white.
It's pretty fattening.
It's quite delicious.
What is it? ______________

8. This thing is quite colorful.
It isn't very common.
It sometimes follows rainstorms.
It is quite a beautiful sight.
What is it? ______________

EXERCISE 8

Ed Toppil continues his interview with Thor. Write an intensifier in each blank. There is more than one possible answer.

Ed: So tell me, Thor, what do you think of our planet?

Thor: Well, Earth is a beautiful planet, but it's (1) ___quite___ a strange place. Many of your leaders are not doing a (2) ________ good job. Some people on Earth are (3) ________ rich. Others are (4) ________ poor. There can be a (5) ________ big difference between people. On Thorax, we are all equal. Money isn't (6) ________ important. Learning is (7) ________ important. That's why we're visiting Earth. Your knowledge can be (8) ________ useful to us. Also, your art and music are (9) ________ beautiful.

Ed: That's (10) ________ interesting. I'm sure we can learn many (11) ________ useful and exciting things from you, too, Thor.

Exercise 8

Many of these sentences have more than one answer, except those with ***quite a*** + ***intensifier*** + ***noun***, and those with ***very*** in a negative context.

ANSWER KEY

Exercise 8
2. very **3.** very/rather/quite **4.** very/rather/quite **5.** very/rather/fairly **6.** very **7.** very/rather/quite **8.** very/rather/quite **9.** very/rather/quite **10.** very/rather/quite **11.** very/rather/quite

EXERCISE 9

How necessary or important is each item to you? Give your opinion using intensifiers. Explain your answers.

▶ **EXAMPLE:** a cellular phone

A cellular phone is very important to me. I can call my friends anytime I want.

1. a computer
2. a life partner
3. a driver's license
4. a university degree
5. children
6. good health
7. a beautiful planet
8. the Internet
9. art and music
10. friends
11. free time
12. a good leader for my country

EXERCISE 10

Read the statements and comments. Fill in an intensifier in each blank. Sometimes, there can be more than one possible answer.

	Statement	Comment
1.	I want to see the movie "Psycho."	Don't! That's a _______ scary movie!
2.	She's planning a birthday party for me.	That's _______ a nice thing to do.
3.	Do you still watch talk shows on TV?	Yes, I do. They're _______ interesting programs.
4.	I like this restaurant very much.	Me too! This is _______ a delicious dinner.
5.	My friends want to stay up all night.	That's not a _______ good idea.
6.	He's working in Vietnam.	Really! That's _______ a fascinating place!
7.	They have eight children.	Wow! That's a _______ large family.
8.	Eric and Tina are doing well in my class.	In mine too. They're _______ bright students.
9.	I'm bored again today.	I'm afraid this is not a _______ exciting vacation.
10.	Do you know Newport, Rhode Island?	Oh, yes. The mansions in Newport are _______ big—just like castles.

Exercise 9

Answers to this exercise will vary.

VARIATION

Add items to this list that are relevant to your particular population. For example: good health, free time, a university degree, children, a life partner, etc.

EXPANSION

Encourage Ss to elaborate by providing clear, detailed reasons for their answers. Example: *A good leader is quite important. A good leader cares about people and the environment.*

Exercise 10

Ss can do these dyads individually or in pairs. If they work individually, have them read the dyads aloud for pratice with stress, intonation, and pronunciation.

Workbook Ex. 7, pp. 133–134.
Answers: TE, p. 537.

ANSWER KEY

Exercise 10

Some of these responses may vary, except for ***quite a*** and ***very*** in negative contexts.
1. pretty/rather/very **2.** quite **3.** pretty/rather/very **4.** quite **5.** very **6.** quite **7.** rather/pretty/very **8.** fairly/rather/pretty/very **9.** very **10.** pretty/rather/very/quite

USE YOUR ENGLISH

For a more complete discussion of how to implement the Use Your English Activities, see p. xxvi of this Teacher's Edition.

Activity 1

1. Model this activity by bringing in a map of your own native country, city, town, or a place you know well. Describe this place using adjective phrases.
2. Then ask Ss to write their sentences, working either individually or in small groups with people from the same place. Check their sentences and have Ss do mini-presentations for the class.

Activity 2

Have Ss write on small strips of paper. Collect these and put them in a hat or a box. Have each student pick one (or several) to read aloud. The class will guess who it is.

Use Your English

ACTIVITY 1: WRITING/SPEAKING

STEP 1 Write ten sentences that give information about your home country or city.

▶ **EXAMPLES:** The beaches in the south are very beautiful.

The market in the center of the city is always crowded.

The coffee in Brazil is delicious.

STEP 2 Now tell the class about your country or city.

ACTIVITY 2: WRITING/SPEAKING

STEP 1 In a group, write sentences about ten students in the class. Use adjective phrases. Do not use names.

STEP 2 Read your sentences to the class. The class guesses the person you are talking about.

▶ **EXAMPLES:** The student from Bogotá has pretty eyes.

The student next to Miyuki wears glasses.

The student with the big smile is from Ecuador.

ACTIVITY 3: SPEAKING/WRITING

STEP 1 Check (✔) the adjectives that describe you, and write *very/quite/rather/pretty/fairly/not very* under **You** in the chart below.

STEP 2 Ask your partner questions to find out which adjectives describe him or her. Then ask questions with how and write *very/quite/rather/pretty/fairly/not very* under **Your Partner** in the same chart.

▶ **EXAMPLE:** **You ask:** Are you shy?

Your partner answers: Yes, I am.

You ask: How shy are you?

Your partner answers: I'm very shy.

	You		Your Partner	
Adjective		**very quite rather pretty fairly not very**		**very quite rather pretty fairly not very**
				very
shy				
lazy				
quiet				
romantic				
friendly				
old-fashioned				
organized				
jealous				
talkative				
athletic				
healthy				

Activity 3

SUGGESTIONS

1. In Step 1, have Ss generate more adjectives to add to this list.
2. In Step 2, encourage Ss to elaborate on their statements. Example: *I'm very organized. I make "To Do" lists every day.* This elaboration will give them more to write about in Activity 4.
3. To recycle adverbs of manner (Unit 12), give Ss certain common expressions with these adjectives. Examples: *insanely jealous, incurably romantic, painfully shy*.

Activity 4

Depending on how much information Ss got in Activity 3, they can do this either at the sentence level or as a short paragraph. If Ss can do this at the paragraph level, take time out to focus on topic/support and coherence.

Example: *My partner is very healthy. He has pretty good eating habits. He's quite athletic ... etc..*

Activity 5 

This activity is similar to Exercise 9, but different in that this is a consensus-building activity that will require much more discussion.

1. Have Ss work in small groups to select the ten most necessary people. Give Ss useful discussion strategies such as agreeing, disagreeing, asking for an opinion, asking for clarification, etc.
2. Then regroup them into larger groups, until all Ss in the class have reached a consensus on the ten people. This will provide Ss with an excellent opportunity to negotiate meaning.

Activity 6  

Ss can select everyday objects or objects of cultural significance. Go around helping pairs or groups with descriptive adjectives. This is a good time to practice circumlocution strategies: they explain to you what they are trying to say; you provide the necessary language.

ACTIVITY 4: WRITING

Use the information in Activity 3 to write five sentences about you or about your partner using *very/quite/rather/pretty/fairly/not very.*

▶ **EXAMPLE:** My partner is a very romantic person. He is pretty old-fashioned, and he is very jealous.

ACTIVITY 5: SPEAKING

Imagine you are starting life on a new planet. Look at the list of people. Then choose only ten people to move to the new planet. Say how necessary each one is and why. Say why the others are not necessary and why

▶ **EXAMPLE:** A doctor is very necessary because we need to stay healthy.

an actor	an artist	a police officer	a political leader
a scientist	a religious leader	a young man	a young woman
a historian	a writer	a musician	a lawyer
a farmer	a teacher	a journalist	a pilot
a doctor	a mechanic	a computer specialist	a dancer
a military person	a stockbroker	an elderly person	an engineer

ACTIVITY 6: WRITING/SPEAKING

Write descriptions of objects using intensifiers like those in Exercise 7. Test your classmates' knowledge of these objects.

ACTIVITY 7: LISTENING/ SPEAKING 

STEP 1 Listen to the three descriptions. Write each name under the correct picture.

______ ______ ______

STEP 2 Work in a group. Each student draws a face. Then, the student describes the face to the rest of the group. The rest of the group draws what the student describes.

Activity 7 

Play textbook audio. The tapescript for this listening appears on p. 547 of this book.

The test for this unit can be found on pp. 495–496 of this book. The answers can be found on p. 497.

Unit 17

UNIT OVERVIEW

The past tense is first introduced here with the past tense of the verb *be*. The general theme of this unit is famous people and events in the past; the mini-theme is texts of different genres: fairy tales, detective stories, personal narrative, and adventure stories. To support this theme, bring in realia from magazines like *Life*, children's fairy tales, detective stories, etc.

UNIT GOALS

To maximize the diagnostic potential of the Opening Task, do not review the Unit Goals with students (Ss) until after they have completed and reviewed the Opening Task.

OPENING TASK
SETTING UP THE TASK

Discuss the meaning of memory, and of the words in the "Occupation" column.

UNIT 17

PAST TENSE OF BE

UNIT GOALS:

- To make affirmative and negative statements with the verb *be* in the past tense
- To ask and answer *yes/no* and *wh*-questions with *be* in the past tense

OPENING TASK
Test Your Memory

Look at the photos and the information about famous people from the past. Make statements about each person. Correct any facts that are not true.

	Nationality	Occupation
1. Martin Luther King, Jr.	African	civil rights leader
2. The Beatles	British	hairdressers
3. Diana	American	actress

ANSWER KEY

Opening Task

1. Martin Luther King wasn't African. He was African-American. He was a civil rights leader. 2. The Beatles were British. They weren't hairdressers. They were singers/a rock group. 3. Princess Diana wasn't American. She was British. She was a British Princess and the wife of Prince Charles. 4. Mahatma Gandhi was Indian. He wasn't a rock singer. He was a political leader. 5. Pierre and Marie Curie were French. They weren't fashion designers. They were scientists. 6. Mao Zedong was Chinese. He was a political leader in the People's Republic of China. 7. Jacqueline Kennedy Onassis wasn't Greek. She was American. She was the wife of John F. Kennedy, president of the U. S., and later of Aristotle Onassis, who was a Greek millionaire. She wasn't a millionaire. 8. Washington, Jefferson, Lincoln, and Roosevelt weren't Canadian. They were American presidents. Their heads are on Mt. Rushmore in South Dakota.

	Nationality	Occupation
4. Mahatma Gandhi	Indian	rock singer
5. Pierre and Marie Curie	French	fashion designers
6. Mao Zedong	Chinese	political leader
7. Jacqueline Kennedy Onassis	Greek	millionaire
8. George Washington, Thomas Jefferson, Abraham Lincoln, Theodore Roosevelt	Canadian	presidents

CONDUCTING THE TASK

Since this task is brief, it can be done as a class. Choose one person you think Ss will know. Elicit statements about this person from the class. Write them on the board. Group Ss' statements on the board by error type: affirmative, negative, article use, etc. Return to these statements when you introduce the form in Focus 1.

VARIATION

Put Ss in multinational groups so they can rely on each other's background knowledge. Walk around and listen. Take notes on statements they make and put them on the board by error type.

REVIEWING THE TASK

SUGGESTIONS

1. Go over the statements on the board. Check first to see that all statements give accurate information. Then analyze the grammar Ss used. If Ss have generated both affirmative and negative statements, do Focuses 1 and 2 together; then do Exercises 1–5. Otherwise, do each focus and set of exercises in a step-by-step manner.
2. Have a representative from each group make statements about the people in the Opening Task and write them on the board. Since the first focus box deals with affirmative statements, present the affirmative form first and have Ss do Exercises 1 and 2. If Ss also produce negative statements, either keep these statements up on one side of the board to deal with later, or present the negative as well.

FOCUS 1

1. Have Ss read the affirmative statements in the box. Point out the similarity between the past form of *be* and the present form. Point out that there are no contractions for *be* in the simple past affirmative. *He was famous*. NOT: *He's famous*.
2. Ss have already seen *there* + *be* in Unit 7. Reiterate that *there* is used for describing and for showing the existence or location of something that represents new information.

Exercise 1

Have Ss do this exercise individually.

FOCUS **1**

FORM

Past Tense of *Be:* Affirmative Statements

SUBJECT	VERB	
I	was	famous.
You	were	
He She It	was	
We You They	were	
There There	was were	a famous actress in that film. many political leaders at the meeting.

EXERCISE 1

Use the past tense of *be* to make correct statements about the famous people in the Opening Task.

1. The Beatles ______________ a famous British rock group in the 1960s.
2. Mahatma Gandhi ______________ a nationalist and Hindu religious leader in India.
3. Marie and Pierre Curie ______________ French scientists.
4. Mao Zedong ______________ a revolutionary and political leader in the People's Republic of China.
5. George Washington, Thomas Jefferson, Abraham Lincoln, and Theodore Roosevelt ______________ presidents of the United States.
6. Martin Luther King, Jr. ______________ an American civil rights leader.
7. Diana ______________ a British princess, the wife of Prince Charles.
8. Jacqueline Kennedy Onassis ______________ the wife of president John F. Kennedy, and then, of Aristotle Onassis, a Greek millionaire.

ANSWER KEY

Exercise 1

1. were 2. was 3. were 4. was
5. were 6. was 7. was 8. was

EXERCISE 2

Fill in the blanks in the postcard. Use *be* in the simple past.

Dear Grandma and Grandpa,

Here we are in Florida. What a place! Yesterday we (1) ___________ at Disneyworld all day. The sun (2) ___________ really strong and it (3) ___________ very hot. The lines (4) ___________ long, but the rides and the shows (5) ___________ fun. Disneyworld (6) ___________ crowded, but all the people (7) ___________ friendly and polite. Our favorite place (8) ___________ Cinderella's palace! The fireworks at night (9) ___________ beautiful! It (10) ___________ great for us, but Dad (11) ___________ really hot and tired at the end of the day!

We miss you! See you soon.

Love, Melanie and Michele

Grandma and Grandpa Henner
Homestead Lane
Harvard, MA 01451

Exercise 2

Before doing the exercise, ask Ss if they have ever been to Disneyworld or Disneyland and what they thought about it. Have them *skim* the postcard: ask who wrote the card and whom they were writing to.

Workbook Exs. 1 & 2, pp. 135–136.
Answers: TE, p. 537.

ANSWER KEY

Exercise 2

1. were 2. was 3. was 4. were
5. were 6. was 7. were 8. was
9. were 10. was 11. was

FOCUS 2

Go over the focus box. Have Ss read the sentences aloud. Point out that, as in present tense, the negative with NOT is more emphatic.

FOCUS 2 FORM

Past Tense of *Be*: Negative Statements

SUBJECT	*BE + NOT*		NEGATIVE CONTRACTIONS		
I	was not	famous.	I	wasn't	famous.
You	were not		You	weren't	
He She It	was not		He She It	wasn't	
We You They	were not		We You They	weren't	
There	was	no time to eat	There	wasn't	any time to eat.
There	were	no good restaurants	There	weren't	any good restaurants.

276 UNIT 17

EXERCISE 3

How do Michael and Carol remember their trip to Disneyworld? Fill in the blanks with the affirmative or negative of *be* in the simple past. Then read the dialogue aloud.

Alice: Oh, hi, Michael. Hi, Carol. How (1) ___was___ your trip to Disneyworld last week?

Carol: Hi, Alice. Oh, it (2) ______ fun.

Michael: Fun! That vacation (3) ______ (not) fun, it (4) ______ terrible!

Carol: But Michael, how can you say that? I think the children and I (5) ______ very satisfied with our vacation.

Michael: Carol, the weather (6) ______ boiling hot.

Carol: It (7) ______ (not) boiling hot, it (8) ______ very comfortable.

Michael: The food (9) ______ (not) very good . . .

Carol: The food (10) ______ fine, Michael.

Michael: The people (11) ______ (not) friendly.

Carol: Of course, they (12) ______ friendly.

Michael: The kids (13) ______ very difficult.

Carol: The kids (14) ______ (not) difficult, Michael. Come on, they (15) ______ great.

Exercise 3

EXPANSION

Have Ss read the dialogue aloud. Correct negatives and contractions. Work on intonation, especially because of the argumentative nature of this interaction.

ANSWER KEY

Exercise 3

2. was 3. wasn't/was not 4. was 5. were 6. was 7. wasn't/was not 8. was 9. wasn't/was not 10. was 11. weren't/were not 12. were 13. were 14. wern't/were not 15. were

Exercise 4

1. Explain the idea of "positive" (optimistic) people and "negative" (pessimistic) people. Use an example relative to your class. Example: *Elena is always happy; she is a very positive person.*
2. Go over time expressions: last summer, yesterday ...

EXPANSION

To make this exercise more open-ended, encourage Ss to make additional statements about the situations given, or to add situations to this list. Encourage them to use other adjectives as well (*The food was awful/overcooked/bland/tasty. The music was sensational.*). After checking the exercise with Ss, ask them to judge themselves as positive or negative people.

Exercise 5

SUGGESTIONS

1. Bring in a children's picture book to familiarize Ss with the Cinderella story.
2. Elicit what Ss know about the story and provide them with some key vocabulary.

Workbook Exs. 3 & 4, pp. 136–138.
Answers: TE, pp. 537–538

EXERCISE 4

A positive person sees the world in a positive way and believes that good things will happen. A negative person usually sees only the bad things in life. Make sentences using *was/were* for the situations below. These adjectives may help you. Use other adjectives you know.

terrible	ugly	romantic	small
rude	friendly	sunny	rainy
delicious	beautiful	polite	spacious
fantastic	loud		

Situation	A positive person says:	A negative person says:
1. Yesterday evening, you were at a restaurant with friends.	a. The place was romantic. c. The food ________. e. The waiters ________.	b. The place was ugly. d. The food ________. f. The waiters ________.
2. Last Saturday, you went to a disco.	a. The music ________. c. The dance floor ________.	b. The music ________. d. The dance floor ________.
3. Last summer, you were on vacation with your friends.	a. The weather ________. c. The scenery ________.	b. The weather ________. d. The scenery ________.

EXERCISE 5

Do you remember the story *Cinderella?* Fill in the blanks with the affirmative or negative form of *be.*

Once upon a time, there (1) ______________ a young woman named Cinderella. She (2) ______________ rich, but she (3) ______________ very beautiful and kind. Her two stepsisters (4) ______________ beautiful. They (5) ______________ jealous of Cinderella. Cinderella's stepmother (6) ______________ good to her.

One day, there (7) ______________ a ball for the Prince at the King's palace. . . .

ANSWER KEY

Exercise 4

Answers will vary. Possible answers are:
1. **c.** was delicious **d.** was terrible **e.** were polite/friendly **f.** were rude
2. **a.** was fantastic **b.** was loud/bad **d.** was spacious **e.** was small/crowded
3. **a.** was sunny **b.** was rainy **c.** was beautiful **d.** was ugly/not interesting

Exercise 5

1. was 2. wasn't 3. was 4. weren't 5. were 6. wasn't 7. was

FOCUS **3**

Yes/No Questions and Short Answers with *Be* in the Simple Past

***YES/NO* QUESTIONS** Verb	Subject		**SHORT ANSWERS** Affirmative		Negative	
Was	I	right?	Yes,	you were.	No,	you were not. you weren't.
Were	you			I was.		I was not. I wasn't.
Was	he she it			he she it was.		he/she/it was not he/she/it wasn't.
Were	we you they			you we they were.		you/we they were not. you/we they weren't.
Was there any good food at Disneyworld?			Yes,	there was.	No, No,	there was not. there wasn't.
Were there long lines at Disneyworld?			Yes,	there were.	No, No,	there were not. there weren't.

EXERCISE 6

Detective Furlock Humes is questioning a police officer about a crime. Fill in the blanks with *there* + *be* in the simple past.

EXAMPLES: ___Was there___ a crime last night?

___Yes, there were___ several police officers at the house.

Police Officer: The body was here, Detective Humes.

Furlock: (1) ______________ a weapon?

Police Officer: Yes, (2) ______________ a gun next to the body.

Furlock: (3) ______________ any fingerprints on the gun?

Police Officer: No, sir, (4) ______________ .

FOCUS 3

SUGGESTIONS

1. To work inductively, use the realia suggested in the Unit Overview. Bring in pictures from special editions of *Life* magazine and ask questions about past events. Or bring in books of children's fairy tales and ask questions about the stories. See if Ss can ask questions about these pictures and give short answers.
2. To work deductively, have Ss study the chart, and then read the questions with *was* and *were* aloud. Encourage Ss to ask additional questions. *Was Minh absent last week? Were you late to class this morning*? Make sure Ss give short answers.

Exercise 6 

EXPANSION

Have pairs practice the dialogue aloud. Work on the rising intonation of yes/no questions.

ANSWER KEY

Exercise 6

1. Was there 2. there was 3. Were there 4. There weren't 5. Was there 6. Were there 7. There was 8. there were

Furlock: (5) _______________ any motive for this crime?

Police Officer: We don't know, sir.

Furlock: How about witnesses? (6) _______________ any witnesses to the crime?

Police Officer: Yes, sir. (7) _______________ one witness—a neighbor. She said (8) _______________ loud noises in the apartment at midnight.

Furlock: Where is she? Bring her to me . . .

Exercise 7  

Ss can work with partners or in groups to help each other try to answer the questions. Have a few Ss write their questions on the board so the whole class can check.

Workbook Ex. 4, p. 138.
Answers: TE, p. 538

EXERCISE 7

Ask your classmates *yes/no* questions about the events below. Give short answers. Correct the facts if necessary.

▶ **EXAMPLE:** Margaret Thatcher/the first female Prime Minister of Great Britain.

Was Margaret Thatcher the first female Prime Minister of Great Britain?

Yes, she was.

1. Tom Hanks/the first man to walk on the moon
2. AIDS/a known disease in 1949
3. Yugoslavia/a country in 1980
4. Europeans/the first people on the American continent
5. Nelson Mandela/in prison for many years in South Africa
6. The Wright Brothers/the first men to cross the Atlantic Ocean by plane
7. a big earthquake/in Kobe, Japan in 1995
8. any women/in the Olympic Games in 1920

ANSWER KEY

Exercise 7

1. Was Tom Hanks the first man to walk on the moon? No, he wasn't. Neil Armstrong was. 2. Was AIDS a known disease in 1949? No, it wasn't. 3. Was Yugoslavia a country in 1980? Yes, it was. 4. Were Europeans the first people on the American continent? No, they weren't. Indians/Native Americans were. 5. Was Nelson Mandela in prison for many years in South Africa? Yes, he was. 6. Were the Wright Brothers the first men to cross the Atlantic Ocean by plane? No , they weren't. 7. Was there a big earthquake in Kobe, Japan in 1995? Yes, there was. 8. Were there any women in the Olympic Games in 1920? No, there weren't.

FOCUS 4

Wh-Questions with *Be*

WH-QUESTION	*BE*	SUBJECT	ANSWERS
When		JFK's assassination?	November 22, 1963
Where		the assassination?	It was in Dallas, Texas.
Who	was	the assassin?	Lee Harvey Oswald, we think.
What		his motive?	There were different theories.
How		the day?	very sad
Why	were	people sad?	because Kennedy was a popular president
Whose gun	was	it?	Lee Harvey Oswald's

EXERCISE 8

Fill in the *wh*-question word and the correct form of *be* to complete each question.

Andrea: (1) ______________ you on the day of Kennedy's assassination?

Helene: I was in school. There was an announcement over the loud speaker.

Andrea: (2) ______________ you with at the time?

Helene: I was with my friend Patty.

Andrea: (3) ______________ it in school that day?

Helene: It was terrible. We were all very upset and silent.

Andrea: (4) ______________ you all silent?

Helene: because it was hard to believe he was dead.

Andrea: And at home? (5) ______________ things at home?

Helene: At home, things were very bad. My parents were in shock too.

Andrea: (6) ______________ their feelings after the assassination?

Helene: They were angry, sad, confused, and afraid.

FOCUS 4

SUGGESTIONS

1. To help contextualize Focus 4 and Exercise 8, bring photographs of John F. Kennedy during his presidency or photos of the assassination.
2. Cover the answers in Focus 4. Ask Ss the *wh*-questions in the box to see if they understand and can answer.
3. If your Ss are old enough (!), ask them where they were on November 22, 1963. If you are old enough, have Ss ask you the question as well!

Exercise 8

Have Ss do this exercise individually.

EXPANSIONS

1. Have Ss read the dialogue aloud. Work on the falling intonation of *wh*-questions.
2. If appropriate, have Ss discuss what people's reactions to this event were in their home countries and/or families.

ANSWER KEY

Exercise 8

1. Where were 2. Who(m) were 3. How was 4. Why were 5. How were 6. What were

Exercise 9 

Ss can do this exercise in pairs or in small groups. Ask Ss to describe the photograph and to guess where the climbers are. Have Ss write the questions on the board to do a final check.

EXERCISE 9

Look at the photo and write a *wh*-question for each answer.

1. ____?
   These people were mountain climbers.
2. ____?
   They were in the Himalayas.
3. ____?
   They were there for the adventure and the challenge.
4. ____?
   They were there in 1996.
5. ____?
   The name of the mountain was Mount Everest.
6. ____?
   It was their idea to take this trip.
7. ____?
   The trip was a disaster; eight people died on this trip.

ANSWER KEY

Exercise 9

1. Who were these people? 2. Where were they? 3. Why were they there? 4. When were they there? 5. What was the name of the mountain? 6. Whose idea was it to take this trip? 7. How was the trip?

EXERCISE 10

Work in a group. Take turns. One student makes a statement about last weekend. The other students ask questions. Use *wh*-questions and the past tense of *be*.

▶ **EXAMPLE:** **Statement:** I was at the movies on Saturday.
Questions: What was the movie? Who were you with?
Who was in the movie? How was the movie?

EXERCISE 11

Correct the mistakes in the following sentences.

1. Do was Mahatma Gandhi a Prime Minister?
2. The Beatles wasn't fashion designers.
3. Was hot the weather at Disneyworld last week?
4. Where the earthquake was in 1996?
5. Why the people were on Mount Everest?
6. Was good the service at the restaurant?
7. No was any good restaurants in Disneyworld.
8. How it was the trip to Disneyworld?

Exercise 10 

As an example, have one student come up in the front of the class and make a statement about last weekend. Elicit questions from all the Ss and write them on the board. Then let Ss do the exercise in groups.

VARIATION

Make this into a team competition by giving one point for each correct question each team makes. The team with the most points at the end wins.

Workbook Ex. 5, pp. 138–139.
Answers: TE, p. 538.

Exercise 11

Ss can do this individually or in pairs

UNIT GOAL REVIEW

Have Ss look at the goals on the opening page of the unit again. Help them understand how much they have accomplished in each area. Ask them if there are any questions they still have about what they have learned so far.

ANSWER KEY

Exercise 11

1. Was Mahatma Gandhi a Prime Minister?
2. The Beatles weren't fashion designers.
3. Was the weather hot at Disneyworld?
4. Where was the big earthquake in 1996?/ Where was there a big earthquake in 1996?
5. Why were the people on Mt. Everest?
6. Was the service good at the restaurant?
7. There weren't any good restaurants in Disneyworld.
8. How was the trip to Disneyworld?

USE YOUR ENGLISH

For a more complete discussion of how to use the activities, see p. xxvi of this Teacher's Edition.

Activity 1

1. Bring in a Cinderella storybook with illustrations to help Ss tell the story. As a pre-writing activity, elicit what Ss already know about the fairy tale and write vocabulary on the board.
2. Have Ss work in groups and write the end of the story on butcher block paper.
3. Post the stories around the room and use these to discuss features of writing (coherence, perhaps direct speech) and to do error correction.

Activity 2

Choose a time frame for this activity—last summer, last vacation, last winter, etc. Encourage Ss to prepare a variety of *wh*-questions in writing so you can check before they ask their partners the questions.

Activity 3

Collect Ss' writing. Evaluate their ability to write a focused, coherent, well-developed paragraph in correct English. Use their papers to focus on writing or grammar problems with the whole class. Have Ss revise and edit their paragraphs. Then ask them to select the two or three best ones. Give a prize for these.

Use Your English

ACTIVITY 1: WRITING/SPEAKING

Work with a partner. Finish writing the story of Cinderella in Exercise 5 (page 278). Then tell your stories to each other.

ACTIVITY 2: SPEAKING

Work with a partner. Ask your partner the questions below and other questions to find out about a special place he or she knows.

QUESTIONS: Where were you last summer? When were you there?
Why were you there? What was special about this place?
How was the weather? Were the people friendly? How was the food?

ACTIVITY 3: SPEAKING/WRITING

With the information from Activity 2, tell the class about your partner's special place, or write a paragraph about it.

▶ **EXAMPLE:** Last summer, my partner was in Greece. She was there with her friend. Greece was very beautiful and interesting.

ACTIVITY 4: SPEAKING

Work in a group.

STEP 1 Write the dates below on pieces of paper. Mix all the papers together.

STEP 2 Pick a piece of paper and say something about your life at that time and your life now. Take turns with the classmates in your group.

▶ **EXAMPLE:** In 1994, I was a doctor in the Philippines, but now I am an ESL student in the United States.

In the summer of 1999 On November 22, 1963 On December 31, 1999	In the 90's In the 80's In the 70's In the 60's	In 1998 1994 1990 1985

ACTIVITY 5: LISTENING/SPEAKING

STEP 1 Listen to the beginning of the stories on tape. Decide what kind of story type each one is. Write the number of the story you hear next to the story type.

A horror story ______ A murder mystery ______
A love story ______ A children's story/fairy tale ______

STEP 2 Finish one of the stories. Tell the story to the class.

Past Tense of *Be* 285

Activity 4

SUGGESTIONS

1. Prepare the slips of paper or index cards in advance.
2. Provide an example by giving Ss a statement about yourself. *In the 1960s I was a hippie. Now, I'm a professor. On November 22, 1963, I was in twelfth grade.*
3. Have Ss work as a whole class or in groups. Designate a notetaker in each group to write down the sentences.
4. Collect the sentences and create an error correction sheet.

Activity 5

Play textbook audio. The tapescript for this listening appears on p. 547 of this book.

SUGGESTION

Step 2:

1. Assign a specific genre to each group of Ss. For example, one group finishes the love story, another the horror story, etc.
2. Without saying what kind of story it is, the group reads or retells its story aloud and the class decides which genre it is. Because of the limitations (only the verb *be*), Ss can only be asked to set the scene; in other words, to create the beginning of the story.

✓

The test for this unit can be found on pp. 498–499 of this book. The answers can be found on p. 500

ANSWER KEY

Activity 5

Horror–2, Love–3, Murder–4, Fairy tale–1

Unit 18

UNIT OVERVIEW

The theme of this unit is how bad luck befalls ordinary people. Many of the characters here—Bookworm Benny, Monique and Daniel, Jinxed Jerry, etc.,—are victims of bad luck. Whether their stories end happily or not, they provide a rich context for practicing the past tense. Because the spelling and pronunciation of regular past tense verbs are so challenging, these aspects are presented separately.

UNIT GOALS

To maximize the diagnostic potential of the Opening Task, do not review the Unit Goals with students (Ss) until after they have completed and reviewed the Opening Task.

OPENING TASK
SETTING UP THE TASK

1. Pre-teach vocabulary such as *videotape, VCR, language lab, tuition, semester, to fail.*
2. Discuss teaching techniques and the feelings Ss may have when they fail in school.

UNIT 18

PAST TENSE

UNIT GOALS:

- To make affirmative and negative statements with regular and irregular past tense verbs
- To know how to spell and pronounce regular past tense verbs
- To understand the meaning and position of past time expressions
- To ask and answer *yes/no* and *wh*-questions in the past tense

OPENING TASK

Solve the Mystery: Who took the VCR?

STEP 1 Read the mystery.

For most students, Ms. Ditto was the best ESL teacher in the English Language Center. Three years ago, she began to use a VCR in her classes. She brought in interesting videotapes for her students to watch every week. The students enjoyed her classes and really liked her.

Only one student, Harry, didn't like Ms. Ditto. Harry's writing wasn't very good, so he failed Ms. Ditto's class twice. Last summer, he got a job in the language lab to help pay the tuition for her class again this semester. Yes, Harry felt angry at Ms. Ditto.

Just before the new semester started, the Director of the English Language Center heard the university didn't have money to pay the teachers. They were not able to give Ms. Ditto a job this semester. Everyone was sad. Harry just laughed!

On the first day of class, Professor Brown wanted to use the VCR. He asked Harry to open the language lab. But when Harry opened the door to the lab, the VCR was not there. In its place, there was a typed note with a signature on it. The note said:

> Today, I very sad. I no can work in English Language Center because there no have money to pay me. What I can do now? How I can live? I take this VCR because I have angry. Please understand my. I sorry . . .
>
> C. Ditto

STEP 2 Read the sentences and check True or False.

	True	False
1. Ms. Ditto's students didn't like her.		
2. Harry needed money.		
3. Harry worked in the language lab.		
4. Ms. Ditto didn't have a job this semester.		
5. Harry disliked Ms. Ditto.		
6. Harry did well in Ms. Ditto's class.		

STEP 3 Solve the mystery. Discuss your answers with the class. Who took the VCR? How do you know?

ANSWER KEY

Opening Task

1. False 2. True 3. True 4. True 5. True 6. False

Step 3. Harry stole the VCR. He worked in the language lab. Harry didn't like Ms. Ditto. Harry was angry at Ms. Ditto because he failed her course twice. Harry wrote the note. (You know because the note contains many grammatical errors.)

CONDUCTING THE TASK

Step 1

First, have Ss read the story individually.

Step 2

In small groups, Ss should check true or false, and mark each answer in the text with the question number.

Step 3

Allow 10 minutes for the groups to solve the mystery. Walk around to see if Ss are focusing on the note or using past tense in their discussions.

REVIEWING THE TASK

1. Assign a notetaker to present the group's hypothesis to the class.
2. Write any past tense statements on the board. Separate affirmative and negative. You will come back to these in Focuses 1, 3, and 5.
3. Even if Ss have trouble solving the mystery, you do *not* have to tell them the answer at this point. They will find the solution in Exercise 4.

FOCUS 1

The form here is quite simple. The difficulty lies in the spelling and pronunciation. You can go through the rules in a deductive presentation, or present the form inductively by giving Ss the base form and *-ed* form and having them come up with the rules. Ss will need lots of practice with this.

FOCUS **1**

Forming and Spelling Regular Past Tense Verbs

SUBJECT	BASE FORM + *-ED*
I You He She It We You They	started three years ago.

Regular verbs can change spelling in the simple past tense.

IF THE VERB ENDS IN:	SPELLING RULE
(a) a consonant **want** **need**	Add *-ed* **wanted** **needed**
(b) a vowel + *y* **enjoy** **play**	Add *-ed* **enjoyed** **played**
(c) a consonant + *e* **like** **smile**	Add *-d* **liked** **smiled**

IF THE VERB ENDS IN:	SPELLING RULE
(d) a consonant + *y* **study** **worry**	Change *-y* to *-i*, add *-ed* **studied** **worried**
(e) consonant + vowel + consonant (one syllable verbs) **stop** **drop**	Double the consonant, add *-ed* **stopped** **dropped**
(f) *-x*, *-w* (one syllable verbs) **show** **fix**	Do not double the consonant, add *-ed* **showed** **fixed**
(g) two-syllable verbs with the stress on the last syllable **oCCUR** **preFER**	Double the consonant, add *-ed* **occurred** **preferred**
(h) two-syllable verbs with the stress on the first syllable **LISten** **VISit**	Do not double the consonant, add *-ed* **listened** **visited**

Exercise 1

Have Ss work on this exercise individually; ask them to give you the base form of each verb ending in *-ed*.

Exercise 2

Have Ss work individually. Ask them which spelling rule from Focus Box 1 applies to each sentence (e.g., *enjoyed* = rule "b"; *used* = "c"), especially for numbers 10–13.

Workbook Ex. 1, pp. 140–141.
Answers: TE, p. 538.

EXERCISE 1

Go back to the Opening Task on page 287 and underline all the regular past tense verbs in the mystery.

▶ **EXAMPLE:** They enjoyed her classes and really liked her.

EXERCISE 2

Fill in the blanks with the past tense of the verbs.

1. Ms. Ditto ___enjoyed___ (enjoy) her classes.
2. Ms. Ditto ________________ (use) interesting videotapes in her classes.
3. She ________________ (help) her students to understand the tapes.
4. The students ________________ (study) new vocabulary.
5. They ________________ (learn) about American life.
6. They ________________ (discuss) the tapes in class.
7. The students ________________ (play) language learning games in class.
8. Many students ________________ (register) for her class every semester.
9. All the students really ________________ (love) her.
10. Ms. Ditto ________________ (stop) teaching because the university didn't have money to pay her.
11. Ms. Ditto's students ________________ (cry).
12. One day, a robbery ________________ (occur) at the English Language Center.
13. A VCR ________________ (disappear) from the language lab.

ANSWER KEY

Exercise 1

Enjoyed, liked, failed, started, laughed, wanted, asked, opened

Exercise 2

2. used **3.** helped **4.** studied **5.** learned **6.** discussed **7.** played **8.** registered **9.** loved **10.** stopped **11.** cried **12.** occurred **13.** disappeared

FOCUS **2**

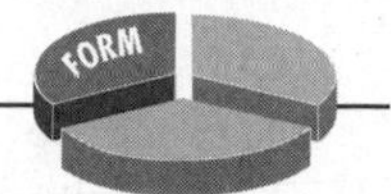

Pronunciation of the -*ed* Ending

VERB END	EXAMPLES
Group I After voiceless sounds,* the final -*ed* is pronounced /t/.	**/t/** *asked* *kissed* *stopped*
Group II After voiced sounds,** the final -*ed* is pronounced /d/.	**/d/** *robbed* *killed* *played*
Group III After /t/ and /d/, the final -*ed* is pronounced /Id/. *Voiceless sounds: p, k, f, s, sh, ch **Voiced sound: b, g, v, z, l, m, n, r, or a vowel	**/Id/** *pointed* *wanted* *waited*

EXERCISE 3

STEP 1 Put each verb in the simple past and read each sentence aloud. Check the column that shows the pronunciation of each verb.

Bookworm Benny was an excellent student.	/t/	/d/	/Id/
1. Teachers always ___liked___ (like) Bookworm Benny.	✔		
2. He __________ (work) hard in school.			
3. He always __________ (finish) his work first.			
4. The teacher always __________ (call) on him.			
5. He always __________ (answer) questions correctly.			

FOCUS 2

The pronunciation of the -*ed* ending in the regular past tense is challenging to Ss at all levels.

SUGGESTIONS

1. Practice the pronunciation of each group. Point out that an extra syllable is added to Group III verbs in the past tense.
2. Then call out additional examples of past tense verbs and tell Ss to raise one finger if the word belongs to group 1, two fingers if it is in group 2, and three fingers if it belongs to group 3. (Call these examples out in random order: Group 1: *liked, worked*; Group 2: *called, used*; Group 3: *decided, started*). You could also put up three signs indicating Group I, II, and III at the front of the room so that when Ss make past tense pronunciation errors, you can easily point to or ask Ss to point to the appropriate sign.

Exercise 3

This exercise can be done in two ways—either starting with Step 1 or with Step 2, depending on how strong your Ss are:

Step 1

1. Have pairs read the sentences aloud to determine which group the verb belongs to.
2. Check pronunciation and the answers with the whole class.

ANSWER KEY

Exercise 3
2. worked /t/ **3.** finished /t/ **4.** called /d/ **5.** answered /d/ **6.** remembered /d/ **7.** talked /t/ **8.** hated /Id/ **9.** decided /Id/ **10.** rolled /d/ **11.** waited /Id/ **12.** landed /Id/ **13.** yelled /d/ **14.** asked /t/ **15.** pointed /Id/ **16.** trusted /Id/ **17.** punished /t/
Step 2: A.3 B.5 C.2 D.1 E.4

	/t/	/d/	/Id/
6. He ___________ (remember) all his lessons.			
7. He never ___________ (talk) out of turn.			
8. The other students ___________ (hate) Benny.			
9. One day, they ___________ (decide) to get him into trouble.			
10. They ___________ (roll) a piece of paper into a ball.			
11. They ___________ (wait) for the teacher to turn his back.			
12. They threw the paper ball at the teacher. It ___________ (land) on the teacher's head.			
13. The teacher was really angry. He ___________ (yell) at the class.			
14. "Who did that?" he ___________ (ask).			
15. All the students ___________ (point) to Benny.			
16. But the teacher ___________ (trust) Benny.			
17. The teacher ___________ (punish) the other students.			

STEP 2 The pictures about Bookworm Benny on the next page are not in the correct order. Number the pictures in the correct order. Then use the pictures to retell Bookworm Benny's story.

Step 2

1. Have Ss study the pictures and reestablish the correct sequence using visual clues and their own experience.

2. Check each pair or group's story. Elicit the story from Ss and put their statements on the board.
3. Have them return to Step 1 and fill in the verbs in past tense and determine the pronunciation.
4. Have Ss retell the story to each other.

EXPANSION

Tape record Ss and play the tape back so that they can give feedback on each other's grammar and pronunciation.

A. Number ______

B. Number ______

C. Number ______

D. Number ______

E. Number ______

EXERCISE 4

The solution to the Ms. Ditto story is in this exercise. Fill in the blanks with the past tense of the verbs in the box.

discuss	look	remember	fire	notice	learn ✔
type	confess	believe	lock	ask	sign

When the Director of the English Language Center (1) ___learned___ about the robbery, she was sad. She (2) ______________ Ms. Ditto was an honest person.

To solve the mystery, the Director (3) ______________ herself in her office alone. She (4) ______________ the problems between Harry and Ms. Ditto. Then, the Director (5) ______________ at the note again. She (6) ______________ all the grammar mistakes! And the signature on the note was not Ms. Ditto's signature.

The Director (7) ______________ Harry to come to her office. She (8) ______________ the problem with him. Finally, Harry (9) ______________ to the crime. Harry said, "I (10) ______________ the note and (11) ______________ Ms. Ditto's name." In the end, the Director (12) ______________ Harry and kicked him out of the school.

Exercise 4

SUGGESTIONS

1. Have Ss read the story first for global comprehension, so that they can choose the correct verbs. Then have them fill in the verb forms.
2. Either in groups or as a class, have Ss retell the conclusion to the Ms. Ditto story using only the verbs in the box. (Put these on the board). This will provide a fairly realistic speaking exercise during which you can focus on pronunciation.

Workbook Exs. 2 & 3 pp. 141–142.
Answers: TE, p. 538.

ANSWER KEY

Exercise 4

2. believed **3.** locked **4.** remembered **5.** looked **6.** noticed **7.** asked **8.** discussed **9.** confessed **10.** typed **11.** signed **12.** fired

FOCUS 3

Irregular past tense verbs have been categorized in this focus box to help learners remember them more easily. Ss will need a great deal of practice.

SUGGESTIONS

1. Put these lists up in the classroom for easy reference.
2. Or, create flash cards by writing the base form of the verbs on one side of an index card and the simple past on the other. Use these flash cards at the beginning of class as a warm-up. Encourage Ss to make their own flashcards or lists. Ask them to discuss their own strategies for remembering these verbs.

FOCUS **3**

Irregular Past-Tense Verbs: Affirmative Statements

Many verbs in the past tense are irregular. They do not have the *-ed* form.

SUBJECT	VERB	
I You He She It We You They	went	to Miami last year.

You can learn irregular past tense forms in groups.

BASE FORM	SIMPLE PAST
/I/ sound	**/æ/ sound**
begin	began
drink	drank
ring	rang
sing	sang
sink	sank
swim	swam

BASE FORM	SIMPLE PAST
	ought/aught
buy	bought
bring	brought
catch	caught
fight	fought
teach	taught
think	thought

BASE FORM	SIMPLE PAST
	Base form and past-tense forms are the same
cost	cost
cut	cut
hit	hit
hurt	hurt
put	put
quit	quit
shut	shut
let	let
-ow	**-ew**
blow	blew
grow	grew
know	knew
throw	threw
/iy/ sound	**/ɛ/ sound**
feed	fed
feel	felt
keep	kept
lead	led
leave	left
meet	met
read	read
sleep	slept
-d	**-t**
lend	lent
send	sent
spend	spent
bend	bent
build	built

BASE FORM	SIMPLE PAST
	Change of vowel
become	became
come	came
dig	dug
draw	drew
fall	fell
forget	forgot
get	got
give	gave
hold	held
hang	hung
run	ran
sit	sat
win	won
	/o/ sound
break	broke
choose	chose
sell	sold
tell	told
speak	spoke
steal	stole
drive	drove
ride	rode
wake	woke
write	wrote

BASE FORM	SIMPLE PAST
	Other
be	was
bite	bit
do	did
eat	ate
find	found
fly	flew
go	went
have	had
hear	heard
hide	hid
lose	lost
make	made
pay	paid
say	said
see	saw
shake	shook
shoot	shot
stand	stood
take	took
tear	tore
understand	understood
wear	wore

(See Appendix 8 for an alphabetical list of common irregular past tense verbs.)

Exercise 5

This is a simple recognition exercise. Have Ss do this individually.

EXERCISE 5

Go back to the Opening Task on page 287. Circle the irregular past tense verbs.

▶ **EXAMPLE:** For most students, Ms. Ditto (was) the best ESL teacher in the English Language Center.

ANSWER KEY

Exercise 5

Was, began, brought, wasn't, got, felt, heard, were not able, was, was not, was, said

EXERCISE 6

Liisa and Kate are from Finland. They had a dream vacation in New York last fall. Fill in the blanks with the past tense of the verbs in parentheses.

1. Liisa and Kate ___flew___ (fly) to New York on Sunday, November 4.
2. They ________ (find) many interesting things to do in the city.
3. They ________ (eat) great food every day.
4. They ________ (go) to the Statue of Liberty.
5. They ________ (take) a ferry to the Immigration Museum at Ellis Island.
6. They ________ (stand) at the top of the World Trade Center.
7. They ________ (spend) an evening at a jazz club.
8. Liisa ________ (buy) gifts for her friends in Finland.
9. They ________ (see) an exhibit at the Museum of Modern Art.
10. They ________ (meet) a nice woman at the museum.
11. They ________ (speak) English with her all afternoon.
12. They ________ (think) New York was a beautiful, friendly city.

EXERCISE 7

Monique and Daniel are from France. Their vacation in New York was a nightmare. Fill in the blanks with the past tense of the verbs in parentheses.

1. On Sunday, November 4, Monique and Daniel's flight to New York was late, so they ___sat___ (sit) in the airport in Paris for four hours.
2. The airline company ________ (lose) all their luggage, so on Monday they ________ (go) shopping for new clothes.
3. On Tuesday, they ________ (get) stuck in the subway when their train ________ (break) down.
4. On Wednesday, they ________ (pay) ninety dollars to rent a car, and ________ (drive) to the Aquarium.
5. They (leave) the car on the street and ________ (get) a fifty-dollar parking ticket!
6. A thief ________ (throw) a rock through the car window and ________ (steal) Monique's camera.

Exercise 6 

SUGGESTIONS

1. Preface Exercises 6 and 7 by talking about New York City, asking Ss what they know about it, or showing photos of famous sights. Have them make predictions: *Describe a dream vacation in New York City. Describe a nightmare vacation.* Write their predictions on the board, and discuss them in terms of content and form. Correct all statements.
2. Have Ss do Exercises 6 and 7 either individually or in groups. Correct all statements.

Workbook Ex. 4, pp. 142–143.
Answers: TE, p. 538.

ANSWER KEY

Exercise 6

2. found 3. ate 4. went 5. took
6. stood 7. spent 8. bought 9. saw
10. met 11. spoke 12. thought

Exercise 7

2. lost, went 3. got, broke 4. paid, drove
5. left, got 6. threw, stole 7. bought
8. went 9. fell, hurt 10. broke
11. caught 12. ate 13. woke, felt
14. took, left

7. On Thursday, they ________________ (buy) a new camera downtown.
8. On Friday, they ________________ (go) ice skating at Rockefeller Center. Monique had the new camera around her neck.
9. Monique ________________ (fall) on the ice ________________ (hurt) her knee.
10. She ________________ (break) her new camera.
11. Monique was wet and frozen, so she ________________ (catch) a cold.
12. On Saturday night, they ________________ (eat) some unusual food in a restaurant.
13. On Sunday morning, they each ________________ (wake) up and ________________ (feel) sick.
14. Later that Sunday, they ________________ (take) a taxi to the airport and finally ________________ (leave) for home.

FOCUS 4

To help Ss understand when to use the prepositions *in*, *on*, and *at*, explain that *in* is more general (in 1988, in the summer), *on* is more specific (on Sunday, on the weekend), and *at* is the most specific (at 4:00, at midnight).

FOCUS 4

FORM MEANING

Time Expressions in the Past

Time expressions tell us when the action occurred in the past.

yesterday morning yesterday afternoon yesterday evening	last night last week last month last year last summer	an hour ago two days ago six months ago a year ago	in 1988 on Sunday at 6:00 the day before yesterday

EXAMPLES	EXPLANATIONS
(a) **On Sunday,** they flew to New York. (b) Liisa and Kate went to Spain **two years ago.**	Time expressions can come at the beginning or at the end of a sentence.
(c) **Yesterday morning,** a VCR disappeared from the English Language Center.	Use a comma after the time expression if it is at the beginning of the sentence.

EXERCISE 8

On Tuesday, November 13, Monique and Daniel meet their friend Colette in Paris to talk about their trip. Complete the sentences with time expressions.

Colette: When did you get home?

Monique: 1. We left New York ________________.

2. We got home ________________ 8:00 yesterday morning.

Colette: So, how was your trip?

Daniel: Well, pretty bad.

3. ________________ week was a week to remember!

4. Our plane arrived in New York four hours late ________________ Sunday.

5. Today's Tuesday, right? Well, exactly a week ________________, we got stuck in the subway for two hours!

6. Then, ________________ Wednesday, we rented a car and got a parking ticket.

7. What else? Oh, ________________ Thursday, we bought a new camera and Monique broke it.

Monique: 8. So you see, we had bad luck every day ________________ week.

9. We were happy to come home ________________.

10. Our trip to New York four years ________________ was much better!

Exercise 8 

Have Ss review the time frame of Monique and Daniel's trip to New York in Exercise 7.

EXPANSION

Have pairs read the dialogue aloud.

ANSWER KEY

Exercise 8

1. two days ago/on Sunday **2.** at **3.** Last **4.** on **5.** ago **6.** on **7.** on **8.** last **9.** on Sunday **10.** ago

Exercise 9

Have Ss do this exercise individually. Write the most interesting responses on the board, and correct. You may want to use these to introduce Focus 6. (Yes/No Questions and Short Answers.)

VARIATION

1. Have Ss work in groups. Write the time expressions on separate index cards and create a set for each group. Ss take turns turning over a card and making a statement using past tense.
2. Have Ss make either true or false statements about themselves using the time expressions. Let the group ask questions, and then decide whether the student is telling the truth or not.

Workbook Exs. 5 & 6 pp. 143–145.
Answers: TE, p. 538.

FOCUS 5

SUGGESTIONS

1. To introduce negative statements in the past, refer to the Opening Task. Write sentences on the board like: *Harry liked Ms. Ditto. Professor Brown stole the VCR.*
2. Ask Ss if the sentences are true or false.
3. See whether they know how to form the negative. If they don't, teach it. Then look at the focus box as a class.

EXERCISE 9

Make true statements about yourself. Use each of the time expressions below.

▶ **EXAMPLE:** Six months ago

Six months ago, I took a trip to Mexico.

1. Two months ago, ______________________________ .
2. In 1988, ______________________________ .
3. Last year, ______________________________ .
4. Last summer, ______________________________ .
5. Two days ago, ______________________________ .
6. On Sunday, ______________________________ .
7. The day before yesterday, ______________________________ .
8. Yesterday morning, ______________________________ .
9. At six o'clock this morning, ______________________________ .
10. An hour ago, ______________________________ .

FOCUS **5**

Past Tense: Negative Statements

SUBJECT	*DID + NOT/DIDN'T*	BASE FORM OF VERB
I You He She It We You They	**did not** **didn't**	work.

ANSWER KEY

Exercise 9
Answers will vary.

EXERCISE 10

Make affirmative or negative statements aloud about the people in this unit.

▶ **EXAMPLE:** the teacher/like Benny

The teacher liked Benny.

the teacher/get angry at Benny.

The teacher didn't get angry at Benny.

1. The other students/like Bookworm Benny
2. The teacher/trust Benny
3. The students/try to get Benny into trouble
4. The students' plan for Benny/succeed
5. Liisa and Kate/lose their luggage
6. Liisa's camera/break
7. Liisa and Kate/get stuck on the subway
8. Liisa and Kate/enjoy their vacation in New York
9. Harry/notice the grammar mistakes in his note
10. Ms. Ditto/sign the note
11. Harry/steal the VCR
12. The Director/believe Harry
13. Monique and Daniel/spend an evening at a jazz club
14. Monique and Daniel/visit the Statue of Liberty
15. Monique and Daniel/enjoy their vacation in New York

Exercise 10

Have Ss do this exercise as a whole class.

Workbook Ex. 7, p. 146.
Answers: TE, p.538.

ANSWER KEY

Exercise 10

1. didn't like 2. trusted 3. tried 4. didn't succeed 5. didn't lose 6. didn't break 7. didn't get stuck 8. enjoyed 9. didn't notice 10. didn't sign 11. stole 12. didn't believe 13. didn't spend 14. didn't visit 15. didn't enjoy

FOCUS 6

SUGGESTIONS

1. One way to present this focus box is to go back to Exercise 9. Refer to the sentences you kept on the board. Ask Ss to refresh their memories about who did what, by asking each other questions. Use Ss' own hypotheses to derive yes/no question and short answer forms, or teach them explicitly, if necessary.
2. Another way to introduce this focus box is to ask Ss yes/no questions related to them *(Did you do your homework last night? Did you take a vacation last summer?)* and teach short answers: *Yes, I did. No, I didn't.* Then have them study the focus box. Point out that the auxiliary *"did"* is the equivalent of *"do,"* but in the past tense.

FOCUS **6**

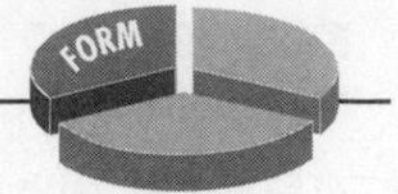

Past Tense: *Yes/No* Questions and Short Answers

Yes/No Questions

DID	SUBJECT	BASE FORM OF THE VERB	
Did	I you he she we you they	visit	New York last year?

Short Answers

AFFIRMATIVE			NEGATIVE		
Yes,	I you he she we you they	did.	No,	I you he she we you they	did not. didn't.

EXERCISE 11

Ask a partner *yes/no* questions about Ms. Ditto and the missing VCR.

▶ **EXAMPLES:** **Q:** understand the mystery

Did you understand the mystery?

A: Yes, I did.

1. like the Ms. Ditto story
2. enjoy being a detective
3. think Ms. Ditto took the VCR
4. guess that Harry was the thief
5. find the grammar mistakes in Harry's note
6. correct the mistakes in the note
7. feel sorry for Harry
8. want to give Harry any advice

Exercise 11

EXPANSION

When going over the answers with the whole class, ask Ss follow-up questions: *Why did you like the Ms. Ditto story? Why did you feel sorry for Harry?*

ANSWER KEY

Exercise 11

Add *"Did you"* in front of each of the phrases in the exercise.

Exercise 12 

SUGGESTIONS

1. Prepare Ss for this exercise by eliciting or providing the necessary vocabulary based on the picture (*deserted island, ax, chop down, tree trunk, palm trees, swim, build a boat, make a sail,* etc.)
2. In Step 1, have Ss work in pairs while you go around helping them. Have them call out the answers to check.
3. Step 2 is a prediction exercise. Ss first ask each other yes/no questions that will guide them in finishing the story. Encourage Ss to ask other questions too. They can make their predictions orally or in writing. Have the class choose the best ending. Ss will be able to write their own ending in Activity 2 on p. 309 and see the actual cartoon ending on p. A-20.

Workbook Ex. 8, p. 147.
Answers: TE, p. 538.

EXERCISE 12

Look at the cartoon about Jinxed Jerry, a man with very bad luck. He left on a two-week Caribbean cruise last winter and there was a big storm at sea.

STEP 1 Ask a partner *yes/no* questions with the words below. The pictures can help you answer the questions.

▶ **EXAMPLE:** Jerry/go on a cruise last winter

Did Jerry go on a cruise last winter?

Yes, he did.

1. Jerry's ship/get to the Caribbean
2. Jerry/know how to swim
3. Jerry/die
4. he/find an island
5. he/meet anyone on the island
6. the island/have stores
7. he/have enough food
8. he/write postcards home
9. he/make tools
10. he/build a good boat

STEP 2 Remember, Jerry has very bad luck. Ask each other *yes/no* questions and guess the end of the story.

11. Jerry's luck/change
12. a helicopter/find Jerry
13. Jerry/find his way back home
14. the story/have a happy ending
15. Jerry/ever take another cruise again

See the Appendix for the conclusion to Exercise 12 (page A-20).

ANSWER KEY

Exercise 12

1. Did Jerry's ship get to . . .? No, it didn't. **2.** Did Jerry know how ...? Yes, he did. **3.** Did Jerry die? No, he didn't. **4.** Did he find ...? Yes, he did. **5.** Did he meet ...? No, he didn't. **6.** Did the island have any stores? No, it didn't. **7.** Did he have ...? Yes, he did. **8.** Did he write ...? No, he didn't. **9.** Did he make ...? Yes, he did. **10.** Did he build ...? Yes, he did.

Step 2: The answers will be based partly on the questions the Ss want to ask; on their version of the story. **11.** Did Jerry's luck change? **12.** Did a helicopter find Jerry? **13.** Did Jerry find ...? **14.** Did the story have ...? **15.** Did Jerry ever take ...?

FOCUS **7**

Past Tense: *Wh-* Questions

WH-WORD	*DID*	SUBJECT	BASE FORM OF VERB	ANSWERS
What		I	do last summer?	You went to Paris.
When		you	make plans?	(I made plans) last month.
Where		he	go last summer?	(He went) to Scotland.
Why		the ship	sink?	(It sank) because there was a storm.
How	**did**	she	get to Paris?	(She got there) by plane.
How long		they	stay in New York?	(They stayed there for) two weeks.
How long ago		you	visit Alaska?	(I visited Alaska) ten years ago.
Who(m)		Liisa and Kate	meet in New York?	(They met) a nice woman.

WH-WORD AS SUBJECT	PAST TENSE VERB	ANSWERS
What	happened to Jerry's ship?	It sank.
Who	had a terrible vacation?	Monique and Daniel (did).

EXERCISE 13

Write *wh*-questions about Jerry. Then ask your partner the questions. Your partner gives an answer or says "I don't know."

EXAMPLES: Jerry/eat on the island?

Q: What did Jerry eat on the island ?

A: (He ate) fruit from the trees and fish from the sea .

1. Jerry/want to go on vacation

Q: Where ______________________ ?

A: ______________________

FOCUS 7

1. Go back again to Exercise 9 and look at the questions Ss asked then. Ask Ss to get more information from each other by using wh-question words. Ss should be familiar with *wh*-questions from Unit 9 on the present tense. Once Ss have generated these questions, you can correct them.

2. To work inductively, ask Ss to work in pairs and write *wh*-questions about Jinxed Jerry right after Exercise 12. Analyze the questions and correct them on the board. If some questions have not been generated (*How long ... How long ago ...*), refer Ss to Focus 7. Review the whole focus box at this point.
3. Point out that in questions with *what* and *who* as subjects, we do not use the auxiliary *did*. Juxtapose two questions: (a) *Who fired Harry? The Director fired him.* (b) *Who(m) did the Director fire? She fired Harry.* Draw an arrow from *"The Director"* to *"Who"* and emphasize its position as subject. In "b," draw an arrow from *"Who(m)"* to *"Harry"* and emphasize its position as the object.

Exercise 13

Ss don't need to answer in complete sentences. Encourage them to answer naturally.

2. Jerry/go on vacation

Q: When ____?

A: ____

3. Jerry/leave home

Q: How long ago ____?

A: ____

4. Jerry's ship/sink

Q: Why ____?

A: ____

5. Jerry/do after the ship sank

Q: What ____?

A: ____

6. Jerry/meet on the island

Q: Who(m) ____?

A: ____

7. Jerry/build the boat

Q: How ____?

A: ____

8. Jerry/put on the boat

Q: What ____?

A: ____

9. Jerry/feel when he finished the boat

Q: How ____?

A: ____

10. the story end (in your opinion)

Q: How ____?

A: ____

ANSWER KEY

Exercise 13

1. Where did Jerry want to go on vacation? He wanted to go to the Caribbean. /He wanted to go on a cruise to the Caribbean. **2.** When did Jerry go on vacation? Last winter **3.** How long ago did he leave home? A couple of months ago **4.** Why did Jerry's ship sink? because it ran into a big storm **5.** What did Jerry do after the ship sank? He swam to a small island. **6.** Who(m) did Jerry meet on the island? Nobody. **7.** How did Jerry build the boat? From trees. **8.** What did Jerry put on the boat? Fresh fish and fruit **9.** How did Jerry feel when be finished the boat? He felt great/hopeful/ optimistic/ happy/excited **10.** In your opinion, how did the story end?

EXERCISE 14

Make questions that ask for the underlined information. Use *who, whom,* or *what.*

▶ **EXAMPLES:** **Q:** What did the students enjoy ________________ ?

A: The students enjoyed Ms. Ditto's classes.

1. **Q:** ________________ ?
   A: The students loved Ms. Ditto.
2. **Q:** ________________ ?
   A: Ms. Ditto used a VCR in her classes.
3. **Q:** ________________ ?
   A: Harry wanted to hurt Ms. Ditto.
4. **Q:** ________________ ?
   A: Harry got hurt in the end.
5. **Q:** ________________ ?
   A: Professor Brown found the note.
6. **Q:** ________________ ?
   A: The Director fired Harry.
7. **Q:** ________________ ?
   A: Harry stole the VCR.
8. **Q:** ________________ ?
   A: The Director fired Harry.
9. **Q:** ________________ ?
   A: The moral of the story was *"crime doesn't pay."*

EXERCISE 15

Information Gap. This is a true story about a very special woman named Doina. Work with a partner. You look at Text A, below. Your partner looks at Text B on page A-20. Take turns asking questions to get the information in the blanks.

▶ **EXAMPLE:** **Your Partner:** (Look at Text B) 1. Where did Diona grow up?

You: (Look at Text A) 1. She grew up in Romania.

TEXT A:

1. Doina grew up in Romania.
2. She married ________________ (who/m)
3. She had a daughter.

Exercise 14

What you want to see here is whether Ss know when to use the auxiliary *did* and when to omit it in questions with *who* or *what*. The questions with *who* or *what* as subject are #4,5, and 6.

Exercise 15

1. To facilitate this information exchange, cues have been provided to indicate the type of question that must be asked. Model this information gap exercise with a student. You ask the first question, *"Where did Doina grow up"* Then have a student ask the second question, *"Whom did she marry?"*
2. Write the questions on the board if you feel this is useful. Have Ss work in pairs and walk around to assist when necessary.

Workbook Ex. 9, pp. 147–148.
Answers: TE, p. 538.

ANSWER KEY

Exercise 14

1. Who(m) did the Ss love? 2. What did Ms. Ditto use in her class? 3. Who(m) did Harry want to hurt? 4. Who got hurt in the end? 5. Who found the note? 6. Who fired Harry? 7. What did Harry steal? 8. Who(m) did the Director fire? 9. What was the moral of the story?

Exercise 15

Text A: 2. Whom did she marry? **5.** What did she think of every day? **7.** Where did she swim to? **9.** Where did Doina and her daughter go? **11.** How did they leave Romania? **13.** Why did Doina go to school?
Text B: 1. Where did Doina grow up? **3.** What happened in 1976? **4.** Why was Doina unhappy? **6.** What did she teach her daughter? **8.** Who caught them? **10.** When did they try to escape? **12.** Where did they go in 1989? **14.** What did she write in her ESL class?

4. Doina was unhappy because she was against the government in Romania.
5. She thought of _______________ (what) every day.
6. She taught her daughter how to swim.
7. On October 9, 1988, she and her daughter swam across the Danube River. They swam to _______________ (where)
8. The police caught them.
9. Doina and her daughter went _______________ (where)
10. They tried to escape several months later.
11. Finally, they left Romania _______________ (how)
12. They flew to New York in 1989.
13. Doina went to school _______________ (why)
14. She wrote the story of her escape from Romania in her ESL class.

Exercise 16

Students can do this exercise individually.

EXERCISE 16

Correct the mistakes in the following sentences.

1. This morning, I waked up early.
2. I saw him yesterday night.
3. Harry didn't felt sad.
4. They don't met the Mayor of New York last week.
5. What Harry wanted?
6. Harry didn't noticed his mistakes.
7. Who did signed the note?
8. What did the Director?
9. What did happen to Harry?
10. Where Liisa and Kate went on vacation?
11. Who did go with Lisa to New York?
12. How Jerry built a boat?
13. They no had dinner in a Greek restaurant.
14. Whom did trust the teacher in the Bookworm Benny story?
15. The ship sank before a long time.

UNIT GOAL REVIEW

Ask Ss to look at the goals on the opening page of the unit again. Help them understand how much they have accomplished in each area. Ask them if there are any questions they still have about what they have learned so far.

ANSWER KEY

Exercise 16

1. This morning, I woke up early. **2.** I saw him last night. **3.** Harry didn't feel sad. **4.** They didn't meet the Mayor of New York. **5.** What did Harry want? **6.** Harry didn't notice his mistakes. **7.** Who signed the note? **8.** What did the Director do? **9.** What happened to Harry? **10.** Where did Liisa and Kate go on vacation? **11.** Who went with Liisa to New York? **12.** How did Jerry build a boat? **13.** They didn't have dinner in a Greek restaurant. **14.** Who(m) did the teacher trust in the Bookworm Benny story? **15.** The ship sank a long time ago.

Use Your English

ACTIVITY 1: SPEAKING

STEP 1 Get into groups. One person in the group thinks of a famous person from the past.

STEP 2 The others in the group can ask up to twenty *yes/no* questions to guess who the person is. After twenty questions the group loses if they haven't guessed.

▶ **EXAMPLES:** Did this person sing?
Did this person live in North America?
Was this person a woman?

ACTIVITY 2: WRITING/SPEAKING

Write your own ending for the story about Jinxed Jerry. Compare your ending with your classmates'. Who has the best ending? When you are finished, look at the cartoons that tell the end of Jerry's story on page A-20. Discuss how your ending compares with the ending in the cartoon.

ACTIVITY 3: SPEAKING

Who is telling the truth?

STEP 1 Work in groups of three. Each person tells a true personal story. The group chooses one story. Then each of you must learn as much as you can about that story.

STEP 2 Each person tells the same beginning to the class. Your classmates ask each of you questions to find out who is telling the truth. Your job is to make the class believe this is your story. (See Example on next page.)

USE YOUR ENGLISH

For a more complete discussion of how to use the activities, see p. xxvi of this Teacher's Edition.

Activity 1

1. Show Ss how to work by telling them you have a famous person in mind (e.g., John Lennon) and they have to ask you yes/no questions to guess who the person is. Guide the class in asking you questions such as, *"Was this person a man? Was he American? British? Did he perform?"*
2. If necessary, generate a list of famous people with the whole class and write the names on the board or on index cards for Ss to choose from. Famous people should show a multicultural perspective: Confucius, Gandhi, Mao, John F. Kennedy, Princess Diana, Mother Theresa, Albert Einstein, Michelangelo, etc ... If you have photographs of famous people, post them around the room to give Ss ideas.
3. Then have Ss work in groups to do the activity. Make it into a competition giving one point for each question asked. The group with the most points wins.

Activity 2

Ss can exchange their endings with a partner or group. Have them compare their conclusions with the actual one in the cartoon on A-20. *Who was optimistic or pessimistic in the class?*

Activity 3

1. This activity can be fun with the whole class. It helps to model this first with two other speakers so that you can show Ss how to work. With the three "speakers" in front of the room, give each student a chance to ask a question to a particular person. At the end of the first round (or about 10–15 questions), the Ss decide who is telling the truth.
2. As Ss continue performing, keep a list of the questions they ask so that you can show them the variety of questions they generated and also work on error correction.

▶ **EXAMPLE:** **Student 1 says:** When I was ten years old, I went on a long trip.

Student 2 says: When I was ten years old, I went on a long trip.

Student 3 says: When I was ten years old, I went on a long trip.

The Class asks each person questions: Student #1, where did you go?

Who(m) did you go with? etc.

ACTIVITY 4: SPEAKING

Interview a partner about a past vacation. Ask as many *wh*-questions as you can. Report back to the class about your partner's trip.

▶ **EXAMPLE:**

Where did you go?	How long did you stay?
When did you go?	With whom did you go?
How did you get there?	Why did you go there?
What did you do there?	

ACTIVITY 5: LISTENING/SPEAKING

STEP 1 Listen to the three students talking about their vacations. Match the students to the titles of the essays they wrote about their vacations.

Names	**Essay Titles**
Pedro	A Great Vacation
Hakim	My Terrible Trip
Angela	A Boring Vacation

STEP 2 In a group discuss why each vacation was good or bad. What is your opinion of each vacation?

Activity 4 

VARIATION

Have Ss write about their partner's trip. Collect these reports to see how Ss have mastered the past tense.

Activity 5 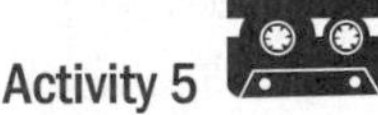

Play textbook audio. The tapescript for this listening appears on p. 547 of this book.

EXPANSION

Have Ss write their own stories or tell the class about their own Great, Boring, or Terrible Vacations.

ACTIVITY 6: SPEAKING

Jeopardy Game. Your teacher will choose one student to be the host. Only the host can look at the complete game board (page A-21). The rest of the class will be divided into two teams. Team 1 chooses a category and an amount of money from the blank game board below. The host reads the answer. Team 1 has one minute to ask a correct question. If Team 1 can't, Team 2 gets a chance to ask a question. There may be more than one correct question for each answer. The team with the most money wins.

▶ **EXAMPLE:** **Team 1 chooses:** People for $10.

Host reads: Ms. Ditto

Team 1 asks: Who lost her job?

Who(m) did Harry hate?

GAME BOARD

$$$	Category 1 PEOPLE	Category 2 WH-QUESTIONS	Category 3 YES/NO QUESTIONS
$10 $20 $30 $40 $50			

ACTIVITY 7: WRITING/SPEAKING

The stories in this unit are about unfair or unlucky things that happen to people. Think about a time when something unfair or unlucky happened to you. Write your story and tell the class what happened. Your classmates can ask you questions.

ANSWER KEY

	People	WH- Questions	Yes/No Questions
$10	Who lost her job? Whom did Harry hate?	What did Harry steal?	Did Ms. Ditto love her job?
$20	Who stole the VCR? Whom did the Director fire?	When did professor Brown want to use the VCR?	Did Harry write the note?
$30	Who solved the mystery of the missing VCR?	Where did Harry work?	Did Professor Brown steal the VCR?
$40	Who wanted to use the VCR?	Why did Harry get a job in the language lab?	Did Harry like Ms. Ditto?
$50	Who loved Ms. Ditto's class?	What did the Director notice in the note?	Did the Ss like Ms. Ditto?

Activity 6

This activity encourages Ss to work on question formation. The fact that Ss are working in groups also encourages them to collaborate and not feel so pressured to come up with the questions on their own. It might turn into a very competitive activity, so try to keep the focus on correctness.

SUGGESTIONS

1. Write up the questions Ss generate as the game goes on so that you can provide Ss with a summary of the questions afterwards.
2. Make sure the Ss who are the "hosts" write the answers in the appropriate column and row when the group chooses the category, so that Ss can see the answers.

Activity 7

This is an engaging topic for Ss. Collect Ss' stories and create a class book of bad luck stories that they can all read. This will also serve as an authentic assessment of how well Ss have mastered the past tense.

The test for this unit can be found on pp. 501–502 of this book. The answers can be found on page 503.

TOEFL Test Preparation exercises for Units 16–18 can be found on pp. 149–151 of the workbook. The answers are on p.539 of this book.

Unit 19

UNIT OVERVIEW

Reflexive pronouns (myself) and the reciprocal pronoun (each other) are introduced and contrasted in this unit in various social, people-oriented contexts such as giving advice and talking about human behavior.

UNIT GOALS

To maximize the diagnostic potential of the Opening Task, do not review the Unit Goals with students (Ss) until after they have completed and reviewed the Opening Task.

OPENING TASK
SETTING UP THE TASK

Have Ss look at or read some real advice columns such as "Dear Abby" from the newspaper to give them an understanding of this context. Try to find samples where reflexive/reciprocal pronouns are used. Read only for global comprehension at this point, but come back to any examples of the target structure when doing Focuses 1 and 3.

CONDUCTING THE TASK

Step 1 

Ss can do Step 1 by reading for general meaning, using a lexical strategy. They do not need to understand the target structure to match the letters to the advice in Part B.

UNIT 19

REFLEXIVE PRONOUNS, RECIPROCAL PRONOUN:

Each Other

UNIT GOALS:

- To use reflexive pronouns correctly
- To know which verbs are commonly used with reflexive pronouns
- To know how to use *each other*

OPENING TASK
Advice Columns

STEP 1 Read the letters to "Dear Darcy" in Part A. Match each one to a "Letter of Advice" in Part B. Fill in the name of the person who wrote each letter in the blanks in Part B.

PART A

Dear Darcy,

I'm married and have two children. I'm trying to be a super-woman. I work outside the home. I also do all of the housework, shopping, and the cleaning. I help my children with their school work. I never have time for myself. I am tired and unhappy. Please help!

—*Supermom in Seattle*

Dear Darcy,

My wife and I never go out anymore. We have a new baby, and my wife doesn't want to get a babysitter. I need a social life. I'm starting to talk to myself! Can you help me?

—*Bored in Boston*

Dear Darcy,

My mom and dad got divorced last month. They fought with each other a lot, and finally, my dad moved out. Maybe I wasn't a good daughter to them. Maybe the break-up was my fault. I can't forgive myself.

—*Guilty in Gainesville*

Part B

A. Dear ______________________________ ,
Don't blame yourself. You did not cause these problems. Your parents need to learn to talk to each other.

B. Dear ______________________________ ,
You need to explain how you feel to her. Tell her you want to go out once a week. Life is short. Find a babysitter. Go out and enjoy yourselves!

C. Dear ______________________________ ,
You need to make time for yourself. Go out with your friends. Do yourself a favor and join a gym. Take care of yourself too. Buy yourself something special.

STEP 2 Now read the last letter from *Lonely in Los Angeles.* Read Darcy's response and circle the correct pronouns.

Dear Darcy:

I'm a rather shy and lonely high school student. I'm doing well in school, but I don't have many friends. The girls in my class always call each other, but they never call me. I don't go out. I don't enjoy myself. I don't even like myself very much anymore.

—*Lonely in Los Angeles*

Dear Lonely in Los Angeles:

Remember, the teenage years are difficult. At 16, many girls don't like (1) (they/them/themselves). You're doing well in school. Be proud of (2) (you/yourself). Try to like (3) (you/yourself) first. Then others will like (4) (you/yourself). Teenage girls need (5) (each other/themselves). Force (6) (you/yourself) to open up to other girls. Relax and try to enjoy (7) (you/yourself).

—*Darcy*

Step 2
Step 2 is the diagnostic phase of this task, where Ss must differentiate between subject, object, reflexive, and reciprocal pronouns. This phase will show you how much Ss know. Ask each pair to compare their answers with another pair.

REVIEWING THE TASK

When going over the answers, write sentences with reflexive pronouns on one side of the board, and those with reciprocals on the other side. Go over the answers to Step 2. Use this context to present the meaning of reflexive vs. reciprocal pronouns. This will lead you into Focus 1 and Focus 3.

ANSWER KEY

Opening Task
Step 1: A. Guilty in Gainesille **B.** Bored in Boston **C.** Supermom in Seattle

Step 2: 1. themselves **2.** yourself **3.** yourself **4.** you **5.** each other **6.** yourself **7.** yourself

FOCUS 1

1. Bring a mirror to class and look at yourself, or have a student do this. Elicit the statement, *"I'm (or He's) looking at myself (himself) in the mirror."* and write it on the board.
2. Underline the reflexive pronoun and ask what it refers to in the sentence.
3. Explain that we use a reflexive pronoun when the subject and object of the sentence are the same.
4. Point out that in imperative sentences, reflexive pronouns refer to the subject "you," which is understood: In example (b); *you* is singular; in example (g), *you* is plural.

Exercise 1

Have Ss work on this exercise individually. Check as a class.

Exercise 2

Have Ss do this exercise individually and then read the conversations aloud with a partner.

Workbook Ex. 1, pp. 152–153.
Answers: TE, p. 539.

FOCUS **1**

Reflexive Pronouns

Use a reflexive pronoun when the subject and object are the same.

▶ **EXAMPLE:** Sara bought **herself** a new car.

NOT: Sara bought Sara a new car.

EXAMPLES	REFLEXIVE PRONOUNS
(a) I bought **myself** a new car.	*myself*
(b) Look at **yourself** in the mirror.	*yourself*
(c) He doesn't take care of **himself.**	*himself*
(d) She blames **herself** for the accident.	*herself*
(e) A cat licks **itself** to keep clean.	*itself*
(f) We enjoyed **ourselves** at the theater.	*ourselves*
(g) Help **yourselves** to some food.	*yourselves*
(h) Babies can't feed **themselves.**	*themselves*

EXERCISE 1

Go back to Step 1 in the Opening Task on page 312. Underline all the reflexive pronouns and the subjects.

▶ **EXAMPLE:** I never have time for myself.

EXERCISE 2

Fill in each blank with a reflexive pronoun.

▶ **EXAMPLE:** I lost my wallet yesterday, and I wanted to kick ___myself___ .

1. **Mary:** Do you sometimes talk to ________________ ?
   Bill: Well, sometimes, when I'm alone.
2. **Monica:** Thanks for such a lovely evening. We really enjoyed (a) ________________ .
   Gloria: Well, thanks for coming. And the children were just wonderful. They really behaved (b) ________________ all evening. I hope you can come back soon.
3. **Jane:** I can't believe my bird flew out the window! It's my fault. I forgot to close the birdcage.
   Margaret: Don't blame ____________ . He's probably happier now. He's free!

314 UNIT 19

ANSWER KEY

Exercise 1

Part A: 1. I never have time for myself **2.** I'm starting to talk to myself **3.** I can't forgive myself.
Part B: A. Don't blame yourself **B.** Go out and enjoy yourselves. **C.** You need to make time for yourself. Do yourself a favor ... Take care of yourself too. Buy yourself something special.

Exercise 2

1. yourself **2.** (a) ourselves (b) themselves **3.** yourself **4.** himself **5.** herself **6.** (a) yourselves (b) yourselves **7.** yourself

4. **Cynthia:** What's the matter with Bobby's leg?
Enrique: He hurt ____________ at the soccer game last night.
5. **Jason:** My girlfriend Judy really knows how to take care of ____________ . She eats well, exercises regularly, and gets plenty of sleep.
6. **Sylvia:** Hello Carol, hello Eugene. Come on in. Make (a) ____________ at home. Help (b) ____________ to some drinks.
7. **Mother:** Be careful! That pot on the stove is very hot. Don't burn ____________ .

FOCUS **2**

Verbs Commonly Used with Reflexive Pronouns/ *By* + Reflexive Pronoun

EXAMPLES	EXPLANATIONS
(a) I fell and **hurt myself.** (b) He **taught himself** to play the guitar. (c) Be careful! Don't **cut yourself** with that knife. (d) Did you **enjoy yourself** at the party?	These verbs are commonly used with reflexive pronouns: *hurt* *cut* *tell* *burn* *blame* *enjoy* *teach* *introduce* *behave* *take care of*
(e) He got up, washed, and shaved.	The verbs *wash, dress,* and *shave* do not usually take reflexive pronouns. In sentence (e) it is clear he washed and shaved *himself* and not another person.
(f) He's only two, but he wants to get dressed **by himself.** (g) I sometimes go to the movies **by myself.**	Use *by* + a reflexive pronoun to show that someone is doing something alone (without help or company).

FOCUS 2

1. Have Ss read the verbs commonly used with reflexive pronouns; and ask them to read the examples aloud.
2. For (e) explain that in English when we talk about routine activities that people obviously do to themselves (dress, shave, wash, etc.), we do not use the reflexive pronoun, In contrast to some languages like French and Spanish where the reflexive pronoun is used in these cases.

Exercise 3 

Most of these pictures can be described in the present progressive; however, #3 and #6 work best in past tense. Ask Ss to write their sentences on the board. Check with the whole class.

Workbook Exs. 2 & 3, pp. 153–154. Answers: TE, p. 539.

EXERCISE 3

Write a sentence describing the action in each picture.

▶ **EXAMPLES:** The woman is introducing herself to the man.

The woman introduced herself to the man.

1.

2.

3.

4.

5. **6.**

7.

8.

cut	dry	enjoy	look at/admire
clean/lick	hurt	talk to	weigh

1. ______________________________
2. ______________________________
3. ______________________________
4. ______________________________
5. ______________________________
6. ______________________________
7. ______________________________
8. ______________________________

ANSWER KEY

Exercise 3

Answers may vary. Possible answers include:
1. The man is weighing himself. **2.** The man is looking at/admiring himself in the mirror. **3.** The woman cut herself with the knife. **4.** The woman is drying herself. **5.** The people are enjoying themselves at a party. **6.** The boy fell off his bicycle and hurt himself. **7.** The old man is sitting on a park bench and talking to himself. **8.** The cat is cleaning/licking itself.

FOCUS **3**

MEANING

Reciprocal Pronoun: *Each Other*

The reciprocal pronoun *each other* is different in meaning from a reflexive pronoun.

(a) John and Ann blamed **themselves** for the accident.

(b) John and Ann blamed **each other** for the accident.

EXERCISE 4

Work with a partner. Draw pictures to show the differences in meaning between the following sentences.

1. **(a)** The weather was very hot. The runners poured water on themselves after the race.
(b) The weather was very hot. The runners poured water on each other after the race.

a.

b.

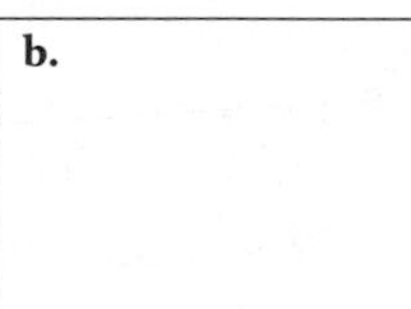

2. **(a)** They love themselves.
(b) They love each other.

a.

b.

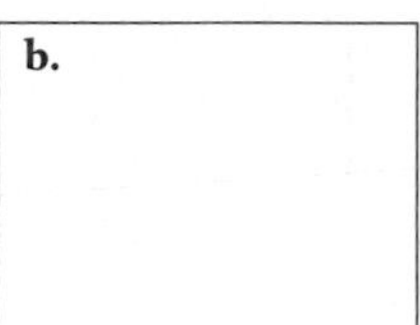

FOCUS 3

1. Refer to the Opening Task and review the difference in meaning between reciprocal and reflexive pronouns. Look at the pictures.
2. Ask Ss to think of situations in which two people would blame themselves (e.g., a married couple having problems with their teenage son) and would blame each other (e.g., 2 children breaking a neighbor's window while playing baseball).
3. Discuss these or have Ss role-play these situations. Write their statements on the board and correct.

Exercise 4

Drawings will vary. Put up Ss' drawings without the captions and have the class provide the appropriate caption.

ANSWER KEY

Exercise 4

1. (a) The drawing should show two runners pouring water on themselves. **(b)** The drawing should show two runners pouring water on each other. **2. (a)** The drawing could show a man looking at himself and a woman looking at herself in the mirror. **(b)** The drawing could be the same man and woman with their arms around each other, affectionately.

Exercise 5 

VARIATION

Put each sentence on an index card. Assign each pair of Ss a scene to act out. Give Ss time to plan and then have them perform in front of the room. The class will then make statements about what they are doing.

Exercise 6

This exercise will teach some new vocabulary while showing you if Ss are able to distinguish reflexive pronouns from reciprocal pronouns. Working in pairs, Ss can pool their background knowledge to better understand the definitions. Go around the room to monitor and assist Ss with both form and meaning. (A few of these statements could be correct in form, but incorrect in meaning. For example, *Young children can't always control themselves.* NOT: *each other.*)

EXERCISE 5

Act out the following sentences to show the difference between *each other* and reflexive pronouns.

1. You and your classmate are looking at yourselves in the mirror.
2. You and your classmate are looking at each other.
3. You and your classmate are talking to yourselves.
4. You and your classmate are talking to each other.
5. You're playing ball with a friend, and you break a neighbor's window. Blame yourself for the accident.
6. You're playing ball with a friend, and you break a neighbor's window. Blame each other for the accident.
7. You introduce yourself to your partner.
8. You and your partner introduce each other to another person.

EXERCISE 6

Choose a reflexive pronoun or each other to complete the statements.

1. An egotistical person loves himself/herself.
2. Divorced people can be friends if they forgive ________.
3. Good friends protect ________.
4. Close friends tell ________ their secrets.
5. A self-confident person believes in ________.
6. In a good relationship, the two people trust ________.
7. A realistic person doesn't lie to ________.
8. Independent people take care of ________.
9. Caring people help ________.
10. Angry people say things to hurt ________.
11. Young children can't always control ________.
12. An insecure person doesn't have confidence in ________.

ANSWER KEY

Exercise 6

2. each other **3.** each other **4.** each other **5.** himself/herself **6.** each other **7.** himself/herself **8.** themselves **9.** each other **10.** each other **11.** themselves **12.** himself/herself

EXERCISE 7

Circle the correct word in the "Dear Darcy" letters below.

▶ **EXAMPLE:** (He,) Him, Himself) cares about (I, (me,) myself).

Dear Darcy,

(1) (I, My, Mine) boyfriend loves himself. (2) (He, His, Him) is very pleased with (3) (he, him, himself). He always looks at (4) (he, him, himself) in store windows when he passes by. (5) (Himself, He, Him) only thinks about (6) (his, himself, him). He never brings (7) (my, me, myself) flowers. The last time he told (8) (my, me, myself) that he loved me was two years ago. He's also very selfish with (9) (he, his, him) things. For example, he never lends me (10) (him, himself, his) car. He says that the car is (11) (himself, him, his), and he doesn't want me to use it. Do (12) (yourself, your, you) have any advice for me?

—*"Unhappy"*

Dear Unhappy:

(13) (You, Your, Yourself) boyfriend certainly is very selfish. (14) (You, Your, Yourself) can't really change (15) (he, himself, him). Get rid of (16) (he, himself, him)! Find (17) (you, yourself, yours) a new guy!

—*Darcy*

EXERCISE 8

Correct the mistakes in the following sentences.

1. I hurt me.
2. They're looking at theirselves in the mirror.
3. I shave myself every morning.
4. I have a friend in Poland. We write to ourselves every month.
5. We enjoyed at the circus.
6. Larry blamed Harry for the accident. Harry blamed Larry for the accident. They blamed themselves for the accident.
7. He did it hisself.

Exercise 7

Have Ss do this exercise individually.

EXPANSION

When reviewing the exercise, ask Ss to identify each item circled; there are subject pronouns (SP), object pronouns (OP), reflexive pronouns (RP), and possessive pronouns (PP); there are also possessive determiners/adjectives (PA).

Exercise 8

Ss can do this error correction individually.

Workbook Ex. 4, p. 155.
Answers: TE, p. 539.

UNIT GOAL REVIEW

Ask Ss to look at the goals on the opening page of the unit again. Help them understand how much they have accomplished in each area. Ask them if there are any questions they still have about what they have learned so far.

ANSWER KEY

Exercise 7

1. My/(PA) **2.** He (SP) **3.** himself (RP) **4.** himself (RP) **5.** He (SP) **6.** himself (RP) **7.** me (OP) **8.** me (OP) **9.** his (PA) **10.** his (PA) **11.** his (PP) **12.** you (SP) **13.** Your (PA) **14.** You (SP) **15.** him (OP) **16.** him (OP) **17.** yourself (RP)

Exercise 8

1. I hurt myself. **2.** They're looking at themselves... **3.** I shave every morning **4.** We write to each other... **5.** We enjoyed ourselves at the circus. **6.** They blamed each other for the accident. **7.** He did it himself.

USE YOUR ENGLISH

For a more complete discussion of how to use the activities, see p. xxvi of this Teacher's Edition.

Activity 1 

This is a common problem of logic that Ss may be familiar with. They can help each other figure it out by posing certain questions such as: *Why is there a puddle of water? Do you think someone else murdered the prisoner?"*

SUGGESTION

Encourage Ss to draw this scene. The visual element may help them find the explanation.

Activity 2 

VARIATIONS

1. Create an even number of groups. Have each group make up questions and combine the best ones in one questionnaire where each item is worth one point (Yes = 1, No = 0). Have half the Ss survey the other half. Then repeat until all Ss have responded to the questionnaire.
2. Generate the survey questions with the whole class and then assign each student a question to ask all the other Ss. Each student then summarizes the results for his question and presents the information to the class.

In either variation, have the class decide which three Ss are the most independent and tell why.

Use Your English

ACTIVITY 1: SPEAKING

Read the following riddle and try to find the answer. Discuss it with a partner.

A prison guard found a prisoner hanging from a rope in his prison cell. Did he hang himself or did someone murder him? There was nothing else in the prison cell but a puddle of water on the floor.

ACTIVITY 2: WRITING/SPEAKING

Who is the most independent person in your class?

Make up a survey with ten questions. Then go around to all the students in your class and ask your questions. Tell the class who the independent people are.

▶ **EXAMPLES:** *Do you like to do things by yourself?*
Do you usually travel by yourself?
Do you ever go to the movies by yourself?

320 UNIT 19

ANSWER KEY

Activity 1

The prisoner stood on a block of ice with the rope around his neck. When the ice melted, his feet didn't touch the ground, so he hanged himself.

ACTIVITY 3: SPEAKING

Interview another classmate, using the questions below.

1. Do you believe in yourself?
2. When you go shopping for clothes, do you like to look at yourself in the mirror?
3. Do you ever compare yourself to other people?
4. Do you ever buy yourself a present?
5. In a new relationship, do you talk about yourself or try to learn about the other person?
6. Do you ever talk to yourself?
7. Do you cook for yourself?
8. Do you blame yourself for your problems or do you blame others?
9. Do you take care of yourself? (Do you eat well? Do you get enough sleep?)
10. Do you ever get angry at yourself?

Add questions of your own.

ACTIVITY 4: LISTENING/SPEAKING

Listen to the people talk about their problems.

STEP 1 Match the problems to the people.

Person #1 _____	(a) Serious
Person #2 _____	(b) Lonely
Person #3 _____	(c) Unhealthy

STEP 2 What advice can you give to each of these people? Tell your classmates.

ACTIVITY 5: WRITING

STEP 1 Write a letter to Dear Darcy about a problem you have.

STEP 2 Work with a partner. Exchange your letters and write a response to the problem.

ANSWER KEY

Activity 4

Person #1-b Person #2-c Person #3-a

Activity 3

SUGGESTION

Print this interview on separate sheets of paper. Give one to each student. Encourage Ss to add their own questions and interview each other.

EXPANSION

1. Ask Ss to write about their partners. You can work on paragraph structure, for example, by getting Ss to see connections in their partners' characteristics. *She believes in herself. She doesn't compare herself to other people. She doesn't get angry at herself.*
2. Using the information from these sentences, Ss need to write some general statements about their partners. *My partner is a mature woman with a positive attitude*. They can then put this paragraph together: topic sentence and support. When they've completed the paragraphs, have them exchange with each other for peer review and feedback.

Activity 4

Play textbook audio. The tapescript for this listening appears on p. 547 of this book. Play the tape more than once if necessary.

Activity 5

Collect Ss' letters to Dear Darcy. Highlight errors and give papers back to be rewritten. Then have them exchange letters so the partners can write responses.

VARIATION

Post all the letters around the room. Ss walk around reading all the letters and writing advice at the bottom. The Ss then take back their original letter and read all the advice they've been given. They can then choose the best piece of advice and share it with the class.

The test for this unit can be found on pp. 504–505 of this book. The answers can be found on p. 506.

Unit 20

UNIT OVERVIEW

This unit prepares students (Ss) to refer to future time events, whether they are purely hypothetical (*will*) or somewhat more predictable within a given context (*be going to*); intentional and planned (*be going to*), or spontaneous (*will*); certain to happen (*will*) or merely possible (*may/might*). Thematically, the unit deals with fortune telling and making predictions about the future in general, and about one's own future in particular.

UNIT GOALS

To maximize the diagnostic potential of the Opening Task, do not review the Unit Goals with Ss until after they have completed and reviewed the Opening Task.

OPENING TASK SETTING UP THE TASK

1. Have Ss look at the photograph of the fortune teller. Elicit Ss' knowledge of and experience with fortune telling (reading tea leaves, palm reading, tarot cards, etc.). Ask Ss what kinds of things fortune tellers might say. At this point, Ss might make statements using *be going to* or *will*.

2. Put all their statements on the board, separating those with *will* from those with *be going to*, separating the correct forms from the incorrect ones. You will come back to these later.

UNIT 20

FUTURE TIME

Will* and *Be Going To*, *May* and *Might

UNIT GOALS:

- To talk about future time using *will, be going to, may,* and *might*
- To understand the meaning and position of future time expressions
- To choose between *will* and *be going* to when
  -talking about future intentions or plans
  -making predictions

OPENING TASK

Looking into Wanda's Crystal Ball

What is Wanda the Fortune Teller saying about each person? Match the phrases to the correct person (or people). Then, make a statement about each person's future.

1. The bald man . . .

2. The homeless man . . .

3. The athlete . . .

4. The young boy . . .

5. The elderly couple . . .

6. The scientist . . .

7. The lifeguard . . .

8. The chef . . .

9. The movie director . . .

10. The writers . . .

a. ____ inherit one million dollars from an uncle
b. ____ win an Olympic gold medal
c. ____ have ten grandchildren
d. ____ open his own restaurant
e. ____ be very successful authors
f. ____ produce a new movie and win an Oscar
g. ____ find a cure for AIDS
h. ____ save someone's life
i. ____ grow hair on his head
j. ____ become a famous rock star

CONDUCTING THE TASK

1. Ask pairs to make predictions by matching the phrases to the correct people. Ss can start with picture #1 of the bald man and try to find the matching phrase (*The bald man/grow hair on his head*). Alternatively, Ss could start with the phrases and find the matching person.
2. Next, have them make statements aloud about each person, or write statements. It is possible that Ss will generate statements using *will* or *be going to* at this point. Try to elicit both forms. Add these statements to the ones on the board, again separating the two and correct and incorrect statements.

REVIEWING THE TASK

This unit is set up so that there is a flow from the Opening Task, where predictions are made, to the first focus box, where two ways of making predictions are outlined: *Will* is used to make predictions of a more hypothetical, abstract nature (like those of a fortune teller) and *be going to* is used to make predictions that are more grounded in a present reality—when something in the present situation allows us to assume that something else is going to happen. At this stage, you are trying to see whether Ss: (1) can refer to future time in any understandable way; (2) know this distinction between *will/be going to*; (3) know the different forms for *will/be going to*; and (4) know anything about *may/might.* Therefore, you will need to analyze the sentences Ss have produced in light of this.

ANSWER KEY

Opening Task

a.(2). The homeless man will inherit... **b.(3).** The athlete will win... **c.(5).** The elderly couple will have... **d.(8).** The chef will open... **e.(10).** The writers will be... **f.(9).** The movie director will produce... **g.(6).** The scientist will find... **h.(7).** The lifeguard will save... **i.(1).** The bald man will grow... **j.(4).** The young boy will become...

FOCUS 1

The meaning and use of *will* and *be going to* are presented in this focus box. Explain that *will* is more hypothetical and abstract, based on feelings and assumptions, whereas *be going to* is more grounded in present reality.

SUGGESTION

To explain this distinction to your Ss, make up examples about them. *This class is going to do very well on the final test.* (Judging by the class' past performance.) vs. *The Ss in this class will all live to be 100 years old.*

Exercise 1 

Ss can do this exercise individually or in pairs. There is a lot of contextual support here. Since this is a use-focused exercise, Ss are not yet producing the forms. However, the use distinction between *will* and *be going to* is crucial here. By looking at each picture, Ss must determine whether there is sufficient indication that something is going to happen (#1-Picture F). If so, they need to use *be going to*. If the picture does not indicate an impending event, they need to choose *will* (#3-Picture g).

Workbook Exs. 1 & 2, pp. 156–157. Answers: TE, p. 539.

FOCUS **1** MEANING USE

Talking about Future Time

Use *will* and *be going to* to make predictions about the future or to say what you think will happen in the future.

EXAMPLES	EXPLANATIONS
(a) One day, he *will* be rich.	Use *will* for a prediction (what we think will happen).
(b) Look at those big black clouds. It **is going to** rain. (c) **NOT:** It will rain.	Use *be going to* for a prediction based on the present situation (what we can see is going to happen).
(d) Teacher to student: Your parents **will** be very upset about this.	*Will* is more formal.
(e) Father to daughter: Your mother**'s going to** be very angry about this.	*Be going to* is less formal.

EXERCISE 1

Match the sentences to the pictures.

a.

b.

c.

d.

e.

f.

g.

1. ____ Look at that waiter! He's going to fall!
2. ____ This marriage isn't going to last.
3. ____ You will find gold on the streets of America!
4. ____ She's going to get a headache.
5. ____ I will always love you.
6. ____ You will grow up and be famous.
7. ____ Be careful, Julian. You're going to fall!

ANSWER KEY

Exercise 1
1. f **2.** c **3.** g **4.** a **5.** b **6.** d
7. e

FOCUS **2**

Will

AFFIRMATIVE STATEMENTS		NEGATIVE STATEMENTS	
I You He She It We You They	**will arrive** next week. **'ll arrive** next week.	I You He She It We You They	**will not arrive** next week. **won't arrive** next week.
There	**will be** peace in the world. **'ll be**	There **will not be** any wars. **won't be**	
Men **will be able** to stay home with their children.		Men **will not be able to** have children. **won't**	

YES/NO QUESTIONS			SHORT ANSWERS					
Will	I you he she it we you they	arrive next week?	Yes,	you I he she it we you they	**will**.	No,	you I he she it we you they	**won't**.

FOCUS 2

All forms of *will* including statements and yes/no questions are presented here. As suggested in Unit 14 for the modal *can*, point out that *will* is a modal verb and that, like *can*, *will* does not change form no matter what the subject. Go over all the forms.

WH-QUESTIONS	ANSWERS
(a) **When will** the scientists discover a cure?	(They **will discover** a cure) in ten years.
(b) **Where will** the couple go on their honeymoon?	(They **will go**) to Hawaii.
(c) **What will** the homeless man do with the money?	He'**ll buy** a new house.
(d) **How will** the couple travel?	(They'**ll travel)** by plane.
(e) **How** long **will** they be on the plane?	(They'**ll be** on the plane) for five hours.
(f) **Who will** get an Olympic medal?	The athlete.
(g) **Who(m) will** the lifeguard save?	(**He'll save**) a lucky person.

Exercise 2

Since all of the statements in the Opening Task are predictions, this is a good context for practicing *will*. Encourage Ss to make additional predictions about the people in the Opening Task. *The scientist will receive a Nobel prize for his work. The chef will write his own cook book.*

EXERCISE 2

Think about the people in the Opening Task on page 323. Make a second prediction for each.

▶ **EXAMPLE:** The scientist *will win a Nobel prize.*

1. The bald man . . .
2. The athlete . . .
3. The teenager . . .
4. The movie director . . .
5. The lifeguard . . .
6. The chef . . .
7. The homeless man . . .
8. The authors . . .
9. The elderly couple . . .

Exercise 3

VARIATION

Have Ss work in pairs or small groups to reach a consensus and then share their answers as a class.

EXPANSION

Ask Ss to support their predictions with specifics: for example, #6: *The traditional family will disappear. People won't get married and have children.* #11: *People won't drive electric cars. They won't be able to go very far in electric cars. They will continue to use gas.*

EXERCISE 3

How will our lives be different in fifty years? Make predictions with *will* or *won't*. Discuss your predictions with a partner.

1. The climate ________________ change.
2. People ________________ take vacations on the moon.
3. Couples ________________ choose the sex of their babies.
4. All countries ________________ share the world's money equally.

ANSWER KEY

Exercise 2
Answers will vary. Be sure answers are appropriate in context and grammatically correct.

Exercise 3
Answers will depend on the Ss' personal views of the future.

5. Most people ________________ move back to the countryside.
6. The traditional family with a husband, wife, and two children ________________ disappear.
7. Men and women ________________ continue to marry.
8. All people of different races ________________ learn to live together peacefully.
9. People ________________ speak the same language.
10. Crime ________________ stop.
11. People ________________ drive electric cars.
12. We ________________ discover life on other planets.
13. Science ________________ continue to be very important.
14. People ________________ live to be 130 years old.
15. A woman ________________ be President of the United States.

EXERCISE 4

Think about the year 2025. Where will you be? What will you be able to do? Write *yes/no* questions with *will.* Interview your classmates and report their answers to the class.

	Classmate 1	Classmate 2
1. be in the United States *Will you be in the United States?*	________	________
2. speak English fluently	________	________
3. be back in your home country	________	________
4. have a good job	________	________
5. earn a living	________	________
6. have a big family	________	________
7. have a nice house	________	________
8. be content	________	________
9. want something different	________	________

Add two questions of your own.

10. ________________________	________	________
11. ________________________	________	________

Exercise 4

Encourage Ss to add several questions at the end.

EXPANSION

Ss could use this information to write a short paragraph about one of their classmates. If they do this, make sure they've had enough time to ask the questions they need to support their topic statements.

ANSWER KEY

Exercise 4

2. Will you speak English fluently?/Will you be able to speak. **3.** Will you be back ... **4.** Will you have ... **5.** Will you earn .../Will you be able to earn ... **6.** Will you have ... **7.** Will you have ... **8.** Will you be ... **9.** Will you want ... **10., 11** Ss answers will vary.

Exercise 5 

Have Ss role-play this exercise. Give copies of Wanda's crystal ball to those Ss role-playing Wanda. Give the question prompts to the Ss playing Janice. This will create a true information gap.

Workbook Exs. 3 & 4, pp. 158–160. Answers: TE, p. 539.

EXERCISE 5

Work with a partner. You are Janice Williams and your partner is Wanda the Fortune Teller. Ask your partner *yes/no* and *wh*-questions with *will* and *will be able to*. Your partner looks into the crystal ball to answer your questions.

▶ **EXAMPLE:** **You:** Will my husband lose his job?

Your Partner: Yes, he will.

Wanda's Crystal Ball

Husband will find another job in 3 months
Daughter will get married to a computer specialist
Husband will lose job
Will have 5 grandchildren
You and your husband will retire to Tahiti!
Son will drop out of high school and get a job

Janice's Questions

1. my husband/lose his job?
2. my husband/be able to find another job?
3. when/my husband/find another job?
4. my daughter/get married?
5. who(m)/she/marry?
6. I/have grandchildren?
7. how many grandchildren/I/have?
8. my son/go to college?
9. what/he/do?
10. my husband and I/be able to retire?
11. where/we/retire?

ANSWER KEY

Exercise 5

1. Will my husband lose his job? Yes, he will. **2.** Will my husband be able to find another job? Yes, he will. **3.** When will my husband find another job? In three months. **4.** Will my daughter get married? Yes, she will. **5.** Whom will she marry? She will marry a computer specialist. **6.** Will I have grandchildren? Yes, you will. **7.** How many grandchildren will I have? Five. **8.** Will my son go to college? No, he won't. **9.** What will he do? He will drop out of high school and get a job. **10.** Will my husband and I be able to retire? Yes, you will. **11.** Where will we retire to? To Tahiti.

FOCUS **3**

Be Going To

AFFIRMATIVE STATEMENTS			NEGATIVE STATEMENTS		
I	**am** **'m**	**going to** leave.	I	**am not** **'m not**	**going to** leave.
You	**are** **'re**		You	**are not** **aren't**	
He She It	**is** **'s**		He She It	**is not** **isn't**	
We You They	**are** **'re**		We You They	**are not** **aren't**	

YES/NO QUESTIONS			SHORT ANSWERS				
Am	I	**going to** leave?	Yes,	you **are**.	No,	you **aren't**.
Are	you			I am.		I'm **not**.
Is	he she it			hc she it **is**.		he she it **isn't**.
Are	we you they			we you they **are**.		we you they **aren't**.

FOCUS 3

Point out that the reduced form of *going to* + verb is "*gonna*," but that "*gonna*" is an oral form, not a written form. Go over affirmative, negative, yes/no, and *wh*-questions and short answers.

WH-QUESTIONS			ANSWERS	
When Where What How How long Who(m)	**are you going to**	leave? go? do there? get there? stay? visit?	**I'm going to**	leave in two weeks. go to Colorado. go skiing. go by car. stay for one week. visit my cousin.
Who**'s**	**going to**	drive?	My friend (is **going to** drive).	

Remember: *Going to* is often pronounced "gonna" when we speak. We do not usually write "gonna."

Exercise 6

SUGGESTIONS

1. Have Ss say the sentences aloud. You may choose not to have Ss repeat *gonna* since it is not a standard form. They should, however, be able to recognize and understand *gonna* since it is so commonly used.
2. Tape-record them and replay so they can hear their own speech and monitor their contractions.

EXERCISE 6

Look at the pictures. Then fill in the blanks with the affirmative or negative form of *be going to*.

1. "Watch out! That bag ______________ fall!"

2. "Hurry up! We ______________ miss the bus."

ANSWER KEY

Exercise 6

1. That bag's going to... **2.** We're going to... **3.** This isn't going to... **4.** I'm going to... **5.** I'm not going to... **6.** What are you going to ... I'm going to... **7.** She's going to... **8.** They're going to... **9.** I'm not going to... **10.** I'm going to ... I'm not going to ... I'm going to...

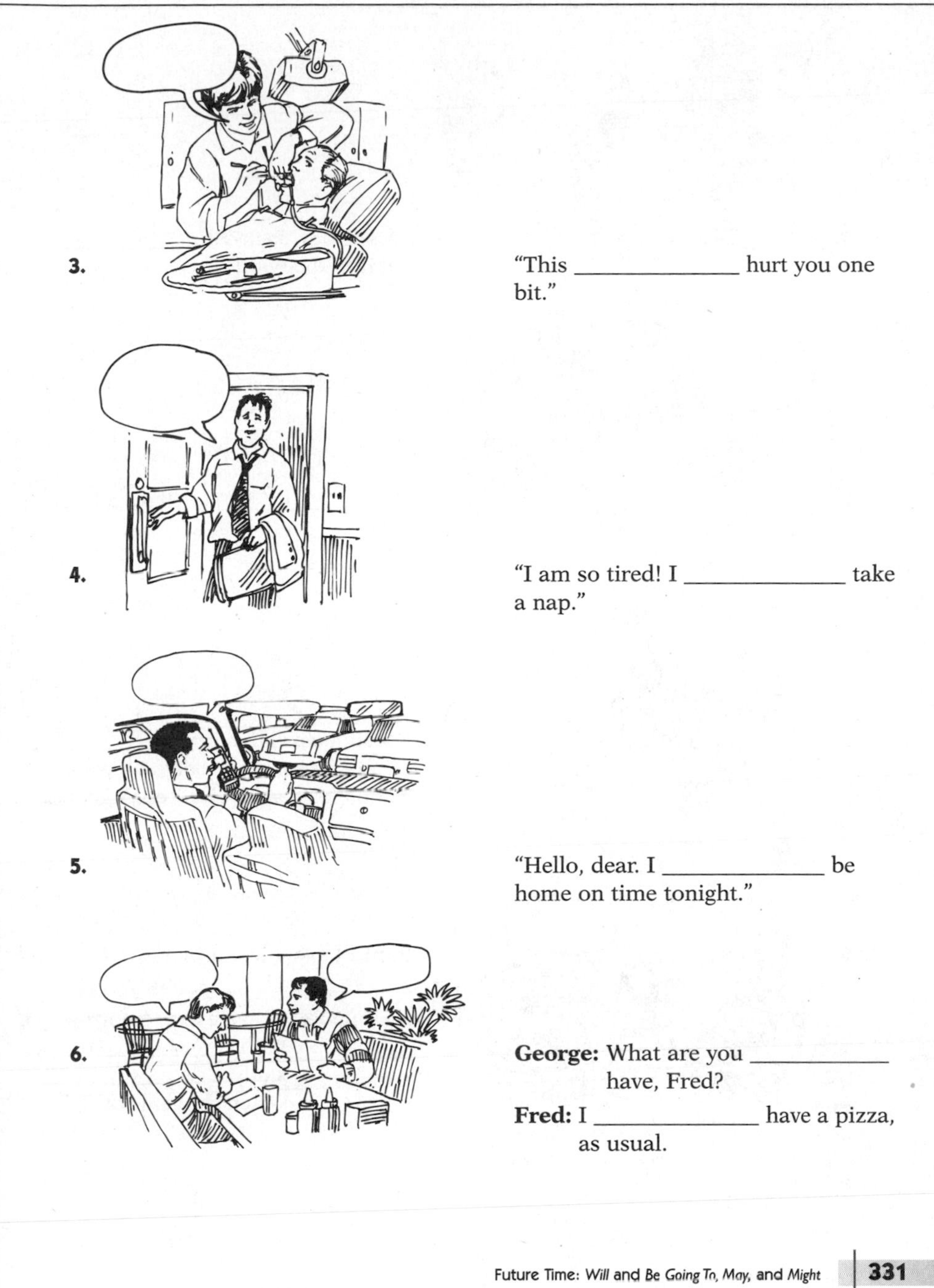

3. "This ______________ hurt you one bit."

4. "I am so tired! I ______________ take a nap."

5. "Hello, dear. I ______________ be home on time tonight."

6. **George:** What are you ____________ have, Fred?

Fred: I ______________ have a pizza, as usual.

7.  "Watch her, Jack! She ______________ fall into the pool!"

8.  "They ______________ have a baby today."

9.  "Hello, boss. I'm sorry, I ____________ be able to come in today. I have a terrible backache and I can't get out of bed."

10.  **Ben:** I have a test tomorrow. I ______________ study.

Roommate: I have a test tomorrow too, but I ______________ study. I ______________ watch the game on TV!

EXERCISE 7

Read the answers. Write a *yes/no* or *wh-* question with *be going to*.

▶ **EXAMPLE:** **Richard:** My doctor says I need to leave my job and get away somewhere.

Robert: Where are you going to go?

Richard: To California.

Robert: (1) ______________________________?
Richard: I don't know (what I'm going to do there).

Robert: (2) ______________________________?
Richard: (I'm going to stay) with some old friends.

Robert: (3) ______________________________?
Richard: For about a month.

Robert: (4) ______________________________?
Richard: By plane.

Robert: (5) ______________________________?
Richard: I don't know (if I'm going to come back to my job).

EXERCISE 8

Use your imagination to answer these questions about the people in the Opening Task on page 323. Use *be going to* in writing your answers. Compare your answers with your classmates'.

▶ **EXAMPLE:** What is going to happen to the elderly people?

They're going to live to a ripe old age.

1. What is the poor person going to do with the million dollars?
2. Who is the lifeguard going to save?
3. What kind of movie is the director going to make?
4. What kind of food is the chef going to serve in his restaurant?
5. How are the authors going to celebrate their success?
6. What is the athlete going to do after the Olympics?
7. What kind of life is the rock star going to have?

Exercise 7

Ss can do this exercise individually. Then have them read the dialogue aloud with a partner.

Exercise 8

Encourage a variety of answers by modeling the example with Ss and calling on their background knowledge. Have them write their answers on the board so you can check. Have the class choose the most creative answers.

Workbook Exs. 5 & 6, p. 161.
Answers: TE, p. 539.

ANSWER KEY

Exercise 7

1. What are you going to do there? **2.** Who(m) are you going to stay with? **3.** How long are you going to stay? **4.** How are you going to go/get there? **5.** Are you going to come back to your job?

FOCUS 4

SUGGESTIONS

1. Put up a large calendar in front of the room. Point to the current day of the week. Then present the different time expressions using the calendar as a reference *(Today is... Tomorrow, Next week, The day after tomorrow, A week from today).*
2. Remind Ss of the movement from general to more specific time with the prepositions *in, on,* and *at.*

FOCUS **4**

Time Expressions in the Future

EXAMPLES	EXPLANATIONS
(a) I'm going to visit you **tomorrow evening.** (b) **A month from now,** Wanda will be on a tropical island.	Future time expressions can come at the beginning or at the end of the sentence. Put a comma (,) after the time expression when it is at the beginning of the sentence.

Future Time Expressions

(Later) this morning afternoon evening	next week month year Sunday weekend	tomorrow morning afternoon evening night	soon later the day after tomorrow a week from today tonight

EXAMPLES		EXPLANATIONS
I'll see you	(c) **in** fifteen minutes. two weeks. March. 2015. (d) **on** Tuesday. May 21st. (e) **at** 4:00. midnight. (general ↕ specific)	We also use prepositional phrases of time to talk about future time.
(f) We are going to go to the Bahamas **for** three weeks.		*For* shows how long the action will last.
(g) I'll be there **until** 3:00 (At 3:00, I will leave. I will not be there after 3:00.) (h) I won't be there **until** Monday. (Before Monday, I won't be there. After Monday, I'll be there.)		*Until* shows the specific time in the future when the action will change.

EXERCISE 9

Make statements about yourself. Use *be going to*.

▶ **EXAMPLE:** In a few days, I'm going to move out of my apartment.

1. In a few days, ______________________________ .
2. Next summer, ______________________________ .
3. The day after tomorrow, ______________________________ .
4. This evening, ______________________________ .
5. Tomorrow night, ______________________________ .
6. This weekend, ______________________________ .
7. At 9:00, ______________________________ .
8. In December, ______________________________ .
9. On Wednesday night, ______________________________ .
10. On New Year's Eve, ______________________________ .

EXERCISE 10

Anthony and Sally are planning a vacation in Europe. They are going to visit four countries in seven days. Sally is telling Anthony about their travel plans. Fill in the blanks with *in, on, at, for,* or *until*.

1. We are going to arrive in London (a) ___at___ 6:00 P.M. (b) ___on___ Sunday.
2. We'll stay in London __________ two days.
3. Then, we'll fly to Paris __________ Tuesday morning.
4. We'll stay in Paris __________ Wednesday afternoon.
5. Then, we'll fly to Rome __________ the evening.
6. We won't leave Rome __________ Friday morning.
7. __________ 10:00 A.M. on Friday morning, we'll fly to our final destination, Athens, Greece.
8. We'll stay in Greece __________ two days.
9. We'll return home __________ Sunday. Then, we'll need a vacation!

Exercise 9

Answers will vary. Have Ss do this exercise orally or in writing and compare answers.

VARIATION

1. Give each student a blank paper. Assign a sentence to each student and have each one write it at the top of the paper.
2. Ask them to complete the sentences and then pass the papers to the people on their left. With the new paper, Ss complete the sentences at the top and then pass them along, etc.
3. The final student gets back his original paper and reads all the responses. Ask Ss to do error correction.

Exercise 10

Ss can do this exercise individually and then read the vacation plans aloud.

ANSWER KEY

Exercise 10

2. for 3. on 4. until 5. in 6. until
7. At 8. for 9. on

Exercise 11

1. Show Wednesday, April 10, on the calendar as the reference point. Have Ss work individually and check their answers with a partner. There may be several answers for each sentence.
2. Write the possibilities on the board to indicate the variety of responses.

EXERCISE 11

Look at Wanda's calendar. Imagine it is now 2 P.M. on Wednesday, April 10. Read the sentences about Wanda's plans and fill in the blanks on the next page with a time expression or a preposition of time. There may be more than one correct answer.

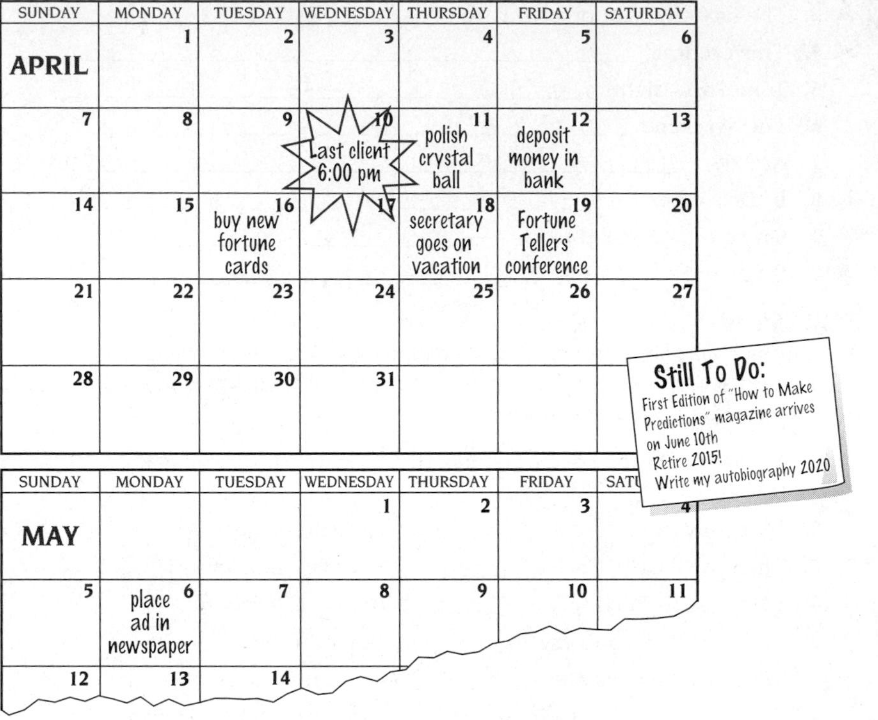

1. Wanda is going to see her last client at 6:00 this evening/in four hours.
2. She's going to attend the Fortune Tellers' Conference ______________.
3. She's going to polish her crystal ball ______________.
4. She's going to deposit all her money in the bank ______________.
5. Her secretary is going to go on vacation ______________.
6. She is going to buy new fortune cards ______________.
7. She's going to put an advertisement about herself in the newspaper ______________.
8. She will read her first *How To Make Predictions* magazine ______________.
9. She will retire to a tropical island ______________.
10. She will write a book called *How to Be a Successful Fortune Teller in 10 Easy Lessons* ______________.

FOCUS **5**

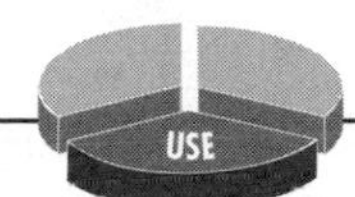

Talking about Future Intentions or Plans

EXAMPLES	EXPLANATIONS
(a) **A:** The phone is ringing. **B:** O.K. **I'll get** it.	Use *will* when you decide to do something **at** the time of speaking.
(b) Mother: Where are you going? Daughter: **I'm going to** take a drive with Richard tonight. Remember, Mom? You said it was okay . . . Mother: I did?	Use *be going to* when you made a plan to do something **before** the time of speaking.

FOCUS 5

This focus box differentiates between *will*, used when the speaker spontaneously decides to do something at the time of speaking, and *be going to*, used to express future plans that have been made prior to the time of speaking. Focuses 1 and 5 present different uses of *will/be going to* since these two forms are not always interchangeable. You might initially decide not to focus on the distinction between *will* and *be going to* for Ss at a low level. However, the distinction is an important one in sounding like native speaker. Exercise 12 is based on this distinction.

ANSWER KEY

Exercise 11

2. on April 19/next week/next Friday/a week from Friday. **3.** tomorrow/on Thursday/this Thursday/on April 11. **4.** on April 12/in two days/this Friday/on Friday. **5.** on April 18/next week/next Thursday/a week from Thursday. **6.** on April 16/next week/next Tuesday. **7.** next month/on May 6/in May/in five weeks. **8.** on June 10/in two months. **9.** in 2015/in __ years. **10.** in 2020/in __ years.

Exercise 12

Let Ss work in pairs to figure out the answers in this exercise.

Workbook Exs. 9 & 10, pp. 164–165.
Answers: TE, p. 540.

EXERCISE 12

Work with a partner. You read the first five statements in Column A aloud. Your partner chooses an answer from Column B. After the first five, your partner reads from Column A and you choose the answer from Column B.

▶ **EXAMPLE:** Do you have any plans for tonight?

A. Yes, we will go to the theater.

(B.) Yes, we're going to the theater.

Column A	Column B
1. Christine called. She's coming over for dinner.	A. Great! I'll cook. B. Great! I'm going to cook.
2. What are you doing with that camera?	A. I'll take your picture. B. I'm going to take your picture.
3. Do you need a ride home today?	A. No, thanks. Jason will take me home. B. No, thanks. Jason's going to take me home.
4. We don't have a thing to eat in the house.	A. I'll call up and order a pizza. B. I'm going to call up and order a pizza.
5. Help! The car died again.	A. Calm down. I'll be right there. B. Calm down. I'm going to be right there.
6. Why are you meeting Jenny in the library tonight?	A. She'll help me with my homework. B. She's going to help me with my homework.
7. Look, those thieves are robbing the bank!	A. I'll call the police. B. I'm going to call the police.
8. Mom, can you brush my hair?	A. I'll do it in a minute, sweetie. B. I'm going to do it in a minute, sweetie.
9. Are you off the phone yet?	A. I'll be off in a minute! B. I'm going to be off in a minute!
10. Why did Maria cancel her date for Saturday night?	A. Her parents will take her away for the weekend. B. Her parents are going to take her away for the weekend.

ANSWER KEY

Exercise 12

1. A **2.** B **3.** B **4.** A **5.** A **6.** B
7. A (or B) **8.** A **9.** A **10.** B

May and *Might*

Use *may* or *might* to say something is possible in the future.

EXAMPLES	EXPLANATIONS
(a) I **will go** to Mexico next year.	(a) Shows certainty. The speaker is 100% sure.
(b) I **may/might go** to Mexico next year.	(b) Shows possibility. The speaker is 50% sure.

AFFIRMATIVE STATEMENTS			NEGATIVE STATEMENTS		
I You He She We You They	**may** **might**	study abroad next year. be able to stay abroad for two years.	I You He She We You They	**may not** **might not**	take a vacation be able to stay for two years.
It		rain later.	It		rain later.
There		be cheap flights to Mexico.	There		be any discounts on flights.

NOTE:
- There are no contractions for *may* or *might*.

FOCUS 6

1. If you have been introducing grammatical metalanguage, tell Ss that *may/might* are also modal verbs. At this point they will have learned *can* and *will*. Like these, the form of *may/might* does not change no matter what the subject. However, *may/might* are not used in *yes/no* questions about future time, or as contractions.
2. Explain that *may* or *might* are used to express future possibilities. Example: *Rosa may apply to university. She might take next semester off*. It's less important to distinguish between *may* and *might* here than to distinguish both of these from *will*, which shows certainty.

Exercise 13
Ss can use *may* or *might* here.

EXERCISE 13

Fill in the blanks with *may* or *might* in the affirmative or negative.

▶ **EXAMPLE:** **Peter:** How are you going to go to Boston next weekend?

Al: I __may__ drive or I __may__ take the train. I won't fly because it's expensive.

1. **Joanne:** Is Ilene going to come to your New Year's Eve party?
   Paula: She (a) ________________ be able to come. She went out of town on business and she (b) ________________ be back in time for the party.

2. **Tamara:** Where are you and Jeff going to go on vacation this summer?
   Susan: Jeff (a) ________________ start a new job in July, so we (b) ________________ be able to go on vacation. We (c) ________________ stay home and go to the beach.

3. **Eugene:** What's Jason going to major in at the university?
   Carol: Well, he really loves the ocean, so he (a) ________________ major in marine biology, or he (b) ________________ major in environmental science.

4. **Priscilla:** Will you go back to your country after you finish college here?
   Arnaldo: I don't know. I (a) ________________ want to go back to visit my family, but I (b) ________________ want to go back to live. There (c) ________________ be more job opportunities for me here in the United States.

ANSWER KEY

Exercise 13
1.a. may not/might not **b.** may not/might not **2.a.** may/might **b.** may not/might not **c.** may/might **3.a.** may/might **b.** may/might **4.a.** may/might **b.** may not/might not **c.** may/might

EXERCISE 14

What are your plans for the future? Complete your chart with a base verb. Exchange charts with your partner. Report your partner's plans to the class.

▶ **EXAMPLES:** He**'s going to/might/may/will go to** see a movie this evening.

He **may/might** study at home this weekend.

	Base Verb	*Will/Be Going to*	*May/Might*
1. This evening,	see a movie	x	
2. This weekend,	study at home		x
3. Tomorrow night,			
4. A week from today,			
5. In 3 months,			
6. Next summer,			
7. In 5 years,			

EXERCISE 15

What is our future in the computer age? Make statements with affirmative or negative forms of *will, be going to, may,* or *might.*

▶ **EXAMPLE:** Computers/always be part of our lives

Computers will always be part of our lives.

1. People/want to go back to a time before computers
2. The number of computers in the world/increase
3. We/all have pocket computers
4. The Internet/connect people in every home all over the world
5. Students in classrooms all around the world/be able to "talk" to each other
6. People/learn languages easily with computers
7. People/prefer to communicate by computer
8. Books/disappear completely
9. People who cannot use computers/be able to find jobs
10. Computers/take away our privacy.

Exercise 14

Ss must distinguish between possibility and certainty in the future.

1. First have Ss complete the chart individually.
2. Have them share with a partner and report to the class.
3. Have Ss write out their answers to see if they are using the forms correctly. Check that they are distinguishing between *may/might* and *will* by asking how certain they are about their plans. *Are you 100% certain you will see a movie this evening? How certain are you about your plans for next summer? For 5 years from today?*

Exercise 15 

This exercise will be more interesting if done in groups. The groups report their answers. Discuss differing attitudes toward computers.

EXPANSION

Encourage Ss to make additional statements of opinion about our future with computers. *Computers will be smarter than people. Computer gadgets will fill our homes.*

Workbook Exs. 11 & 12, pp. 165–166. Answers: TE, p. 540.

UNIT GOAL REVIEW

Ask Ss to look at the goals on the opening page of the unit again. Help them understand how much they have accomplished in each area. Ask them if there are any questions they still have about what they have learned so far.

USE YOUR ENGLISH

For a more complete discussion of how to use the activities, see p. xxvi of this Teacher's Edition.

Activity 1

SUGGESTION

Have groups write their predictions on butcher block paper so you can post them around the room and discuss them with the class. Decide which group is the most optimistic, the most pessimistic, the most imaginative, serious, realistic, etc.

Activity 2

Encourage Ss to be as creative, as specific and as funny as they can.

SUGGESTION

Bring in pictures to give Ss ideas of the variety of the things they can say, or have Ss bring in pictures, catalogues, travel brochures, etc.

Activity 3

Encourage Ss to fill in many activities on their calendars first, to make it more challenging for them to plan a date with their partner.

Use Your English

ACTIVITY 1: WRITING/SPEAKING

What do you think the world will be like in 2050? Think about changes in travel, the home, food, technology, and people, etc. With your group, write down ten changes. Discuss your group's ideas with the rest of the class.

ACTIVITY 2: SPEAKING

Imagine that you and your partner win $10,000 in the lottery. You have one day to spend it. What are you going to do together? Give details of your activities. For example, if you rent a car, say what kind of car you are going to rent (a sports car, a limousine, a jeep?). Share your plans with the class. Decide which pair has the most interesting plans.

ACTIVITY 3: SPEAKING

Make a weekly calendar and fill in your schedule for next week. Write different activities for each day. Try to make a date to do something with your partner in the future.

▶ **EXAMPLES:** What are you going to do on Sunday?

I'm going to go jogging along River Walk.

342 UNIT 20

ACTIVITY 4: LISTENING/SPEAKING

You are a group of tourists going to Europe. You are at the airport and the tour guide is giving you some information.

STEP 1 Listen to the tour guide, and complete the travel plan below.

Day	Place	Number of Days/Nights
Sunday	Paris	
		3 nights
	Milan	
Saturday		
	Vienna	
Thursday		
Saturday		

STEP 2 Compare your plan with a partner's.

STEP 3 Tell the class your travel plans, real or imaginary. Say when you are going to go, how you are going to go there, where you are going to stay, etc.

▶ **EXAMPLE:** In June, I'm going to go to Vancouver. I'm going to fly there. I'm going to visit my uncle.

ACTIVITY 5: WRITING/SPEAKING

STEP 1 Sit in a circle with your whole class or a group of six to eight people. On the top of a blank piece of paper write:

On ________________ *in the year 2015,* ________________
(today's date) (your name)

STEP 2 Pass the sheet of paper to the person on your left. This person writes a prediction about you for the year 2015. Then he or she passes the paper to the left for the next person to write a second prediction.

STEP 3 Continue until everyone has written their predictions. At the end of the activity, you will have a list of predictions. Read the predictions and choose the best one. Read them aloud to the class.

Activity 4

Play textbook audio. The tapescript for this listening appears on p. 548 of this book. Play the tape more than once. The first time, Ss can listen for main ideas; after that, they can listen for details and complete the chart.

Activity 5

Ss should know each other fairly well by this time and will be able to make pertinent, funny, pointed predictions about each other. Collect the Ss' papers and use them for error correction.

VARIATION

If there is a strong sense of group cohesion in your class, ask Ss to write one prediction for each student on a piece of paper. Collect all papers and put them in a hat. Have each student pull a prediction out of the hat, read it, and guess who it's about.

The test for this unit can be found on pp. 507–509 of this book. The answers can be found on p.510.

Unit 21

UNIT OVERVIEW

Phrasal verbs are difficult for students (Ss) since the meanings are often not transparent (i.e., The meaning of "run into," for example, is not "run" + "into," but a new meaning created by the combination of a verb and a particle); in addition, this type of verb form may not exist in the Ss' native languages. However, since they are so common in English, they need to be addressed, even at a beginning level. The main challenge in phrasal verbs is meaning, so it is especially important to present phrasal verbs in context. This unit gives Ss the tools to talk about everyday events in informal, more colloquial language.

UNIT GOALS

To maximize the diagnostic potential of the Opening Task, do not review the Unit Goals with Ss until after they have completed and reviewed the Opening Task.

OPENING TASK
SETTING UP THE TASK

Ask Ss if they have ever given a speech. Were they nervous about it? What did they do to prepare for the speech?

CONDUCTING THE TASK

Step 1

1. Ask Ss to imagine they are giving a talk. Have them look at the pictures of Nervous Nellie and explain what she's doing in each one. Do this with the whole class so that you can hear whether or not Ss are using phrasal verbs, or have Ss do this in groups while you walk around and monitor.

2. Put any statements containing phrasal verbs (correct or incorrect) on the board.

UNIT 21

PHRASAL VERBS

UNIT GOALS:

- To understand the meaning of common phrasal verbs
- To use separable and inseparable phrasal verbs
- To know how to use direct objects with phrasal verbs
- To learn phrasal verbs that do not take objects

OPENING TASK
Nervous Nelly Gives a Lecture

Nelly is nervous about the lecture she is going to give.

STEP 1 Look at the pictures and describe the steps in Nelly's lecture.

STEP 2 Nelly has index cards to help her remember what to do. Complete each index card with appropriate expressions from the box. Then read each card aloud.

sit down	calm down	take out
call up	call on	stand up
put on		slow down

1. Take a deep breath and ________.

2. ________ and introduce myself.

3. ________ my glasses.

4. ________ my notes.

5. Don't talk too fast. Remember to ________.

6. ________ people with questions.

7. ________ and relax.

8. ________ all my friends and tell them it's over.

Step 2

Have pairs read each card aloud to check.

REVIEWING THE TASK

Compare these answers to the Ss-generated statements on the board. Ask Ss if they know what all these verbs mean and how they are formed. This will allow you to bridge to Focus 1, which shows the form and meanings of phrasal verbs, and Exercise 1, which is a simple recognition exercise. Ask Ss if they know any other verbs that are formed in this way. You could even present new combinations of verb + particle, in context, using the same verbs. For example: *Put on/off/down Call on/up/out/back*

VARIATION

Write the steps to the lecture on separate index cards and have Ss put them in the correct order. Tape the cards on the board to check on the order and then present the meaning and form.

ANSWER KEY

Opening Task

1. calm down **2.** Stand up **3.** Put on
4. Take out **5.** Slow down **6.** Call on
7. Sit down **8.** Call up

FOCUS 1 

The term "particle" is difficult to explain. Point out that the verb + particle is not the same as verb + preposition. Write the following on the board:

	Subject	Phrasal Verb	Object
A.	Subject	Phrasal Verb	Object
	I	looked up	the word...
B.	Subject	Verb	Prep. Phrase
	I	looked	up the street, but I didn't see her.

In A, *looked up* has a new meaning: to find information in a reference book. In B, *looked* does not change meaning. This will be clearer if you have given examples of phrasal verbs in reviewing the Opening Task.

Exercise 1

Have Ss do this exercise individually.

FOCUS **1**

Phrasal Verbs

EXAMPLES	EXPLANATIONS
(a) **Turn on** the lights.	A phrasal verb is: a verb + a particle *turn + on* *sit + down* *stand + up*
(b) Plants grow. (grow = to increase in size) Children **grow up.** (grow up = to become an adult)	The verb + particle together have a specific meaning

EXERCISE 1

Look at Nelly's index cards from the Opening Task on page 345 and circle all the phrasal verbs.

1. Take a deep breath and (calm down.)
2. Stand up and introduce myself.
3. Put on my glasses.
4. Take out my notes.
5. Don't talk too fast. Remember to slow down.
6. Call on people with questions.
7. Sit down and relax.
8. Call up all my friends and tell them it's over!

ANSWER KEY

Exercise 1

1. calm down 2. Stand up 3. Put on
4. Take out 5. Slow down 6. Call on
7. Sit down 8. Call up

EXERCISE 2

Read each statement on the left to your partner. Your partner chooses a response from the right.

Statement	Response
1. I don't want to cook tonight.	a. Calm down.
2. It's hot in here.	b. Call up a friend.
3. It's so quiet in here.	c. Stand up for a few minutes.
4. I can't read the map. The print's too small.	d. Sit down for a while.
5. I can't do my homework with the TV on.	e. Lie down and take a nap.
6. I'm bored.	f. Take off your jacket.
7. My feet hurt.	g. Put on your glasses.
8. I'm sleepy.	h. Turn off the TV.
9. I'm really upset about our argument today.	i. Let's eat out.
10. I'm tired of sitting on this plane.	j. Turn on the radio.

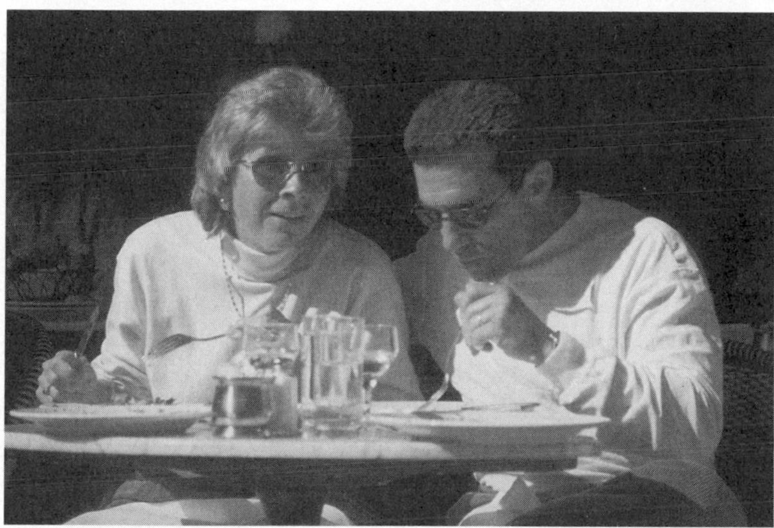

Exercise 2

VARIATION

Do this exercise with the whole class. Prepare index cards with one statement on one card and the response on another card. Mix up the cards and give one to each student. Have them walk around the room trying to find their match. When everyone is finished, have the pairs say the statements and responses aloud to check.

EXPANSION

To increase the challenge, you can add statements and responses using other phrasal verbs. For example:
Statement: *It's freezing in here!*
Response: *Put on a sweater.*
Statement: *I can't hear the music.*
Response: *Turn up the radio.*

Workbook Ex. 1, p. 167.
Answers: TE, p. 540.

ANSWER KEY

Exercise 2

1. i 2. f 3. j 4. g 5. h 6. b 7. d
8. e 9. a 10. c

FOCUS 2

Provide additional examples of phrasal verbs in context using the verbs in Exercise 2 or others, along with the corresponding one-word verbs: *take after* = *resemble in behavior or appearance; take over* = *take control; turn up* = *make louder; turn down* = *make lower.*

FOCUS **2**

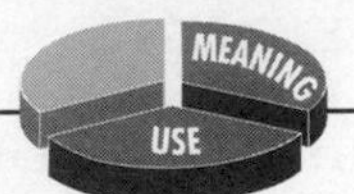

Phrasal Verbs

EXAMPLES	EXPLANATIONS
(a) I **hung up** the picture.	Sometimes the meaning of a phrasal verb is clear from the verb + particle combination.
(b) I **ran into** Joe on the street the other day.	Sometimes it is difficult to guess the meaning of a phrasal verb. The meaning of *ran into* is not the combination of *ran* and *into*. *Run into* means "to meet someone by chance."
(c) Please **put out** your cigarette, Jake. (d) Please **extinguish** your cigarettes, ladies and gentlemen.	In informal English, phrasal verbs are more frequent than one-word verbs with the same meaning. In (c), you are talking to a friend. In (d), an announcer is speaking to passengers at a train station.

Exercise 3

Have Ss do this exercise individually or in pairs.

EXERCISE 3

Circle the phrasal verbs. Then match each phrasal verb with a one-word verb.

Sentences with phrasal verbs	One-word verb with same meaning
1. I called 911 Emergency. The firefighters will be here soon to put out the fire. d	**a.** raise
2. Don't just stand at the door. Come in. _____	**b.** remove
3. Fill out the application. _____	**c.** telephone
4. We're going to practice some phrasal verbs. Henry, can you please hand out this exercise? _____	**d.** extinguish
5. I left my book at school. I don't remember the homework for tonight. I'll call up Manny and ask him. _____	**e.** enter
6. I can't talk to you now. Come back in fifteen minutes. _____	**f.** distribute

ANSWER KEY

Exercise 3

2. (e) enter **3.** (g) complete **4.** (f) distribute
5. (c) telephone **6.** (j) return **7.** (i) lower
8. (a) raise **9.** (b) remove **10.** (h) wait

7. I can't concentrate! Would you please turn down the music! _____
8. I am freezing in this house. Please turn up the heat. _____
9. Please take off your wet shoes. _____
10. Hold on a minute. I'm not ready yet. _____

g. complete
h. wait
i. lower
j. return

EXERCISE 4

Fill in the blanks with the phrasal verbs below.

put away	turn on	pick up	throw away	turn off

DIRECTIONS FOR LANGUAGE LAB ASSISTANTS

When you leave the language lab, there are several things you must do. First, (1) ________________ all the trash from the floor. Then (2) ________________ all the equipment—tape recorders, VCRs, etc. (3) ________________ all the cassettes students used. (4) ________________ any coffee cups or trash students left in the room. Finally, (5) ______________ the alarm system before you lock the doors.

Exercise 4

Be sure that Ss know what a language lab is and what the function of a lab assistant is.

Workbook Ex. 2, p. 168.
Answers: TE, p. 540.

ANSWER KEY

Exercise 4

1. pick up **2.** turn off **3.** Put away
4. Throw away **5.** turn on

FOCUS 3

Most of the phrasal verbs presented here are of the separable type.

SUGGESTION

Help Ss develop a sense of the particle movement rule by involving them in visual sentence scramble activities like this:

1. Put each word of sentence (*a*) and (*b*) on a large index card or piece of paper. (You can also use a magnetic board.)
2. Have Ss unscramble sentence (*a*) and put it up on the board.
3. Have Ss identify the parts of speech (subject = *The teacher*, phrasal verb = *hand out*, object = *the exercise*)
4. Do the same with (*b*) and show Ss the movement of the particle with phrasal verbs that can be separated.
5. Look at examples (*c*) and (*d*), using the same visual sentence scramble technique. Remind Ss that a direct object pronoun must precede the particle.

FOCUS **3** FORM

Separable and Inseparable Phrasal Verbs

Separable Phrasal Verbs

EXAMPLES	EXPLANATIONS
Verb **Particle** **(a)** The teacher **handed out** the exercise. **Verb** **Direct Object** **Particle** **(b)** The teacher **handed** the exercise **out.**	When the direct object is a noun, it can go: • after the particle (*out*) • between the verb (*handed*) and the particle (*out*)
(c) The teacher handed **it** out. **(d)** NOT: The teacher handed out **it.**	When the direct object is a pronoun, it always goes between the verb and the particle.

Inseparable Phrasal Verbs

EXAMPLES	EXPLANATIONS
(e) I **ran into** an old friend on the street. **(f)** I **ran into** her on the street. **(g)** **NOT:** I **ran** an old friend **into** on the street. **(h)** **NOT:** I **ran** her **into** on the street.	The direct object—noun or pronoun—goes after the particle.

EXERCISE 5

Sergeant Strict is giving orders to his new soldiers. He's losing his patience. Repeat the Sergeant's orders in a different way each time.

1. (a) "Take off your civilian clothes."
   (b) *"I said,* take your civilian clothes off *."*
   (c) *"Come on,* take them off *!"*
2. (a) "Hand out these uniforms."
   (b) "I said, ______________________."
   (c) "Come on, ______________________!"
3. (a) "Put on your new Army clothes."
   (b) "I said, ______________________."
   (c) "Come on, ______________________!"
4. (a) "Turn down that radio."
   (b) "I said, ______________________."
   (c) "Come on, ______________________!"
5. (a) "Put away your old clothes."
   (b) "I said, ______________________."
   (c) "Come on, ______________________!"
6. (a) "Throw out that junk food from home."
   (b) "I said, ______________________."
   (c) "Come on, ______________________!"
7. (a) "Clean up this mess."
   (b) "I said, ______________________."
   (c) "Come on, ______________________!"
8. (a) "Turn off the lights!"
   (b) "I said, ______________________."
   (c) "Come on, ______________________!"

Exercise 5

SUGGESTION

1. Before doing this exercise, ask if any of your Ss have served time in the military. Let Ss describe their experiences with their superior officers. Elicit the types of orders they were given.

2. Put these orders on the board. Compare them to the orders in Exercise 5.
3. Have Ss role-play the situations in groups. Choose a drill sergeant and soldiers. Have soldiers add the line
   (1) *"Okay—I'm taking them off!"*
   (2) *"Okay—I'm putting them on!"*

Workbook Ex. 3, p. 169.
Answers: TE, p. 540.

ANSWER KEY

Exercise 5

2.b. Hand these uniforms out. **c.** hand them out. **3.b.** Put your new Army clothes on. **c.** Put them on. **4.b.** Turn that radio down. **c.** Turn it down. **5.b.** Put your old clothes away. **c.** Put them away. **6.b.** Throw that junk food from home out. **c.** Throw it out. **7.b.** Clean this mess up. **c.** Clean it up. **8.b.** Turn the lights off. **c.** Turn them off.

FOCUS 4

1. Have Ss cover the meaning column in the chart and encourage them to read the examples and derive the meanings from context.
2. Note that all meanings of these phrasal verbs have not been presented here. (e.g., pick up—*He picked up a woman in the bar./My friend picks me up at school every day.*). You may decide to expand on these meanings, or at least inform Ss that there are many other meanings. They will need to understand the meanings in context.
3. Introduce the inseparable phrasal verbs and stress that the particle does not move.

EXPANSION

To help Ss develop a "feel" for phrasal verbs, have them create flash cards with a phrasal verb on one side and the meaning and example(s) on the other. Use these as a warm-up; for reinforcement, have Ss create sentences or mini-dialogues using the phrasal verbs. Have them look for new phrasal verbs in authentic texts

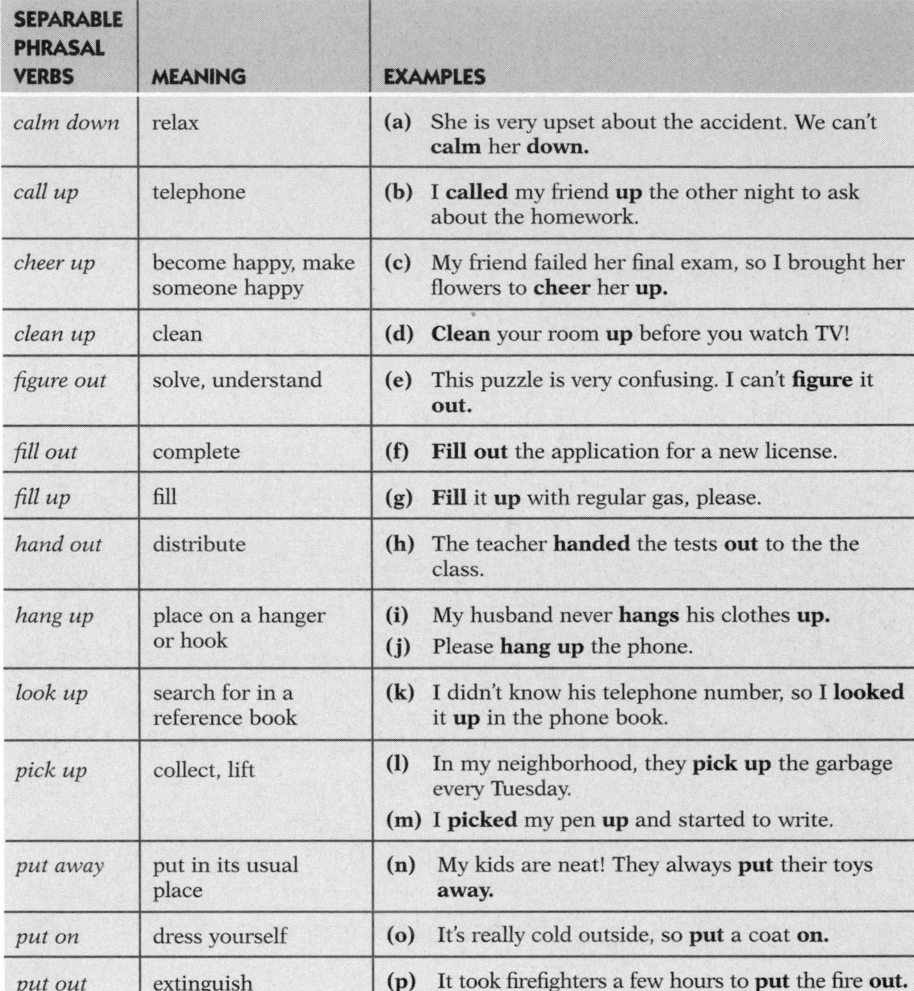

FOCUS 4

MEANING

Common Separable and Inseparable Phrasal Verbs

Separable Phrasal Verbs

SEPARABLE PHRASAL VERBS	MEANING	EXAMPLES
calm down	relax	(a) She is very upset about the accident. We can't **calm** her **down.**
call up	telephone	(b) I **called** my friend **up** the other night to ask about the homework.
cheer up	become happy, make someone happy	(c) My friend failed her final exam, so I brought her flowers to **cheer** her **up.**
clean up	clean	(d) **Clean** your room **up** before you watch TV!
figure out	solve, understand	(e) This puzzle is very confusing. I can't **figure** it **out.**
fill out	complete	(f) **Fill out** the application for a new license.
fill up	fill	(g) **Fill** it **up** with regular gas, please.
hand out	distribute	(h) The teacher **handed** the tests **out** to the the class.
hang up	place on a hanger or hook	(i) My husband never **hangs** his clothes **up.** (j) Please **hang up** the phone.
look up	search for in a reference book	(k) I didn't know his telephone number, so I **looked** it **up** in the phone book.
pick up	collect, lift	(l) In my neighborhood, they **pick up** the garbage every Tuesday. (m) I **picked** my pen **up** and started to write.
put away	put in its usual place	(n) My kids are neat! They always **put** their toys **away.**
put on	dress yourself	(o) It's really cold outside, so **put** a coat **on.**
put out	extinguish	(p) It took firefighters a few hours to **put** the fire **out.**

352 UNIT 21

SEPARABLE PHRASAL VERBS	MEANING	EXAMPLES
take off	remove	(q) **Take** your shoes **off** before you come into the house.
take out	put something outside	(r) Will you please **take** the garbage **out**?
throw out/ away	put in the garbage	(s) I have a lot of old things in the garage. I need to **throw** them **out.**
turn down	lower the volume	(t) It's 2:00 in the morning. **Turn** that stereo **down!**
turn off	stop the power	(u) There aren't any good programs on TV tonight. **Turn** it **off.**
turn on	start the power	(v) I always **turn on** the radio in the morning.
turn up	increase the volume	(w) When I hear my favorite song, I **turn** the volume **up.**
wake up	to open your eyes; to finish sleeping; to interrupt someone's sleep	(x) Be quiet! Don't **wake** the baby **up.**

Inseparable Phrasal Verbs

INSEPARABLE PHRASAL VERBS	MEANING	EXAMPLES
get in *get out of**	enter and leave a vehicle (car, taxi, truck)	(y) I **got in** my car and drove away. (z) I dropped my bag when I **got out of** the cab.
get on *get off*	enter and leave other forms of transportation (bus, plane, train)	(aa) I **got on** the train at 42nd Street. (bb) I **got off** the bus in front of the school.
go over	review	(cc) I **went over** my notes before the test.
run into	meet by chance	(dd) I **ran into** an old friend the other day.

*Sometimes phrasal verbs have three parts.

Exercise 6

Have Ss pairs read these short interactions aloud.

EXERCISE 6

Fill in the blanks with the phrasal verbs below. Use a pronoun in the second blank of each dialogue.

▶ **EXAMPLE:** (clean up)

Mother: Danny, don't forget to (a) _clean up_ the mess in your bedroom.

Danny: Mom, I (b) _cleaned it up_ this morning.

pick up	cheer up	hand out	throw out	fill out

1. **Counselor:** You need to (a) ________________ this application for college.

   Abdul: Can I (b) ________________ at home?

2. **Susie:** Danny, I think it's time to (a) ________________ all these old newspapers.

   Danny: I'm (b) ________________ right now.

3. **Jackie:** Could you please (a) ________________ that paper on the floor for me?

   Mark: I'll (b) ________________ in a minute!

4. **Ms. Wagner:** Can you help me (a) ________________ these exams, John?

   John: Sure, I'll (b) ________________ right now.

5. **Mom:** Please try to (a) ________________ your sister. She's in a bad mood!

   Bobbie: No one can (b) ________________. She's always in a bad mood.

ANSWER KEY

Exercise 6

1.a. fill out **b.** fill it out **2.a.** throw out **b.** throwing them out **3.a.** pick up **b.** pick it up **4.a.** hand out **b.** hand them out **5.a.** cheer up **b.** cheer her up

EXERCISE 7

Sylvia is working late tonight. She's calling her husband, Abe, to see if he has done all the things on her list. Role-play the dialogue with a partner.

▶ **EXAMPLE:** **Sylvia:** Did you pick up the children at school?

Abe: Yes, dear. I picked them up.

1. pick up your shirts at the cleaners
2. clean up the kitchen
3. put away the clean laundry
4. take out the dog
5. throw out the old flowers in the vase
6. fill up the car with gas
7. pick up a pizza for dinner
8. turn on the movie for the children
9. call up Warren to invite him to dinner

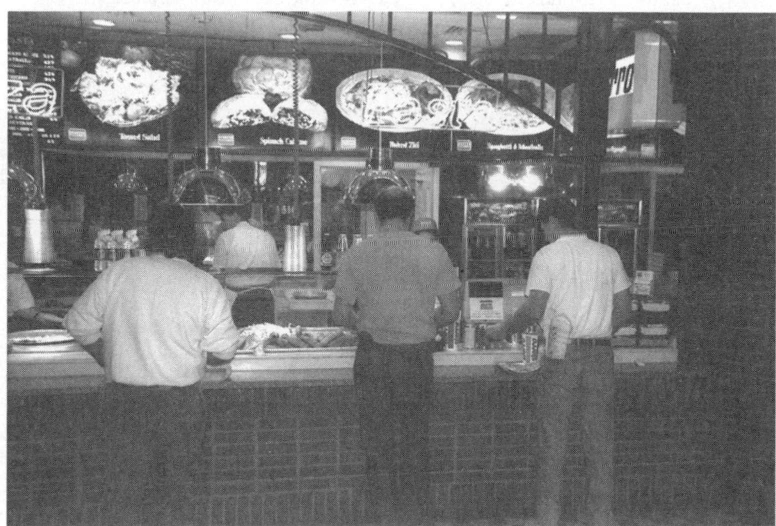

Exercise 7 

This exercise is supposed to evoke the hen-pecked husband. Have Ss role-play accordingly and embellish the dialogue if they can. Pay attention to stress and intonation. If some Ss are uncomfortable with this role-play situation, an alternative could be to have them be roommates.

Workbook Exs. 4&5, pp. 170–172. Answers: TE, p. 540.

ANSWER KEY

Exercise 7

1. Did you pick up... Yes, I picked them up.
2. Did you clean up... Yes, I cleaned it up.
3. Did you put away... Yes, I put it away.
4. Did you take out... Yes, I took her/him out.
5. Did you throw out... Yes, I threw them out.
6. Did you fill up... Yes, I filled it up. **7.** Did you pick up... Yes, I picked it up. **8.** Did you turn on... Yes, I turned it on. **9.** Did you call up... Yes, I called him up.

FOCUS 5

1. Common phrasal verbs without objects should also be learned in context. As in Focus 4, have Ss cover up the "meaning" column, read the examples, and derive meaning through context.
2. Have Ss generate other examples with these phrasal verbs. *My computer always breaks down. I invited them to my party, but they never showed up.*
3. Ask Ss questions and have them use the phrasal verbs in their answers. *How often do you eat out? How often does your car break down? In your home country, do Ss stand up when a teacher walks into a room?*

Exercise 8

Have Ss do this exercise individually or in pairs.

FOCUS **5** FORM MEANING

Common Phrasal Verbs without Objects

Some phrasal verbs do not take an object.

PHRASAL VERBS WITHOUT OBJECTS	MEANING	EXAMPLES
break down	stop working	**(a)** My car **broke down** last night, so I walked home.
come back	return	**(b)** He left home and never **came back**.
come in	enter	**(c)** **Come in** and make yourself comfortable.
eat out	eat in a restaurant	**(d)** I hate to cook, so I often **eat out**.
grow up	become an adult	**(e)** I **grew up** in the United States.
show up	appear	**(f)** After two hours, he finally **showed up**.
sit down	sit	**(g)** I feel tired, so I think I'll **sit down** for a while.
stand up	stand	**(h)** In some countries, students **stand up** to show respect when the teacher enters the room.

EXERCISE 8

Fill in the blanks with a phrasal verb from the box.

stand up	sit down	break down	eat out
show up	come in	come back	grow up

What do you say when . . . ?

1. you are very late for an important date:
   "Oh, I'm so sorry. Please forgive me, my car ________________."
2. your friend's dog runs away from home:
   "Don't worry, Elliot; I'm sure she'll ________________ home very soon."

ANSWER KEY

Exercise 8

1. broke down 2. come back 3. Stand up
4. grow up 5. come in 6. eat out
7. show up 8. sit down

3. a child is sitting and an elderly man is standing on the bus. The child's mother says: "________________ and give that man your seat."
4. your thirty-year-old friend is acting like a child:
"Come on, Matt, ________________. You're not a child anymore."
5. you are a car salesperson and you are trying to get people into your showroom:
"Please ________________, folks. We have many new models and great prices this year."
6. you and your roommate are hungry, but you're too tired to cook:
"Let's ________________."
7. your friend is crying about her date last night:
Tammy: "What happened, Cheryl? Don't tell me your date didn't ________________ last night."
Cheryl: "Oh, he did! That's why I'm crying!"
8. you are a receptionist in a very busy doctor's office and an angry patient is complaining about waiting so long:
"Please ________________, Mr. Brody. The doctor will be with you in a few minutes."

Exercise 9 

This is a cartoon about human nature. All Ss can understand and probably relate to this experience.

SUGGESTION

1. Have Ss describe each picture first before trying to put the pictures in order.
2. Have Ss generate possible stories by looking at the pictures. This will provide them with some background vocabulary and help them read the story in this exercise.
3. Ss can do the exercise individually or in groups.

Workbook Ex. 6, p. 173.
Answers: TE, p. 540–541.

UNIT GOAL REVIEW

Ask Ss to look back at the goals on the opening page of the unit and evaluate their own levels of progress and determine their own areas of weakness. If common problems persist, reteach or continue to practice these items in class or for homework. If individual problems persist, make recommendations to those Ss having problems.

EXERCISE 9

Make a story by puting the pictures in the correct order. Write the number of each picture next to the letter. Then fill in each blank with a phrasal verb from the box below.

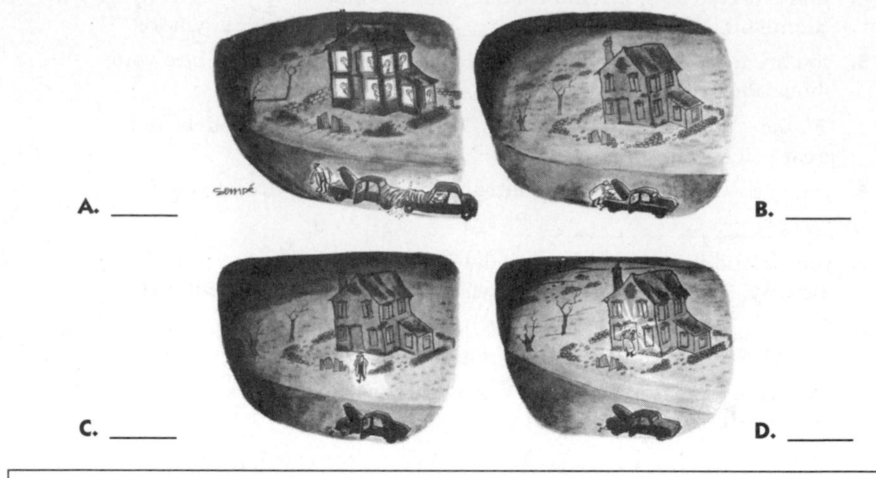

fill up	look up	break down
figure out	wake up	calm down
turn on	get out of	take out

It was a cold and lonely night. Forgetful Phil was on his way to visit his mother when his car suddenly (1) ______________. He was angry and upset, but after a while, he (2) ______________. It was dark, so Phil (3) ______________ a flashlight from the glove compartment. Then he took out his car manual. He tried to (4) ______________, *"What to do when your car breaks down in the middle of nowhere,"* but he didn't find anything in the manual. Next, he (5) ______________ the car and looked under the hood. He wasn't able to (6) ______________ what the problem was. Then Phil began to understand. He asked himself, "Did I (7) ______________ my tank with gas?" The answer, of course, was no.

Luckily there was a house near by. He knocked on the door and shouted, but nobody answered. There were no other houses. There was no telephone. "What now??" thought Phil. Then, just as he turned around to go back to his car, another car crashed into the back of his car. Suddenly, the people in the house (8) ______________ and (9) ______________ the lights. Poor Phil felt like crying.

358 UNIT 21

ANSWER KEY

Exercise 9

Order of pictures: A.4 B.1 C.3 D.2

1. broke down 2. calmed down 3. took out 4. look up 5. got out of 6. figure out 7. fill up 8. woke up 9. turned on

Use Your English

ACTIVITY 1: WRITING/SPEAKING

Work with a partner. Write a story or dialogue about the situation below, using the phrasal verbs in the box. Then role-play the situation for the class.

Situation: It is 11:00 P.M. You are sleeping very deeply. Suddenly, you hear some noise coming from the apartment downstairs. Your neighbor's stereo is very loud.

wake up	throw out	turn down	turn off
turn on	go back	calm down	call up

ACTIVITY 2: SPEAKING

Work in a group or as a whole class. The first person begins a story. He or she says, "I woke up . . ." and completes the sentence. The second person repeats the first sentence and adds a second sentence using a phrasal verb. The third person repeats the first two sentences and then adds a third, and so on. Try not to write anything down. Use your memory! Refer to the phrasal verbs in this unit.

▶ **EXAMPLES:** **Player #1:** I woke up early.

Player #2: I woke up early, and turned off the alarm clock.

Player #3: I woke up early, turned off the alarm clock, and took off my pajamas.

USE YOUR ENGLISH

For a more complete discussion of how to use the activities, see p. xxvi of this Teacher's Edition.

Activity 1

Contextualizing phrasal verbs around specific situations like this makes the meanings more accessible to Ss.

VARIATIONS

1. Allow Ss to write a dialogue, story, narrative, letter of complaint, etc., with these phrasal verbs. Let them share their texts with the class.
2. Have Ss write their texts on butcher block paper or transparencies (or an OHP). These can be posted in front of the room, read by the class, and used for correction. Encourage Ss to be creative, to use their imagination or their own personal experience.

EXPANSION

Have groups act out their stories for the class.

Activity 2

SUGGESTION

1. First, have the class brainstorm a list of phrasal verbs they remember from the unit and write them on the board. As Ss use a particular phrasal verb for the story, put a check next to the verb on the board. Ss may use the phrasal verb more than once if they wish.
2. Tape-record Ss telling the story. Then have them transcribe the tape and correct themselves.

Activity 3 

Step 1: Ss can work in a group or as a whole class.

Step 2: Have Ss write the actions on the board so the class can check the sentences. Encourage Ss to make a second sentence separating the particle if possible. *(Jose turned off the light. Jose turned the light off.)*

EXPANSION

Have Ss create their own phrasal verb grid and play the game again.

ACTIVITY 3: SPEAKING/WRITING

STEP 1 Work in a group. Put numbers 1 to 12 in a bag. Pick a number from the bag. Read the sentence in the box that corresponds to your number and then do the action.

STEP 2 After the group has done all the actions, write sentences about the things you did.

▶ **EXAMPLES:** Mario put on Marcela's cap.
José turned off the light.

1. Put on a piece of a classmate's clothing or jewelry.	2. Turn off the light.	3. You spill a cup of hot coffee on yourself and on the floor. Clean it up.
4. Call up a friend and tell him or her you are sick.	5. Draw a picture of yourself on a piece of paper and hang it up on the wall.	6. Stand up. Put your hands on your head. Then sit down.
7. Cheer a classmate up.	8. Hand your telephone number out to all the people in the group.	9. Take something out of your pocket and throw it away.
10. Take off an article of clothing and put it on someone else.	11. Turn on something electrical (tape recorder, radio, light, etc.) and then turn it off.	12. Pretend you find a word whose meaning you don't know. Look it up in the dictionary.

360 UNIT 21

ACTIVITY 4: LISTENING/SPEAKING

Amy wants to buy a jacket. She goes to a store.

STEP 1 Listen to the conversation. Then look at the statements below. Check (✔) True or False.

	True	False
1. The store doesn't have any size ten jackets.	____	____
2. The jacket Amy tries on fits perfectly.	____	____
3. Amy thinks the jacket is too expensive.	____	____
4. Amy doesn't like the pink jacket she is wearing.	____	____
5. Amy will return to the store.	____	____

STEP 2 Listen to the conversation again and complete the phrasal verbs you hear below:

take_____ put_____ throw_____ come_____ come_____

STEP 3 Compare the phrasal verbs you found with those your partner found. Now make a dialogue on a similar topic with your partner. Use the five phrasal verbs in the dialogue and others from this unit.

STEP 4 Role-play your dialogue in front of the class.

Activity 4 

Play textbook audio. The tapescript for this listening appears on p. 548 of this book.

EXPANSION

After doing the Activity, have Ss listen to the tape focusing on pronunciation and intonation.

The test for this unit can be found on pp. 511–512 of this book. The answers can be found on p. 513

TOEFL Test Preparation Exercises for Units 19–21 can be found on pp. 174–176 of the workbook.
The answers are on p. 541 of this book.

ANSWER KEY

Activity 4
Step 1
1. False **2.** True **3.** False **4.** True
5. True

Unit 22

UNIT OVERVIEW

In this unit, Students (Ss) will be using adjectives to realize the function "comparing." They will be expressing similarities and differences in both standard and more tactful ways. Ss generally enjoy discovering their similarities, so this unit will lead to interesting and lively discussions.

UNIT GOALS

To maximize the diagnostic potential of the Opening Task, do not review the Unit Goals with Ss until after they have completed and reviewed the Opening Task.

OPENING TASK
SETTING UP THE TASK

1. Elicit the kinds of things Ss would look for in an apartment (space, light, low rent, prime location, quiet environment, proximity to transportation, etc.). List new vocabulary on the board, especially key words such as *furnished, utilities, square feet, spacious, convenient, far, close,* which appear in the Opening Task.
2. Bring in advertisements for apartments from the classified section of the newspaper.

UNIT 22

COMPARISON WITH ADJECTIVES

UNIT GOALS:

- To use the (regular and irregular) comparative form of adjectives in statements
- To ask questions using comparative adjectives
- To express similarities and differences with adjectives using *as . . . as*
- To make polite comparisons

OPENING TASK
Comparison Shopping for an Apartment

You are a college student and are looking for an apartment. You study during the day and have a part-time job at night.

FOR RENT
Studio Apartment. 200 square feet. Central location. Close to bus stop and market. Fully furnished. $500/month plus utilities.

FOR RENT
One-bedroom apartment. 900 square feet. Quiet. Lots of light. $800/month including utilities.

STEP 1 Look at the apartment ads. Read the statements below about the studio apartment. Check (✓) *Yes, No,* or *I Don't Know.*

			YES	NO	I DON'T KNOW
	1. smaller				
	2. closer to the bus stop				
	3. farther away from the downtown area				
The studio apartment is	4. more expensive	than the one-bedroom apartment.			
	5. more spacious				
	6. noisier				
	7. safer				
	8. more convenient				
	9. sunnier				
	10. quieter				

STEP 2 Which apartment is better? Give reasons for your choice.

I think the ______________________ is better because . . .

CONDUCTING THE TASK

Step 1

Be sure Ss understand that the task is to compare the two apartments. Have Ss read the two ads. Go around the room as they work, to ensure that they understand each point of comparison. Then have Ss check the answers in the chart.

Step 2

Ss are asked to produce the target structure. Have pairs present their opinions. Write their answers on the board.

REVIEWING THE TASK

Use the Ss' statements as a bridge to the comparative form of adjectives in Focus Box 1.

ANSWER KEY

Opening Task

Step 1

1. Yes **2.** Yes **3.** I don't know
4. No **5.** No **6.** Yes **7.** I don't know
8. Yes **9.** No **10.** No

FOCUS 1

Deciding when to use *more* vs. *-er* is complicated for Ss.

1. First, see if Ss can generate the spelling rules for *a, b, c, d* by looking at the adjectives and the comparative forms. Present one-syllable adjectives and adjectives ending in *-y*. Give additional examples (*wide, hot, easy, tall*).
2. Have Ss read *e* and *f* and count out the number of syllables in the adjectives. Present additional examples if needed (comfortable, intelligent, difficult) and count the syllables. Note that some two-syllable adjectives can take either form: handsomer, more handsome; (cleverer, more clever—but not nervouser!). Tell Ss to use *more* if they are in doubt.
3. Present the examples and rules for irregular comparatives (*g, h,* and *i*). Remind Ss that these adjectives do not agree in number with the nouns they modify. In other words, we say: *These apartments are more convenient than those apartments.* NOT: *These apartments are more convenients than those apartments.*
4. Expect Ss to overgeneralize and produce sentences such as "*This is more better.*" Emphasize that there cannot be two markers (*more* + *er*) for a comparative form. Point out the use of *much* to make comparisons stronger.
5. Explain that we always compare things of the same nature. Put these two sentences on the board: "*Joe's feet are bigger than Jay's (feet).* NOT: "*Joe's feet are bigger than Jay.*"

FOCUS **1**

Comparative Form of Adjectives

Regular Comparatives

There are two regular comparative forms of adjectives in English.

1. For adjectives with one syllable or those ending in *-y*:

X *is* ______________*er than* Y.

EXAMPLE	ADJECTIVE	COMPARATIVE	RULE
(a) This neighborhood is **safer than** that one.	*safe*	*safer than*	For adjectives ending in *-e*, add *-r*.
(b) The one-bedroom apartment is **bigger than** the studio.	*big*	*bigger than*	For adjectives that end in consonant-vowel-consonant, double the consonant, add *-er*.
(c) The studio is **noisier than** the one bedroom.	*noisy*	*noisier than*	For adjectives ending in *-y*, change the *-y* to *i*, add *-er*.
(d) The studio is **smaller than** the one-bedroom.	*small*	*smaller than*	For all other adjectives, add *-er*.

2. For adjectives with two or more syllables:

X *is (more/less)* ______________ *than* Y.

EXAMPLE	ADJECTIVE	COMPARATIVE	RULE
(e) The studio is **more economical than** the one-bedroom.	*economical*	*more economical than*	Use *more* or *less* before the adjective.
(f) The studio is **less expensive than** the one-bedroom.	*expensive*	*less expensive than*	

NOTES:

- Some adjectives with two syllables can take either *-er* or *more/less*. For example: *quiet—quieter* or *more quiet.*
- In formal English we say: Joe is taller than **I** (am).
- In informal English we sometimes say: Joe is taller than **me**.
- Be sure to compare two like things: My hair is longer than Rita's (hair). NOT: My hair is longer than Rita.

Irregular Comparatives

EXAMPLES	EXPLANATIONS
(g) This neighborhood is **better than** that one. (h) This year's winter was **worse than** last year's (winter). (i) The one-bedroom is **farther** away from the bus stop **than** the studio is.	The comparative forms of good, bad, and far are irregular. *good—better* *bad—worse* *far—farther*
(j) This apartment is **much better than** that one. (k) This apartment is **much farther than** the other one.	Use *much* to make a comparison stronger.

EXERCISE 1

Make statements using the comparative form of each adjective in parentheses + *than*. Make a logical conclusion for each set of sentences.

EXAMPLES: Dog lovers say:

a. Dogs are (smart) smarter than cats.

b. Dogs are (obedient) more obedient than cats.

c. Therefore, dogs are (good) better than cats.

1. **a.** A small car is (easy) ________________ to drive ________________ a big car.
   b. A small car is (economical) ________________ a big car.
   c. A big car is (practical) ________________ a small car.
2. **a.** The weather in Spain is (hot) ________________ the weather in Sweden.
   b. The food in hot countries is (spicy) ________________ the food in cold countries.

Exercise 1

This exercise presents sets of facts that lead to logical conclusions.

SUGGESTION

1. Encourage Ss to draw other logical conclusions in this context: "*A small car is more practical than a big car.*"
2. Or, have them read the first two sentences (*a* & *b*) and draw a logical conclusion before they actually read "*c*".

ANSWER KEY

Exercise 1

1.a. easier to drive than **b.** more economical than **c.** less practical than **2.a.** hotter than **b.** spicier than **c.** less spicy than **3.a.** less nervous than **b.** more talkative than **c.** more comfortable than **4.a.** more expensive than **b.** more crowded than **c.** more difficult to travel during holidays than

Exercise 2

Have Ss do this exercise individually and then role-play the dialogue with a partner to check their answers.

VARIATION

To vary their responses, assign different role relationships to each pair—in one case they could be friends; in others, they could be boyfriend/girlfriend, parent and child, etc. Tape or videotape them. Let the class judge how the relationship affects intonation and body language when these role-plays are performed.

c. Therefore, the food in Sweden is (spicy) ________________ the food in Spain.

3. a. Outgoing people are often (nervous) ________________ shy people.
   b. They are (talkative) ________________ shy people.
   c. Therefore, they are (comfortable) ________________ shy people in social situations.
4. a. During a holiday season, airline tickets are (expensive) ________________ they are off season.
   b. During a holiday season, hotels are (crowded) ________________ they are off season.
   c. It's (difficult) ________________ to travel during holidays ________________ off season.

EXERCISE 2

Fill in the blanks with the comparative form of the adjective.

Jane: Kevin, I found these two apartment ads in the newspaper this morning. There's a studio and a one-bedroom. I think the one-bedroom sounds nice. What do you think?

Kevin: Well, the one-bedroom is definitely (1) (large) ________________ than the studio, but the studio is (2) (cheap) ________________ . You know you only have a part-time job. How can you afford to pay $800 a month for rent?

Jane: I know the one-bedroom is (3) (expensive) ________________ , but I have so much furniture. The one-bedroom is (4) (big) ________________ and I want to have guests visit and it will be much (5) (comfortable) ________________ . Besides, maybe someday I'll have a roommate, and I'll need a (6) (spacious) ________________ apartment, Kevin. Right?

Kevin: Well, maybe, but you need to be realistic. The studio is in the center of town. You'll be (7) (close) ________________ to transportation, stores, the library, and the college.

Jane: You're much (8) (practical) ________________ than I am, Kevin. But the studio is directly over a nightclub, so it will be (9) (noisy) ________________ than the one-bedroom. I will need peace and quiet so I can study.

ANSWER KEY

Exercise 2

1. larger 2. cheaper 3. more expensive 4. bigger 5. more comfortable 6. more spacious 7. closer 8. more practical 9. noisier 10. cozier 11. safer 12. better

Kevin: Listen,—the studio is small, but it's much (10) (cozy) _______________ than the one-bedroom and you'll spend much less time cleaning it!

Jane: True, but I think the one-bedroom will be much (11) (safe) _______________ and (12) (good) _______________ for me than the studio.

Kevin: It seems to me your mind is made up.

Jane: Yes, it is. By the way, Kevin, I'm going to see the one-bedroom later today. Can you come with me?

Kevin: Sure.

EXERCISE 3

Write an advertisement for each product on the left. Compare it to the product on the right. Use the adjectives below.

▶ **EXAMPLE:** *"Double Chocolate" cake tastes richer than "Chocolate Surprise."*

1. **Product:** Double Chocolate Cake Mix
   Compare with Chocolate Surprise Cake Mix.
   Adjectives: rich, creamy, delicious, sweet, thick, fattening

   ____
   ____
   ____

2. **Product:** Genie Laundry Detergent
   Compare with Bubbles Laundry Detergent.
   Adjectives: strong, effective, expensive, gentle, concentrated

   ____
   ____
   ____

3. **Product:** Save-a-Watt Space Heater
   Compare with Consumer Space Heater.
   Adjectives: efficient, safe, reliable, big, economical, practical

   ____
   ____
   ____

Exercise 3  

Have Ss work in pairs or in groups.

SUGGESTIONS

1. Encourage them to add their own adjectives, and create new names for these products.
2. Have each pair present an ad as if they were on TV. Ask the class to decide which presentation was the most convincing. If you have access to a videocamera, videotape the presentations and analyze them for effectiveness, creativity and for errors.

EXPANSION

1. Cut out products from magazines or catalogues and ask Ss to create advertisements for these. Use unusual items from catalogues such as The Sharper Image, Home Depot, the Pottery Barn (e.g., an electric towel warmer). Use audio or video recordings of commercials for listening strategy practice.
2. Devise listening comprehension activities in which Ss have to (1) identify the product being sold, (2) identify the comparative form(s), (3) identify the seller's strategy. This will prepare Ss for Activity 4.

ANSWER KEY

Exercise 3

1. Double Chocolate Cake is richer than; creamier than; more delicious than; sweeter than; thicker than; more fattening than Chocolate Surprise Cake Mix. **2.** Genie laundry detergent is stronger than; more effective than; less expensive than; more gentle (gentler) than Bubbles laundry detergent, more concentrated than. **3.** Save-Watt Space Heater is more efficient than; safer than; more reliable than; bigger than; more economical than; more practical than Consumer Space Heater.

Exercise 4

SUGGESTIONS

1. To make this exercise more concrete and interesting, bring in a map of the U.S. and pictures of Brattleboro, Vermont (or of small towns in New England) and of Los Angeles (or of a big city). Have Ss make statements about where they would prefer to live and why. This will generate some useful vocabulary and help them do the exercise.
2. Have Ss work in pairs or groups and generate as many statements as possible in this pre-phase.
3. Since this exercise is a bit more open-ended, anticipate Ss' errors here, especially those which fail to compare two things of a similar nature. Example: Ss might say, *Public transportation in L.A. is better than Brattleboro, instead of: Public transportation in L.A. is better than (it is) in Brattleboro.* *Or, L.A.'s public transportation (system) is better than Brattleboro's.*

Workbook Exs. 1&2, pp. 177–180
Answers: TE, p. 541.

EXERCISE 4

Yoko wants to study English in the United States. She knows about an English program in Brattleboro, a small town in Vermont. She also knows about a program in Los Angeles, a big city in California. She needs to decide where she wants to live. Here is some information about the two places.

	Brattleboro, Vermont	**Los Angeles, California**
1. Rent for a one-bed apartment	$450 a month	$1,000 a month
2. Population	12,000	3 million
3. Weather	cold in winter hot in summer	warm in winter hot in summer
4. Public transportation	not good	good
5. Quality of life		
a. the environment	clean	not so clean
b. the crime rate	low	high
c. lifestyle	relaxed	busy
d. the streets	quiet	noisy

Make comparative statements about Brattleboro and Los Angeles.

1. crime rate (low/high) *The crime rate is lower in Brattleboro than in Los Angeles. The crime rate is higher in Los Angeles than in Brattleboro.*
2. (populated) __________
3. (cheap/expensive) __________
4. public transportation (good/bad) __________
5. winters (cold) __________
6. (dangerous/safe) __________
7. (clean/dirty) __________
8. (quiet/noisy) __________
9. (relaxed/busy) __________
10. In your opinion, which place is better for Yoko? Why?

ANSWER KEY

Exercise 4

Answers may vary.
2. Brattleboro is less populated than L.A./L.A is more populated than Brattleboro. **3.** A one-bedroom apartment in Brattleboro is cheaper than a one-bedroom apartment in L.A./A one-bedroom apartment is more expensive in L.A. than in Brattleboro.
4. Public transportation in L.A. is better than in Brattleboro. **5.** Winters are colder in Brattleboro than in L.A./Winters in L.A. are warmer than in Brattleboro. **6.** L.A. is more dangerous than Brattleboro/Brattleboro is safer than L.A. **7.** Brattleboro is cleaner than L.A./L.A. is dirtier than Brattleboro.
8. Brattleboro is quieter than L.A./L.A. is noisier than Brattleboro. **9.** Brattleboro is more relaxed than L.A./L.A. is busier than Brattleboro.

FOCUS 2

Questions with Comparative Adjectives

EXAMPLES

(a)	Is the one-bedroom **more expensive than** the studio?
(b)	Are studios **better than** apartments?
(c)	Are studios **less practical than** one bedroom apartments?
(d)	**Who** is **older**, you or your brother?
(e)	**Which** is **more difficult**, English or Chinese?
(f)	**Whose** apartment is **more comfortable**, yours or hers?

EXERCISE 5

Refer to the Opening Task on pages 362–363 and ask a partner *yes/no* questions about the studio and the one-bedroom apartment. Answer the questions.

EXAMPLE: economical

Is the studio more economical than the one-bedroom?

Yes, it is.

1. practical
2. far from the downtown area
3. small
4. cheap
5. sunny
6. comfortable
7. economical
8. roomy
9. quiet
10. convenient
11. close to the bus stop
12. pretty
13. large
14. good

FOCUS 2

Review yes/no questions with *be* and questions with *who, which, whose*, reminding Ss that questions with *whose* require responses with possessives (*my apartment, mine*).

Exercise 5 

Have Ss work in pairs and alternate asking questions and giving answers.

ANSWER KEY

Exercise 5

Ss will generate a variety of questions. Check answers to ensure that they are true in the context of these two apartments. Possible questions: **1.** Is the studio more practical than the one-bedroom? **2.** Is the studio farther from the downtown area than the one-bedroom? **3.** smaller than– **4.** cheaper than– **5.** sunnier than– **6.** more comfortable than– **7.** more economical than– **8.** roomier than– **9.** quieter than– **10.** more convenient than– **11.** closer to the bus stop than– **12.** prettier than– **13.** larger than– **14.** better than–

Exercise 6 

This exercise is more open-ended, designed to provoke interesting discussion. After pairwork, ask Ss to share their answers with the class to open up the discussion.

Exercise 7  

Have Ss work in pairs or small groups. Some of these questions should generate lively discussion. Encourage Ss to justify their answers by making additional comparative statements.

Workbook Exs. 3&4, p. 180.
Answers: TE, p. 541.

EXERCISE 6

Interview your partner. Answer each other's questions.

▶ **EXAMPLE:** **Question:** Is a theater ticket more expensive than a movie ticket?

Answer: Yes, it is. No, it isn't. **OR** I'm not sure.

1. people in the United States/friendly/people in other countries
2. English grammar/difficult/the grammar of your native language
3. a house/good/an apartment
4. a single person's life/exciting/a married person's life
5. reading/interesting/watching TV
6. electric heat/economical/gas heat
7. men/romantic/women
8. a Japanese watch/expensive/a Swiss watch
9. the American population/diverse/the population in your native country

EXERCISE 7

Ask a partner questions with *who, which,* or *whose* and the words in parentheses. Answer each other's questions.

▶ **EXAMPLES:** (popular) Who is more popular, Elton John or Ricky Martin?

(practical) Which is less practical, a cordless phone or a regular phone?

1. (funny) Steven Martin or Jim Carrey?
2. (difficult) speaking English or writing English?
3. (hard) a man's life or a woman's life?
4. (bad) ironing or vacuuming?
5. (cheap) a public college or a private college?
6. (interesting) a taxi cab driver's job or a scientist's job?
7. (powerful) a four-cylinder car or a five-cylinder car?
8. (dangerous) a motorcycle or a car?
9. (sensitive) a man or a woman?
10. (good) Celine Dion's voice or Barbara Streisand's voice?
11. (delicious) Chinese food or Italian food?
12. (spicy) Indian food or Japanese food?

ANSWER KEY

Exercise 6

1. Are people in the U.S. friendlier than...
2. Is English grammar more difficult than...
3. Is a house better than...
4. Is a single person's life more exciting than...
5. Is reading more interesting than...
6. Is electric heat more economical than...
7. Are men more romantic than...
8. Is a Japanese watch more expensive than...
9. Is the American population more diverse than...

Exercise 7

1. Who is funnier? 2. Which is more difficult... 3. Which is harder... 4. Which is worse... 5. Which is cheaper... 6. Whose job is more interesting... 7. Which is more powerful... 8. Which is more dangerous 9. Who is more sensitive... 10. Whose voice is better... 11. Which is more delicious... 12. Which is spicier...

FOCUS **3**

Expressing Similarities and Differences with *As . . . As*

EXAMPLES	EXPLANATIONS
(a) Mark is **as tall as** Sam. (b) Tokyo is **as crowded as** Hong Kong.	To say two things are equal or the same, use *as* + adjective + *as*.
(c) Mark **isn't as tall as** Steve. (= Steve is taller than Mark.) (d) The studio **isn't as expensive as** the one-bedroom.	To say there is a difference between two things, use *not as* + adjective + *as*.

EXERCISE 8

Here is a dialogue between teenage Tommy and his mother. Write the correct form of the comparative in the blanks. Use *-er, more than, less than,* and *as . . . as.*

Mother: Tommy, I don't want you to buy a motorcycle. Why don't you buy a car instead? A car is (1) more convenient than (convenient) a motorcycle and it's (2) ______________ (practical), too.

Tommy: Maybe it is, Mom, but a car isn't (3) ______________ (economical) a motorcycle. I can get fifty miles to a gallon with a motorcycle! And a motorcycle's (4) ______________ (cheap) a car.

Mother: Listen to me. You live in a big city. There are a lot of crazy people out there on the streets. A car is (5) ______________ (safe) a motorcycle.

Tommy: Mom, I'm a good driver. I'm (6) ______________ (good) you are! Besides that, it's (7) ______________ (easy) to park a motorcycle in the city than it is to park a car.

Mother: Well, you're right about that. But I'm still your mother and you live in my house, so you will do as I say! When you are (8) ______________ (old), you can do whatever you want.

FOCUS 3

Ask two Ss of about the same height to stand up. Then elicit the statement: (a)__*is as tall as*__. Do the same with two Ss whose hair is about the same length and elicit "__*'s hair is as long/short as*__*'s hair*. Remember to point out that we must compare two things of the same nature. (*My hair is as long as Rita's*. NOT: *as long as Rita*)

Exercise 8

Have several pairs role-play this dialogue. Focus on stress and intonation. Ask Ss to decide which Ss played their roles most convincingly.

ANSWER KEY

Exercise 8
2. more practical **3.** as economical as **4.** cheaper than **5.** safer than **6.** better than/as good as **7.** easier **8.** older **9.** as cool as **10.** as nervous as **11.** as concerned as

Tommy: But all my friends are getting motorcycles, Mom. I won't look (9) ______________ (cool) my friends.

Mother: I don't care, Tommy. Maybe their mothers aren't (10) ______________ (nervous) I am, or (11) ______________ (concerned) I am. My answer is "no" and that's final!

Exercise 9 

Try to mix nationalities in the pairs or groups. Encourage Ss to share their experiences with the class. Keep track of errors produced and review these at the end of the discussion.

Workbook Ex. 5, p. 181.
Answers: TE, p. 541.

EXERCISE 9

Work with a partner. Make *yes/no* questions with *as . . . as*. Compare the city/town you are living in now with a city/town in your native country.

▶ **EXAMPLE:** city/crowded

Is Quito as crowded as Philadelphia?

1. capital city/big
2. foreign cars in . . . /expensive
3. the school year in . . . /long
4. soccer in . . . /popular
5. your hometown/safe
6. teenagers in your country/interested in rock music
7. beaches/crowded
8. foreign films/popular
9. air/polluted

FOCUS 4

Have Ss read the examples and explanations. Elicit certain characteristics that people might be particularly sensitive about, such as age. Try to have Ss generate examples: *He's not as young as his friends.* vs. *He's older than his friends.* Additional adjectives: *ugly/pretty; fat/thin; sloppy/neat.* Discuss this strategy for putting a positive or polite "spin" on things.

FOCUS **4**

USE

Making Polite Comparisons

EXAMPLES	EXPLANATIONS
(a) Hamid is **shorter than** Marco. (b) Hamid is **not as tall as** Marco.	Sentence (b) is more polite. To make a polite comparison, use not *as* + adjective + *as*.

ANSWER KEY

Exercise 9

Answers will vary.
1. Is the capital city of ____ as big as Washington, D.C.?**2.** Are foreign cars in... as expensive as **3.** Is the school year in... as long as in **4.** Is soccer as popular in.... as.... in **5.** Is your hometown as safe as in **6.** Are teenagers in your country as interested in rock music as in **7.** Are beaches in... as crowded as in **8.** Are foreign films in... as popular as in **9.** Is the air in... as polluted as the air in

EXERCISE 10

You are "Blunt Betty." Your statements are very direct and a little impolite. Read a statement from Column A. Your partner, "Polite Polly," makes a statement with *not as + adjective + as* to make your statement more polite. The first one has been done for you.

Column A Blunt Betty	Column B Polite Polly
1. Marco is fatter than Jonathan.	(thin) Marco is not as thin as Jonathan.
2. London is dirtier than Geneva.	(clean)
3. Science class is more boring than math.	(interesting)
4. Your child is lazier than mine.	(ambitious)
5. Your car is slower than ours.	(fast)
6. Her eyesight is worse than mine.	(good)
7. Your apartment is smaller than ours.	(big)
8. Miguel's pronunciation is worse than Maria's.	(good)
9. American coffee is weaker than Turkish coffee.	(strong)
10. Your salary is lower than mine.	(high)

EXERCISE 11

Make true statements about yourself. Use each of the categories below. Add more categories of your own.

EXAMPLES: My partner's older than I am. My partner's older than me.
I'm not as old as he is. I'm not as old as him.

Categories	Me	My Partner
1. Age	19	24
2. Height		
3. Hair length		
4. Hair color		
5. Personality		
6. Other		

EXERCISE 12

Correct the errors in the following sentences.

1. John is more tall than Mary.
2. Seoul is more safer than Los Angeles.
3. Paul is as intelligent than Robert.

Exercise 10

Explain the meaning of "blunt" — "to be frank," e.g., *She is blunt because she tells people exactly what she thinks.*

Exercise 11

This exercise is more open-ended and a good way for Ss to practice making polite and tactful comparisons. Because these categories might all represent sensitive issues, it is important for Ss to be able to talk about them in a socially appropriate way. Add to this list categories that are relevant to your Ss.

If Ss are comfortable with each other, have them report the information to the class. You can also ask Ss to write their comparisons.

Exercise 12

Have Ss do this exercise individually or in pairs. It can also be done as homework.

ANSWER KEY

Exercise 10

2. not as clean as **3.** not as interesting as **4.** not as ambitious as **5.** not as fast as **6.** not as good as **7.** not as big as **8.** not as good as **9.** not as strong as **10.** not as high as

Exercise 12

1. John is taller than Mary. **2.** Seoul is safer (much safer) than Los Angeles. **3.** Paul is as intelligent as Robert. **4.** Mary is not as beautiful as Kim. **5.** My test scores were (much) worse than Margaret's. **6.** Lorraine's eyes are darker than mine (my eyes). **7.** Jeff is handsomer/more handsome than Jack. **8.** My parents' life was harder than mine. **9.** Is New York as exciting as Paris? **10.** Is Lake Ontario cleaner than Lake Erie? **11.** The Hudson River is not as polluted as the Volga River. **12.** Mexico's capital city is more crowded than America's capital city.

UNIT GOAL REVIEW

Ask Ss to look back at the goals on the opening page of the unit and evaluate their own levels of progress and determine their own areas of weakness. If common problems persist, reteach or continue to practice these items in class or for homework. If individual problems persist, make recommendations to those Ss having problems.

USE YOUR ENGLISH

For a more complete discussion of how to use the activities, see p. xxvi of this Teacher's Edition.

Activity 1 

This activity will provoke a lot of discussion. Have Ss work individually first to fill in the column "Your Country" and to add items to the list. Then, ask Ss to work in pairs.

VARIATIONS

1. Ss can complete this as a "Find Someone Who" activity where they all move around the room asking each other for information. They then make summary statements using comparatives.
2. This activity can also be done as a whole class. Create one large chart with all the countries represented in your class. Have Ss complete the chart and make a variety of comparative statements. This chart can also be used when you introduce superlatives (*Gas is the cheapest in Mexico.*)

4. Mary is not beautiful as Kim.
5. My test scores were more worse than Margaret's.
6. Lorraine's eyes are darker than me.
7. Jeff is more handsomer than Jack.
8. My parents' life was hard than mine.
9. Is New York exciting as Paris?
10. Is Lake Ontario cleaner that Lake Erie?
11. The Hudson River is not polluted as the Volga River.
12. Mexico's capital city is more crowded than the United States.

Use Your English

ACTIVITY 1: SPEAKING

How much do the following things cost in your country? Write the cost in United States dollars for each thing in your country. Ask a classmate the prices of the same things in his or her country. Add three items of your own. Present your comparisons to the class.

▶ **EXAMPLE:** A gallon of gas is more expensive in Malaysia than in Indonesia.

	Your Country	Classmate's Country
1. a gallon of gas		
2. a movie ticket		
3. bus fare		
4. a pair of jeans		
5. a cup of coffee		
6. rent for a one-bedroom apartment		
7. a newspaper		
8.		
9.		
10.		

ACTIVITY 2: WRITING/SPEAKING

Work in a group. Write six statements comparing cities, countries, or other places in the world. Make three statements that are true and three statements that are false. Read the statements to the class. The class guesses if they are true or false.

▶ **EXAMPLES:** *Canada is larger than the People's Republic of China.* (False)

The Pacific Ocean is bigger than the Atlantic Ocean. (True)

ACTIVITY 3: WRITING/SPEAKING

STEP 1 Look at the list of adjectives. Think about yourself and check *Very, Average,* or *Not Very* for each adjective.

STEP 2 Compare yourself with a partner. Write a comparative sentence for each adjective.

STEP 3 Tell the class about you and your partner.

▶ **EXAMPLES:** I'm more talkative than my partner.

He's less practical than I am.

I'm as athletic as he is.

	Very	*Average*	*Not Very*
1. talkative	______	______	______
2. friendly	______	______	______
3. shy	______	______	______
4. neat	______	______	______
5. practical	______	______	______
6. optimistic	______	______	______
7. moody	______	______	______
8. lazy	______	______	______
9. funny	______	______	______
10. athletic	______	______	______
11. jealous	______	______	______
12. serious	______	______	______
13. ______	______	______	______
14. ______	______	______	______
15. ______	______	______	______

Activity 2 

This is an opportunity for Ss to apply their background knowledge. Make this into a contest or game. Give points for each correct guess.

Activity 3 

This activity encourages Ss to compare their personalities. Most of these adjectives have already appeared in previous units, but review them first. Ask Ss to add other adjectives (*pessimistic, modest, studious, hard-working*). Have Ss write comparative sentences. Check them in class or collect and check.

Activity 4 

Ss were prepared for this advertising campaign in Exercise 7. Encourage them to come up with creative, relevant, and interesting products or services: a new soft drink, a cultural service for foreign Ss, a new method for learning English, a language school. Have them present their ads. The class decides which ad was the most convincing, the funniest, the most original.

Activity 5 

Do Step 1 with the whole class. When adding statements, try to elicit ideas that lend themselves to discussion. Examples: *Work is more interesting. People are less selfish.* Explain to Ss that these are implicit comparisons: "*Life is more difficult*" implies life is more difficult today than it was 50 years ago. In context, it is not necessary to make each comparison explicit.

EXPANSION

When Ss work individually, ask them to write one or two statements to support their views. Example: *Life is more difficult. (a) Life is more stressful. (b) People are busier.*

ACTIVITY 4: WRITING/SPEAKING

Work with a partner. Find a product or service you want to sell. Create a name for it. Then write a thirty-second radio or TV commercial for the product or service. Present your commercials to the class.

ACTIVITY 5: WRITING/SPEAKING

STEP 1 Compare life today with life fifty years ago. Read the first four sentences on the chart below and then add six statements of your own. Check *Agree* or *Disagree* under *You*. Then ask your partner and check *Agree* or *Disagree* under *Your Partner*.

	You		Your Partner	
	Agree	Disagree	Agree	Disagree
1. Life is more difficult.				
2. People are happier.				
3. Families are stronger.				
4. Children are more intelligent.				
5.				
6.				
7.				
8.				
9.				
10.				

STEP 2 Compare your answers with your partner's. Then write six sentences that compare life today with life fifty years ago.

▶ **EXAMPLE:** Today, children are more intelligent. They are more independent.

ACTIVITY 6: LISTENING/SPEAKING

STEP 1 Look at the three different apartment ads below. Listen and say which apartment, A, B, or C, each person is talking about.

A. FOR RENT: Studio apartment. 200 square feet. Close to bus stop and supermarket. Fully furnished. $500/month plus utilities.

B. FOR RENT: One-bedroom apartment. 900 square feet. Quiet. Lots of light. $800/month including utilities.

C. FOR RENT: Two-bedroom apartment. 1,500 square feet. Close to subway. Quiet area. $1,000/month plus utilities.

STEP 2 Which apartment is it? Work in a group. Each person gives two facts about one of the apartments and the others guess which apartment it is.

▶ **EXAMPLE:** It's more expensive than the studio. It's closer to the subway.

Is it the ______________________ ?

Yes, it is. No, it isn't.

Activity 6

Play textbook audio. The tapescript for this listening appears on p. 548 of this book. Play the tape more than once if necessary.

The test for this unit can be found on pp. 514–515 of this book. The answers can be found on p. 516.

Unit 23

UNIT OVERVIEW

Gender differences, a provocative topic, constitutes the main theme of this unit. There are many exercises and activities here that will incite discussion. As in Unit 22 (comparison with adjectives), Students (Ss) will learn not only how to make comparisons wirh adverbs, but also how to use equatives (*as...as*) with adverbs.

UNIT GOALS

To maximize the diagnostic potential of the Opening Task, do not review the Unit Goals with Ss until after they have completed and reviewed the Opening Task.

OPENING TASK
SETTING UP THE TASK

Introduce the topic of gender; tell Ss they are going to be comparing men and women, boys and girls. Have Ss generate some statements comparing men and women, as examples. Put these on the board, or on butcher block paper. Then make sure Ss understand the questions about men and women.

UNIT 23

COMPARISON WITH ADVERBS

UNIT GOALS:

- To use the (regular and irregular) comparative form of adverbs in statements
- To express similarities and differences with adverbs using *as . . . as*
- To ask questions with *how*

OPENING TASK
Comparing Men and Women

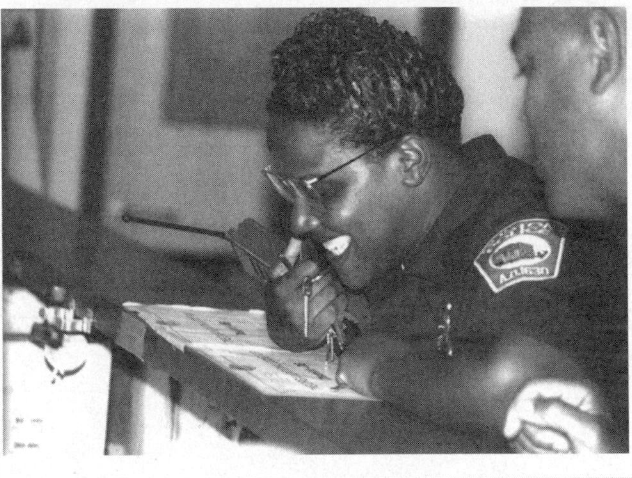

What are your opinions about men and women? Check *Yes, No,* or *Maybe* for each question. Then talk about your answers with your classmates.

	Yes	No	Maybe
1. Do women work harder than men?			
2. Do men drive more safely than women?			
3. Do women communicate better than men?			
4. Do men dance less gracefully than women?			
5. Do women take care of children more patiently than men?			
6. Do men express their feelings more openly than women?			
7. Do women learn math less easily than men?			
8. Do men spend money more freely than women?			
9. Do women learn languages more easily than men?			
10. Do women think less clearly in emergencies than men?			

CONDUCTING THE TASK

1. Ss should first answer the questions individually, taking time to think about their personal opinions on these questions.

2. Put Ss in mixed gender groups. Have them discuss their opinions and justify their way of thinking. As Ss are working, go around and eavesdrop to see how well they can make comparisons with adverbs.

REVIEWING THE TASK

Choose a few questions to focus on. Have a representative from each group present the group's opinions. Add these statements to the list already on the board and begin focusing on form, bridging to the first part of Focus 1.

ANSWER KEY

Opening Task

Answers will vary according to Ss' opinions. Example: #6: Women express their feelings more openly than men. Women talk more intimately than men. They reveal their secrets more willingly than men.

FOCUS 1

Have Ss study the chart. Point out the following:

1. Comparisons with adverbs are similar to comparisons with adjectives.
2. The informal statement, "*I run faster than him*" is more common than the form, "*I run faster than he (does).*"
3. We use *much* to make a comparative stronger—*I raise my hand much more often than you (do).*

FOCUS 1

Comparative Forms of Adverbs

FORM USE

EXAMPLES	ADVERB/COMPARATIVE		RULE
(a) Women live **longer than** men.	*long*	*longer than*	For short adverbs, add *-er* + *than*.
(b) Do women drive **more safely than** men? (c) Do men drive **less carefully than** women?	*safely* *carefully*	*more/less safely than* *carefully than*	For adverbs with two or more syllables, use *more/less* + adverb + *than*.
(d) Eugene and Carol eat out much **more often than** Warren and Harriet.	*often*	*more/less often than*	With adverbs of frequency, use *more/less* + adverb + *than*.
(e) Do women **cook better than** men? (f) Do boys do **worse** in school **than** girls? (g) Can a man throw a ball **farther than** a woman?	*well* *badly* *far*	*better than* *worse than* *farther than*	With irregular adverbs, use the irregular form + *than*.

EXAMPLES	EXPLANATIONS
(h) Jason can climb higher than his brother **(can).** (i) She's better in school than I **(am).**	Sometimes, the auxiliary verb, for example *can, be,* or *will*, follows the subject after *than*.
(j) I type faster than my friend **(does).** (k) We speak Spanish better than they **(do).**	If there is no *be* or auxiliary verb, you can use *do*.
(l) I type faster than she **(does).** (m) I type faster than **her.**	In formal English, the subject pronoun follows *than*. In informal English, the object pronoun (*me, you, him, her, us, them*) follows *than*.

EXERCISE 1

Go back to the questions in the Opening Task on page 379 and underline the comparatives with adverbs.

▶ **EXAMPLE:** Do women live longer than men?

EXERCISE 2

Write sentences comparing yourself with your partner. Use the verbs and adverbs in the chart.

Verb	Adverb	Comparisons
1. cry	easily	My partner cries more easily than I (*do*).
2. drive	carefully	
3. speak English	fluently	
4. exercise	regularly	
5. travel	often	
6. study	hard	
7. laugh	loudly	
8. participate in class	actively	
9. take exams	calmly	
10. read	fast	

Exercise 1

Have Ss do this exercise individually.

Exercise 2

These questions are of a general nature. However, you could change the questions depending on the pairs you set up. If these are mixed-gender pairs, focus on gender issues in the questions. If they are mixed-nationality pairs, focus on national or cultural habits. *The French take food more seriously than the Americans.*

Ss will first need to ask each other yes/no questions with the verbs: *Do you cry easily*? They also might have to ask additional questions to be able to make the comparisons. Do a couple with the whole class to demonstrate. If two Ss respond in the same way and cannot make comparative statements, take advantage of the opportunity to try to elicit a statement expressing similarity, using *as.... as*.

For example, if they both say they don't drive carefully, elicit the statement: Cheung drives as poorly/carelessly as I do. This structure will be recycled in Focus 2. Have pairs report their similarities and differences to the class.

Workbook Exs. 1 & 2, pp. 182–183. Answers: TE, p. 541.

ANSWER KEY

Exercise 1

1. harder than **2.** more safely than **3.** better than **4.** less gracefully than **5.** more patiently than **6.** more openly than **7.** less easily than **8.** more freely than **9.** more easily than **10.** less clearly (in emergencies) than

Exercise 2

Answers will vary.

FOCUS 2

If you have elicited this structure in Exercise 2, you'll make a smooth transition to Focus 2. If not, have Ss read the examples and explanations. Refer them back to Exercise 2 and have them generate more sentences. For example, if two Ss both said they travel often, elicit the sentence, "*Paolo travels as often as Yoshi (does.).*" You might also point out that the statement "*Amaya doesn't speak as clearly as Lily (does)*" is more tactful than "*Lily speaks more clearly than Amaya (does).*"

Exercise 3

Have Ss write the sentences on the board. Check them as a class.

FOCUS 2

Expressing Similarities and Differences with *As . . . As*

EXAMPLES	EXPLANATIONS
(a) A woman can work **as hard as** a man. (b) A man can dance **as gracefully as** a woman.	To show similarities, use *as* + adverb + *as*.
(c) He does**n't** speak **as clearly as** I (do). (d) = I speak more clearly than he (does). (e) = He speaks less clearly than I (do).	To show differences, use *not as* + adverb + *as*. Remember that (c) is more polite, more tactful than (d) or (e). (See Focus 4 in Unit 22 on p. 372.)

EXERCISE 3

Sally Miller and Bill Benson are applying for a job as director of an art company. Decide who is better for the job. Make comparative statements about each person.

EXAMPLES: Sally works as hard as Bill.

Bill draws better than Sally./Sally doesn't draw as well as Bill.

Work Habits	Sally Miller	Bill Benson
1. works hard	X	X
2. draws well		X
3. thinks creatively	X	✔
4. communicates openly	X	
5. plans carefully		X
6. works well with others	X	X
7. treats the staff fairly	X	
8. solves problems calmly		X
9. deals with clients successfully	X	✔
10. works fast		X

382 UNIT 23

ANSWER KEY

Exercise 3

1. Sally works as hard as Bill (does). **2.** Bill draws better than Sally./Sally doesn't draw as well as Bill. **3.** Sally thinks more creatively than Bill (does). Bill doesn't think as creatively as Sally (does). **4.** Sally communicates more openly than Bill./Bill doesn't communicate as openly as Sally (does). **5.** Bill plans work more carefully than Sally./Sally doesn't plan work as carefully as Bill (does). **6.** Sally works with others as well as Bill (does). **7.** Sally treats the staff more fairly than Bill (does). Bill doesn't treat the staff as fairly as Sally (does). **8.** Bill solves problems more calmly than Sally (does). Sally doesn't solve problems as calmly as Bill (does). **9.** Sally deals with clients more successfully than Bill (does). Bill doesn't deal with clients as successfully as Sally (does). **10.** Bill works faster than Sally (does)./Sally doesn't work as fast as Bill (does).

EXERCISE 4

Imagine you are the president of the art company. You want to compare Sally and Bill. Write some questions to ask about them.

▶ **EXAMPLES:** *Does Sally work as hard as Bill?*

Does Bill draw better than Sally?

EXERCISE 5

Discuss these questions before you read.

1. Do you think boys and girls grow up differently? In what ways do they grow up differently?
2. Do you think boys and girls talk to each other differently?
3. In what ways do you think boys and girls play differently?

Now, read the following:

Boys and girls grow up in different worlds. Research studies show that boys and girls act very differently. For example, when boys and girls play, they don't play together. Some of their activites are similar, but their favorite games are different. Also, the language they use in games is different.

Boys usually play outside in large groups. The group has a leader. The leader gives orders. There are winners and losers in boys' games. Boys frequently brag about how good they are at something and argue about who is the best.

Girls, on the other hand, play in small groups or pairs. The most important thing for a girl is her best friend. Closeness is very important to girls. Girls like to sit together and talk. In their games, like jump rope, everyone gets a turn. In many of their activities, such as playing together with their dolls, there are no winners or losers. Girls don't brag about how good they are at something. They don't give orders. They usually make suggestions.

Does this text say the same things you said in your discussion? What information is the same? What information is different?

Exercise 4

SUGGESTION

You may want to include *Wh*-questions here as well: Example: *Who thinks more creatively?*

EXPANSION

Have Ss role-play this as a conversation between the president and the current director of the company who is helping choose his successor.

Exercise 5

1. Discussing the pre-reading questions as a class will allow Ss to access and share their experience and background knowledge of this topic. Write what they say on the board to set down some vocabulary and expectations. This framework will help Ss read and understand a text that might otherwise seem daunting.
2. Have Ss read the text silently. Ask them to underline what they don't understand. Encourage them to use the context and their own expectations to guess the meanings of words they don't know.
3. After the reading, ask Ss whether the text matched their expectations. Go over any problematic parts of the text. Provide explanations when necessary and guidance in guessing in context whenever possible. Explain to Ss that good readers use these strategies.

ANSWER KEY

Exercise 4

Have Ss generate their own questions about Sally and Bill, or recycle the statements from Exercise 3. Possible questions:

1. Does Sally work as hard as Bill? **2.** Does Sally draw better than Bill? **3.** Does Bill think as creatively as Sally? **4.** Does Sally communicate more openly than Bill?

Exercise 6

This comprehension exercise challenges Ss to call upon higher order thinking skills. Because these statements are not phrased to be identical to the text, Ss must think, interpret, and make connections in order to respond correctly. Have Ss do this individually. Then check, in groups or as a class.

Exercise 7

VARIATION

To make this exercise more fun, have Ss "boast" about themselves, using exaggerated intonation. If possible, have them demonstrate the abilities they're boasting about! Encourage Ss to add statements to this list. A variety of answers is acceptable. If you think that Ss from some cultures might feel uncomfortable "boasting" about themselves, suggest that Ss pretend they are someone else.

EXERCISE 6

To test your understanding of the reading, check *True* or *False* for the statements below.

	True	False
1. Boys and girls play differently.		
2. Boys and girls usually play with each other.		
3. Girls act more aggressively than boys.		
4. Girls play more competitively than boys do.		
5. Boys brag about how good they are at something more frequently than girls.		
6. Girls talk to each other more intimately than boys do.		
7. Girls give suggestions more frequently than boys.		
8. Boys play more cooperatively than girls do.		

EXERCISE 7

For each statement you read, your partner says how he or she is similar or different.

▶ **EXAMPLE:** **You say:** I (can) cook well.

Your partner says: I can cook as well as you.
I can't cook as well as you.
I can cook better than you.

1. speak clearly
2. dance gracefully
3. sing sweetly
4. jump high
5. run far
6. add numbers quickly
7. meet new people easily
8. tell a joke well
9. study hard
10. learn English fast

ANSWER KEY

Exercise 6

1. True **2.** False **3.** False **4.** False **5.** True **6.** True **7.** True **8.** False

Exercise 7

Answers will vary.
1. I speak English more clearly than you./I can speak as clearly as you./I can't speak as clearly as you. **2.** I dance more gracefully than you./I dance as gracefully as you./I don't dance as gracefully as you. **3.** I sing more sweetly than you./I (don't) sing as sweetly as you. **4.** I can jump higher than you./You can't jump as high as I can. **5.** I can run farther than you... I can't run as fast as you can. **6.** I can add numbers more quickly than you./I can't add numbers as quickly as you. **7.** I meet new people more (less) easily than you (do). **8.** I can tell a joke better than you./I can tell a joke as well as you. **9.** I study harder than you./I study as hard as you. **10.** I can learn English faster than you. I can learn English as fast as you (can).

EXERCISE 8

Write statements comparing men and women. Use *more/less/as . . . as*. Discuss your answers with the class.

1. think creatively

   Men think more creatively than women.
   Women think as creatively as men (do).

2. run fast
3. behave responsibly
4. act aggressively
5. ask for directions willingly
6. listen supportively
7. act independently
8. think logically
9. make friends quickly
10. cry easily

Add two statements of your own.

11. ______________________________

12. ______________________________

Exercise 8  

Ss can do this individually, in pairs, or as a class.

SUGGESTIONS

1. If done in pairs, encourage Ss to support their opinions. Example (For # 9): *Women open up to others more readily than men (do). Women care more deeply about people's personal lives.* Have them share their ideas with the class.

2. If done as a class, put three columns on the board: *Men, Women,* and *Both.*

Have Ss read each statement and place it in one of the columns.

Men	Both	Women
Run fast	Behave responsibly	Listen supportively

Once the diagram is filled out, Ss can easily see the differences and similarities and make comparative statements. Example: *Men behave as responsibly as women.*

Workbook Ex. 3, pp. 183–184.
Answers: TE, p. 541.

ANSWER KEY

Exercise 8

Answers will vary according to the views of the students.

FOCUS 3

Ask your Ss *how*-questions to clarify meaning first; then have them read the box.

Exercise 9 

After pairs have completed the exercise, have Ss report one interesting thing they learned about their partners.

FOCUS **3**

Questions with *How*

EXAMPLES	EXPLANATIONS
(a) **How old** are you? (b) **How well** do you speak English?	An adjective (*old, tall*) or an adverb (*well, far*) is often used in a *how* question.
(c) **How far** is it from here to the park? It's about five blocks.	*How far* asks about distance.
(d) **How long does it take** to fly from New York to Saigon? It takes about twenty-four hours. (e) **How long does it take** you to prepare dinner? It takes me an hour.	*How long does it take* asks about time.

EXERCISE 9

Ask a partner questions with *how*. Fill in your partner's answers on the right. Your partner asks you the same questions, and fills in your answers on the left.

▶ **EXAMPLES:** How far do you live from school?

How well can you cook?

	You	Your Partner
1. how far/live from school	5 miles	4 blocks
2. how well/cook	very well	very well
3. how easily/fall asleep at night		
4. how far/run		
5. how hard/study		
6. how fast/type		
7. how late/stay up at night		
8. how early/get up in the morning		
9. how well/know your classmates		
10. how often/speak to your best friend		

ANSWER KEY

Exercise 9

1. How far do you... 2. How well can you... 3. How easily do you... 4. How far can you... 5. How hard do you... 6. How fast can you... 7. How late do you... 8. How early do you... 9. How well do you... 10. How often do you...

EXERCISE 10

Compare yourself with your partner for each of the questions in Exercise 9.

1. I live farther away from school than my partner (does).
2. My partner cooks as well as I (do).
3. ______________________.
4. ______________________.
5. ______________________.
6. ______________________.
7. ______________________.
8. ______________________.
9. ______________________.
10. ______________________.

EXERCISE 11

Fill in the chart. Say how much time it takes you to do each of the activities below. Then interview a partner. Write statements with the comparative form of adverbs.

▶ **EXAMPLES:** It takes me longer to do my homework.

I get dressed faster than you (do) in the morning.

	You	Your Partner
1. do your homework	1 hour	45 minutes
2. get dressed in the morning		
3. get to school		
4. clean your room/apartment/house		
5. have breakfast		
6. take a shower		
7. cook dinner		
8. fall asleep at night		

Exercise 10

In this exercise, Ss will need to use all the comparative forms they have learned in this unit. Collect Ss' papers and review any problems they might still be having.

Exercise 11

Ss first complete the chart individually. Then they work with a partner asking questions with *How long does it take...* Practice having Ss make questions first. Have one or two pairs write their sentences on the board so that you can check with the whole class.

Workbook Ex. 4, pp. 185–186.
Answers: TE, p. 542.

UNIT GOAL REVIEW

Ask Ss to look back at the goals on the opening page of the unit and evaluate their own levels of progress and determine their own areas of weakness. If common problems persist, reteach or continue to practice these items in class or for homework. If individual problems persist, make recommendations to those Ss having problems.

ANSWER KEY

Exercise 10

Ss generate their own sentences. Answers will vary.

USE YOUR ENGLISH

For a more complete discussion of how to use the activities, see p. xxvi of this Teacher's Edition.

Activity 1 

Pair up Ss from different countries, if possible. Have them ask each other questions first. Examples: *Do trains run smoothly in Bangladesh? How smoothly/often do they run? Do people work hard? How hard do they work? How many hours a day do they work*? Practice doing a few of these with the whole class before pairing Ss up. Have pairs share their answers with the class.

Use Your English

ACTIVITY 1: WRITING

Write sentences comparing two cities or places that you know.

▶ **EXAMPLE:** The trains run more smoothly in Montreal than in New York.

1. trains/run smoothly
2. buses/run efficiently
3. people/work hard
4. taxi drivers/drive recklessly
5. traffic/move slowly
6. people/talk quickly
7. people/talk to foreigners politely
8. stores/stay open late
9. people/drive fast
10. families/take vacations frequently

Add two sentences of your own:

11. ______________________________
12. ______________________________

ACTIVITY 2: SPEAKING/MIMING

STEP 1 Here is a list of adverbs and a list of actions. Write each adverb and each action on a separate card.

Adverbs	**Actions**
Slowly	Eat spaghetti
Sadly	Put on your clothes
Nervously	Make the bed
Angrily	Cook dinner
Fast	Type a letter
Carefully	Brush your teeth
Seriously	Comb your hair
Happily	Paint a picture
Loudly	Play tennis
Enthusiastically	Shake someone's hand
Shyly	Look at someone

STEP 2 Mix up each group of cards separately. With a partner, take one adverb card and one action card.

STEP 3 Both of you mime the same action and adverb. The class guesses the action and the adverb.

STEP 4 The class compares your two performances.

▶ **EXAMPLE:** Angrily/Eat spaghetti

Paola ate spaghetti more angrily than Maria.

Activity 2

This activity can be done with the whole class and will give Ss a chance to relax and express themselves nonverbally. If possible, videotape these performances so that Ss can compare them.

SUGGESTIONS

1. Have Ss add their own adverbs and actions.
2. Make two groups: one group to mime the actions and the other group to compare their performances. Put sentences on the board to check.

Activity 3 

1. Spend some time familiarizing Ss with the national parks on the map (using photos, realia, etc.) and explaining the mileage chart.
2. As Ss are working, walk around making sure they are asking questions with *How far...?* and *how long does it take...?*
   To vary this activity, have pairs make up their own itineraries, and present them to the class. Decide who has the best itinerary.

ACTIVITY 3: SPEAKING

Planning a Vacation

Here is a map of the southwestern United States. You and your friend want to take a two-week vacation to visit four national parks. You will start and end your trip in Las Vegas, Nevada.

Approximate Mileage Between National Parks and Las Vegas

	Las Vegas	Bryce Canyon	Death Valley	Grand Canyon	Zion National Park
Las Vegas		245	130	275	145
Bryce Canyon	(245)		365	300	100
Death Valley	130	365		405	275
Grand Canyon	275	300	405		250
Zion National Park	145	100	275	250	

STEP 1 Use the map and the mileage chart. Ask each other questions to find out the distances between parks. Fill in the information in the chart below.

▶ **EXAMPLE:** How far is it from Las Vegas to Death Valley?
It's 130 miles.

Depart from Las Vegas	Distance	Time
Stop 1: Death Valley	130 miles	2 hours
Stop 2: Zion National Park		
Stop 3: Bryce Canyon		
Stop 4: Grand Canyon		

STEP 2 Calculate the time required to go from one place to another and fill in the information in the chart. Remember you will travel by car and the average speed limit is 65 MPH. All distances are in miles.

▶ **EXAMPLE:** How long does it take to get from Las Vegas to Death Valley?
It takes about two hours.

ACTIVITY 4: WRITING

Compare yourself with someone you know—a family member, a friend, your boyfriend/girlfriend, etc. Write ten sentences.

▶ **EXAMPLES:** *I dance better than my sister (does).*

I can make friends more easily than she (does).

ACTIVITY 5: LISTENING/ SPEAKING

What does Richard like about London, England?

STEP 1 Listen to the tape and look at the list below. Check the things he thinks are good.

Richard likes . . .

1. _______ the people
2. _______ the hotel
3. _______ the buses
4. _______ the taxi drivers
5. _______ the subway
6. _______ English cooking
7. _______ the restaurants

STEP 2 Listen again and say why Richard likes or dislikes the things.

STEP 3 Tell the class about a place you visited. Use adverbs of comparison.

Activity 4

Depending on your class, this can be written as individual statements or as a coherent paragraph with topic and support. For the latter, allow Ss some prewriting time to think, make connections, and prepare their ideas. Collect Ss' papers and analyze them for target structure and topic/support. Use these errors as a basis for a succeeding writing lesson.

Activity 5 

Play textbook audio. The tapescript for this listening appears on p. 548 of this book.

The test for this unit can be found on pp. 517–518 of this book. The answers can be found on p.519.

ANSWER KEY

Activity 5

Step 1: Richard likes: 1, 4

Unit 24

UNIT OVERVIEW

Since the superlative is more difficult for most students (Ss), it is presented separately here. A major challenge for Ss is dealing with regular and irregular superlative forms. Much of the content in this unit comes from the *Guinness Book of World Records* and calls upon Ss' background knowledge.

UNIT GOALS

To maximize the diagnostic potential of the Opening Task, do not review the Unit Goals with Ss until after they have completed and reviewed the Opening Task.

OPENING TASK
SETTING UP THE TASK

Have Ss discuss the photo at the beginning of the unit. Try to elicit superlative statements. Put them on the board.
If possible, use photos to introduce the places, paintings and other items mentioned in Step 1.

UNIT 24

SUPERLATIVES

UNIT GOALS:

- To understand the meaning of superlatives
- To know how to form regular and irregular superlatives
- To use the expression *one of the* + superlative + plural noun

OPENING TASK
General Knowledge Quiz

STEP 1 Check the correct answer. Then compare your answers with your classmates'.

1. What is the largest ocean?
   a. Pacific b. Atlantic c. Indian
2. What's the most valuable painting in the world?
   a. Van Gogh's "Sunflowers"
   b. Leonardo da Vinci's "Mona Lisa"
   c. Rembrandt's "Self Portrait"
3. What's the most widely spoken language in the world?
   a. English b. Spanish c. Chinese
4. What's the hottest place in the world?
   a. Australia b. Israel c. Ethiopia
5. What's the tallest office building in the world?
   a. the Sears Tower, Chicago
   b. the World Trade Center, New York
   c. the Petronas Tower, Kuala Lumpur
6. What's the most crowded city in the world?
   a. Shanghai b. Mexico City c. Tokyo
7. What's the most expensive university in the United States?
   a. Harvard b. Yale c. M.I.T.
8. What's the wettest place in the world?
   a. Hawaii b. India c. Jamaica
9. What's the most nutritious fruit?
   a. banana b. avocado c. orange
10. What's the hardest gem?
   a. ruby b. diamond c. emerald

STEP 2 Now write similar questions. Quiz your classmates.

11. ______________________________
12. ______________________________
13. ______________________________
14. ______________________________
15. ______________________________

ANSWER KEY

Opening Task

1. a 2. b 3. a 4. c 5. c 6. b
7. c 8. b 9. b 10. b

CONDUCTING THE TASK

Step 1

Have Ss work in small groups to help each other answer these trivia questions. Ask groups why they chose certain answers to see if they can use comparative and superlative forms correctly and appropriately.

Step 2

This step constrains Ss to generate questions using superlatives, and will give you a chance to see if they can do it correctly. Have each group ask the other groups their questions. Make it into a game where the group that answers the most questions correctly wins.

REVIEWING THE TASK

Ask a representative from each group to give answers. Write their statements on the board, "*The Pacific is the largest ocean.*" Use them later to present the form.

FOCUS 1

1. Point out that superlatives can apply to both positive and negative distinctions—*The most popular food* vs. *the least popular food*.
2. Point out the use of "*the*" and prepositional phrases with superlatives.

Exercise 1

Have Ss do this exercise individually, in pairs or small groups.

Workbook Exs. 1 & 2, pp. 177.
Answers: TE, p. 542.

FOCUS 1

Superlatives

EXAMPLES	EXPLANATIONS
(a) **The tallest** building in the world is the Petronas Tower. (b) **The least expensive** food on the menu is a hamburger. (c) Rosa writes **the most beautifully** of all.	Superlatives compare one thing or person to all the others in a group.
(d) Dr. Diaz is the most respected teacher **at the school.** (e) M.I.T. is the most expensive university **in the United States.** (f) Etsuko performs the best **of all the dancers.**	Use prepositional phrases after superlatives to identify the group.

EXERCISE 1

Go back to the Opening Task on page 393. Underline all the superlative forms in the questions.

▶ **EXAMPLE:** What is the largest ocean?

ANSWER KEY

Exercise 1
2. the most valuable 3. the most widely spoken 4. the hottest 5. the tallest 6. the most crowded 7. the most expensive 8. the wettest 9. the most nutritious 10. the hardest

FOCUS **2**

Regular and Irregular Superlative Forms

Regular Forms

EXAMPLES	ADJECTIVE/ADVERB	SUPERLATIVE FORM	RULE
(a) The Sears Tower in Chicago is **the tallest** building in the United States. (b) My grandfather worked **the hardest** of his three brothers.	*tall* *hard*	*the tallest* *the hardest*	One-syllable adjectives or adverbs: *the* + adjective/adverb + *-est*
(c) Jupiter is **the largest** planet. (d) I get up **the latest** in my family	*large* *late*	*the largest* *the latest*	Adjectives/adverbs ending in *-e:* add *-st.*
(e) **The hottest** place in the world is Ethiopia.	*hot*	*the hottest*	One-syllable adjectives ending in consonant-vowel-consonant: double the final consonant, add *-est.*
(f) **The easiest** subject for me is geography. (g) She arrived **the earliest.**	*easy* *early*	*the easiest* *the earliest*	Two-syllable adjectives/adverbs ending in *-y:* change *-y* to *-i:* add *-est.*
(h) **The most nutritious** fruit is the avocado. (i) **The least expensive** food on the menu is a hamburger. (j) Of all his friends, he drives **the most carefully.** (k) She danced **the least gracefully** of all the students.	*nutritious* *expensive* *carefully* *gracefully*	*the most nutritious* *the least expensive* *the most carefully* *the least gracefully*	Adjectives/adverbs with two or more syllables: use *the* + *most/least.*

FOCUS 2

Both regular and irregular superlative forms of adjectives and adverbs are presented in this box. Have Ss identify the adjectives and adverbs (and also identify the verbs—e.g., (*b*) *worked* is the verb).

SUGGESTIONS

1. To present this form box inductively, copy and enlarge Focus 2 and put it on the board or an OHP, covering the rules, or write the adjectives/adverbs and superlative forms on the board. Ask Ss to formulate the rules.
2. To present it deductively, have Ss read the rules and try to come up with additional examples.

Exercise 2

SUGGESTION

Have Ss say which rule governs each sentence (e.g., #1 = the largest = rule (c).)

VARIATION

Have Ss tape record these sentences and pretend they are producing a radio show called "Did you know that ...?"

Irregular Forms

EXAMPLES	ADJECTIVE/ADVERB	ADVERB	SUPERLATIVE
(l) That college has **the best** professors.	good	well	the best
(m) That was **the worst** movie I saw last year.	bad	badly	the worst
(n) He ran **the farthest.**	far	far	the farthest

EXERCISE 2

Here are some interesting facts from the *Guinness Book of World Records.* Write the superlative form of the adjective/adverb in parentheses in the blanks.

▶ **EXAMPLE:** (cold) Antarctica is ___the coldest___ place on earth.

1. ______________ (large) cucumber weighed sixty-six pounds.
2. ______________ (popular) tourist attraction in the United States is Disneyworld in Florida.
3. ______________ (successful) pop group of all time was the Beatles.
4. ______________ (heavy) baby at birth was a boy of twenty-two pounds eight ounces. He was born in Italy in 1955.
5. ______________ (fat) person was a man in New York City. He weighed almost 1,200 pounds.
6. ______________ (prolific) painter was Pablo Picasso. He produced about 13,500 paintings; 100,00 prints; 34,000 book illustrations; and 300 sculptures.
7. ______________ (long) attack of hiccups lasted sixty-seven years.
8. ______________ (big) omelet was made of 54,763 eggs with 531 pounds of cheese in Las Vegas, Nevada in 1986.
9. ______________ (hot) city in the United States is Key West, Florida.
10. Mexico City is now the world's (fast)-growing ______________ city.

ANSWER KEY

Exercise 2

1. the largest **2.** The most popular **3.** The most successful **4.** The heaviest **5.** The fattest **6.** The most prolific **7.** The longest **8.** The biggest **9.** The hottest **10.** the world's fastest-growing

EXERCISE 3

Fill in the name of a student in your class and the superlative form of each adverb.

	Name		Superlative	
1.	Juan	does the homework	the most carefully	(carefully).
2.	________	writes	____________	(well).
3.	________	arrives in class	____________	(early).
4.	________	guesses new words	____________	(fast).
5.	________	makes us laugh	____________	(often).
6.	________	expresses opinions	____________	(open).
7.	________	communicates in English	____________	(effectively).
8.	________	participates in class	____________	(actively).

Add two statements of your own.

9. ____

10. ____

EXERCISE 4

Information Gap. Work with a partner. One person looks at Chart A on the next page, and the other person looks at Chart B on page A-21. Ask your partner questions to find out the missing information in your chart. Write the answers in the chart.

▶ **EXAMPLE:** **Student A:** What is the longest river in North America?
Student B: The Mississippi.

Exercise 3

Students can work individually or in groups. The names in the subject position will vary depending on the Ss in your class. Have each student or group present their answers so that the class can arrive at a consensus.

Exercise 4

1. Elicit and practice the following questions Ss need to ask, to ensure that they proceed successfully: *What's the longest river in...? What's the largest country in...? What's the most populated country in...? What's the highest mountain in...? What's the smallest country in...?*
2. Bring in a world map so Ss can see all these places when checking their answers.

EXPANSION

Ask Ss to do mini-research projects on these places or on places with similar characteristics in their home countries. Working in small groups, they can find information in the library, or on the Internet, read and prepare a short report to present to the class.

ANSWER KEY

Exercise 3

2. the best **3.** the earliest **4.** the fastest
5. the most often **6.** the most openly
7. the most effectively **8.** the most actively

CHART A

	North America	South America	Asia	Europe	Africa	The World
long river		The Amazon		The Volga		The Nile
large country	Canada		The People's Republic of China		Sudan	
populated country		Brazil		Germany		The People's Republic of China
high mountain	Mt. McKinley		Mt. Everest		Mt. Kilimanjaro	
small country		French Guiana		Vatican City		Vatican City

EXERCISE 5

Play this modified Jeopardy game in two teams. Look at the gameboard on page 399. Team 1 chooses a category and a dollar amount. Choose one person in the class to read the questions under the CATEGORIES column aloud. Team 1 has one minute to choose an answer from the Answer Box. If the answer is correct, they "win" the money. If the answer is not correct, Team 2 answers the question and wins the money. The team with the most money at the end wins.

▶ **EXAMPLE:** **Team 1:** "Animals" for $20.
Reader: What's the most dangerous animal?
Team 1: Mosquitoes (They can give you malaria.)

Exercise 5

SUGGESTIONS

1. Put a large jeopardy gameboard up in front of the room and leave blanks in the boxes.
2. Bring in play money.

GAMEBOARD

$$$	Planets	Animals	Other
$10			
$20			
$30			
$40			
$50			

CATEGORIES

Planets

$10 What is the largest planet in the solar system?
$20 What is the fastest planet?
$30 What is the hottest planet?
$40 What is the farthest planet from the sun?
$50 What is the closest planet to Earth?

Animals

$10 What is the tallest animal?
$20 What is the most dangerous animal?
$30 What is the fastest land animal?
$40 What is the most valuable animal?
$50 What is the largest and heaviest animal?

Other

$10 What is the hardest gem?
$20 What is the largest desert in the world?
$30 What is the highest court in the United States?
$40 What is the oldest country in the world?
$50 What is the shortest day of the year?

ANSWER BOX (Choose the answers to the questions from this box.)

Planets	Animals	Other
Pluto Mercury Venus Jupiter Mars	mosquitoes the blue whale giraffe cheetah race horse	the Supreme Court the Sahara the winter solstice (first day of winter) diamond Iraq

3. Choose one person in the class to be the host who asks the "CATEGORIES" questions. Also allow the host to have the answers.
4. Proceed by having Team 1 pick a category and an amount. The host reads the question to Team 1. They get one minute to talk to each other and choose in answer from the answer box. If Team 1 answers correctly, the host writes the answer in the appropriate box. If the answer is incorrect, then Team 2 has a chance to give the correct answer.
5. As a follow-up, ask Ss to write sentences for each category; Example: *Mosquitoes are the most dangerous animals in the world.*

VARIATION

To make this exercise more challenging, do not let students look at the answer box. The host asks the questions, and each group tries to answer.

Workbook Exs. 3 & 4, pp. 188–189.
Answers: TE, p.542.

FOCUS 3

1. This meaning of the superlative can also be represented visually for clarification: *Category*: *Greatest Composers*

Mozart	*Handel*
Bach	*Vivaldi*
Beethoven	

2. Point out the use of the plural noun in these superlatives. Example: *Bach is one of the greatest composers.* This shows that Bach is not in a category of his own, but shares that category with other composers.
3. Ask Ss to provide examples of their own. (*one of the best restaurants, one of the easiest grammar points to learn,* etc.).

Exercise 6

Have Ss do this exercise individually or in pairs and compare their answers.

FOCUS **3**

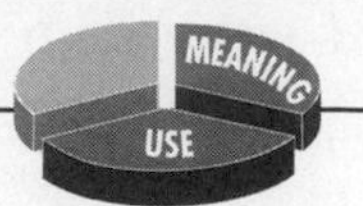

One Of The + Superlative + Plural Noun

EXAMPLES	EXPLANATION
(a) Bach was **one of the greatest composers** of all time.	*One of the* + superlative + plural noun is common with the superlative form. Example (a) means that there are several composers we think of as the greatest composers of all time. Bach is one of them.
(b) He is **one of the least popular** students in the school.	

EXERCISE 6

Fill in the blanks with *one of the* + superlative + plural noun. Use the words in parentheses.

1. That's *one of the most expensive cars* you can buy. (expensive car)

2. In my opinion, wrestling is ______________ you can play. (exciting sport)

3. Graduation was ______________ of my life. (proud moment)

4. That was ______________ in the city. (expensive hotel)

ANSWER KEY

Exercise 6

Answers may vary depending on Ss' viewpoints. **2.** one of the most/least exciting sports **3.** one of the proudest moments **4.** one of the least expensive hotels **5.** one of the worst things **6.** one of the best desserts **7.** one of the finest doctors **8.** one of the greatest jazz musicians **9.** one of the most beautiful sculptures **10.** one of the most tragic deaths

5.  Drinking and driving is _______________ you can do. (bad thing)

6.  The chocolate ice cream is _______________ on the menu. (good dessert)

7.  Dr. Jones is _______________ in the hospital. (fine doctor)

8.  Louis Armstrong was _______________ in America. (great jazz musicians)

9.  This is _______________ in the museum. (beautiful sculpture)

10.  Sergei Grinkov, the Olympic ice skater, died in 1995. He was twenty-nine years old. This was _______________ in the history of ice skating. (tragic death)

Exercise 7

Have Ss write their sentences on the board so they can compare their ideas. Ask them to support their answers, using more superlatives. Example: *Prague is one of the most beautiful cities in the world. It has the most interesting architecture. It is one of the cleanest cities.*

Workbook Exs. 5 & 6, pp. 190–191. Answers: TE, p. 542.

UNIT GOAL REVIEW

Ask Ss to look back at the goals on the opening page of the unit and evaluate their own levels of progress and determine their own areas of weakness. If common problems persist, reteach or continue to practice these items in class or for homework. If individual problems persist, make recommendations to those Ss having problems.

USE YOUR ENGLISH

For a more complete discussion of how to use the activities, see p. xxvi of this Teacher's Edition.

Activity 1

SUGGESTIONS

1. Turn this into a game with either teams or individuals. Correct each group's questions as they are working. Then collect all of the questions. Choose one student to ask the questions. The team, or individual, who answers the most questions correctly, wins.
2. Bring in the *Guinness Book of World* records for more information.

EXPANSION

Have Ss peruse the *Guinness Book of World Records* and select ten facts to teach the class.

EXERCISE 7

Make sentences with *one of the* + superlative + plural noun. Compare your answers with your classmates'.

▶ **EXAMPLE:** 1. *Prague is one of the most beautiful cities in the world.*

1. a beautiful city in the world
2. an interesting place (in the city you are living in)
3. a good restaurant (in the city you are in)
4. a famous leader in the world today
5. a dangerous disease of our time
6. a serious problem in the world
7. a popular food (in the country you come from)
8. a funny show on television

Use Your English

ACTIVITY 1: WRITING/SPEAKING

Work in a group. Write five questions in the superlative form like the ones in the Opening Task on page 393. Then ask the class the questions.

▶ **EXAMPLES:** *What's the most expensive car in the world?*
What is the largest island?

ANSWER KEY

Exercise 7

2. ___ is one of the most interesting places in ___. 3. ___ is one of the best restaurants in ___. 4. ___ is one of the most famous leaders in ___. 5. ___ is one of the most dangerous diseases ... 6. ___ is one of the most serious problems in the world. 7. ___ is one of the most popular foods in ___. 8. ___ is one of the funniest shows on television.

ACTIVITY 2: WRITING/SPEAKING

Write ten questions to ask another student in the class about his or her home country or a country he or she knows. Use the superlative form of the words below or add your own.

▶ **EXAMPLES:** *What's the most crowded city in . . . ?*
What's the most popular sport in your country?
What's the most unusual food in your city?

crowded city	popular sport	popular food
polluted city	dangerous sport	unusual food
beautiful city	expensive sport	cheap food
important holiday	hot month	other
important monument	cold month	

ACTIVITY 3: SPEAKING

In groups, discuss the following statements. Say if you agree or disagree and why.

1. Money is the most important thing in life.
2. AIDS is the worst disease in the world today.
3. English is the most difficult language to learn.
4. Baseball is the most boring sport.
5. Democracy is the best form of government.

Activity 2  

After Ss have worked individually, list their questions on the board. Correct any mistakes and then have Ss interview each other.

Activity 3 

SUGGESTION

Tape-record groups as they speak on each subject. Make error correction lists for Ss to work on.

VARIATION

Have Ss choose one of these statements to write about. If you do this in class, encourage Ss to do some free-writing or listing to generate ideas for a paragraph.

Activity 4

VARIATION

1. Ss can work in groups answering only one of the questions. For example, they could all discuss the most embarrassing moment in their lives.
2. Have the group choose one student's story and act it out for the class.

Activity 5

1. Give Ss time for pre-writing activities. Besides needing time to think, they may need help with vocabulary. Go around the room during this phase to provide assistance.
2. Collect Ss' writing. Check their stories for clarity, focus, and development. Use some of their stories as examples of good/or problematic writing. Give them time to revise their stories.
3. Check their mastery of the superlative or other forms. This can be done through peer editing or use of a correction guide—whichever system you are using to focus on writing.

ACTIVITY 4: SPEAKING

Interview a partner about his or her life experience. Use the adjectives below to write questions with superlatives. Tell the class about the most interesting things you learned about your partner.

▶ **EXAMPLES:** What was the best experience you had this year?
What was the most embarrassing moment in your life?

Adjectives to describe experiences:

unusual	sad	exciting
embarrassing	interesting	frightening
happy	dangerous	beautiful
funny	good	bad

ACTIVITY 5: WRITING

Write a paragraph on one of the topics below:

a. The most embarrassing moment in my life.
b. The most frightening moment in my life.
c. The funniest moment in my life.

ACTIVITY 6: WRITING/ SPEAKING 

STEP 1 Listen to the quiz show. Circle the letter of the correct answer.

Quiz Choices:

	a.	b.	c.
1.	North America	Asia	Africa
2.	the elephant	the turtle	the bear
3.	New York	Los Angeles	Chicago
4.	Chinese	French	English
5.	North America	Asia	Antarctica
6.	The United States	China	Canada
7.	Tokyo	Paris	Hong Kong
8.	The Himalayas	The Andes	The Rockies
9.	Spain	The United States	Italy
10.	Islam/Muslim	Christian	Hindu

STEP 2 Discuss your answers with your classmates.

Activity 6

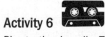

Play textbook audio. The tapescript for this listening appears on p. 548 of this book. Play the tape more than once if necessary.

The test for this unit can be found on pp. 520–521 of this book. The answers can be found on p. 522.

ANSWER KEY

Activity 6

1. B **2.** B **3.** A **4.** C **5.** C **6.** A
7. C **8.** B **9.** C **10.** B

Unit 25

UNIT OVERVIEW

Factual conditionals are rarely introduced in beginning level texts; however, they are commonly used and relatively simple to master. They also provide an opportunity to introduce the *if*-clause/main clause structure needed for the more complex conditionals introduced later in the Grammar Dimensions series.

UNIT GOALS

To maximize the diagnostic potential of the Opening Tasks, do not review the Unit Goals with Students (Ss) until after they have completed and reviewed the Opening Task.

OPENING TASK
SETTING UP THE TASK

Have Ss look at the photograph in the introduction of the unit and read the caption, *"If you read a lot, you learn a lot."* Ask Ss whether they agree with that statement and why. Ask other related questions, *What happens if you watch too much TV? If you never do homework? ...*

UNIT 25

FACTUAL CONDITIONALS

If

UNIT GOALS:

- To use factual conditionals to express facts and habitual relationships
- To understand the order of clauses in factual conditionals

OPENING TASK
That's Life

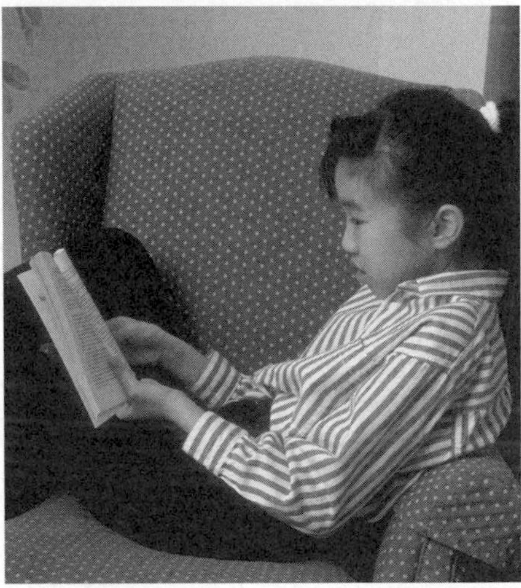

If you read a lot, you learn a lot.

Find a match for each statement on the left. Write the letter in the blank next to the number.

____ **1.** If you read a lot,	**a.** you get sick more often.
____ **2.** If you play with fire,	**b.** you don't smoke.
____ **3.** If you speak two languages,	**c.** people respect you.
____ **4.** If you don't wash your hands,	**d.** you have money problems.
____ **5.** If you care about your health,	**e.** you succeed.
____ **6.** If you eat too much,	**f.** you can communicate with more people.
____ **7.** If you respect people,	**g.** people listen to you.
____ **8.** If you spend more money than you earn,	**h.** you live longer.
____ **9.** If you work hard,	**i.** you gain weight.
____ **10.** If you speak well,	**j.** you get burned.
____ **11.** If you think positively,	**k.** you learn a lot.

Now make two similar true statements of your own.

12. ____

13. ____

ANSWER KEY

Opening Task

1. k **2.** j **3.** f **4.** a **5.** b **6.** i
7. c **8.** d **9.** e **10.** g **11.** h

CONDUCTING THE TASK

While Ss are working, go around offering assistance and checking to see that they understand these cause-effect relationships. Check their sentences for correct verb form and plausible meaning.

REVIEWING THE TASK

Have Ss write their sentences on the board and use these to introduce the form. Encourage Ss to provide alternative main clauses—*If you care about your health, you eat good foods/ you exercise/ you see a doctor regularly.*

FOCUS 1

This focus box presents the *if* clause/main clause structure for factual conditionals. Explain to Ss that the "if" clause states a condition and the "main" clause states the result. Each clause has a subject and a verb, but only the main clause is a complete sentence. The tense is the same in both clauses because these conditionals are generalizations; about relationships that always hold true.

Exercise 1

VARIATION

Have Ss do this exercise first as a sentence completion without looking at the multiple choice answers to see if they can produce the form and understand the relationship between the two parts of the sentence.

FOCUS **1**

Expressing Facts

Factual conditionals tell about things that are always true and never change.

EXAMPLES			EXPLANATIONS
	Clause 1 (*If* Clause)	**Clause 2 (Main Clause)**	
(a)	If you heat water to 212° (degrees) Fahrenheit,	it boils.	Use the simple present in both clauses.
(b)	If you don't water a house plant,	it dies.	
(c)	When (ever) you mix black and white,	you get gray.	You can use *when* or *whenever* in place of *if*.

EXERCISE 1

Test your knowledge. Circle the correct clause on the right. Discuss your answers with a partner.

1. If you put oil and water together,
   a. the oil stays on top.
   b. they mix.
2. If the temperature outside drops below 32° (degrees) Fahrenheit,
   a. water freezes.
   b. ice melts.
3. If you stay in the sun a lot,
   a. your skin stays young and smooth.
   b. your skin looks old.
4. If you smoke,
   a. you have health problems.
   b. you stay in good health.
5. If you don't refrigerate milk,
   a. it stays fresh.
   b. it goes bad.
6. If you fly west,
   a. the time is earlier.
   b. the time is later.
7. If you fly east,
   a. the time is earlier
   b. the time is later.
8. If your body temperature is 103° (degrees) Fahrenheit,
   a. you are well.
   b. you are sick.

ANSWER KEY

Exercise 1

1. a **2.** a **3.** b **4.** a **5.** b **6.** a
7. b **8.** b

EXERCISE 2

Think of the definitions of the words in italics. Find the definition on the right that completes each statement. Say your statements aloud.

1. If you live in a *democracy,* you can	**a.** want to be independent.
2. If you're *patient,* you don't	**b.** go to bed late.
3. If you're a *night owl,* you	**c.** teach in a school or college.
4. If you're a *teenager,* you	**d.** lose your temper.
5. If you're a *member of the faculty,* you	**e.** work in a factory.
6. If you're a *pediatrician,* you	**f.** have any money.
7. If you're a *blue-collar worker,* you may	**g.** treat sick children.
8. If you're *broke,* you don't	**h.** vote in elections.

FOCUS **2**

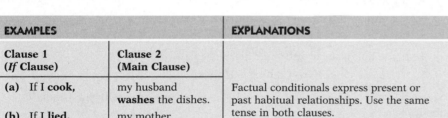

Expressing Habitual Relationships

EXAMPLES		EXPLANATIONS
Clause 1 (*If* Clause)	**Clause 2 (Main Clause)**	
(a) If I **cook,**	my husband **washes** the dishes.	Factual conditionals express present or past habitual relationships. Use the same tense in both clauses.
(b) If I **lied,**	my mother **punished** me.	
(c) When(ever) it **snowed,**	we **stayed** home from school.	You can use *when* or *whenever* in place of *if.*

ANSWER KEY

Exercise 2

1. h **2.** d **3.** b **4.** a **5.** c **6.** g
7. e **8.** f

Exercise 2 

This exercise will also teach Ss new vocabulary, idioms, and concepts. Ss can do this individually or in pairs.

Workbook Ex. 1, pp. 192–193.
Answers: TE, p. 542.

FOCUS 2

This focus box shows that factual conditionals express habitual conditional–result relationships in both present and past time. Example: *If A happens—B happens. If A happened—B happened.*

Have Ss make sentences about themselves and their families using the models in the box.

Exercise 3
Have Ss do this exercise individually and then compare their sentences in pairs.

Exercise 4 
Encourage Ss to share old wives' tales from their own cultures. Have Ss write their tales on the board or on butcher block paper so the class can read them and discuss the similarities and differences.

Exercise 5
Have Ss work individually first, then in pairs or small groups to read their answers to each other and compare.

EXERCISE 3

Make sentences with *if, when,* or *whenever* with the words below. Say your sentences aloud and compare your answers.

▶ **EXAMPLE:** I drive to school/take
If I drive to school, it takes about twenty minutes.

1. I drive to school/take
2. I take the bus to school/take
3. you have elderly parents/worry
4. you live with a roommate/share
5. you buy things on credit/pay
6. you take a vacation every year/feel
7. you never take a vacation/feel
8. exercise regularly/stay
9. someone sneezes/say
10. I don't want to cook/eat

EXERCISE 4

In some cultures, people say, "If you go out with wet hair, you get sick." We call these kinds of statements "old wives' tales." They are not always true, but people believe them and repeat them. Read the following "old wives' tales" and decide in your group if they are true or not.

1. If you go out with wet hair, you catch a cold.
2. If your ears are ringing, someone is talking about you.
3. If you eat chicken soup, your cold gets better.
4. If you hold your breath, your hiccups go away.
5. If you eat spinach, you get big and strong.

Now add a few old wives' tales from your home country and tell your group about them.

EXERCISE 5

Complete the *if* clauses with a statement of your own.

▶ **EXAMPLE:** If I feel very tired when I come home, I take a nap for ten minutes.

1. If I don't get enough sleep, ______________________.
2. If I get angry, ______________________.
3. If I get a headache, ______________________.

ANSWER KEY

Exercise 3
Possible answers include:
1. If... it takes... **2.** If..., it takes... **3.** If...., you worry a lot. **4.** If...., you share expenses. **5.** If..., you pay a lot of interest. **6.** If..., you feel great/relaxed/happy. **7.** If..., you feel unhappy/stressed/sad. **8.** If..., you stay in good health/healthy. **9.** If..., you say "God bless you". **10.** If..., I go out to eat/ I eat out.

4. If I am late, ____.
5. If I gain weight, ____.
6. If I fail an exam, ____.
7. If I have money to spend, ______________________________________.
8. If I can't sleep at night, ______________________________________.
9. If I eat too much, ____.
10. If I get very worried, ____.

EXERCISE 6

Work with a partner. Ask each other questions about your childhood.

▶ **EXAMPLE:** When you were a child, what happened if/when you . . . told a lie?

If I told a lie, my mother yelled at me.

1. told a lie?
2. got sick?
3. disobeyed your parents?
4. did well in school?
5. got a bad grade on your report card?
6. came home very late?
7. had a serious personal problem?
8. fought with your brother or sister?

Exercise 6

Ss generate their own answers. Have pairs report what they learned about their partners to the class.

Workbook Exs. 2 & 3, pp. 193–195.
Answers: TE, p. 542.

ANSWER KEY

Exercise 5

Answers will very. Check for correct form.

FOCUS 3

The order of clauses in factual conditionals is determined by the discourse rule governing given-new information. New information is postponed until the end of the sentence. Therefore, when the *if* clause contains the new information, it can occur in second position. Point out the need to include a comma when the *if* clause comes first.

Exercise 7

In this exercise, Ss practice both present and past factual conditionals. Have Ss do this individually and spend a couple of minutes making sure the tenses are correct in each sentence. Then have them share their responses with a partner or a small group.

UNIT GOAL REVIEW

Ask Ss to look back at the goals on the opening page of the unit and evaluate their own levels of progress and determine their own areas of weakness. If common problems persist, reteach or continue to practice these items in class or for homework. If individual problems persist, make recommendations to those Ss having problems.

FOCUS **3**

Order of Clauses in Factual Conditionals

EXAMPLES	EXPLANATIONS
(a) If you study hard, you get good grades.	The *if* clause is usually first.
(b) How do you get an A in this class? You get an A **if you do all the work.**	When the *if* clause contains new information, the *if* clause can be second. When it is second, there is no comma between the two clauses.
(c) How do you get the color gray? You get gray **when(ever) you mix black and white.**	With *when* or *whenever,* you can also change the order of the clauses.

EXERCISE 7

Answer the questions below.

EXAMPLES: When do you feel nervous?
I feel nervous if I have many things to do and little time.
I feel nervous whenever I have a test.

1. When do you feel nervous?
2. When do you get a headache?
3. How do you catch a cold?
4. When do you have trouble sleeping?
5. When did your parents punish you?
6. When were your parents pleased with you?
7. When do you listen to music?
8. When do you get angry?
9. When do you feel happy?
10. How do you know if you're in love?

ANSWER KEY

Exercise 7

Answers will vary. Possible answers:
1. I feel nervous whenever I take a test. **2.** I get a headache if I don't have a cup of coffee in the morning. **3.** I catch a cold if I come into contact with a sick person. **4.** I have trouble sleeping whenever I feel anxious. **5.** My parents punished me whenever I did something wrong. **6.** My parents were pleased with me whenever I got good grades. **7.** I listen to music whenever I want to relax. **8.** I get angry if I see people treating others badly. **9.** I feel happy whenever I get a letter from home. **10.** I know I'm in love if I think about my girlfriend/boyfriend all the time.

Use Your English

ACTIVITY 1: WRITING/SPEAKING

Psychologists say there are two personality types: A and B. "Type A" people worry, get nervous, and are under stress all the time. "Type B" people are calm and try to enjoy life.

STEP 1 Which personality type are you? Complete the statements.

1. Whenever there is a change in my life, I . . .
2. If I have a test, I . . .
3. When I get stuck in traffic, I . . .
4. When I enter a room with people I don't know, I . . .
5. When another driver on the road makes a mistake, I . . .
6. If a friend hurts my feelings, I . . .
7. If I don't hear from my family and friends, I . . .
8. When I have a lot of things to do in one day, I . . .
9. When I don't succeed at something, I . . .
10. When someone criticizes me, I . . .

STEP 2 Discuss your results in your group. Decide which students in the group are "Type A" personalities and which are "Type B." Explain why. Fill in the chart below.

Name	Type A Personality	Name	Type B Personality
Stefan	If he has a test, he worries a lot. When he doesn't succeed at something, he gets angry at himself.		

USE YOUR ENGLISH

For a more complete discussion of how to use the activities, see p. xxvi of this Teacher's Edition.

Activity 1 

1. Introduce the concepts of Type A and Type B personalities. Ask Ss to describe some typical behaviors for each personality type.
2. Have Ss do Step 1 individually. Show Ss the variety of sentences they can write by eliciting examples for #1 *(Whenever there is a change in my life, I feel happy/I feel stress/I write in my journal)*. Ask Ss to evaluate themselves. Are they Type A or Type B personalities?

3. Step 2: 

After group discussions, have a representative from each group report the A and B personality types to the class.

Activity 2

Ss can refer to Exercises 5 or 7 for ideas. Have them work individually. Then group Ss and have them share their sentences with each other. Have each group present the person with the most unusual habits.

Activity 3

Collect Ss' writing to check for errors with the factual conditionals or other structures.

VARIATION

Depending on the abilities of your Ss, this activity can be written either as separate sentences or as a coherent paragraph with topic and support. For example: Topic: *I was a difficult child.* Support: *When my parents talked to me, I didn't listen.* Topic: *I had a very happy childhood.* Support: *Whenever my parents spoke to me, I always felt their support and love.* You can provide the generalizations for Ss and have them try to support the topic sentence. Or, you can have Ss generate statements about their childhood, then group the statements in some meaningful way, and try to write appropriate topic sentences. Have pairs read their paragraphs together to work on clarity, focus, and development.

Activity 4

This activity will encourage Ss to share information about cultural habits. If possible, put Ss in cross-cultural groups. Have groups present their information to the class.

EXPANSION

Have Ss create a culture manual comparing American culture to the cultures represented by the students.

ACTIVITY 2: WRITING/SPEAKING

Do you have any special problems or unusual habits? Write down any habits you have. Share your statements with your group. Try to find the person with the most unusual habits.

▶ **EXAMPLES:** If I eat chocolate, I get a headache.
Whenever I feel anxious, I clean my apartment.

ACTIVITY 3: WRITING

Think about your childhood. Write five sentences with *if* clauses about past habits in your childhood.

▶ **EXAMPLES:** If my sister hit me, I hit her back.
If my mother yelled at me, I felt miserable.

ACTIVITY 4: SPEAKING

STEP 1 Compare habits in different countries. Write the name of a country in the left column and complete each *if/when(ever)* clause.

▶ **EXAMPLE:** In Canada, when you have dinner in a restaurant, you leave a tip.

Country	If/When(ever) Clause 1	Clause 2
Canada	you have dinner in a restaurant	you leave a tip
	someone gives you a compliment	
	someone gives you a gift	
	you greet an old friend	
	a baby is born	
	someone sneezes	
	someone invites you to dinner	
	you want to refuse someone's invitation	

STEP 2 Add two more habits to the list and make sentences about them.

ACTIVITY 5: LISTENING/SPEAKING

Marcia and Eduardo are having a conversation about what they do if they can't sleep.

STEP 1 Listen to the conversation and then check the box if the statements below are true or false.

Read the statements. Check **True** or **False.**

	True	False
1. If Eduardo can't sleep, he takes a sleeping pill.		
2. If Marcia can't sleep, she drinks a glass of milk.		
3. If Eduardo can't sleep, he reads a boring book.		
4. If Eduardo drinks milk in the evening, he feels sick.		
5. If Marcia reads a boring book, she falls asleep.		

STEP 2 What conditions make people have problems with sleep? Tell the class.

Activity 5 

Play textbook audio. The tapescript for this listening appears on p. 549 of this book.

The test for this unit can be found on pp. 523–524 of this book. The answers can be found on p. 525.

TOEFL Test Preparation exercises for Units 22–25 can be found on pp. 196–198 of the work book.
The answers are on p. 543 of this book

Appendices

APPENDIX 1 Forming Verb Tenses

Appendix 1A *Be:* Present Tense

<table>
<tr><td>I</td><td>am</td><td rowspan="3">from Japan.</td></tr>
<tr><td>He
She
It</td><td>is</td></tr>
<tr><td>We
You
They</td><td>are</td></tr>
<tr><td>There</td><td>is</td><td>a student from Japan in our class.</td></tr>
<tr><td>There</td><td>are</td><td>students from all over the world in this class.</td></tr>
</table>

Appendix 1B *Be:* Past Tense

<table>
<tr><td>I
He
She
It</td><td>was</td><td rowspan="2">happy.</td></tr>
<tr><td>We
You
They</td><td>were</td></tr>
<tr><td>There</td><td>was</td><td>a party yesterday.</td></tr>
<tr><td>There</td><td>were</td><td>a lot of people there.</td></tr>
</table>

Appendix 1C Simple Present

I You We They	work.
He She It	works.

Appendix 1D Present Progressive

I	am	working.
He She It	is	
We You They	are	

Appendix 1E Simple Past

I He She It We You They	worked	yesterday.

Appendix 1F Future Tense with *Will*

I He She It We You They	will work	tomorrow.

Appendix 1G Future Tense with *Be Going To*

<table>
<tr><td>I</td><td>am</td><td rowspan="3">going to work in a few minutes.</td></tr>
<tr><td>He
She
It</td><td>is</td></tr>
<tr><td>We
You
They</td><td>are</td></tr>
</table>

Appendix 1H *Can/Might/May*

<table>
<tr><td>I
He
She
It
We
You
They</td><td>can
might
may</td><td>work.</td></tr>
</table>

Appendix 1I *Be Able To*

<table>
<tr><td>I</td><td>am</td><td rowspan="3">able to dance.</td></tr>
<tr><td>He
She
It</td><td>is</td></tr>
<tr><td>We
You
They</td><td>are</td></tr>
</table>

APPENDIX 2 Spelling Rules

Appendix 2A Plural Nouns

Nouns	Singular	Plural
Regular	book table	books tables
Ends in vowel + *y*	toy	toys
Ends in vowel + *o*	radio	radios
Ends in consonant + *o*	potato tomato	potatoes tomatoes
Ends in −*y*	city	cities
Ends in *f, fe*	thief wife	thieves wives
(Except)	chief chef	chiefs chefs
Ends in *ss, ch, sh, x,* and *z*	class sandwich dish box	classes sandwiches dishes boxes
Irregular plural nouns	man woman child foot tooth mouse	men women children feet teeth mice
Plurals that stay the same	sheep deer fish	sheep deer fish
No singular form		scissors pants shorts pajamas glasses clothes

Appendix 2B Simple Present: Third Person Singular

Rule	Example
1. Add *-s* to form the third person singular of most verbs.	My brother **sleeps** 8 hours a night.
2. Add *-es* to verbs ending in *sh, ch, x, z,* or *ss.*	She **watches** television every evening.
3. When the verb ends in a consonant + *y,* change the *y* to *i* and add *-es.*	He **hurries** to class every morning.
4. When the verb ends in a vowel + *y,* do not change the *y.* Add *-s.*	My sister **plays** the violin.
5. Irregular Forms: have go do	 He **has** a good job. He **goes** to work every day. He **does** the laundry.

Appendix 2C Present Progressive

1. Add *-ing* to the base of the verb.	talk study do agree	talking studying doing agreeing
2. If the verb ends in a single *-e,* drop the *-e* and add *-ing.*	drive	driving
3. If a one-syllable verb has a consonant, a vowel, and a consonant (c-v-c), double the last consonant and add *-ing.*	(c-v-c) s i t r u n	 sitting running
Do not double the consonant if the verb ends in *w, x,* or *y.*	s h o w f i x p l a y	showing fixing playing
4. In two-sylllable verbs that end in a consonant, a vowel, and a consonant (c-v-c), double the last consonant only if the last syllable is stressed.	beGIN LISten	beginning listening
5. If the verb ends in *-ie,* drop the *-ie,* add *-y* and *-ing.*	lie die	lying dying

Appendix 2D Simple Past of Regular Verbs

1. Add *-ed* to most regular verbs.	start	started
2. If the verb ends in an *-e*, add *-d*.	like	liked
3. If the verb ends in a consonant + *y*, change the *y* to *i* and add *-ed*.	study	studied
4. If the verb ends in a vowel + *y*, don't change the *y* to *i*. Add *-ed*.	enjoy play	enjoyed played
5. If a one-syllable verb ends in a consonant, a vowel, and a consonant (c-v-c), double the last consonant and add *-ed*.	stop	stopped
Do not double the last consonant if it is *w*, *x*, or *y*.	show fix play	showed fixed played
6. If a two-syllable word ends in a consonant, a vowel, and a consonant (c-v-c), double the last consonant if the stress is on the last syllable.	ocCUR LISten	occurred listened

APPENDIX 3 Pronunciation Rules

Appendix 3A Regular Plural Nouns

/s/	/z/		/ɪz/
After voiceless sounds (*p, t, k, f, th*)	After voiced sounds (*b, d, g, v, m, n, l, r, ng*) and vowel sounds		After *s, z, sh, ch, ge/dge* sounds. (This adds another syllable to the word.)
maps	jobs	pens	classes
pots	beds	schools	exercises
books	rugs	cars	dishes
cuffs	leaves	rings	sandwiches
months	rooms	days	colleges

Appendix 3B Simple Present Tense: Third Person Singular

/s/	/z/	/ɪz/
After voiceless sounds *(p, t, k, f)*	After voiced final sounds *(b, d, g, v, l, r, m, n, ng)*	Verbs ending in *sh, ch, z, s.* (This adds another syllable to the word.)
He sleeps. She works.	She drives a car. He prepares dinner.	He teaches English. She rushes to class.

Appendix 3C Simple Past Tense of Regular Verbs

/t/	/d/	/td/Id/
After voiceless sounds *(p, k, f, s, sh, ch)*	After voiced final sounds *(b, g, v, l, r, m, n)*	Verbs ending in *t* or *d.* (This adds another syllable to the word.)
He kissed her once. She asked a question.	We learned a song. They waved goodbye.	She painted a picture. The plane landed safely.

APPENDIX 4 Time Expressions

Appendix 4A Simple Present

Adverbs of Frequency	Frequency Expressions	Time Expressions
always often frequently usually sometimes seldom rarely never	every { morning, afternoon, night, summer, winter, spring, fall, day, week, year all the time once a week twice a month 3 times a year once in a while	in { 1997, October, the fall on { Monday, Sundays, January 1st, the weekend at { 6:00, noon, night, midnight

Appendix 4B Present Progressive

now right now at the moment today these days nowadays	this semester this evening this week this year

Appendix 4C Past

yesterday	last	ago	in/on/at
yesterday { morning afternoon evening	last { night week month year summer	an hour two days 6 months a year } ago	in { 1988 June the evening on { Sunday December 1 weekends at { 6:00 night midnight

Appendix 4D Future

this	next	tomorrow	other	in/on/at
this { morning afternoon evening	next { week month year Sunday weekend summer	tomorrow { morning afternoon evening night	soon later a week from today tonight for 3 days until 3:00	in { 15 minutes a few days 2 weeks March 2005 on { Tuesday May 21 at { 4:00 midnight

APPENDIX 5 Pronouns

Appendix 5A Subject Pronouns

Subject Pronouns		
I	am	
You	are	
He She It	is	happy.
We You They	are	

Appendix 5B Object Pronouns

		Object Pronouns
She	loves	me. you. him. her. it. us. you. them.

Appendix 5C Demonstrative Pronouns

This That	is a list of subject pronouns.
These Those	are object pronouns.

Appendix 5D Possessive Pronouns

This book is	mine. his. hers. * ours. yours. theirs.

* "It" does not have a possessive pronoun.

Appendix 5E Reflexive Pronouns

I You We You They	love	myself. yourself. ourselves. yourselves. themselves.
He She It	loves	himself. herself. itself.

Appendix 5F Reciprocal Pronoun

Friends help each other.

APPENDIX 6 Possessives

Appendix 6A Possessive Nouns

Bob's Thomas' Thomas's The teacher's The students' The children's Bob and Andrea's	house is big.

Appendix 6B Possessive Determiners (Adjectives)

My Your His Her Its Our Your Their	eyes are big.

Appendix 6C Possessive Pronouns

The house is	mine. yours. his. hers. * ours. yours. theirs.

* "It" does not have a possessive pronoun.

APPENDIX 7 Comparisons with Adjectives and Adverbs

Appendix 7A Comparative Form (to compare two people, places, things or actions)

Betsy	is	older bigger busier later more punctual less talkative	than	Judy.
	plays the violin	faster more beautifully better		

Appendix 7B Superlative Form (to compare one thing or person to all the others in a group)

Betsy	is	the oldest the biggest the busiest the most practical the most punctual	of all her sisters.
	plays the violin	the fastest more beautifully the best	

Appendix 7C *As...As* (to say that two people, places, or things are the same)

Betsy	is	as	old big busy practical punctual	as	Judy.
	plays the violin		fast beautifully well		

APPENDIX 8 Past-Tense Forms of Common Irregular Verbs

Simple Form	Past-Tense Form	Past Participle	Simple Form	Past-Tense Form	Past Participle
be	was	been	leave	left	left
become	became	became	lend	lent	lent
begin	began	begun	let	let	let
bend	bent	bent	lose	lost	lost
bite	bit	bitten	make	made	made
blow	blew	blown	meet	met	met
break	broke	broken	pay	paid	paid
bring	brought	brought	put	put	put
build	built	built	quit	quit	quit
buy	bought	bought	read	read*	read*
catch	caught	caught	ride	rode	ridden
choose	chose	chosen	ring	rang	rung
come	came	come	run	ran	run
cost	cost	cost	say	said	said
cut	cut	cut	see	saw	seen
dig	dug	dug	sell	sold	sold
do	did	done	send	sent	sent
draw	drew	drawn	shake	shook	shaken
drink	drank	drunk	shoot	shot	shot
drive	drove	driven	shut	shut	shut
eat	ate	eaten	sing	sang	sung
fall	fell	fallen	sit	sat	sat
feed	fed	fed	sleep	slept	slept
feel	felt	felt	speak	spoke	spoken
fight	fought	fought	spend	spent	spent
find	found	found	stand	stood	stood
fly	flew	flown	steal	stole	stolen
forget	forgot	forgotten	swim	swum	swum
get	got	gotten	take	took	taken
give	gave	given	teach	taught	taught
go	went	gone	tear	tore	torn
grow	grew	grown	tell	told	told
hang	hung	hung	think	thought	thought
have	had	had	throw	threw	thrown
hear	heard	heard	understand	understood	understood
hide	hid	hidden	wake	woke	woken
hit	hit	hit	wear	wore	worn
hold	held	held	win	won	won
hurt	hurt	hurt	write	wrote	written
keep	kept	kept			
know	knew	known			
lead	led	led			

* Pronounce the base form: /rid/; pronounce the past-tense form and the past participle: red.

Exercises (second parts)

UNIT 1

Unit 1

Exercise 5 (page 5)

List B

Men	Country	Nationality
1. Mario		Peruvian
2. Mohammed	Morocco	
3. Hideki and Yoshi		Japanese
4. Leonardo	The Dominican Republic	
5. Oumar		Senegalese
Women		
6. Lilik	Indonesia	
7. Krystyna		Polish
8. Liisa and Katja	Finland	
9. Belén		Spanish
10. Margarita and Dalia	Brazil	

UNIT 2

Exercise 4 (page 18)

Example:

1. 

2. 

3. 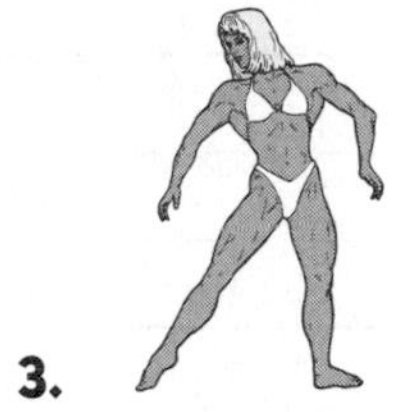

4. 

5. 

6. 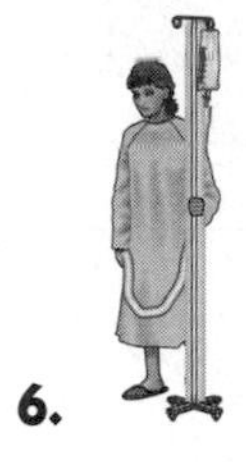

7. 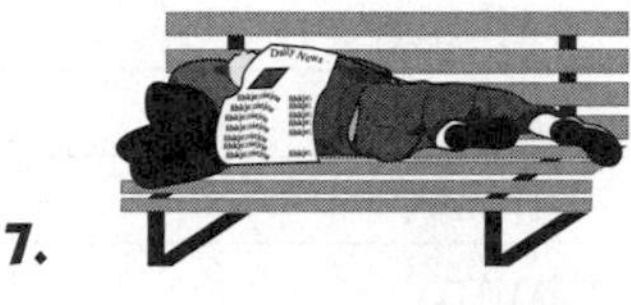

8. 

9. 

10. 

Exercise 6 (page 20)

Chart B

Name: **Age:**	**Cindy** **24**	**Shelly** **30**
1. Height		
tall		✔
average height		
short		
2. Weight		
thin		
average weight		✔
heavy		
3. Personality		
shy		✔
friendly		
quiet		✔
talkative		
neat		✔
messy		
funny		
serious		✔
nervous		
calm		✔

Exercise 6 (page 34)

MAP B

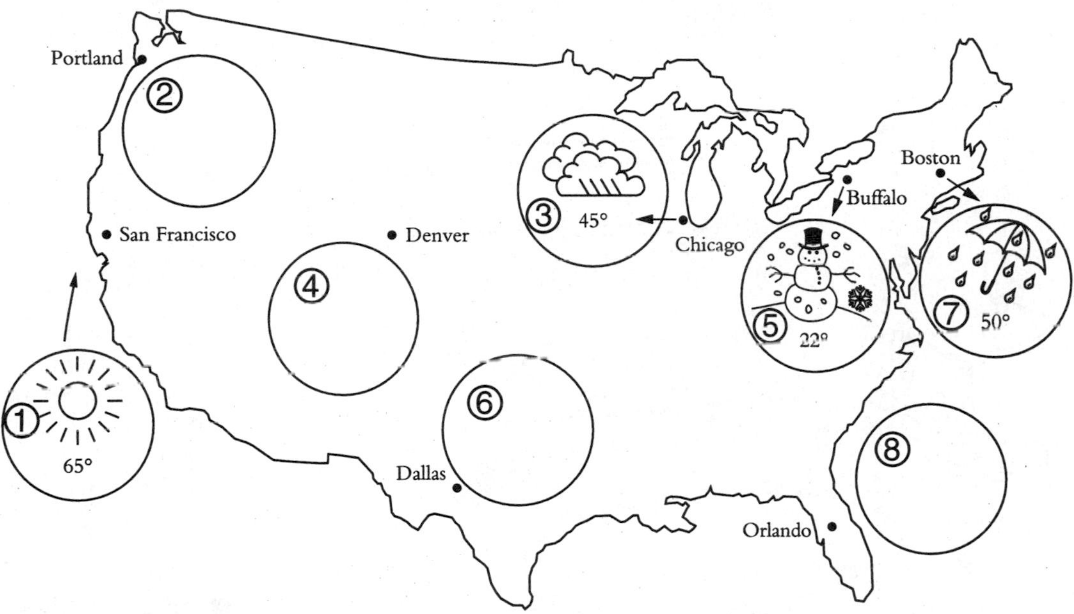

UNIT 3

Exercise 7 (page 36)

Chart B

1. 11:30	**2.** 8:15	**3.** 7:35	**4.** 9:45
5. 1:55	**6.** 3:10	**7.** 2:40	**8.** 5:20

UNIT 3

Exercise 10 (page 40)

Exercise 2 (page 141)

Student B

	Nahal		Sang-Woo	
	Yes	No	Yes	No
1. like to learn English			✔	
2. want to meet English-speaking people	✔			
3. feel nervous when speaking English			✔	
4. like to work in groups	✔			
5. need grammar rules to learn English			✔	
6. learn by speaking and listening to English	✔			
7. learn by reading and writing English			✔	
8. learn slowly, step by step		✔		
9. try new ways of learning				✔

UNIT 18

Answers to Exercise 15 (page 307)

Text B

1. Doina grew up in ____________________ (where).
2. She married a government official.
3. She was pregnant in 1976. She had ____________________ (what).
4. Doina was unhappy ____________________ (why).
5. She thought of ways to escape.
6. She taught her daughter ____________________ (what).
7. On October 9, 1988, she and her daughter swam across the Danube River to Serbia.
8. ____________________ caught them (who).
9. Doina and her daughter went to jail.
10. They tried to escape ____________________ from jail (when).
11. Finally, they left Romania on foot in the middle of the night.
12. They flew to ____________________ in 1989 (where).
13. Doina went to school to learn English.
14. She wrote ____________________ (what) in her ESL class.

Activity 2: Conclusion to Exercise 12 (page 309)

Activity 6: (page 311)

Only the Host looks at this game board.

GAME BOARD

$$$	Category 1 PEOPLE	Category 2 WH-QUESTIONS	Category 3 YES/NO QUESTIONS
$10	Ms. Ditto	a VCR	Yes, she did.
$20	Harry	on the first day of classes	Yes, he did.
$30	the Director	in the language lab	No, he didn't.
$40	Professor Brown	because he needed to pay for the ESL classes again this semester	No, he didn't.
$50	the students	she noticed grammar mistakes in the note	Yes, they did.

UNIT 24

Exercise 4 (page 397)

CHART B

	North America	Central and South America	Asia	Europe	Africa	The World
long river	The Mississippi		The Yangtze		The Nile	
large country		Brazil		France		The People's Republic of China
populated country	The United States		The People's Republic of China		Nigeria	
high mountain		Mt. Aconcagua		Mt. Elbrus		Mt. Everest
small country	Bermuda		Macao		the Seychelles	

Credits

Text Credits

Unit 8, Exercise 4: Permission is granted by JAG Publications to reprint cartoons from COMICS AND CONVERSATION and MORE COMICS AND CONVERSATION. Cartoons copyright © 1974, 1981, 1983 by Sergio Aragones.

Unit 18, Exercise 3: Permission is granted by JAG Publications to reprint cartoons from COMICS AND CONVERSATION and MORE COMICS AND CONVERSATION. Cartoons copyright © 1974, 1981, 1983 by Sergio Aragones.

Unit 21, Exercise 9: Permission is granted by Cambridge University Press to reprint cartoons from THE MIND'S EYE. Cartoons copyright © 1980 by Sempé.

Photo Credits

Page 1: Upper left, © The Stock Market/Julie Harrington; upper middle, © The Stock Market/Rob Lewine; upper right, © The Stock Market/Harvey Lloyd; lower left, © The Stock Market/Marco Cristofori; lower middle, © The Stock Market/Vince Streano; lower right, © The Stock Market/Roy Morsch. Page 9: (Top to bottom) © The Stock Market/Vivianne Holbrooke; © The Stock Market/Claudia Park. Page 11: © The Stock Market/Roy Morsch. Page 28: Upper left, © Corbis/Yannn Arthus-Bertrand; upper right, © The Stock Market/Ned Gillette; lower left, © The Stock Market/J. Messerschmidt; lower right, © Corbis/Vittoriano Rastelli. Page 46: © The Stock Market/Jeff Zaruba. Page 64: © Corbis/Richard A. Cooke. Page 65: Left, © Corbis/Michael T. Sedam; middle, © Corbis/Perry Conway; © Corbis/Wolfgang Kaehler. Page 69: Upper left, © The Stock Market/Frank P. Rossotto; upper right, © The Stock Market/Ray Shaw; lower left, © Corbis/David Turnley. Page 74: Top, © The Stock Market/Jon Feingersh. Page 107: © The Stock Market/Anne Heimann. Page 116: Left, © Heinle & Heinle, photograph by Jonathan Stark; right, © The Stock Market/David Pollack. Page 129 © Heinle & Heinle, photograph by Jonathan Stark. Page 130 © Heinle & Heinle, photograph by Jonathan Stark. Page 138: Left, © Heinle & Heinle, photograph by Jonathan Stark; right, © The Stock Market/John Henley. Page 153 © Heinle & Heinle, photograph by Jonathan Stark. Page 168 © Heinle & Heinle, photograph by Jonathan Stark. Page 172: © The Stock Market/Gabe Palmer. Page 188: © The Stock Market/David Woods. Page 198: Left, © The Stock Market/Chuck Savage; right, © The Stock Market/Jon Feingersh. Page 199: Top left, © The Stock Market/Peter Steiner; top middle, © The Stock Market/Jon Feingersh; middle left, © The Stock Market/David Frazier; middle middle, © Corbis/Gianni Orti; middle right, © The Stock Market/Michael Tamboririno; lower left, © The Stock Market/Chris Jones. Page 202: Left, © Heinle & Heinle, photograph by Jonathan Stark; middle, © The Stock Market/Peter Steiner; right, © The Stock Market/Rob & Sas. Page 228 © Heinle & Heinle, photograph by Jonathan Stark. Page 232: © The Stock Market/Gabe Palmer. Page 251: © The Stock Market/Nancy Ney. Page 258 © Heinle & Heinle, photograph by Jonathan Stark. Page 272: Top, © Corbis/Flip Schulke; middle, © Corbis/ Hulton-Deutsch Collection; bottom, © Corbis/Hulton-Deutsch Collection. Page 273: (Top to bottom) © Corbis/Hulton-Deutsch Collection; © Corbis/Underwood & Underwood; © Corbis/Robert Maass; © Corbis/Richard T. Nowitz. Page 283: photograph by Jonathan Stark. Page 286: © Corbis/Owen Franken. Page 288: © Corbis/Steve Chenn. Page 303 © Heinle & Heinle, photograph by Jonathan Stark Page 312: © Corbis/Roger Ressmeyer. Page 322: © Archive Photos/Curry. Page 347 © Heinle & Heinle, photograph by Jonathan Stark. Page 355 © Heinle & Heinle, photograph by Jonathan Stark. Page 362: Left, © Corbis/Michael Boys; right, © Corbis/Christpher Cormack. Page 378 © Heinle & Heinle, photograph by Jonathan Stark. Page 406: © Corbis/Laura Dwight.

Index

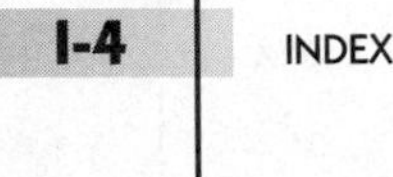

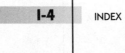

TESTS AND ANSWERS

Grammar Dimensions Book 1

Unit 1 The Verb *Be:* Affirmative Statements, Subject Pronouns

Name ________________________

Score ____________
100

10-minute quiz (20 items at 5 points each = 100%)

A. Review the continents/regions listed below. Then fill in the blanks with *is* or *are* and the correct continent/region.

Europe *Africa* *The Middle East* *Asia* *North America*
Central America *The Caribbean* *South America*

1. Arabia ________________ in ______________________________________ .
2. Chile and Argentina ________________ in ___________________________ .
3. The United States ________________ in ______________________________ .
4. England and France ________________ in ___________________________ .
5. My country, ________________ , ________________ in ______________ .

B. Fill in the blanks of Franz's letter to Jane's parents. Use subject pronouns and contractions with *be.*

Dear Mr. and Mrs. Smith,

Hi! (6) ________________ Franz. (7) ________________ in love with your

daughter, Jane. (8) ________________ wonderful! (9) ________________

beautiful! (10) ________________ lucky parents. (11)

crazy about me, and (12) ________________ crazy about her.

(13) ________________ very happy together.

Hope to meet you soon.

Love, Franz

C. Study the information below. Then write six complete sentences describing the famous people.

Person:	**Country:**	**Occupation:**	**Marital Status:**
Pele	Brazil	soccer player	married
Sophia Loren	Italy	actress	married
Michael & Janet Jackson	United States	singers	divorced/single

Pele:

14. (country) ______________________________

15. (occupation) ______________________________

16. (marital status) ______________________________

Sophia Loren:

17. (marital status) ______________________________

18. (occupation) ______________________________

Michael & Janet Jackson:

19. (nationality) ______________________________

20. (occupation) ______________________________

UNIT 1 ANSWERS

A. 1. is; the Middle East
2. are; South America
3. is; North America
4. are; Europe
5. (varies)

B. 6. I'm
7. I'm
8. She's
9. She's
10. You're
11. She's
12. I'm
13. We're

C. 14. Pele is from Brazil.
15. He's a soccer player.
16. He's married.
17. Sophia Loren is married.
18. She's an actress.
19. Michael and Janet Jackson are American.
20. They are singers.

Grammar Dimensions Book 1 Name ______________

Unit 2 The Verb *Be: Yes/No* Questions Score ________ / 100

Be + Adjective, Negative Statements

15-minute quiz (25 items at 4 points each = 100%)

A. Cindy is interested in Mark Heller. Complete her letter to Mark. Use contractions where possible.

Hi Mark!

(1) ______________ 22 years old. (2) ______________ (negative) tall, but

(3) ______________ thin.

(4) ______________ you friendly and talkative? (5) ______________ you

ready for marriage?

Please call me soon at (718)-245-1926. Love, Cindy

B. Ask *yes/no* questions about the women who are interested in Mark. Then write the correct short answer.

6.–7. (Shelly/tall) ______________________________?

Yes, ______________________________.

8.–9. (Cindy/quiet) ______________________________?

No, ______________________________.

10.–11. (Shelly/messy) ______________________________?

No, ______________________________.

12.–13. (Cindy/under 30) ______________________________?

Yes, ______________________________.

C. Lisa Gomez calls the New English Language School for information. Complete the dialogue. Use the correct form of the verb *be* and subject pronouns where necessary.

14. Lisa: Hello, ______________ this the New English Language School?
15. Mary: Yes, ______________. May I help you? Lisa: I'd like some information

    about your program.

    Mary: Of course.
16. Lisa: ______________ the classes small?
17. Mary: No, ______________. We have about 25 people in a class.
18. Lisa: ______________ the teachers experienced?
19. Mary: Yes, ______________. They are excellent.
20. Lisa: ______________ the tuition expensive?
21. Mary: Yes, ______________.

    Lisa: Thank you very much.
22. Mary: ______________ welcome.

D. Give the opposite adjective to describe these famous people.

23. Barbara Streisand isn't outgoing. She's ______________.
24. Robin Williams isn't serious. He's ______________.
25. The president and his wife aren't lazy. They're ______________.

UNIT 2 ANSWERS

A.
1. I'm
2. I'm not
3. I'm
4. Are
5. Are

B.
6. Is Shelly tall?
7. Yes, she is.
8. Is Cindy quiet?
9. No, she isn't.
10. Is Shelly messy?
11. No, she isn't.
12. Is Cindy under 30?
13. Yes, she is

C.
14. is
15. it is
16. Are
17. they aren't
18. Are
19. they are
20. Is
21. it is
22. You're
23. shy
24. funny
25. hardworking

Name ____________________

Unit 3 The Verb *Be: Wh*-Question Words, *It* with Time and Weather, and Prepositions of Location

Score ________
100

15-minute quiz (25 items at 4 points each = 100%)

A. It's cloudy today! Choose the correct preposition from those given below to describe the plane and the clouds.

1. 

2. 

3. 

4. 

5. 

6. 

in *on* *in back of* *next to* *between* *in front of* *opposite* *above* *under*

1. The plane is ______________ the clouds.
2. It's ______________ the clouds.
3. It's ______________ the clouds.
4. It's ______________ the clouds.
5. It's ______________ the clouds.
6. It's ______________ the clouds.

B. Answer these questions about TIME and WEATHER. Write <u>complete</u>, true sentences.

7. Q: Where are you now? A: ______________ in ______________ (city name).
8. Q: What time is it? A: ______________________________.
9. Q: How's the weather today? A: ______________________________.
10. Q: What city are you from? A: ______________________________.
11. Q: What time is it there? A: ______________________________.
12. Q: How's the weather in your city in the summer? A: ______________________________.
13. Q: How's the weather in your city in the winter? A: ______________________________.

C. Imagine you are having a conversation and the underlined information isn't clear. Ask for that information with the correct *wh*-question word from the words given below.

(*Note:* Teacher should count 4 points for the correct *wh?* word and 4 points for the correct question structure with *be.*)

What *Where* *Who* *How* *When* *What time* *How old* *Why*

Example: My best friend is *in the hospital.*

Q. Where is your best friend?

14.–15. *The Pope* is the head of the Catholic Church.

Q: ____?

16.–17. The Pyramids of Egypt are *about 4700 years old*.

Q: ____?

18.–19. *Washington, D.C.* is the capital of the United States.

Q: ____?

20.–21. Independence Day in the U.S. is *July 4th*.

Q: ____?

22.–23. We are here *because we want to learn English*.

Q: ____?

24.–25. The meaning of "shy" is "*timid*."

Q: ____?

UNIT 3 ANSWERS

A. **1.** above
2. in front of
3. under
4. between
5. in
6. in back of

B. **7.** I'm . . .
8. It's . . .
9. It's . . .
10. I'm from . . .
11. It's . . .
12. It's . . .
13. It's . . .

C. **14.** Who
15. is the head of the Catholic Church?
16. How old
17. are the Pyramids of Egypt?
18. What
19. is the capitol of the United States?
20. When
21. is Independence Day in the U.S.
22. Why
23. are you here?
24. What
25. is the meaning of shy?

Grammar Dimensions Book 1 — Name ____________________

Unit 4 Nouns: Count and Noncount Nouns, — Score ________ / 100

Be + Adjective + Noun

15-minute quiz (25 items at 4 points each = 100%)

A. Today you are going shopping and to school. You need to get many things. Look at the list below. 1) Add *a/an* to indicate singular; OR 2) make the base noun plural; OR 3) make no changes for noncount nouns.

Grocery Store:	Stationary Store:	Teacher's Office
1. some potato	6. some pencil	11. some advice
2. some cheese	7. ____ eraser	12. some homework
3. ____ birthday cake	8. some scissors	13. some exercise
4. some match	9. two dictionary	14. ____ extra copy of the handout
5. some coffee	10. some new bookshelf	15. some help

B. Answer the following questions in <u>complete</u> sentences. Choose from the nouns given below. Add "*very*" when possible.

large continent *popular island* *hot desert* *long river* *famous museum* *university*
big clock in London *hour* *expensive car* *unusual airplane* *tall mountain*

16. Q: What's the Louvre?

    A: *It's* ____.

17. Q: What's Harvard?

    A: ____.

18. Q: What's the Concorde?

    A: ____.

19. Q: What's 60 minutes?

    A: ____.

20. Q: What's the Sahara?

    A: ____.

C. Ask a question with the expressions "*how much is* . . ." or "*how much are* . . ." about a particular country or city.

Example: *How much is coffee in Mexico City?*

21. a one-bedroom apartment ____________________________?
22. clothing ____________________________?
23. sneakers ____________________________?
24. meat ____________________________?
25. movies ____________________________?

UNIT 4 ANSWERS

A.
1. -es
2. no change
3. a
4. -es
5. no change
6. -s
7. an
8. no change
9. -ies
10. -ves
11. no change
12. no change
13. -s
14. an
15. no change

B.
16. It's a (very) famous museum.
17. It's a university.
18. It's an unusual airplane./It's a very unusual plane.
19. It's an hour.
20. It's a (very) hot desert.

C.
21. How much is a one-bedroom apartment in . . .
22. How much is clothing in . . .
23. How much are sneakers in . . .
24. How much is meat in . . .
25. How much are movies in . . .

Grammar Dimensions Book 1

Unit 5 The Verb *Have:* Affirmative and Negative Statements, Questions and Short Answers, *Some/Any*

Name ________________________

Score ____________
100

15-minute quiz (25 items at 4 points each = 100%)

A. Think about your family and select a relative to describe.

Relative's name: ________________ Relationship to you: ________________
Write complete, true sentences, negative or affirmative. Use the correct form of the verb *have*.

1. (a dog) ____.
2. (a bicycle) ____.
3. (hair length) ____.
4. (eye color) ____.
5. (other) ____.

B. Complete each question with the correct verb forms. Then give the short answer you think is correct. Use the verb *have*.

6. Q: ________________ traditional Eskimo men ________________ cordless telephones?
7. A: ____.
8. Q: ________________ modern Eskimo houses ________________ electricity?
9. A: ____.
10. Q: ________________ Nilaulaq ________________ a traditional Eskimo name?
11. A: ____.
12. Q: ________________ you ________________ any more questions?
13. A: ____.

C. Write the correct form of *have*, affirmative or negative (–).

Amish Americans (14) ______________ freedom to practice their religion in the United States. They (15) ______________ a very simple life-style. They (16) (–) ______________ expensive clothes. The women (17) ______________ plain, dark dresses. They (18) (–) ______________ jewelry.

John Lapp is a traditional Amish farmer. He (19) ______________ a horse. John (20) (–) ______________ modern machines for his farm.

D. ERROR DETECTION
Circle the letter of the *INCORRECT* underlined word or phrase.

21. (A) Does she is (B) an Eskimo? Maybe she (C) is. She was born (D) in Alaska.
22. My teacher (A) doesn't has three (B) children. She (C) isn't (D) married.
23. (A) I'm sorry. I (B) no have (C) any change (D) right now.
24. Big (A) cities such as Los Angeles (B) have (C) any (D) traffic problems.
25. We (A) don't have (B) some videos. We prefer to see (C) movies (D) at the theater.

UNIT 5 ANSWERS

A. **1.–5.** Answers vary, but every sentence must include the verb "have".

B. **6.** Do/have
7. No, they don't.
8. Do/have
9. Yes, they do.
10. Does/have
11. Yes, she does.
12. Do/have
13. Yes, I do./No, I don't.

C. **14.** have
15. have
16. don't have
17. have
18. don't have
19. has
20. doesn't have

D. **21.** A
22. A
23. B
24. C
25. B

Grammar Dimensions Book 1 Name ______________________

Unit 6 *This/That/These/Those,* Possessives Score __________
100

15-minute quiz (25 items at 4 points each = 100%)

A. Maria is new to the United States. She is asking many questions about food. For example, she asks, "What is that?" Her American friend responds, "It's a hot dog." Fill in the blanks below with the correct forms.

(is/are) (this/that/these/those)

1. Q: What ______________________________ ? (*near*)
2. A: ______________________________ muffins.
3. Q: What ______________________________ ? (*far*)
4. A: ______________________________ doughnuts.
5. Q: What ______________________________ ? (*near*)
6. A: ______________________________ cheese.
7. Q: What ______________________________ ? (*far*)
8. A: ______________________________ a peanut.

B. Complete these sentences about Nancy and her family. Fill in the blanks with the possessive form of the nouns in parentheses.

9. Nancy has a husband. ________________ husband is Jordan. (Nancy)
10. Her husband has shoes. Her ________________ shoes are on the floor. (husband)
11. Her sons have a stereo. Her ________________ stereo is loud. (sons)
12. Her daughter has a lot of clothes. Her ________________ clothes are dirty. (daughter)
13. Her dog has a nose. Her ________________ nose is wet. (dog)

C. The city shopping mall is a popular place. Many people work there. Complete the statements below with the correct form of <u>be</u> + <u>possessive pronoun</u>.

14. John is a hairdresser at the salon. The hairbrush ______________________.

15. Pierre and Daniel are cooks at the food court. The frying pans ______________.

16. Jackie is a secretary at the mall headquarters. The paper clips ______________.

17. I am a customer who loves to shop. The shopping bag ____________________.

D. Fill in the blanks with <u>*Whose*</u> or <u>*Who's*</u>.

18. ________________ shopping bag is that?

19. ________________ at the counter?

20. ________________ next in line?

E. ERROR DETECTION
Circle the letter of the *INCORRECT* <u>underlined</u> word or phrase.

21. Andrea (A) <u>is</u> married. Fred is (B) <u>his</u> (C) <u>husband</u>. They (D) <u>have</u> a new baby.

22. (A) <u>Andrea and Freds'</u> house (B) <u>has</u> three (C) <u>large</u> (D) <u>bedrooms</u>.

23. (A) <u>The Andrea's</u> new car is (B) <u>expensive</u>. She (C) <u>has</u> a (D) <u>white Jaguar</u>.

24. (A) <u>Today</u> (B) <u>they're</u> going to the shopping mall to buy some new (C) <u>furniture</u> for (D) <u>her</u> baby.

25. In the parking lot, they tell another driver, (A) "<u>That</u> isn't (B) <u>your</u> parking (C) <u>space</u>! It is (D) <u>our</u>!"

UNIT 6 ANSWERS

A. 1. are these
2. They're
3. are those
4. They're
5. is this
6. It's
7. is that
8. It's

B. 9. Nancy's
10. husband's
11. sons'
12. daughter's
13. dog's

C. 14. is his
15. are theirs
16. are hers
17. is mine

D. 18. Whose
19. Who's
20. Who's

E. 21. B
22. A
23. A
24. D
25. D

Name ______________________

Unit 7 *There is/There Are, A/An Versus The*

Score __________
100

15-minute quiz (25 items at 4 points each = 100%)

A. Read this description of the Amazon River. Fill in the blanks with *there is/are,* or *there isn't/aren't* (2). (−) indicates that a negative sentence is needed.

The Amazon is a fascinating river. It is about 6400 kilometers (4000 miles) long. Most of the river is in Brazil. (1) ______________ 1100 small rivers that move into the Amazon. Near the Amazon River (2) ______________ a large rain forest.

(3) (−) ______________ any streets next to the river.

(4) ______________ many enormous plants and trees.

(5) ______________ many animals. (6) ______________ big cats like jaguars, cougars, and ocelots. (7) ______________ monkeys. The animals live free.

(8) (−) ______________ a zoo. (9) (−) ______________ many people living in the rain forest. The Amazon River is a beautiful, wild place.

B. Ask questions about the area near the Amazon. Use *there* in each question.

10. (a city) ____?
11. (an airport) ____?
12. (public transportation) ____?
13. (parks) ____?
14. (pollution) ____?
15. (dangerous insects) ____?

C. Write TRUE sentences about your classroom (affirmative or negative). Use *there* in each sentence.

16. (a TV) ______________________________.
17. (some chairs) ______________________________.
18. (exercise equipment) ______________________________.
19. (plants) ______________________________.
20. (computers) ______________________________.

D. Give TRUE answers about YOUR home. Your address: ______________

21. Q: Is there a movie theater across the street?

    A: ______________________________.

22. Q: Are there any banks nearby?

    A: ______________________________.

23. Q: How many parks are there?

    A: ______________________________.

E. Fill in the blank with *a, an,* or *the*.

24. Customer: Good evening. Can I buy ______________ ticket for tonight's show?
25. Clerk: I'm sorry, sir. ______________ theater is full. We're sold out.

UNIT 7 ANSWERS

A. **1.** There are
2. there is
3. There aren't
4. There are
5. There are
6. There are
7. There are
8. There isn't
9. There aren't

B. **10.** Is there a city near the Amazon River
11. Is there an airport
12. Is there public transportation
13. Are there parks
14. Is there pollution
15. Are there dangerous insects

C. & D. 16.–23. Answers will vary.

E. **24.** a
25. the

Grammar Dimensions Book 1

Name ______________________

Unit 8 Simple Present Tense: Affirmative and Negative Statements, Time Expressions: *In/On/At, Like/Want/Need*

Score ____________ / 100

15-minute quiz (25 items at 4 points each = 100%)

A. Write the correct simple tense forms of the verbs in parentheses, affirmative or negative (−).

Dolphins are friendly animals. Many people like to study their habits.

Dolphins (1) ________________ (swim) together in groups called "schools." They (2) ________________ (play) with each other, and they (3) ________________ (look) for food together. They (4) ________________ (−) (take) classes, and they (5) ________________ (−) (study) books in their school!

Dolphins (6) ________________ (have) their own communication system. A mother dolphin (7) ________________ (call) her baby when she is worried. She (8) ________________ (make) a high sound. She (9) ________________ (−) (shout). The baby (10) ________________ (come) to its mother. It (11) ________________ (−) (go) very far away.

People (12) ________________ (tell) stories about dolphins. Sometimes dolphins (13) ________________ (help) people who are in trouble in the ocean. Dolphins are very intelligent. People (14) ________________ (−) (eat) dolphins. They (15) ________________ (admire) this animal.

B. Fill in the blanks with the correct preposition of time: <u>*at*</u>, <u>*in*</u>, or <u>*on*</u>

16. Lazy Louie snores ________________ night.
17. His wife, Hannah, wakes him up early ________________ the morning.
18. Sometimes she lets him sleep late ________________ Saturdays.
19. Their wedding anniversary is ________________ December.
20. It is ________________ December 15th.

C. **MULTIPLE CHOICE: Circle the letter of the CORRECT word or phrase.**

21. Lazy Louie ________________ to work every morning.

    A) hurrys B) doesn't hurry C) drive D) rushs

22. Jane and Fred want ________________ tennis together on the weekends.

    A) playing B) don't playing C) play D) to play

23. Jane often skips dinner. She ________________ dinner.

    A) doesn't like to eat B) takes C) likes have D) is eating

24. I am a stressed person. I ________________.

    A) everyday worry a lot. B) worry a lot everyday. C) am worry a lot. D) worry at noon.

25. My cousin and I ________________ to watch football games on TV.

    A) are liking B) aren't like C) like D) likes

UNIT 8 ANSWERS

A. 1. swim
2. play
3. look
4. don't take
5. don't study
6. have
7. calls
8. makes
9. doesn't shout
10. comes
11. doesn't go
12. tell
13. help
14. don't eat
15. admire

B. 16. at
17. in
18. on
19. in
20. on

C. 21. B
22. D
23. A
24. B
25. C

Grammar Dimensions Book 1 Name ______________________

Unit 9 Simple Present Tense: *Yes/No* Questions, Score __________ / 100

Adverbs of Frequency, *Wh*-Questions

15-minute quiz (25 items at 4 points each = 100%)

A. Ask and answer questions about Sophia. Use the verb phrases given below.

feel bad about her mistakes *have American friends*

1. ____?
2. No, ____.
3. ____?
4. Yes, ____.

Ask and answer questions about Sophia and her classmates. Use the verb phrases given below.

study in groups *speak English perfectly*

5. ____?
6. Yes, ____.
7. ____?
8. No, ____.

B. Read the following story about a student named Henry.

Henry is a Nicaraguan student in Dallas. He speaks Spanish and English. He wants to be a math teacher at an elementary school. He studies at the community college. His writing in English is very good, but sometimes he feels nervous when he has to give oral presentations. He is worried about that because he knows that it is an important skill for teachers. Do you have any advice for Henry?

Now go back and look at the underlined phrases. Write *wh*-questions about Henry.

9. (Henry/come from) ____?
10. (he/want to be) ____?

11. (he/study) ____?

12. (he/feel nervous) ____?

C. Use *who* or *whom* in the questions below.

13. ________________ dreams in English?

14. ________________ do you dream about?

15. ________________ wakes you up in the morning?

D. Imagine you are interviewing a roommate. Create a dialogue using the words and expressions below.

16. Q: ____ (smoke?)

17. A: ____ (never)

18. Q: ____ (TV a lot?)

19. A: ____ (rarely)

20. Q: ____ (wake up?)

21. A: ____ (usually/7:00 o'clock)

E. ERROR DETECTION: Circle the letter of the INCORRECT underlined word or phrase.

22. (A) Children in China (B) go usually to (C) primary school for (D) four years.

23. (A) They (B) are always learn (C) how to read (D) Chinese characters.

24. Q: (A) What (B) does mean "characters"? A: Characters (C) are pictures that represent (D) whole words.

25. Q: (A) How many characters (B) are the (C) children (D) need to know? A: More than 2,300 characters.

UNIT 9 ANSWERS

A. 1. Does Sophia feel bad about her mistakes?
2. No, she doesn't.
3. Does she have American friends?
4. Yes, she does.
5. Do they study in groups?
6. Yes, they do.
7. Do they speak English perfectly?
8. No, they don't.

B. 9. Where does Henry come from?
10. What does he want to be?
11. Where does he study?
12. When does he feel nervous?

C. 13. Who
14. Whom
15. Who

D. 16. Do you smoke?
17. I never smoke.
18. Do you watch TV a lot?
19. I rarely watch TV
20. What time do you wake up?
21. I usually wake up at 7:00 o'clock.

E. 22. B
23. B
24. B
25. B

Grammar Dimensions Book 1 Name ______________________

Unit 10 Imperatives and Prepositions of Direction

Score ____________
100

15-minute quiz (25 items at 4 points each = 100%)

A. Imagine a police officer is talking to you about a traffic violation. Create a dialogue using a verb in the imperative and the expressions below.

1. Police officer: ____. (out of the car) You: Yes, sir. What's wrong?
2. Police officer: You were speeding. ________________________. (your driver's license)
   You: Here you are.

   Police officer: Okay. This time I'll just give you a warning, but from now on

3. ____. (more slowly)
4. ____. (the speed limit)
5. ____. (careful)
6. ____. (attention)
7. ____. (that again)

B. Complete the story below with prepositions from those given below. Use each word or phrase only one time. *Note:* there are some extra expressions given.

to away from in into out of up down straight left right
around through across along past over

"Little Red Riding Hood" is a story about a young girl who goes to visit her grandmother. In the morning, she walks (8) ______________ the door and (9) ______________ the house. She walks (10) ______________ the driveway (11) ______________ the road. She walks (12) ______________ the road, (13) ______________ her neighbors' houses. She doesn't turn (14) ______________, and she doesn't turn (15) ______________. She just walks (16) ______________. Soon, she sees a river. Fortunately, there is a bridge. Little Red Riding Hood walks (17) ________________ the bridge,

(18) ________________ the river. She doesn't walk (19) ________________

the river. Finally, she sees her grandmother's house. Little Red Riding Hood

knocks on the door, walks (20) ________________ the house, and then . . .

C. Circle yes if the imperative is appropriate in the situations below. Circle no if it is not appropriate.

21. yes no A student says to a teacher, "Give me my test."

22. yes no A teacher says to a student, "Don't talk during the test."

23. yes no A student says to a classmate, "Don't worry about the test. Relax."

24. yes no A teacher says to his/her boss, "Give me my paycheck."

25. yes no A boss says to a teacher, "Be sure to begin your classes on time."

UNIT 10 ANSWERS

A.
1. Get out of the car.
2. Show me your driver's license.
3. Drive more slowly.
4. Obey the speed limit.
5. Be careful.
6. Pay attention.
7. Don't do that again.

B.
8. through (out of)
9. out of (away from)
10. down
11. to
12. along
13. past
14. right (left)
15. left (right)
16. straight
17. over (across)
18. across (over)
19. around (in)
20. into (in)

C.
21. no
22. yes
23. yes
24. no
25. yes

Grammar Dimensions Book 1 Name ______________________

Unit 11 Quantifiers Score ____________ / 100

15-minute quiz (25 items at 4 points each = 100%)

A. Read this description of Miami. Circle the correct quantifier from the underlined choices.

Miami is a large city in the southeastern part of the United States. (1) some, few, many, a lot of immigrants live in Miami. There are people from (2) not any, no, many, much different countries. Miami is a modern city. It has (3) some, a little, few, much international banks and international businesses.

People from Miami like to go to the beach on the weekends and enjoy (4) a lot, a little, many, few sunshine. There aren't (5) few, some, no, any mountains in Miami. There is (6) little, a few, many, a lot of pollution. Usually, the weather is nice. There are (7) little, a little, one, few cold days.

B. Complete these questions about Miami. Use *How much* or *How many*.

8. ________________ crime is there in Miami?
9. ________________ skyscrapers are there in Miami?
10. ________________ universities are there in Miami?
11. ________________ traffic is there in Miami?
12. ________________ poor people are there in Miami?

C. You need to complete the shopping list below. Fill in with correct measure/container words to express quantity.

(Note: for some, various answers are possible.)

13. a ________________ sugar
14. a ________________ eggs
15. a ________________ lettuce
16. a ________________ tuna
17. a ________________ milk
18. a ________________ bread
19. a ________________ onions
20. a ________________ toothpaste

D. Study the food chart below.

Food:	**calories**	**% fat**	**cholesterol (mg)**	**sodium (mg)**
white rice (1/2 cup)	102	2%	0	2
apple (1)	81	5%	0	1
yogurt (1 cup: low-fat)	231	9%	10	133
eggs (2 scrambled)	202	66%	430	342
doughnut	205	49%	13	117

Write five quantifiers to correctly describe the foods listed above.

21. White rice has ________________ fat.
22. Apples have ________________ cholesterol.
23. Yogurt has ________________ calories.
24. Eggs have ________________ cholesterol.
25. Doughnuts have ________________ sodium.

UNIT 11 ANSWERS

A. 1. a lot
2. many
3. some
4. a little
5. any
6. little
7. few

B. 8. How much
9. How many
10. How many
11. How much
12. How many

C. 13. bag of
14. dozen
15. head of
16. can of
17. gallon of
18. loaf of
19. pound of/bag of
20. tube of

D. 21. little
22. no
23. some
24. a lot of
25. some

Name ____________________

Unit 12 Quantifiers

Score ________
100

15-minute quiz (20 items at 5 points each = 100%)

A. Fill in the correct form of the adverb indicated below.

1. (slow) Camels walk ______________ in the hot deserts of Arabia.
2. (quick) Polar bears catch fish ______________ for dinner.
3. (sweet) Mother monkeys take care of their babies ______________.
4. (loud) Dogs bark ______________ when a stranger comes to the door.
5. (patient) Cats wait ______________ for mice.

B. Do you have a job right now, or are you only a student? Write five sentences that describe your performance at work or at school. Use adverbs of manner.

Job title: ______________ Student only ______________

6. ____.
7. ____.
8. ____.
9. ____.
10. ____.

C. Write another sentence about each famous person below. Include an adverb of manner made from the adjective form in parentheses.

11. Ayrton Senna is a famous car racer.

    (quick) ____.

12. Mikhail Baryshnikov is a famous dancer.

    (graceful) ____.

13. Monica Seles is a famous tennis player.

    (good) ____.

14. Mariah Carey is a famous singer.

    (beautiful) ____.

15. Mike Tyson is a famous boxer.

    (skillful) ____.

D. Do the following sentences talk about the person or action? Circle the correct word, person or action.

16. person action My lawyer defends her clients well.
17. person action My lawyer is fantastic.
18. person action My doctor gives medical treatment carefully.
19. person action My doctor works hard.
20. person action I am a good student. My teacher likes me.

UNIT 12 ANSWERS

A. **1.** slowly
2. quickly
3. sweetly
4. loudly
5. patiently

B. **6.–10.** Answers will vary.

C. **11.** He drives quickly.
12. He dances gracefully.
13. She plays tennis well.
14. She sings beautifully.
15. He boxes skillfully.

D. **16.** action
17. person
18. action
19. action
20. person

Grammar Dimensions Book 1 Name ____________________

Unit 13 Direct and Indirect Objects, Object Pronouns Score ________ / 100

15-minute quiz (25 items at 4 points each = 100%)

A. Read the story. Fill in the blanks with the correct subject or object pronoun.

(Note: Each line here = 4 points, each blank = 2 points.)

1. I love my grandfather a lot. ______________ is a mailman.

   ______________ delivers

2. letters everyday. ______________ puts ______________ in people's

   mailboxes. My

3. grandfather's name is Joseph. People are usually happy to see ______________.

   ______________ rides a bicycle.

4. Joseph keeps ______________ in good condition. When people notice that

   Joseph is hot, ______________ offer

5. ______________ a cool drink. He always accepts ______________ and

   says, "Thank you!" Joseph is a very friendly mailman.

B. Answer these questions. Include an *object pronoun* and *time expression* or *adverb of frequency*. Example: How often do you drive your car? *I drive it everyday.*

6. Q: How often do you study your English books?

   A: ____.

7. Q: How often does your teacher see you and your classmates?

   A: ____.

8. Q: How often does your mom call you?

   A: ____.

9. Q: How often do you visit the dentist?

   A: ____.

10. Q: How often do you brush your teeth?

A: ____.

C. Write statements about customs in your country. Country name: ______________ Use the verbs given.

make give buy send prepare throw bring get

When a baby is born . . .

11. ____.

12. ____.

13. ____.

When a couple gets married...

14. ____.

15. ____.

D. Teachers arc helpful people. They are always doing something for you. Match the verbs and objects below to make statements about teachers.

VERBS: prepare, introduce, solve, explain **OBJECTS:** grammar points, new ideas, problems, lessons **OBJECTS:** to/for us

16. *Teachers* ____

17. *Teachers* ____

18. *Teachers* ____

19. *Teachers* ____

E: Circle the letter of the CORRECT/BEST sentence.

20. You are waiting at the bus stop, and you want to know the fare. You ask another person:
    A) Could you please tell me the fare? B) Could you please tell the fare to me?

21. Now you need change. You ask:
    A) Could you give me change for a dollar? B) Could you change me a dollar?

22. You put your fare in the box, and you need a transfer ticket for the next bus. You tell the driver:
    A) Please give a transfer ticket to me. B) Please give me a transfer ticket.

23. You want to sit down, but one of the passengers put packages on an empty seat. You say:
    A) Do me a favor. Please move your packages. B) Do a favor for me. Please move your packages.

24. The bus driver gave you a schedule to find out about the next bus, but you don't understand it. You ask:
    A) Can you please explain this schedule to me? B) Can you explain me this schedule?

25. Now you want to get off the bus. You say to the driver:
    A) Please open me the door. B) Please open the door for me.

UNIT 13 ANSWERS

A.
1. He; He
2. He; them
3. him; He
4. it; they
5. him; it

B. (6–10, adverbs of frequency will vary)
6. I study them . . .
7. S/he sees us . . .
8. She (never) calls me . . .
9. I visit him/her . . .
10. I brush them . . .

C. 11.–15. Answers will vary.

D.
16. Teachers prepare lessons for us.
17. Teachers introduce new ideas to us.
18. Teachers solve problems for us.
19. Teachers explain grammar points to us.

E.
20. A
21. A
22. B
23. A
24. A
25. B

Grammar Dimensions Book 1 Name ______________________

Unit 14 *Can, Know How To, Be Able To, And/But/So/Or* Score __________ / 100

15-minute quiz (25 items at 4 points each = 100%)

A. Write true statements about the animals below. Use *can*, affirmative (+) or negative (−), to describe ability.

a cat 1. swim in the ocean 2. purr 3. walk from China to Mexico

1. (−) ____.
2. (+) ____.
3. (−) ____.

mice 1. eat cheese 2. prepare fondue 3. hide in small places

4. (+) ____.
5. (−) ____.
6. (+) ____.

B. Write questions and short answers about the animals below. Use <u>can</u>. Give true answers, affirmative or negative (−).

a dog 7. sit on command 8. give kisses 9. meow

Question: 7. ____?

Short answer: 7. ____.

Q: 8. ____?

A: 8. ____?

Q: 9. ____?

A: 9. (−) ____.

deer 10. speak English 11. run faster than men 12. dance the Tango

Question: 10. ______________________________?

Short answer: 10. (−) ______________________________.

Q: 11. ______________________________?

A: 11. ______________________________.

Q: 12. ______________________________?

A: 12. (−) ______________________________.

C. The embassy secretary wants to finalize plans for the function this Saturday night. She has asked you several questions. Write sentences to describe *your* situation. Use *be able to*, affirmative (+) or negative (−).

able to 13. (+) give a speech 14. (−) arrive exactly at eight

13. (+) ______________________________.

14. (−) ______________________________.

Now write sentences to describe <u>*the ambassador.*</u>

able to 15. (+) to introduce the new president 16. (−) stay until 4:00 A.M.

15. <u>*The ambassador*</u> ______________________________.

16. (−) ______________________________.

D. Write true statements with *know how to*, affirmative (+) or negative (−).

17. an artist/draw (+) 18. a baby/drive a car (−) 19. doctors/cure AIDS (−)
20. second language students/mime (+)

17. ______________________________.

18. ______________________________.

19. ______________________________.

20. ______________________________.

E. MULTIPLE CHOICE: Circle the letter of the correct word.

21. I can dance, ________________ I can't sing.
    A) and B) but C) so D) or

22. I can speak English ________________ Spanish. Which do you prefer?
    A) and B) but C) so D) or

23. The Olympic games are very popular, ________________ the stadium is full.
    A) and B) but C) so D) or

24. Bob and Andrea love movies, ________________ they can't go on Saturday.
    A) and B) but C) so D) or

25. Andrea has to visit her mom, ________________ Bob has to prepare a report.
    A) and B) but C) so D) or

UNIT 14 ANSWERS

A.
1. A cat can't swim in the ocean.
2. A cat can purr.
3. A cat can't walk from China to Mexico.
4. Mice can eat cheese.
5. Mice can't prepare fondue.
6. Mice can hide in small places.

B.
7. Can a dog sit on command? Yes, it can.
8. Can a dog give kisses? Yes, it can.
9. Can a dog meow? No, it can't.
10. Can deer speak English? No, they can't.
11. Can deer run faster than men? Yes, they can.
12. Can deer dance the Tango? No, they can't.

C.
13. I am able to give a speech.
14. I'm not able to arrive exactly at eight.
15. The ambassador is able to introduce the new president.
16. He isn't able to stay until 4:00 a.m.

D.
17. An artist knows how to draw.
18. A baby doesn't know how to drive a car.
19. Doctors don't know how to cure AIDS.
20. Second language students know how to mime.

E.
21. B
22. D
23. C
24. B
25. A

Grammar Dimensions Book 1 Name ______________________

Unit 15 Present Progressive Tense Score ________
100

15-minute quiz (25 items at 4 points each = 100%)

A. Write questions and true short answers about things that are happening in your classroom right now.

1. students/take/a grammar test
2. teacher/sit/on top of the desk
3. a mosquito/bite/my knee
4. the lights/turn/off and on
5. the sun/shine/outside
6. I/think/about this question

Question:	Short answer:
1. ______________________________?	7. ______________________________.
2. ______________________________?	8. ______________________________.
3. ______________________________?	9. ______________________________.
4. ______________________________?	10. ______________________________.
5. ______________________________?	11. ______________________________.
6. ______________________________?	12. ______________________________.

B. Fill in the blanks with the correct form of the *present progressive* or *simple present*, affirmative (+) or negative (−)

At the moment, Regis Harrison (7) _______________ (+) (try) to be a good househusband. This afternoon, his wife, Robin, (8) _______________ (+) (attend) a special meeting. She usually (9) _______________ (+) (stay) home with the children, but Robin (10) _______________ (−) (take) care of them today. Now, Regis is very busy. He (11) _______________ (+) (prepare) dinner with his son, Jimmy. They (12) _______________ (+) (cook) some chicken noodle soup. It (13) _______________ (+) (smell) good. Regis (14) _______________ (+) (need) a lot of patience because Jimmy (15) _______________ (+) (be) curious about everything. He always (16) _______________ (+) (ask) a lot of questions.

At the same time the other children, Suzy and Baby Frankie are busy too. They (17) ______________ (−) (fight) now. Suzy (18) ______________ (+) (read) a book to Baby Frankie. He (19) ______________ (+) (like) that. They (20) ______________ (+) (have) a good time.

C. ERROR DETECTION: Circle the letter of the INCORRECT word or phrase.

Somedays the house is NOT peaceful when Regis takes care of the children.

21. Today (A) the children (B) are behave (C) like (D) wild animals.
22. Baby Frankie (A) is no listening to (B) his sister. He (C) is screaming and making a lot of (D) noise.
23. Suzy (A) loves to rollerskate (B) in the house when (C) her dad isn't looking, but she (D) can to rollerblade.
24. (A) For what is Regis (B) taking (C) some aspirin (D) right now?
25. Robin (A) is calling home to check on everybody, (B) but Regis (C) isn't answering the phone. What (D) Robin is thinking?

UNIT 15 ANSWERS

A. 1. Are students taking a grammar test?
Yes, they are.
2. Is the teacher sitting on top of the desk?
No, she/he isn't.
3. Is a mosquito biting my knee?
No, it isn't.
4. Are the lights turning off and on?
No, they aren't.
5. Is the sun shining outside?
Yes, it is./No, it isn't.
6. Are you thinking about this question?
Yes, I am.

B. 7. is trying
8. is attending
9. stays
10. isn't taking
11. is preparing
12. are cooking
13. smells
14. needs
15. is
16. asks
17. aren't fighting
18. is reading
19. likes
20. are having

C. 21. B
22. A
23. D
24. A
25. D

Grammar Dimensions Book 1 **Name** ____________________

Unit 16 Adjective Phrases: *Another, The Other, Other*(s), *The Other*(s), Intensifiers **Score** __________ / 100

15-minute quiz (25 items at 4 points each = 100%)

A. Here we are at the new space station. There are many families in the waiting area. Combine each of the sentence pairs below to write one sentence with an adjective phrase.

1. The baby is on his mother's lap. He is crying.

   ____.

2. The girl has a braid. She is fighting with her brother.

   ____.

3. The children are at the window. They are watching the space traffic.

   ____.

4. The man is in line. He is waiting to get his boarding pass.

   ____.

5. The security officer is wearing a uniform. He is standing near the gate.

   ____.

B. Fill in the blanks with *another* , *other(s)* , or the *other(s)*.

Thor is having (6) ________________ interview with Ed Toppil.

Ed: So, Thor, we're very curious about life on (7) ________________ planets. Tell us, how big is Thorax? How many (8) ________________ live there?

Thor: Thorax is smaller than Earth, and we control our population size. Each couple has only one or two children.

Ed: Can they have (9) ________________ child?

Thor: No, because that isn't fair to (10) ________________.

Ed: I see. Can I ask you (11) ________________ question?

Thor: Of course.

Ed: How many (12) ______________ people from Thorax came with you to visit Earth?

Thor: There are no (13) ______________ with me at this time.

Ed: Okay, Thor. That's all for now. It's time for (14) ______________ commercial.

C. On TV they are selling some beautiful clothes. Ask questions with *which*.

There is a black coat or a red coat . . .

15. ____?

There are some tennis shoes or some dress shoes . . .

16. ____?

D. Use the intensifiers listed below to describe a classmate, another friend, or a relative. Write complete sentences.

Person's name: ______________ Relationship: ______________

very *quite* *rather* *pretty* *fairly* *not*

17. (romantic) ____
18. (old-fashioned) ____
19. (shy) ____
20. (athletic) ____

E. MULTIPLE CHOICE: Circle the letter of the CORRECT word.

21. Spaghetti is ______________ long and thin.
    A) very B) sometimes C) not D) tall

22. It is ______________ popular in Italy.
    A) fairly B) not C) much D) very

23. Coffee is usually ______________ hot.
    A) not B) very C) a lot of D) cool

24. It has a ______________ strong smell.
    A) rather B) so so C) black D) cream

25. It's not ______________ expensive.
    A) pretty B) rather C) very D) fairly

UNIT 16 ANSWERS

A. 1. The baby on his mother's lap is crying.
2. The girl with a braid is fighting with her brother.
3. The children at the window are watching the space traffic.
4. The man in line is waiting to get his boarding pass.
5. The security officer near the gate is wearing a uniform.

B. 6. another
7. other
8. others
9. another
10. the others
11. another
12. other
13. others
14. another

C. 15. Which coat do you like? (Which one do you like?)
16. Which shoes do you like? (Which ones do you like?)

D. 17.–20. Answers will vary.

E. 21. A.
22. D
23. B
24. A
25. C

 Name ____________________

 Score ________ 100

15-minute quiz (25 items at 4 points each = 100%)

A. Write five sentences describing a special event in your past that you can clearly remember (for example: your high school graduation day, your wedding day, your last birthday). Write complete TRUE affirmative (+) or negative (–) sentences. Include the verb *be* in the past tense. Select from the topics below.

year, place, weather, food, service, friends, parents, decorations, YOU *event:* ________

1. (+) ____
2. (+) ____
3. (+) ____
4. (–) ____
5. (–) ____

B. Imagine you are having a conversation with your teacher about King Tut. Fill in the correct *wh*-question word, and the correct form of *be* to complete each question.
(Note: Teacher should count 4 points for the correct *wh*? word, and 4 points for the correct form of *be*.)

6.–7. Q: ______________ King Tut?
A: He was a famous Egyptian King.

8.–9. Q: ______________ his things?
A: Archeologists discovered King Tut's things in his tomb. He had possessions made of gold and jewels there.

10.–11. Q: ______________ he when he died?
A: He was only 18 years old when he died.

12.–13. Q: ______________ his real name?
A: His real name was Tutankhamen. Tut was his nickname.

C. Imagine you are having a conversation with a friend about a car accident. Fill in the blanks with *there* + *be* in the simple past tense.

Q: Was anyone hurt?

A: No. Fortunately, no one was hurt.

14. Q: How about the cars? How many cars ______________ ______________?

15. A: ______________ ______________ three cars involved in the accident.

16. Q: ______________ ______________ a lot of damage?

17. Q: No, ______________ ______________. We were lucky.

18. Q: ______________ ______________ any witnesses?

19. Q: Yes, ______________ ______________. Two pedestrians saw the accident.

D. ERROR DETECTION: Circle the letter of the INCORRECT underlined word or phrase.

20. (A) Were the Beatles a (B) famous British rock group? Yes, (C) they (D) are.

21. (A) Whose was that gun? (B) It was Lee Harvey (C) Oswald's gun. (D) He assassinated President Kennedy.

22. AIDS (A) no was a known disease (B) in 1900. Now (C) doctors (D) are working hard to find a cure for AIDS by the year 2000.

23. They (A) were not famous (B) French fashion designers. Pierre and Marie Curie (C) was famous (D) scientists.

24. How (A) was your weekend? It (B) was fantastic! We (C) was at the beach, and the weather (D) was perfect.

25. (A) Were you (B) happy to finish (C) this quiz? Yes, I (D) were. Now I feel great, and I can relax.

UNIT 17 ANSWERS

A. **1.–5.** Answers will vary.

B. **6.** Who
7. was
8. Where
9. were
10. How old
11. was
12. What
13. was

C. **14.** were there
15. There were
16. Was there
17. there wasn't
18. Were there
19. there were

D. **20.** D
21. A
22. A
23. C
24. C
25. D

Grammar Dimensions Book 1 Name ______________________

Unit 18 Past Tense Score ____________ 100

15-minute quiz (25 items at 4 points each = 100%)

A. Write five sentences about a past vacation or trip. Write complete TRUE affirmative (+) or negative (−) sentences. Select from the verbs in the box below:

go, fly, drive, see, meet, speak, rent, stay, buy, swim

1. (+) ____.
2. (+) ____.
3. (+) ____.
4. (−) ____.
5. (−) ____.

B. Imagine you are having a conversation, but the <u>underlined information</u> isn't clear. Ask for that information with the correct *wh*-question word. Write the correct question.

6. Harry hated Ms. Ditto <u>because he received bad grades in her class</u>.

   Q: ____?

7. He felt <u>angry</u> about her class.

   Q: ____?

8. <u>Harry</u> stole the VCR from the language lab.

   Q: ____?

9. The robbery occurred <u>four days ago</u>.

   Q: ____?

10. Harry reported the robbery to <u>the program director</u>.

    Q: ____?

C. Write the correct past tense form, affirmative (+) or negative (−).

Cinderella's mother (11) ______________ (+) (die) when she (12) ______________ (+) (be) very young. Later, her father (13) ______________ (+) (remarry). Unfortunately, Cinderella's new stepmother and stepsisters (14) ______________ (−) (be) nice. They (15) ______________ (+) (order) her around, and they (16) ______________ (+) (make) her do all of the housework. Cinderella (17) ______________ (+) (clean) the furniture and (18) ______________ (+) (mop) the floor. She (19) ______________ (+) (have) to be polite. She (20) ______________ (−) (fight) with her stepsisters.

D. MULTIPLE CHOICE: Circle the letter of the CORRECT word or phrase.

21. Harry wrote the note. Did he notice his mistakes?

    A) He didn't noticed them B) Yes, he didn't. C) No, he didn't.
    D) No, he doesn't.

22. Lisa and Kate went to New York . . .

    A) a month ago. B) next month. C) right now. D) since last year.

23. Who ______________ the paper at the teacher when he turned around?

    A) did throw B) threw C) throwed D) hitted

24. Our teacher told us a funny story. She said she ______________ a Martian last night.

    A) was met B) meeted C) met D) meets

25. We ______________ lunch at an Italian restaurant yesterday.

    A) spent B) one day ago ate C) took D) had

UNIT 18 ANSWERS

A. 1.–5. Answers will vary.

B. 6. Why did Harry hate Ms. Ditto?
7. How did he feel about her class?
8. Who stole the VCR from the language lab?
9. When did the robbery occur?
10. (To) Whom did Harry report the robbery to?

C. 11. died
12. was
13. remarried
14. weren't
15. ordered
16. made
17. cleaned
18. mopped
19. had
20. didn't fight

D. 21. C
22. A
23. B
24. C
25. D

Grammar Dimensions Book 1 — Name ______________________

Unit 19 Reflexive Pronouns, Reciprocal Pronouns: *Each Other* — Score ________ / 100

10-minute quiz (20 items at 5 points each = 100%)

A. Fill in each blank with a reflexive pronoun.

One evening Jason and his friend Rick were driving to a party at their friend's house. Unfortunately, they ran out of gas. Jason was angry at (1) ______________. He blamed (2) ______________ because he forgot to stop at the last gas station. He and Rick had to walk to the party.

When they arrived, their friend Sylvia said, "Come on in. Make (3) ______________ at home. Help (4) ______________ to some drinks and food."

Jason and Rick were feeling sorry for (5) ______________. They were hot and tired. They weren't enjoying (6) ______________ at the party.

Finally Sylvia said, "Hey, Jason, just look at (7) ______________. Cheer up! You two should be proud of (8) ______________. You arrived safely, and now you don't have to solve the problem by (9) ______________. We can help each other."

Jason said, "You're right, Sylvia. I need to learn to laugh at (10) ______________!"

B. Choose a <u>reflexive pronoun</u> or <u>*each other*</u> to complete these statements.

11. Successful people believe in ______________.
12. Sometimes people hurt ______________ when they are angry. They are mean to the other person.
13. Later they tell ______________ that they are sorry.
14. An honest person doesn't lie to ______________.
15. We need to be honest with ______________.

C. Read the "Dear Darcy" letter and circle the correct pronoun.

Dear Darcy,

Our two-year-old daughter is causing a lot of problems. She never behaves (16. her, herself, herselves, us) when we go out to restaurants. She plays with everything on the table, including knives and candles. I'm afraid she will hurt (17. we, himself, she, herself). I tell (18. myself, me, him, her) that everything will be okay, but my husband says that we can't enjoy (19. us, himself, ourselves, ourself) any more. He thinks we should just eat at home until she's older. (20. Our, me, myself, I) hope that you have a good suggestion.

"Hungry Mom"

UNIT 19 ANSWERS

A.
1. himself
2. himself
3. yourselves
4. yourselves
5. themselves
6. themselves
7. yourself
8. yourselves
9. yourself (yourselves)
10. myself

B.
11. themselves
12. each other
13. each other
14. himself/herself
15. ourselves/each other

C.
16. herself
17. herself
18. myself
19. ourselves
20. I

Name ____________________

Unit 20 Future Time: *Will* and *Be Going To*, *May*, and *Might*

Score ________
100

15-minute quiz (25 items at 4 points each = 100%)

A. Read the conversation below. Fill in the blanks with appropriate subjects and future forms: *will, be going to, may* or *might*. (Note: Sometimes more than one answer is possible.)

Freddy: Hi, Christine. What are you doing?

Christine: I'm thinking about my future education goals.

Freddy: (1) ________________ (you/study) English next semester?

Christine: Yes, of course (2) ________________, but I'm thinking about the more distant future. (3) ____________________ (you/stay) here after you finish the English classes, or (4) ________________ (you/go) back to your country?

Freddy: I'm not sure. (5) ________________ (I/continue) here, or (6) ________________ (I/return).

Christine: I think (7) ________________ (transfer) to the university here, but I know (8) ________________ (the regular classes/be) easy. (9) ________________ (I/have) to work very hard.

Freddy: You have to be patient with yourself, Christine. (10) ________________ (Your English/get) better, and (11) ________________ (it/seem) as difficult as it does now.

Christine: Thanks, Freddy.

B. Janice is worried about her son Mark. She is talking with Wanda the Fortune Teller, but the underlined information isn't clear. Ask for that information with the correct *wh*-question word. Write the correct question.

12. Mark is going to move to California.

    Q: ______________________________?

13. He'll live with an attractive roommate.

    Q: ______________________________?

14. They're going to participate in a game show in three weeks.

    Q: ______________________________?

15. They'll win $10,000.

    Q: ______________________________?

16. I will feel very proud of Mark because he's going to donate some of the money to a charity.

    Q: ______________________________?

C. Make some predictions about the future. How will the world be 20 years from now?

17. Technological Changes: ______________________________.
18. Social Changes: ______________________________.
19. Environmental Changes: ______________________________.

Make some predictions about YOU and/or your family. How will you be 20 years from now?

20. ______________________________.
21. ______________________________.

D. Choose the BETTER response. Circle A or B.

22. Max is coming over for dinner.
    A) Super! I'll go to the store and get some beer.
    B) Super! I'm going to the store and get some beer.

23. There's someone at the door!
    A) I'll open it.
    B) I'm going to open it.

24. Why is George talking to the travel agent?
    A) He'll go back to Argentina for vacation this year.
    B) He's going to go back to Argentina for vacation this year.

25. Look at those big black clouds.
    A) It will rain.
    B) It is going to rain.

UNIT 20 ANSWERS

A. 1. Are you going to study
2. I am
3. Are you going to stay
4. will you go (are you going to go)
5. I may continue (might)
6. I might return (may)
7. I'm going to transfer (may/might)
8. the regular classes won't be easy
9. I will have
10. Your English is going to get (will)
11. it won't seem

B. 12. Where is Mark going to move?
13. (With) Whom will he live with?
14. When are they going to participate in a game show?
15. How much will they win?
16. How will you feel?

C. 17.–21. Answers will vary.

D. 22. A
23. A
24. B
25. B

Grammar Dimensions Book 1

Name ______________________

Unit 21 Phrasal Verbs

Score ____________
100

15-minute quiz (25 items at 4 points each = 100%)

A. Match the phrasal verbs with the one-word verbs with the same meaning.

remove *enter* *complete* *wait* *telephoned* *lower*

1. Today I called up my doctor because I wasn't feeling well. ______________
2. The receptionist who answered the phone asked me to hold on for a minute.______________
3. Then, she told me to come in at noon.______________
4. When I arrived, I had to fill out a form.______________
5. A child in the waiting room had a loud radio. I asked him to turn it down.______________
6. Finally, I was able to see the doctor. She asked me to take off my shirt.______________

Then, she listened to my chest. She told me that I had the flu and prescribed some antibiotics.

B. Complete the dialogue below with phrasal verbs from the box.

calm down *come on* *get out of* *hang up* *cheer up*
throw out *get up* *put away* *clean up*

Mom: Good morning, Mariah. It's time to (7) ______________.

Mariah: No, Mom! I'm tired!

Mom: (8) ______________, Mariah. It's Saturday. We need to (9) ______________ the house. (10) ______________ bed.

Mariah: My room is clean.

Mom: No, it isn't. You need to (11) ______________ those clothes, (12) ______________ the trash, and (13) ______________ your CDs.

Mariah: (14) ________________, Mom. I'll do it later.

Mom: (15) ________________, honey. I'll help, and we'll be finished before you know it.

C. Repeat Sergeant Strict's orders in a different way each time.

"Turn on the ignition."

16. I said, "____."
17. "Come on. ____!"

"Turn off the ignition."

18. I said, "____."
19. "Come on. ____!"

"Fill up the car with gas."

20. I said, "____."
21. "Come on. ____!"

D. Write your own sentences Use the phrasal verbs in parentheses.

22. (eat out) ____.
23. (break down) ____.
24. (come back) ____.
25. (grow up) ____.

UNIT 21 ANSWERS

A. 1. telephoned
2. wait
3. enter
4. complete
5. lower
6. remove

B. 7. get up
8. Come on
9. clean up
10. get out of
11. hang up
12. throw out
13. put away
14. Calm down
15. Cheer up

C. 16. Turn the ignition on.
17. Turn it on.
18. Turn the ignition off.
19. Turn it off.
20. Fill the car up with gas.
21. Fill it up.

D. 22.–25. Answers will vary.

Grammar Dimensions Book 1 Name ____________________

Unit 22 Comparison with Adjectives Score ________
100

10-minute quiz (20 items at 5 points each = 100%)

A. Compare yourself to a classmate, friend or relative. Use *more, -er,* or *as . . . as* expressions. Write complete sentences.

Name: ____________________ Relationship: ____________________

1. (tall) ____.
2. (strong) ____.
3. (independent) ____.
5. (practical) ____.

Now write two questions about the two of you.

6. (energetic/who) ____?
7. (long hair/whose) ____?

B. Compare big cities and small towns. Use *more, -er,* or *as . . . as* expressions.

8. (dangerous) Big cities are ______________ small towns.
9. (expensive) Small towns are ______________ big cities.
10. (exciting) Big cities are ______________ small towns.
11. (polluted) Small towns are ______________ big cities.
12. (friendly) Big city people aren't ______________ small town people.

Now write two questions about cities and towns.

13. (convenient/which) ______________?
14. (good/which) ______________?

C. Think about your bedroom when you were a child. Compare it to your bedroom now. Choose from the adjectives below.

comfortable *pretty* *small* *roomy* *nice* *large* *sunny* *spacious*

My old bedroom (15) ______________ my new bedroom.

(16) ____.

(17) ____.

(18) ____.

(19) ____.

(20) ____.

UNIT 22 ANSWERS

A. 1.–5. Answers will vary.
6. Who is more energetic?
7. Whose hair is longer?

B. 8. more dangerous than
9. less expensive than
10. more exciting than
11. less polluted than
12. as friendly as
13. Which are more convenient, cities or towns?
14. Which are better, cities or towns?

C. 15.–20. Answers will vary.

Name ______________________

Unit 23 Comparison with Adverbs

Score ____________
100

10-minute quiz (20 items at 5 points each = 100%)

A. Ann Roemer and Charles Widmar are applying for a job as a bank teller. Use the information in parentheses to come up with comparative adverb phrases for each sentence below. Include *more, -er,* or *as . . . as*.

Ann's positive qualities:

1. (does careful calculations) Ann ______________________ Charles.
2. (creative problem solver) Ann ______________________ Charles.
3. (open communicator) Ann ______________________ Charles.

Charles' positive qualities:

4. (fast worker) Charles ______________________ Ann.
5. (calm reactor in emergencies) Charles ______________________ Ann.
6. (effective writer) Charles ______________________ Ann.

Qualities they both share:

7. (hard workers) Ann ______________________ Charles.
8. (polite speakers) Charles ______________________ Ann.

B. In Unit 23 you participated in some interesting discussions about differences between boys and girls. What are your conclusions? Choose from the verbs below and write four sentences comparing the actions of boys and girls. Include *more, -er,* or *as . . . as* adverb expressions.

act *play* *talk* *learn languages* *study* *express feelings*

9. ____.
10. ____.
11. ____.
12. ____.

C. "ANYTHING YOU CAN DO, I CAN DO BETTER . . ."
Write four sentences about things that you can do better than others in your family (brother, sister, mother, father).

13. ______________________________.

14. ______________________________.

15. ______________________________.

16. ______________________________.

D. Imagine you're having a conversation with your friend, and you want more specific information.
Ask questions with <u>*How* + adverb or adjective.</u>

17. It takes a long time to learn English.

    Q: ______________________________?

18. My grandfather is very old.

    Q: ______________________________?

19. I can walk very far.

    Q: ______________________________?

20. The Concorde can fly fast.

    Q: ______________________________?

UNIT 23 ANSWERS

A. 1. does calculations more carefully than
2. solves problems more creatively than
3. communicates more openly than
4. works faster than
5. reacts more calmly in emergencies than
6. writes more effectively
7. works as hard as
8. speaks as politely as

B. 9.–16. Answers will vary.

C. 17. How long does it take to learn English?
18. How old is your grandfather?
19. How far can you walk?
20. How fast can it fly?

Grammar Dimensions Book 1 Name ______________________

Unit 24 Superlatives Score ____________ 100

10-minute quiz (20 items at 5 points each = 100%)

A. Fill in the correct superlative form in the contest questions below. Then check the clues below to help you answer correctly and win the contest. Good luck!

1. (far/planet) *What's* ______________________ *from the sun?* ______________
2. (large/ocean) *What's* ______________________ *in the world?* ______________
3. (high/mountain) *What's* ______________________ *in the world?* ______________
4. (small/country) *What's* ______________________ *in the world?* ______________
5. (big/city) *What's* ______________________ *in the world?* ______________

Mt. Everest *Mexico City* *Pluto* *The Vatican* *The Pacific*

B. Ask superlative questions about the students in your class. Use *who + superlative adverb phrase.*

6. (speak English/fluently) *Who* ______________________________________?
7. (ask questions/often) ______________________________________?
8. (arrive/early) ______________________________________?
9. (work/cooperatively) ______________________________________?
10. (sit/close to the teacher) ______________________________________?

C. Make sentences with *one of the + superlative + plural noun.*

11. (great idea) ______________________ I ever had was ______________________.
12. (happy day) ______________________ I ever had was ______________________.
13. (good experience) ______________________ I ever had was ______________________.
14. (proud moment) ______________________ I ever had was ______________________.
15. (difficult exam) ______________________ I ever took was ______________________.

D. ERROR DETECTION: Circle the letter of the INCORRECT word or phrase.

16. Disney World is the (A) most fun (B) tourist (C) attraction in (D) the United States.

17. (A) There are four (B) children in my (C) family. I am (D) the smarter.

18. My (A) older brother can run (B) fast, but he isn't (C) as fastest as (D) I am.

19. My (A) younger brother is (B) more lazy (C) than a lizard. He (D) always lies on the couch and watches TV.

20. I guess you're happy this is (A) the (B) last question. I hope it will be (C) the (D) most easiest one for you.

UNIT 24 ANSWERS

A. 1. the farthest planet; Pluto
2. the largest ocean; The Pacific
3. the highest mountain; Mt. Everest
4. the smallest country; Vatican city
5. the biggest city; Mexico City

B. 6. Who speaks English the most fluently?
7. Who asks questions the most often?
8. Who arrives the earliest?
9. Who works the most cooperatively?
10. Who sits the closest to the teacher?

C. 11. One of the greatest ideas . . .
12. One of the happiest days . . .
13. One of the best experiences . . .
14. One of the proudest moments . . .
15. One of the most difficult exams . . .

D. 16. A
17. D
18. C
19. B
20. D

Grammar Dimensions Book 1 Name ______________________

Unit 25 Factual Conditionals: *If* Score ________
100

10-minute quiz (20 items at 5 points each = 100%)

A. Sometimes people do unusual things because of unusual circumstances. Give a reason why people might do the following. Write compound sentences with *when*.

1. When do people speed?

   A: ____.

2. When do people run out of their houses in their pajamas?

   A: ____.

3. When do people sleep outside?

   A: ____.

4. When do people steal?

   A: ____.

5. When do people cheat on a test?

   A: ____.

B. Every culture has its superstitions. Make *"if"* statements by combining the ideas below.

6. (break a mirror/seven years bad luck)

   ____.

7. (knock on wood/good luck)

   ____.

8. (scratch left hand/lose money)

   ____.

9. (see a spider/get money)

   ____.

10. (get a room on the thirteenth floor/not take it)

____.

C. Remember when you were a child, and your mom or someone special helped you? How did they help you? What did they do? Write past sentences with <u>*if,*</u> <u>*when,*</u> or <u>*whenever*</u> and the words below.

11. (felt hungry) ____.

12. (had the flu) ____.

13. (missed the school bus) ____.

14. (didn't understand my homework) ____.

15. (needed a friend) ____.

D. MULTIPLE CHOICE: Circle the letter of the CORRECT word or phrase.

16. When I ______________ in Spain, I learned about another culture.
    A) am living B) live C) lived D) will live

17. If I wanted to communicate, I ______________ to speak in Spanish.
    A) had B) was C) may D) thought

18. In the United States, we shake hands when we ______________ someone new.
    A) are meeting B) met C) know D) meet

19. We ______________ each other on the cheeks when we greet each other.
    A) always kiss B) don't kiss C) aren't kissing D) didn't kiss

20. If you leave your native country and live in another place, you ______________ a lot about other cultures and your own.
    A) are learn B) learned C) can learn D) do not learn

UNIT 25 ANSWERS

A. 1. People (might) speed when . . .
2. People (might) run out of their houses in their pajamas when . . .
3. People (might) sleep outside when . . .
4. People (might) steal when . . .
5. People (might) cheat on a test when . . .

B. 6. If you break a mirror, you have seven years of bad luck.
7. If you knock on wood, you have good luck.
8. If you scratch your left hand, you lose money.
9. If you see a spider, you get money.
10. If you get a room on the thirteenth floor, you don't take it.

C. 11.–15. Answers will vary.

D. 16. C
17. A
18. D
19. B
20. C

WORKBOOK ANSWER KEY

Unit 1

The Verb *Be:* Affirmative Statements, Subject Pronouns

EXERCISE 1

1. Rosa is divorced. **2.** Yumiko is Japanese. **3.** Juan and Julia are single. **4.** The engineer is 35. **5.** The German is a student. **6.** The teacher is from Puerto Rico. **7.** Juan and Julia are 19 years old. **8.** The Mexican is a student. **9.** Yumiko is Asian. **10.** The students are single.

EXERCISE 2

1. is **2.** is **3.** is **4.** are **5.** are

EXERCISE 3

1. She **2.** They **3.** She **4.** He **5.** It **6.** I **7.** We **8.** It **9.** He **10.** She

EXERCISE 4

Answers will vary.

EXERCISE 5

1. They're **2.** She's **3.** She's **4.** She's **5.** They're **6.** I'm **7.** We're **8.** They're **9.** She's **10.** He's

EXERCISE 6

Answers will vary.

EXERCISE 7

1. formal or informal **2.** informal **3.** informal **4.** informal **5.** formal **6.** formal

Unit 2

The Verb *Be: Yes/No* Questions, *Be* + Adjective, Negative Statements

EXERCISE 1

Guess the Place

Is; it is; Is it; it isn't; Is it; Yes; Is it; it is; Is it; it is; the Louvre

Guess Who I Am

you aren't; Am I; No; Am I; you aren't. Am I; Yes; Am I; you are. Am I; Pele

Guess Who We Are

No; Are we; you aren't; Are we; you are; Are we; Yes; Prince William and Prince Harry?

EXERCISE 2

Questions and answers will vary.

EXERCISE 3

Sentences will vary.

EXERCISE 4

Questions and answers will vary.

EXERCISE 5

Sentences will vary.

EXERCISE 6

1. The mouse isn't small. It's big. **2.** The speaker isn't interesting. He's boring. **3.** The baby isn't quiet. He's/She's crying. **4.** Santa isn't thin. He's fat. **5.** The woman isn't old. She's young. **6.** The man isn't ugly. He's handsome. **7.** The toy isn't hard. It's soft. **8.** The bees aren't lazy. They're busy. **9.** The problem isn't difficult. It's easy. **10.** The children aren't awake. They're sleepy.

Unit 3

The Verb *Be: Wh*-Question Words, *It* with Time and Weather, and Prepositions of Location

EXERCISE 1

how are; What is; Who is; why are; how old are; when is; Where is; how much is; who is; Where is; When is

EXERCISE 2

What is the meaning of . . .

EXERCISE 3

Possible answers:
1. It's sunny and warm. **2.** It's twenty-two degrees. **3.** It's rainy. **4.** It's thirty degrees. **5.** It's rainy. **6.** It's foggy.
7. It's twenty degrees. **8.** It's cold and snowy.
9. It's rainy. **10.** It's seventy-one degrees.

EXERCISE 4

Questions and answers will vary.

EXERCISE 5

1. It's 8 A.M. **2.** It's 10 A.M. **3.** It's 11 A.M. **4.** It's 11 A.M.
5. It's noon.
Questions and answers will vary.

EXERCISE 6

Sentences may vary.
2. The triangle is above the square. **3.** The rectangles are under the square./The square is above the rectangles. **4.** The face is on the square. **5.** The circle is behind the square./The square is in front of the circle.
In the next two sets.
1.–5. Answers will vary.
1.–5. Answers will vary.

EXERCISE 7

Answers will vary.

EXERCISE 8

1. Where are the keys? On the dresser. **2.** Where is the shirt? On the floor. **3.** Where are the pants? On the floor, next to the shirt.
4. Where are the books? On the dresser, next to the towels (behind the jewelry box). **5.** Where are the shoes? Under the bed.
6. Where is the sweater? In the drawer. **7.** Where is the jewelry? In the box on the dresser. **8.** Where are the glasses? On the books. (On top of the books.) **9.** Where is the pillow? On the bed.
10. Where is the brush? On the towels. (On top of the towels.)

Exercises for the TOEFL® Test

Units 1–3

1. C	**4.** C	**7.** A	**10.** B	**13.** A	**16.** D	**19.** C	**22.** C	**24.** C
2. B	**5.** C	**8.** B	**11.** D	**14.** D	**17.** D	**20.** C	**23.** B	**25.** A
3. D	**6.** A	**9.** A	**12.** D	**15.** C	**18.** A	**21.** D		

Unit 4

Nouns: Count and Noncount Nouns, *Be* + Adjective + Noun

EXERCISE 1

Noncount nouns: **1.** money **2.** change **5.** clothing **6.** pants

EXERCISE 2

Clothes: a tie, a sweater, a blouse, a uniform, an undershirt
Transportation: an airplane, a truck, a train, a helicopter, an automobile
Vegetables: a pea, an herb, a carrot, a potato, a radish
Time: a day, a month, a year, a week, an hour

EXERCISE 3

countries; babies; witches; monsters; knives; axes; boys; heroes; Fairies; wishes; princesses; stories; girls; cats; bats; parties; classes; doors; houses; treats; candies; oranges; toys; tricks.

EXERCISE 4

/z/: holidays, countries, babies, monsters, knives, boys, heroes, fairies, stories, girls, parties, doors, candies, toys

/s/: cats, bats, treats, tricks

/iz/: witches, axes, wishes, princesses, classes, houses, oranges

EXERCISE 5

Taped pronunciation practice.

EXERCISE 6

Humans: people, men, women, children
Animals: moose, deer, fish, oxen, geese, mice, sheep
Body Parts: feet, teeth, hooves, hair

EXERCISE 7

Informations; A news; informations; Computers; homeworks; advices; mails; an electricity

Information is easier to get with today's new technology. News is transmitted around the world by TV satellites. Computers also make information easier to get. A computer can help a person do his homework. Computer networks allow people to tell some news and give some advice. With computer mail a person can send a message with electricity and a phone line.

foods; furnitures; a coffee; a tea; a milk; jewelrys; clothings; musics; luggages; a bread; a rice; a sugar; a fruit; moneys; the love.

There is a new kind of store in the United States now. Superstores are a combination of supermarkets and discount stores. Superstores have everything from food to furniture. At a superstore you can buy beverages like coffee, tea, or milk. In the same store you can buy jewelry, clothing, music, and luggage. You can also buy things like bread, rice, sugar, or fruit. You should bring lots of money with you when you go to a superstore because there is a lot to buy. But one thing you can't buy at a superstore is love.

EXERCISE 8

Information gap; questions and answers will vary.

EXERCISE 9

Questions and answers will vary.

EXERCISE 10

Sentences will vary.

Unit 5

The Verb *Have:* Affirmative and Negative Statements, Questions and Short Answers, *Some/Any*

EXERCISE 1

1. Both families have a pet. /Both families have pets. **2.** Jill Johnson has a warm coat. /The Johnsons have warm coats. **3.** The Johnson family has a snow shovel. **4.** The Sunshine family has a hammock. **5.** The Sunshine family has a swimming pool. **6.** Both families have a porch./Both families have porches. **7.** Both families have a child./Both families have children. **8.** The Sunshine family has a daughter. **9.** The Johnson family has a son. **10.** The Sunshine family has palm trees. **11.** The Johnson family has a fireplace. **12.** The Johnson family has a woodpile. **13.** Jill and Jack Johnson have scarves. **14.** Jan Johnson and Ray Sunshine both have a wife./Jan Johnson and Ray Sunshine both have wives. **15.** Ray and Malibu Sunshine have sunglasses.

EXERCISE 2

Sentences will vary.

EXERCISE 3

Answers will vary.

EXERCISE 4

1. Do the Sunshines have . . . **2.** Does Jack Johnson have . . . **3.** Do the Sunshines have . . . **4.** Does Malibu Sunshine have . . . **5.** Do the Johnsons have . . . **6.** Do the Sunshines have . . . **7.** Does California have . . . **8.** Does Wisconsin have . . . **9.** Do the Sunshines have . . . **10.** Does Jack have . . . **11.** Does Malibu Sunshine have . . .

EXERCISE 5

(1) some **(2)** any **(3)** any **(4)** any **(5)** some **(6)** any **(7)** some **(8)** some **(9)** some **(10)** any

EXERCISE 6

All begin with "Excuse me, do you have . . ."
1. any pencils? **2.** a telephone? **3.** any fountain pens? **4.** any basketballs? **5.** any restrooms? **6.** a photocopier? **7.** any Ashland University t-shirts? **8.** any notebooks? **9.** any computer disks? **10.** any comic books?

EXERCISE 7

Questions and answers will vary.

EXERCISE 8

Sentences will vary.

Unit 6

This/That/These/Those, Possessives

EXERCISE 1

1. This is **2.** That is **3.** This is **4.** These are **5.** This is **6.** These are **7.** That is **8.** Those are **9.** This is **10.** That is **11.** That is

EXERCISE 2

1. What are those? Those are kinds of furniture. **2.** What is this? This is meat. **3.** What is that? That is a doll. **4.** What are these? These are computers. **5.** What are those? Those are colors. **6.** What are these? These are trees. **7.** What is this? This is fruit. **8.** What are those? Those are places to live. **9.** What are these? These are kitchen appliances. **10.** What is this? This is bedding.

EXERCISE 3

Follow pictures left to right on each page to match answers.
3. Maya's car is a compact. **8.** The secretaries' desks are neat. **1.** Mark's computer is new. **6.** Paulo's homework is finished.

2. Erle's homework is incomplete. **10.** The secretaries' desks are messy. **4.** Mexico's flag has an eagle and a snake on it. **9.** Canada's flag has a maple leaf on it. **5.** Monique's car is luxurious. **7.** James's computer is old.

EXERCISE 4

1. is Marie's niece. **2.** is Marie's grandmother. **3.** is Marie's uncle. **4.** is Marie's husband. **5.** is Marie's nephew. **6.** is Marie's father. **7.** is Marie's daughter. **8.** is Marie's son. **9.** is Marie's grandfather. **10.** is Marie's sister-in-law. **11.** is Marie's brother-in-law. **12.** are Marie's grandparents. **13.** is Marie's aunt. **14.** is Marie's niece.

EXERCISE 5

Sentences will vary.

EXERCISE 6

Lee: My
Lee: Our
Sun: Her; our
Sun: our
Sun: My
Sun: its
Lee: Our; His; his; your; Our; Its

EXERCISE 7

Sentences will vary.

EXERCISE 8

2. **(I)** The truck is his. **3.** **(D)** The fire hose is theirs. **4.** **(K)** The wrench is his. **5.** **(H)** The music is hers. **6.** **(E)** The dog leash is hers. **7.** **(F)** The police badges are theirs. **8.** **(A)** The book bag is hers. **9.** **(C)** The cash register is his. **10** **(G)** The plans for a house are his. **11.** **(J)** The football is his.

EXERCISE 9

1. Whose mother is this? She's Ashley's mother. She's hers. **2.** Whose notebooks are these? They're Ginette's and Jasmine's notebooks. They're theirs. **3.** Whose boyfriends are these? They're Ginette's and Jasmine's boyfriends. They're theirs. **4.** Whose rocking chair is this? It's James's rocking chair. It's his. **5.** Whose tie is this? It's James's tie. It's his. **6.** Whose bottle is this? It's Ashley's bottle. It's hers. **7.** Whose cane is this? It's James's cane. It's his. **8.** Whose tape players are these? They're Ginette's and Jasmine's tape players. They're theirs. **9.** Whose toy is this? It's Ashley's toy. It's hers. **10.** Whose cassette tapes are these? They're Ginette's and Jasmine's cassette tapes. They're theirs. **11.** Whose glasses are these? They're James's glasses. They're his. **12.** Whose diaper is this? It's Ashley's diaper. It's hers.

Exercises for the TOEFL® Test

Units 4–6

1. A	4. D	7. D	10. D	13. C	16. C	19. A	22. A	24. B
2. B	5. D	8. B	11. D	14. B	17. D	20. D	23. B	25. C
3. C	6. C	9. B	12. A	15. B	18. B	21. B		

Unit 7

There Is/There Are, A/An Versus *The*

EXERCISE 1

1. There is a pig in the mud. **2.** There is a horse in the barn. **3.** There are chickens in the coop. **4.** There is hay in the barn. **5.** There's a goat beside the barn. **6.** There's a farmer in the truck. **7.** There are ducks on the pond. **8.** There's a rooster on the chicken coop. **9.** There is some corn in the field. **10.** There are two cows in the barn.

EXERCISE 2

1. There's a pig in the doghouse. **2.** There are chickens on Farmer McDonald's hat. **3.** There's corn in Farmer McDonald's pockets. **4.** There are a goat, a duck, and a rooster in Farmer McDonald's truck. **5.** There's a TV in the chicken coop. **6.** There's electricity in the barn and the chicken coop. **7.** There are cows talking on the telephone. **8.** There's a hat on one of the cows. **9.** There are glasses on the horse. **10.** There's a dog dancing on the fence. **11.** There's furniture in the barn.

EXERCISE 3

1. There's no gym at New College. **2.** There aren't any job counselors at New College. **3.** There isn't a college radio station. **4.** There isn't any public transportation into town. **5.** There aren't any cultural events. **6.** There isn't a language lab. **7.** There isn't a math tutor. **8.** There isn't a drugstore close to campus. **9.** There aren't any quiet places to study. **10.** There isn't a soccer team.

EXERCISE 4

1. Are there any academic counselors? **2.** Is there a library? **3.** Are there any scholarships? **4.** Is there any financial aid money? **5.** Are there any sports teams? **6.** Is there a bookstore? **7.** Are there any student clubs? **8.** Are there any tutors? **9.** Are there any dorms? **10.** Is there any entertainment?

EXERCISE 5

The; The; a
The; the;
a; the; an; an; a;
the; an; a; a; the;
the; the; a

Unit 8

Simple Present Tense: Affirmative and Negative Statements, Time Expressions: *Like/Need/Want*

EXERCISE 1

goes; checks; cuts out; uses; dries; is; conserves; turns off; leaves

spends; buys; looks; forgets; eats out; wastes; washes; forgets; leaves; dries

EXERCISE 2

live; likes; walks; works; goes; walks; goes; thinks; prefers; enjoys; camp; complains; hates; want; work

EXERCISE 3

Answers will vary.

EXERCISE 4

Sentences will vary.

EXERCISE 5

hurries; enjoys; worries; has
works; tests; has; empties; looks; plays; tries sees; does; writes; says; tells; sends

EXERCISE 6

Sentences will vary.

EXERCISE 7

Sentences will vary.

EXERCISE 8

Answers will vary.

EXERCISE 9

1. Ron doesn't work inside. 2. Don doesn't live in a house. 3. Don and Ron don't smoke. 4. Ron doesn't have a sports car. 5. Don doesn't play volleyball. 6. Don and Ron don't like jogging. 7. Don doesn't drive a pickup truck. 8. Ron doesn't live in an apartment. 9. Don and Ron don't like movies. 10. Ron doesn't like basketball.

EXERCISE 10

1. no; Good parents don't let their children . . . 2. yes; Good parents . . . 3. yes; Good parents . . . 4. no; Good parents don't . . . 5. no; Good parents don't . . . 6. no; Good parents don't . . . 7. yes; Good parents . . . 8. yes; Good parents . . . 9. yes; Good parents . . . 10. yes; Good parents . . .

EXERCISE 11

Sentences will vary.

Unit 9

Simple Present Tense: *Yes/No* Questions, Adverbs of Frequency, *Wh*-Questions

EXERCISE 1

Answers will vary. They will begin with "Do you . . ."

EXERCISE 2

Answers will vary. They will begin with "Does (name of partner or he/she) . . ."

EXERCISE 3

Answers will vary.

EXERCISE 4

Sentences will vary.

EXERCISE 5

Chris Crash
2. do you like skateboarding? 3. do you live? 4. do you practice skateboarding? 5. do you practice skateboarding? 6. do you learn new skateboard tricks? 7. do you want to do?

Suzy Flex
1. do you like to do? 2. do you practice hard? 3. do you rehearse your gymnastic routines? 4. do you rehearse your gymnastic routines? 5. do you practice? 6. do you learn new routines? 7. do you practice?

EXERCISE 6

1. How often do you call your parents? 2. What do your parents do? 3. Why do they wait? 4. What time (When) do you call? 5. Where does your brother live? 6. What does he do? 7. Where does he work? 8. Where do your parents live? 9. Why does your brother live in Brasilia? 10. What does your brother do on holidays?

EXERCISE 7

1. Who shares an apartment? 2. Who goes to school? 3. Who drives the car? 4. Whom does Jill drive to school every day? 5. Who cooks dinner on Tuesday? 6. Who prepares dinner on the weekends? 7. Who takes out the trash? 8. Who puts out the recycling? 9. Who washes Jill's car? 10. Whom do Jill, Mandy and Joy meet on Saturday night? 11. Who plays tennis?

EXERCISE 8

1. I 2. F 3. I 4. I 5. I 6. I 7. F 8. I

EXERCISE 9

1. C 2. How do you say . . . 3. How do you pronounce . . . 4. What does "illogical" mean? 5. What does the word . . . mean 6. How do you say the opposite of "freedom"? 7. How

do you spell . . . **8.** How do you pronounce . . . **9.** What does "ethical" mean? **10.** How do you say "a little wet"?

EXERCISE 10

Q. What is the opposite of relaxed? **A.** Tense.
Q. What is the opposite of winter? **A.** Summer.
Q. How do you spell your name? **A.** (Answers will vary.)
Q. How do you spell the capital of the United States?
A. W-a-s-h-i-n-g-t-o-n, D. C.
Q. How do you spell the President's name?
A. C-l-i-n-t-o-n.
Q. How do you pronounce "through"?
A. (Listen for correct pronunciation.)
Q. How do you pronounce "Illinois"?
A. (Listen for correct pronunciation.)
Q. How do you pronounce your name?
A. (Listen for correct pronunciation.)
Q. What does "neither" mean? **A.** Not the one or the other.
Q. What does "annoy" mean? **A.** Disturb.
Q. What does "obligatory" mean? **A.** Not optional.
Q. What do you call a thing that a baby drinks from? **A.** A bottle.
Q. What do you call the square thing you put into a computer?
A. A disk.
Q. What do you call a chair with no back, just legs? **A.** A stool.

Exercises for the TOEFL® Test

Units 7–9

1. B **2.** A **3.** D **4.** C **5.** D **6.** A **7.** A **8.** D **9.** C **10.** D **11.** B **12.** D **13.** C **14.** D **15.** C **16.** B **17.** B **18.** C **19.** B **20.** C **21.** B **22.** D **23.** B **24.** A **25.** C

Unit 10

Imperatives and Prepositions of Direction

EXERCISE 1

1. Open the door./Please open the door. **2.** Hand in your homework./Please hand in your homework. **3.** Turn right./Don't turn left. **4.** Carry my bags./Please carry my bags. **5.** Help me with the groceries./Please help me with the groceries. **6.** Eat your dinner./Don't waste food. **7.** Have some cake./Please have some cake. **8.** Walk./Please don't run.

EXERCISE 2

1. Giving directions **2.** Warning of danger **3.** Giving an order **4.** Politely offering something **5.** Making a polite request **6.** Giving advice

EXERCISE 3

1. yes **2.** no **3.** no **4.** depends **5.** no **6.** yes **7.** yes

EXERCISE 4

2. Please tell me the answer. **3.** Please fill out these insurance forms. **5.** Please give me the report.

EXERCISE 5

1. C **2.** **(I)** Debbie's office is on the seventh floor. **3.** **(I)** Every morning Debbie is late for work, so she runs out of her house. **4.** C **5.** C **6.** **(I)** Debbie gets off the freeway when she gets downtown. **7.** C **8.** **(I)** She runs to the elevator. **9.** C **10.** **(I)** When her boss arrives, Debbie is at her desk.

EXERCISE 6

Answers will vary.

EXERCISE 7

Unit 11

Quantifiers

EXERCISE 1

COUNT: crackers, chicken, sausage, steak, fish, bagels, watermelon, apples, oranges, pears, cucumbers, potatoes, beans, peas, carrots, mushrooms, tomatoes

NONCOUNT: milk, yogurt, ice cream, cheese, shortening, butter, oil, rice, bread, flour, cereal, lettuce (can be either: chicken, sausage, steak, fish)

EXERCISE 2

(1) a lot of/some **(2)** some **(3)** some **(4)** a lot of/some **(5)** much **(6)** some/a little **(7)** some/a little **(8)** a little **(9)** a lot of **(10)** some/a lot of **(11)** some/a few **(12)** some/a lot of **(13)** any **(14)** some/a little **(15)** some/a little **(16)** some/a few **(17)** some/a little

EXERCISE 3

Sentences will vary.

EXERCISE 4

(1) a little **(2)** a little **(3)** little **(4)** a few **(5)** a little **(6)** a little **(7)** little **(8)** little **(9)** few **(10)** a few **(11)** a little **(12)** a little **(13)** a little **(14)** a few

EXERCISE 5

1. How many cups of coffee did Sarah drink for breakfast?
2. How many hot dogs did Wendy have for lunch?
3. How much orange juice did Wendy drink for breakfast?
4. How much did Sarah eat for breakfast? **5.** How much vegetable soup did Sarah have? **6.** How many apples did Wendy eat for lunch?. **7.** How many grapes did Wendy eat for lunch? **8.** How much soup did Wendy have for lunch?
9. How much yogurt did Sarah eat for breakfast?
10. How much milk did Sarah have at lunch?

EXERCISE 6

2. a quart of ice cream **3.** a bag of candy **4.** a dozen eggs/a carton of eggs **5.** three sticks of butter **6.** a jar of jelly **7.** a jar of peanut butter **8.** two boxes of cereal **9.** two heads of lettuce **10.** two ears of corn. **11.** two bottles of soda **12.** a slice of pizza

Unit 12

Adverbs of Manner

EXERCISE 1

1. I'm happy when I get my grades. / I'm sad when I . . .
2. I'm grumpy when I wake up in the morning. / I'm cheerful when I . . . **3.** My clothes are loose. / My clothes are tight.
4. I'm a heavy exerciser. / I'm a light exerciser. **5.** I'm shy when I meet a new person. / I'm outgoing when I . . . **6.** I'm slow when I walk somewhere. / I'm quick when I . . . **7.** I'm careful when I drive. / I'm careless when I . . .

EXERCISE 2

1. Yes he/she gets grades happily. / No, he/she doesn't get . . . He/she gets grades unhappily. **2.** Yes, he/she wakes up grumpily. / No, he/she doesn't wake . . . He/she wakes up cheerfully. **3.** Yes, his/her clothes fit loosely. / No, his/her clothes don't . . . They fit tightly. **4.** Yes, he/she exercises heavily. / No, he/she doesn't exercise . . . He/she exercises lightly. **5.** Yes, he/she meets new people easily. / No, he/she doesn't meet . . . He/she meets new people shyly. **6.** Yes, he/she walks quickly. / No, he/she doesn't walk . . . He/she walks slowly. **7.** Yes, he/she drives carelessly. / No, he/she doesn't drive . . . He/she drives carefully.

EXERCISE 3

terribly; enthusiastically; terribly; loosely; tightly; carelessly; carefully; anxiously; shyly; gladly; unsuccessfully; bravely; calmly; neatly; quickly

EXERCISE 4

Sentences will vary.
1. A teacher is creative. / . . . teaches classes creatively.
2. A waitress is quick to serve customers. / . . . serves customers quickly. **3.** A nurse is calm in an emergency. / . . . handles emergencies calmly. **4.** A truck driver is careful on the road. / . . . drives carefully. **5.** A mechanic does messy

work. / works messily. **6.** A race car driver is fast./drives fast. **7.** A scientist is systematic in the laboratory. / . . . works systematically in the laboratory. **8.** A pilot is cautious when he files. / . . . flies cautiously. **9.** A construction worker is often noisy. / . . . often works noisily. **10.** The president is diplomatic in speaking to other leaders. / . . . speaks diplomatically to other leaders.

EXERCISE 5

Sentences will vary.
1. Michael Jordan jumps very high. **2.** Gail Devers runs very well. **3.** _______ reads very quickly. **4.** _______ works very sloppily. **5.** Placido Domingo sings very beautifully. **6.** A cactus grows very slowly. **7.** _______ shops very carefully. **8.** Kathleen Turner speaks very softly. **9.** You can buy good food at _______ very cheaply. **10.** _______ writes very poetically. **11.** A cheetah runs very quickly.

EXERCISE 6

Sentences will vary.

Exercises for the TOEFL® Test

Units 10–12

1. B	**4.** D	**7.** B	**10.** C	**13.** A	**16.** C	**19.** A	**22.** D
2. C	**5.** C	**8.** D	**11.** A	**14.** B	**17.** C	**20.** C	**23.** D
3. A	**6.** B	**9.** A	**12.** B	**15.** C	**18.** D	**21.** B	**24.** A

Unit 13

Direct and Indirect Objects, Object Pronouns

EXERCISE 1

1. music. **2.** strings. **3.** note. **4.** notes. **5.** string **6.** string **7.** note. **8.** guitar **9.** pick **10.** guitars **11.** folk music. **12.** guitars.

EXERCISE 2

he; he; He; him; he; her; She; She; him; me; I; I; me; me; me; me

EXERCISE 3

them: my family; them: flowers; me: I; me: I; her: mother; him: father; them: my family; him: Ruff; it: milk; you: you

EXERCISE 4

First word is direct object; second is indirect object.
1. songs; friends **2.** party; Josh **3.** cake; Josh **4.** decorations; party **5.** present; him **6.** money; guitar **7.** money; Len **8.** guitar; Josh **9.** gift; Josh **10.** guitar **11.** song; friends

EXERCISE 5

1. Gwen makes Josh a cake. **2.** They all give Len some money. **3.** The man hands Len the new guitar. **4.** Len gives Josh the guitar. **5.** Josh gives Gwen his old guitar. **6.** On the weekends, Josh gives the children in his building guitar lessons. **7.** He teaches the children music. **8.** He also finds the children used guitars. **9.** After the lessons, Josh buys the children sodas. **10.** In his free time, Josh writes his friends special songs.

EXERCISE 6

Pete gives
2. the neighbors a screwdriver set **3.** the hairbrush to Cecelia **4.** the mail carrier dog repellent **5.** his girlfriend a hairbrush **6.** the dictionary to his secretary **7.** his dad a flashlight **8.** the dish towels to his mom **9.** the car wax to Angela and Bob **10.** his secretary a dictionary **11.** the screwdriver set to the neighbors

EXERCISE 7

Sentences will vary.

EXERCISE 8

2. I hand my teacher the homework. **4.** He teaches the students algebra. **6.** He shows the students the solution. **7.** Angel offers Gretchen help.

Unit 14

Can, Know How To, Be Able To, And/But/So/Or

EXERCISE 1

Sentences will vary.
Mr. Sierra: **2.** . . . can scrape the old paint. **3.** . . . can repair the window screens.
Mrs. Sierra: **1.** . . . can't install a hot-water heater. **2.** . . . can paint the walls. **3.** . . . can wallpaper the hallway.
Carpenter: **1.** . . . can't install a ceiling fan. **2.** . . . can build kitchen cabinets. **3.** . . . can repair the cracked plaster.
Sisi: **1.** . . . can't repair light switches. **2.** . . . can mow the grass. **3.** . . . can rake the leaves.
Plumber: **1.** . . . can't build kitchen cabinets **2.** . . . can fix the shower. **3.** . . . can install a hot-water heater.
Electrician: **1.** . . . can't repair the cracked plaster. **2.** . . . can install a ceiling fan. **3.** . . . can repair light switches.

EXERCISE 2

Answers will vary.

EXERCISE 3

Answers will vary. They will begin with "Can you . . ."

EXERCISE 4

1. What time can I pick up the papers? **2.** Where can I meet you? **3.** How long can we rent the TV camera? **4.** How often can my father take the medicine? **5.** Where can I find the butter? **6.** Who can show me how to fix this? **7.** Where can we find the right size? **8.** Who can drive me to the store? **9.** What can help me understand the words better? **10.** When can I find the best fruit?

EXERCISE 5

1. A. . . . Can I say, "They can sing very beautiful". **B.** No. you can't. The correct way to say that is, "They can sing very beautifully." **2. A.** . . . "I know how to breath"? **B.** No, you can't. The correct way to say this is, "I know how to breathe." **3. A.** . . . "You can speak English very well"? **B.** Yes, you can. **4. A.** . . . "You can fishing from this bridge?" **B.** No, you can't. The correct way to say that is," Can you fish from this bridge?" **5. A.** . . . "Do you know how to play a card game?" **B.** Yes, you can. **6. A.** . . . "I can no finish in time"? **B.** No, you can't. The correct way to say that is, "I can't finish in time."

EXERCISE 6

Learned abilities: speaking English; riding a bike; flying an airplane; reading; swimming; writing

EXERCISE 7

Answers will vary.

EXERCISE 8

Sentences will vary.
2. Ali can float, but he can't dive. **3.** Ali can paint and draw. **4.** Ali can't make jewelry or pottery. **5.** Ali can't dive or stay underwater a long time. **6.** Ali can ice skate, but he can't ski. **7.** Ali can ride a sled, but he can't drive a snowmobile. **8.** Ali can drive a car, but he can't repair the engine. **9.** Ali can fix a flat tire, but he can't replace a broken headlight. **10.** Ali can wash clothes, but he can't sew. **11.** Ali can remove stains, but he can't iron. **12.** Ali can't sew or iron. **13.** Ali can wash clothes and remove stains. **14.** Ali can swim, and he can float, too. **15.** Ali can drive a car, but he can't drive a snowmobile.

Unit 15

Present Progressive Tense

EXERCISE 1

2. is eating **3.** is watching **4.** are sitting **5.** is jumping **6.** is buying **7.** is sleeping **8.** is wading **9.** am sliding **10.** are burning **11.** are spilling

EXERCISE 2

2. Tito is eating a hot dog right now./At the moment, Tito is eating a hot dog. **3.** The lifeguard is watching the swimmers and blowing his whistle right now./At the moment, the lifeguard is . . . .

4. Carmen and Margarita are sitting in the sand right now./At he moment, Carmen and Margarita are . . . 5. The man is jumping in the water right now./At the moment, the man is . . .
6. Mom is buying the hot dogs and hamburgers right now./At the moment, Mom is . . . 7. Dad is sleeping on the sand right now./At the moment, Dad is . . . 8. Ricky is wading right now./At the moment, Ricky is . . . 9. I'm sliding down the water slide right now./At the moment, I'm . . . 10. The hot dogs are burning right now./At the moment, the hot dogs are . . . 11. The drinks are spilling right now./At the moment, the drinks are . . .

EXERCISE 3

1. Jennifer's looking at the lifeguard. 2. Tito's eating a hot dog.
3. The lifeguard's watching the swimmers and blowing his whistle.
4. They're sitting in the sand. 5. The man's jumping in the water.
6. Mom's buying the hot dogs and hamburgers. 7. Dad's sleeping on the sand. 8. Ricky's wading. 9. I'm sliding down the water slide. 10. They're burning. 11. They're spilling.

EXERCISE 4

2. Dad is getting a sunburn. 3. Carmen is digging in the sand.
4. The swimmers are splashing in the water. 5. The girls are burying their dad. 6. The hot dogs are burning. 7. I'm sliding down the water slide. 8. The lifeguard is blowing his whistle.
9. Dad is lying in the sand. 10. Mom is buying food.
11. Jennifer is smiling at the lifeguard. 12. Tito is eating a hot dog.

EXERCISE 5

2. The family is not having fun. 3. Dad is not driving carefully.
4. Carmen and Margarita are not sitting still. 5. Mom is not agreeing with Dad. 6. The air conditioning is not working.
7. I am not talking to my family. 8. Traffic is not moving.
9. Jennifer is not smiling. 10. Ricky is not sleeping.
11. Dad is not watching the road.

EXERCISE 6

Answers same as above with "isn't" replacing "is not"; "aren't" replacing "are not."

EXERCISE 7

Sentences will vary.

EXERCISE 8

Sentences will vary. The following are possible answers.
2. but today I'm staying home. 3. My dad is usually at work, but 4. but she's making them today. 5. My sister seldom sees her boyfriend, and 6. but now he's playing. 7. My brother Tito eats fruit, but 8. My sisters don't fight much, but
9. but at the moment she's baking cookies. 10. but now he's putting up the Christmas lights.

EXERCISE 9

Sentences will vary.

EXERCISE 10

2. prefers; is not eating 3. is getting; belongs 4. forgets; looks 5. smell; are burning 6. have; have/am having
7. is eating; loves 8. seems; are having 9. belongs; is having 10. believe; are going

EXERCISE 11

Questions and answers will vary.
1. Do you like this class? 2. Is your English getting better?
3. Do you and your classmates work hard? 4. Do you practice English at home? 5. Do you understand English grammar? 6. Is English grammar easier than the grammar of your first language?/Is English grammar getting easier? 7. Are you having a good day?
8. Am I asking these questions correctly? 9. Does your mother live in the United States? 10. Am I speaking clearly?

EXERCISE 12

Questions and answers will vary.
1. What are Grandma and Grandpa bringing? They're bringing potato salad. 2. How are Grandma and Grandpa coming? They're coming by car. 3. Where are Grandma and Grandpa sleeping? They're sleeping in the twins' room. 4. When is Uncle Manuel arriving? He's arriving at 7:00 A.M. on Friday. 5. What is Uncle Manuel bringing? He's bringing drinks. 6. How is Uncle Manuel coming? He's taking the train. (He's coming by train.) 7. Where is Uncle Manuel sleeping? He's sleeping in the living room. 8. Who is bringing fresh fruit? Cousin Carla and her husband are bringing fresh fruit.
9. When are cousin Carla and her husband arriving? They're arriving on Friday at noon. 10. How are cousin Carla and her husband getting here? They're flying. /They're taking a plane. 11. Where are cousin Carla and her husband sleeping? They're sleeping in Jose's room. 12. When is Aunt Luz coming? She's coming Friday evening.
13. What is Aunt Luz bringing? She's bringing cake. 14. How is Aunt Luz getting here? She's coming by car. (She's driving.)
15. Where is Aunt Luz sleeping? She's sleeping in the guest room.
16. When is Uncle Raul arriving? He's arriving Friday morning.
17. What is Uncle Raul bringing? He's bringing chips. 18. How is Uncle Raul getting here? He's coming by bus./He's taking the bus.
19. Where is Uncle Raul sleeping? He's sleeping in the garage.

Exercises for the TOEFL® Test

Units 13–15

1. B	4. C	7. C	10. C	13. B	16. D	19. C	22. D	25. C	28. A
2. B	5. C	8. D	11. A	14. C	17. D	20. A	23. D	26. C	29. D
3. A	6. B	9. D	12. A	15. A	18. C	21. A	24. C	27. B	30. B

Unit 16

Adjective Phrases: *Another, The Other, Other(s), The Other(s)*, Intensifiers

EXERCISE 1

2. f **3.** k **4.** a **5.** e **6.** g **7.** b **8.** i **9.** h **10.** c **11.** j

EXERCISE 2

1. in the ambulance **2.** on the skateboard **3.** at the traffic light **4.** on the highway **5.** with the red light on top **6.** with the squeaky wheel **7.** parked at the grocery store **8.** with the ladder **9.** with the woman driver **10.** on the country road **11.** with the chauffeur

EXERCISE 3

Sentences will vary.

1. The man in the apron drives the bread truck. **2.** The sports car belongs to the man with a pipe. **3.** The men with the stretcher drive the ambulance. **4.** The woman in the uniform drives the police car. **5.** The skateboard belongs to the boy in the helmet. **6.** The tricycle belongs to the little girl with the balloon. **8.** The woman in the hard hat drives the bulldozer. **9.** The man with the fire hose drives the fire engine. **10.** The limousine belongs to the woman with the cigarette. **11.** The man with the briefcase drives the convertible.

EXERCISE 4

1. Which skirt does Cheryl want to get? **2.** Which shoes does Rachel like? **3.** Which earrings does Rachel prefer? **4.** Which sweater does Cheryl want to buy? **5.** Which skirt does Rachel like? **6.** Which earrings does Cheryl prefer? **7.** Which blouse does Rachel like? **8.** Which sweater does Rachel want to buy? **9.** Which shoes does Cheryl want to buy?

EXERCISE 5

Answers will vary.

EXERCISE 6

other; other; Another; Other; another; Another; others; the others; the other

EXERCISE 7

Answers will vary.

Unit 17

Past Tense of *Be*

EXERCISE 1

2. Ernest Hemingway and Mark Twain were American writers. **3.** Napoleon Bonaparte was a French general. **4.** Winston Churchill was a British prime minister. **5.** The Soviet Union and East Germany were eastern European nations. **6.** Eva Peron was the wife of the president of Argentina. **7.** Muhammad Ali was an Olympic boxer. **8.** Rhodesia and Upper Volta were African nations. **9.** Arthur Ashe was a professional tennis player. **10.** Elvis Presley, Jimi Hendrix, and Jim Morrison were American rock singers.

EXERCISE 2

Sentences will vary.

EXERCISE 3

1. There were trains 100 years ago. **2.** There were horses 100 years ago. **3.** There weren't any jet airplanes . . . **4.** There weren't any skateboards . . . **5.** There wasn't a United Nations . . . **6.** There was a country called China . . . **7.** There weren't two countries on the Korean peninsula . . . **8.** There were Olympic Games . . .

9. There weren't any computers . . . 10. There was a prime minister of Canada . . . 11. There was a queen of Great Britain . . . 12. There was a president of the United States . . .

EXERCISE 4

Answers will vary.
1. Were you neat when you were a child? 2. Were you helpful when you were a child? 3. Were you happy . . . 4. Were you sad . . . 5. Were you good in school . . . 6. Were you funny . . . 7. Were you messy . . .

EXERCISE 5

1. Where was Eva Peron from? 2. Who was the author of *Tom Sawyer*? 3. When was Muhammad Ali in the Olympics? 4. What were Rhodesia and Upper Volta? 5. Whose house was in Tennessee? 6. When was Ernest Hemingway born? 7. Where were the Soviet Union and East Germany? 8. Why was Napoleon arrested? 9. What was one of the Marx Brothers' movies? 10. When was Winston Churchill prime minister of Great Britain?

Unit 18

Past Tense

EXERCISE 1

planned; arrived; studied; covered; tripped; entered; turned; looked; pointed; demanded; filled; handed; robbed; tried; ripped; dropped; hopped; remembered; wanted; worried; arrived

EXERCISE 2

Group 1/T/: discussed, asked, walked, fixed, locked, worked, typed, talked, polished, baked, washed, brushed, bounced, jumped, tripped, skipped, hopped, kissed

Group 2/D/: learned, studied, answered, listened, named, remembered, delivered, filed, vacuumed, ironed, changed, cleaned, scrubbed, played, enjoyed, climbed

Group 3/ID/: corrected, printed, started, pointed, dusted, skated

EXERCISE 3

Sentences will vary.

EXERCISE 4

got; saw; looked; broke; went; looked; found; put; looked; began; took; found; heated; made; ate; drank; felt; sat; fell; slept; came; saw; called; heard; woke; stood; ran; caught; went

EXERCISE 5

Sentences will vary.

EXERCISE 6

2. David raked the leaves, mowed the grass, planted flowers, and repaired the sprinklers last week./Last week, David . . .
3. David raked the leaves two days ago./Two days ago, David . . .
4. David checked his tools on Monday./On Monday, David . . .
5. David trimmed the hedges yesterday morning./Yesterday morning, David . . . 6. David set up the president's party last night./Last night, David . . . 7. David raked the leaves the day before yesterday./The day before yesterday, David . . . 8. David trimmed the hedges two weeks ago./Two weeks ago, David . . .
9. David repaired the sprinklers last Friday./Last Friday, David . . .
10. David mowed the grass yesterday afternoon./Yesterday afternoon, David . . .

EXERCISE 7

2. Bernie didn't wear . . .
3. Bernie didn't get away . . .
4. Bernie didn't learn . . .
5. Bernie didn't open . . .
6. Bernie didn't buy any . . .
7. Bernie didn't steal . . .
8. Bernie didn't eat . . .
9. Bernie didn't drink . . .
10. Bernie didn't sleep . . .
11. Mr. Chan didn't call . . .
12. Bernie didn't drive . . .
13. Bernie didn't escape . . .

EXERCISE 8

Answers will vary. 1. Did you wear . . . 2. Did you help . . . 3. Did you study . . . 4. Did you ride . . . 5. Did you get . . . 6. Did you sing . . . 7. Did you like your . . . 8. Did you play . . . 9. Did you buy your . . . 10. Did you say . . .

EXERCISE 9

2. Where did you put the money? 3. What happened to the money? 4. What did the police do? 5. Where did the police catch Bernie? 6. What happened? 7. How did he get in? 8. Who found him? 9. Where did you find him? 10. What did you do? 11. How long did he sleep?

Exercises for the TOEFL® Test

Units 16–18

1. C	**4.** D	**7.** B	**10.** D	**13.** B	**16.** C	**19.** A	**22.** A	**25.** D	**28.** C
2. A	**5.** B	**8.** A	**11.** C	**14.** B	**17.** A	**20.** D	**23.** D	**26.** D	**29.** A
3. D	**6.** A	**9.** D	**12.** A	**15.** B	**18.** B	**21.** D	**24.** D	**27.** C	**30.** D

Unit 19

Reflexive Pronouns, Reciprocal Pronoun: *Each Other*

EXERCISE 1

Paul: myself Charlotte: yourself; itself; myself Paul: themselves; himself Charlotte: yourselves; themselves Paul: themselves; ourselves Charlotte: ourselves; myself.

EXERCISE 2

Charlotte: x; myself Paul: x; x; ourselves; themselves; x. *Later* . . . Paul: themselves; himself; himself Charlotte: themselves Paul: herself

EXERCISE 3

Sentences will vary.

EXERCISE 4

Following from left to right 1, 10, 2   9, 3, 4   6, 5, 7, 8

Unit 20

Future Time: *Will* and *Be Going To, May* and *Might*

EXERCISE 1

Following left to right: Monday (car insurance); Friday (arm) Saturday (clumsy); Sunday (exterminator) Wednesday (lottery); Thursday (knee)

EXERCISE 2

Answers will vary.

EXERCISE 3

Sentences will vary.
2. Alicia and the other musicians will form a rock band.
3. Alberta will get her Ph.D. in physics. **4.** Alberta will teach and do research at a university. **5.** Dana will become a high school football coach. **6.** Dana's team will win the state championship. **7.** Grace will become a mechanic. **8.** Grace will open her own garage. **9.** Clara will go to New York.
10. Clara will work as a waitress and take more ballet classes.
11. Ross will become a vice president of his dad's business.
12. Ross will invest his money carefully. **13.** Con will study architecture. **14.** Con will build his own house. **15.** Brian will go to medical school. **16.** Brian will work for a pharmaceutical company. **17.** Cull will buy a small farm. **18.** Cull will grow vegetables and fruit.

EXERCISE 4

2. When will Alberta win . . . **3.** Where will Grace open . . . **4.** Will Clara become . . . **5.** Why will Cull . . . **6.** Where will Brian . . . **7.** How long will it take Con . . . **8.** Where will Dana . . . **9.** Who will discover . . .

EXERCISE 5

Paul: isn't going to; is going to Helen: isn't going to; is going to Paul: is going to; are going to; are going to; are we going to; Helen: are going to Paul: is going to; am not going; is going to; isn't going to; is going to

EXERCISE 6

1. What grade are you going to get in this class? **2.** When is the sun going to set tonight? **3.** Who is going to be the next person to walk into our classroom?
Answers will vary.

EXERCISE 7

Answers may vary.
2. She'll meet with her study group in three weeks. **3.** She'll go to the dentist in two weeks. **4.** She'll get paid next week.
5. She'll have a vacation from work in three weeks. **6.** She'll have a conference with her advisor on Friday morning. **7.** She'll have a date with Ned in two weeks. **8.** She'll take her first exam next month. **9.** She will take her dog to the vet tomorrow.
10. She'll have to work all weekend next week.

EXERCISE 8

Suggested answers:
1. The study group meets at 5:00 P.M. **2.** Suzy's vacation from work is one week. **3.** She'll start school in September.
4. She'll have a date with Ned on Friday night, September 17.
5. Her dental appointment is at 3:00. P.M. **6.** She should see her advisor between 8:00 and 12:00. **7.** It's one week until school begins. **8.** It's ten days until she has to work all weekend. **9.** She'll take her dog to the vet tomorrow. **10.** She can register for classes until September 7.

EXERCISE 9

Aunt Polly: am not going to; will; are going to Tom: are going to Aunt Polly: are going to Ben: are you going to Tom: am going to Ben: are you going to; am going to; aren't going to Tom: am going to; won't Tom: are you going to

EXERCISE 10

are going to paint/I; am not going to stand/I; will cause/P; are going to do/I; are going to go/I; are going to do/I; are you going to do/I; am going to paint/I; are you going to do/I; am going to go/I; aren't going to have any fun/P; am going to have/I; won't like/P; are you going to give/P

EXERCISE 11

Sentences will vary.

EXERCISE 12

Explanations will vary.

Unit 21

Phrasal Verbs

EXERCISE 1

calm down; slow down; Come in; sat down; came in; stood up; figure out; stood up; stand up; sit down; handed out; fill out; call up; filled out; handed out; went over; put away

EXERCISE 2

Sentences will vary.
2. When he came in, he saw students sitting in small groups.
3. He told himself to calm down. **4.** He stood up when the teacher came in. **5.** The teacher handed out information cards.
6. The students filled them out.

EXERCISE 3

1. He takes the trash out. **2.** He takes it out. **3.** He throws the trash away. **4.** He throws it away. **5.** It's time to turn the TV off. **6.** It's time to turn it off. **7.** Please come in. Take your coat off. **8.** Take it off. **9.** I will hang your coat up. **10.** I will hang it up.

EXERCISE 4

picked up; threw it away; stacked up; cleaned up; put them away; hung up; turned off

turn up; woke up; put on; got on; got off; figure out; ran into; got in

EXERCISE 5

First she picked all the trash up and threw it away. Then she washed up. She cleaned the kitchen up. Next she washed all the family's dirty clothes. She folded them and put them away—she hung all of the shirts, blouses, and dresses up. Then she vacuumed the rugs. By the time she turned the vacuum cleaner off she was exhausted.

My day started poorly. Last night I forgot to turn my radio alarm clock up. So this morning I woke up late. I quickly put my clothes on and ran to catch the bus. I was in such a hurry that I got on the wrong bus. The bus went several blocks before I realized my mistake. I got off the bus, and then I tried to figure out how to get to the right bus. Luckily, while I was standing there I ran into one of my coworkers. He offered to give me a ride to work. I gladly accepted. I got in his car. In the end, I got to work on time.

EXERCISE 6

1. In your country, do men stand up when women come into a room? **2.** . . . do people usually eat out? **3.** . . . do people cross their legs when they sit down? **4.** . . . do children do household chores when they grow up? **5.** . . . do people usually show up late at parties? **6.** . . . do people call a repairman when appliances break down? **7.** . . . do people go back to the same place for vacation each year? **8.** . . . do people knock before they come in?

Exercises for the TOEFL® Test

Units 19–21

1. B	**4.** C	**7.** A	**10.** C	**13.** D	**16.** A	**19.** D	**22.** B	**25.** C	**28.** C
2. D	**5.** B	**8.** C	**11.** A	**14.** C	**17.** B	**20.** B	**23.** C	**26.** C	**29.** C
3. C	**6.** B	**9.** A	**12.** B	**15.** C	**18.** C	**21.** C	**24.** D	**27.** A	**30.** B

Unit 22

Comparison with Adjectives

EXERCISE 1

Answers will vary.

1. Felicia's shoes are dressier than Bob's shoes. **2.** Bob's / Felicia's shoes are more expensive than Felicia's / Bob's shoes. **3.** Felicia's shoes are newer than Bob's shoes. **4.** Bob's shoes are older than Felicia's shoes. **5.** Bob's shoes are more casual than Felicia's shoes. **6.** Bob's shoes are bigger than Felicia's shoes. **7.** Felicia's favorite movies are more emotional than Bob's favorite movies. **8.** Bob's favorite movies are more exciting than Felicia's favorite movies. **9.** Felicia's favorite movies are more sensitive than Bob's favorite movies. **10.** Felicia's favorite movies are sadder than Bob's favorite movies. **11.** Bob's favorite movies are funnier than Felicia's favorite movies. **12.** Bob's favorite movies are sillier than Felicia's favorite movies.

EXERCISE 2

Sentences will vary.

EXERCISE 3

Sentences will vary.

EXERCISE 4

Answers will vary.

EXERCISE 5

2. Sheri is less action oriented than people from the U.S./Sheri is more "being" oriented . . . **3.** Sheri is less individualistic than people from the U.S./Sheri is more group oriented . . . **4.** Sheri is more cooperative than people from the U.S./Sheri is not as competitive as . . . **5.** Sheri is as future oriented as people from the U.S.

Unit 23

Comparison with Adverbs

EXERCISE 1

Answers will vary.

EXERCISE 2

Sentences will vary.

EXERCISE 3

Answers will vary.

1. Dan spells as well as Pia. **2.** Pia grows more quickly than Dan. **3.** Pia writes as neatly as Dan. **4.** Pia talks more quietly than Dan. **5.** Pia answers more politely than Dan. **6.** Nathan jumps as high as Ned. **7.** Nathan runs as fast as Ned. **8.** Nathan throws as far as Ned. **9.** Nathan practices more frequently than Ned. **10.** Nathan practices harder than Ned.

EXERCISE 4

2. How well do you swim? 3. How well do you kayak? 4. How long have you been kayaking? 5. How often do you plan to kayak? 6. How far do you to plan kayak? 7. How far do you live from here? 8. How long a membership are you interested in? 9. How do you want to pay for your membership? 11. How well does your daughter swim? 12. How well does she kayak? 13. How long has she been kayaking? 14. How often does she plan to kayak? 15. How far does she plan to kayak?

Unit 24

Superlatives

EXERCISE 1

1. C 2. E 3. J 4. I 5. F 6. D 7. A 8. B 9. H 10. K 11. G

EXERCISE 2

1. Mount Logan is the tallest mountain in Canada. 2. Della Falls is the highest waterfall in Canada. 3. Lake Superior is the largest lake in Canada. 4. Toronto is the biggest city in Canada. 5. The CN Tower is the tallest building in Canada. 6. Montreal is the oldest city in Canada. 7. The prime minister is the highest government official in Canada. 8. Alert, the Northwest Territories, is the town that is the farthest north. 9. Jacques Cartier was the earliest European explorer. 10. The United States is Canada's biggest trading partner.

EXERCISE 3

Sentences will vary. Superlative forms to be used are
1. the silliest 2. the sleepiest 3. runs the fastest/fastest runner 4. the most helpful 5. sleeps the most lightly/is the lightest sleeper 6. the most pleasant 7. the heaviest 8. the busiest 9. the saddest 10. drives the most slowly/is the slowest driver 11. the best musician 12. the most graceful dancer 13. has the bluest eyes 14. works the hardest 15. drives the farthest

EXERCISE 4

Sentences will vary. Superlative forms to be used are
1. the worst writer 2. the least shy 3. the least interesting 4. the least busy 5. the worst singer

EXERCISE 5

Answers will vary.
1. What is one of the most famous landmarks in your country? 2. What are the best restaurants . . . 3. What are the most interesting sights . . . 4. What are the least expensive places to shop . . . 5. What are the longest rivers . . . 6. What are the most common foods . . . 7. What are the biggest industries . . . 8. What are the warmest places to visit . . . 9. Who are the greatest artists or entertainers . . . 10. When are the best times to visit . . . 11. What are the most beautiful cities . . .

EXERCISE 6

Answers will vary.

Unit 25

Factual Conditionals: *If*

EXERCISE 1

2. T 3. F If you don't get enough sleep, you get sick. 4. F If a tadpole grows up, it becomes a frog. 5. T 6. T 7. F If you eat too many fatty foods, you gain weight. 8. T 9. F If plants have sunlight, they grow faster./If plants don't have sunlight, they grow slowly. 10. F If it is fall, ducks migrate for the winter. 11. T

EXERCISE 2

Sentences will vary.

EXERCISE 3

Sentences will vary.

Exercises for the TOEFL® Test

Units 22–25

1. C
2. A
3. B
4. C
5. A
6. D
7. B
8. C
9. B
10. C
11. B
12. D
13. C
14. A
15. C
16. D
17. D
18. B
19. B
20. D
21. B
22. A
23. D
24. D
25. B
26. B
27. D
28. A
29. B
30. B

TAPESCRIPT

Unit 1 (Activity 5)

1. **Bank Manager:** Good morning, Mr. Blake. I'm Maxwell Forbes, the Bank Manager.
Mr. Blake: Hi, Max. How are you doing today?

2. **Bank Manager:** Good morning, Ms. Robbins. I'm Maxwell Forbes, the Bank Manager.
Ms. Robbins: Hello, Mr. Forbes. It's nice to meet you.

3. **Bank Manager:** Good morning, Mr. Dobbs. I'm Maxwell Forbes, the Bank Manager.
Kevin Dobbs: How's everything, Mr.?

Unit 2 (Activity 5)

Man: Hello. May I help you?
Consuela: Yes. My name is Consuela. I'd like to register English classes.
Man: OK. Are you a new student?
Consuela: Yes, I am.
Man: And are you intermediate-level?
Consuela: No, I'm advanced, I think. I studied English for five years.
Man: All right. Hmmm . . . are you interested in evening classes?
Consuela: No, I'd like morning classes.
Man: Morning . . . let me see . . . Yes, we have a 10 o'clock advanced class.

Unit 3 (Activity 3)

Secretary: Hello, Glenwood College. How can I help you?
Student: Hi, I'm coming to campus this morning to register for my classes. Can you tell where's the best parking in the morning?
Secretary: Do you have a campus map?
Student: Yes, I do, It's in front of me.
Secretary: The best parking in the morning is Parking B. Go in Entrance Gate A on Hill Street. Parking B is behind Parking A.
Student: Where do I register for classes?
Secretary: In the Administration Building. It is in front of Parking A.
Student: And where's the bookstore?
Secretary: Opposite the Administration building is the library. The bookstore is in the back of library.
Student: Is there a big ESL department?
Secretary: Yes, there is. Next to the library is Bunch Hall. The ESL Department is in that building.
Student: One more thing. Where's the cafeteria?
Secretary: Next to Bunch Hall is the Auditorium. The cafeteria is between the Administration Building and the Auditorium.
Secretary: Anything else?
Student: No. That's it. Well, thanks a lot.

Unit 4 (Activity 4)

Man: Tony's Pizza Delivery. What can I do for you?
Woman: I'd like a medium pizza with cheese, tomatoes, and mushrooms, No pepperoni.
Man: Anchovies?
Woman: No thanks.
Man: Olives?
Woman: Oh, yes please.
Man: Is that it?
Woman: Yes.
Man: Address?
Woman: 66 Park Place.
Man: Your pizza will be there in 20 minutes.
Woman: Thanks.

Unit 5 (Activity 5)

Good Evening. This is Tina Thomson for the 5 o'clock news in Zorlik. Things are very bad here after the earthquake this week. People don't have any gas or electricity. And they don't have any water. Today, some airplanes from the United States are here with some medicine, food and doctors. But they need more help here in Zorlik. The next report from Zorlik is at eleven. This is Tina Thomson reporting from Zorlik for *World News Today.*

Unit 6 (Activity 5)

Carol: What an interesting room!
Dave: Thanks. Well, I have things from all over the world in this room.
Carol: Really?
Dave: Yeah, these chairs are Chinese and the-uh-this table is from Mexico. That lamp over there is from Peru.
Carol: How about those pictures on the wall?
Dave: They're from Indonesia. And that statue is from India.
Carol: This sofa is nice. Where's it from?
Dave: It's from England, and those cushions are from France.

Unit 7 (Activity 6)

My apartment is on Wood Street. There's a big tree in front of my apartment building. Across from my apartment, there's a laundromat. Next to the laundromat, there's a mini-market for groceries. There's a gas station next to the market. The gas station is on the corner of Wood Street and State Street. There aren't any banks on Wood Street, but there is a bank on State Street. There's a parking lot across from the gas station. The bank is next to it. There are no schools in my neighborhood.

Unit 8 (Activity 6)

Man: I start work at five. I'm a farmer. We stop and have breakfast at eight. We work all day. We finish at six or seven in the evening. Do we have days off? No, we don't! We work seven days a week. We work Sundays mornings from six to nine and then from four to seven. We have 100 cows and the cows don't have days off!

Woman: I'm a computer programmer. I work at home. I go to the office one or two times a week for a meeting. I do all my work at home. I have a computer at home. I work about 40 hours a week. Sometimes I work one or two hours a day, and some days I work fourteen hours. I don't work on Saturdays and Sundays. I don't work from four to six because I get the children from school.

Unit 9 (Activity 6)

Pedro: What do you do on Sundays?
Yuko: I usually stay home and watch TV. What do you do?
Pedro: I usually play tennis in the morning. Then I meet my friends and we go out for a meal.
Yuko: When do you do your homework?
Pedro: Sunday night when I watch TV. How about you?
Yuko: I do it in the morning when I think better.

Unit 10 (Activity 6)

Speaker 1 (male): Take two aspirin every four hours. Drink lots of liquid, umm, rest. Chicken soup or other clear soup helps too.
Speaker 2 (female): Put cold water or ice on it immediately. Leave it there for five minutes or until the pain goes away. Take some aspirin to stop the pain. Do not use butter, cream or Vaseline. See a doctor if pain does not stop after two days.
Speaker 3 (female): Take some aspirin or similar medicine. Massage the back of your neck. Lie down and close your eyes. Relax.

Unit 11 (Activity 6)

Man: Hello. Don's supermarket.
Sara: This is Sara Jones.
Man: Oh, hi, Mrs. Jones.
Sara: I would like to order some groceries. groceries. (Man knows her. She does this regularly)
Man: Hi. Mrs. jones. We'll get it to you in about an hour. Same address?
Sara: Yes. Are you ready to write it down?
Man: Yes. Go ahead.
Sara: OK. A bag of potatoes.
Man: A five pound bag or a ten pound bag?
Sara: Five pounds, please, and a five pound bag of yellow onions. Some low fat milk.
Man: A quart or a half gallon?
Sara: A half gallon, please, and a two pound carton of non-fat plain yogurt, one head of white cabbage, a bunch of carrots, two cans of tuna, a dozen eggs—large, and a bottle of olive oil.
Man: OK. I think I've got it. I'll see you in about an hour.

Unit 12 (Activity 4)

Speaker 1 (male): I want people to buy things from me. So I always dress neatly for work and smile and speak politely. Sometimes when people are not happy with what they get from me, they speak angrily.
Speaker 2 (female): I usually greet people caringly. People usually have problems when they come to me. I examine them carefully to find out their problem. When I find a problem I explain it to them seriously.
Speaker 3 (male): I'm always perfectly dressed in my uniform. I take care of people happily and get what they need immediately. I travel frequently from place to place.

Unit 13 (Activity 6)

Amy: It's Mother's Day soon, I don't know what to get my mother. What are you going to give your mother, Linda?
Linda: Well, every year I give her flowers and a small gift like her favorite perfume. It's perfume again this year. Every time I ask her what she wants she tells me she has everything.
Amy: My mother is the same. She never tells me. Are you going to take her out to a restaurant?
Linda: Not me, My father takes us out to a really nice restaurant for brunch. She really likes that. And he buys her an expensive gift. So, any ideas on what to give her, Amy?
Amy: Well, not yet.

Unit 14 (Activity 6)

Janet: Hello Ken. My name is Janet Green and I'm president of International TX Computers.
Ken: Nice to meet you.
Janet: I see from your application that you can speak several languages.
Ken: Yes, I can speak Spanish, French and German.
Janet: That's great! We need someone to visit our international offices in France, Spain and Germany. Are you able to stay in another country for some time?
Ken: I can stay for a few months, but I can't stay for a year. I have three small children at home.
Janet: I see from your application you can drive. That's important for this job. There is a lot of travel. Oh, by the way, can you repair computers? My computer seems to have a problem.
Ken: I can use them and sell them, but I can't repair them.
Janet: That's fine. We just need you to sell them.

Unit 15 (Activity 3)

Worried Mother: Hello, is this the police station?
Officer: Yes, ma'am.
Mother: My daughter is missing. I'm so worried.
Officer: Calm down ma'am. Just give me a description of your daughter.
Mother: She's 10 years old. She's about 4 foot 10. She has long brown hair. Her name is Christine. She's wearing a white T-shirt and jeans. She's wearing her sneakers and carrying her school bag. Oh, I don't know what to do . . .
Officer: Calm down, ma'am. There are a few other questions I have to ask you.

Unit 16 (Activity 7)

Man: He has a very long face and rather small eyes. He has a fairly long, straight nose.
Woman: His face is rather long and thin. His eyes are somewhat small. He has a very big nose.
Man: He has rather big, round eyes. His face is somewhat round. He has a very long nose.

Unit 17 (Activity 5)

Woman: A long, long time ago in a faraway country, there was an old man. He was a very kind and good man. He loved the plants and animals around him. They were his friends.
Woman: It was dark. My watch was on the table next to my bed. Three o'clock. Then there was a noise. What was it?
Man: Tony was in the office on Monday to pick up some papers. There was a new receptionist that day. Her name was Jamie. She was a very beautiful young woman. Tony wasn't able to take his eyes off of her.
Man: John Harrington was a millionaire. He was 65 years old. There was a dinner at this big house last night. His wife Emily was there, and their two sons Jason and Robert. John Harrington's brother David was there too. After, dinner John was suddenly very sick.

Unit 18 (Activity 5)

Speaker 1: My parents and I went on vacation last year. They decided to go to a Greek island. They rented a house by the beach. It was beautiful but it was far away from the other houses. The weather was hot. My parents and I went swimming. We went to the market and bought food. There weren't any stores there-just one grocery store. I don't have any brothers or sister, so I was stuck with my parents. I didn't have any friends there and didn't speak Greek. I just swam, ate, slept, and talked to my parents.
Speaker 2: I went to Paris with my wife two years ago. We stayed at a very small hotel—not expensive. The owner was an old lady. We became good friends. Her son works in my hometown. She made wonderful meals for us every evening. The week was not long enough for us to see everything. We went to the Louvre museum, took a trip on the River Seine, walked on the big boulevards, sat in cafes, went up the Eiffel Tower. There were so many things to see and do. We need to go back there again soon.
Speaker 3: I went on a camping trip with my brother a few years ago. The weather was nice when we left. We had a tent, food and sleeping bags with us. But we didn't know very much about camping. We walked for four hours when suddenly it started to rain. It rained very heavily. I fell and hurt my leg. We sat under a tree for a few hours. The rain didn't stop. My brother put up the tent. We got in and stayed in the tent the next day. The rain did not stop. We decided to pack our things and go back home.

Unit 19 (Activity 4)

Speaker 1 (man): After my girlfriend left me, I became depressed. I don't go out anymore. Every evening, I sit by myself and watch TV. I eat by myself and sometimes talk to myself.
Speaker 2 (woman): I'm 50 pounds overweight and have trouble breathing. I smoke and sometimes get pains in my chest. The doctor told me to lose weight and to stop smoking. But I love to eat and smoke. I don't have anything else to enjoy.
Speaker 3 (woman): I'm a 16-year-old high school student. I work very hard in school, and I'm doing very well. But all my friends are having fun. They're always calling each other and making exciting plans. I want to enjoy myself too! What can I do?

Unit 20 (Activity 4)

Tour Guide: Good morning folks. My name is Angela and I will be your tour guide for your trip. I just want to give you some details of our travel plans. Out fight to Paris today will take about nine hours. We will stay in Paris for two nights. Then on Monday mornings we will fly to Rome. We'll stay there for three nights at the Hotel Roma. I will give you more details about the hotel and what we see later. On Thursday we will take the train to Milan. We will stay there for two nights. On Saturday, we will take a morning fight to Geneva, Switzerland. We'll stay two night there. On Monday, we'll go to Vienna for three nights. Vienna is a wonderful city and I know you'll enjoy it. Then early on Thursday morning we'll fly to London and stay there for two nights. On Saturday, we'll fly back to New York from London. It'll be a great vacation and I'm sure you'll remember it for the rest of your lives.

Unit 21 (Activity 4)

Salesperson: Hi, can I help you?
Amy: Yes, I'd like to have a look at your jackets.
Salesperson: What size are you?
Amy: I'm a size 10.
Salesperson: Well, our size ten jackets are all here.
Amy: This is a nice jacket.
Salesperson: Yes, it only arrived yesterday. Why don't you take off your jacket and put this one on?
Amy: Oh, it's great. And it fits perfectly. What's the price?
Salesperson: Seventy-six dollars.
Amy: OK, I'll take it. Now I can throw out this terrible pink jacket my husband got for me.
Salesperson: There you are, ma'am. Thanks for coming in.
Amy: Thanks. I'll come back when I need another jacket.

Unit 22 (Activity 6)

Man: This is great apartment for us. It's larger than the other one we saw today, and it's quieter. I really like this apartment. There's so much light, but it is more expensive.
Woman: This is the apartment for me. It's so much bigger than the other apartments we saw today. It's quieter and closer to the subway too. But it is more expensive.

Unit 23 (Activity 5)

Janet: How was London, Richard?
Richard: It was great! The people were really friendly. They talk to you so politely. In fact they do everything politely, calmly and patiently.
Janet: Where did you stay?
Richard: I stayed in a small hotel. The owner didn't run the hotel very well. Everything was slow or didn't work, and it was expensive.
Janet: How did you get around?
Richard: I took the bus. But the buses didn't run efficiently. So then I took the subway which took where you wanted pretty quickly. And if you are in a hurry you can always take a taxi. They're very good. The drivers drive fast but carefully.
Janet: How was the food Richard? I know that's important to you.
Richard: You can find everything in the supermarkets, but I don't think the English cook very well, personally. The restaurants were expensive, so I didn't go out to eat very often. Maybe twice and that was pretty bad. But food isn't everything you know. I had a great time.

Unit 24 (Activity 6)

Hello listeners. I'm Don Maxwell and welcome to today's Get It Right Quiz Show. I will be asking you questions. Look at your choices. You have 10 seconds to circle the right answer. Good luck!
Question Number 1: What is the largest continent?
Question Number 2: Which animal lives the longest?
Question Number 3: Which is the largest city in the U.S.?
Question Number 4: What language has the greatest number of words?
Question Number 5: What continent has the lowest temperature?
Question Number 6: What is the largest country in the world?
Question Number 7: In what city is land the most expensive?
Question Number 8: What is the longest mountain range?
Question Number 9: What country is the most popular for tourists to visit?
And now your final question,
Number 10: Which religion has the greatest number of members?

Unit 25 (Activity 5)

Marcia: You look tired today, Eduardo.
Eduardo: I know. I feel tired too. I didn't sleep well. If I have too many things on my mind, I can't sleep, And I don't want to take a sleeping pill. What do you do, Marcia, if you can't sleep?
Marcia: Well, if I can't sleep, I drink a glass of milk. If the glass of milk doesn't help, I read a boring book. That always works for me.
Eduardo: Well, if I drink milk in the evening, I feel sick. I'll try a boring book next time.